LAUGHED
THEN ON
ONE HA
LOST
INVULNER
AW!

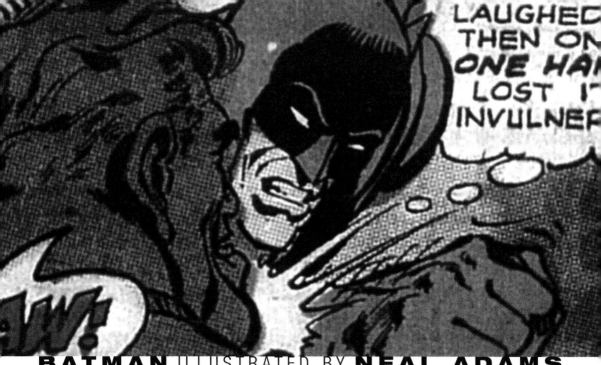

BATMAN ILLUSTRATED BY **NEAL ADAMS**

1

DC Comics New York, New York

BATMAN ILLUSTRATED BY NEAL ADAMS
VOLUME ONE

Published by DC Comics.
Cover, introduction, and compilation
copyright © 2003 DC Comics.
All Rights Reserved.

Originally published in single magazine form as
BATMAN 200, 203, 210; THE BRAVE AND THE BOLD 75-76,
79-85; DETECTIVE COMICS 370, 372, 385, 389, 391,
392; and WORLD'S FINEST COMICS 174-176, 178-180,
182-183, 185, 186. Copyright © 1967, 1968, 1969
DC Comics. All Rights Reserved.

All characters, the distinctive likenesses thereof and
related elements are trademarks of DC Comics.
The stories, characters and incidents featured in this
publication are entirely fictional. DC Comics does not
read or accept unsolicited submissions of ideas,
stories or artwork.

DC Comics
1700 Broadway
New York, NY 10019
A Warner Bros. Entertainment Company.

Printed in China. Fourth Printing.
ISBN: 1-4012-0041-9
ISBN 13: 978-1-4012-0041-1

Cover illustration by Neal Adams.
Interior color reconstruction by
Continuity Associates, Rob Ro &
Alex Bleyaert and Jamison Services.

BATMAN CREATED BY BOB KANE.

TABLE OF CONTENTS

5 Introduction by **Neal Adams**

11 DETECTIVE COMICS #370 Cover
December 1967
Pencils: Carmine Infantino
Inks: Neal Adams

12 THE BRAVE AND THE BOLD #75 Cover
December-January 1968
Pencils and inks: Neal Adams

13 DETECTIVE COMICS #372 Cover
February 1968
Pencils and inks: Neal Adams

14 THE BRAVE AND THE BOLD #76 Cover
February-March 1968
Pencils and inks: Neal Adams

15 BATMAN #200 Cover
March 1968
Pencils and inks: Neal Adams

16 WORLD'S FINEST COMICS #174 Cover
March 1968
Pencils and inks: Neal Adams

17 WORLD'S FINEST COMICS #175
April 1968
Cover: Neal Adams
"The Superman-Batman Revenge Squad"
Story: Leo Dorfman
Pencils: Neal Adams
Inks: Dick Giordano

35 WORLD'S FINEST COMICS #176
June 1968
Cover: Neal Adams
"The Superman-Batman Split"
Story: Cary Bates
Pencils: Neal Adams
Inks: Dick Giordano

54 BATMAN #203 Cover
July-August 1968
Layout: Carmine Infantino
Inks: Neal Adams

55 THE BRAVE AND THE BOLD #79
August-September 1968
Cover: Neal Adams
"The Track of The Hook"
Story: Bob Haney
Pencils and inks: Neal Adams

80 WORLD'S FINEST COMICS #178 Cover
September 1968
Pencils and inks: Neal Adams

81 WORLD'S FINEST COMICS #179 Cover
October 1968
Pencils and inks: Neal Adams

82 WORLD'S FINEST COMICS #180 Cover
November 1968
Pencils and inks: Neal Adams

83 THE BRAVE AND THE BOLD #80
October-November 1968
Cover: Neal Adams
"And Hellgrammite Is His Name"
Story: Bob Haney
Pencils: Neal Adams
Inks: Dick Giordano

107 THE BRAVE AND THE BOLD #81
December-January 1969
Cover: Neal Adams
"But Bork Can Hurt You"
Story: Bob Haney
Pencils: Neal Adams
Inks: Dick Giordano and Vince Colletta

132 WORLD'S FINEST COMICS #182 Cover
February 1969
Pencils: Curt Swan
Inks: Neal Adams

133 WORLD'S FINEST COMICS #183 Cover
March 1969
Layout: Carmine Infantino
Inks: Neal Adams

134 THE BRAVE AND THE BOLD #82
February-March 1969
Cover: Neal Adams
"The Sleepwalker from the Sea"
Story: Bob Haney
Pencils and inks: Neal Adams

158 BATMAN #210 Cover
March 1969
Pencils and inks: Neal Adams

159 DETECTIVE COMICS #385 Cover
March 1969
Pencils and inks: Neal Adams

160 THE BRAVE AND THE BOLD #83
April-May 1969
"Punish Not My Evil Son"
Story: Bob Haney
Pencils and inks: Neal Adams

185 WORLD'S FINEST COMICS #185 Cover
June 1969
Pencils and inks: Neal Adams

186 THE BRAVE AND THE BOLD #84
June-July 1969
Cover: Neal Adams
"The Angel, The Rock, and the Cowl"
Story: Bob Haney
Pencils and inks: Neal Adams
(page 19 inked by Joe Kubert)

211 DETECTIVE COMICS #389 Cover
July 1969
Pencils and inks: Neal Adams

212 WORLD'S FINEST COMICS #186 Cover
August 1969
Layout: Carmine Infantino
Inks: Neal Adams

213 THE BRAVE AND THE BOLD #85
August-September 1969
Cover: Neal Adams
"The Senator's Been Shot"
Story: Bob Haney
Pencils and inks: Neal Adams

237 DETECTIVE COMICS #391 Cover
September 1969
Pencils and inks: Neal Adams

238 DETECTIVE COMICS #392
October 1969
Pencils and inks: Neal Adams

239 Biographies

Stories in this collection were lettered by Ben Oda,
Milt Snapinn and Morris Waldinger.

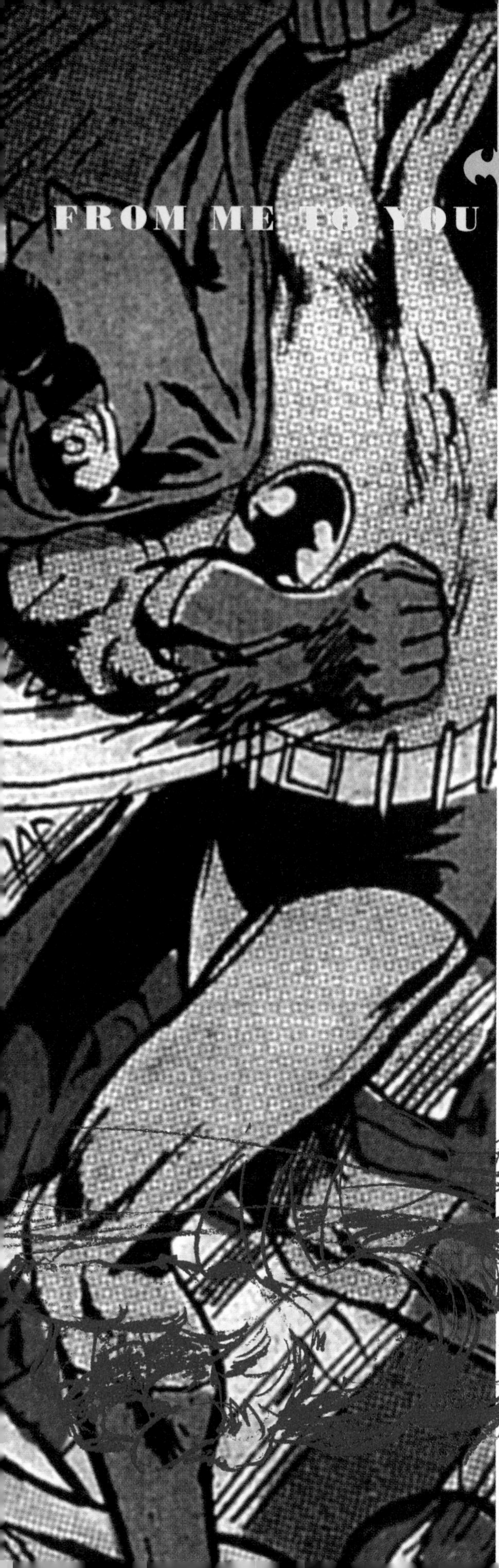

FROM ME TO YOU AN INTRODUCTION

I feel it is somehow incumbent upon me to explain, though I can't really, how it is that you are holding in your hand a fifty-dollar reprint book of my Batman work.

In fact, it is only the first of three such volumes.

Who am I, for heaven's sake, to be worthy of such a high-ticket item?

I have to say I'm not worth it — no matter what anyone says, it just isn't so. Yet here this volume sits, in your hand, joining two similar volumes of my DEADMAN and my GREEN LANTERN/ GREEN ARROW work, each selling for an outrageous price. Believe me, if it was me selling a book at this price it would have to tell you how the whole Universe works. Still, if you bought this, I humbly thank you.

First off, let me say that without the incredible Denny O'Neil, the GL/GA volume would not have seen the light of day. Denny somehow saw a void in the history of comics that no one had filled or probably could fill, and at exactly the right moment he stepped in with the right stuff.

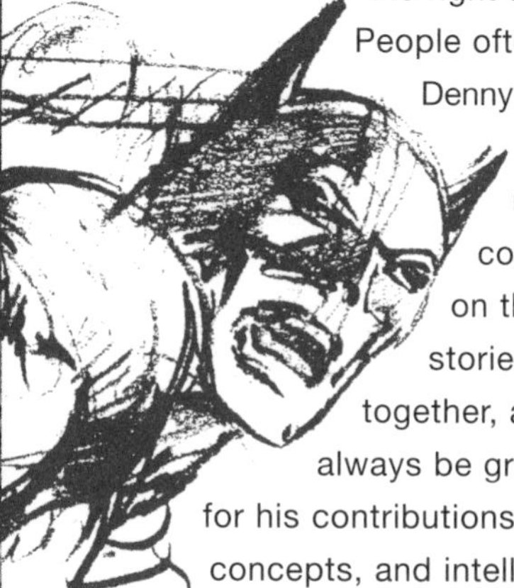

People often overlook Denny's sensitivity and commitment to collaboration on the Batman stories we did together, and I will always be grateful for his contributions, ideas, concepts, and intelligent presentation in usable story form.

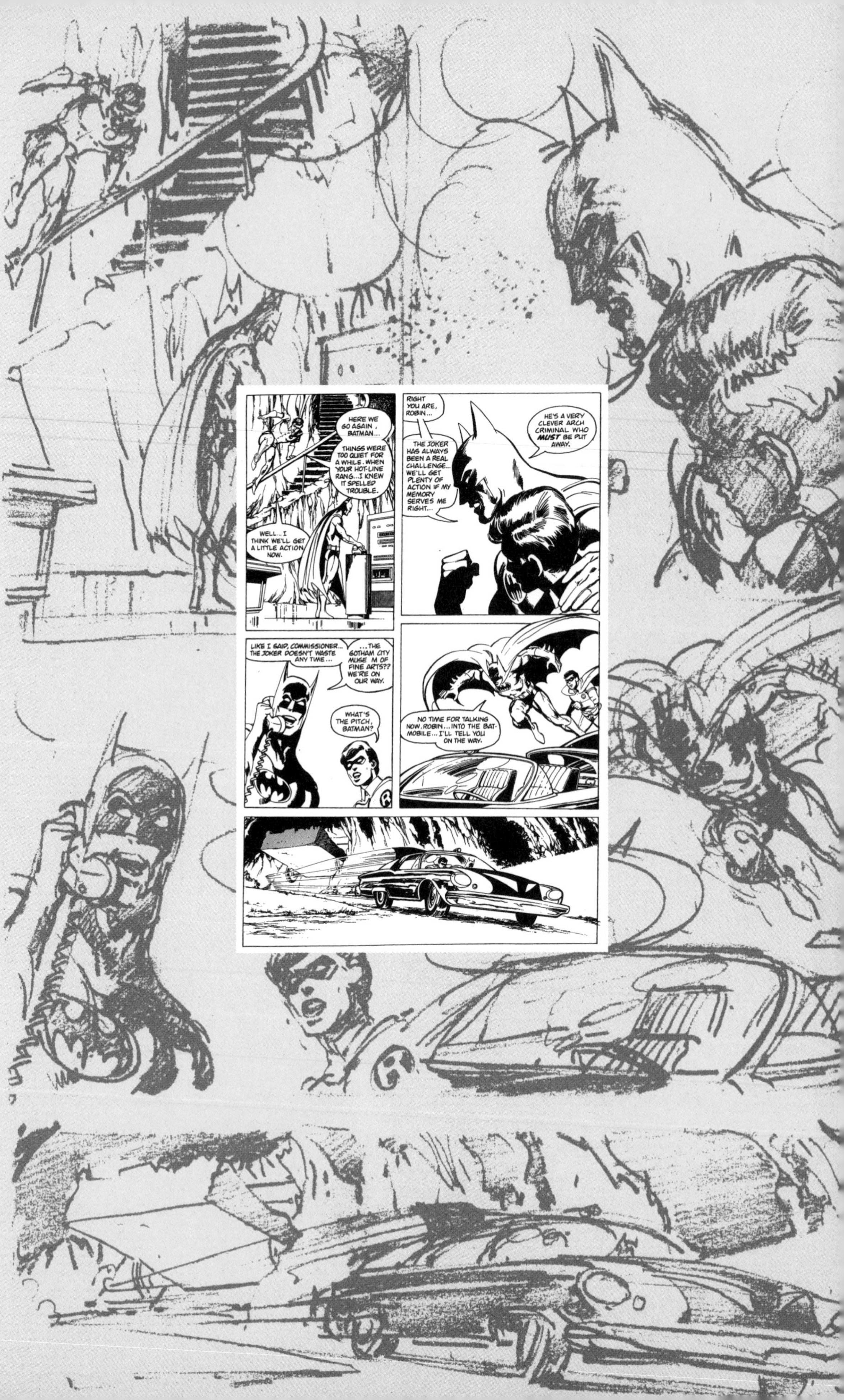
HERE WE GO AGAIN, BATMAN...
THINGS WERE TOO QUIET FOR A WHILE. WHEN YOUR HOT-LINE RANG... I KNEW IT SPELLED TROUBLE.
WELL... I THINK WE'LL GET A LITTLE ACTION NOW.
RIGHT YOU ARE, ROBIN...
THE JOKER HAS ALWAYS BEEN A REAL CHALLENGE... WE'LL GET PLENTY OF ACTION IF MY MEMORY SERVES ME RIGHT...
HE'S A VERY CLEVER ARCH CRIMINAL WHO MUST BE PUT AWAY.
LIKE I SAID, COMMISSIONER... THE JOKER DOESN'T WASTE ANY TIME...
...THE GOTHAM CITY MUSE M OF FINE ARTS?? WE'RE ON OUR WAY.
WHAT'S THE PITCH, BATMAN?
NO TIME FOR TALKING NOW, ROBIN... INTO THE BAT-MOBILE... I'LL TELL YOU ON THE WAY.

When you have all three volumes of this series, I bid you, in one sitting, to read through Denny's Batman stories. There is an evolution there, a growing in power and ownership of the work that is unmistakable. Who could have done it better? I say *no one*!

Then there's the (I would argue) overlooked Bob Haney. Though they have not gotten the recognition they deserve, Bob Haney's stories are classics of good old comic-book drama, and dense in plot, incident, and twists. Haney will never be paid enough in money and honor in his lifetime for his contributions to the medium, and that's a shame.

Then there are the others: Editor Julie Schwartz, cranky and cantankerous, but shepherd to a massive number of memorable stories, including about three Spectre stories I wrote and the Superman-Muhammad Ali book that Denny and I wrote. Julie is, simply, a legend.

Dick Giordano, inker and friend. A legend, yes, but to me a friend and also a partner in our business for several years, until DC made him VP-Executive Editor.

Editor Murray Boltinoff. A sensitive and caring man who herded his flock of creatives like a mother.

Len Wein and Marv Wolfman. Tsimis and Tsuris. Stirring the pot. The first of the Silver Age writers and revolutionaries, predating even Denny.

And the others.

And me? Unwilling mother hen to a pack of radical upstarts. All the new young writers and artists who came to DC Comics in the sixties gravitated to my little borrowed room to hide from the editors. I was the scout. The first line of defense. The first to make it through the thrown-up barrier around DC.

And maybe that's what these three books are about. They span the revolution. Perhaps that's their value.

I did my first WORLD'S FINEST comic-book story before there was a glint of the revolution. I did my last when they were finally sick of me and I was fomenting a revolution of another sort — a revolution of and for creator's rights. Between the two stories, DC Comics went from a company that had not hired a new writer or artist for about 12 years to a company whose staff was two-thirds new people: artists and writers, drawn from all over the world, from Spain to the Philippines.

Can you see this evolution in the stories in these three books?

Well, sort of. If you know what to look for.

You must remember, when I began at DC I had already had a history, a life, a career. When I went into the art field straight out of high school I couldn't get work from DC Comics. (DC was the only regular comic-book company at the time that did what I considered to be "good" comics.) It was 1959. In 1953 Congress had opened hearings on the causes of

juvenile delinquency, surveying radio, television, movies, and comic books. Those hearings turned into an attack on comic books based on Dr. Frederic Wertham's book *Seduction of the Innocent*, and the medium was almost driven underground. There were still Archie Comics, of course, Harvey Comics with Casper, Li'l Dot, Audrey and the like. There was Dell, a tower of boredom, Atlas (*née* Timely), with those six-page Stan Lee stories (Mogog the Gogog, that sort of thing). Besides DC, that was pretty much it.

DC turned me down flat. A production guy kept me at the lobby reception desk, then in a sad, fatherly way sent me away. I never even got through the door.

I got work at Archie Comics instead, first as an assistant and background artist, then as a penciller for Howard Nostrand on a comic strip based on the *Bat Masterson* TV show. Then I did slide films, black and white illustration, some fashion, some movie poster comps, storyboards, and comics for advertising. I had become a professional artist. I landed, with Jerry Capp (Al Capp's brother), a syndicated comic strip based on the *Ben Casey* TV show — a coup since I was only 20 years old. I had hurtled completely past comics work.

As my career advanced, I voluntarily ended the comic strip (we were in 161 newspapers around the world right up to the last day). I spent six months preparing an exclusively illustration-oriented portfolio, which I left at an advertising agency. A week later I came back to get it. It was gone!

Desperate now, I hoped to augment my advertising work with some comic-book work — something I never thought I'd have to do.

I first got work at Warren Publishing. Then I went back to DC. Now, finally, they gave me work.

Times had changed. Jack Kirby had teamed up with Stan Lee, and they were turning out *The Fantastic Four, Iron Man, The Hulk, Spider-Man,* etc. In other words, Timely had stirred and awakened and begun doing real comic books. They had become Marvel.

This scared the heck out of DC Comics. That's when I showed up. Bright-eyed and bushy-tailed, ready to work for a few months and then head back out again to go on with my "real" career.

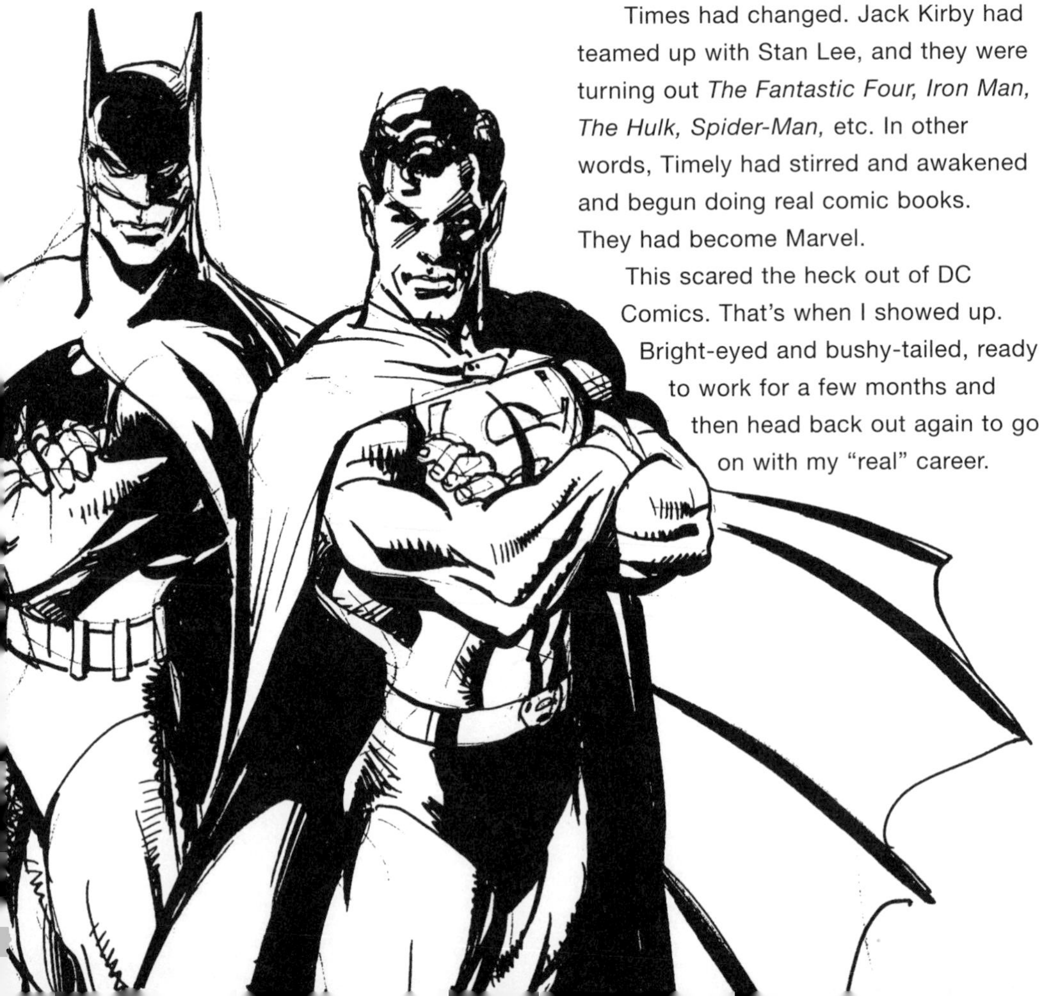

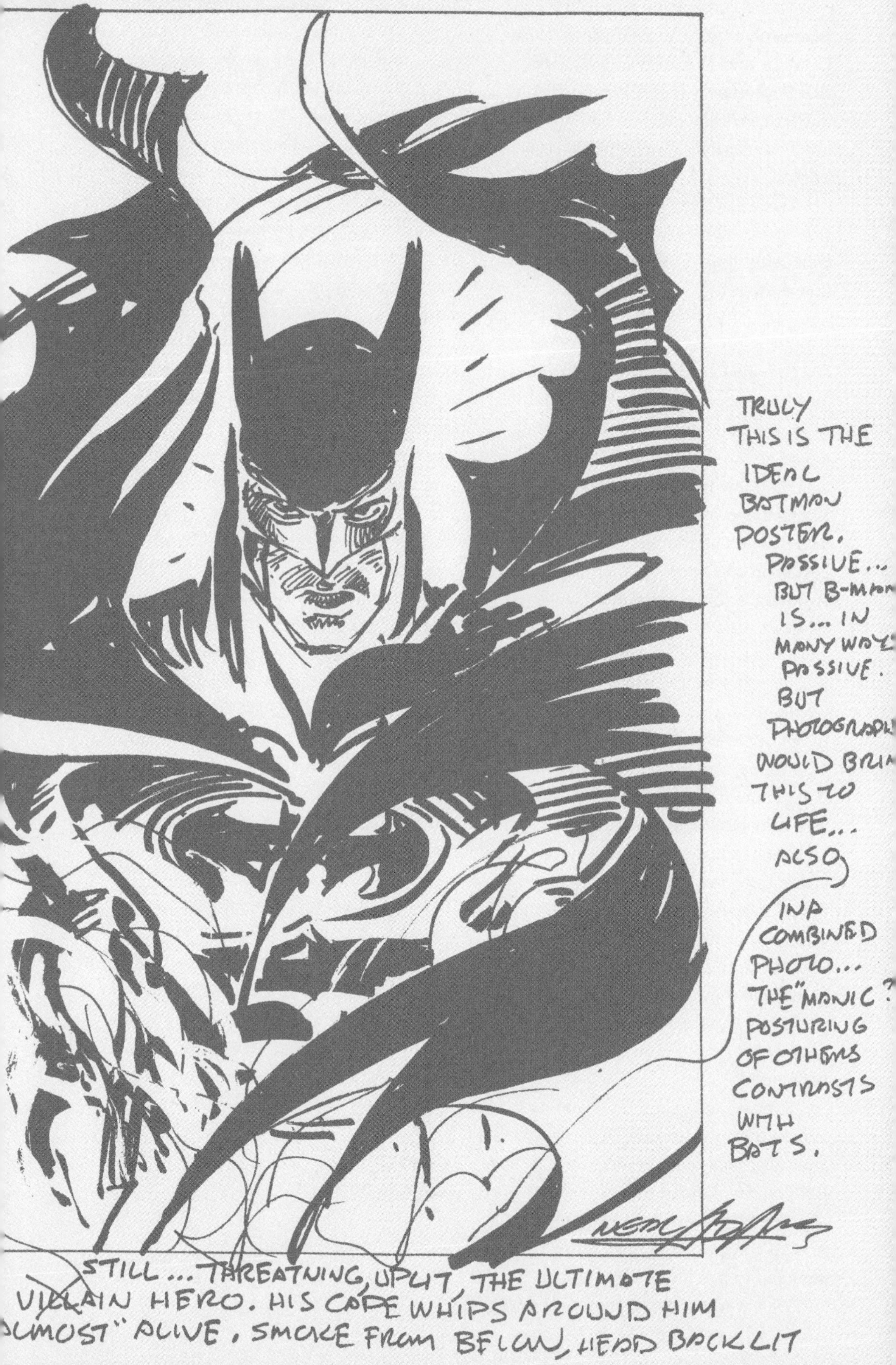
NEAL ADAMS

TRULY THIS IS THE IDEAL BATMAN POSTER. PASSIVE... BUT B-MAN IS... IN MANY WAYS PASSIVE. BUT PHOTOGRAPH WOULD BRIN THIS TO LIFE... ALSO, IN A COMBINED PHOTO... THE "MANIC" POSTURING OF OTHERS CONTRASTS WITH BATS.

STILL... THREATNING, UPLIT, THE ULTIMATE VILLAIN HERO. HIS CAPE WHIPS AROUND HIM LMOST" ALIVE. SMOKE FROM BELOW, HEAD BACKLIT

Then a funny thing happened. Somewhere between WORLD'S FINEST COMICS and THE BRAVE AND THE BOLD (or maybe THE ADVENTURES OF JERRY LEWIS) something had changed.

I had fallen in love with doing comic books.

Don't ask. I really don't know what it was. It was something... *transporting*. It was better than advertising, better than comic strips.

Two things happened. Well, a lot of things happened, but two in particular. First, I realized I was drawing Batman and Superman and doing a lousy job of it. Here was a missed opportunity that I would no longer overlook. The trouble was that now I wanted to get into Batman (and maybe Superman), but I was busy doing the Spectre and Deadman and a ton of other stuff. How to get back to doing Batman? Julie Schwartz, the Batman editor, was ticked when I was switched from his SPECTRE to Jack Miller's DEADMAN, so when I mentioned my doing Batman he told me to get out of his office.

The second thing that happened was that I came to the realization that DC was working in the Dark Ages, stuck in 1953 and hiding behind the safety of the status quo. Yes, it's true, Marvel had begun to kick ass and DC Comics didn't like it. Problem was, they didn't quite know what to do about it. After ten years in the Dark Ages, they were stalled. The world had gone on. The question was, what could I do to kick-start this behemoth?

Even if I could come up with a course of action, the old guard would inevitably fight me every step of the way. But you see, I didn't really have any choice — I'd fallen in love with comics. And so comics would have to be changed to suit me. (Heh.)

Well, it was a bad plan but it worked.

There were already people in place who wanted to try new things. There were young artists out there whose talents could stir things up, if I could prod them along and challenge them. Even in the production room, where things were worst of all, there were one or two people who had done experimental work ten or twenty years before. There was Jack Adler, who pioneered 3-D work at DC. There was Sol Harrison, who had more opportunities to do creative work for charities than he did for DC Comics. And the great Carmine Infantino was getting tired of just drawing Batman and wanted more of a challenge. The pieces were all there. It only took a little friendly persuasion — that and someone prepared to take risks.

I went to see Murray Boltinoff, the editor of THE BRAVE AND THE BOLD. At that time Boltinoff, because of the *Batman* TV show, was teaming up Batman with any other character that struck his fancy. Maybe Julie Schwartz wouldn't use me on BATMAN because I was already doing DEADMAN, I thought, but Boltinoff said he would use me on any of his titles. I asked if I could do THE BRAVE AND THE BOLD and he said yes. Now I was going to do Batman again, and this time I would try to do it right.

In this volume, you can see that process.

I made a lot of mistakes. But I was trying to learn how to do good comic books. Some of you saw it happen at the time, and to you I say, "Welcome back." To the others — I hope you enjoy this journey.

— Neal Adams
January, 2003

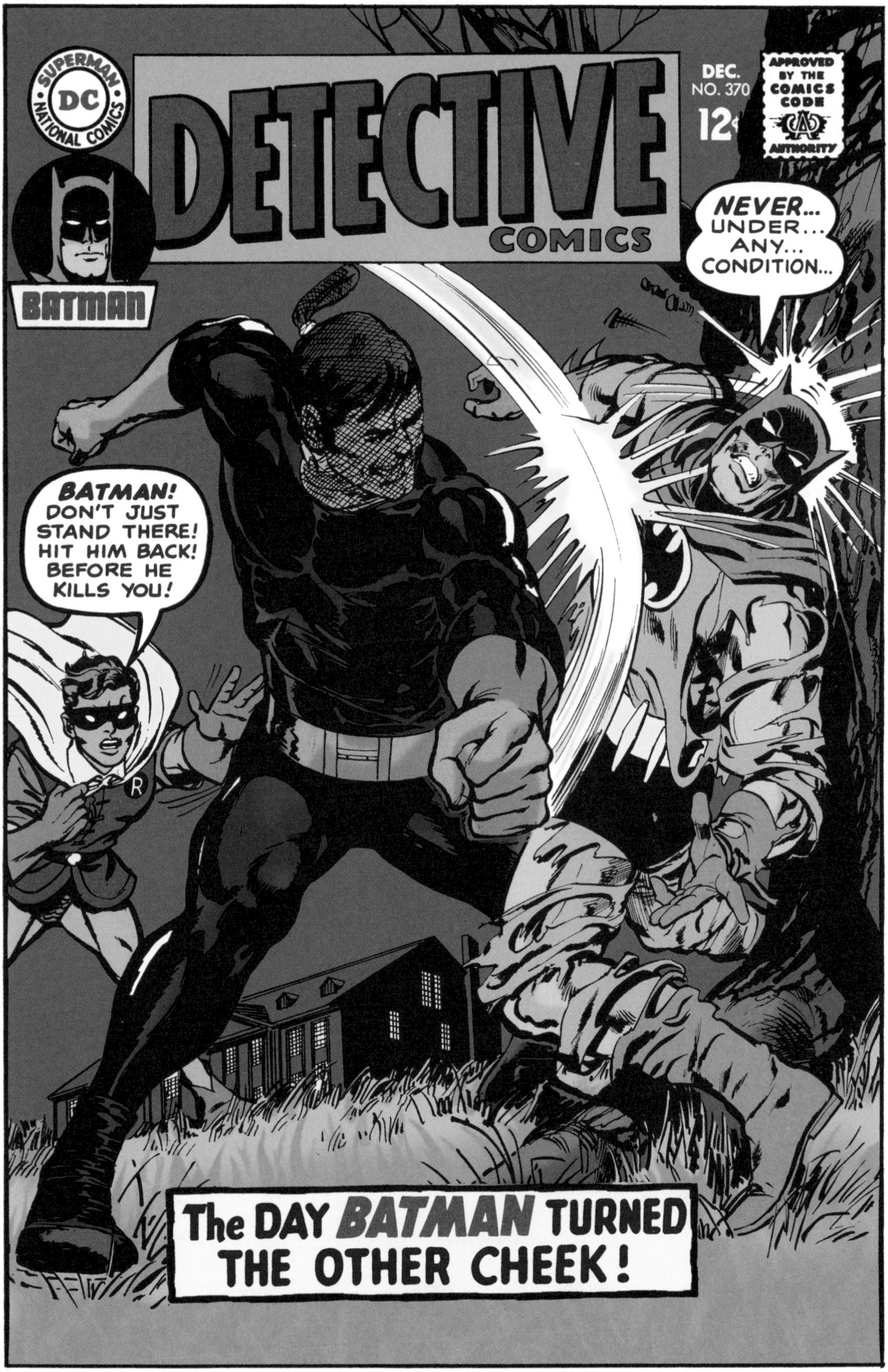
SUPERMAN DC NATIONAL COMICS
DETECTIVE COMICS
DEC. NO. 370 12¢
APPROVED BY THE COMICS CODE AUTHORITY
BATMAN
NEVER... UNDER... ANY... CONDITION...
BATMAN! DON'T JUST STAND THERE! HIT HIM BACK! BEFORE HE KILLS YOU!
The DAY BATMAN TURNED THE OTHER CHEEK!

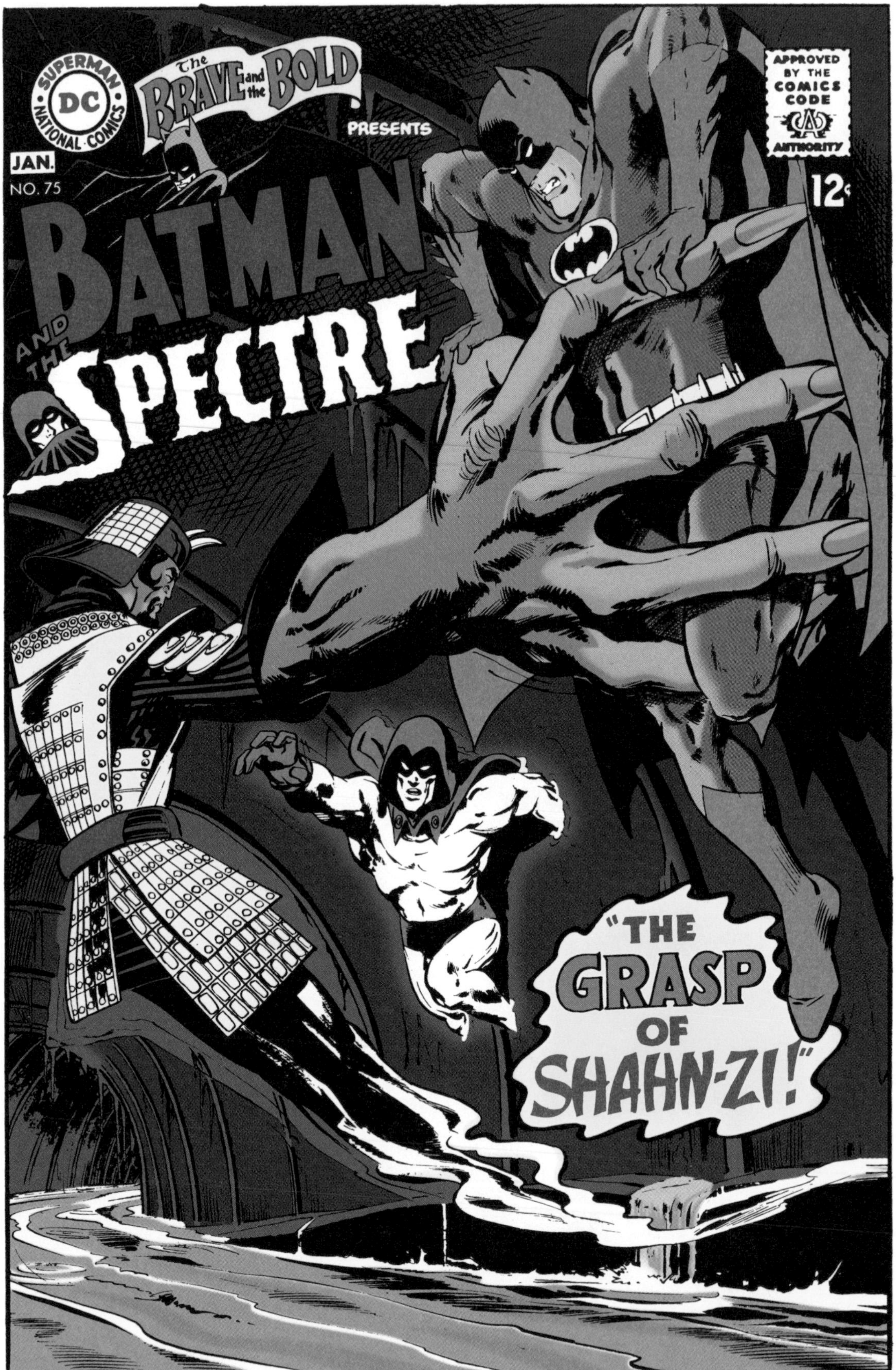
SUPERMAN DC NATIONAL COMICS
The BRAVE and the BOLD
PRESENTS
APPROVED BY THE COMICS CODE AUTHORITY
JAN.
NO. 75
12¢
BATMAN AND THE SPECTRE
"THE GRASP OF SHAHN-ZI!"

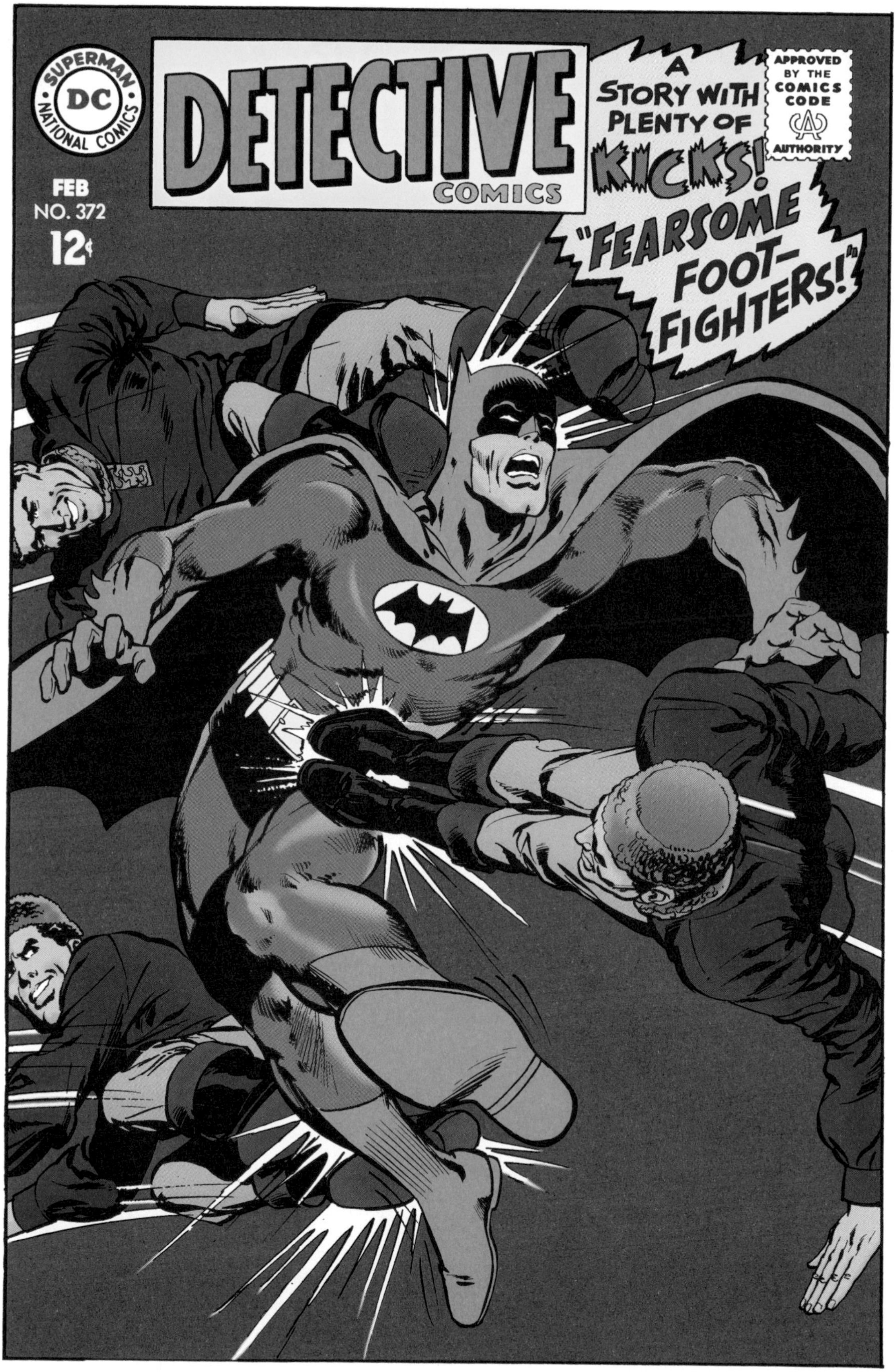
SUPERMAN
DC
NATIONAL COMICS
DETECTIVE
COMICS
FEB
NO. 372
12¢
A STORY WITH PLENTY OF KICKS!
APPROVED BY THE COMICS CODE AUTHORITY
"FEARSOME FOOT-FIGHTERS!"

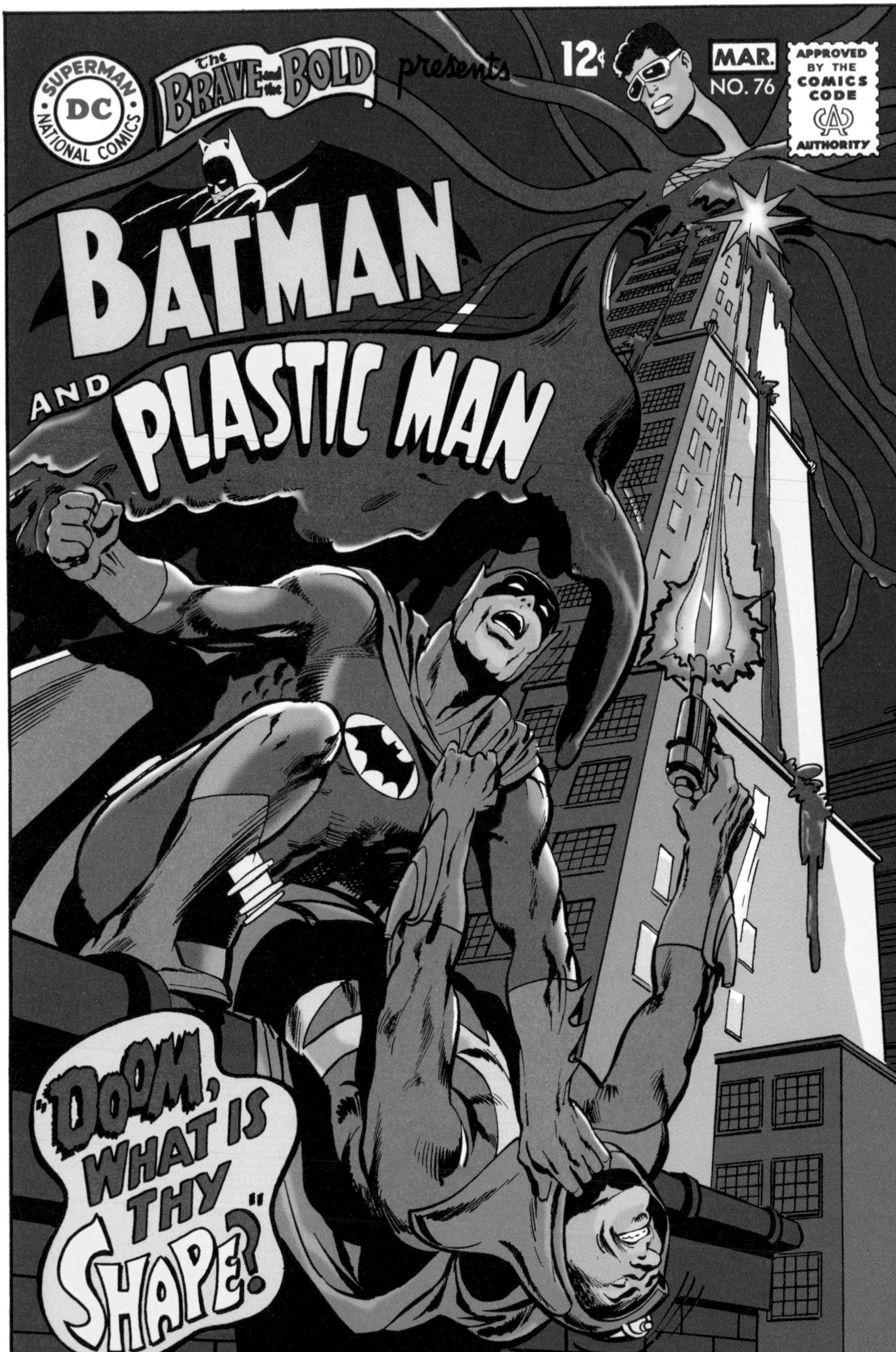
SUPERMAN DC NATIONAL COMICS
The BRAVE and the BOLD presents
12¢
MAR. NO. 76
APPROVED BY THE COMICS CODE AUTHORITY
BATMAN
AND PLASTIC MAN
"DOOM, WHAT IS THY SHAPE?"

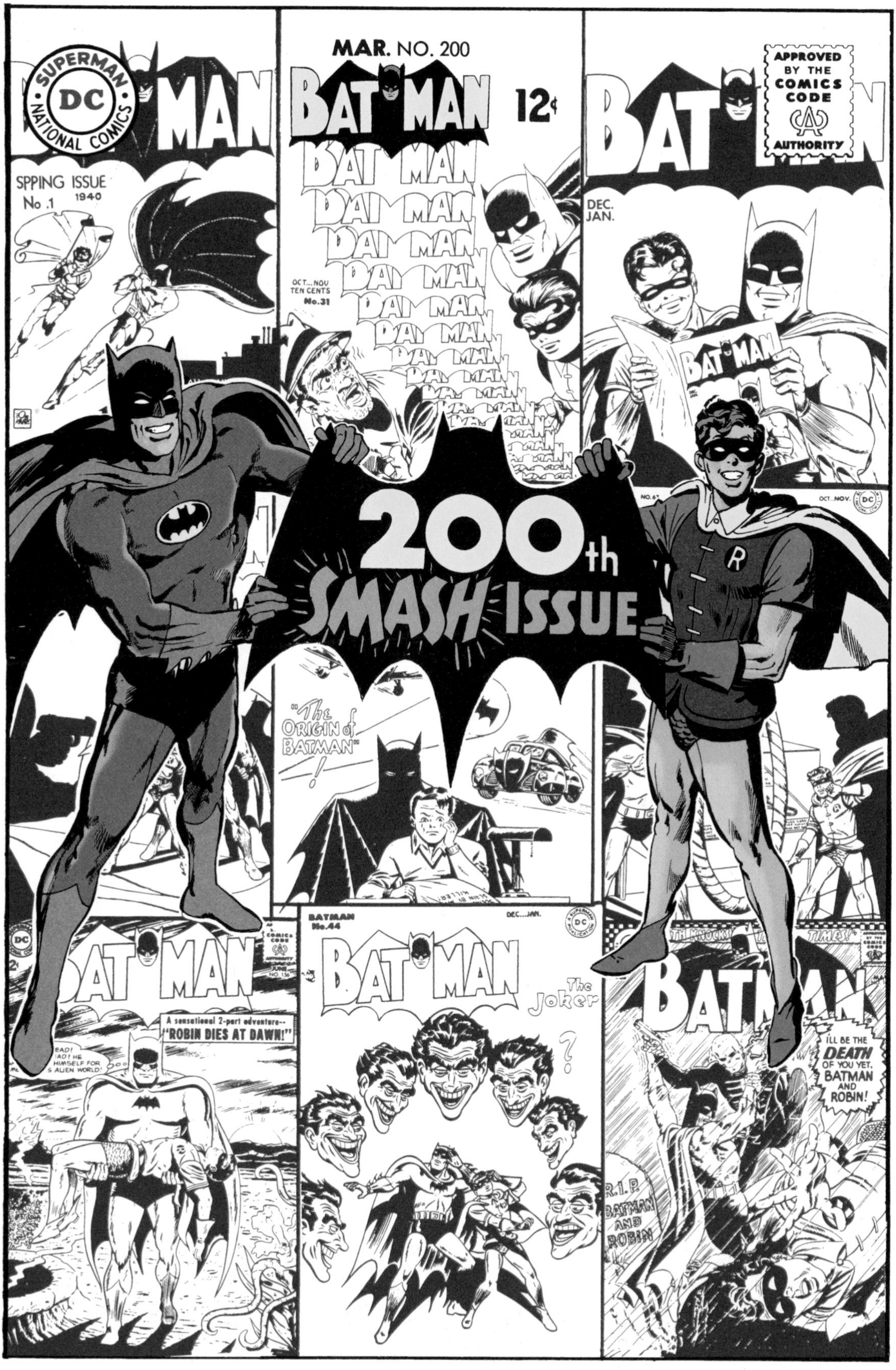

BATMAN
SPPING ISSUE
No.1 1940
MAR. NO. 200
BATMAN
12¢
APPROVED BY THE COMICS CODE AUTHORITY
DEC. JAN.
OCT...NOU TEN CENTS No.31
200th SMASH ISSUE
"The ORIGIN of BATMAN"!
A sensational 2-part adventure-- "ROBIN DIES AT DAWN!"
BATMAN No.44
DEC...JAN.
The Joker
I'LL BE THE DEATH OF YOU YET, BATMAN AND ROBIN!
R.I.P. BATMAN AND ROBIN

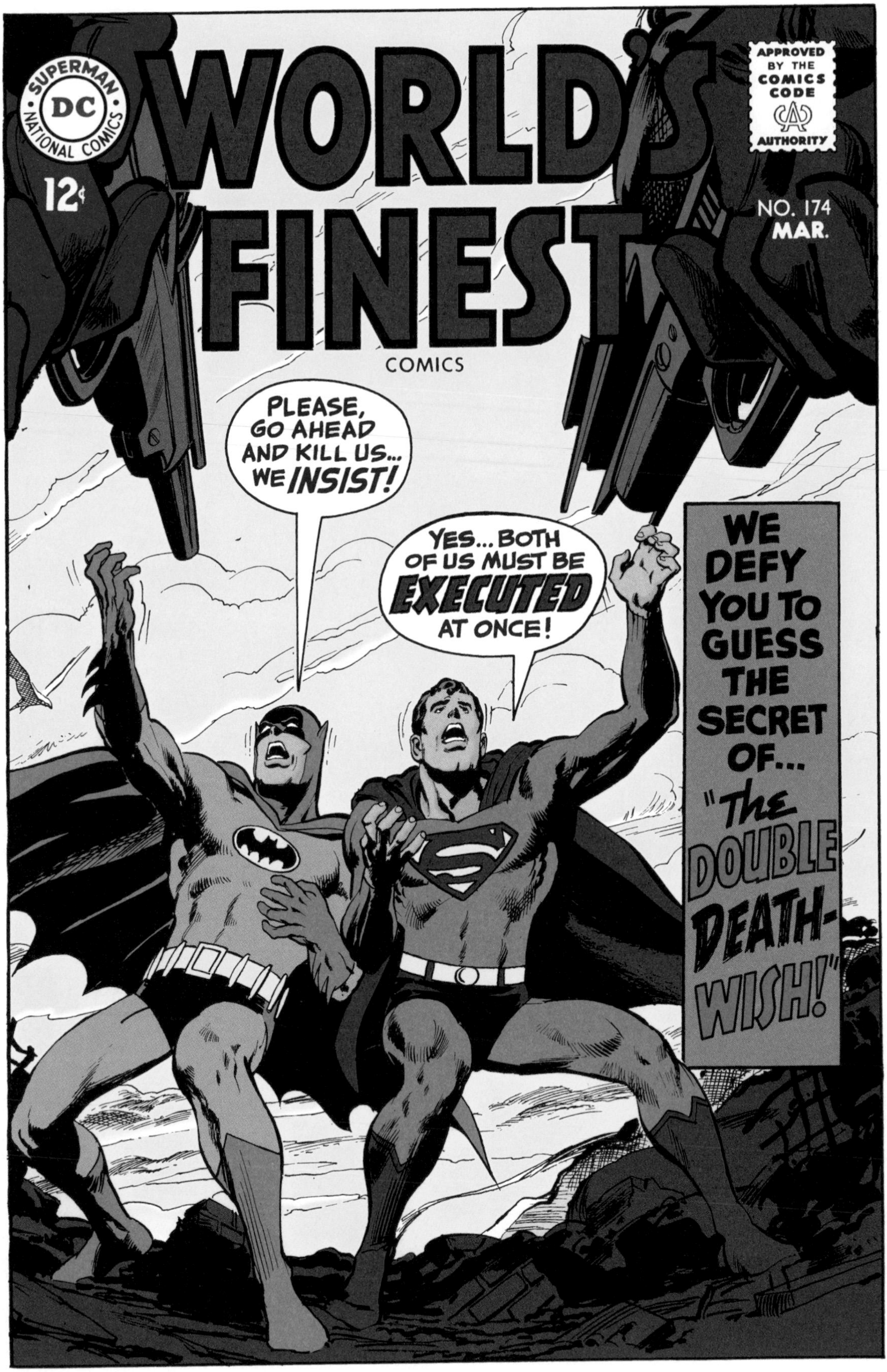
SUPERMAN
DC
NATIONAL COMICS
12¢
WORLD'S FINEST
COMICS
APPROVED BY THE COMICS CODE AUTHORITY
NO. 174
MAR.
PLEASE, GO AHEAD AND KILL US... WE INSIST!
YES... BOTH OF US MUST BE EXECUTED AT ONCE!
WE DEFY YOU TO GUESS THE SECRET OF... "The DOUBLE DEATH-WISH!"

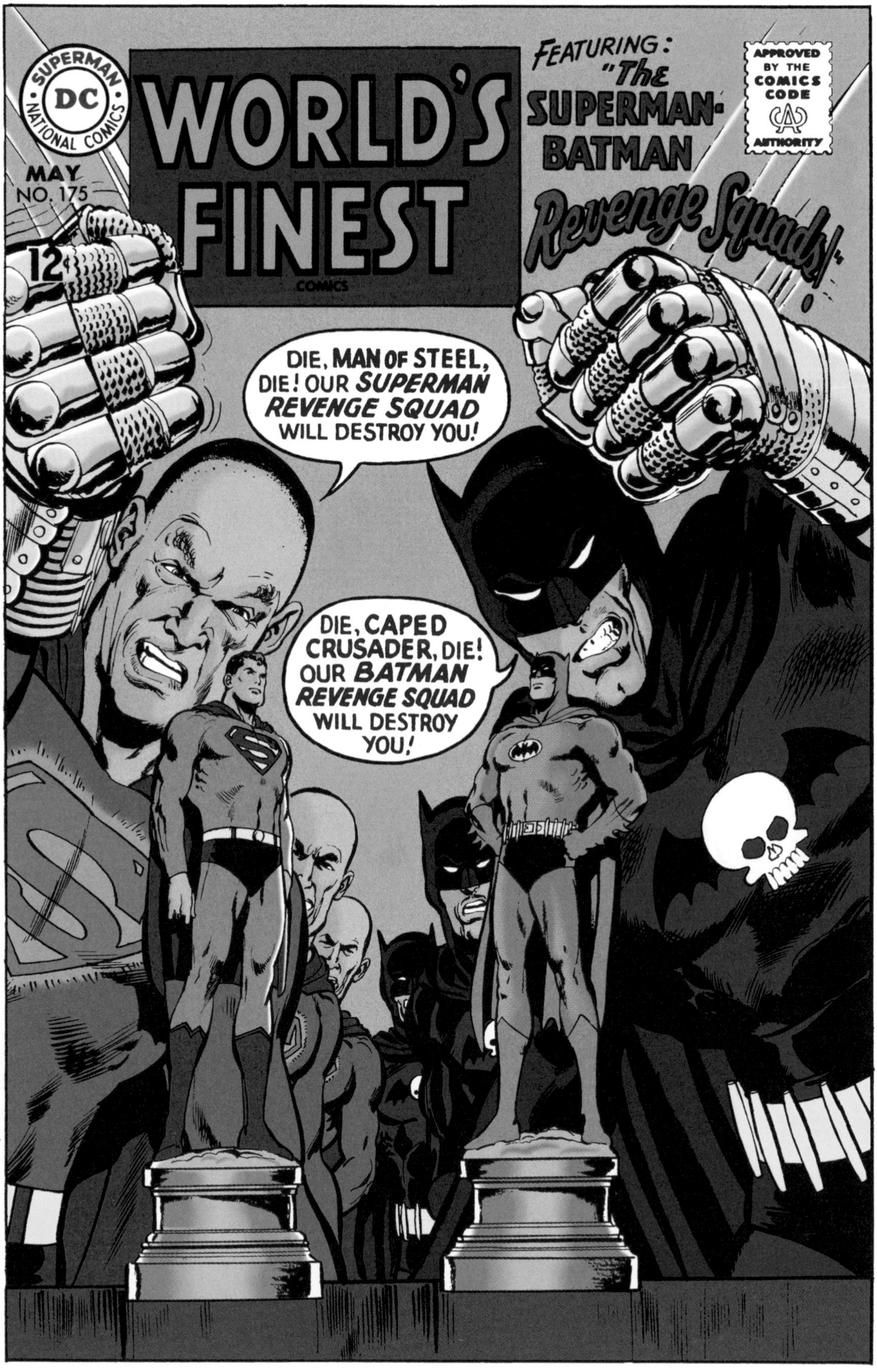
SUPERMAN DC NATIONAL COMICS
MAY NO. 175
12¢
WORLD'S FINEST COMICS
FEATURING: "The SUPERMAN-BATMAN Revenge Squads!"
APPROVED BY THE COMICS CODE AUTHORITY
DIE, MAN OF STEEL, DIE! OUR SUPERMAN REVENGE SQUAD WILL DESTROY YOU!
DIE, CAPED CRUSADER, DIE! OUR BATMAN REVENGE SQUAD WILL DESTROY YOU!

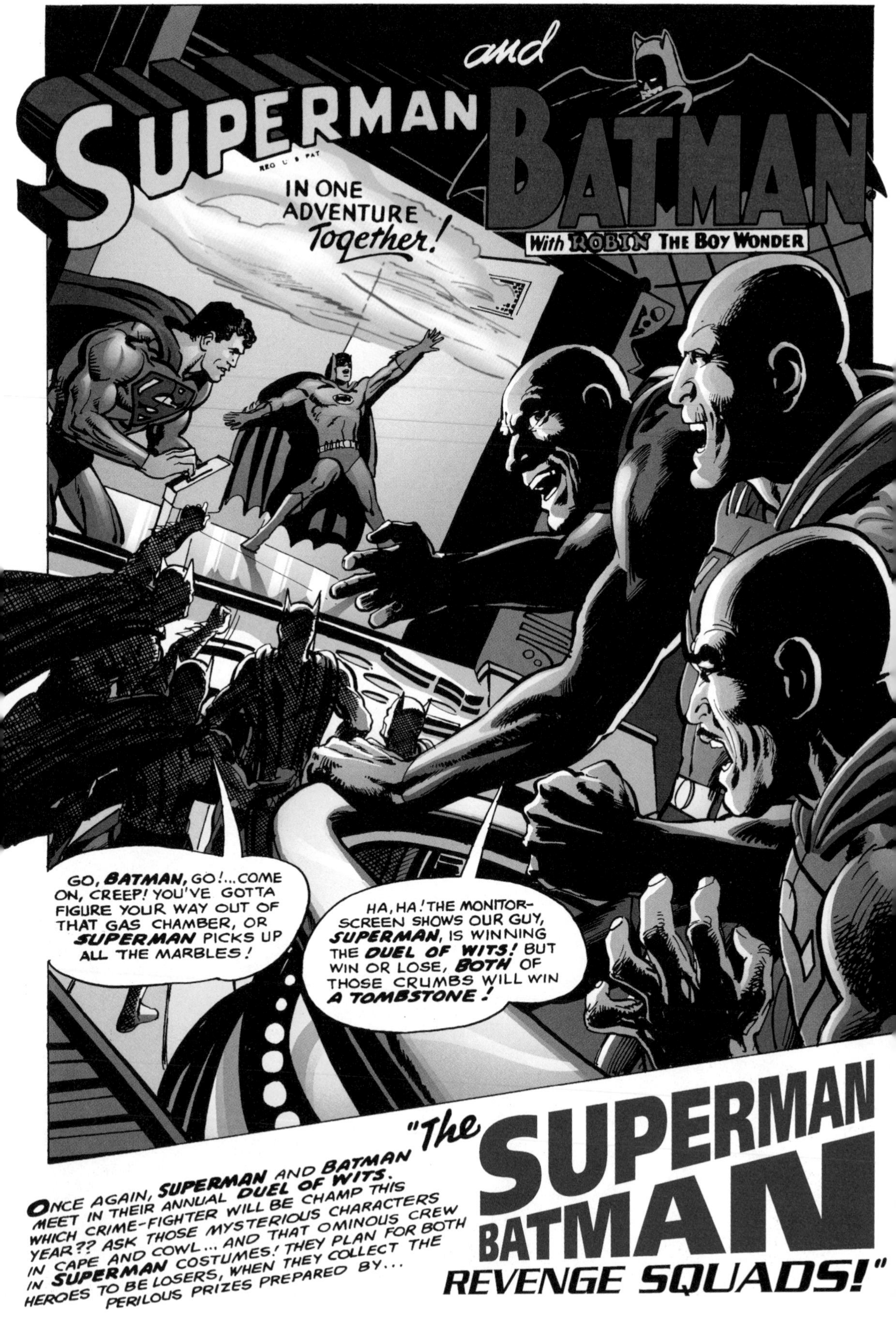

SUPERMAN and BATMAN
REG U.S. PAT
IN ONE ADVENTURE Together!
With ROBIN THE BOY WONDER
GO, BATMAN, GO!...COME ON, CREEP! YOU'VE GOTTA FIGURE YOUR WAY OUT OF THAT GAS CHAMBER, OR SUPERMAN PICKS UP ALL THE MARBLES!
HA, HA! THE MONITOR-SCREEN SHOWS OUR GUY, SUPERMAN, IS WINNING THE DUEL OF WITS! BUT WIN OR LOSE, BOTH OF THOSE CRUMBS WILL WIN A TOMBSTONE!
ONCE AGAIN, SUPERMAN AND BATMAN MEET IN THEIR ANNUAL DUEL OF WITS. WHICH CRIME-FIGHTER WILL BE CHAMP THIS YEAR?? ASK THOSE MYSTERIOUS CHARACTERS IN CAPE AND COWL... AND THAT OMINOUS CREW IN SUPERMAN COSTUMES! THEY PLAN FOR BOTH HEROES TO BE LOSERS, WHEN THEY COLLECT THE PERILOUS PRIZES PREPARED BY...
"The SUPERMAN BATMAN REVENGE SQUADS!"

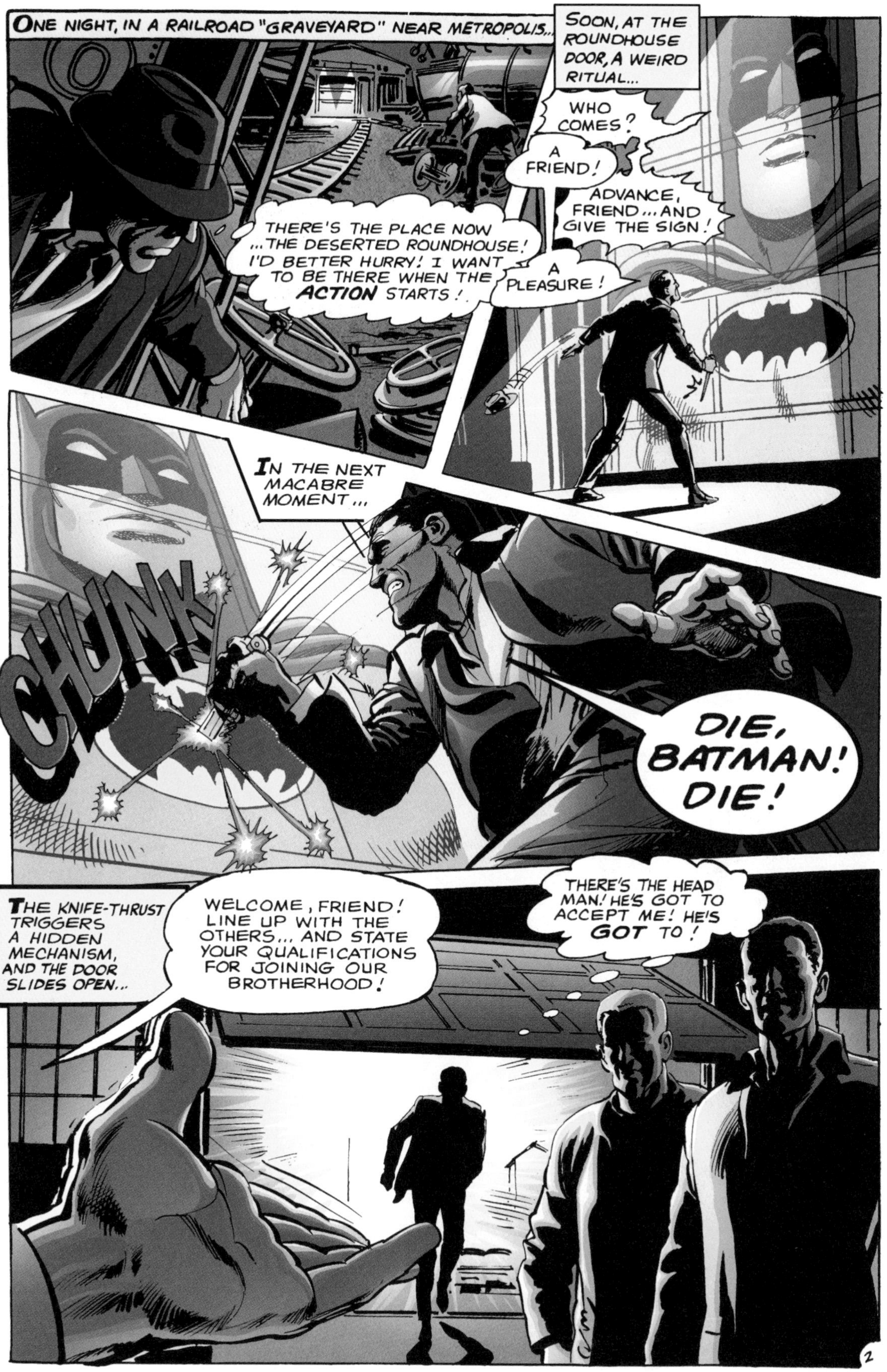
ONE NIGHT, IN A RAILROAD "GRAVEYARD" NEAR METROPOLIS...
THERE'S THE PLACE NOW ...THE DESERTED ROUNDHOUSE! I'D BETTER HURRY! I WANT TO BE THERE WHEN THE ACTION STARTS!
SOON, AT THE ROUNDHOUSE DOOR, A WEIRD RITUAL...
WHO COMES?
A FRIEND!
ADVANCE, FRIEND... AND GIVE THE SIGN!
A PLEASURE!
IN THE NEXT MACABRE MOMENT...
CHUNK
DIE, BATMAN! DIE!
THE KNIFE-THRUST TRIGGERS A HIDDEN MECHANISM, AND THE DOOR SLIDES OPEN...
WELCOME, FRIEND! LINE UP WITH THE OTHERS... AND STATE YOUR QUALIFICATIONS FOR JOINING OUR BROTHERHOOD!
THERE'S THE HEAD MAN! HE'S GOT TO ACCEPT ME! HE'S GOT TO!
2

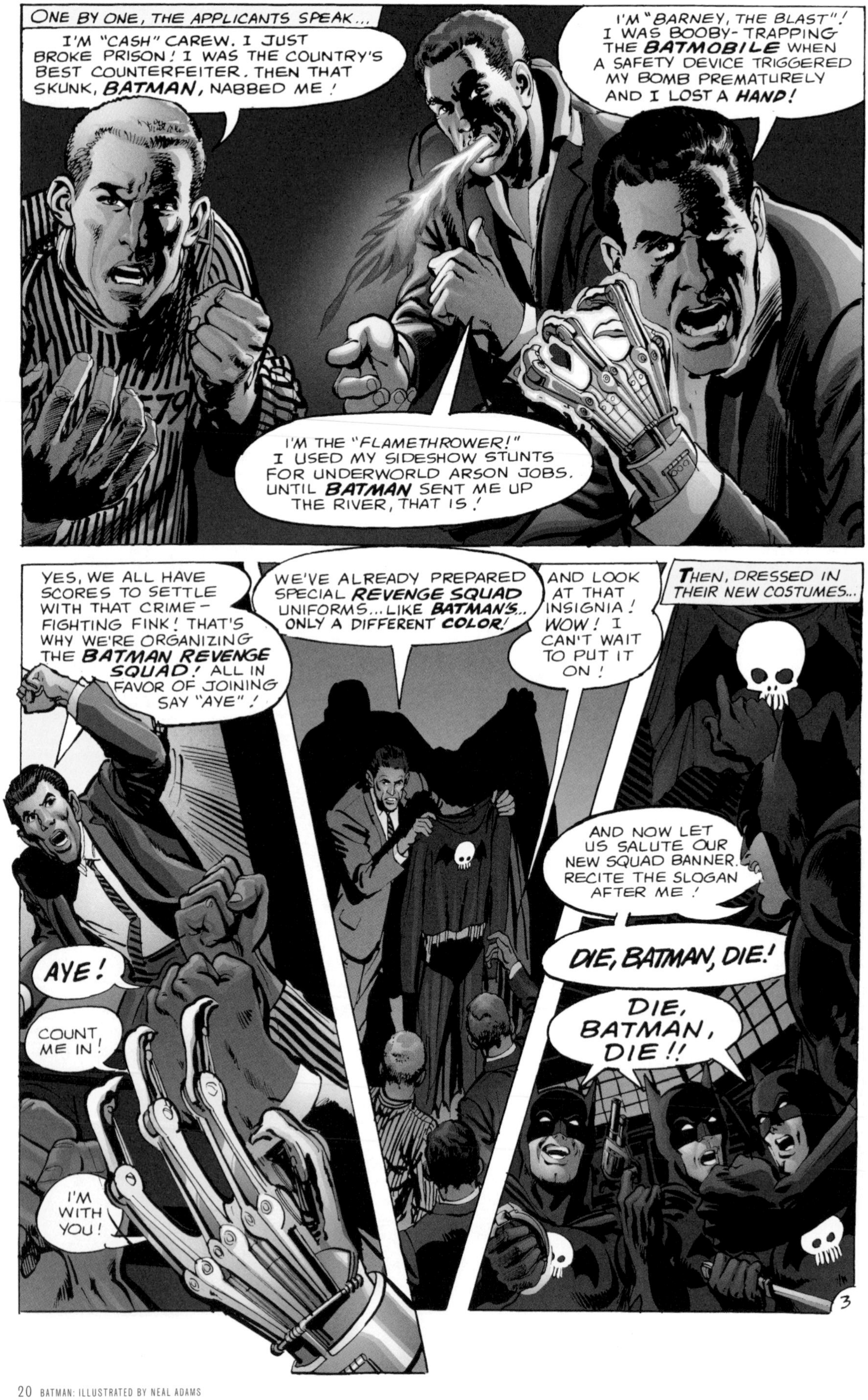
ONE BY ONE, THE APPLICANTS SPEAK...
I'M "CASH" CAREW. I JUST BROKE PRISON! I WAS THE COUNTRY'S BEST COUNTERFEITER. THEN THAT SKUNK, BATMAN, NABBED ME!
I'M "BARNEY, THE BLAST"! I WAS BOOBY-TRAPPING THE BATMOBILE WHEN A SAFETY DEVICE TRIGGERED MY BOMB PREMATURELY AND I LOST A HAND!
I'M THE "FLAMETHROWER!" I USED MY SIDESHOW STUNTS FOR UNDERWORLD ARSON JOBS, UNTIL BATMAN SENT ME UP THE RIVER, THAT IS!
YES, WE ALL HAVE SCORES TO SETTLE WITH THAT CRIME-FIGHTING FINK! THAT'S WHY WE'RE ORGANIZING THE BATMAN REVENGE SQUAD! ALL IN FAVOR OF JOINING SAY "AYE"!
AYE!
COUNT ME IN!
I'M WITH YOU!
WE'VE ALREADY PREPARED SPECIAL REVENGE SQUAD UNIFORMS... LIKE BATMAN'S... ONLY A DIFFERENT COLOR!
AND LOOK AT THAT INSIGNIA! WOW! I CAN'T WAIT TO PUT IT ON!
THEN, DRESSED IN THEIR NEW COSTUMES...
AND NOW LET US SALUTE OUR NEW SQUAD BANNER. RECITE THE SLOGAN AFTER ME!
DIE, BATMAN, DIE!
DIE, BATMAN, DIE!!
3

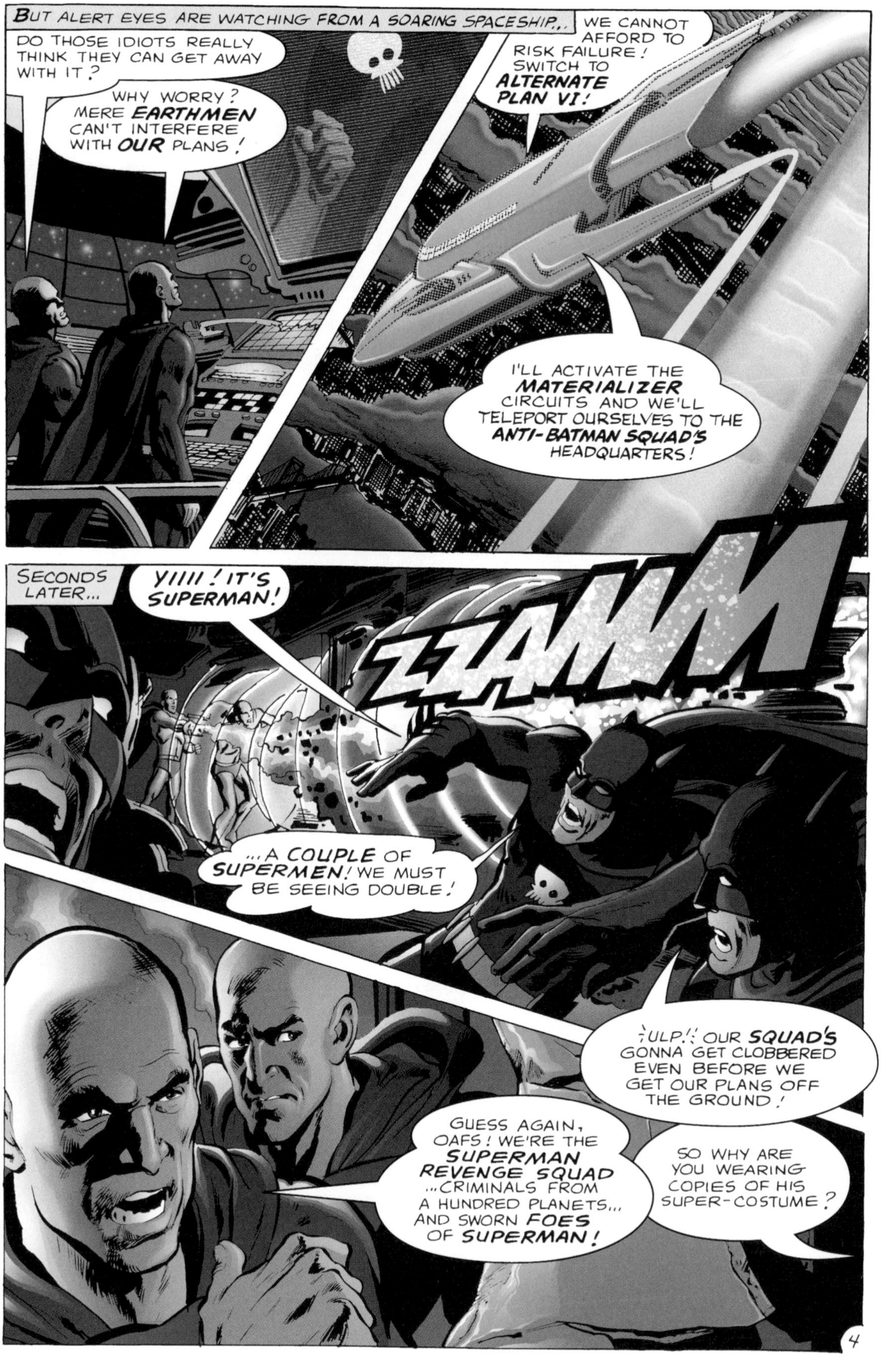

BUT ALERT EYES ARE WATCHING FROM A SOARING SPACESHIP...
DO THOSE IDIOTS REALLY THINK THEY CAN GET AWAY WITH IT?
WHY WORRY? MERE EARTHMEN CAN'T INTERFERE WITH OUR PLANS!
WE CANNOT AFFORD TO RISK FAILURE! SWITCH TO ALTERNATE PLAN VI!
I'LL ACTIVATE THE MATERIALIZER CIRCUITS AND WE'LL TELEPORT OURSELVES TO THE ANTI-BATMAN SQUAD'S HEADQUARTERS!
SECONDS LATER...
YIIII! IT'S SUPERMAN!
ZZAMM
...A COUPLE OF SUPERMEN! WE MUST BE SEEING DOUBLE!
ULP! OUR SQUAD'S GONNA GET CLOBBERED EVEN BEFORE WE GET OUR PLANS OFF THE GROUND!
GUESS AGAIN, OAFS! WE'RE THE SUPERMAN REVENGE SQUAD ...CRIMINALS FROM A HUNDRED PLANETS... AND SWORN FOES OF SUPERMAN!
SO WHY ARE YOU WEARING COPIES OF HIS SUPER-COSTUME?
4

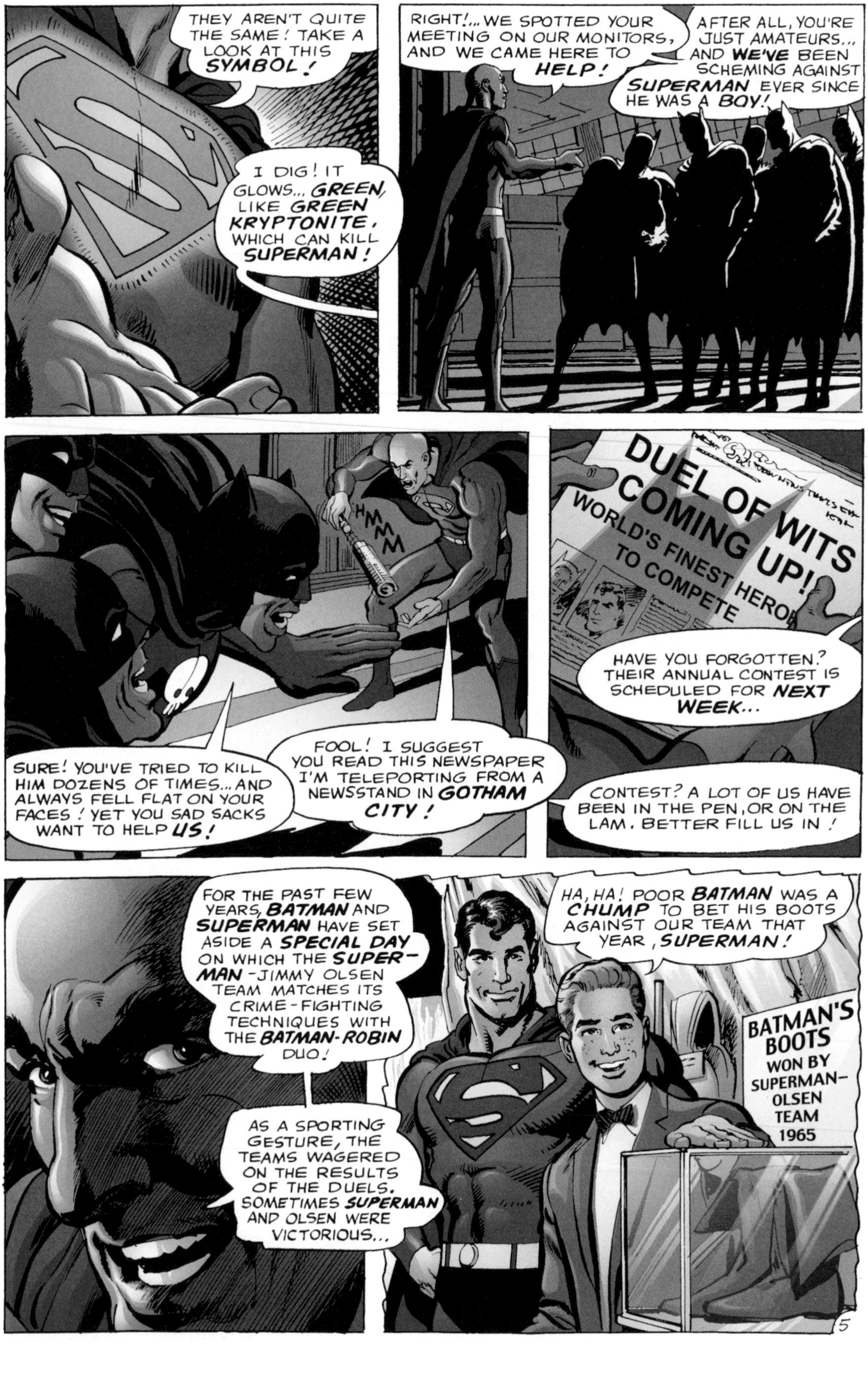
THEY AREN'T QUITE THE SAME! TAKE A LOOK AT THIS SYMBOL!
I DIG! IT GLOWS... GREEN, LIKE GREEN KRYPTONITE, WHICH CAN KILL SUPERMAN!
RIGHT!... WE SPOTTED YOUR MEETING ON OUR MONITORS, AND WE CAME HERE TO HELP!
AFTER ALL, YOU'RE JUST AMATEURS... AND WE'VE BEEN SCHEMING AGAINST SUPERMAN EVER SINCE HE WAS A BOY!
HMMM
SURE! YOU'VE TRIED TO KILL HIM DOZENS OF TIMES... AND ALWAYS FELL FLAT ON YOUR FACES! YET YOU SAD SACKS WANT TO HELP US!
FOOL! I SUGGEST YOU READ THIS NEWSPAPER I'M TELEPORTING FROM A NEWSSTAND IN GOTHAM CITY!
DUEL OF WITS COMING UP!
WORLD'S FINEST HERO
TO COMPETE
HAVE YOU FORGOTTEN? THEIR ANNUAL CONTEST IS SCHEDULED FOR NEXT WEEK...
CONTEST? A LOT OF US HAVE BEEN IN THE PEN, OR ON THE LAM. BETTER FILL US IN!
FOR THE PAST FEW YEARS, BATMAN AND SUPERMAN HAVE SET ASIDE A SPECIAL DAY ON WHICH THE SUPERMAN-JIMMY OLSEN TEAM MATCHES ITS CRIME-FIGHTING TECHNIQUES WITH THE BATMAN-ROBIN DUO!
AS A SPORTING GESTURE, THE TEAMS WAGERED ON THE RESULTS OF THE DUELS. SOMETIMES SUPERMAN AND OLSEN WERE VICTORIOUS...
HA, HA! POOR BATMAN WAS A CHUMP TO BET HIS BOOTS AGAINST OUR TEAM THAT YEAR, SUPERMAN!
BATMAN'S BOOTS WON BY SUPERMAN-OLSEN TEAM 1965
5

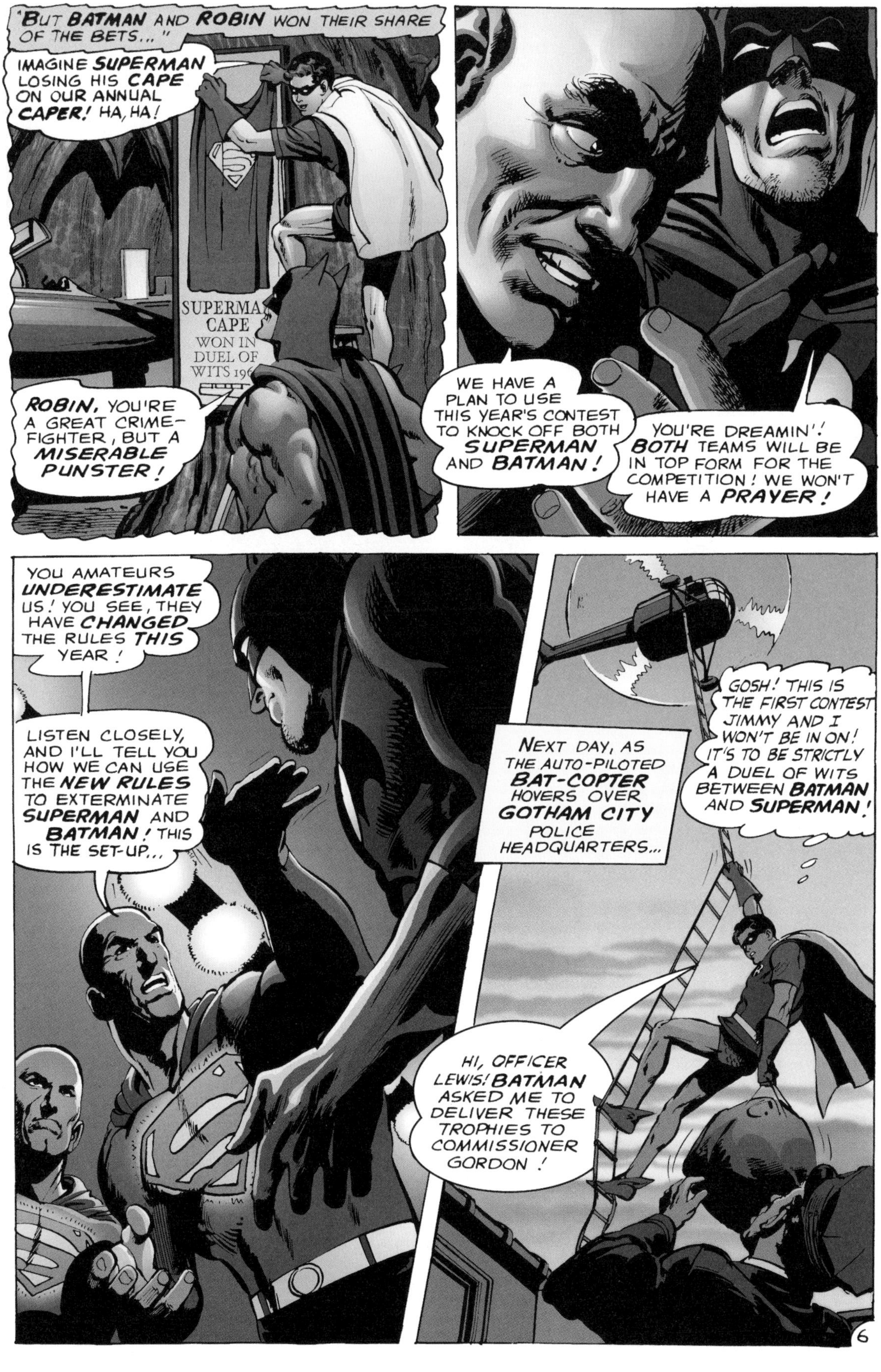

"BUT BATMAN AND ROBIN WON THEIR SHARE OF THE BETS..."
IMAGINE SUPERMAN LOSING HIS CAPE ON OUR ANNUAL CAPER! HA, HA!
SUPERMA CAPE WON IN DUEL OF WITS 196
ROBIN, YOU'RE A GREAT CRIME-FIGHTER, BUT A MISERABLE PUNSTER!
WE HAVE A PLAN TO USE THIS YEAR'S CONTEST TO KNOCK OFF BOTH SUPERMAN AND BATMAN!
YOU'RE DREAMIN'! BOTH TEAMS WILL BE IN TOP FORM FOR THE COMPETITION! WE WON'T HAVE A PRAYER!
YOU AMATEURS UNDERESTIMATE US! YOU SEE, THEY HAVE CHANGED THE RULES THIS YEAR!
LISTEN CLOSELY, AND I'LL TELL YOU HOW WE CAN USE THE NEW RULES TO EXTERMINATE SUPERMAN AND BATMAN! THIS IS THE SET-UP...
NEXT DAY, AS THE AUTO-PILOTED BAT-COPTER HOVERS OVER GOTHAM CITY POLICE HEADQUARTERS...
GOSH! THIS IS THE FIRST CONTEST JIMMY AND I WON'T BE IN ON! IT'S TO BE STRICTLY A DUEL OF WITS BETWEEN BATMAN AND SUPERMAN!
HI, OFFICER LEWIS! BATMAN ASKED ME TO DELIVER THESE TROPHIES TO COMMISSIONER GORDON!
6

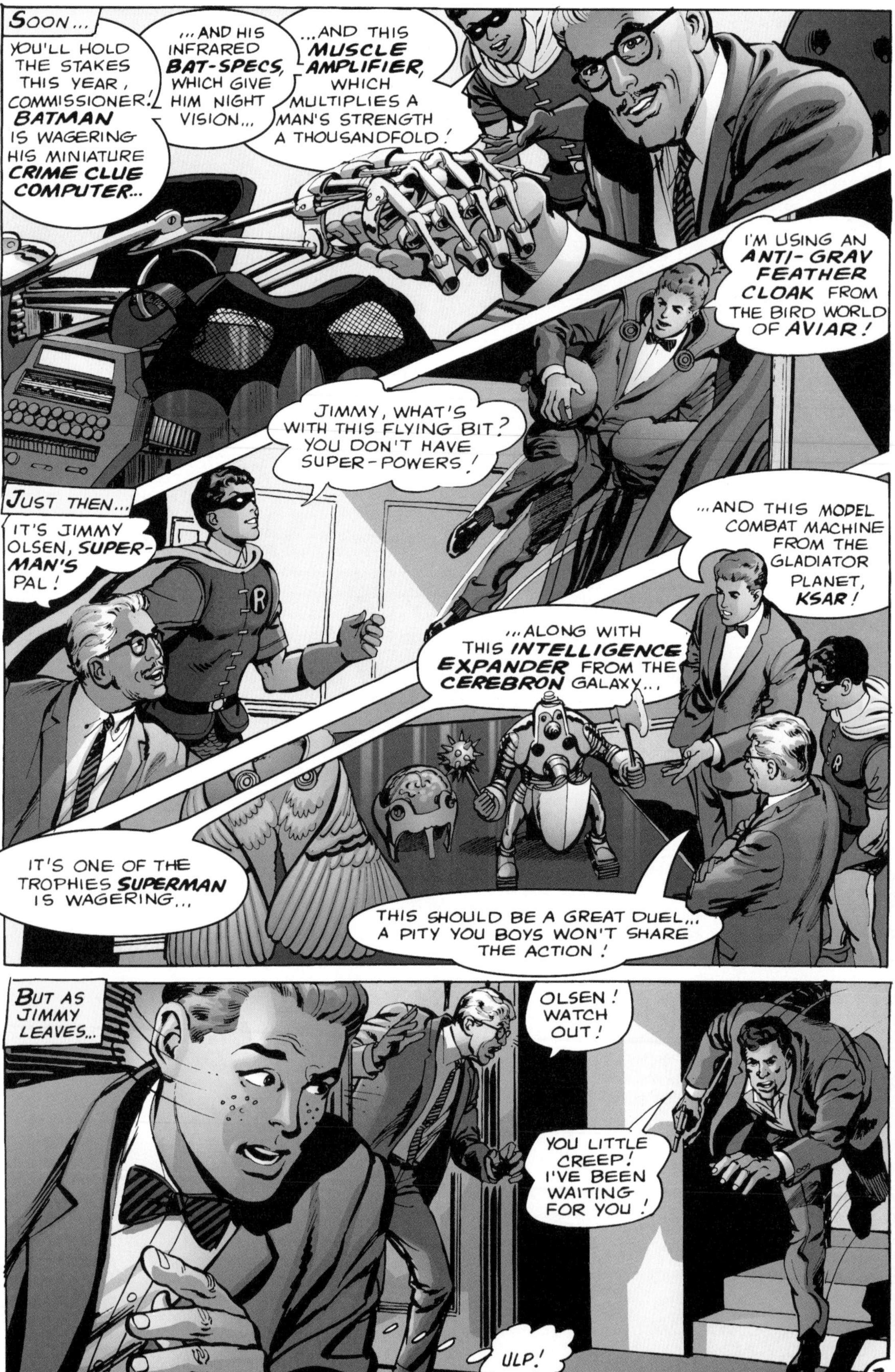
SOON...
YOU'LL HOLD THE STAKES THIS YEAR, COMMISSIONER! BATMAN IS WAGERING HIS MINIATURE CRIME CLUE COMPUTER...
...AND HIS INFRARED BAT-SPECS, WHICH GIVE HIM NIGHT VISION...
...AND THIS MUSCLE AMPLIFIER, WHICH MULTIPLIES A MAN'S STRENGTH A THOUSANDFOLD!
I'M USING AN ANTI-GRAV FEATHER CLOAK FROM THE BIRD WORLD OF AVIAR!
JIMMY, WHAT'S WITH THIS FLYING BIT? YOU DON'T HAVE SUPER-POWERS!
JUST THEN...
IT'S JIMMY OLSEN, SUPERMAN'S PAL!
...AND THIS MODEL COMBAT MACHINE FROM THE GLADIATOR PLANET, KSAR!
...ALONG WITH THIS INTELLIGENCE EXPANDER FROM THE CEREBRON GALAXY...
IT'S ONE OF THE TROPHIES SUPERMAN IS WAGERING...
THIS SHOULD BE A GREAT DUEL... A PITY YOU BOYS WON'T SHARE THE ACTION!
BUT AS JIMMY LEAVES...
OLSEN! WATCH OUT!
YOU LITTLE CREEP! I'VE BEEN WAITING FOR YOU!
ULP!
7

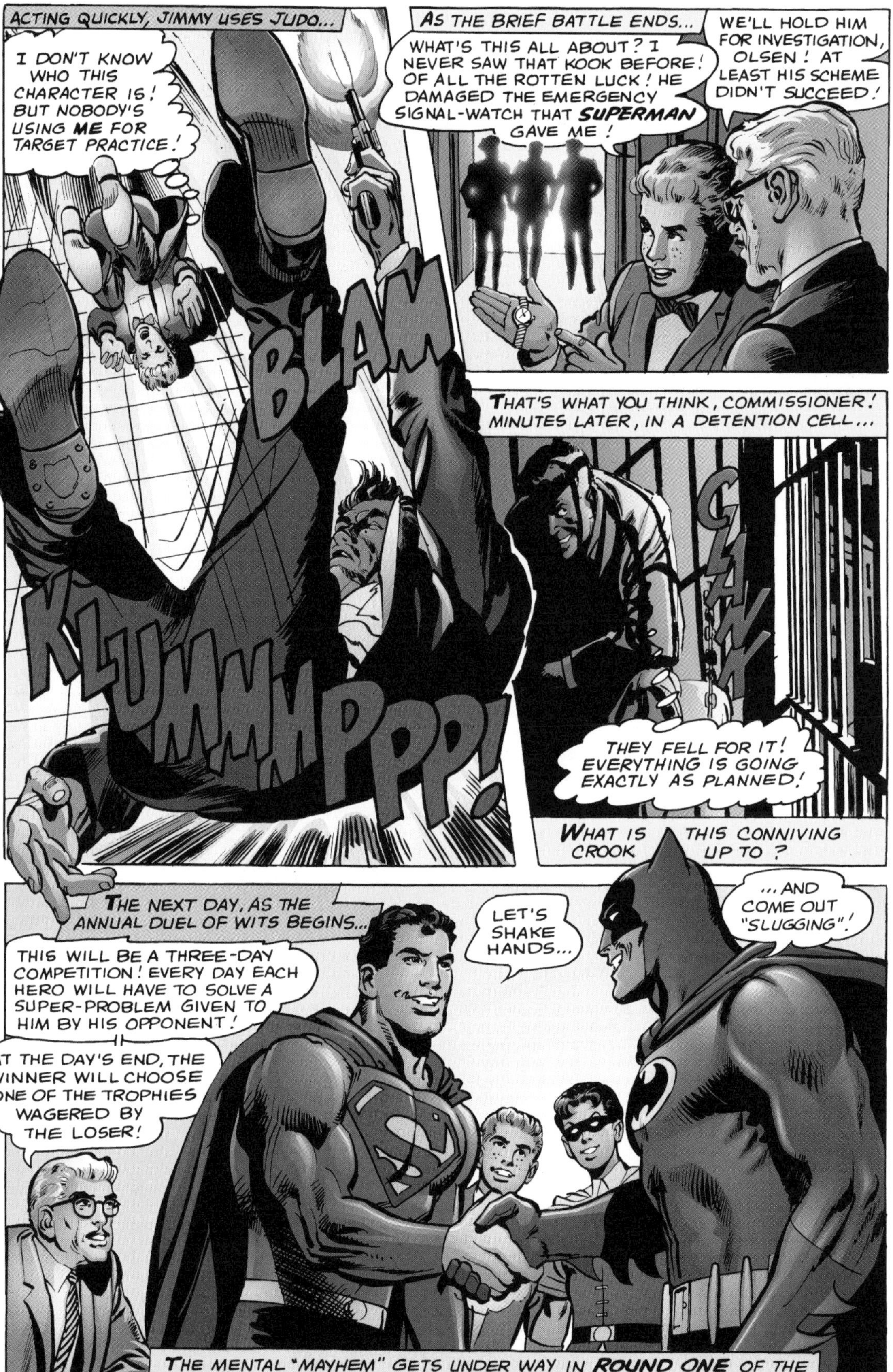
ACTING QUICKLY, JIMMY USES JUDO...
I DON'T KNOW WHO THIS CHARACTER IS! BUT NOBODY'S USING **ME** FOR TARGET PRACTICE!
BLAM
KLUMMMPPP!
AS THE BRIEF BATTLE ENDS...
WHAT'S THIS ALL ABOUT? I NEVER SAW THAT KOOK BEFORE! OF ALL THE ROTTEN LUCK! HE DAMAGED THE EMERGENCY SIGNAL-WATCH THAT **SUPERMAN** GAVE ME!
WE'LL HOLD HIM FOR INVESTIGATION, OLSEN! AT LEAST HIS SCHEME DIDN'T SUCCEED!
THAT'S WHAT YOU THINK, COMMISSIONER! MINUTES LATER, IN A DETENTION CELL...
CLANK
THEY FELL FOR IT! EVERYTHING IS GOING EXACTLY AS PLANNED!
WHAT IS THIS CONNIVING CROOK UP TO?
THE NEXT DAY, AS THE ANNUAL DUEL OF WITS BEGINS...
THIS WILL BE A THREE-DAY COMPETITION! EVERY DAY EACH HERO WILL HAVE TO SOLVE A SUPER-PROBLEM GIVEN TO HIM BY HIS OPPONENT!
AT THE DAY'S END, THE WINNER WILL CHOOSE ONE OF THE TROPHIES WAGERED BY THE LOSER!
LET'S SHAKE HANDS...
...AND COME OUT "SLUGGING"!
THE MENTAL "MAYHEM" GETS UNDER WAY IN **ROUND ONE** OF THE **DUEL OF WITS**, IN **PART II**!
8

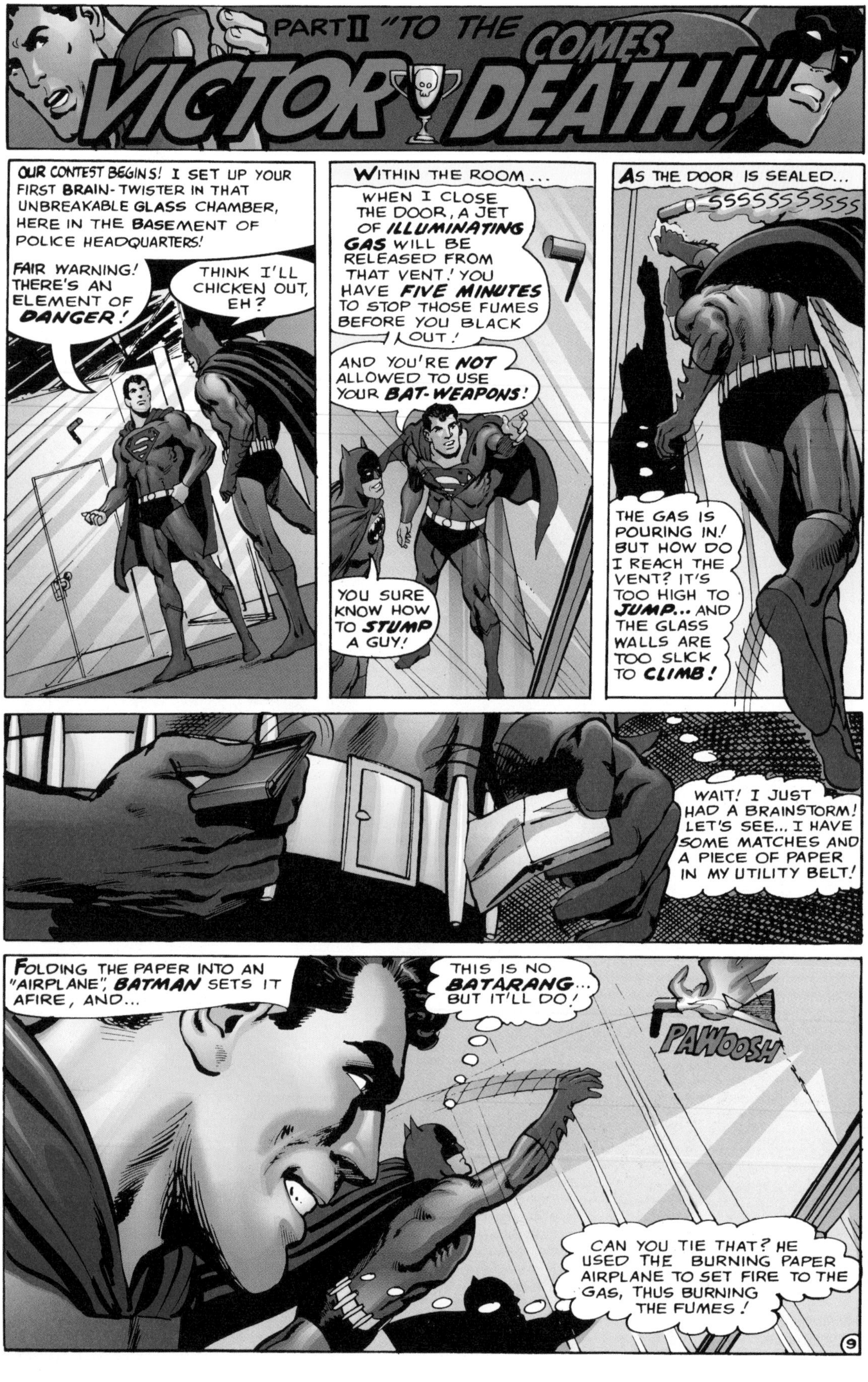
PART II "TO THE VICTOR COMES DEATH!"
OUR CONTEST BEGINS! I SET UP YOUR FIRST BRAIN-TWISTER IN THAT UNBREAKABLE GLASS CHAMBER, HERE IN THE BASEMENT OF POLICE HEADQUARTERS!
FAIR WARNING! THERE'S AN ELEMENT OF DANGER!
THINK I'LL CHICKEN OUT, EH?
WITHIN THE ROOM...
WHEN I CLOSE THE DOOR, A JET OF ILLUMINATING GAS WILL BE RELEASED FROM THAT VENT! YOU HAVE FIVE MINUTES TO STOP THOSE FUMES BEFORE YOU BLACK OUT!
AND YOU'RE NOT ALLOWED TO USE YOUR BAT-WEAPONS!
YOU SURE KNOW HOW TO STUMP A GUY!
AS THE DOOR IS SEALED...
SSSSSSSSSSS
THE GAS IS POURING IN! BUT HOW DO I REACH THE VENT? IT'S TOO HIGH TO JUMP... AND THE GLASS WALLS ARE TOO SLICK TO CLIMB!
WAIT! I JUST HAD A BRAINSTORM! LET'S SEE... I HAVE SOME MATCHES AND A PIECE OF PAPER IN MY UTILITY BELT!
FOLDING THE PAPER INTO AN "AIRPLANE", BATMAN SETS IT AFIRE, AND...
THIS IS NO BATARANG... BUT IT'LL DO!
PAWOOSH
CAN YOU TIE THAT? HE USED THE BURNING PAPER AIRPLANE TO SET FIRE TO THE GAS, THUS BURNING THE FUMES!
9

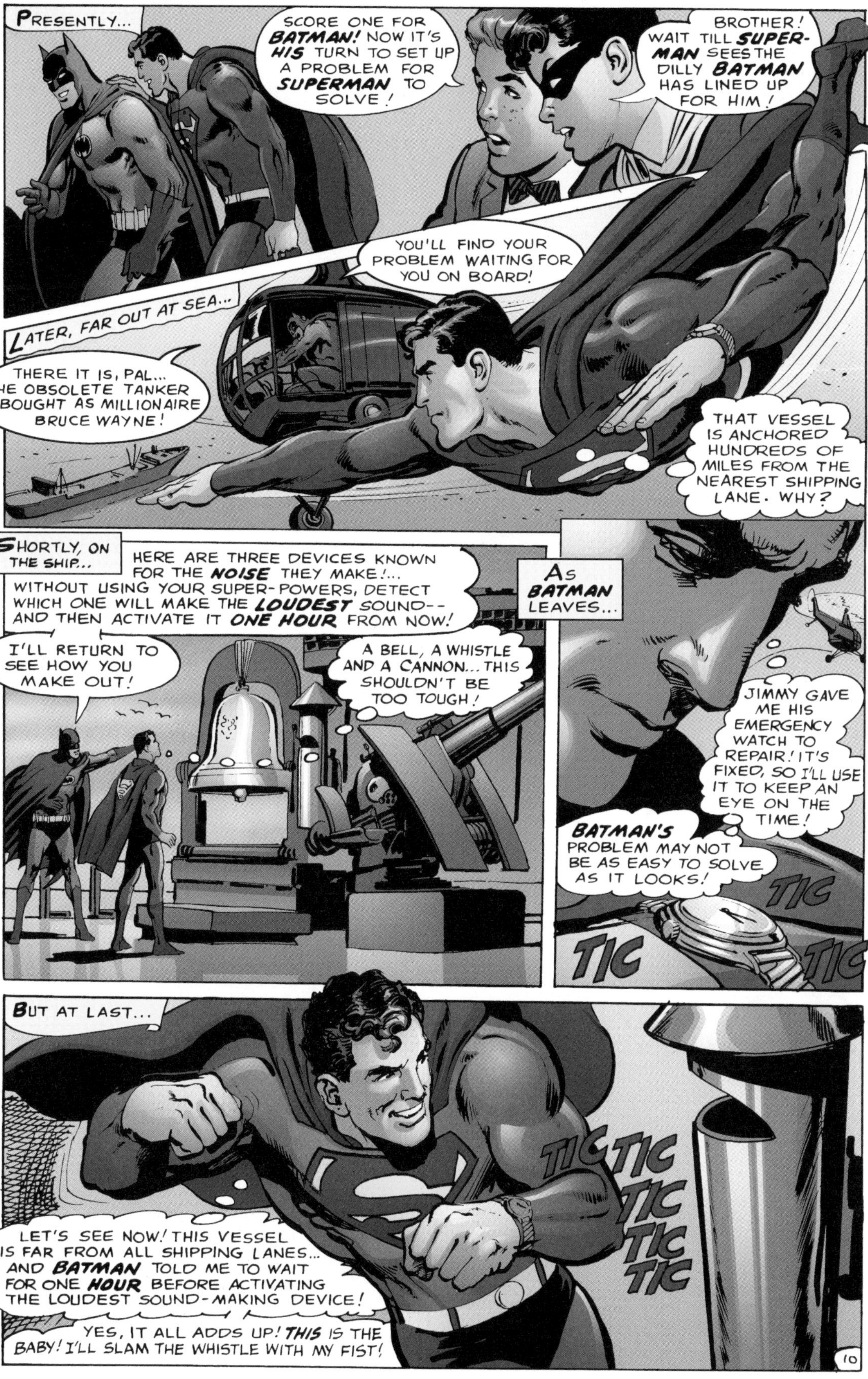
PRESENTLY...
SCORE ONE FOR BATMAN! NOW IT'S HIS TURN TO SET UP A PROBLEM FOR SUPERMAN TO SOLVE!
BROTHER! WAIT TILL SUPERMAN SEES THE DILLY BATMAN HAS LINED UP FOR HIM!
YOU'LL FIND YOUR PROBLEM WAITING FOR YOU ON BOARD!
LATER, FAR OUT AT SEA...
THERE IT IS, PAL... THE OBSOLETE TANKER I BOUGHT AS MILLIONAIRE BRUCE WAYNE!
THAT VESSEL IS ANCHORED HUNDREDS OF MILES FROM THE NEAREST SHIPPING LANE. WHY?
SHORTLY, ON THE SHIP...
HERE ARE THREE DEVICES KNOWN FOR THE NOISE THEY MAKE!... WITHOUT USING YOUR SUPER-POWERS, DETECT WHICH ONE WILL MAKE THE LOUDEST SOUND-- AND THEN ACTIVATE IT ONE HOUR FROM NOW!
I'LL RETURN TO SEE HOW YOU MAKE OUT!
A BELL, A WHISTLE AND A CANNON... THIS SHOULDN'T BE TOO TOUGH!
AS BATMAN LEAVES...
JIMMY GAVE ME HIS EMERGENCY WATCH TO REPAIR! IT'S FIXED, SO I'LL USE IT TO KEEP AN EYE ON THE TIME!
BATMAN'S PROBLEM MAY NOT BE AS EASY TO SOLVE AS IT LOOKS!
TIC
TIC
TIC
BUT AT LAST...
TIC TIC TIC TIC TIC TIC
LET'S SEE NOW! THIS VESSEL IS FAR FROM ALL SHIPPING LANES... AND BATMAN TOLD ME TO WAIT FOR ONE HOUR BEFORE ACTIVATING THE LOUDEST SOUND-MAKING DEVICE!
YES, IT ALL ADDS UP! THIS IS THE BABY! I'LL SLAM THE WHISTLE WITH MY FIST!
10

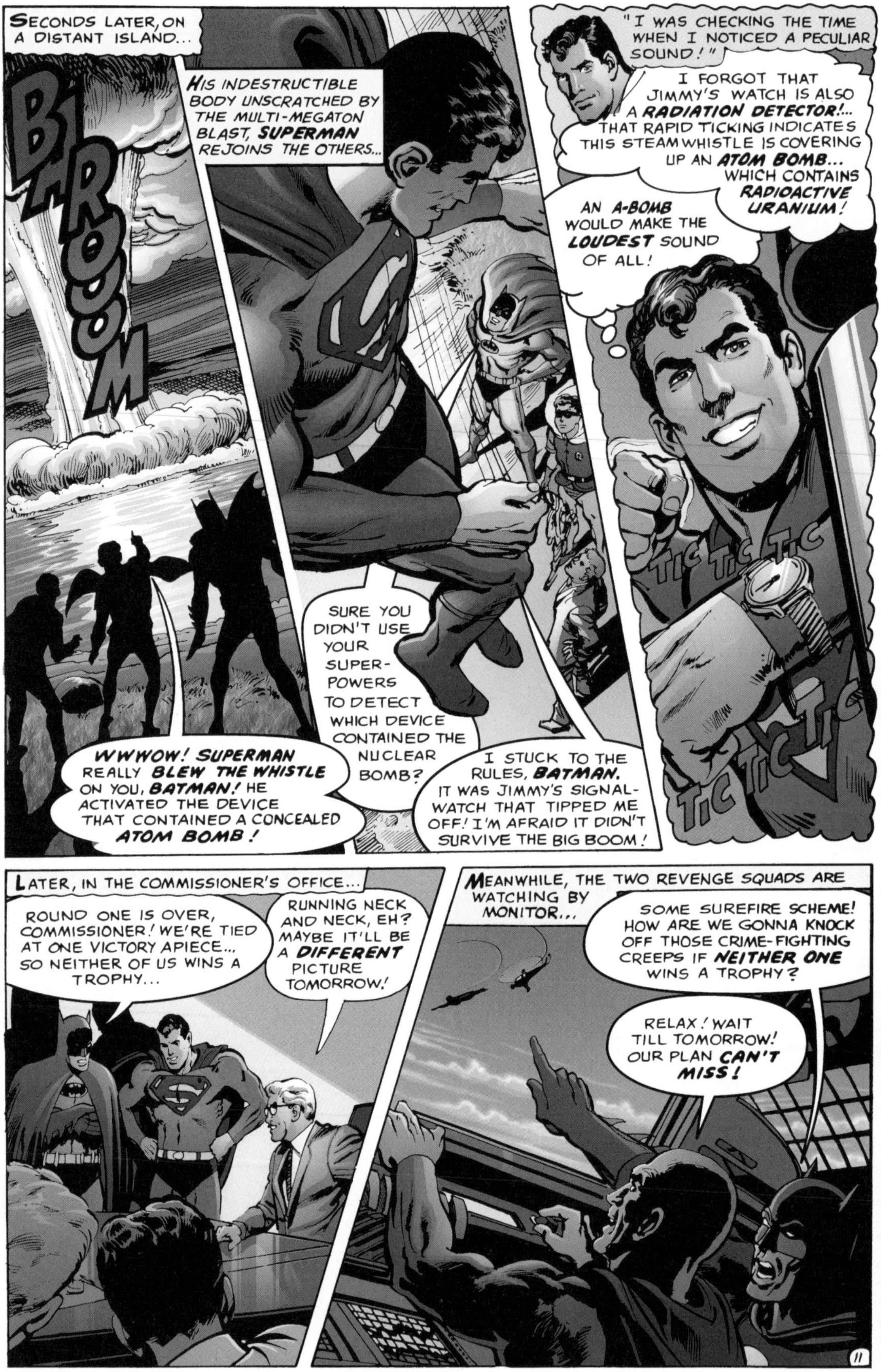

SECONDS LATER, ON A DISTANT ISLAND...
BAROOOM
HIS INDESTRUCTIBLE BODY UNSCRATCHED BY THE MULTI-MEGATON BLAST, SUPERMAN REJOINS THE OTHERS...
WWWOW! SUPERMAN REALLY BLEW THE WHISTLE ON YOU, BATMAN! HE ACTIVATED THE DEVICE THAT CONTAINED A CONCEALED ATOM BOMB!
SURE YOU DIDN'T USE YOUR SUPER-POWERS TO DETECT WHICH DEVICE CONTAINED THE NUCLEAR BOMB?
I STUCK TO THE RULES, BATMAN. IT WAS JIMMY'S SIGNAL-WATCH THAT TIPPED ME OFF! I'M AFRAID IT DIDN'T SURVIVE THE BIG BOOM!
"I WAS CHECKING THE TIME WHEN I NOTICED A PECULIAR SOUND!"
I FORGOT THAT JIMMY'S WATCH IS ALSO A RADIATION DETECTOR!... THAT RAPID TICKING INDICATES THIS STEAM WHISTLE IS COVERING UP AN ATOM BOMB... WHICH CONTAINS RADIOACTIVE URANIUM!
AN A-BOMB WOULD MAKE THE LOUDEST SOUND OF ALL!
TIC TIC TIC
TIC TIC TIC
LATER, IN THE COMMISSIONER'S OFFICE...
ROUND ONE IS OVER, COMMISSIONER! WE'RE TIED AT ONE VICTORY APIECE... SO NEITHER OF US WINS A TROPHY...
RUNNING NECK AND NECK, EH? MAYBE IT'LL BE A DIFFERENT PICTURE TOMORROW!
MEANWHILE, THE TWO REVENGE SQUADS ARE WATCHING BY MONITOR...
SOME SUREFIRE SCHEME! HOW ARE WE GONNA KNOCK OFF THOSE CRIME-FIGHTING CREEPS IF NEITHER ONE WINS A TROPHY?
RELAX! WAIT TILL TOMORROW! OUR PLAN CAN'T MISS!
11

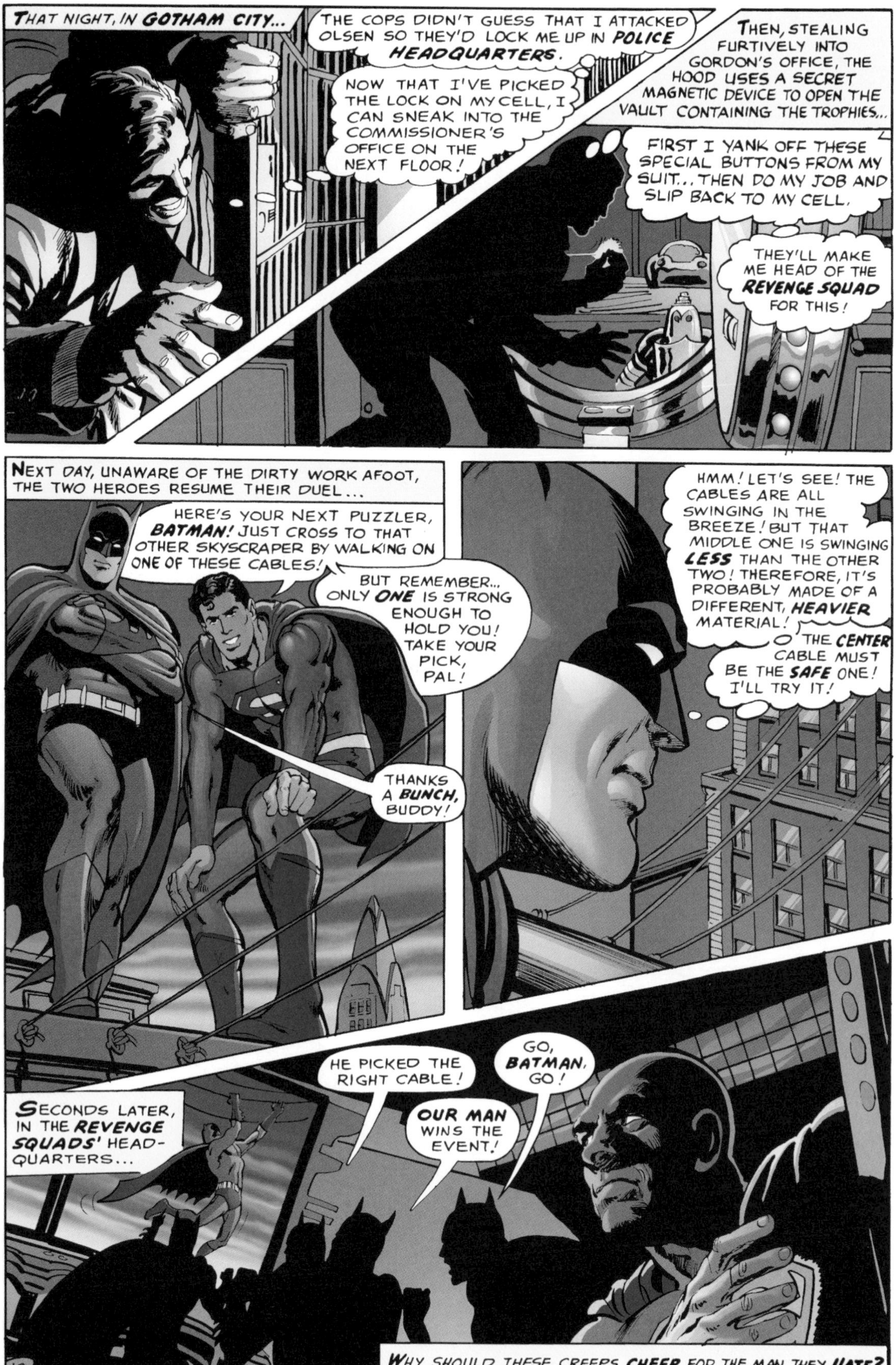
THAT NIGHT, IN GOTHAM CITY...
THE COPS DIDN'T GUESS THAT I ATTACKED OLSEN SO THEY'D LOCK ME UP IN POLICE HEADQUARTERS.
NOW THAT I'VE PICKED THE LOCK ON MY CELL, I CAN SNEAK INTO THE COMMISSIONER'S OFFICE ON THE NEXT FLOOR!
THEN, STEALING FURTIVELY INTO GORDON'S OFFICE, THE HOOD USES A SECRET MAGNETIC DEVICE TO OPEN THE VAULT CONTAINING THE TROPHIES...
FIRST I YANK OFF THESE SPECIAL BUTTONS FROM MY SUIT... THEN DO MY JOB AND SLIP BACK TO MY CELL.
THEY'LL MAKE ME HEAD OF THE REVENGE SQUAD FOR THIS!
NEXT DAY, UNAWARE OF THE DIRTY WORK AFOOT, THE TWO HEROES RESUME THEIR DUEL...
HERE'S YOUR NEXT PUZZLER, BATMAN! JUST CROSS TO THAT OTHER SKYSCRAPER BY WALKING ON ONE OF THESE CABLES!
BUT REMEMBER... ONLY ONE IS STRONG ENOUGH TO HOLD YOU! TAKE YOUR PICK, PAL!
THANKS A BUNCH, BUDDY!
HMM! LET'S SEE! THE CABLES ARE ALL SWINGING IN THE BREEZE! BUT THAT MIDDLE ONE IS SWINGING LESS THAN THE OTHER TWO! THEREFORE, IT'S PROBABLY MADE OF A DIFFERENT, HEAVIER MATERIAL!
THE CENTER CABLE MUST BE THE SAFE ONE! I'LL TRY IT!
SECONDS LATER, IN THE REVENGE SQUADS' HEAD-QUARTERS...
HE PICKED THE RIGHT CABLE!
GO, BATMAN, GO!
OUR MAN WINS THE EVENT!
12
WHY SHOULD THESE CREEPS CHEER FOR THE MAN THEY HATE?

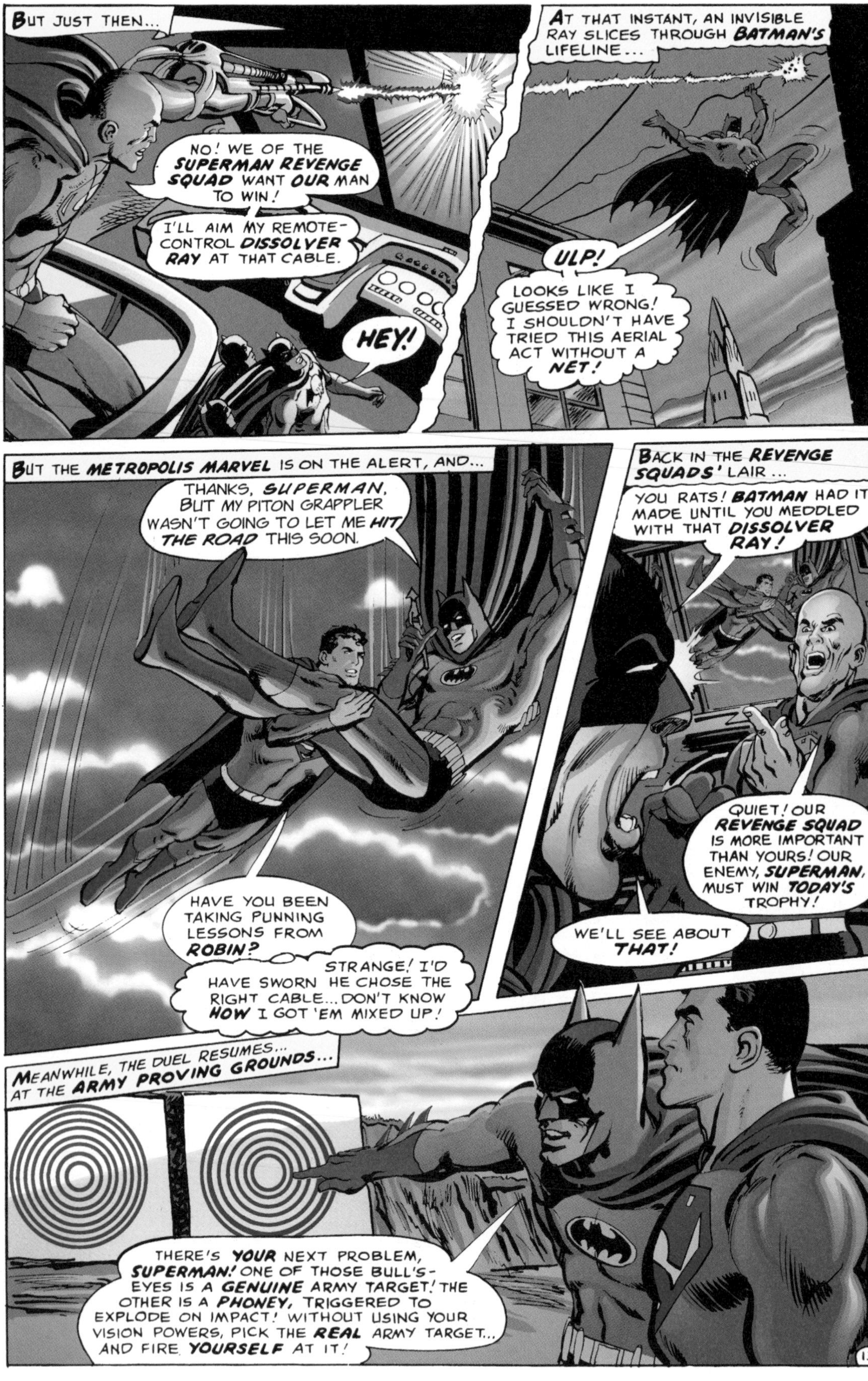

BUT JUST THEN...
NO! WE OF THE SUPERMAN REVENGE SQUAD WANT OUR MAN TO WIN!
I'LL AIM MY REMOTE-CONTROL DISSOLVER RAY AT THAT CABLE.
HEY!
AT THAT INSTANT, AN INVISIBLE RAY SLICES THROUGH BATMAN'S LIFELINE...
ULP!
LOOKS LIKE I GUESSED WRONG! I SHOULDN'T HAVE TRIED THIS AERIAL ACT WITHOUT A NET!
BUT THE METROPOLIS MARVEL IS ON THE ALERT, AND...
THANKS, SUPERMAN, BUT MY PITON GRAPPLER WASN'T GOING TO LET ME HIT THE ROAD THIS SOON.
HAVE YOU BEEN TAKING PUNNING LESSONS FROM ROBIN?
STRANGE! I'D HAVE SWORN HE CHOSE THE RIGHT CABLE... DON'T KNOW HOW I GOT 'EM MIXED UP!
BACK IN THE REVENGE SQUADS' LAIR...
YOU RATS! BATMAN HAD IT MADE UNTIL YOU MEDDLED WITH THAT DISSOLVER RAY!
QUIET! OUR REVENGE SQUAD IS MORE IMPORTANT THAN YOURS! OUR ENEMY, SUPERMAN, MUST WIN TODAY'S TROPHY!
WE'LL SEE ABOUT THAT!
MEANWHILE, THE DUEL RESUMES... AT THE ARMY PROVING GROUNDS...
THERE'S YOUR NEXT PROBLEM, SUPERMAN! ONE OF THOSE BULL'S-EYES IS A GENUINE ARMY TARGET! THE OTHER IS A PHONEY, TRIGGERED TO EXPLODE ON IMPACT! WITHOUT USING YOUR VISION POWERS, PICK THE REAL ARMY TARGET... AND FIRE YOURSELF AT IT!
13

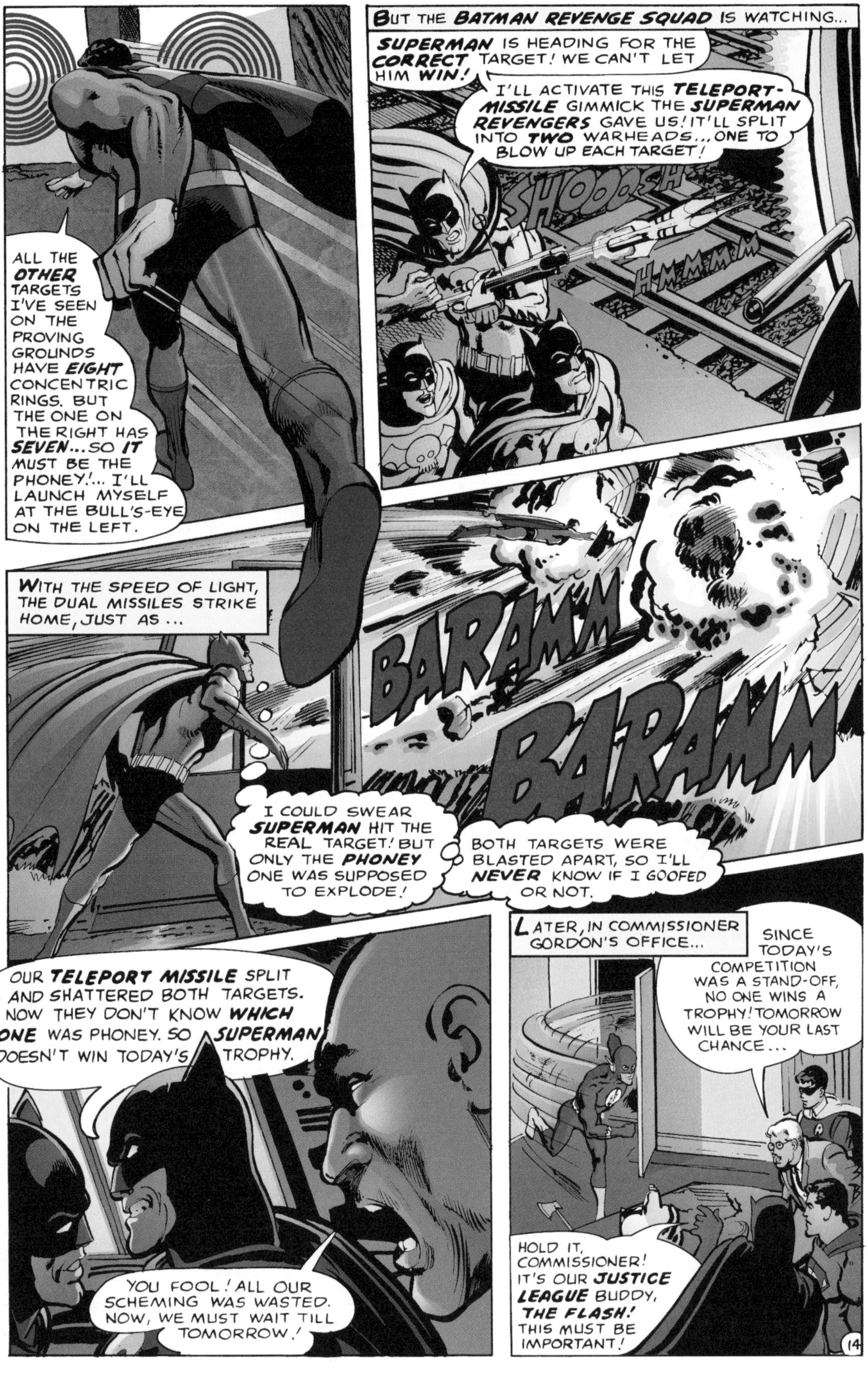
ALL THE OTHER TARGETS I'VE SEEN ON THE PROVING GROUNDS HAVE EIGHT CONCENTRIC RINGS. BUT THE ONE ON THE RIGHT HAS SEVEN... SO IT MUST BE THE PHONEY!... I'LL LAUNCH MYSELF AT THE BULL'S-EYE ON THE LEFT.
BUT THE BATMAN REVENGE SQUAD IS WATCHING...
SUPERMAN IS HEADING FOR THE CORRECT TARGET! WE CAN'T LET HIM WIN!
I'LL ACTIVATE THIS TELEPORT-MISSILE GIMMICK THE SUPERMAN REVENGERS GAVE US! IT'LL SPLIT INTO TWO WARHEADS... ONE TO BLOW UP EACH TARGET!
SHOOOSH
HMMMMM
WITH THE SPEED OF LIGHT, THE DUAL MISSILES STRIKE HOME, JUST AS...
BARAMM
BARAMM
I COULD SWEAR SUPERMAN HIT THE REAL TARGET! BUT ONLY THE PHONEY ONE WAS SUPPOSED TO EXPLODE!
BOTH TARGETS WERE BLASTED APART, SO I'LL NEVER KNOW IF I GOOFED OR NOT.
OUR TELEPORT MISSILE SPLIT AND SHATTERED BOTH TARGETS. NOW THEY DON'T KNOW WHICH ONE WAS PHONEY. SO SUPERMAN DOESN'T WIN TODAY'S TROPHY.
YOU FOOL! ALL OUR SCHEMING WAS WASTED. NOW, WE MUST WAIT TILL TOMORROW!
LATER, IN COMMISSIONER GORDON'S OFFICE...
SINCE TODAY'S COMPETITION WAS A STAND-OFF, NO ONE WINS A TROPHY! TOMORROW WILL BE YOUR LAST CHANCE...
HOLD IT, COMMISSIONER! IT'S OUR JUSTICE LEAGUE BUDDY, THE FLASH! THIS MUST BE IMPORTANT!
14

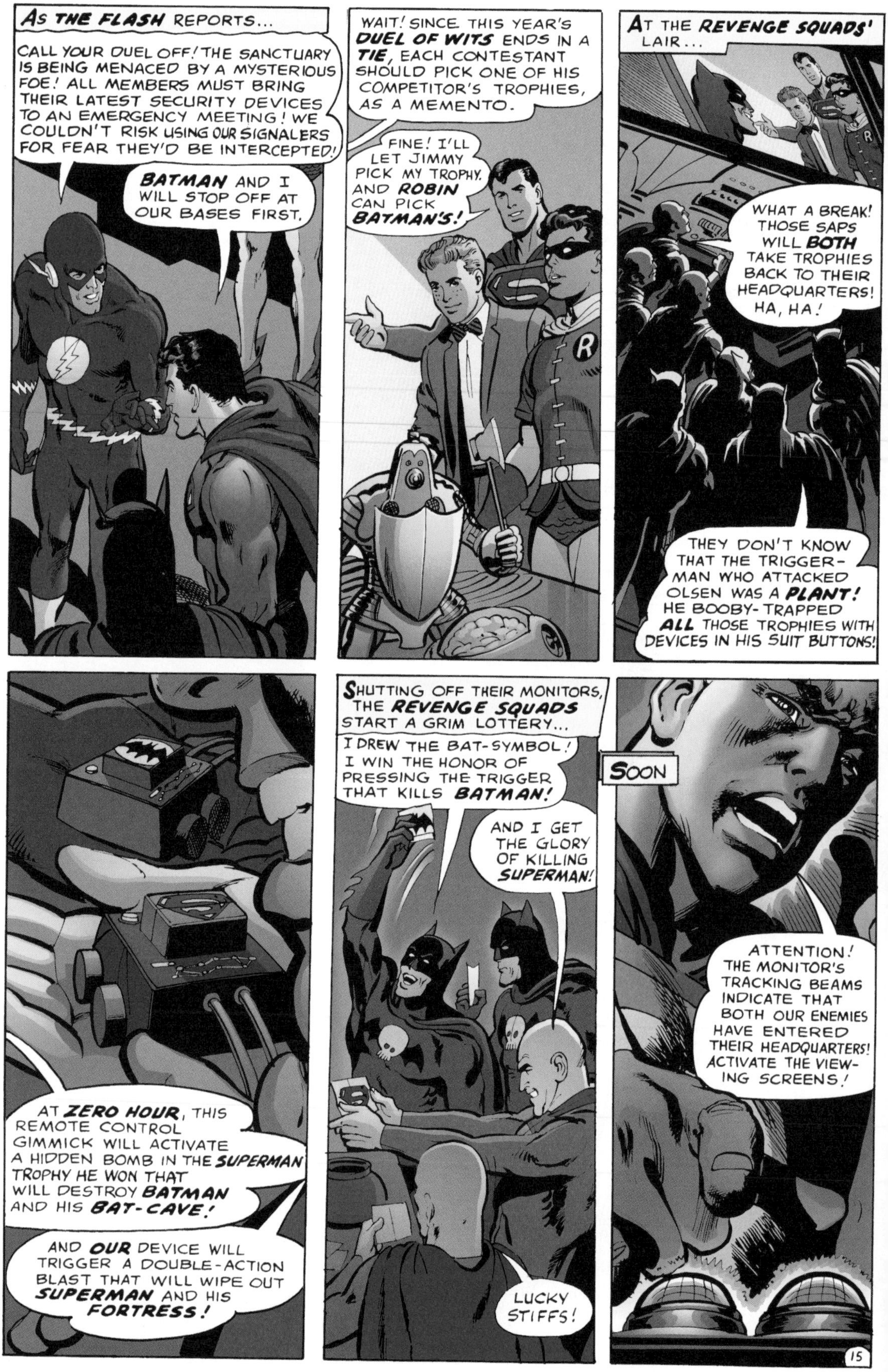
AS THE FLASH REPORTS...
CALL YOUR DUEL OFF! THE SANCTUARY IS BEING MENACED BY A MYSTERIOUS FOE! ALL MEMBERS MUST BRING THEIR LATEST SECURITY DEVICES TO AN EMERGENCY MEETING! WE COULDN'T RISK USING OUR SIGNALERS FOR FEAR THEY'D BE INTERCEPTED!
BATMAN AND I WILL STOP OFF AT OUR BASES FIRST.
WAIT! SINCE THIS YEAR'S DUEL OF WITS ENDS IN A TIE, EACH CONTESTANT SHOULD PICK ONE OF HIS COMPETITOR'S TROPHIES, AS A MEMENTO.
FINE! I'LL LET JIMMY PICK MY TROPHY, AND ROBIN CAN PICK BATMAN'S!
AT THE REVENGE SQUADS' LAIR...
WHAT A BREAK! THOSE SAPS WILL BOTH TAKE TROPHIES BACK TO THEIR HEADQUARTERS! HA, HA!
THEY DON'T KNOW THAT THE TRIGGER-MAN WHO ATTACKED OLSEN WAS A PLANT! HE BOOBY-TRAPPED ALL THOSE TROPHIES WITH DEVICES IN HIS SUIT BUTTONS!
AT ZERO HOUR, THIS REMOTE CONTROL GIMMICK WILL ACTIVATE A HIDDEN BOMB IN THE SUPERMAN TROPHY HE WON THAT WILL DESTROY BATMAN AND HIS BAT-CAVE!
AND OUR DEVICE WILL TRIGGER A DOUBLE-ACTION BLAST THAT WILL WIPE OUT SUPERMAN AND HIS FORTRESS!
SHUTTING OFF THEIR MONITORS, THE REVENGE SQUADS START A GRIM LOTTERY...
I DREW THE BAT-SYMBOL! I WIN THE HONOR OF PRESSING THE TRIGGER THAT KILLS BATMAN!
AND I GET THE GLORY OF KILLING SUPERMAN!
LUCKY STIFFS!
SOON
ATTENTION! THE MONITOR'S TRACKING BEAMS INDICATE THAT BOTH OUR ENEMIES HAVE ENTERED THEIR HEADQUARTERS! ACTIVATE THE VIEWING SCREENS!
15

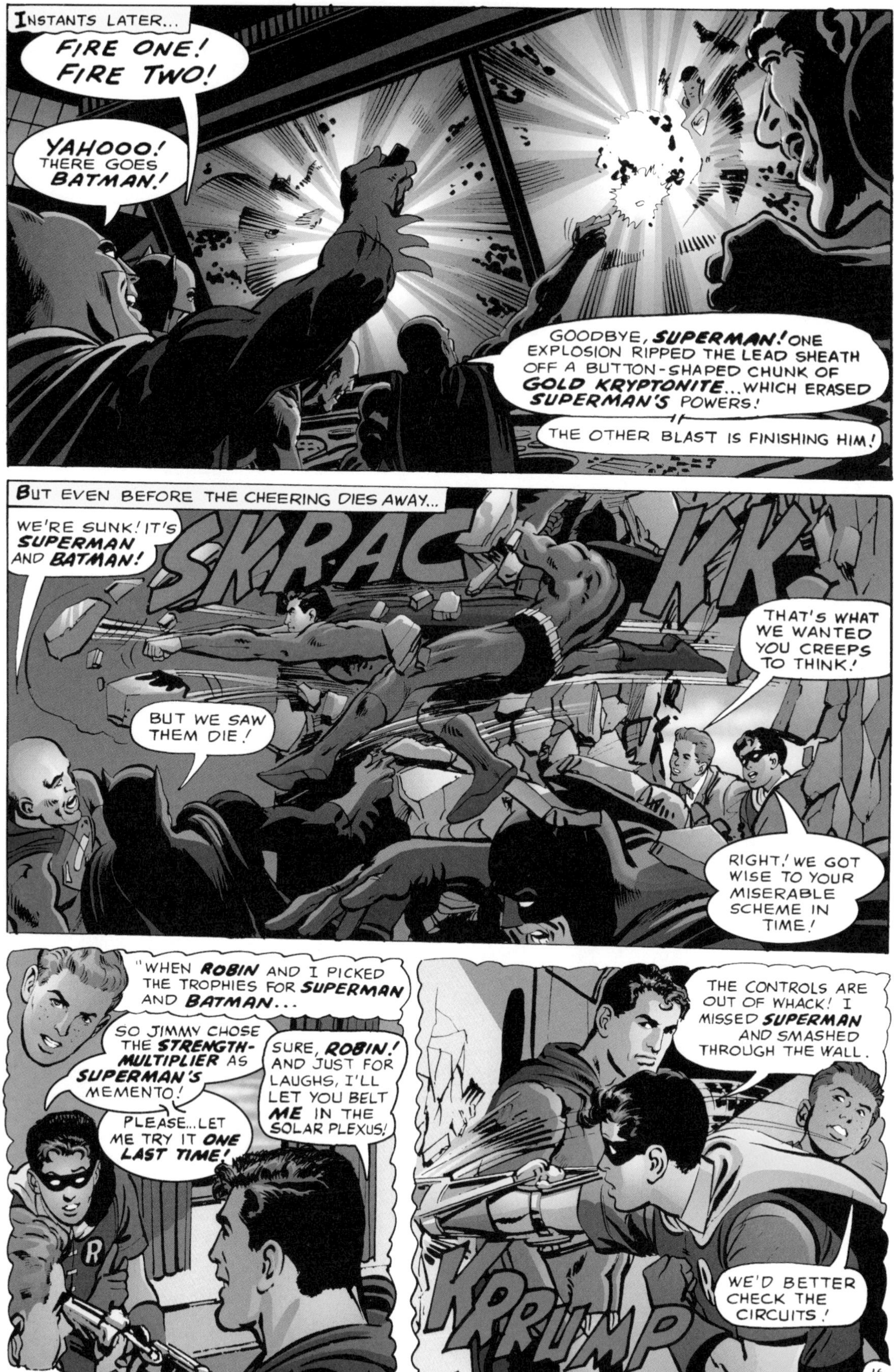
INSTANTS LATER...
FIRE ONE! FIRE TWO!
YAHOOO! THERE GOES BATMAN!
GOODBYE, SUPERMAN! ONE EXPLOSION RIPPED THE LEAD SHEATH OFF A BUTTON-SHAPED CHUNK OF GOLD KRYPTONITE... WHICH ERASED SUPERMAN'S POWERS!
THE OTHER BLAST IS FINISHING HIM!
BUT EVEN BEFORE THE CHEERING DIES AWAY...
WE'RE SUNK! IT'S SUPERMAN AND BATMAN!
SKRACKK
THAT'S WHAT WE WANTED YOU CREEPS TO THINK!
BUT WE SAW THEM DIE!
RIGHT! WE GOT WISE TO YOUR MISERABLE SCHEME IN TIME!
"WHEN ROBIN AND I PICKED THE TROPHIES FOR SUPERMAN AND BATMAN...
SO JIMMY CHOSE THE STRENGTH-MULTIPLIER AS SUPERMAN'S MEMENTO!
SURE, ROBIN! AND JUST FOR LAUGHS, I'LL LET YOU BELT ME IN THE SOLAR PLEXUS!
PLEASE... LET ME TRY IT ONE LAST TIME!
THE CONTROLS ARE OUT OF WHACK! I MISSED SUPERMAN AND SMASHED THROUGH THE WALL.
KRRUMP
WE'D BETTER CHECK THE CIRCUITS!
16

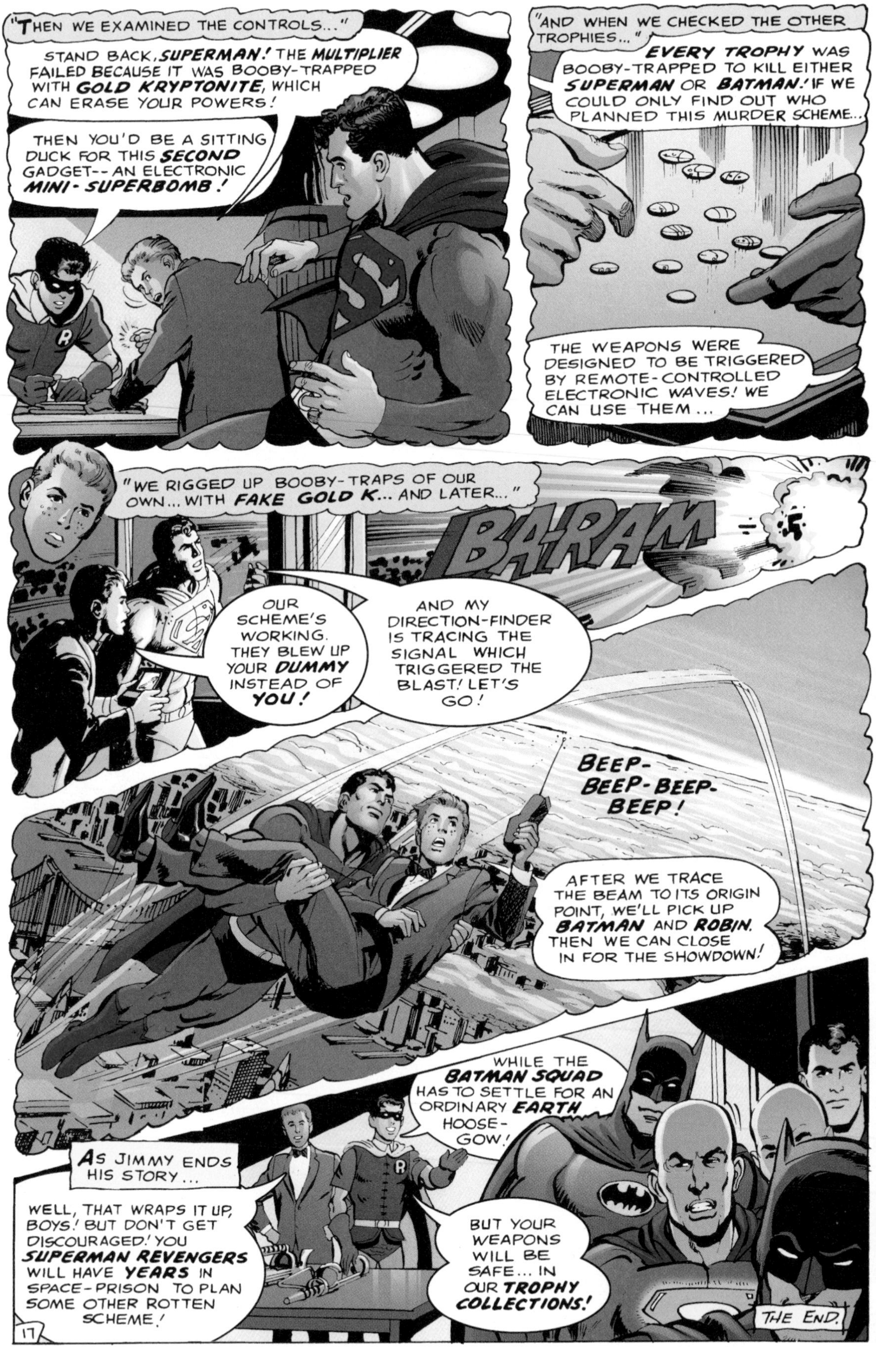
"THEN WE EXAMINED THE CONTROLS..."
STAND BACK, SUPERMAN! THE MULTIPLIER FAILED BECAUSE IT WAS BOOBY-TRAPPED WITH GOLD KRYPTONITE, WHICH CAN ERASE YOUR POWERS!
THEN YOU'D BE A SITTING DUCK FOR THIS SECOND GADGET-- AN ELECTRONIC MINI-SUPERBOMB!
"AND WHEN WE CHECKED THE OTHER TROPHIES..."
EVERY TROPHY WAS BOOBY-TRAPPED TO KILL EITHER SUPERMAN OR BATMAN! IF WE COULD ONLY FIND OUT WHO PLANNED THIS MURDER SCHEME...
THE WEAPONS WERE DESIGNED TO BE TRIGGERED BY REMOTE-CONTROLLED ELECTRONIC WAVES! WE CAN USE THEM...
"WE RIGGED UP BOOBY-TRAPS OF OUR OWN... WITH FAKE GOLD K... AND LATER..."
BA-RAM
OUR SCHEME'S WORKING. THEY BLEW UP YOUR DUMMY INSTEAD OF YOU!
AND MY DIRECTION-FINDER IS TRACING THE SIGNAL WHICH TRIGGERED THE BLAST! LET'S GO!
BEEP-BEEP-BEEP-BEEP!
AFTER WE TRACE THE BEAM TO ITS ORIGIN POINT, WE'LL PICK UP BATMAN AND ROBIN. THEN WE CAN CLOSE IN FOR THE SHOWDOWN!
AS JIMMY ENDS HIS STORY...
WELL, THAT WRAPS IT UP, BOYS! BUT DON'T GET DISCOURAGED! YOU SUPERMAN REVENGERS WILL HAVE YEARS IN SPACE-PRISON TO PLAN SOME OTHER ROTTEN SCHEME!
WHILE THE BATMAN SQUAD HAS TO SETTLE FOR AN ORDINARY EARTH HOOSE-GOW!
BUT YOUR WEAPONS WILL BE SAFE... IN OUR TROPHY COLLECTIONS!
THE END.
17

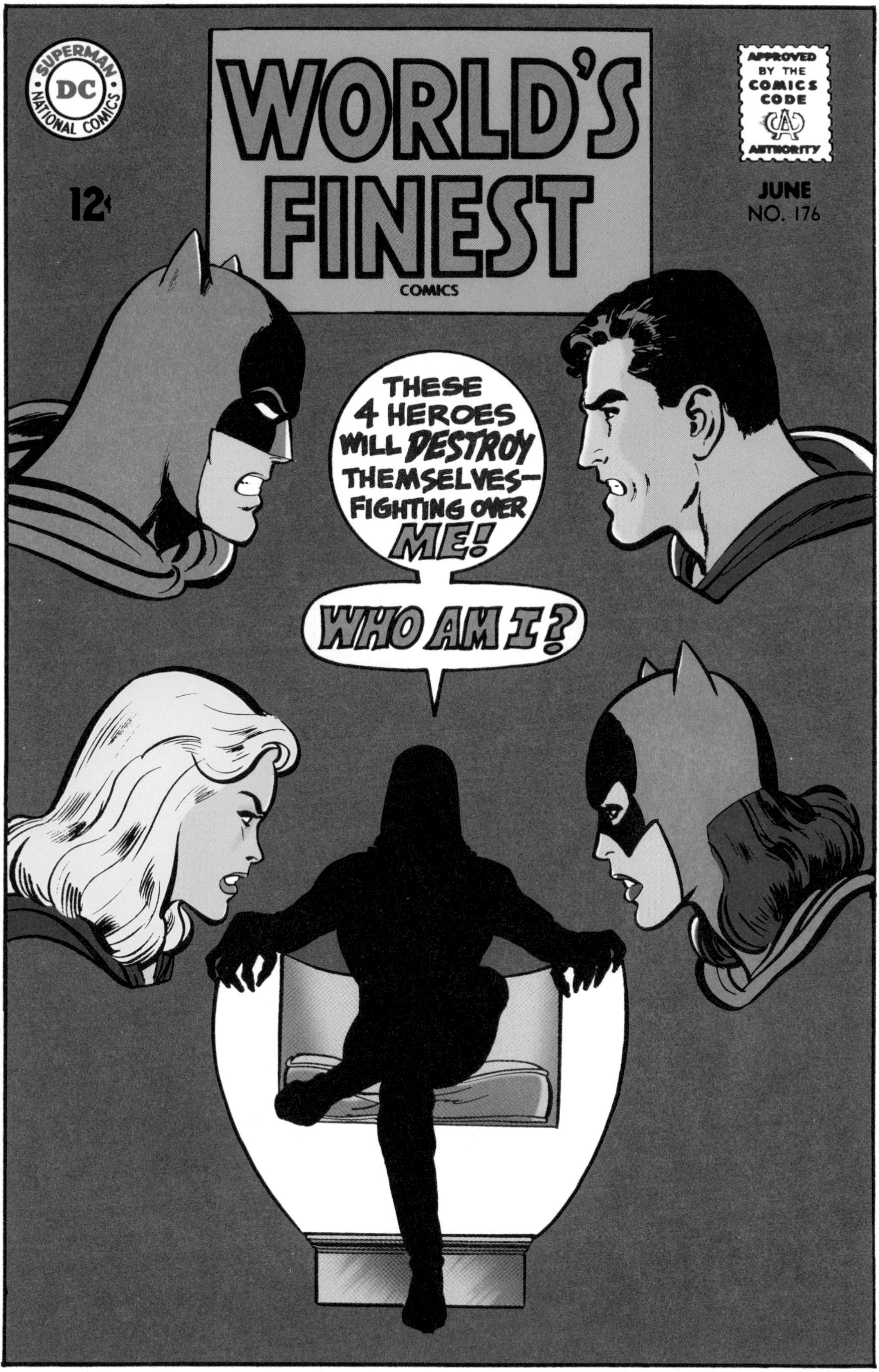
SUPERMAN DC NATIONAL COMICS
WORLD'S FINEST COMICS
APPROVED BY THE COMICS CODE AUTHORITY
12¢
JUNE NO. 176
THESE 4 HEROES WILL DESTROY THEMSELVES-- FIGHTING OVER ME!
WHO AM I?

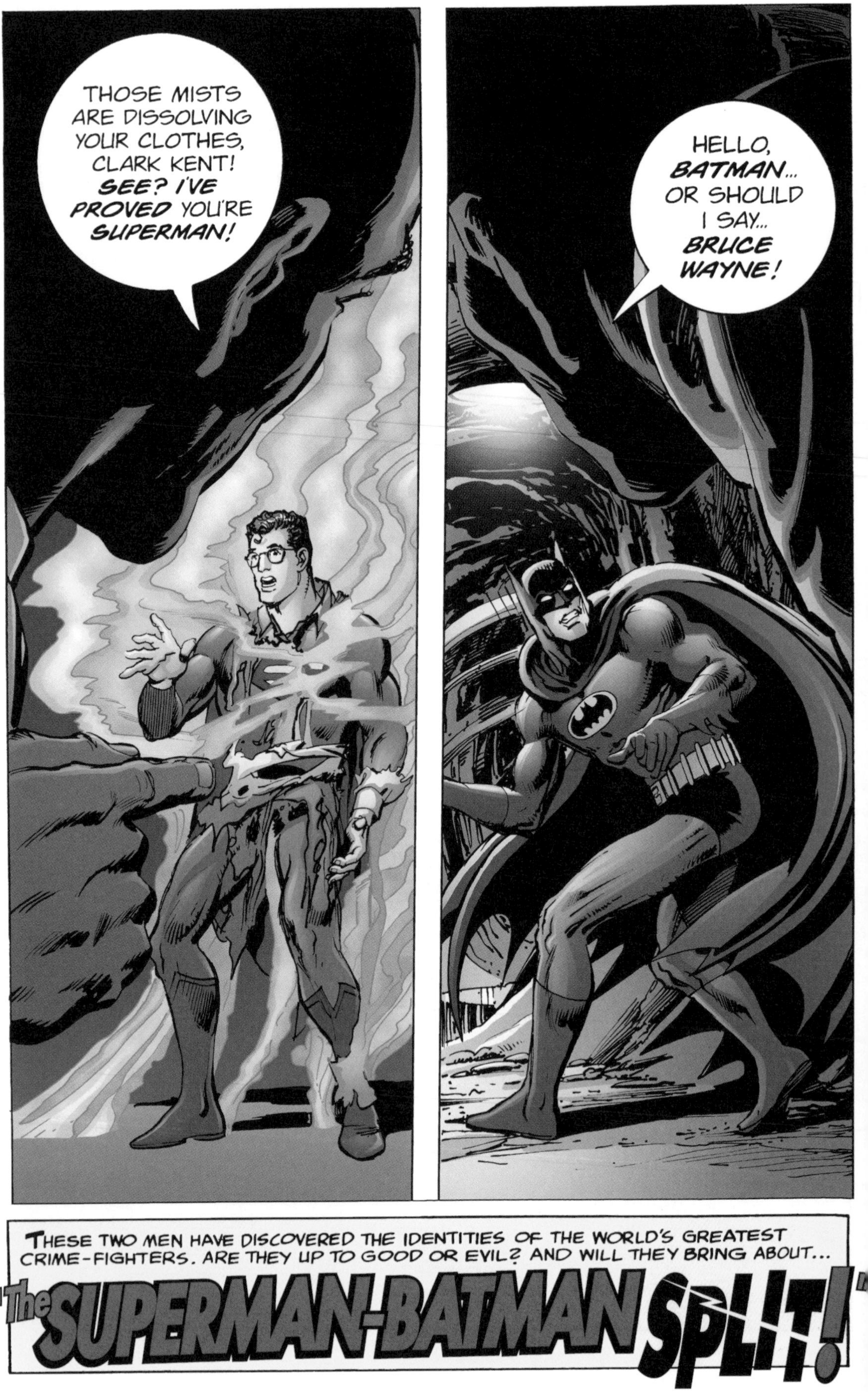
THOSE MISTS ARE DISSOLVING YOUR CLOTHES, CLARK KENT! SEE? I'VE PROVED YOU'RE SUPERMAN!
HELLO, BATMAN... OR SHOULD I SAY... BRUCE WAYNE!
THESE TWO MEN HAVE DISCOVERED THE IDENTITIES OF THE WORLD'S GREATEST CRIME-FIGHTERS. ARE THEY UP TO GOOD OR EVIL? AND WILL THEY BRING ABOUT...
"The SUPERMAN-BATMAN SPLIT!"

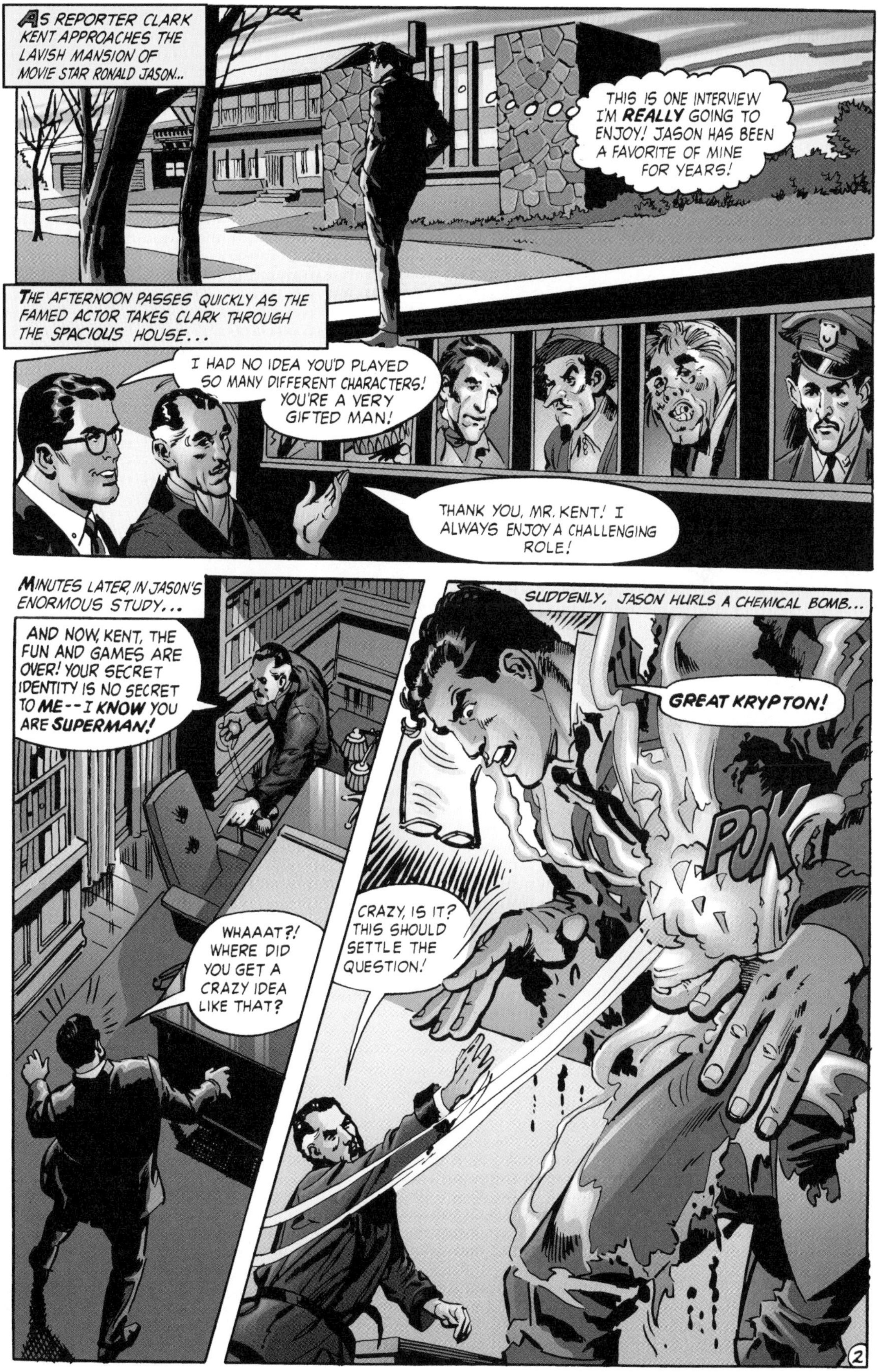

AS REPORTER CLARK KENT APPROACHES THE LAVISH MANSION OF MOVIE STAR RONALD JASON...
THIS IS ONE INTERVIEW I'M REALLY GOING TO ENJOY! JASON HAS BEEN A FAVORITE OF MINE FOR YEARS!
THE AFTERNOON PASSES QUICKLY AS THE FAMED ACTOR TAKES CLARK THROUGH THE SPACIOUS HOUSE...
I HAD NO IDEA YOU'D PLAYED SO MANY DIFFERENT CHARACTERS! YOU'RE A VERY GIFTED MAN!
THANK YOU, MR. KENT! I ALWAYS ENJOY A CHALLENGING ROLE!
MINUTES LATER, IN JASON'S ENORMOUS STUDY...
AND NOW, KENT, THE FUN AND GAMES ARE OVER! YOUR SECRET IDENTITY IS NO SECRET TO ME--I KNOW YOU ARE SUPERMAN!
WHAAAT?! WHERE DID YOU GET A CRAZY IDEA LIKE THAT?
SUDDENLY, JASON HURLS A CHEMICAL BOMB...
GREAT KRYPTON!
POK
CRAZY, IS IT? THIS SHOULD SETTLE THE QUESTION!
2

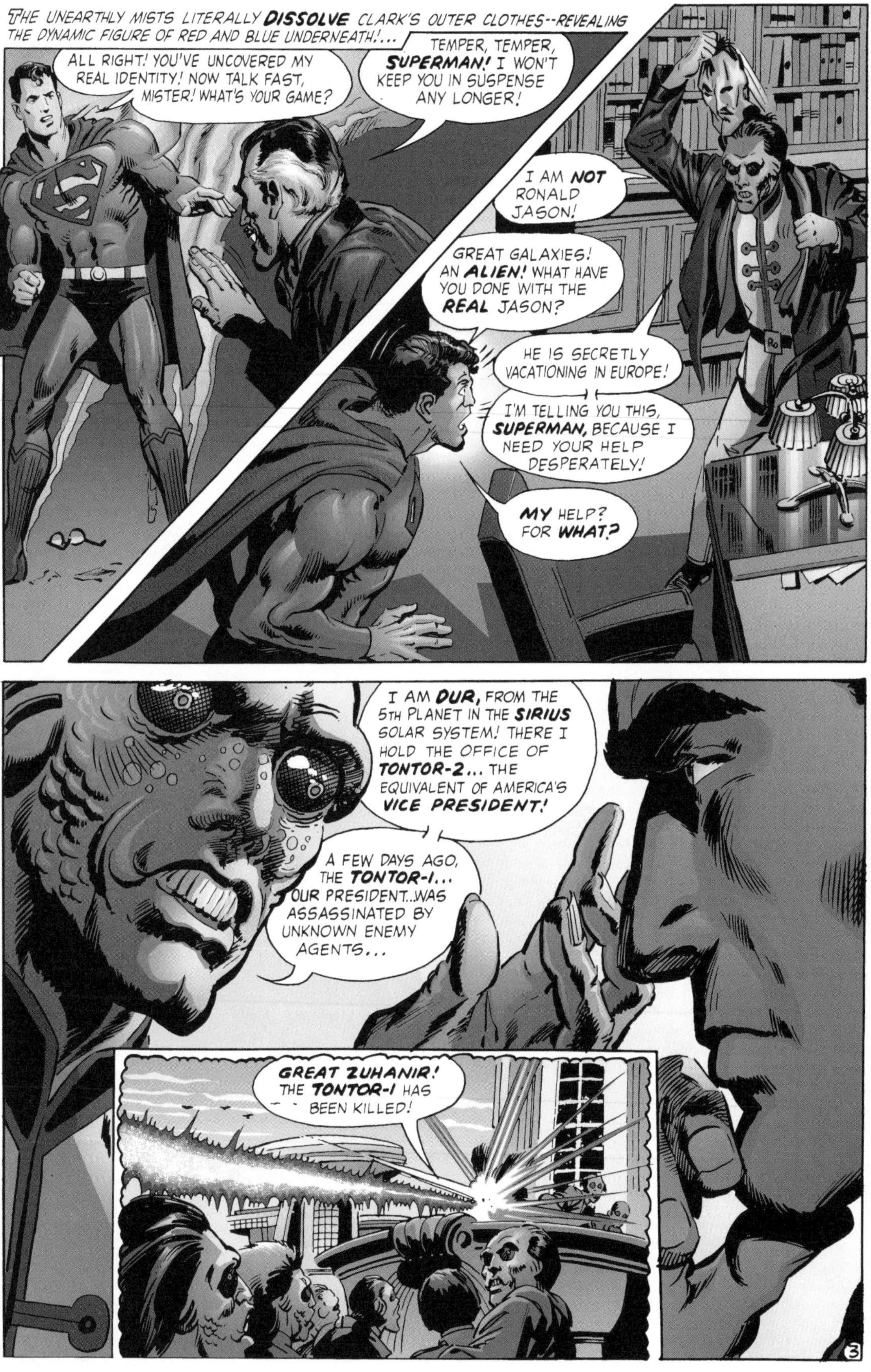
THE UNEARTHLY MISTS LITERALLY DISSOLVE CLARK'S OUTER CLOTHES--REVEALING THE DYNAMIC FIGURE OF RED AND BLUE UNDERNEATH!...
ALL RIGHT! YOU'VE UNCOVERED MY REAL IDENTITY! NOW TALK FAST, MISTER! WHAT'S YOUR GAME?
TEMPER, TEMPER, SUPERMAN! I WON'T KEEP YOU IN SUSPENSE ANY LONGER!
I AM NOT RONALD JASON!
GREAT GALAXIES! AN ALIEN! WHAT HAVE YOU DONE WITH THE REAL JASON?
HE IS SECRETLY VACATIONING IN EUROPE!
I'M TELLING YOU THIS, SUPERMAN, BECAUSE I NEED YOUR HELP DESPERATELY!
MY HELP? FOR WHAT?
I AM DUR, FROM THE 5TH PLANET IN THE SIRIUS SOLAR SYSTEM! THERE I HOLD THE OFFICE OF TONTOR-2... THE EQUIVALENT OF AMERICA'S VICE PRESIDENT!
A FEW DAYS AGO, THE TONTOR-1... OUR PRESIDENT...WAS ASSASSINATED BY UNKNOWN ENEMY AGENTS...
GREAT ZUHANIR! THE TONTOR-1 HAS BEEN KILLED!
3

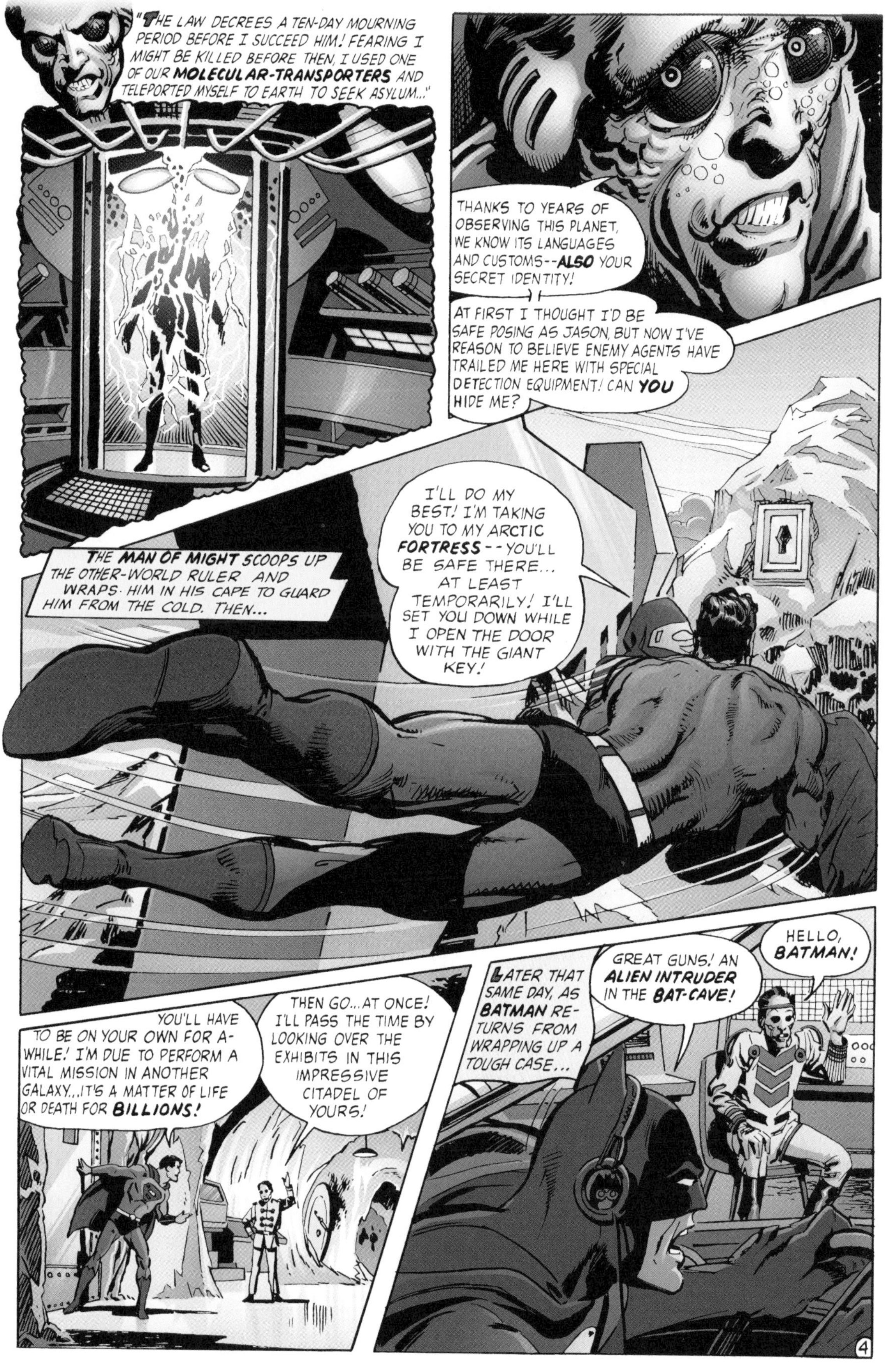
"THE LAW DECREES A TEN-DAY MOURNING PERIOD BEFORE I SUCCEED HIM! FEARING I MIGHT BE KILLED BEFORE THEN, I USED ONE OF OUR MOLECULAR-TRANSPORTERS AND TELEPORTED MYSELF TO EARTH TO SEEK ASYLUM..."
THANKS TO YEARS OF OBSERVING THIS PLANET, WE KNOW ITS LANGUAGES AND CUSTOMS--ALSO YOUR SECRET IDENTITY!
AT FIRST I THOUGHT I'D BE SAFE POSING AS JASON, BUT NOW I'VE REASON TO BELIEVE ENEMY AGENTS HAVE TRAILED ME HERE WITH SPECIAL DETECTION EQUIPMENT! CAN YOU HIDE ME?
THE MAN OF MIGHT SCOOPS UP THE OTHER-WORLD RULER AND WRAPS HIM IN HIS CAPE TO GUARD HIM FROM THE COLD. THEN...
I'LL DO MY BEST! I'M TAKING YOU TO MY ARCTIC FORTRESS--YOU'LL BE SAFE THERE... AT LEAST TEMPORARILY! I'LL SET YOU DOWN WHILE I OPEN THE DOOR WITH THE GIANT KEY!
YOU'LL HAVE TO BE ON YOUR OWN FOR A-WHILE! I'M DUE TO PERFORM A VITAL MISSION IN ANOTHER GALAXY...IT'S A MATTER OF LIFE OR DEATH FOR BILLIONS!
THEN GO...AT ONCE! I'LL PASS THE TIME BY LOOKING OVER THE EXHIBITS IN THIS IMPRESSIVE CITADEL OF YOURS!
LATER THAT SAME DAY, AS BATMAN RETURNS FROM WRAPPING UP A TOUGH CASE...
GREAT GUNS! AN ALIEN INTRUDER IN THE BAT-CAVE!
HELLO, BATMAN!
4

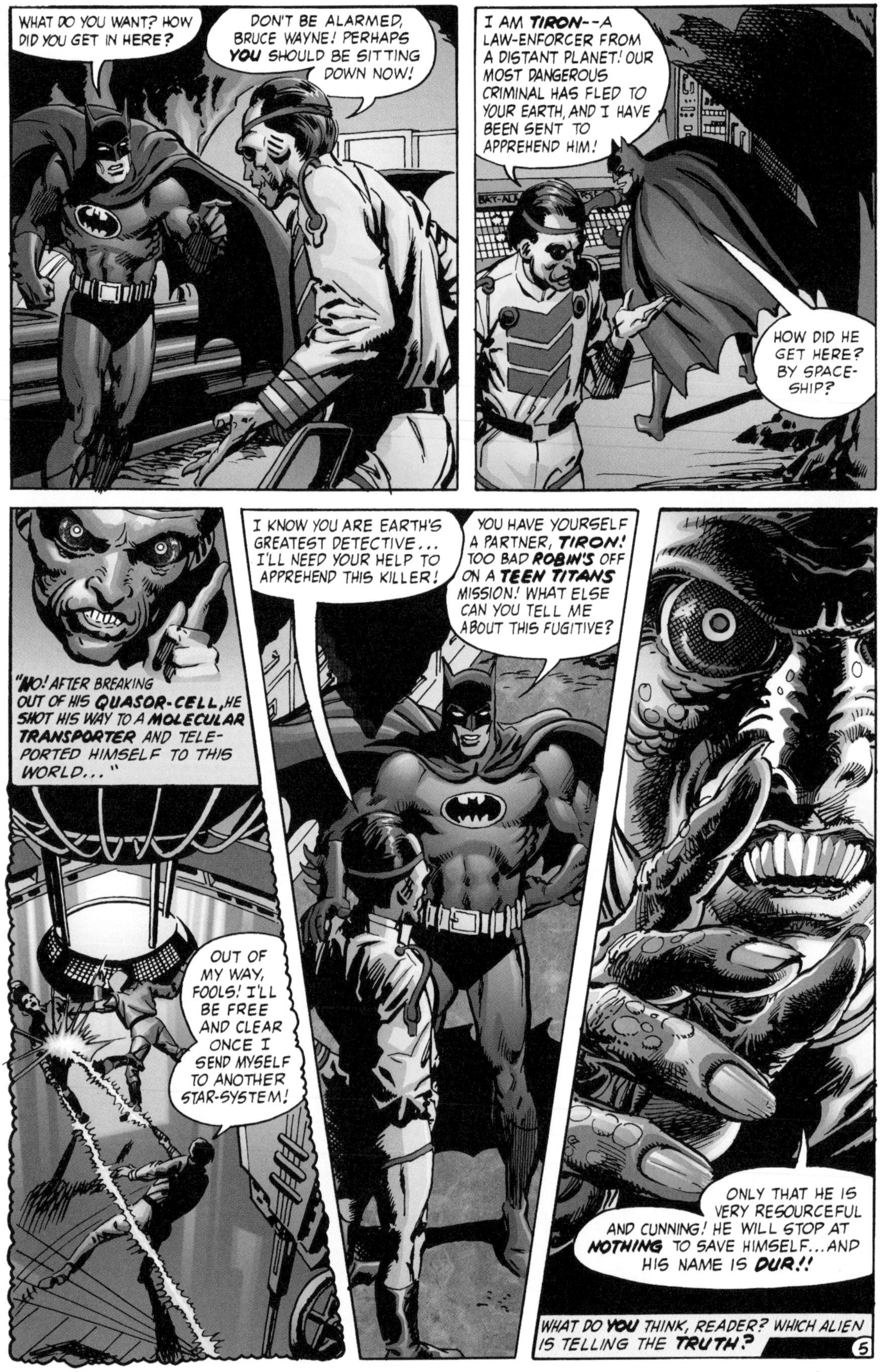

WHAT DO YOU WANT? HOW DID YOU GET IN HERE?
DON'T BE ALARMED, BRUCE WAYNE! PERHAPS YOU SHOULD BE SITTING DOWN NOW!
I AM TIRON--A LAW-ENFORCER FROM A DISTANT PLANET! OUR MOST DANGEROUS CRIMINAL HAS FLED TO YOUR EARTH, AND I HAVE BEEN SENT TO APPREHEND HIM!
HOW DID HE GET HERE? BY SPACE-SHIP?
"NO! AFTER BREAKING OUT OF HIS QUASOR-CELL, HE SHOT HIS WAY TO A MOLECULAR TRANSPORTER AND TELE-PORTED HIMSELF TO THIS WORLD..."
OUT OF MY WAY, FOOLS! I'LL BE FREE AND CLEAR ONCE I SEND MYSELF TO ANOTHER STAR-SYSTEM!
I KNOW YOU ARE EARTH'S GREATEST DETECTIVE... I'LL NEED YOUR HELP TO APPREHEND THIS KILLER!
YOU HAVE YOURSELF A PARTNER, TIRON! TOO BAD ROBIN'S OFF ON A TEEN TITANS MISSION! WHAT ELSE CAN YOU TELL ME ABOUT THIS FUGITIVE?
ONLY THAT HE IS VERY RESOURCEFUL AND CUNNING! HE WILL STOP AT NOTHING TO SAVE HIMSELF...AND HIS NAME IS DUR!!
WHAT DO YOU THINK, READER? WHICH ALIEN IS TELLING THE TRUTH?
5

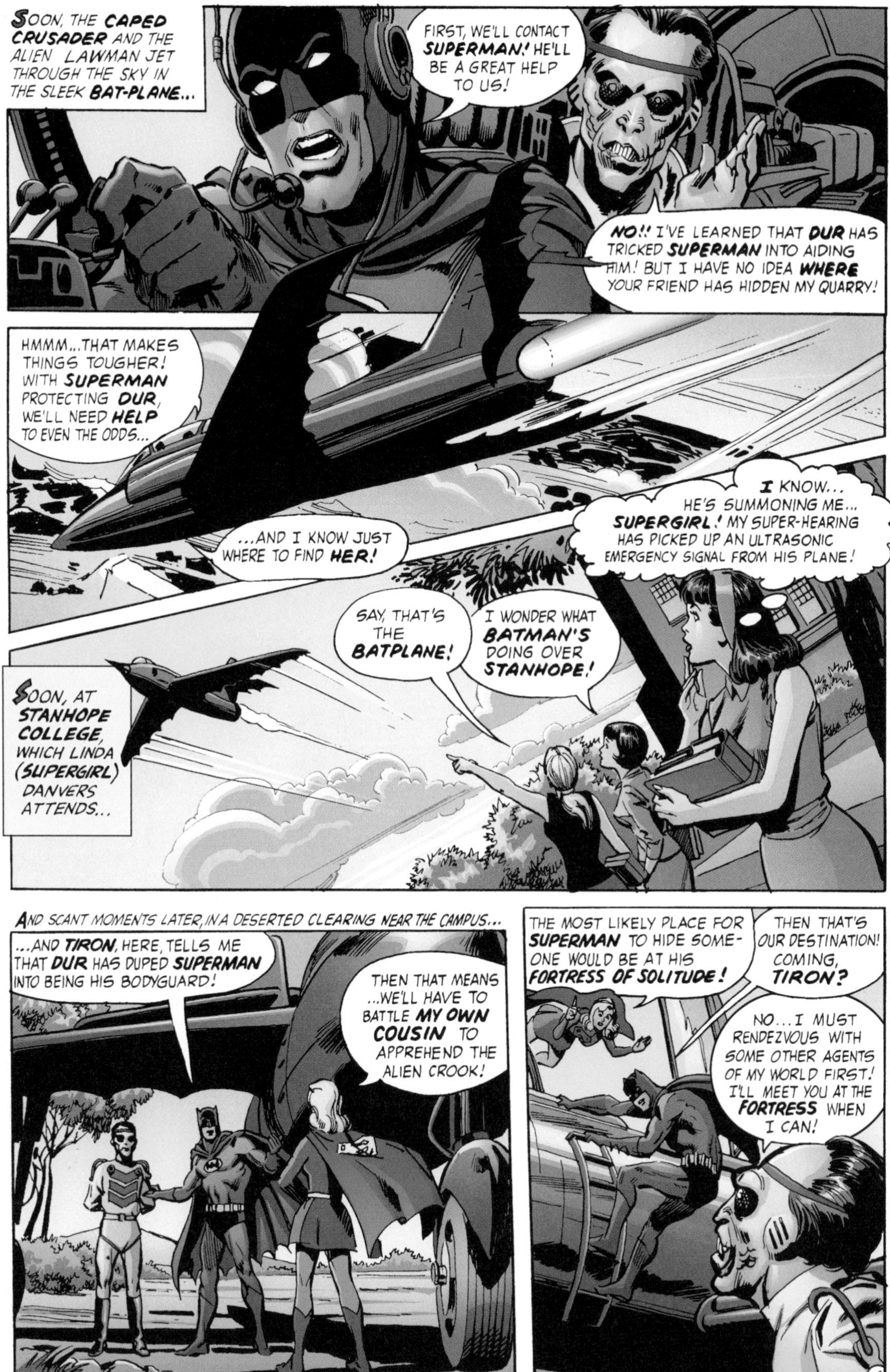
SOON, THE CAPED CRUSADER AND THE ALIEN LAWMAN JET THROUGH THE SKY IN THE SLEEK BAT-PLANE...
FIRST, WE'LL CONTACT SUPERMAN! HE'LL BE A GREAT HELP TO US!
NO!! I'VE LEARNED THAT DUR HAS TRICKED SUPERMAN INTO AIDING HIM! BUT I HAVE NO IDEA WHERE YOUR FRIEND HAS HIDDEN MY QUARRY!
HMMM...THAT MAKES THINGS TOUGHER! WITH SUPERMAN PROTECTING DUR, WE'LL NEED HELP TO EVEN THE ODDS...
...AND I KNOW JUST WHERE TO FIND HER!
I KNOW... HE'S SUMMONING ME... SUPERGIRL! MY SUPER-HEARING HAS PICKED UP AN ULTRASONIC EMERGENCY SIGNAL FROM HIS PLANE!
SOON, AT STANHOPE COLLEGE, WHICH LINDA (SUPERGIRL) DANVERS ATTENDS...
SAY, THAT'S THE BATPLANE!
I WONDER WHAT BATMAN'S DOING OVER STANHOPE!
AND SCANT MOMENTS LATER, IN A DESERTED CLEARING NEAR THE CAMPUS...
...AND TIRON, HERE, TELLS ME THAT DUR HAS DUPED SUPERMAN INTO BEING HIS BODYGUARD!
THEN THAT MEANS ...WE'LL HAVE TO BATTLE MY OWN COUSIN TO APPREHEND THE ALIEN CROOK!
THE MOST LIKELY PLACE FOR SUPERMAN TO HIDE SOME-ONE WOULD BE AT HIS FORTRESS OF SOLITUDE!
THEN THAT'S OUR DESTINATION! COMING, TIRON?
NO...I MUST RENDEZVOUS WITH SOME OTHER AGENTS OF MY WORLD FIRST! I'LL MEET YOU AT THE FORTRESS WHEN I CAN!
6

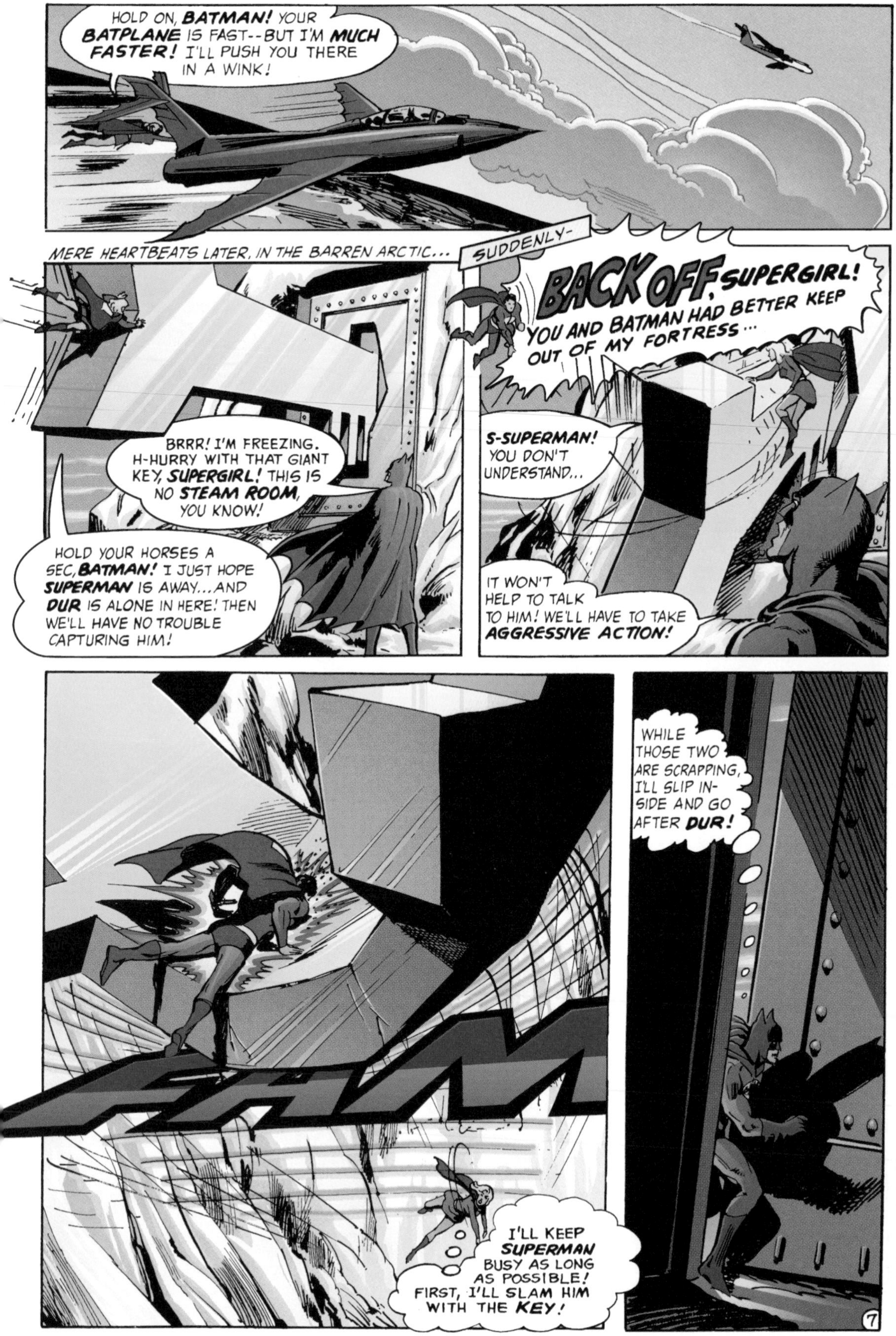
HOLD ON, BATMAN! YOUR BATPLANE IS FAST--BUT I'M MUCH FASTER! I'LL PUSH YOU THERE IN A WINK!
MERE HEARTBEATS LATER, IN THE BARREN ARCTIC...
BRRR! I'M FREEZING. H-HURRY WITH THAT GIANT KEY, SUPERGIRL! THIS IS NO STEAM ROOM, YOU KNOW!
HOLD YOUR HORSES A SEC, BATMAN! I JUST HOPE SUPERMAN IS AWAY... AND DUR IS ALONE IN HERE! THEN WE'LL HAVE NO TROUBLE CAPTURING HIM!
SUDDENLY-
BACK OFF, SUPERGIRL! YOU AND BATMAN HAD BETTER KEEP OUT OF MY FORTRESS...
S-SUPERMAN! YOU DON'T UNDERSTAND...
IT WON'T HELP TO TALK TO HIM! WE'LL HAVE TO TAKE AGGRESSIVE ACTION!
I'LL KEEP SUPERMAN BUSY AS LONG AS POSSIBLE! FIRST, I'LL SLAM HIM WITH THE KEY!
WHILE THOSE TWO ARE SCRAPPING, I'LL SLIP INSIDE AND GO AFTER DUR!
7

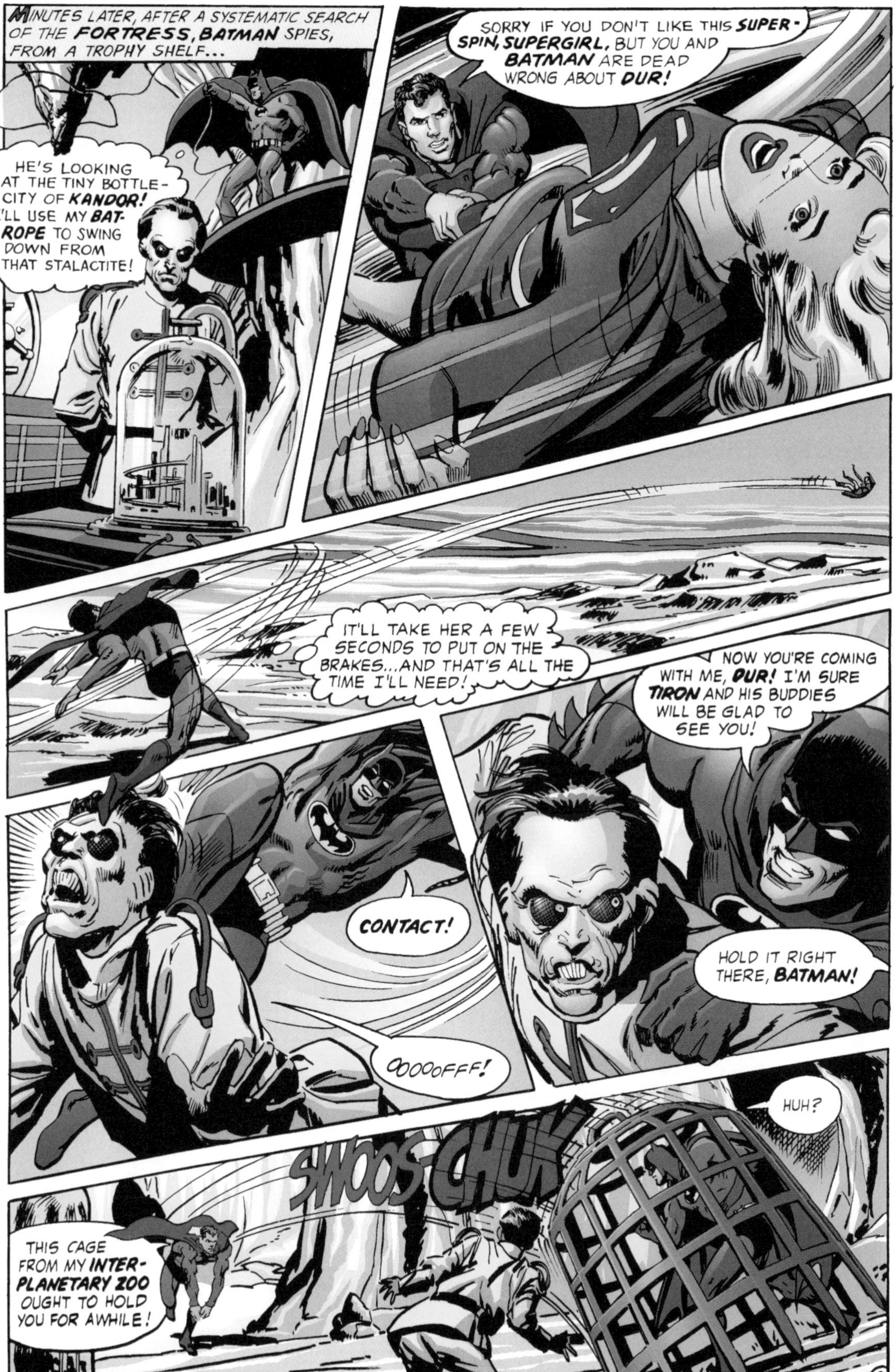
MINUTES LATER, AFTER A SYSTEMATIC SEARCH OF THE FORTRESS, BATMAN SPIES, FROM A TROPHY SHELF...
HE'S LOOKING AT THE TINY BOTTLE-CITY OF KANDOR! I'LL USE MY BAT-ROPE TO SWING DOWN FROM THAT STALACTITE!
SORRY IF YOU DON'T LIKE THIS SUPER-SPIN, SUPERGIRL, BUT YOU AND BATMAN ARE DEAD WRONG ABOUT DUR!
IT'LL TAKE HER A FEW SECONDS TO PUT ON THE BRAKES...AND THAT'S ALL THE TIME I'LL NEED!
CONTACT!
OOOOOFFF!
NOW YOU'RE COMING WITH ME, DUR! I'M SURE TIRON AND HIS BUDDIES WILL BE GLAD TO SEE YOU!
HOLD IT RIGHT THERE, BATMAN!
HUH?
SWOOS-CHUK
THIS CAGE FROM MY INTER-PLANETARY ZOO OUGHT TO HOLD YOU FOR AWHILE!
8

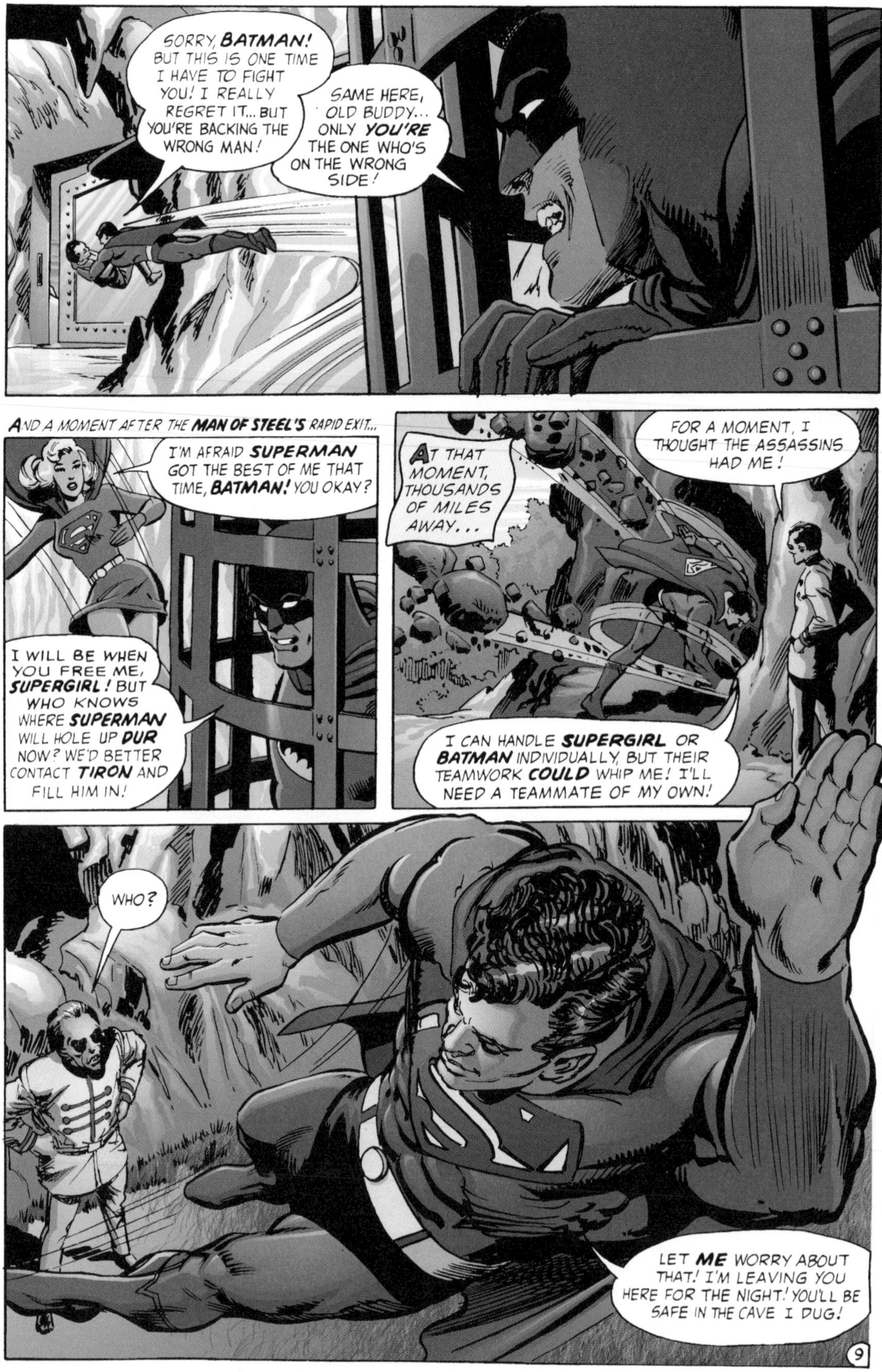
SORRY, BATMAN! BUT THIS IS ONE TIME I HAVE TO FIGHT YOU! I REALLY REGRET IT... BUT YOU'RE BACKING THE WRONG MAN!
SAME HERE, OLD BUDDY... ONLY YOU'RE THE ONE WHO'S ON THE WRONG SIDE!
AND A MOMENT AFTER THE MAN OF STEEL'S RAPID EXIT...
I'M AFRAID SUPERMAN GOT THE BEST OF ME THAT TIME, BATMAN! YOU OKAY?
I WILL BE WHEN YOU FREE ME, SUPERGIRL! BUT WHO KNOWS WHERE SUPERMAN WILL HOLE UP DUR NOW? WE'D BETTER CONTACT TIRON AND FILL HIM IN!
AT THAT MOMENT, THOUSANDS OF MILES AWAY...
FOR A MOMENT, I THOUGHT THE ASSASSINS HAD ME!
I CAN HANDLE SUPERGIRL OR BATMAN INDIVIDUALLY, BUT THEIR TEAMWORK COULD WHIP ME! I'LL NEED A TEAMMATE OF MY OWN!
WHO?
LET ME WORRY ABOUT THAT! I'M LEAVING YOU HERE FOR THE NIGHT! YOU'LL BE SAFE IN THE CAVE I DUG!
9

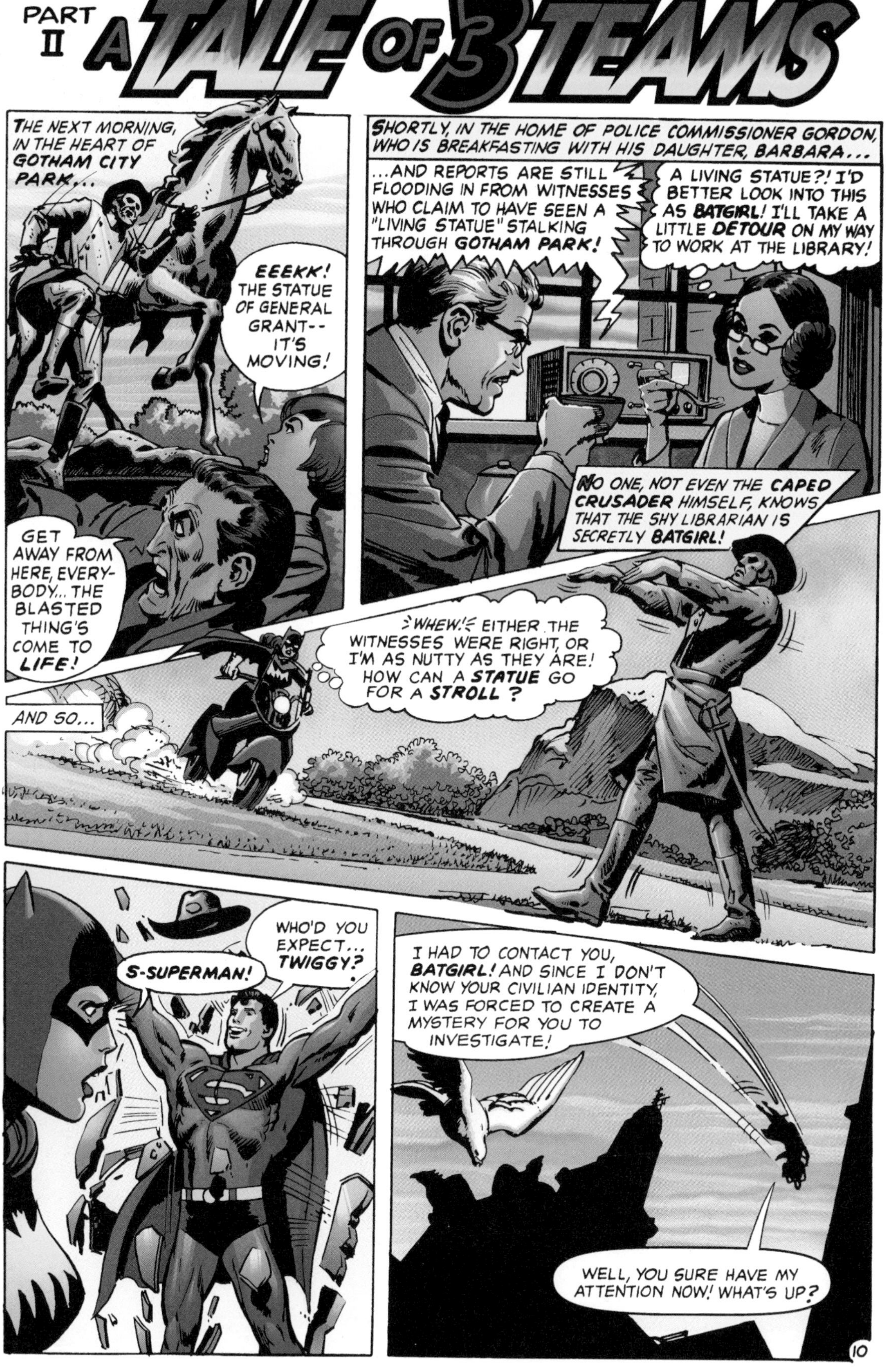
PART II A TALE OF 3 TEAMS
THE NEXT MORNING, IN THE HEART OF GOTHAM CITY PARK...
EEEKK! THE STATUE OF GENERAL GRANT-- IT'S MOVING!
GET AWAY FROM HERE, EVERYBODY... THE BLASTED THING'S COME TO LIFE!
SHORTLY, IN THE HOME OF POLICE COMMISSIONER GORDON, WHO IS BREAKFASTING WITH HIS DAUGHTER, BARBARA...
...AND REPORTS ARE STILL FLOODING IN FROM WITNESSES WHO CLAIM TO HAVE SEEN A "LIVING STATUE" STALKING THROUGH GOTHAM PARK!
A LIVING STATUE?! I'D BETTER LOOK INTO THIS AS BATGIRL! I'LL TAKE A LITTLE DETOUR ON MY WAY TO WORK AT THE LIBRARY!
NO ONE, NOT EVEN THE CAPED CRUSADER HIMSELF, KNOWS THAT THE SHY LIBRARIAN IS SECRETLY BATGIRL!
AND SO...
WHEW! EITHER THE WITNESSES WERE RIGHT, OR I'M AS NUTTY AS THEY ARE! HOW CAN A STATUE GO FOR A STROLL ?
S-SUPERMAN!
WHO'D YOU EXPECT... TWIGGY?
I HAD TO CONTACT YOU, BATGIRL! AND SINCE I DON'T KNOW YOUR CIVILIAN IDENTITY, I WAS FORCED TO CREATE A MYSTERY FOR YOU TO INVESTIGATE!
WELL, YOU SURE HAVE MY ATTENTION NOW! WHAT'S UP?
10

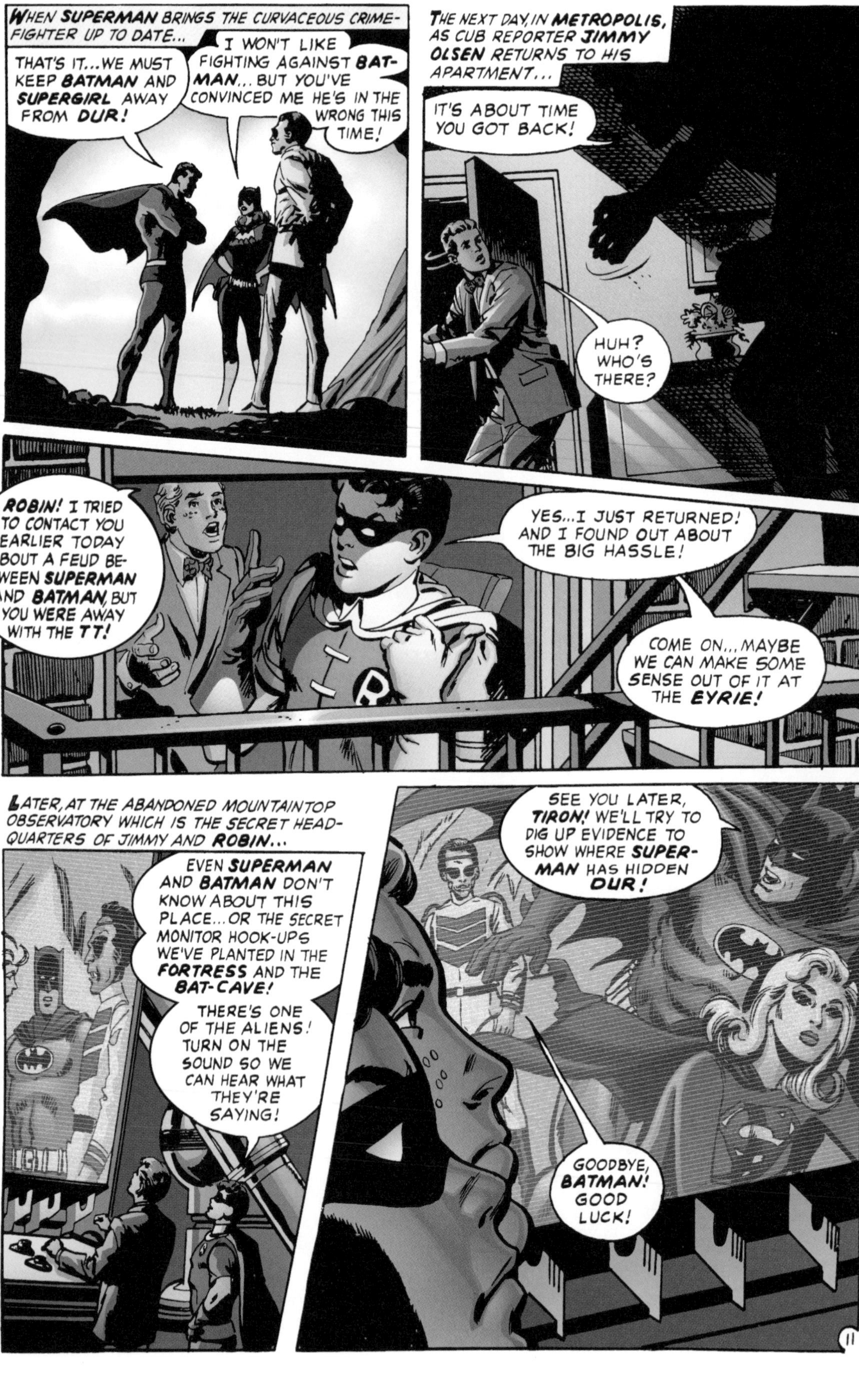
WHEN SUPERMAN BRINGS THE CURVACEOUS CRIME-FIGHTER UP TO DATE...
THAT'S IT...WE MUST KEEP BATMAN AND SUPERGIRL AWAY FROM DUR!
I WON'T LIKE FIGHTING AGAINST BATMAN... BUT YOU'VE CONVINCED ME HE'S IN THE WRONG THIS TIME!
THE NEXT DAY, IN METROPOLIS, AS CUB REPORTER JIMMY OLSEN RETURNS TO HIS APARTMENT...
IT'S ABOUT TIME YOU GOT BACK!
HUH? WHO'S THERE?
ROBIN! I TRIED TO CONTACT YOU EARLIER TODAY ABOUT A FEUD BETWEEN SUPERMAN AND BATMAN, BUT YOU WERE AWAY WITH THE TT!
YES...I JUST RETURNED! AND I FOUND OUT ABOUT THE BIG HASSLE!
COME ON... MAYBE WE CAN MAKE SOME SENSE OUT OF IT AT THE EYRIE!
LATER, AT THE ABANDONED MOUNTAINTOP OBSERVATORY WHICH IS THE SECRET HEADQUARTERS OF JIMMY AND ROBIN...
EVEN SUPERMAN AND BATMAN DON'T KNOW ABOUT THIS PLACE...OR THE SECRET MONITOR HOOK-UPS WE'VE PLANTED IN THE FORTRESS AND THE BAT-CAVE!
THERE'S ONE OF THE ALIENS! TURN ON THE SOUND SO WE CAN HEAR WHAT THEY'RE SAYING!
SEE YOU LATER, TIRON! WE'LL TRY TO DIG UP EVIDENCE TO SHOW WHERE SUPERMAN HAS HIDDEN DUR!
GOODBYE, BATMAN! GOOD LUCK!
11

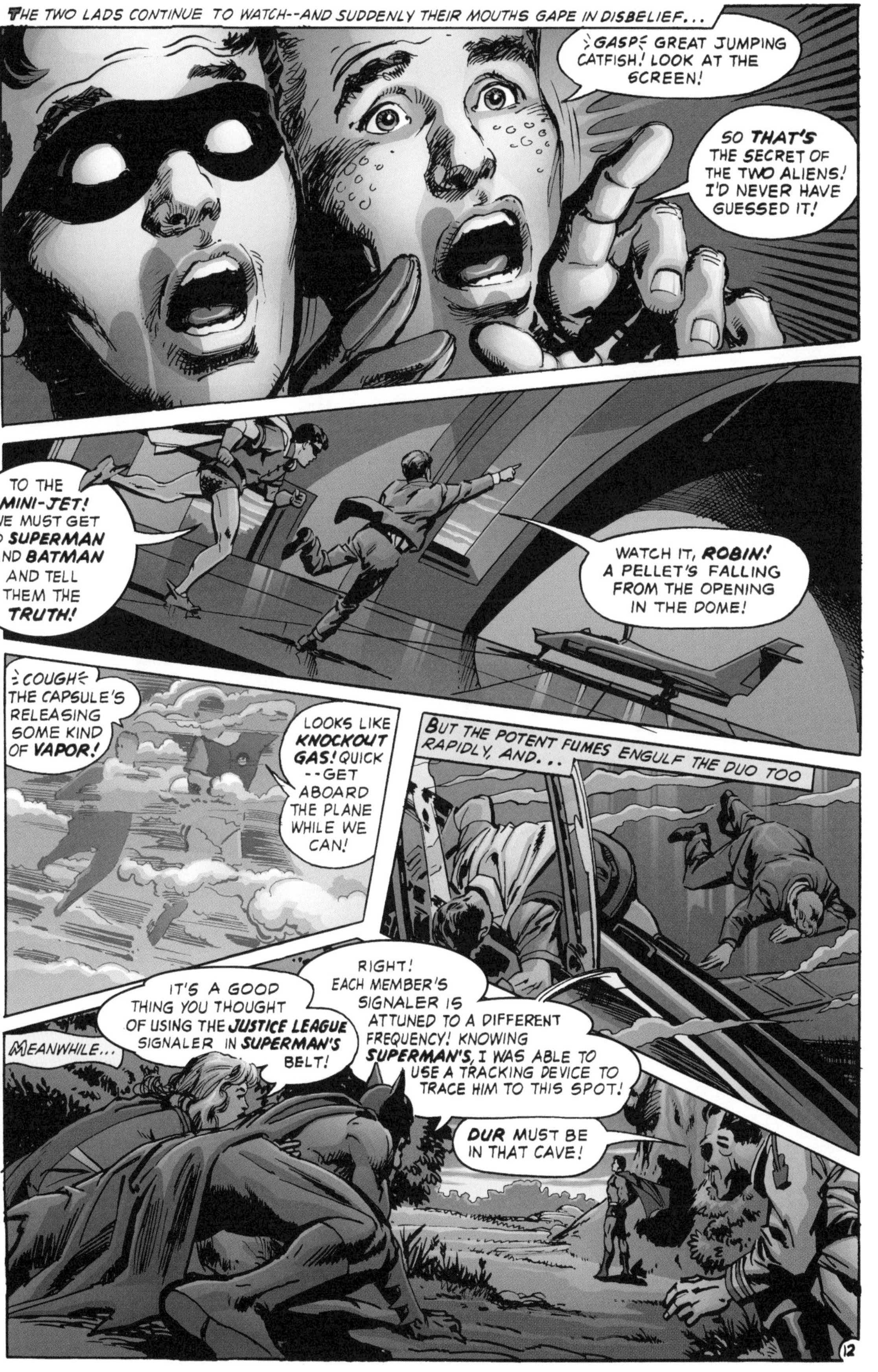
THE TWO LADS CONTINUE TO WATCH--AND SUDDENLY THEIR MOUTHS GAPE IN DISBELIEF...
GASP GREAT JUMPING CATFISH! LOOK AT THE SCREEN!
SO THAT'S THE SECRET OF THE TWO ALIENS! I'D NEVER HAVE GUESSED IT!
TO THE MINI-JET! WE MUST GET TO SUPERMAN AND BATMAN AND TELL THEM THE TRUTH!
WATCH IT, ROBIN! A PELLET'S FALLING FROM THE OPENING IN THE DOME!
COUGH THE CAPSULE'S RELEASING SOME KIND OF VAPOR!
LOOKS LIKE KNOCKOUT GAS! QUICK --GET ABOARD THE PLANE WHILE WE CAN!
BUT THE POTENT FUMES ENGULF THE DUO TOO RAPIDLY, AND...
MEANWHILE...
IT'S A GOOD THING YOU THOUGHT OF USING THE JUSTICE LEAGUE SIGNALER IN SUPERMAN'S BELT!
RIGHT! EACH MEMBER'S SIGNALER IS ATTUNED TO A DIFFERENT FREQUENCY! KNOWING SUPERMAN'S, I WAS ABLE TO USE A TRACKING DEVICE TO TRACE HIM TO THIS SPOT!
DUR MUST BE IN THAT CAVE!
12

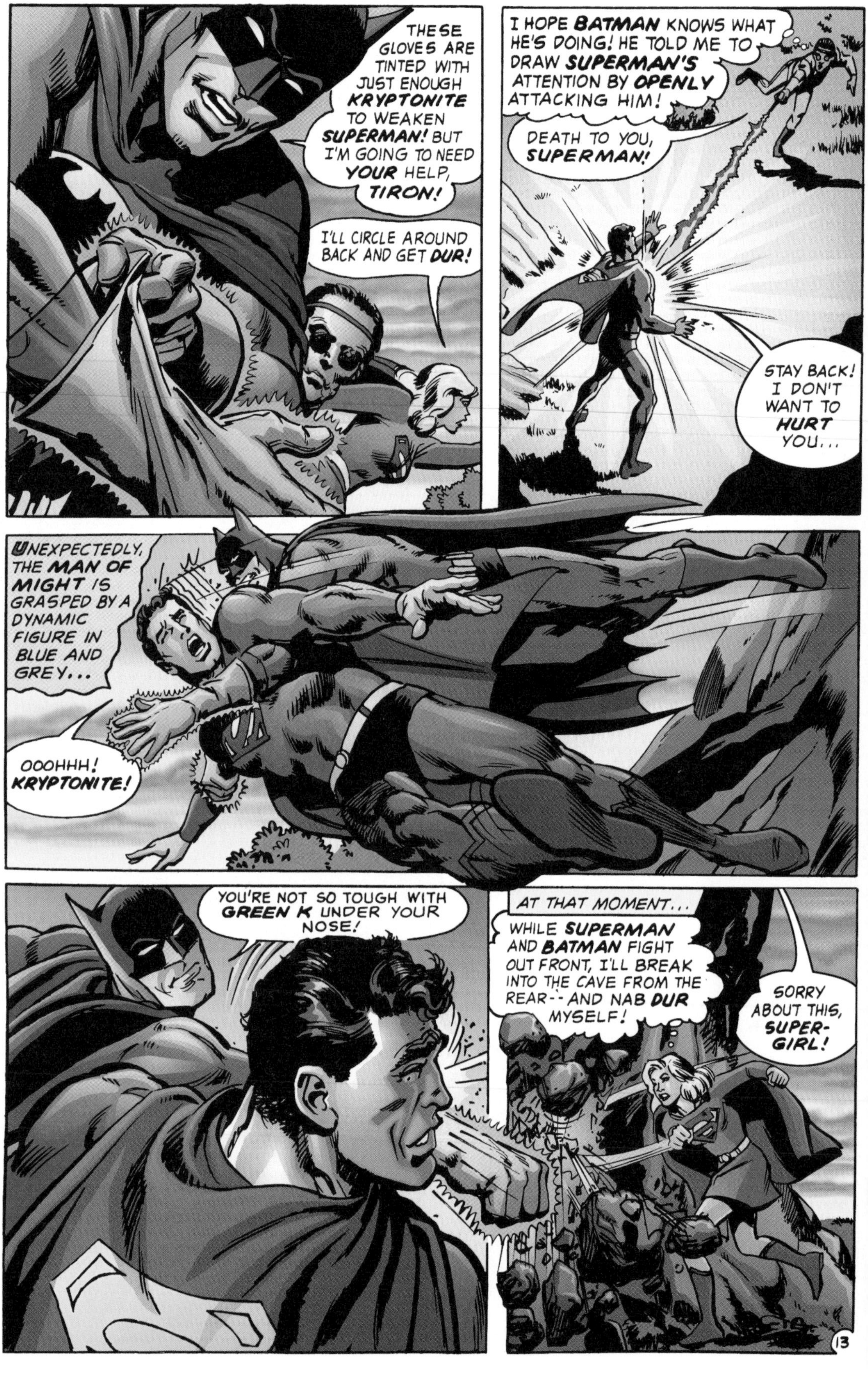
THESE GLOVES ARE TINTED WITH JUST ENOUGH KRYPTONITE TO WEAKEN SUPERMAN! BUT I'M GOING TO NEED YOUR HELP, TIRON!
I'LL CIRCLE AROUND BACK AND GET DUR!
I HOPE BATMAN KNOWS WHAT HE'S DOING! HE TOLD ME TO DRAW SUPERMAN'S ATTENTION BY OPENLY ATTACKING HIM!
DEATH TO YOU, SUPERMAN!
STAY BACK! I DON'T WANT TO HURT YOU...
UNEXPECTEDLY, THE MAN OF MIGHT IS GRASPED BY A DYNAMIC FIGURE IN BLUE AND GREY...
OOOHHH! KRYPTONITE!
YOU'RE NOT SO TOUGH WITH GREEN K UNDER YOUR NOSE!
AT THAT MOMENT...
WHILE SUPERMAN AND BATMAN FIGHT OUT FRONT, I'LL BREAK INTO THE CAVE FROM THE REAR--AND NAB DUR MYSELF!
SORRY ABOUT THIS, SUPER-GIRL!
13

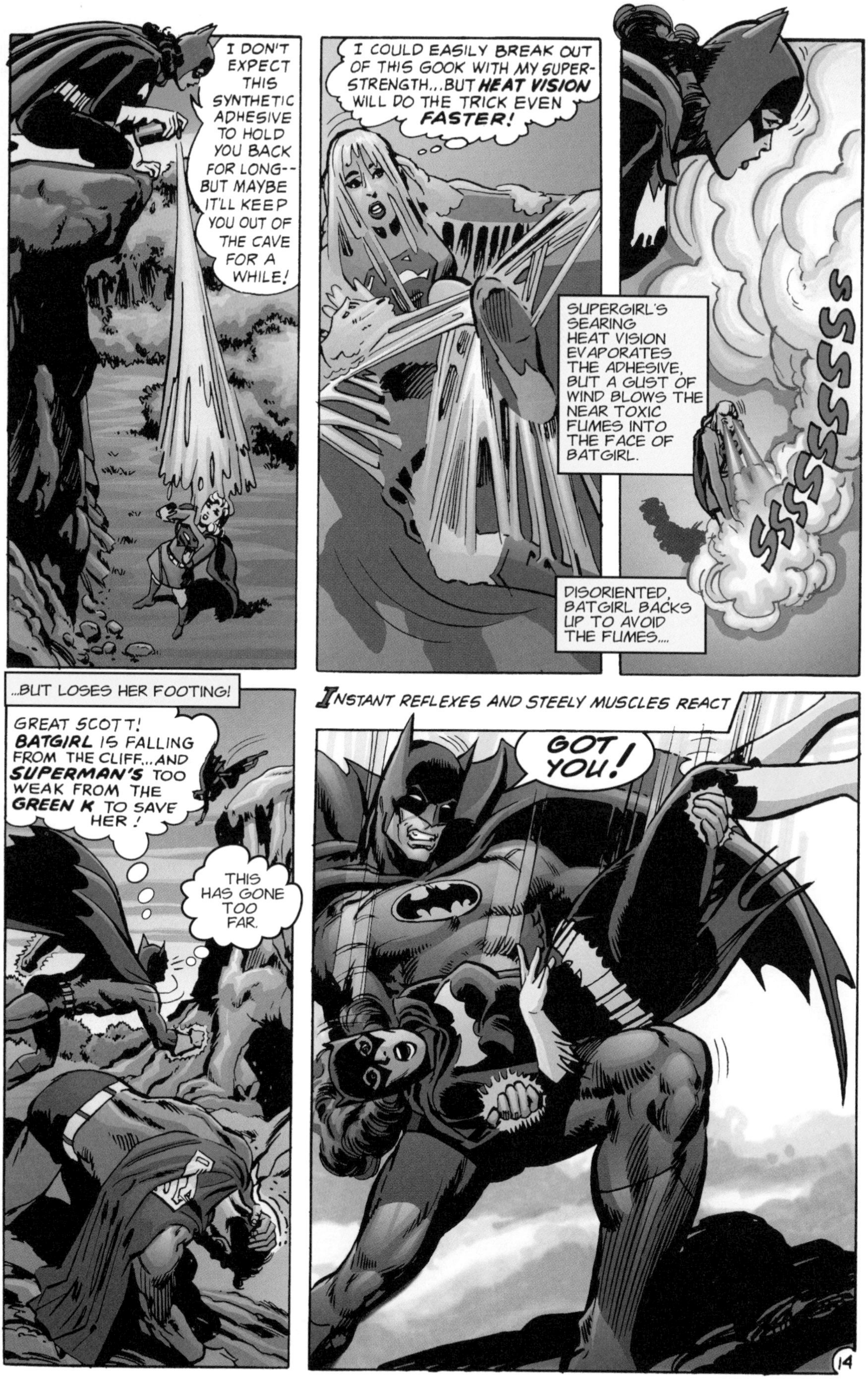
I DON'T EXPECT THIS SYNTHETIC ADHESIVE TO HOLD YOU BACK FOR LONG-- BUT MAYBE IT'LL KEEP YOU OUT OF THE CAVE FOR A WHILE!
I COULD EASILY BREAK OUT OF THIS GOOK WITH MY SUPER-STRENGTH...BUT HEAT VISION WILL DO THE TRICK EVEN FASTER!
SUPERGIRL'S SEARING HEAT VISION EVAPORATES THE ADHESIVE, BUT A GUST OF WIND BLOWS THE NEAR TOXIC FUMES INTO THE FACE OF BATGIRL.
SSSSSSSSS
DISORIENTED, BATGIRL BACKS UP TO AVOID THE FUMES....
...BUT LOSES HER FOOTING!
GREAT SCOTT! BATGIRL IS FALLING FROM THE CLIFF...AND SUPERMAN'S TOO WEAK FROM THE GREEN K TO SAVE HER!
THIS HAS GONE TOO FAR.
INSTANT REFLEXES AND STEELY MUSCLES REACT
GOT YOU!
14

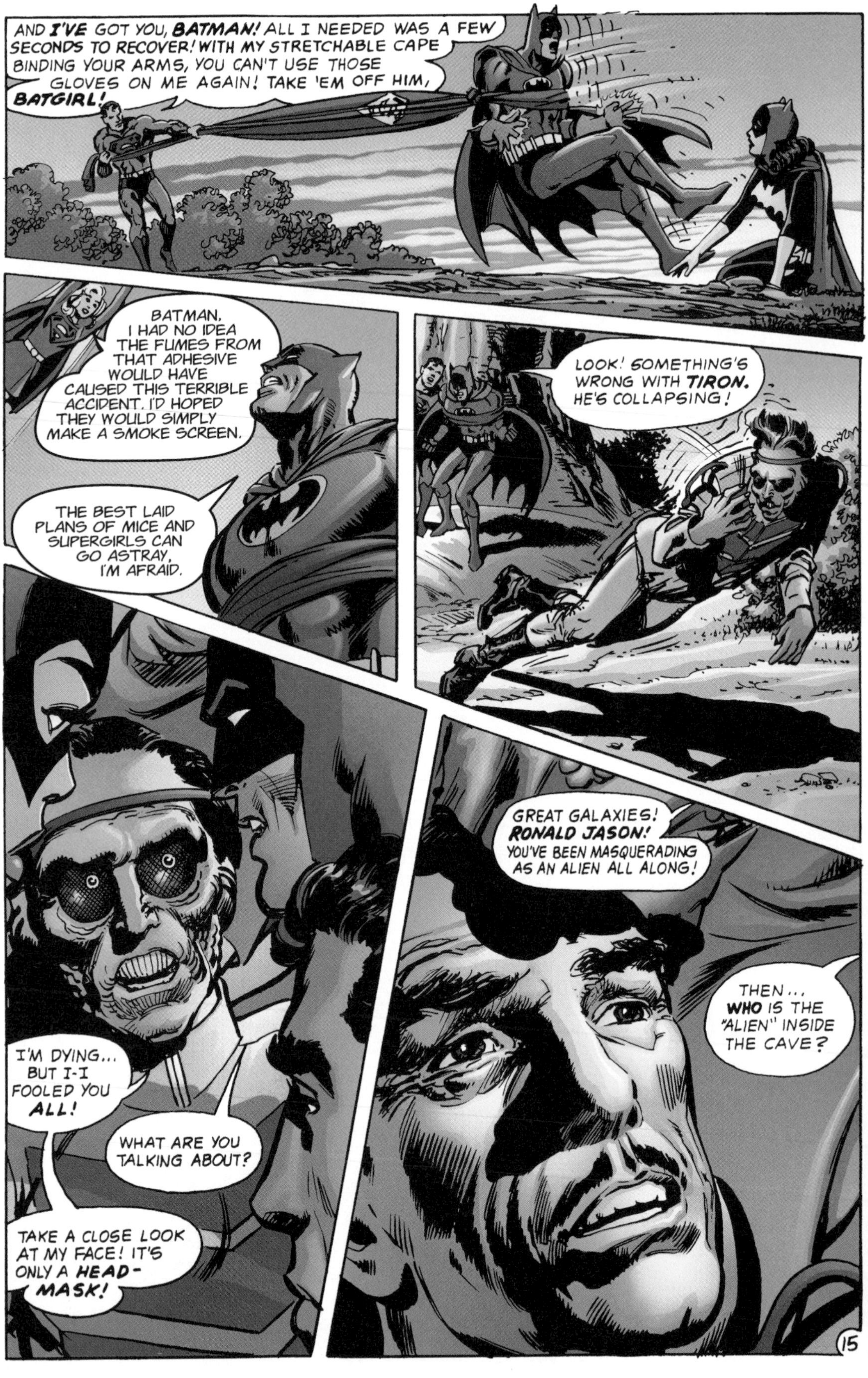
AND I'VE GOT YOU, BATMAN! ALL I NEEDED WAS A FEW SECONDS TO RECOVER! WITH MY STRETCHABLE CAPE BINDING YOUR ARMS, YOU CAN'T USE THOSE GLOVES ON ME AGAIN! TAKE 'EM OFF HIM, BATGIRL!
BATMAN, I HAD NO IDEA THE FUMES FROM THAT ADHESIVE WOULD HAVE CAUSED THIS TERRIBLE ACCIDENT. I'D HOPED THEY WOULD SIMPLY MAKE A SMOKE SCREEN.
THE BEST LAID PLANS OF MICE AND SUPERGIRLS CAN GO ASTRAY, I'M AFRAID.
LOOK! SOMETHING'S WRONG WITH TIRON. HE'S COLLAPSING!
I'M DYING... BUT I-I FOOLED YOU ALL!
WHAT ARE YOU TALKING ABOUT?
TAKE A CLOSE LOOK AT MY FACE! IT'S ONLY A HEAD-MASK!
GREAT GALAXIES! RONALD JASON! YOU'VE BEEN MASQUERADING AS AN ALIEN ALL ALONG!
THEN... WHO IS THE "ALIEN" INSIDE THE CAVE?
15

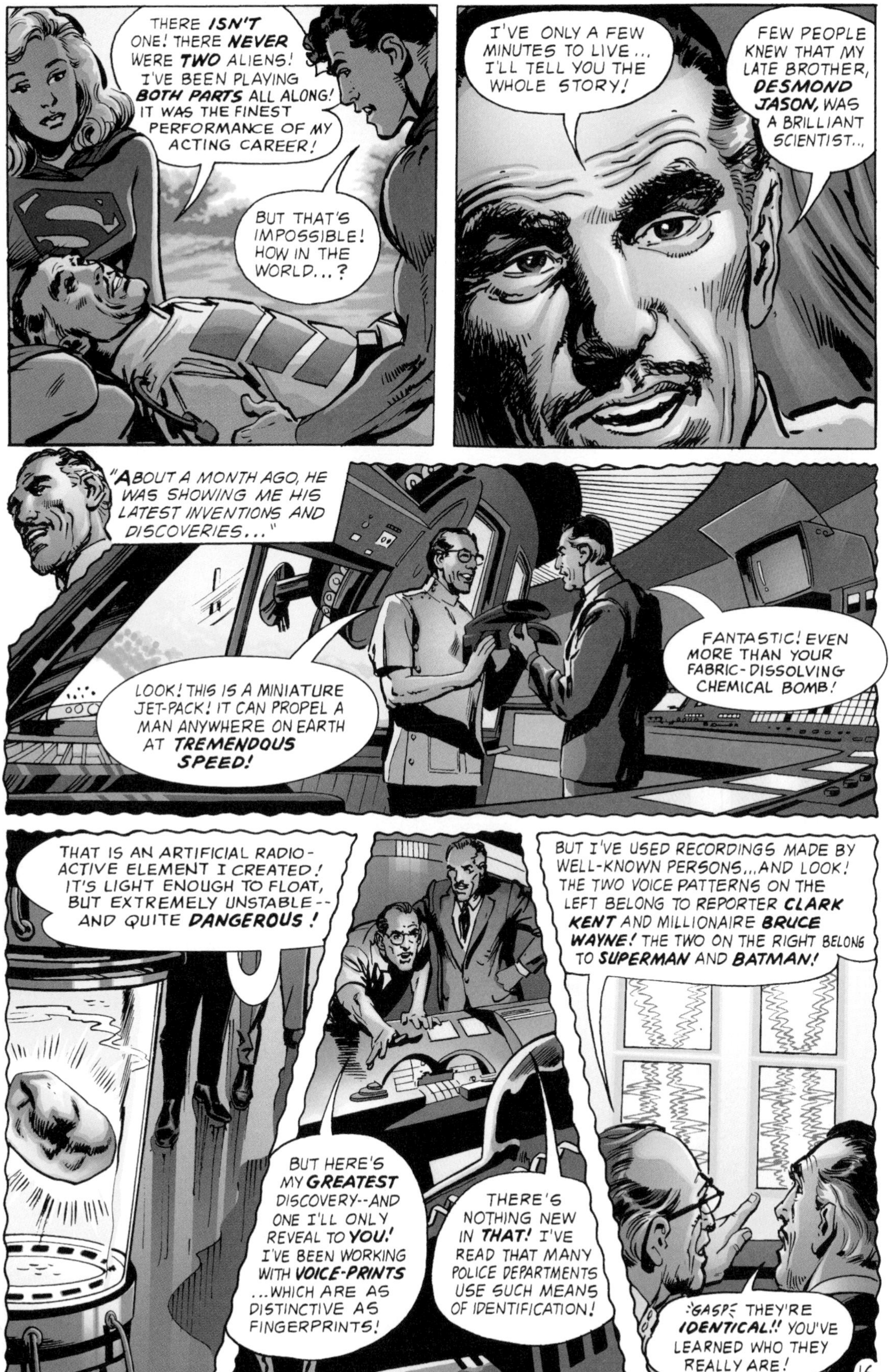
THERE ISN'T ONE! THERE NEVER WERE TWO ALIENS! I'VE BEEN PLAYING BOTH PARTS ALL ALONG! IT WAS THE FINEST PERFORMANCE OF MY ACTING CAREER!
BUT THAT'S IMPOSSIBLE! HOW IN THE WORLD...?
I'VE ONLY A FEW MINUTES TO LIVE... I'LL TELL YOU THE WHOLE STORY!
FEW PEOPLE KNEW THAT MY LATE BROTHER, DESMOND JASON, WAS A BRILLIANT SCIENTIST...
"ABOUT A MONTH AGO, HE WAS SHOWING ME HIS LATEST INVENTIONS AND DISCOVERIES..."
LOOK! THIS IS A MINIATURE JET-PACK! IT CAN PROPEL A MAN ANYWHERE ON EARTH AT TREMENDOUS SPEED!
FANTASTIC! EVEN MORE THAN YOUR FABRIC-DISSOLVING CHEMICAL BOMB!
THAT IS AN ARTIFICIAL RADIO-ACTIVE ELEMENT I CREATED! IT'S LIGHT ENOUGH TO FLOAT, BUT EXTREMELY UNSTABLE--AND QUITE DANGEROUS!
BUT HERE'S MY GREATEST DISCOVERY--AND ONE I'LL ONLY REVEAL TO YOU! I'VE BEEN WORKING WITH VOICE-PRINTS ...WHICH ARE AS DISTINCTIVE AS FINGERPRINTS!
THERE'S NOTHING NEW IN THAT! I'VE READ THAT MANY POLICE DEPARTMENTS USE SUCH MEANS OF IDENTIFICATION!
BUT I'VE USED RECORDINGS MADE BY WELL-KNOWN PERSONS,...AND LOOK! THE TWO VOICE PATTERNS ON THE LEFT BELONG TO REPORTER CLARK KENT AND MILLIONAIRE BRUCE WAYNE! THE TWO ON THE RIGHT BELONG TO SUPERMAN AND BATMAN!
GASP THEY'RE IDENTICAL!! YOU'VE LEARNED WHO THEY REALLY ARE!
16

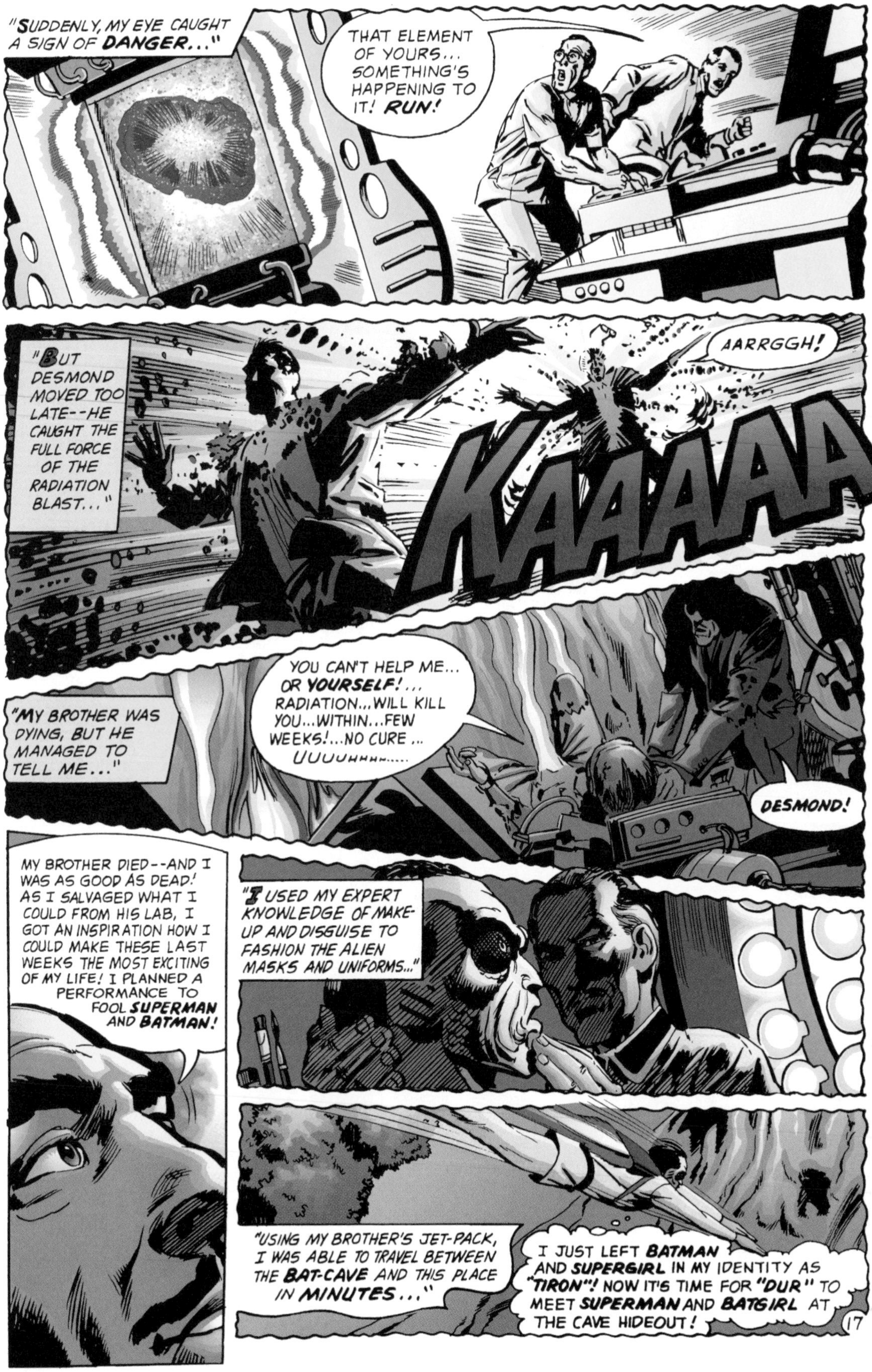
"SUDDENLY, MY EYE CAUGHT A SIGN OF DANGER..."
THAT ELEMENT OF YOURS... SOMETHING'S HAPPENING TO IT! RUN!
"BUT DESMOND MOVED TOO LATE--HE CAUGHT THE FULL FORCE OF THE RADIATION BLAST..."
AARRGGH!
KAAAAA
"MY BROTHER WAS DYING, BUT HE MANAGED TO TELL ME..."
YOU CAN'T HELP ME... OR YOURSELF!... RADIATION...WILL KILL YOU...WITHIN...FEW WEEKS!...NO CURE... UUUUHHHH.....
DESMOND!
MY BROTHER DIED--AND I WAS AS GOOD AS DEAD! AS I SALVAGED WHAT I COULD FROM HIS LAB, I GOT AN INSPIRATION HOW I COULD MAKE THESE LAST WEEKS THE MOST EXCITING OF MY LIFE! I PLANNED A PERFORMANCE TO FOOL SUPERMAN AND BATMAN!
"I USED MY EXPERT KNOWLEDGE OF MAKE-UP AND DISGUISE TO FASHION THE ALIEN MASKS AND UNIFORMS..."
"USING MY BROTHER'S JET-PACK, I WAS ABLE TO TRAVEL BETWEEN THE BAT-CAVE AND THIS PLACE IN MINUTES..."
I JUST LEFT BATMAN AND SUPERGIRL IN MY IDENTITY AS "TIRON"! NOW IT'S TIME FOR "DUR" TO MEET SUPERMAN AND BATGIRL AT THE CAVE HIDEOUT!
17

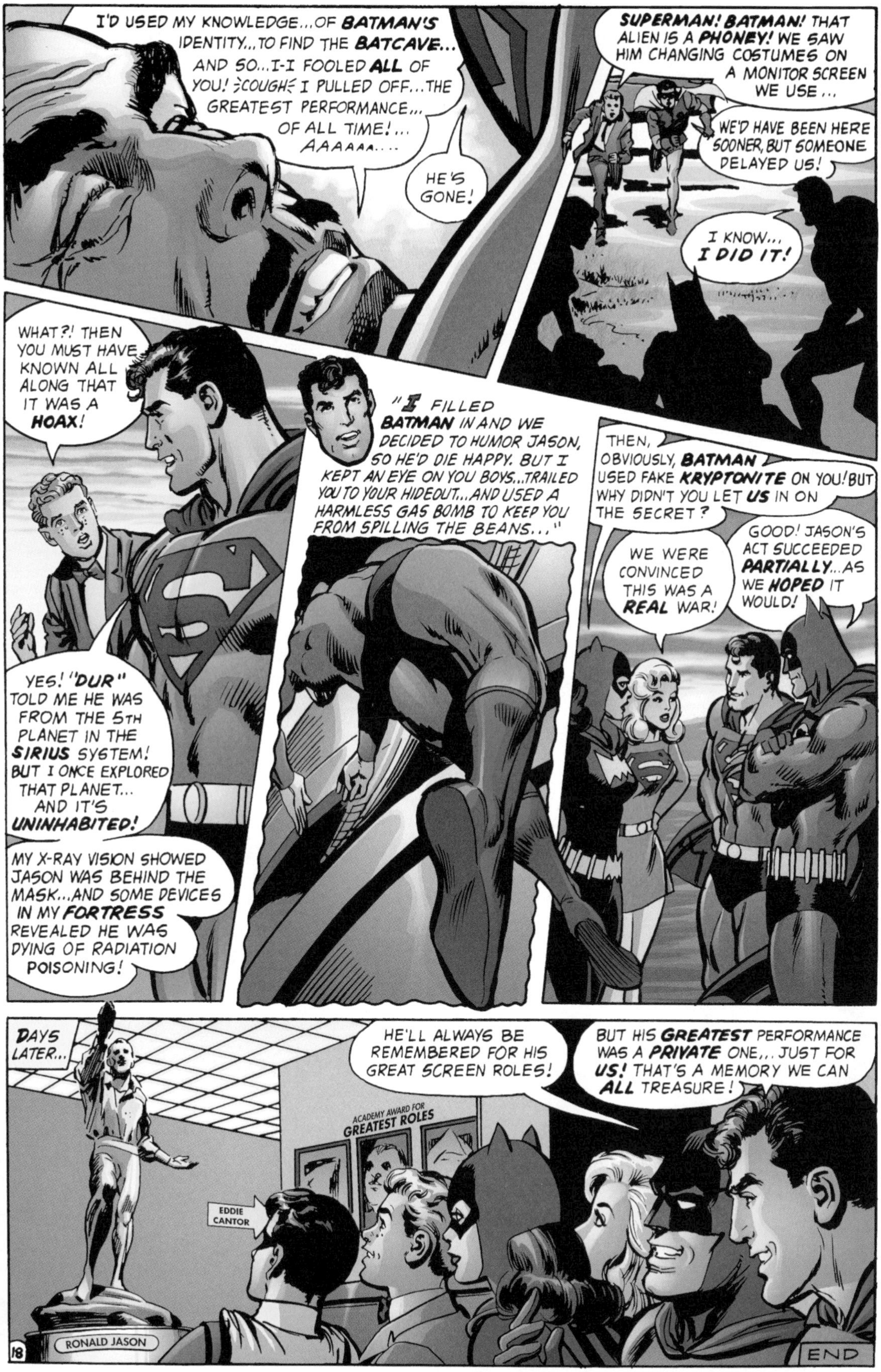
I'D USED MY KNOWLEDGE... OF BATMAN'S IDENTITY... TO FIND THE BATCAVE... AND SO... I-I FOOLED ALL OF YOU! ≷COUGH≶ I PULLED OFF... THE GREATEST PERFORMANCE... OF ALL TIME!... AAAAAA....
HE'S GONE!
SUPERMAN! BATMAN! THAT ALIEN IS A PHONEY! WE SAW HIM CHANGING COSTUMES ON A MONITOR SCREEN WE USE...
WE'D HAVE BEEN HERE SOONER, BUT SOMEONE DELAYED US!
I KNOW... I DID IT!
WHAT?! THEN YOU MUST HAVE KNOWN ALL ALONG THAT IT WAS A HOAX!
YES! "DUR" TOLD ME HE WAS FROM THE 5TH PLANET IN THE SIRIUS SYSTEM! BUT I ONCE EXPLORED THAT PLANET... AND IT'S UNINHABITED!
MY X-RAY VISION SHOWED JASON WAS BEHIND THE MASK... AND SOME DEVICES IN MY FORTRESS REVEALED HE WAS DYING OF RADIATION POISONING!
"I FILLED BATMAN IN AND WE DECIDED TO HUMOR JASON, SO HE'D DIE HAPPY. BUT I KEPT AN EYE ON YOU BOYS... TRAILED YOU TO YOUR HIDEOUT... AND USED A HARMLESS GAS BOMB TO KEEP YOU FROM SPILLING THE BEANS..."
THEN, OBVIOUSLY, BATMAN USED FAKE KRYPTONITE ON YOU! BUT WHY DIDN'T YOU LET US IN ON THE SECRET?
WE WERE CONVINCED THIS WAS A REAL WAR!
GOOD! JASON'S ACT SUCCEEDED PARTIALLY... AS WE HOPED IT WOULD!
DAYS LATER...
HE'LL ALWAYS BE REMEMBERED FOR HIS GREAT SCREEN ROLES!
BUT HIS GREATEST PERFORMANCE WAS A PRIVATE ONE... JUST FOR US! THAT'S A MEMORY WE CAN ALL TREASURE!
ACADEMY AWARD FOR GREATEST ROLES
EDDIE CANTOR
RONALD JASON
18
END

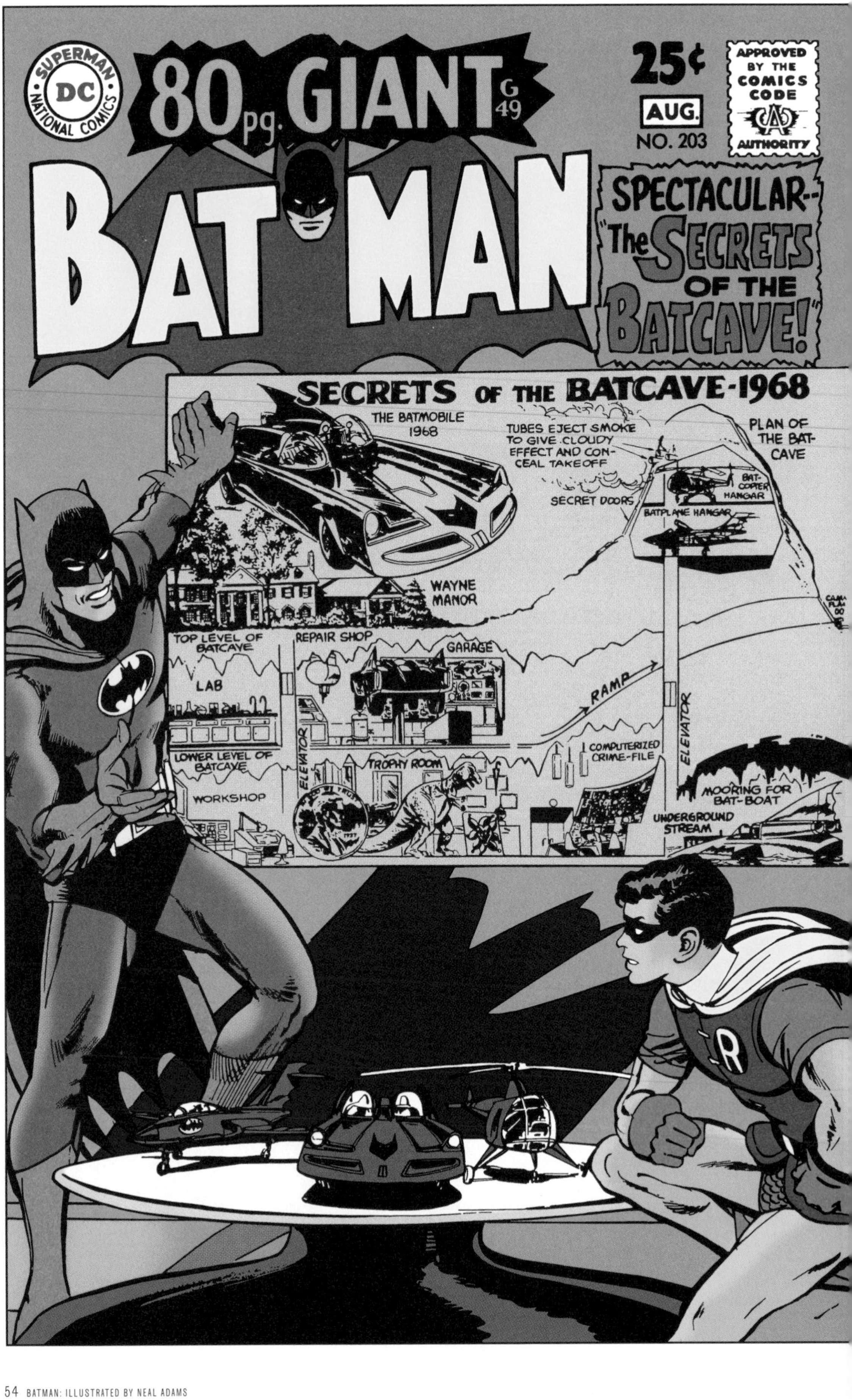
SUPERMAN DC NATIONAL COMICS
80 pg. GIANT G 49
25¢
AUG.
NO. 203
APPROVED BY THE COMICS CODE AUTHORITY
BATMAN
SPECTACULAR-- "The SECRETS OF THE BATCAVE!"
SECRETS OF THE BATCAVE-1968
THE BATMOBILE 1968
TUBES EJECT SMOKE TO GIVE CLOUDY EFFECT AND CONCEAL TAKEOFF
PLAN OF THE BAT-CAVE
BAT-COPTER HANGAR
SECRET DOORS
BATPLANE HANGAR
WAYNE MANOR
TOP LEVEL OF BATCAVE
REPAIR SHOP
GARAGE
LAB
RAMP
ELEVATOR
LOWER LEVEL OF BATCAVE
TROPHY ROOM
COMPUTERIZED CRIME-FILE
MOORING FOR BAT-BOAT
WORKSHOP
UNDERGROUND STREAM

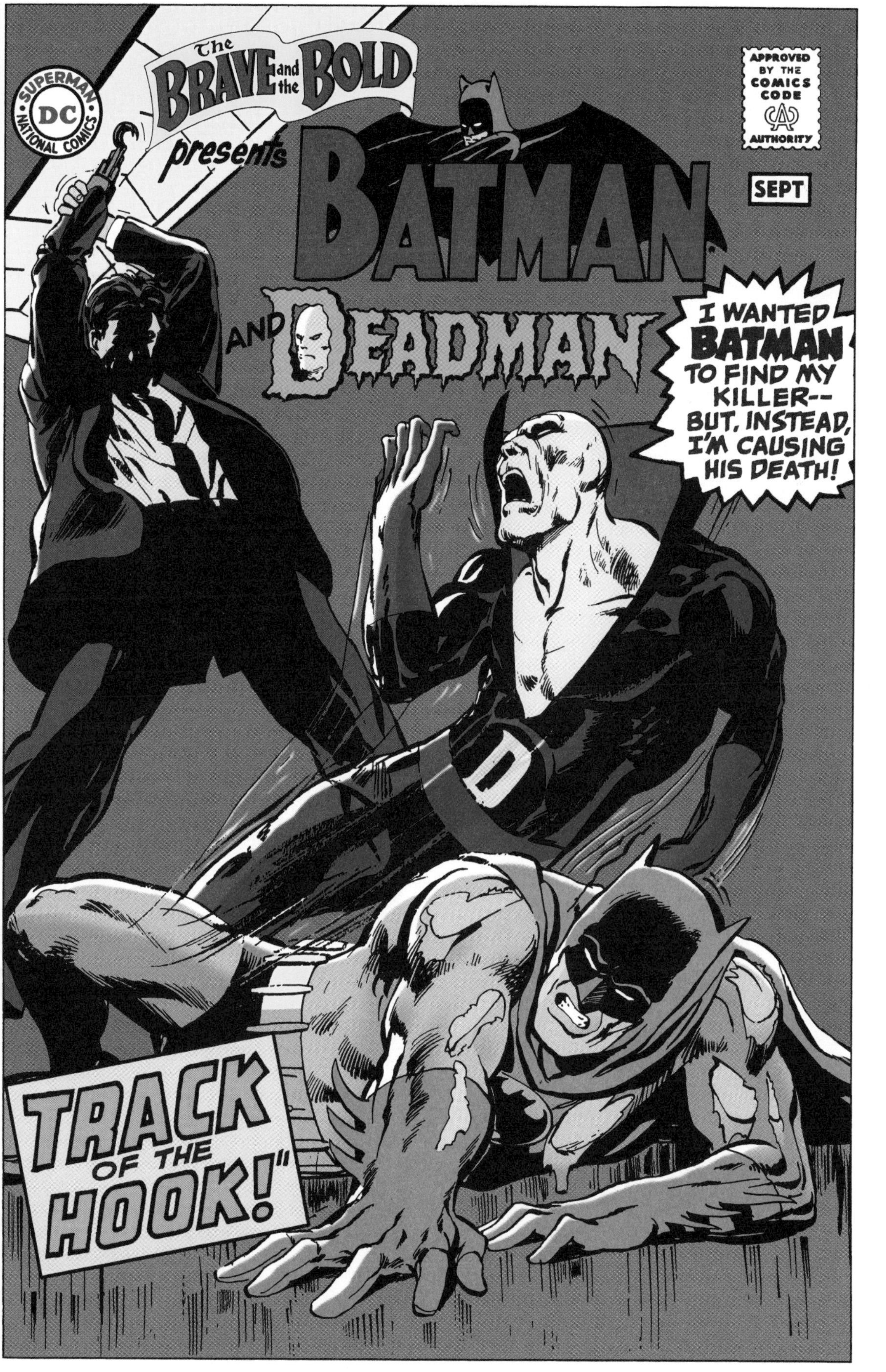
SUPERMAN DC NATIONAL COMICS
The BRAVE and the BOLD
presents
BATMAN
AND DEADMAN
APPROVED BY THE COMICS CODE AUTHORITY
SEPT
I WANTED BATMAN TO FIND MY KILLER-- BUT, INSTEAD, I'M CAUSING HIS DEATH!
"TRACK OF THE HOOK!"

THE TRACK OF THE HOOK

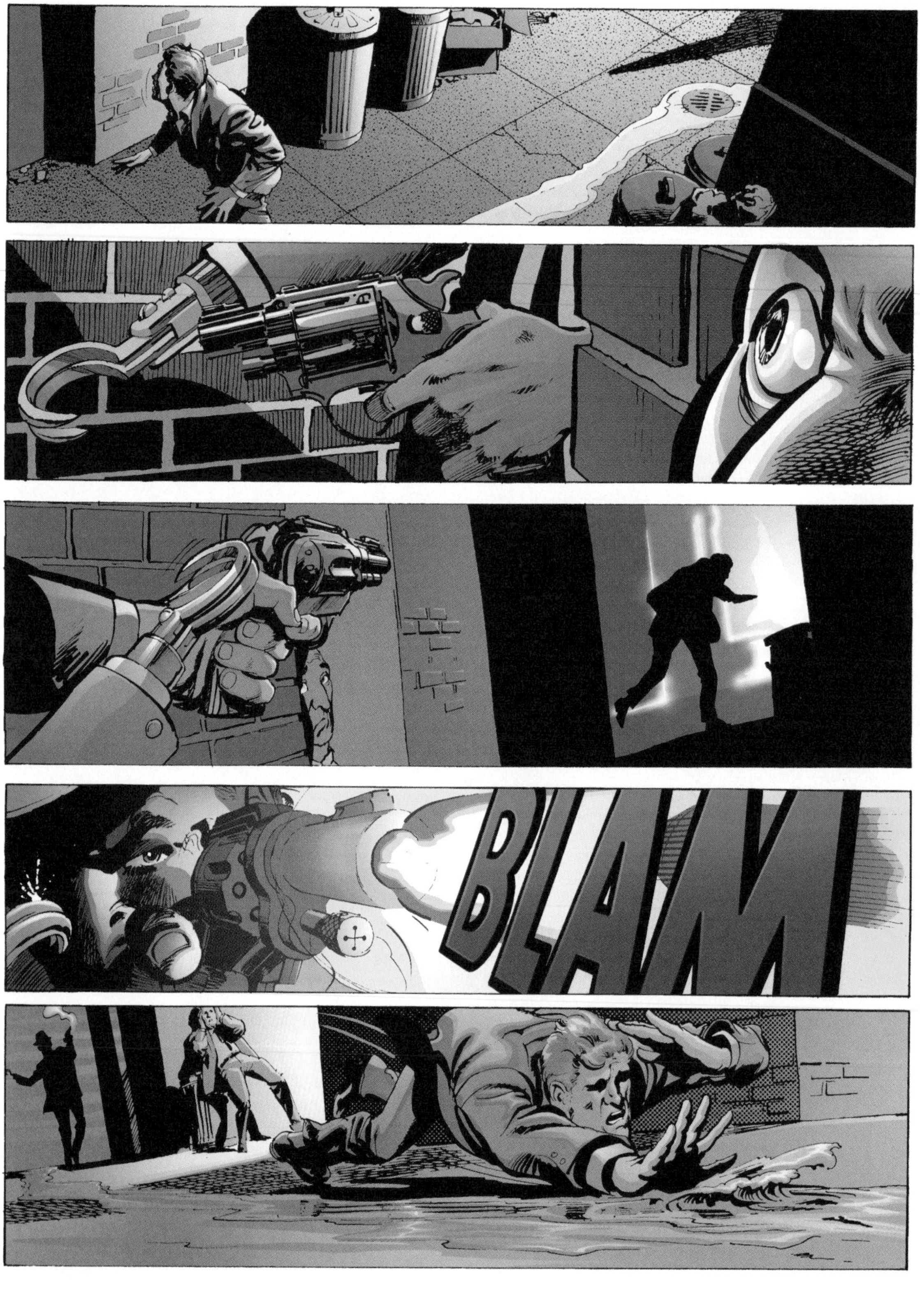
BLAM

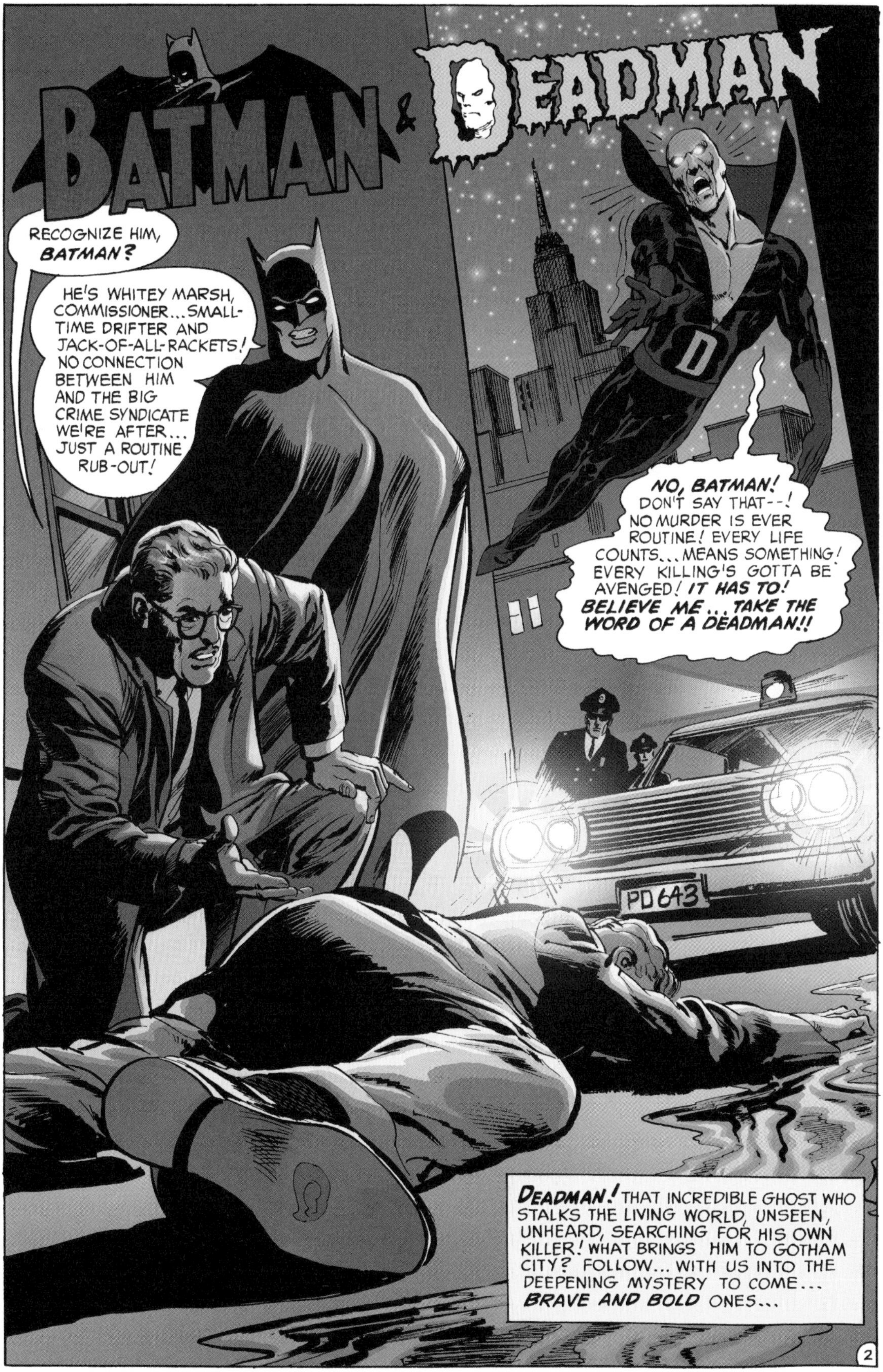
BATMAN & DEADMAN
RECOGNIZE HIM, BATMAN?
HE'S WHITEY MARSH, COMMISSIONER... SMALL-TIME DRIFTER AND JACK-OF-ALL-RACKETS! NO CONNECTION BETWEEN HIM AND THE BIG CRIME SYNDICATE WE'RE AFTER... JUST A ROUTINE RUB-OUT!
NO, BATMAN! DON'T SAY THAT--! NO MURDER IS EVER ROUTINE! EVERY LIFE COUNTS... MEANS SOMETHING! EVERY KILLING'S GOTTA BE AVENGED! IT HAS TO! BELIEVE ME... TAKE THE WORD OF A DEADMAN!!
PD 643
DEADMAN! THAT INCREDIBLE GHOST WHO STALKS THE LIVING WORLD, UNSEEN, UNHEARD, SEARCHING FOR HIS OWN KILLER! WHAT BRINGS HIM TO GOTHAM CITY? FOLLOW... WITH US INTO THE DEEPENING MYSTERY TO COME... BRAVE AND BOLD ONES...
2

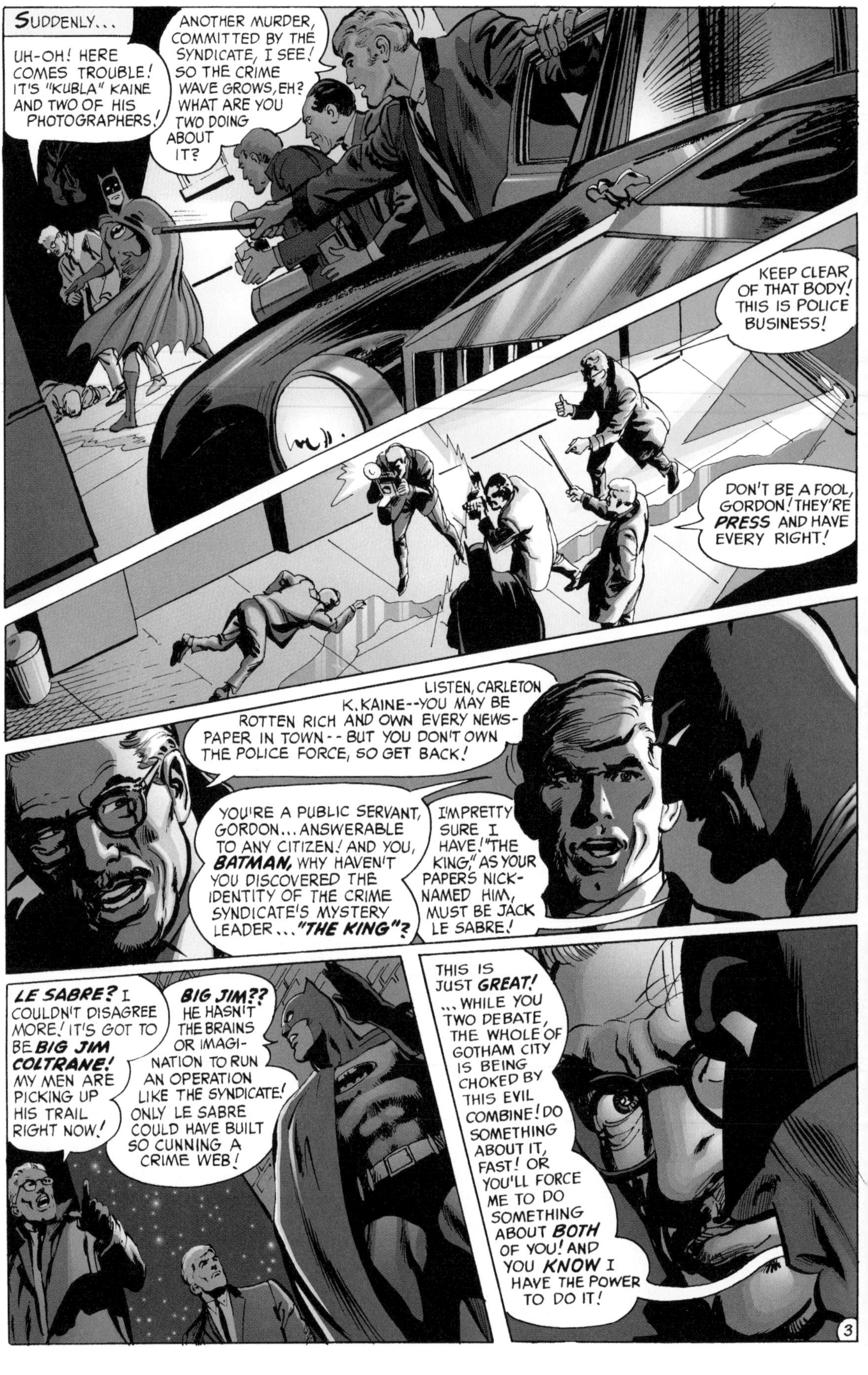

SUDDENLY...
UH-OH! HERE COMES TROUBLE! IT'S "KUBLA" KAINE AND TWO OF HIS PHOTOGRAPHERS!
ANOTHER MURDER, COMMITTED BY THE SYNDICATE, I SEE! SO THE CRIME WAVE GROWS, EH? WHAT ARE YOU TWO DOING ABOUT IT?
KEEP CLEAR OF THAT BODY! THIS IS POLICE BUSINESS!
DON'T BE A FOOL, GORDON! THEY'RE PRESS AND HAVE EVERY RIGHT!
LISTEN, CARLETON K. KAINE--YOU MAY BE ROTTEN RICH AND OWN EVERY NEWSPAPER IN TOWN--BUT YOU DON'T OWN THE POLICE FORCE, SO GET BACK!
YOU'RE A PUBLIC SERVANT, GORDON... ANSWERABLE TO ANY CITIZEN! AND YOU, BATMAN, WHY HAVEN'T YOU DISCOVERED THE IDENTITY OF THE CRIME SYNDICATE'S MYSTERY LEADER... "THE KING"?
I'M PRETTY SURE I HAVE! "THE KING," AS YOUR PAPERS NICKNAMED HIM, MUST BE JACK LE SABRE!
LE SABRE? I COULDN'T DISAGREE MORE! IT'S GOT TO BE BIG JIM COLTRANE! MY MEN ARE PICKING UP HIS TRAIL RIGHT NOW!
BIG JIM?? HE HASN'T THE BRAINS OR IMAGINATION TO RUN AN OPERATION LIKE THE SYNDICATE! ONLY LE SABRE COULD HAVE BUILT SO CUNNING A CRIME WEB!
THIS IS JUST GREAT! ...WHILE YOU TWO DEBATE, THE WHOLE OF GOTHAM CITY IS BEING CHOKED BY THIS EVIL COMBINE! DO SOMETHING ABOUT IT, FAST! OR YOU'LL FORCE ME TO DO SOMETHING ABOUT BOTH OF YOU! AND YOU KNOW I HAVE THE POWER TO DO IT!
3

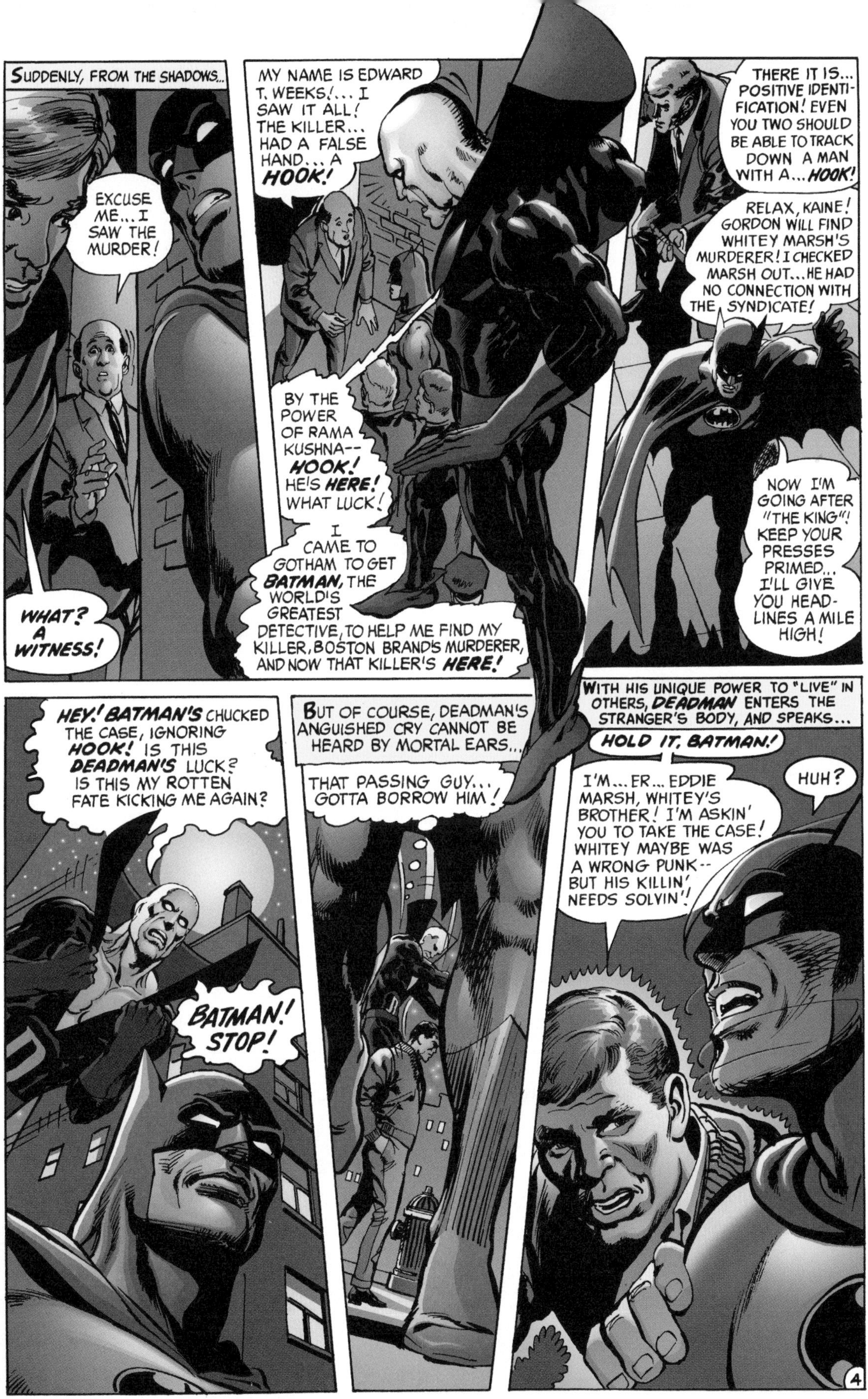
SUDDENLY, FROM THE SHADOWS...
EXCUSE ME... I SAW THE MURDER!
WHAT? A WITNESS!
MY NAME IS EDWARD T. WEEKS!... I SAW IT ALL! THE KILLER... HAD A FALSE HAND... A HOOK!
BY THE POWER OF RAMA KUSHNA-- HOOK! HE'S HERE! WHAT LUCK!
I CAME TO GOTHAM TO GET BATMAN, THE WORLD'S GREATEST DETECTIVE, TO HELP ME FIND MY KILLER, BOSTON BRAND'S MURDERER, AND NOW THAT KILLER'S HERE!
THERE IT IS... POSITIVE IDENTIFICATION! EVEN YOU TWO SHOULD BE ABLE TO TRACK DOWN A MAN WITH A... HOOK!
RELAX, KAINE! GORDON WILL FIND WHITEY MARSH'S MURDERER! I CHECKED MARSH OUT... HE HAD NO CONNECTION WITH THE SYNDICATE!
NOW I'M GOING AFTER "THE KING"! KEEP YOUR PRESSES PRIMED... I'LL GIVE YOU HEADLINES A MILE HIGH!
HEY! BATMAN'S CHUCKED THE CASE, IGNORING HOOK! IS THIS DEADMAN'S LUCK? IS THIS MY ROTTEN FATE KICKING ME AGAIN?
BATMAN! STOP!
BUT OF COURSE, DEADMAN'S ANGUISHED CRY CANNOT BE HEARD BY MORTAL EARS...
THAT PASSING GUY... GOTTA BORROW HIM!
WITH HIS UNIQUE POWER TO "LIVE" IN OTHERS, DEADMAN ENTERS THE STRANGER'S BODY, AND SPEAKS...
HOLD IT, BATMAN!
I'M... ER... EDDIE MARSH, WHITEY'S BROTHER! I'M ASKIN' YOU TO TAKE THE CASE! WHITEY MAYBE WAS A WRONG PUNK-- BUT HIS KILLIN' NEEDS SOLVIN'!
HUH?
4

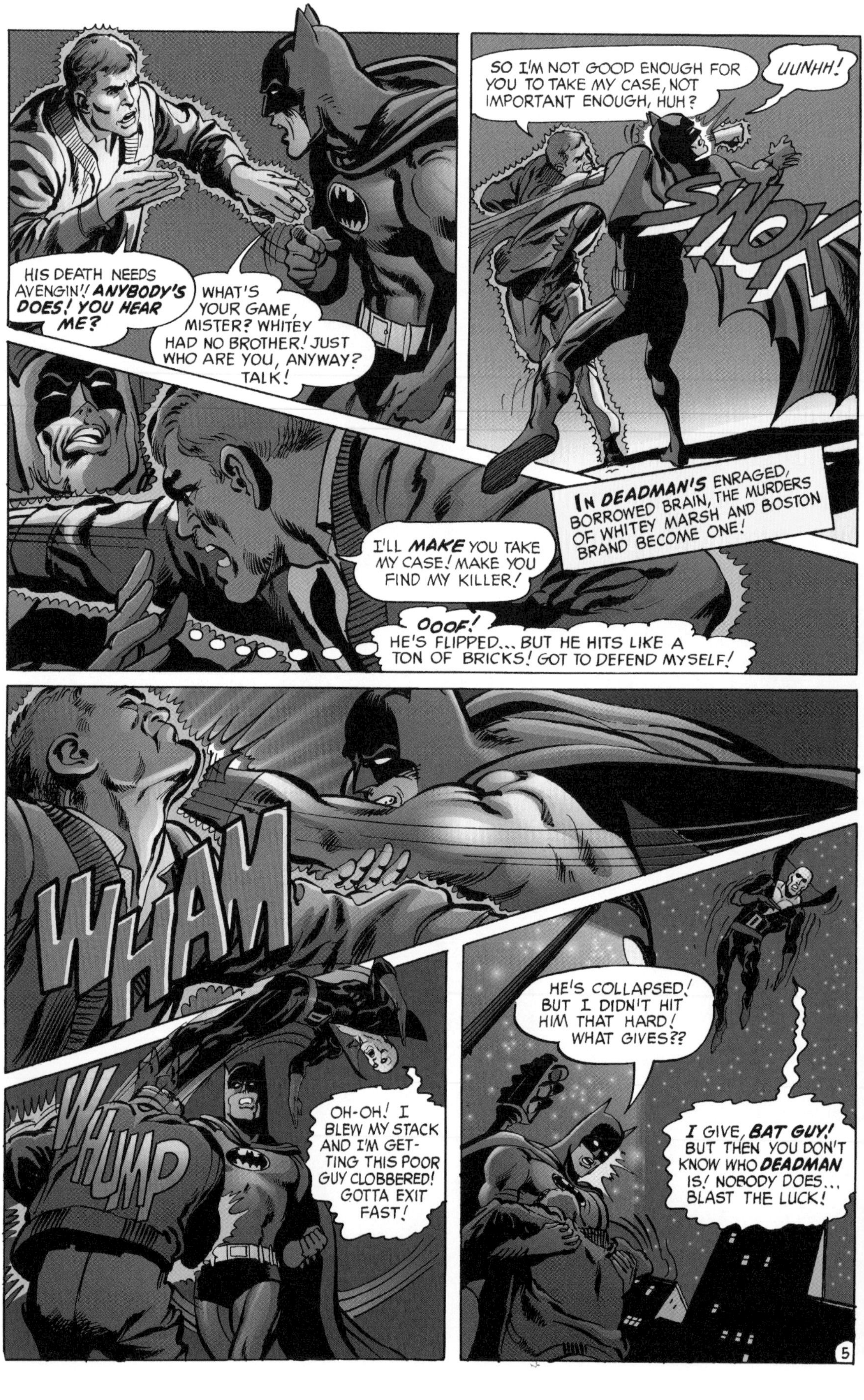
HIS DEATH NEEDS AVENGIN'! ANYBODY'S DOES! YOU HEAR ME?
WHAT'S YOUR GAME, MISTER? WHITEY HAD NO BROTHER! JUST WHO ARE YOU, ANYWAY? TALK!
SO I'M NOT GOOD ENOUGH FOR YOU TO TAKE MY CASE, NOT IMPORTANT ENOUGH, HUH?
UUNHH!
SNOK
IN DEADMAN'S ENRAGED, BORROWED BRAIN, THE MURDERS OF WHITEY MARSH AND BOSTON BRAND BECOME ONE!
I'LL MAKE YOU TAKE MY CASE! MAKE YOU FIND MY KILLER!
OOOF! HE'S FLIPPED... BUT HE HITS LIKE A TON OF BRICKS! GOT TO DEFEND MYSELF!
WHAM
WHUMP
OH-OH! I BLEW MY STACK AND I'M GETTING THIS POOR GUY CLOBBERED! GOTTA EXIT FAST!
HE'S COLLAPSED! BUT I DIDN'T HIT HIM THAT HARD! WHAT GIVES??
I GIVE, BAT GUY! BUT THEN YOU DON'T KNOW WHO DEADMAN IS! NOBODY DOES... BLAST THE LUCK!
5

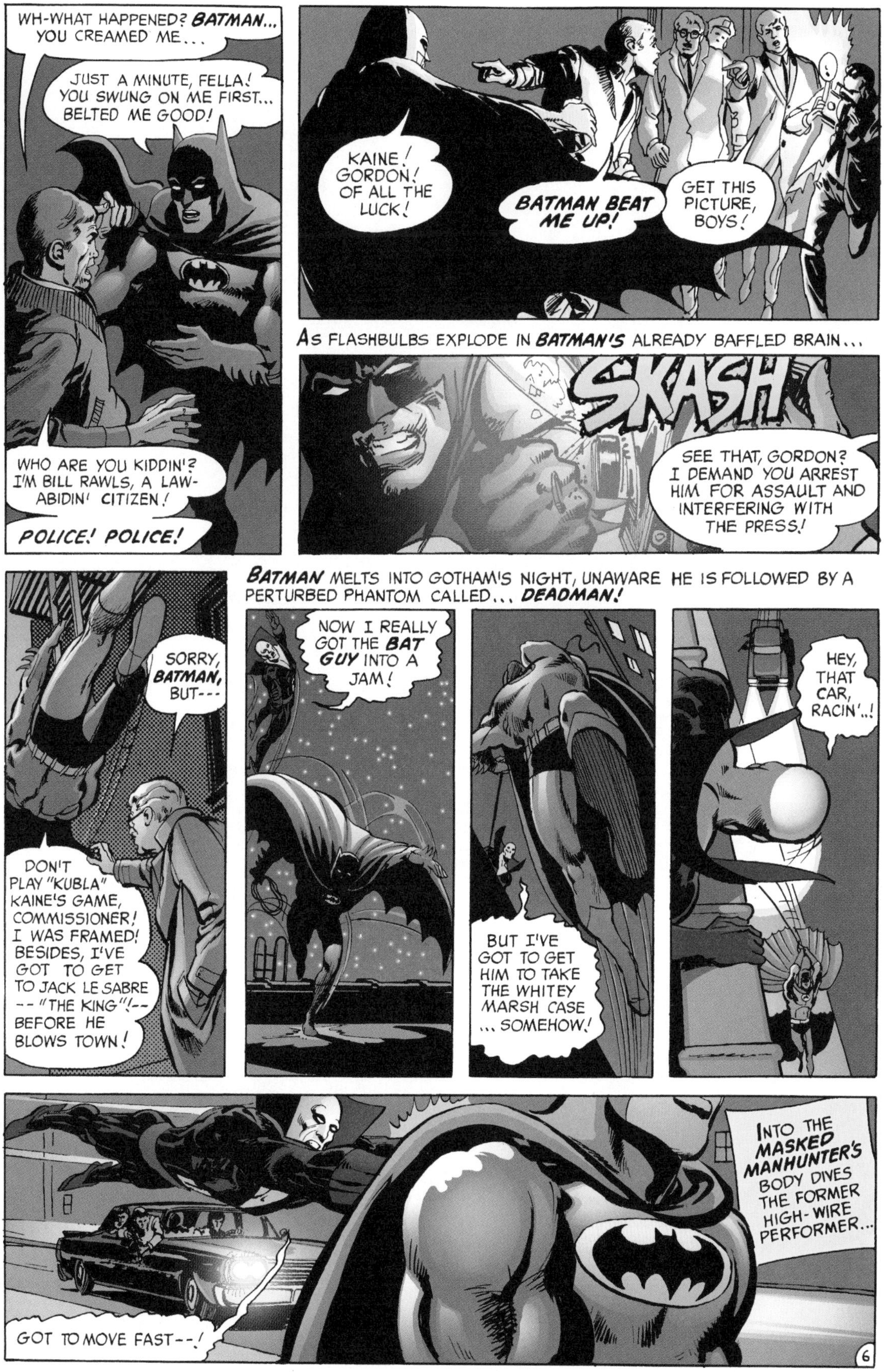
WH-WHAT HAPPENED? BATMAN... YOU CREAMED ME...
JUST A MINUTE, FELLA! YOU SWUNG ON ME FIRST... BELTED ME GOOD!
WHO ARE YOU KIDDIN'? I'M BILL RAWLS, A LAW-ABIDIN' CITIZEN!
POLICE! POLICE!
KAINE! GORDON! OF ALL THE LUCK!
BATMAN BEAT ME UP!
GET THIS PICTURE, BOYS!
AS FLASHBULBS EXPLODE IN BATMAN'S ALREADY BAFFLED BRAIN...
SKASH
SEE THAT, GORDON? I DEMAND YOU ARREST HIM FOR ASSAULT AND INTERFERING WITH THE PRESS!
SORRY, BATMAN, BUT---
DON'T PLAY "KUBLA" KAINE'S GAME, COMMISSIONER! I WAS FRAMED! BESIDES, I'VE GOT TO GET TO JACK LE SABRE -- "THE KING"!-- BEFORE HE BLOWS TOWN!
BATMAN MELTS INTO GOTHAM'S NIGHT, UNAWARE HE IS FOLLOWED BY A PERTURBED PHANTOM CALLED... DEADMAN!
NOW I REALLY GOT THE BAT GUY INTO A JAM!
BUT I'VE GOT TO GET HIM TO TAKE THE WHITEY MARSH CASE ... SOMEHOW!
HEY, THAT CAR, RACIN'..!
GOT TO MOVE FAST--!
INTO THE MASKED MANHUNTER'S BODY DIVES THE FORMER HIGH-WIRE PERFORMER...
6

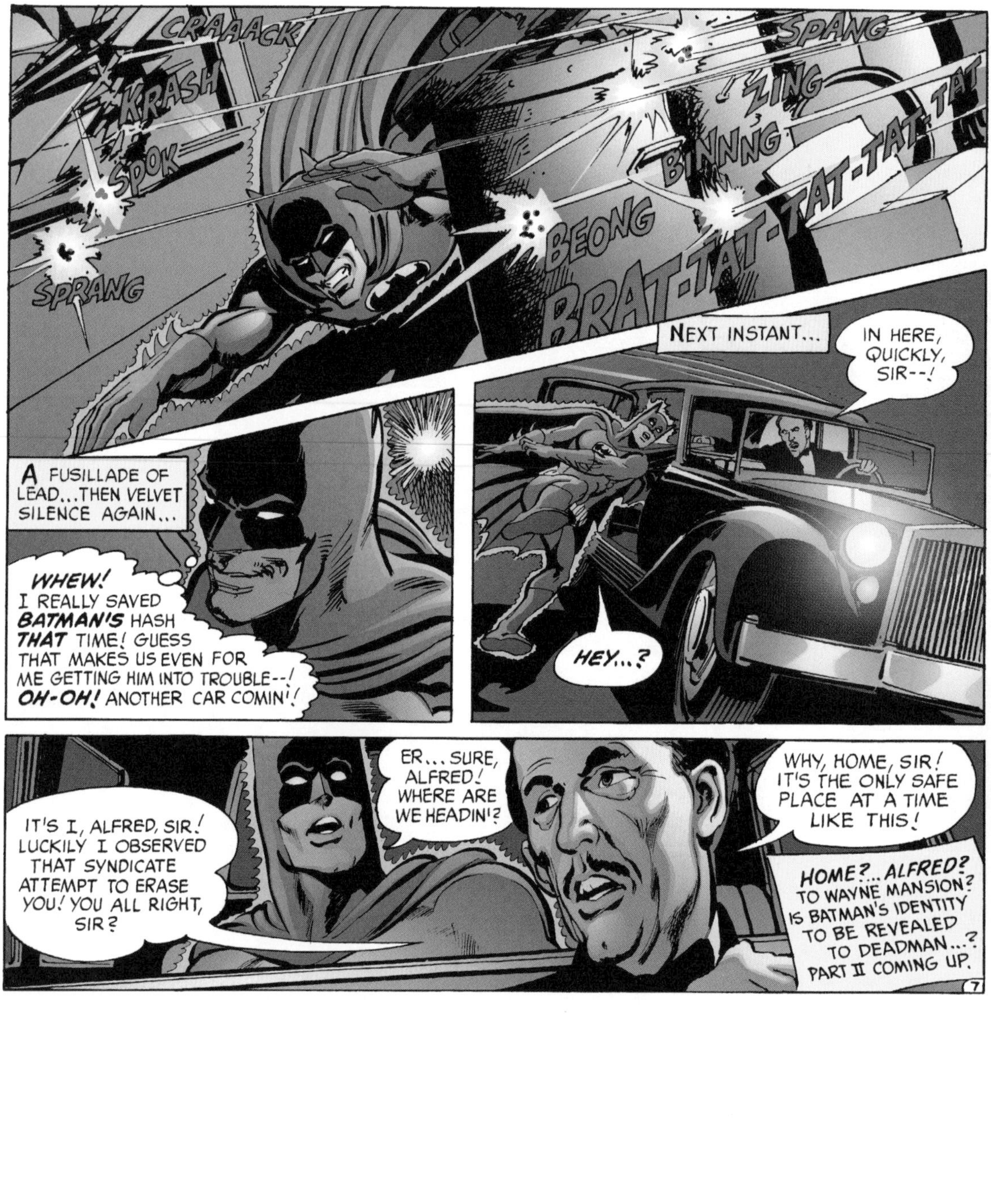
CRAAACK
KRASH
SPOK
SPRANG
SPANG
ZING
BINNNG
BEONG
BRAT-TAT-TAT-TAT-TAT-TAT
NEXT INSTANT...
IN HERE, QUICKLY, SIR--!
HEY...?
A FUSILLADE OF LEAD...THEN VELVET SILENCE AGAIN...
WHEW! I REALLY SAVED BATMAN'S HASH THAT TIME! GUESS THAT MAKES US EVEN FOR ME GETTING HIM INTO TROUBLE--! OH-OH! ANOTHER CAR COMIN'!
IT'S I, ALFRED, SIR! LUCKILY I OBSERVED THAT SYNDICATE ATTEMPT TO ERASE YOU! YOU ALL RIGHT, SIR?
ER... SURE, ALFRED! WHERE ARE WE HEADIN'?
WHY, HOME, SIR! IT'S THE ONLY SAFE PLACE AT A TIME LIKE THIS!
HOME?...ALFRED? TO WAYNE MANSION? IS BATMAN'S IDENTITY TO BE REVEALED TO DEADMAN...? PART II COMING UP.
7

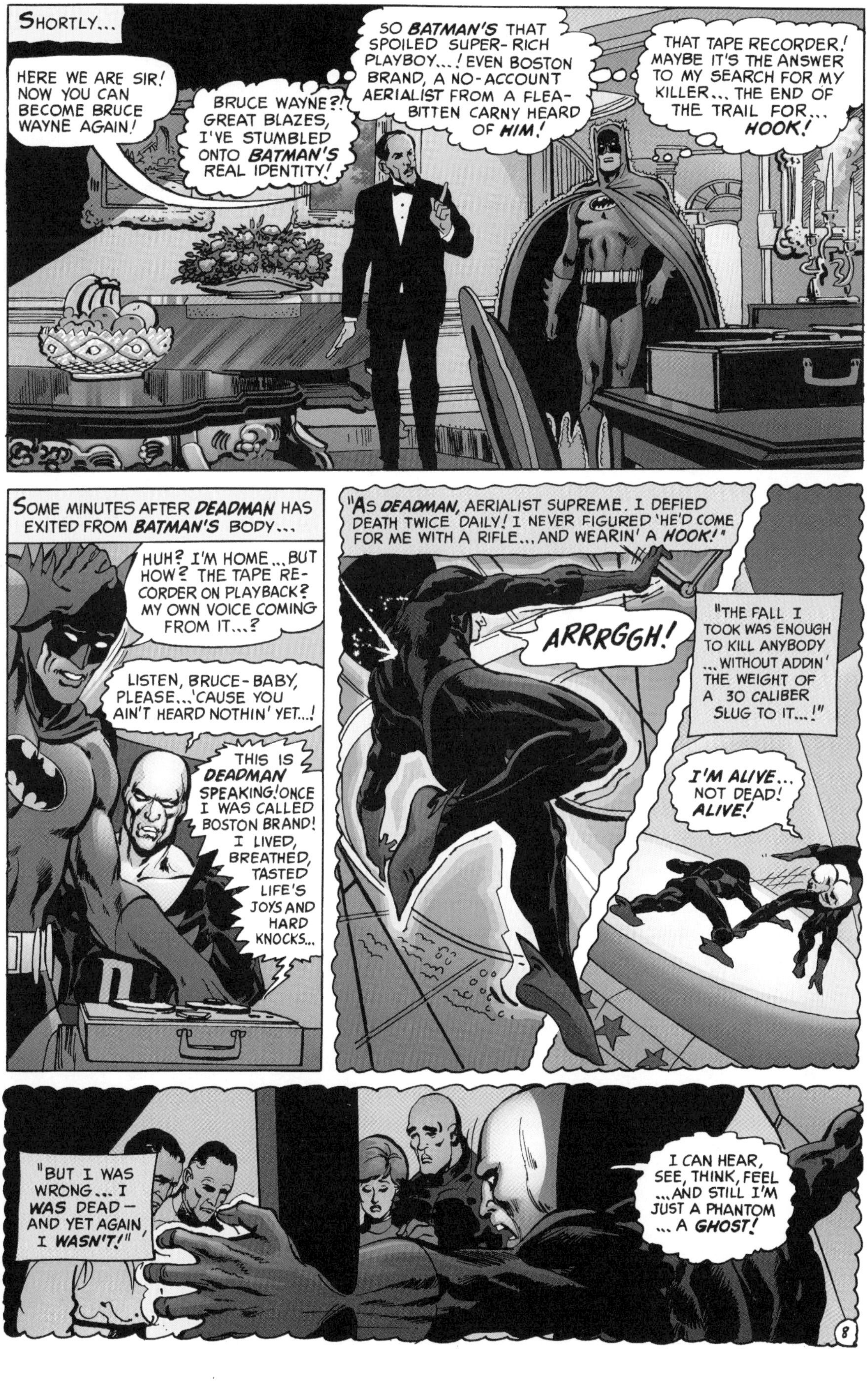

SHORTLY...
HERE WE ARE SIR! NOW YOU CAN BECOME BRUCE WAYNE AGAIN!
BRUCE WAYNE?! GREAT BLAZES, I'VE STUMBLED ONTO BATMAN'S REAL IDENTITY!
SO BATMAN'S THAT SPOILED SUPER-RICH PLAYBOY...! EVEN BOSTON BRAND, A NO-ACCOUNT AERIALIST FROM A FLEA-BITTEN CARNY HEARD OF HIM!
THAT TAPE RECORDER! MAYBE IT'S THE ANSWER TO MY SEARCH FOR MY KILLER... THE END OF THE TRAIL FOR... HOOK!
SOME MINUTES AFTER DEADMAN HAS EXITED FROM BATMAN'S BODY...
HUH? I'M HOME... BUT HOW? THE TAPE RECORDER ON PLAYBACK? MY OWN VOICE COMING FROM IT...?
LISTEN, BRUCE-BABY, PLEASE...'CAUSE YOU AIN'T HEARD NOTHIN' YET...!
THIS IS DEADMAN SPEAKING! ONCE I WAS CALLED BOSTON BRAND! I LIVED, BREATHED, TASTED LIFE'S JOYS AND HARD KNOCKS...
"AS DEADMAN, AERIALIST SUPREME, I DEFIED DEATH TWICE DAILY! I NEVER FIGURED 'HE'D COME FOR ME WITH A RIFLE... AND WEARIN' A HOOK!"
ARRRGGH!
"THE FALL I TOOK WAS ENOUGH TO KILL ANYBODY ... WITHOUT ADDIN' THE WEIGHT OF A 30 CALIBER SLUG TO IT...!"
I'M ALIVE... NOT DEAD! ALIVE!
"BUT I WAS WRONG... I WAS DEAD— AND YET AGAIN, I WASN'T!"
I CAN HEAR, SEE, THINK, FEEL ...AND STILL I'M JUST A PHANTOM ... A GHOST!
8

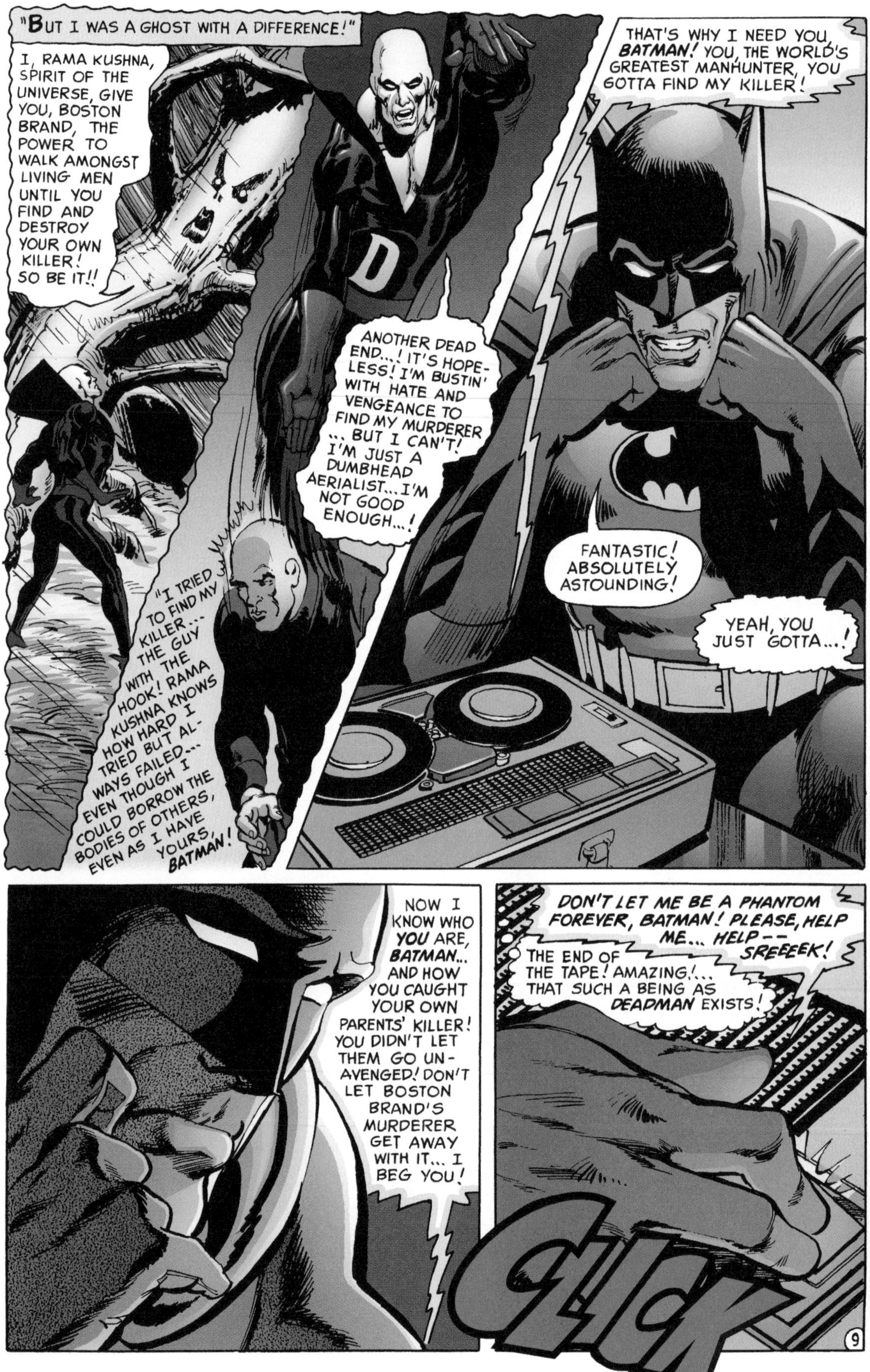
"BUT I WAS A GHOST WITH A DIFFERENCE!"
I, RAMA KUSHNA, SPIRIT OF THE UNIVERSE, GIVE YOU, BOSTON BRAND, THE POWER TO WALK AMONGST LIVING MEN UNTIL YOU FIND AND DESTROY YOUR OWN KILLER! SO BE IT!!
ANOTHER DEAD END...! IT'S HOPE-LESS! I'M BUSTIN' WITH HATE AND VENGEANCE TO FIND MY MURDERER ... BUT I CAN'T! I'M JUST A DUMBHEAD AERIALIST... I'M NOT GOOD ENOUGH...!
"I TRIED TO FIND MY KILLER-- THE GUY WITH THE HOOK! RAMA KUSHNA KNOWS HOW HARD I TRIED BUT AL-WAYS FAILED-- EVEN THOUGH I COULD BORROW THE BODIES OF OTHERS, EVEN AS I HAVE YOURS, BATMAN!
THAT'S WHY I NEED YOU, BATMAN! YOU, THE WORLD'S GREATEST MANHUNTER, YOU GOTTA FIND MY KILLER!
FANTASTIC! ABSOLUTELY ASTOUNDING!
YEAH, YOU JUST GOTTA...!
NOW I KNOW WHO YOU ARE, BATMAN... AND HOW YOU CAUGHT YOUR OWN PARENTS' KILLER! YOU DIDN'T LET THEM GO UN-AVENGED! DON'T LET BOSTON BRAND'S MURDERER GET AWAY WITH IT... I BEG YOU!
DON'T LET ME BE A PHANTOM FOREVER, BATMAN! PLEASE, HELP ME... HELP-- SREEEEK!
THE END OF THE TAPE! AMAZING!... THAT SUCH A BEING AS DEADMAN EXISTS!
CLICK
9

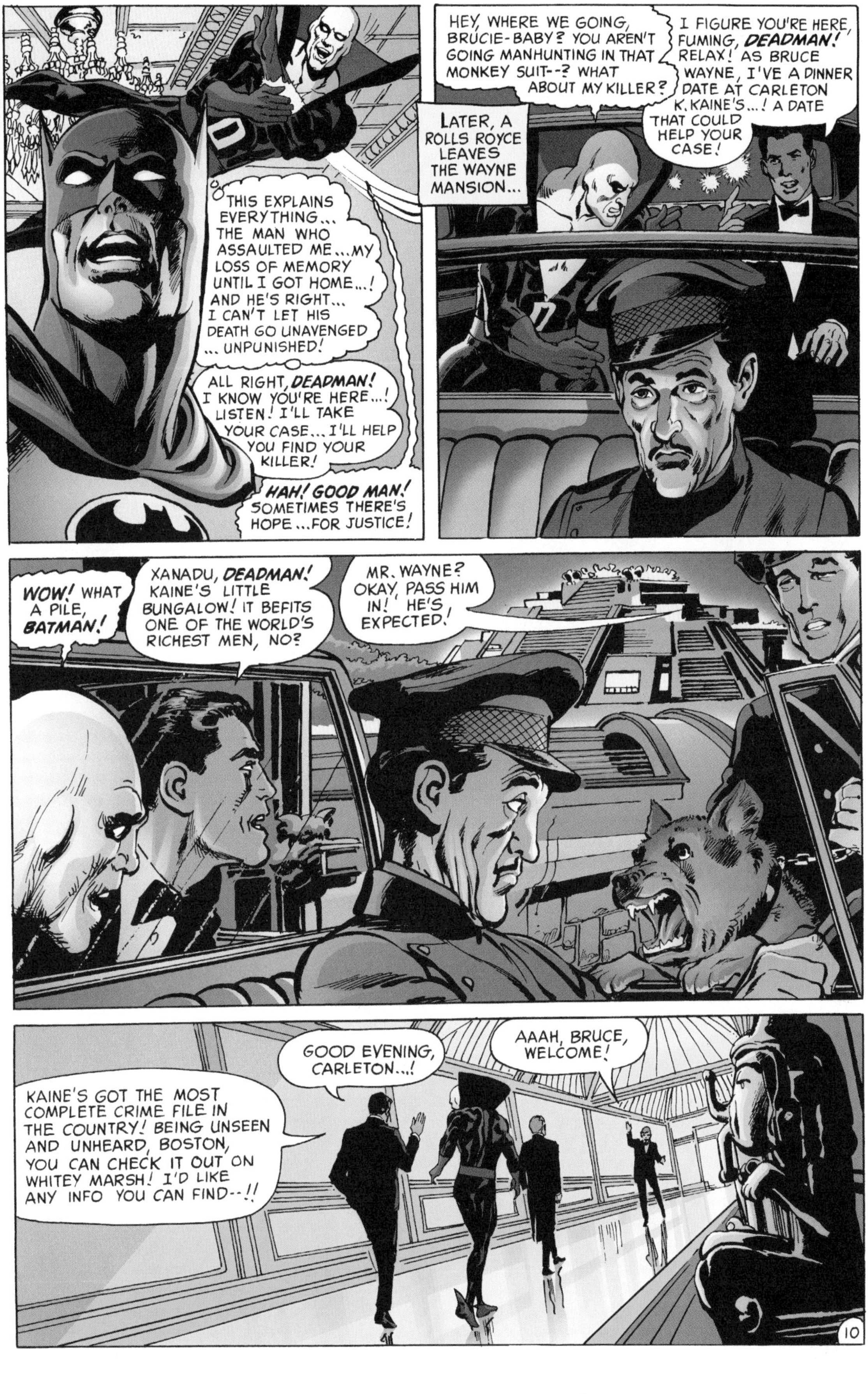

THIS EXPLAINS EVERYTHING... THE MAN WHO ASSAULTED ME...MY LOSS OF MEMORY UNTIL I GOT HOME...! AND HE'S RIGHT... I CAN'T LET HIS DEATH GO UNAVENGED ...UNPUNISHED!
ALL RIGHT, DEADMAN! I KNOW YOU'RE HERE...! LISTEN! I'LL TAKE YOUR CASE... I'LL HELP YOU FIND YOUR KILLER!
HAH! GOOD MAN! SOMETIMES THERE'S HOPE...FOR JUSTICE!
LATER, A ROLLS ROYCE LEAVES THE WAYNE MANSION...
HEY, WHERE WE GOING, BRUCIE-BABY? YOU AREN'T GOING MANHUNTING IN THAT MONKEY SUIT--? WHAT ABOUT MY KILLER?
I FIGURE YOU'RE HERE, FUMING, DEADMAN! RELAX! AS BRUCE WAYNE, I'VE A DINNER DATE AT CARLETON K. KAINE'S...! A DATE THAT COULD HELP YOUR CASE!
WOW! WHAT A PILE, BATMAN!
XANADU, DEADMAN! KAINE'S LITTLE BUNGALOW! IT BEFITS ONE OF THE WORLD'S RICHEST MEN, NO?
MR. WAYNE? OKAY, PASS HIM IN! HE'S EXPECTED!
KAINE'S GOT THE MOST COMPLETE CRIME FILE IN THE COUNTRY! BEING UNSEEN AND UNHEARD, BOSTON, YOU CAN CHECK IT OUT ON WHITEY MARSH! I'D LIKE ANY INFO YOU CAN FIND--!!
GOOD EVENING, CARLETON...!
AAAH, BRUCE, WELCOME!
10

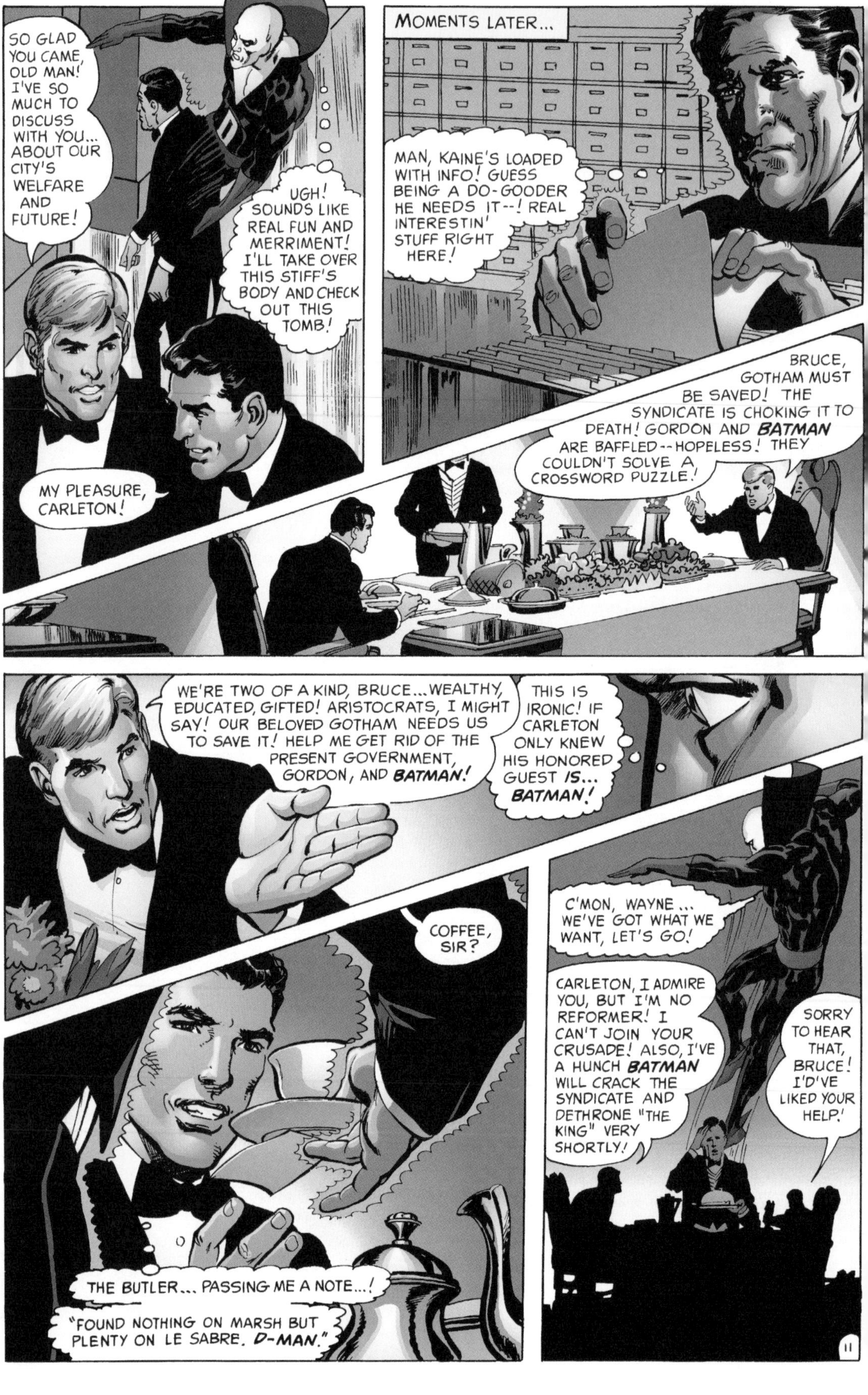
SO GLAD YOU CAME, OLD MAN! I'VE SO MUCH TO DISCUSS WITH YOU... ABOUT OUR CITY'S WELFARE AND FUTURE!
UGH! SOUNDS LIKE REAL FUN AND MERRIMENT! I'LL TAKE OVER THIS STIFF'S BODY AND CHECK OUT THIS TOMB!
MY PLEASURE, CARLETON!
MOMENTS LATER...
MAN, KAINE'S LOADED WITH INFO! GUESS BEING A DO-GOODER HE NEEDS IT--! REAL INTERESTIN' STUFF RIGHT HERE!
BRUCE, GOTHAM MUST BE SAVED! THE SYNDICATE IS CHOKING IT TO DEATH! GORDON AND BATMAN ARE BAFFLED--HOPELESS! THEY COULDN'T SOLVE A CROSSWORD PUZZLE!
WE'RE TWO OF A KIND, BRUCE...WEALTHY, EDUCATED, GIFTED! ARISTOCRATS, I MIGHT SAY! OUR BELOVED GOTHAM NEEDS US TO SAVE IT! HELP ME GET RID OF THE PRESENT GOVERNMENT, GORDON, AND BATMAN!
THIS IS IRONIC! IF CARLETON ONLY KNEW HIS HONORED GUEST IS... BATMAN!
COFFEE, SIR?
THE BUTLER... PASSING ME A NOTE...!
"FOUND NOTHING ON MARSH BUT PLENTY ON LE SABRE. D-MAN."
C'MON, WAYNE... WE'VE GOT WHAT WE WANT, LET'S GO!
CARLETON, I ADMIRE YOU, BUT I'M NO REFORMER! I CAN'T JOIN YOUR CRUSADE! ALSO, I'VE A HUNCH BATMAN WILL CRACK THE SYNDICATE AND DETHRONE "THE KING" VERY SHORTLY!
SORRY TO HEAR THAT, BRUCE! I'D'VE LIKED YOUR HELP.
11

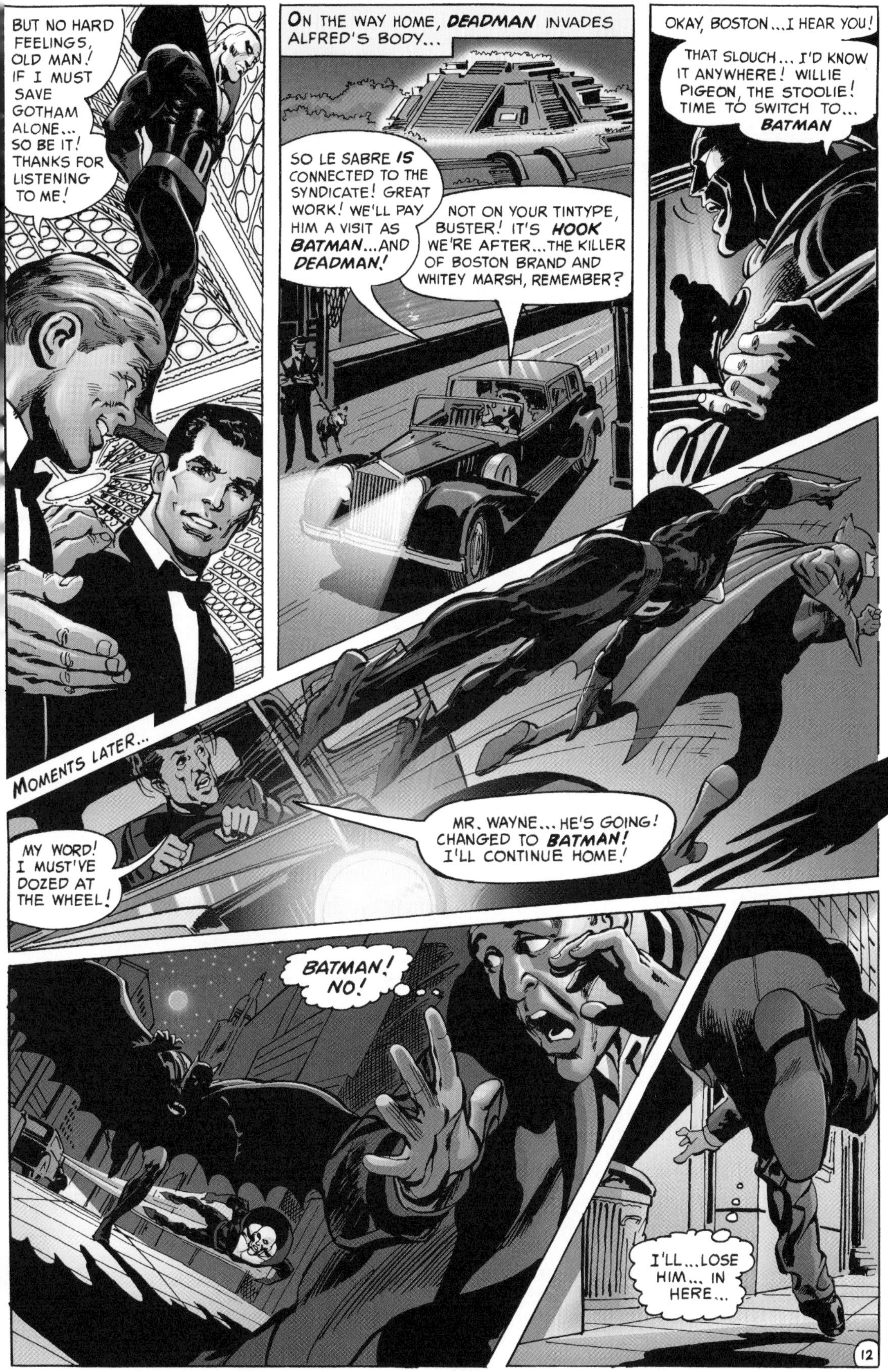

BUT NO HARD FEELINGS, OLD MAN! IF I MUST SAVE GOTHAM ALONE... SO BE IT! THANKS FOR LISTENING TO ME!
ON THE WAY HOME, DEADMAN INVADES ALFRED'S BODY...
SO LE SABRE IS CONNECTED TO THE SYNDICATE! GREAT WORK! WE'LL PAY HIM A VISIT AS BATMAN...AND DEADMAN!
NOT ON YOUR TINTYPE, BUSTER! IT'S HOOK WE'RE AFTER...THE KILLER OF BOSTON BRAND AND WHITEY MARSH, REMEMBER?
OKAY, BOSTON...I HEAR YOU!
THAT SLOUCH... I'D KNOW IT ANYWHERE! WILLIE PIGEON, THE STOOLIE! TIME TO SWITCH TO... BATMAN
MOMENTS LATER...
MY WORD! I MUST'VE DOZED AT THE WHEEL!
MR. WAYNE... HE'S GOING! CHANGED TO BATMAN! I'LL CONTINUE HOME!
BATMAN! NO!
I'LL...LOSE HIM... IN HERE...
12

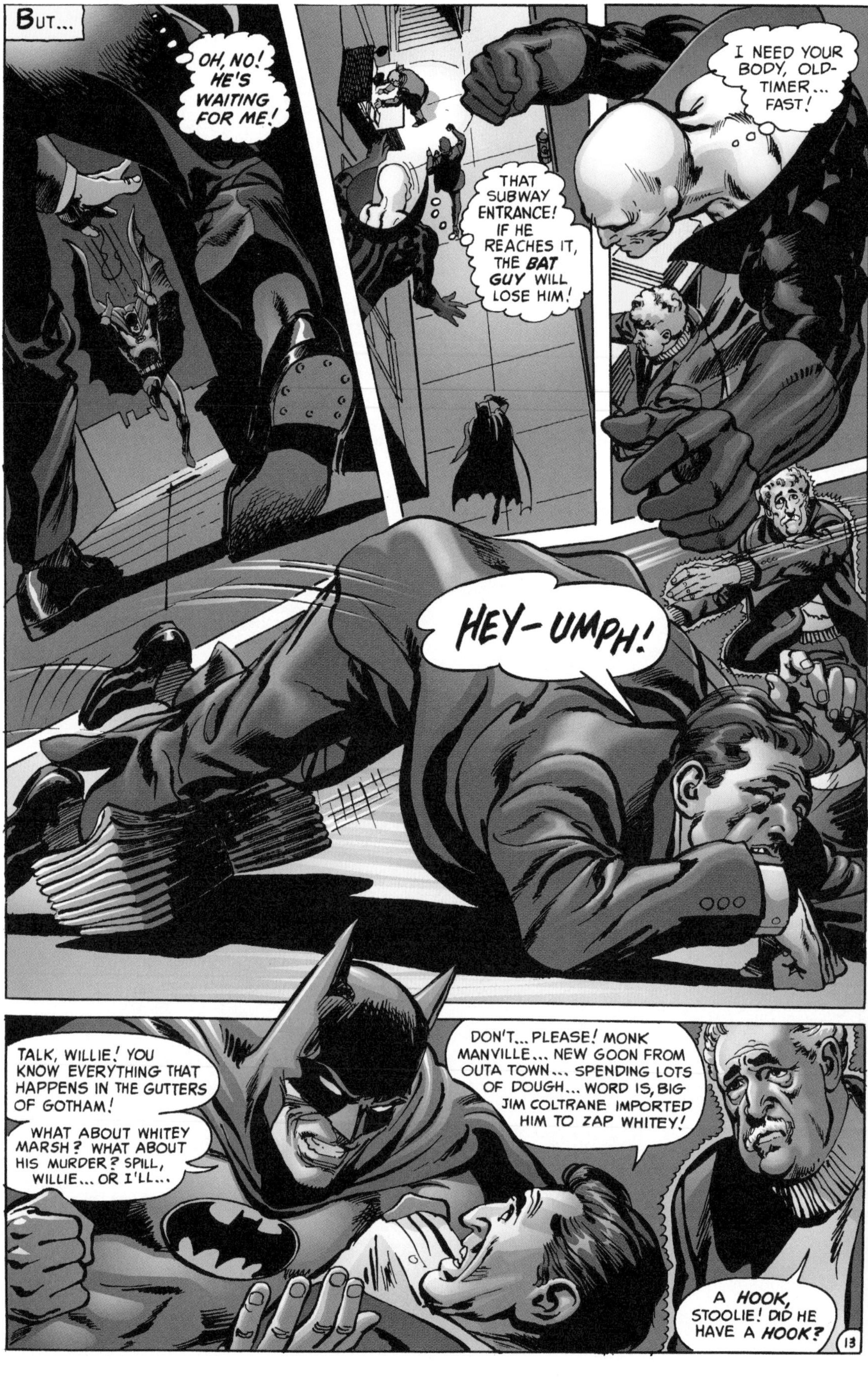
BUT...
OH, NO! HE'S WAITING FOR ME!
THAT SUBWAY ENTRANCE! IF HE REACHES IT, THE BAT GUY WILL LOSE HIM!
I NEED YOUR BODY, OLD-TIMER... FAST!
HEY-UMPH!
TALK, WILLIE! YOU KNOW EVERYTHING THAT HAPPENS IN THE GUTTERS OF GOTHAM!
WHAT ABOUT WHITEY MARSH? WHAT ABOUT HIS MURDER? SPILL, WILLIE... OR I'LL...
DON'T... PLEASE! MONK MANVILLE... NEW GOON FROM OUTA TOWN... SPENDING LOTS OF DOUGH... WORD IS, BIG JIM COLTRANE IMPORTED HIM TO ZAP WHITEY!
A HOOK, STOOLIE! DID HE HAVE A HOOK?
13

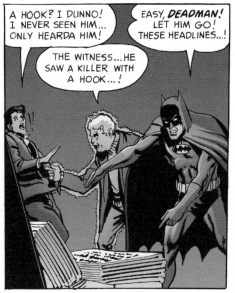

A HOOK? I DUNNO! I NEVER SEEN HIM... ONLY HEARDA HIM!

EASY, **DEADMAN!** LET HIM GO! THESE HEADLINES...!

THE WITNESS...HE SAW A KILLER WITH A HOOK...!

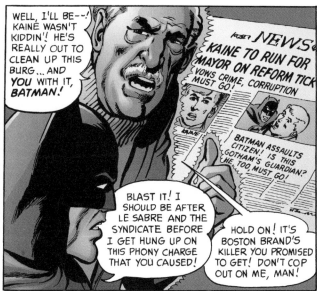

WELL, I'LL BE--! KAINÉ WASN'T KIDDIN'! HE'S REALLY OUT TO CLEAN UP THIS BURG... AND **YOU** WITH IT, **BATMAN!**

NEWS KAINE TO RUN FOR MAYOR ON REFORM TICK VOWS CRIME, CORRUPTION MUST GO!

BATMAN ASSAULTS CITIZEN! IS THIS GOTHAM'S GUARDIAN? HE, TOO, MUST GO!

BLAST IT! I SHOULD BE AFTER LE SABRE AND THE SYNDICATE BEFORE I GET HUNG UP ON THIS PHONY CHARGE THAT YOU CAUSED!

HOLD ON! IT'S BOSTON BRAND'S KILLER YOU PROMISED TO GET! DON'T COP OUT ON ME, MAN!

ALL RIGHT, ALL RIGHT, YOU CRAZY GHOST! GET OFF MY BACK!

WAIT! WILLIE JUST SAID BIG JIM COLTRANE HIRED MONK MANVILLE! GORDON INSISTS BIG JIM'S "THE KING!" MAYBE HE'S RIGHT! AND I THINK I KNOW HOW I CAN FIND HIM! LET'S GO!

AN EX-CON HELPS **BATMAN** LOCATE THE SUSPECTED KILLER...

FIRST DOOR ON THE LEFT, AT THE TOP OF THE STAIRS...

HE'S GONE... OUR BIRD'S FLOWN THE COOP! THE TRAIL'S COLD...! WHAT'S THAT, **DEADMAN,** IN THE CORNER...?

THIS PHOTO OF MONK! HE HAS NO **HOOK!** HEAR THAT, DEADMAN? NO... HOOK!

GET IT, **DEADMAN?** IF MONK DID SHOOT MARSH, HE COULDN'T HAVE KILLED BOSTON BRAND! EVEN IF THAT WITNESS WAS WRONG ABOUT THE HOOK! SO WE'RE STYMIED ... NOWHERE!

THERE'S GOTTA BE AN ANSWER ...THERE MUST!

HOOK! I'LL GET YOU YET... SOME-HOW... SOME WAY... YOU CAN'T CHEAT DEADMAN!

14

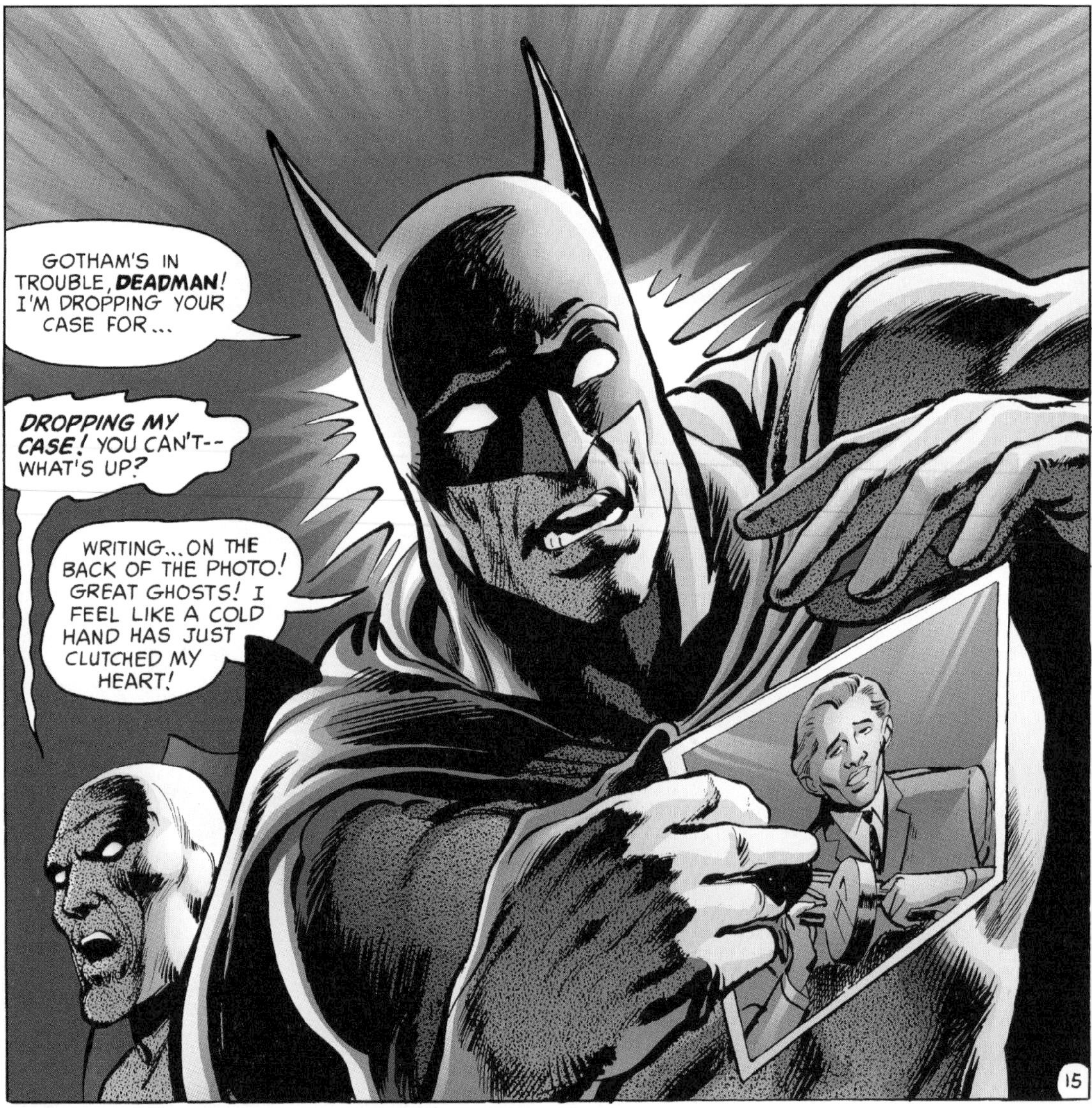
GOTHAM'S IN TROUBLE, **DEADMAN**! I'M DROPPING YOUR CASE FOR...
DROPPING MY CASE! YOU CAN'T-- WHAT'S UP?
WRITING...ON THE BACK OF THE PHOTO! GREAT GHOSTS! I FEEL LIKE A COLD HAND HAS JUST CLUTCHED MY HEART!
15

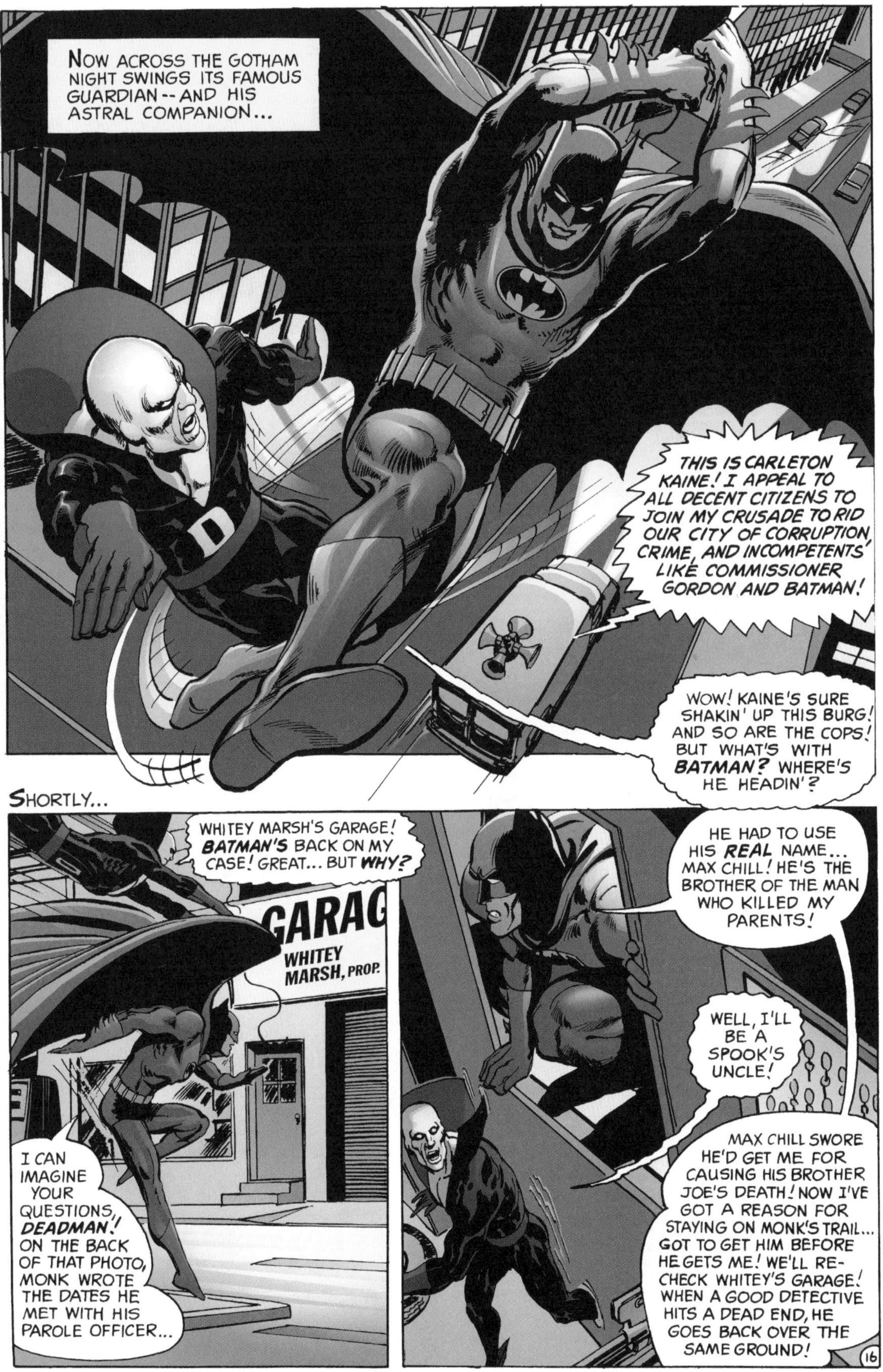
NOW ACROSS THE GOTHAM NIGHT SWINGS ITS FAMOUS GUARDIAN -- AND HIS ASTRAL COMPANION...
THIS IS CARLETON KAINE! I APPEAL TO ALL DECENT CITIZENS TO JOIN MY CRUSADE TO RID OUR CITY OF CORRUPTION, CRIME, AND INCOMPETENTS LIKE COMMISSIONER GORDON AND BATMAN!
WOW! KAINE'S SURE SHAKIN' UP THIS BURG! AND SO ARE THE COPS! BUT WHAT'S WITH BATMAN? WHERE'S HE HEADIN'?
SHORTLY...
WHITEY MARSH'S GARAGE! BATMAN'S BACK ON MY CASE! GREAT... BUT WHY?
GARAG
WHITEY MARSH, PROP.
I CAN IMAGINE YOUR QUESTIONS, DEADMAN! ON THE BACK OF THAT PHOTO, MONK WROTE THE DATES HE MET WITH HIS PAROLE OFFICER...
HE HAD TO USE HIS REAL NAME... MAX CHILL! HE'S THE BROTHER OF THE MAN WHO KILLED MY PARENTS!
WELL, I'LL BE A SPOOK'S UNCLE!
MAX CHILL SWORE HE'D GET ME FOR CAUSING HIS BROTHER JOE'S DEATH! NOW I'VE GOT A REASON FOR STAYING ON MONK'S TRAIL... GOT TO GET HIM BEFORE HE GETS ME! WE'LL RE-CHECK WHITEY'S GARAGE! WHEN A GOOD DETECTIVE HITS A DEAD END, HE GOES BACK OVER THE SAME GROUND!
16

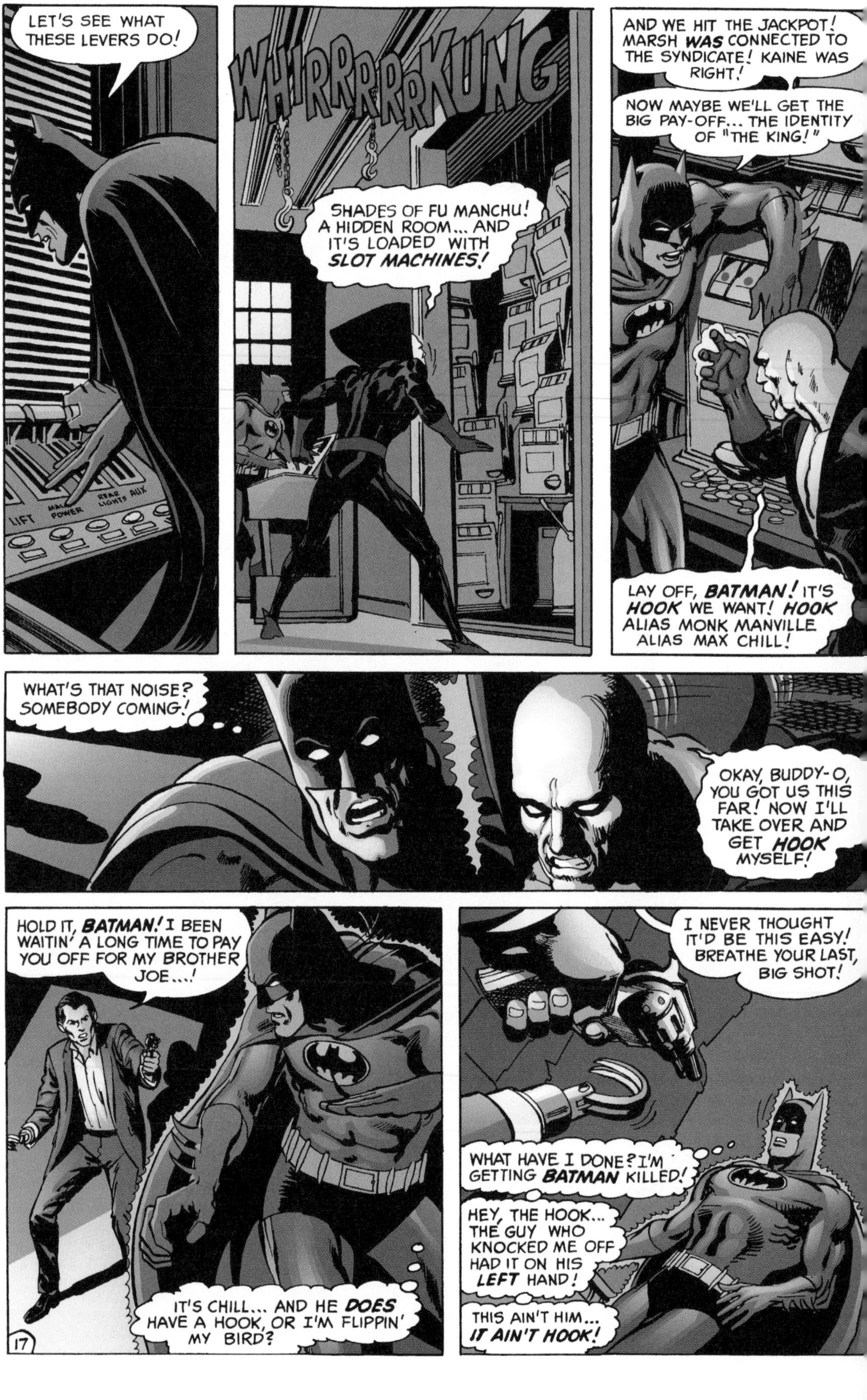
LET'S SEE WHAT THESE LEVERS DO!
LIFT
MAX POWER
REAR LIGHTS
AUX
WHIRRRRRKUNG
SHADES OF FU MANCHU! A HIDDEN ROOM... AND IT'S LOADED WITH SLOT MACHINES!
AND WE HIT THE JACKPOT! MARSH WAS CONNECTED TO THE SYNDICATE! KAINE WAS RIGHT!
NOW MAYBE WE'LL GET THE BIG PAY-OFF... THE IDENTITY OF "THE KING!"
LAY OFF, BATMAN! IT'S HOOK WE WANT! HOOK ALIAS MONK MANVILLE ALIAS MAX CHILL!
WHAT'S THAT NOISE? SOMEBODY COMING!
OKAY, BUDDY-O, YOU GOT US THIS FAR! NOW I'LL TAKE OVER AND GET HOOK MYSELF!
HOLD IT, BATMAN! I BEEN WAITIN' A LONG TIME TO PAY YOU OFF FOR MY BROTHER JOE...!
IT'S CHILL... AND HE DOES HAVE A HOOK, OR I'M FLIPPIN' MY BIRD?
17
I NEVER THOUGHT IT'D BE THIS EASY! BREATHE YOUR LAST, BIG SHOT!
WHAT HAVE I DONE? I'M GETTING BATMAN KILLED!
HEY, THE HOOK... THE GUY WHO KNOCKED ME OFF HAD IT ON HIS LEFT HAND!
THIS AIN'T HIM... IT AIN'T HOOK!

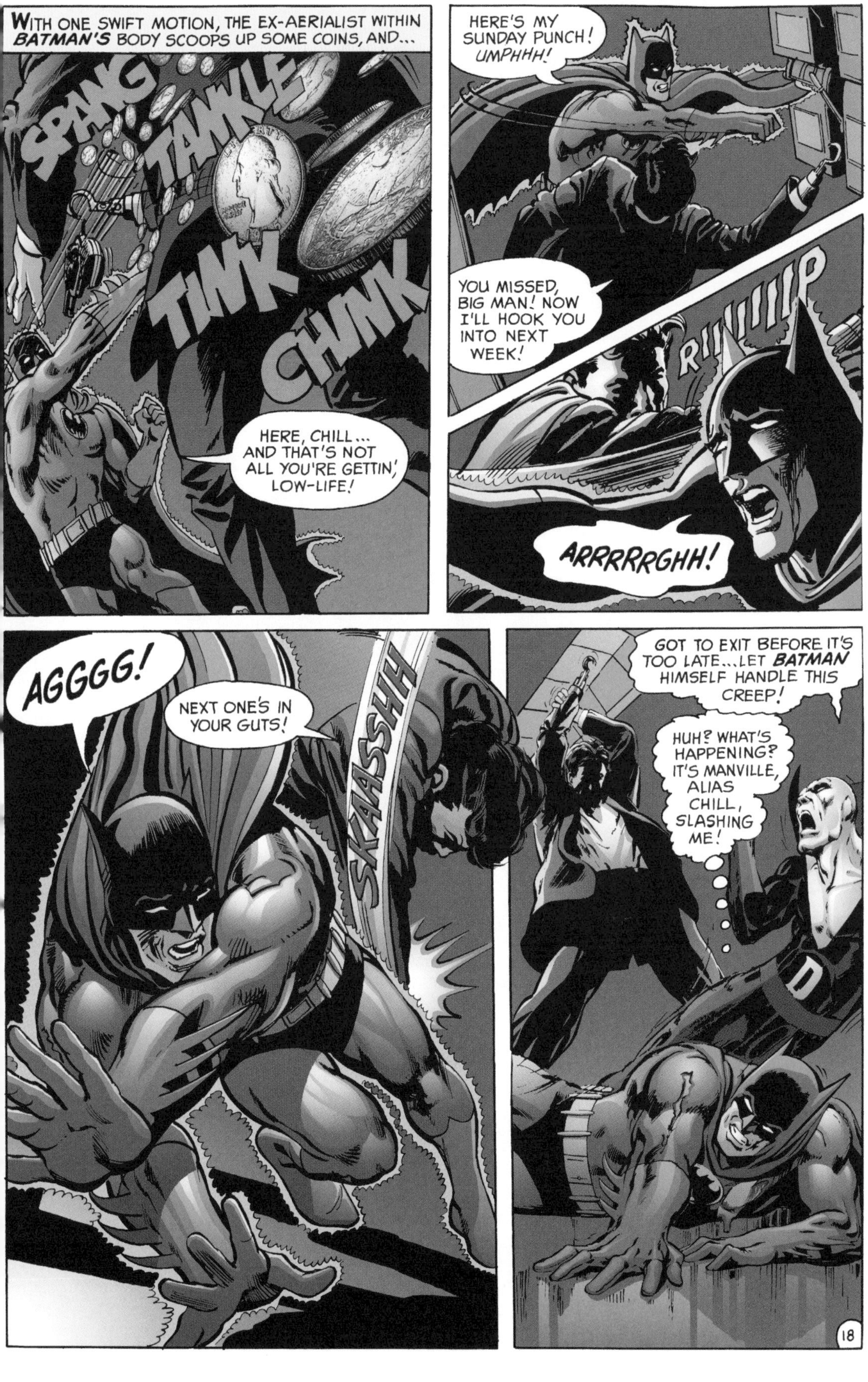

WITH ONE SWIFT MOTION, THE EX-AERIALIST WITHIN BATMAN'S BODY SCOOPS UP SOME COINS, AND...
SPANG
TANKLE
TINK
CHUNK
HERE, CHILL... AND THAT'S NOT ALL YOU'RE GETTIN', LOW-LIFE!
HERE'S MY SUNDAY PUNCH! UMPHHH!
YOU MISSED, BIG MAN! NOW I'LL HOOK YOU INTO NEXT WEEK!
RIIIIIIP
ARRRRRGHH!
AGGGG!
NEXT ONE'S IN YOUR GUTS!
SKAASSHH
GOT TO EXIT BEFORE IT'S TOO LATE...LET BATMAN HIMSELF HANDLE THIS CREEP!
HUH? WHAT'S HAPPENING? IT'S MANVILLE, ALIAS CHILL, SLASHING ME!
18

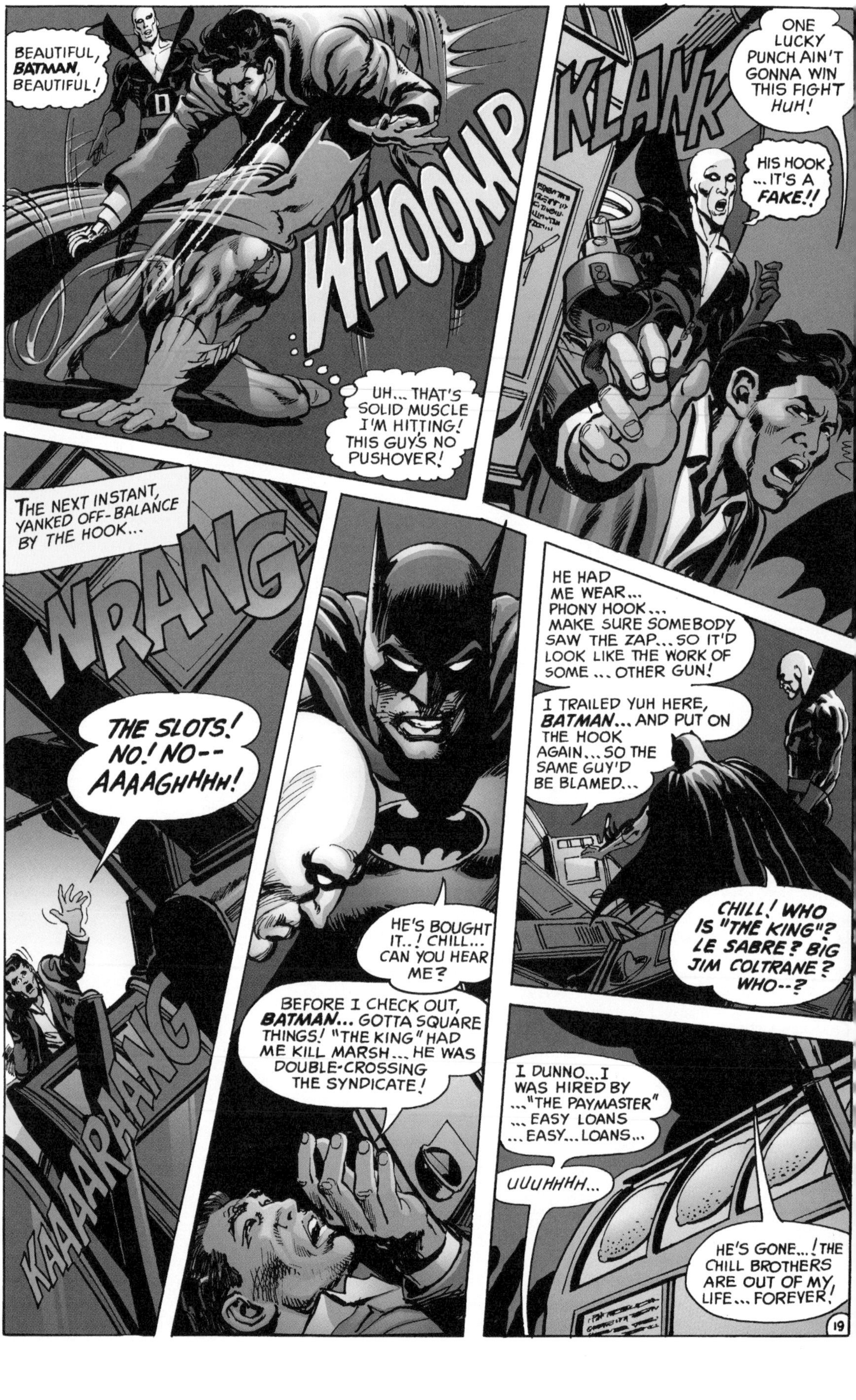

BEAUTIFUL, BATMAN, BEAUTIFUL!
WHOOMP
UH... THAT'S SOLID MUSCLE I'M HITTING! THIS GUY'S NO PUSHOVER!
KLANK
ONE LUCKY PUNCH AIN'T GONNA WIN THIS FIGHT HUH!
HIS HOOK ...IT'S A FAKE!!
THE NEXT INSTANT, YANKED OFF-BALANCE BY THE HOOK...
WRANG
THE SLOTS! NO! NO-- AAAAGHHHH!
KAAARAANG
HE'S BOUGHT IT..! CHILL... CAN YOU HEAR ME?
BEFORE I CHECK OUT, BATMAN... GOTTA SQUARE THINGS! "THE KING" HAD ME KILL MARSH... HE WAS DOUBLE-CROSSING THE SYNDICATE!
HE HAD ME WEAR... PHONY HOOK... MAKE SURE SOMEBODY SAW THE ZAP... SO IT'D LOOK LIKE THE WORK OF SOME... OTHER GUN!
I TRAILED YUH HERE, BATMAN... AND PUT ON THE HOOK AGAIN... SO THE SAME GUY'D BE BLAMED...
CHILL! WHO IS "THE KING"? LE SABRE? BIG JIM COLTRANE? WHO--?
I DUNNO...I WAS HIRED BY ..."THE PAYMASTER" ... EASY LOANS ... EASY... LOANS...
UUUHHHH...
HE'S GONE...! THE CHILL BROTHERS ARE OUT OF MY LIFE... FOREVER!
19

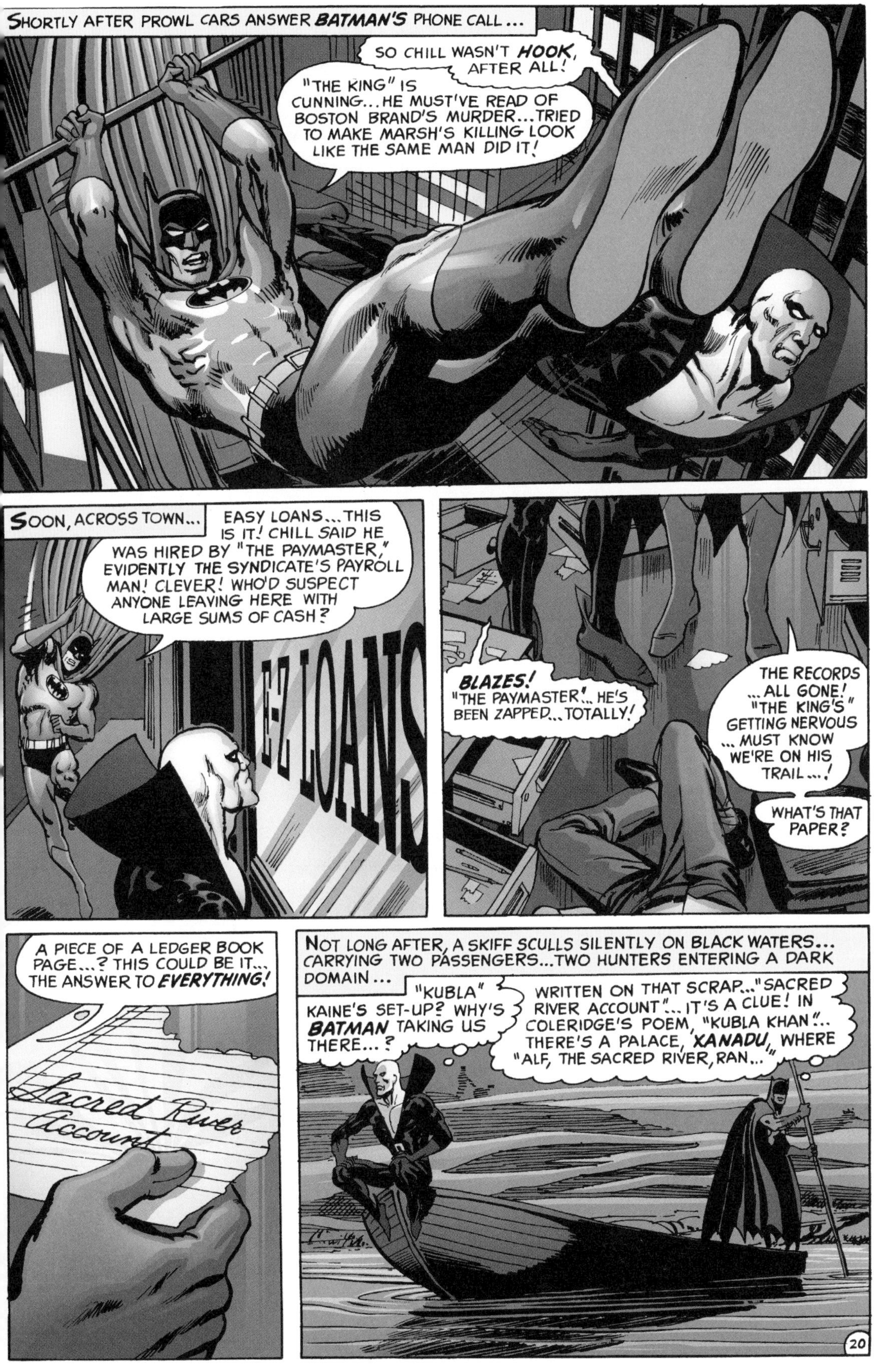
SHORTLY AFTER PROWL CARS ANSWER BATMAN'S PHONE CALL...
SO CHILL WASN'T HOOK, AFTER ALL!
"THE KING" IS CUNNING... HE MUST'VE READ OF BOSTON BRAND'S MURDER... TRIED TO MAKE MARSH'S KILLING LOOK LIKE THE SAME MAN DID IT!
SOON, ACROSS TOWN...
EASY LOANS... THIS IS IT! CHILL SAID HE WAS HIRED BY "THE PAYMASTER," EVIDENTLY THE SYNDICATE'S PAYROLL MAN! CLEVER! WHO'D SUSPECT ANYONE LEAVING HERE WITH LARGE SUMS OF CASH?
E-Z LOANS
BLAZES! "THE PAYMASTER"... HE'S BEEN ZAPPED... TOTALLY!
THE RECORDS ... ALL GONE! "THE KING'S" GETTING NERVOUS ... MUST KNOW WE'RE ON HIS TRAIL...!
WHAT'S THAT PAPER?
A PIECE OF A LEDGER BOOK PAGE...? THIS COULD BE IT... THE ANSWER TO EVERYTHING!
Sacred River Account
NOT LONG AFTER, A SKIFF SCULLS SILENTLY ON BLACK WATERS... CARRYING TWO PASSENGERS...TWO HUNTERS ENTERING A DARK DOMAIN...
"KUBLA" KAINE'S SET-UP? WHY'S BATMAN TAKING US THERE...?
WRITTEN ON THAT SCRAP..."SACRED RIVER ACCOUNT"... IT'S A CLUE! IN COLERIDGE'S POEM, "KUBLA KHAN"... THERE'S A PALACE, XANADU, WHERE "ALF, THE SACRED RIVER, RAN..."
20

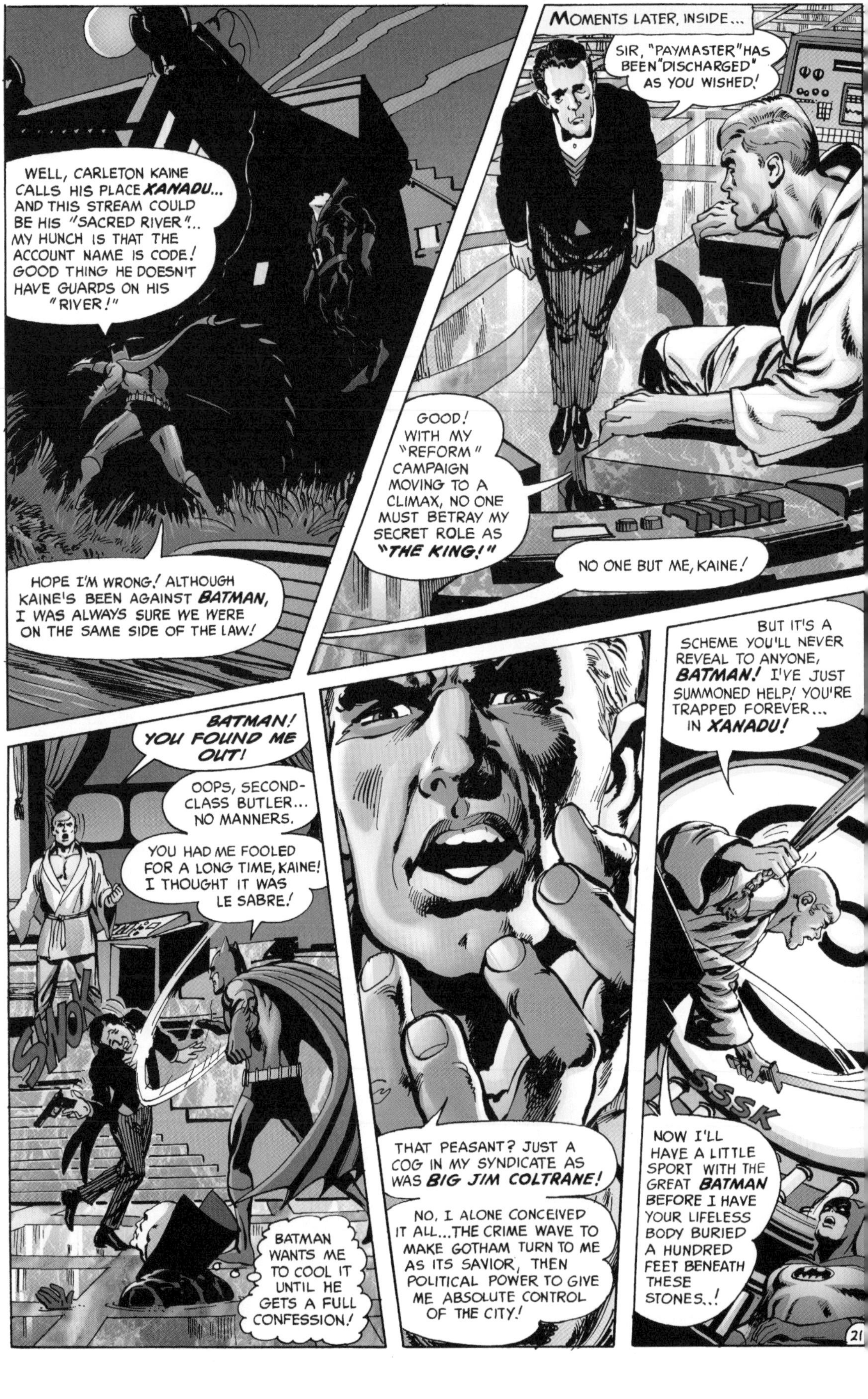
WELL, CARLETON KAINE CALLS HIS PLACE XANADU... AND THIS STREAM COULD BE HIS "SACRED RIVER"... MY HUNCH IS THAT THE ACCOUNT NAME IS CODE! GOOD THING HE DOESN'T HAVE GUARDS ON HIS "RIVER!"
HOPE I'M WRONG! ALTHOUGH KAINE'S BEEN AGAINST BATMAN, I WAS ALWAYS SURE WE WERE ON THE SAME SIDE OF THE LAW!
MOMENTS LATER, INSIDE...
SIR, "PAYMASTER" HAS BEEN "DISCHARGED" AS YOU WISHED!
GOOD! WITH MY "REFORM" CAMPAIGN MOVING TO A CLIMAX, NO ONE MUST BETRAY MY SECRET ROLE AS "THE KING!"
NO ONE BUT ME, KAINE!
BATMAN! YOU FOUND ME OUT!
OOPS, SECOND-CLASS BUTLER... NO MANNERS.
YOU HAD ME FOOLED FOR A LONG TIME, KAINE! I THOUGHT IT WAS LE SABRE!
SWOK
BATMAN WANTS ME TO COOL IT UNTIL HE GETS A FULL CONFESSION!
THAT PEASANT? JUST A COG IN MY SYNDICATE AS WAS BIG JIM COLTRANE!
NO, I ALONE CONCEIVED IT ALL...THE CRIME WAVE TO MAKE GOTHAM TURN TO ME AS ITS SAVIOR, THEN POLITICAL POWER TO GIVE ME ABSOLUTE CONTROL OF THE CITY!
BUT IT'S A SCHEME YOU'LL NEVER REVEAL TO ANYONE, BATMAN! I'VE JUST SUMMONED HELP! YOU'RE TRAPPED FOREVER... IN XANADU!
SSSK
NOW I'LL HAVE A LITTLE SPORT WITH THE GREAT BATMAN BEFORE I HAVE YOUR LIFELESS BODY BURIED A HUNDRED FEET BENEATH THESE STONES..!
21

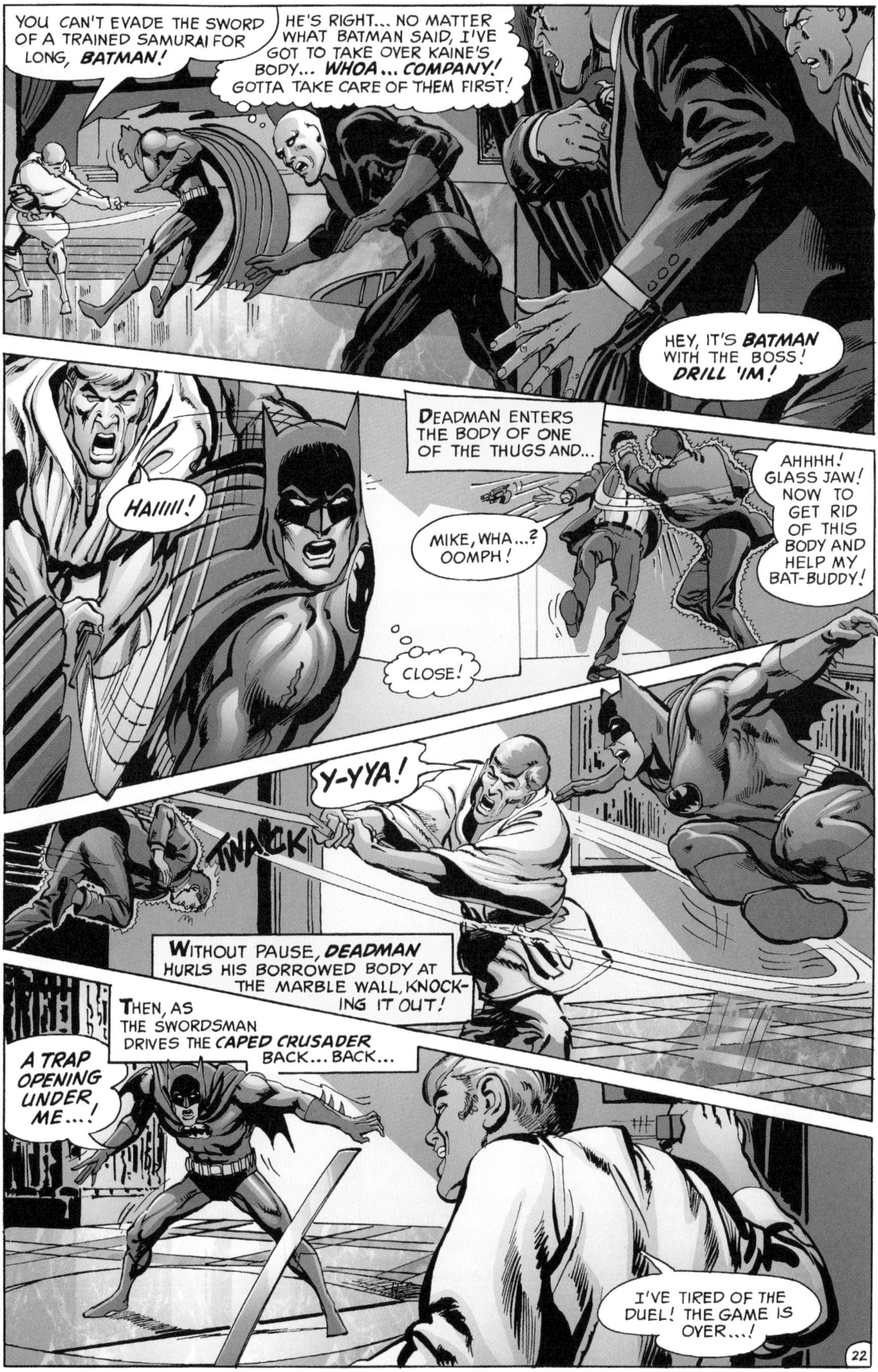
YOU CAN'T EVADE THE SWORD OF A TRAINED SAMURAI FOR LONG, BATMAN!
HE'S RIGHT... NO MATTER WHAT BATMAN SAID, I'VE GOT TO TAKE OVER KAINE'S BODY... WHOA... COMPANY! GOTTA TAKE CARE OF THEM FIRST!
HEY, IT'S BATMAN WITH THE BOSS! DRILL 'IM!
DEADMAN ENTERS THE BODY OF ONE OF THE THUGS AND...
HAIIII!
MIKE, WHA...? OOMPH!
AHHHH! GLASS JAW! NOW TO GET RID OF THIS BODY AND HELP MY BAT-BUDDY!
CLOSE!
Y-YYA!
TWACK
WITHOUT PAUSE, DEADMAN HURLS HIS BORROWED BODY AT THE MARBLE WALL, KNOCKING IT OUT!
THEN, AS THE SWORDSMAN DRIVES THE CAPED CRUSADER BACK... BACK...
A TRAP OPENING UNDER ME...!
I'VE TIRED OF THE DUEL! THE GAME IS OVER...!
22

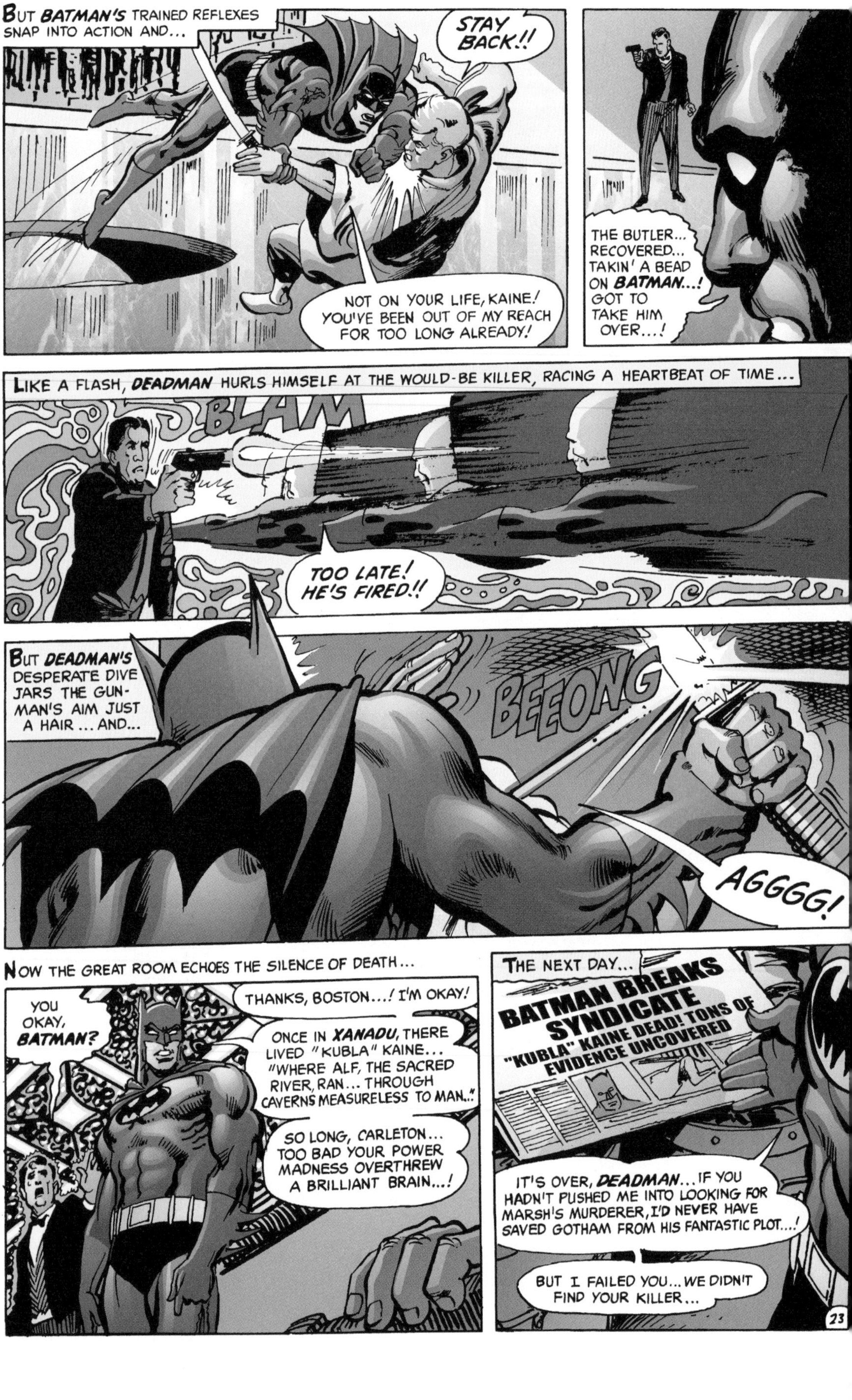
BUT BATMAN'S TRAINED REFLEXES SNAP INTO ACTION AND...
STAY BACK!!
NOT ON YOUR LIFE, KAINE! YOU'VE BEEN OUT OF MY REACH FOR TOO LONG ALREADY!
THE BUTLER... RECOVERED... TAKIN' A BEAD ON BATMAN...! GOT TO TAKE HIM OVER...!
LIKE A FLASH, DEADMAN HURLS HIMSELF AT THE WOULD-BE KILLER, RACING A HEARTBEAT OF TIME...
BLAM
TOO LATE! HE'S FIRED!!
BUT DEADMAN'S DESPERATE DIVE JARS THE GUN-MAN'S AIM JUST A HAIR... AND...
BEEONG
AGGGG!
NOW THE GREAT ROOM ECHOES THE SILENCE OF DEATH...
YOU OKAY, BATMAN?
THANKS, BOSTON...! I'M OKAY!
ONCE IN XANADU, THERE LIVED "KUBLA" KAINE... "WHERE ALF, THE SACRED RIVER, RAN... THROUGH CAVERNS MEASURELESS TO MAN.."
SO LONG, CARLETON... TOO BAD YOUR POWER MADNESS OVERTHREW A BRILLIANT BRAIN...!
THE NEXT DAY...
BATMAN BREAKS SYNDICATE
"KUBLA" KAINE DEAD! TONS OF EVIDENCE UNCOVERED
IT'S OVER, DEADMAN... IF YOU HADN'T PUSHED ME INTO LOOKING FOR MARSH'S MURDERER, I'D NEVER HAVE SAVED GOTHAM FROM HIS FANTASTIC PLOT...!
BUT I FAILED YOU... WE DIDN'T FIND YOUR KILLER...
23

LISTEN, DEADMAN... MAYBE SOME OTHER TIME I'LL BE ABLE TO HELP YOU IF ANOTHER LEAD TURNS UP... I WON'T FAIL NEXT TIME...!
HEY! I CAN'T LET BATMAN GO ON THIS WAY! I'LL JUST HOP INSIDE HIM A SEC... AND...
NOW ONE MAN'S ARM SCRAWLS ANOTHER MAN'S MESSAGE... A MESSAGE FROM... A DEADMAN!
ADIOS, DEADMAN! MAYBE SOME DAY YOU'LL FIND YOUR KILLER, "THE HOOK"... AND PEACE!
NEXT TIME WE'LL GET HIM!! THANKS, BUDDY! ADIOS, DEADMAN
24
YES, MAYBE SOMEDAY DEADMAN WILL REACH THE END OF HIS FANTASTIC HUNT... AND PERHAPS BATMAN WILL BE THERE! BUT THAT'S ANOTHER STORY... NEVER, THE END!

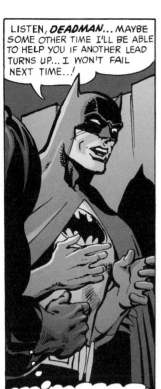

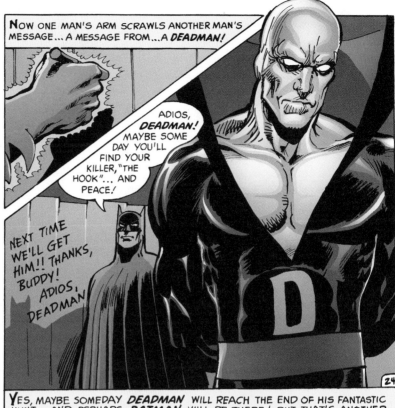

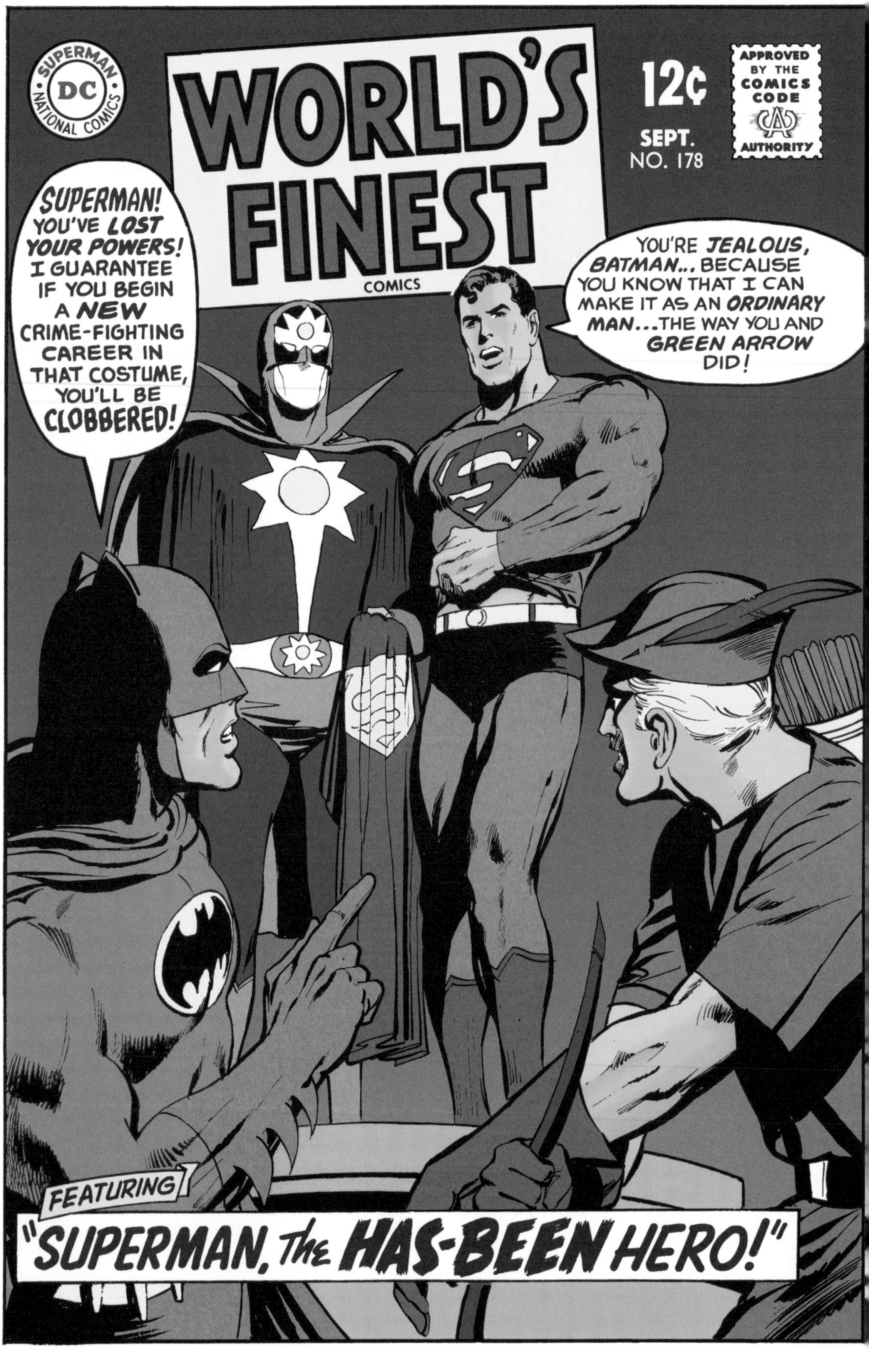
SUPERMAN DC NATIONAL COMICS
WORLD'S FINEST COMICS
12¢
SEPT. NO. 178
APPROVED BY THE COMICS CODE AUTHORITY
SUPERMAN! YOU'VE LOST YOUR POWERS! I GUARANTEE IF YOU BEGIN A NEW CRIME-FIGHTING CAREER IN THAT COSTUME, YOU'LL BE CLOBBERED!
YOU'RE JEALOUS, BATMAN... BECAUSE YOU KNOW THAT I CAN MAKE IT AS AN ORDINARY MAN...THE WAY YOU AND GREEN ARROW DID!
FEATURING
"SUPERMAN, The HAS-BEEN HERO!"

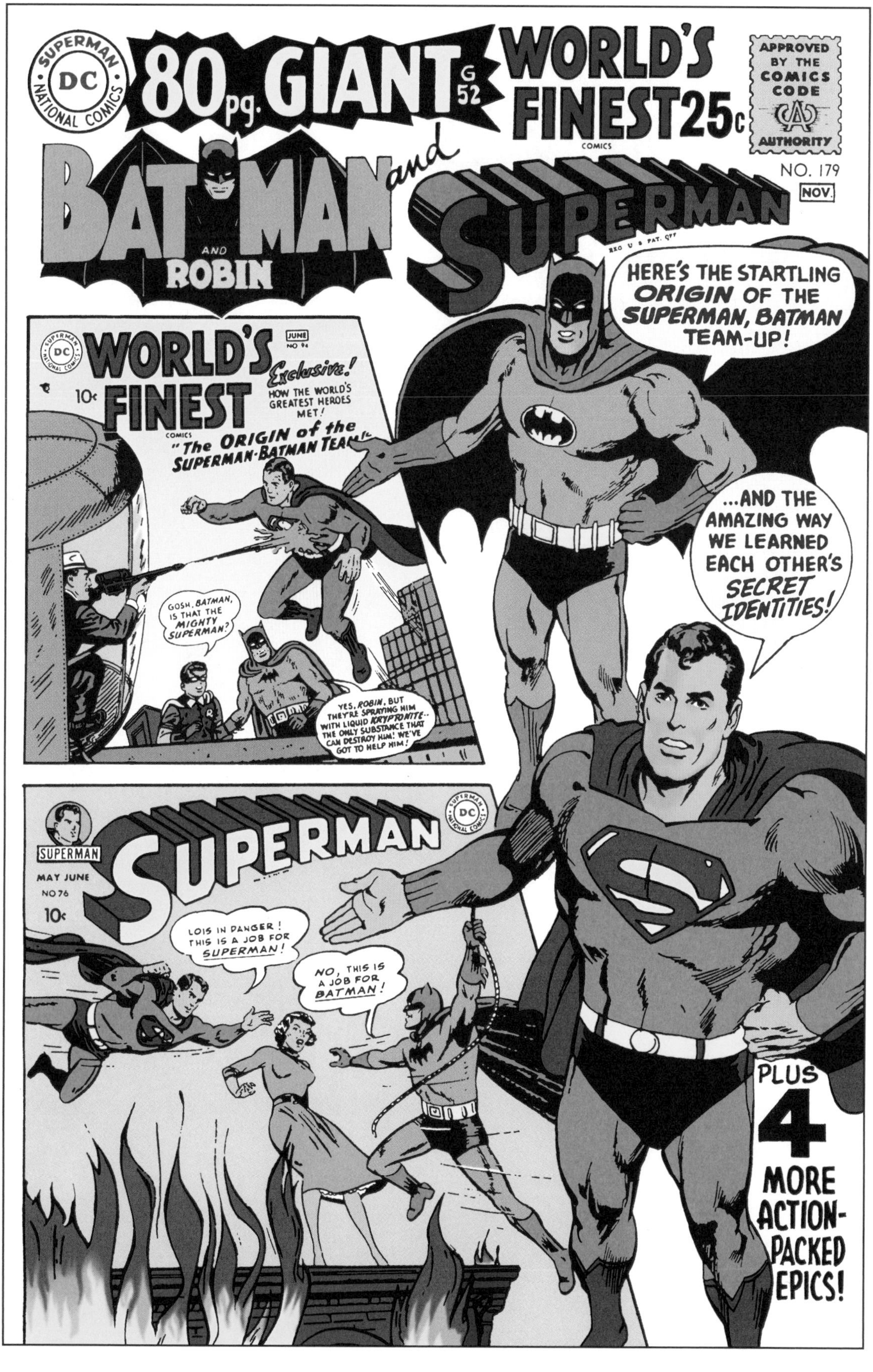
80 pg. GIANT G 52
WORLD'S FINEST COMICS 25c
APPROVED BY THE COMICS CODE AUTHORITY
NO. 179
NOV.
BATMAN AND ROBIN and SUPERMAN
HERE'S THE STARTLING ORIGIN OF THE SUPERMAN, BATMAN TEAM-UP!
...AND THE AMAZING WAY WE LEARNED EACH OTHER'S SECRET IDENTITIES!
WORLD'S FINEST COMICS
JUNE
10¢
Exclusive! HOW THE WORLD'S GREATEST HEROES MET!
"The ORIGIN of the SUPERMAN-BATMAN TEAM!"
GOSH, BATMAN, IS THAT THE MIGHTY SUPERMAN?
YES, ROBIN, BUT THEY'RE SPRAYING HIM WITH LIQUID KRYPTONITE-- THE ONLY SUBSTANCE THAT CAN DESTROY HIM! WE'VE GOT TO HELP HIM!
SUPERMAN
MAY JUNE
NO 76
10¢
LOIS IN DANGER! THIS IS A JOB FOR SUPERMAN!
NO, THIS IS A JOB FOR BATMAN!
PLUS 4 MORE ACTION-PACKED EPICS!

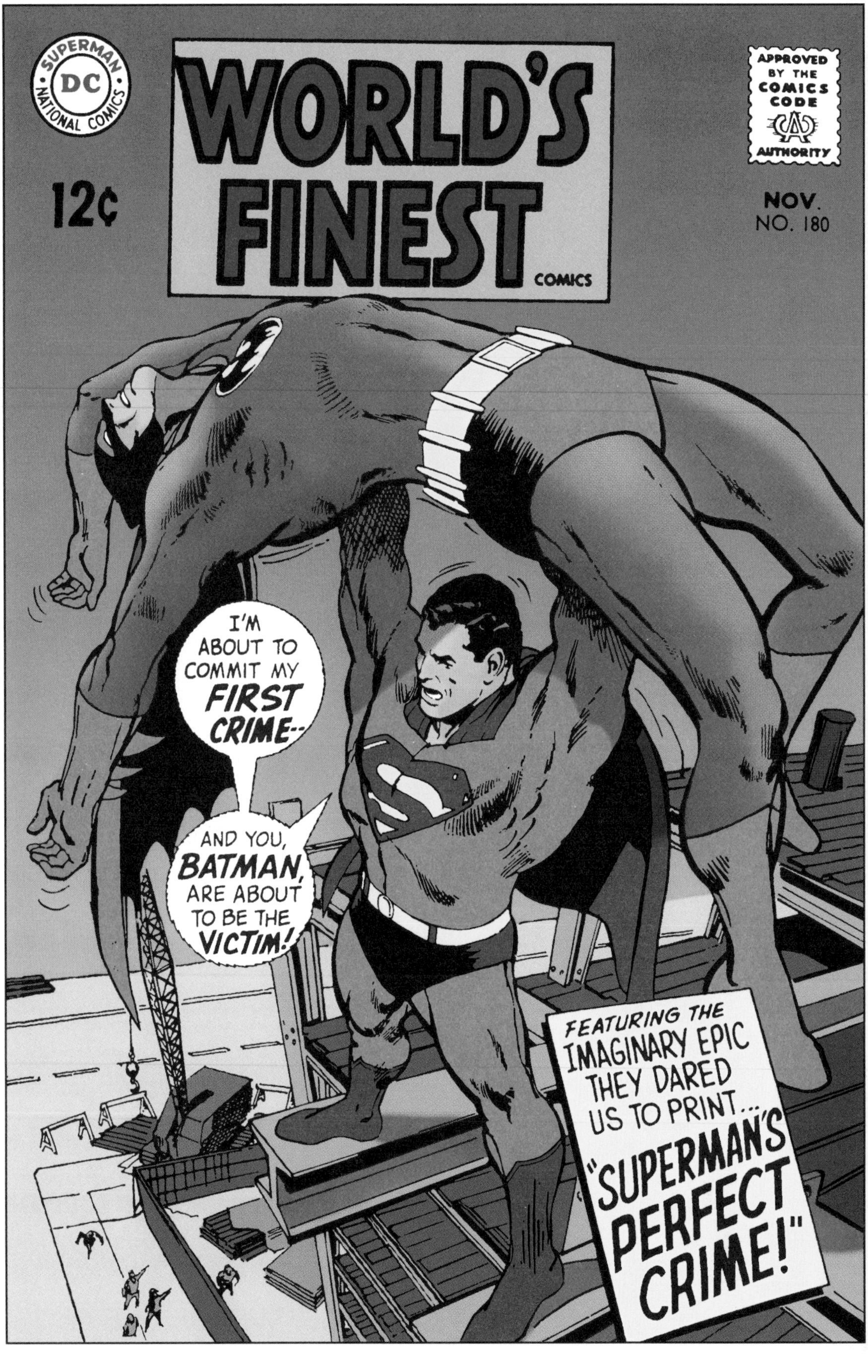
SUPERMAN DC NATIONAL COMICS
WORLD'S FINEST COMICS
APPROVED BY THE COMICS CODE AUTHORITY
12¢
NOV. NO. 180
I'M ABOUT TO COMMIT MY FIRST CRIME--
AND YOU, BATMAN, ARE ABOUT TO BE THE VICTIM!
FEATURING THE IMAGINARY EPIC THEY DARED US TO PRINT... "SUPERMAN'S PERFECT CRIME!"

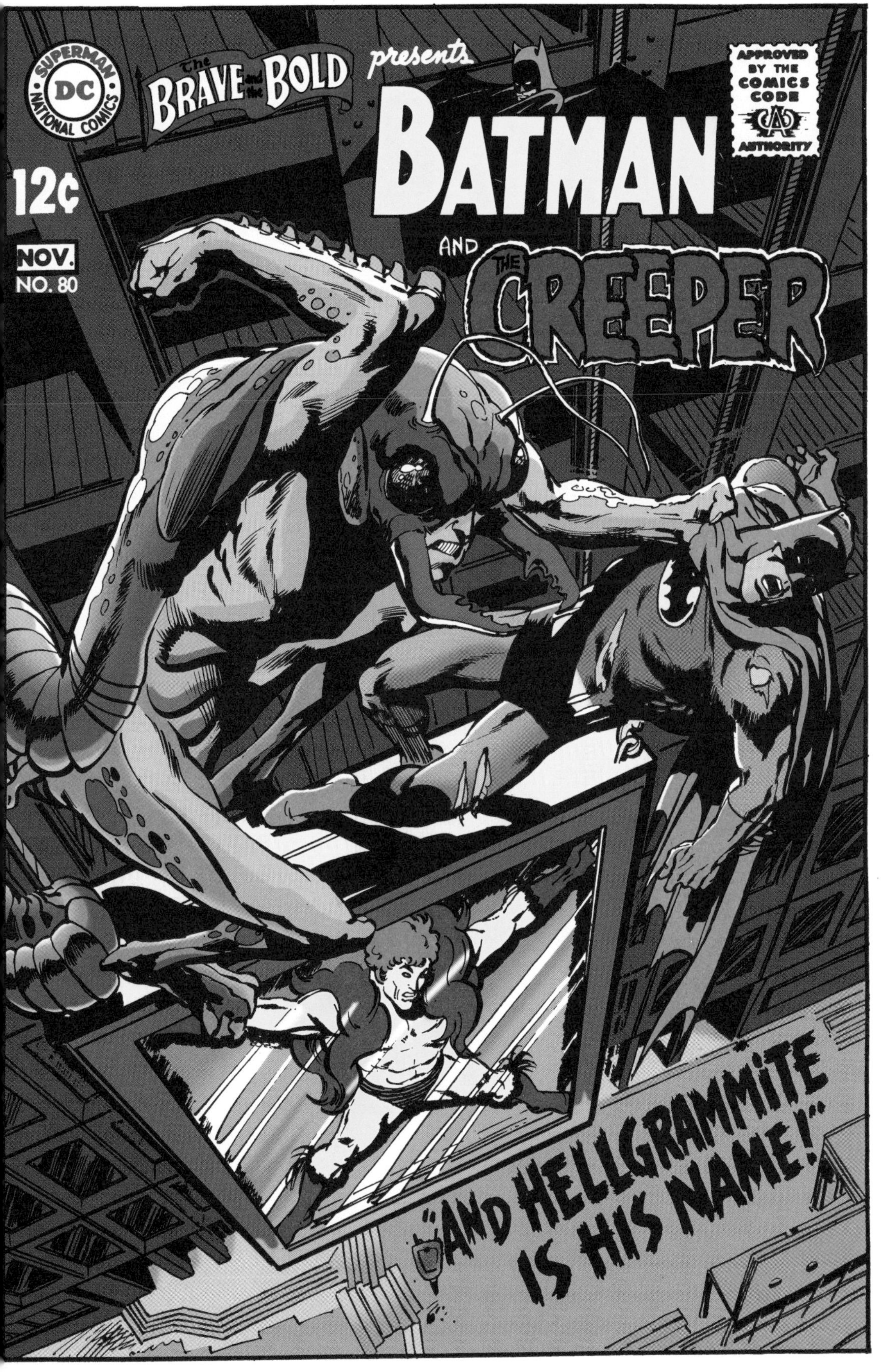
SUPERMAN DC NATIONAL COMICS
The BRAVE and the BOLD presents
BATMAN
AND THE CREEPER
APPROVED BY THE COMICS CODE AUTHORITY
12¢
NOV. NO. 80
"AND HELLGRAMMITE IS HIS NAME!"

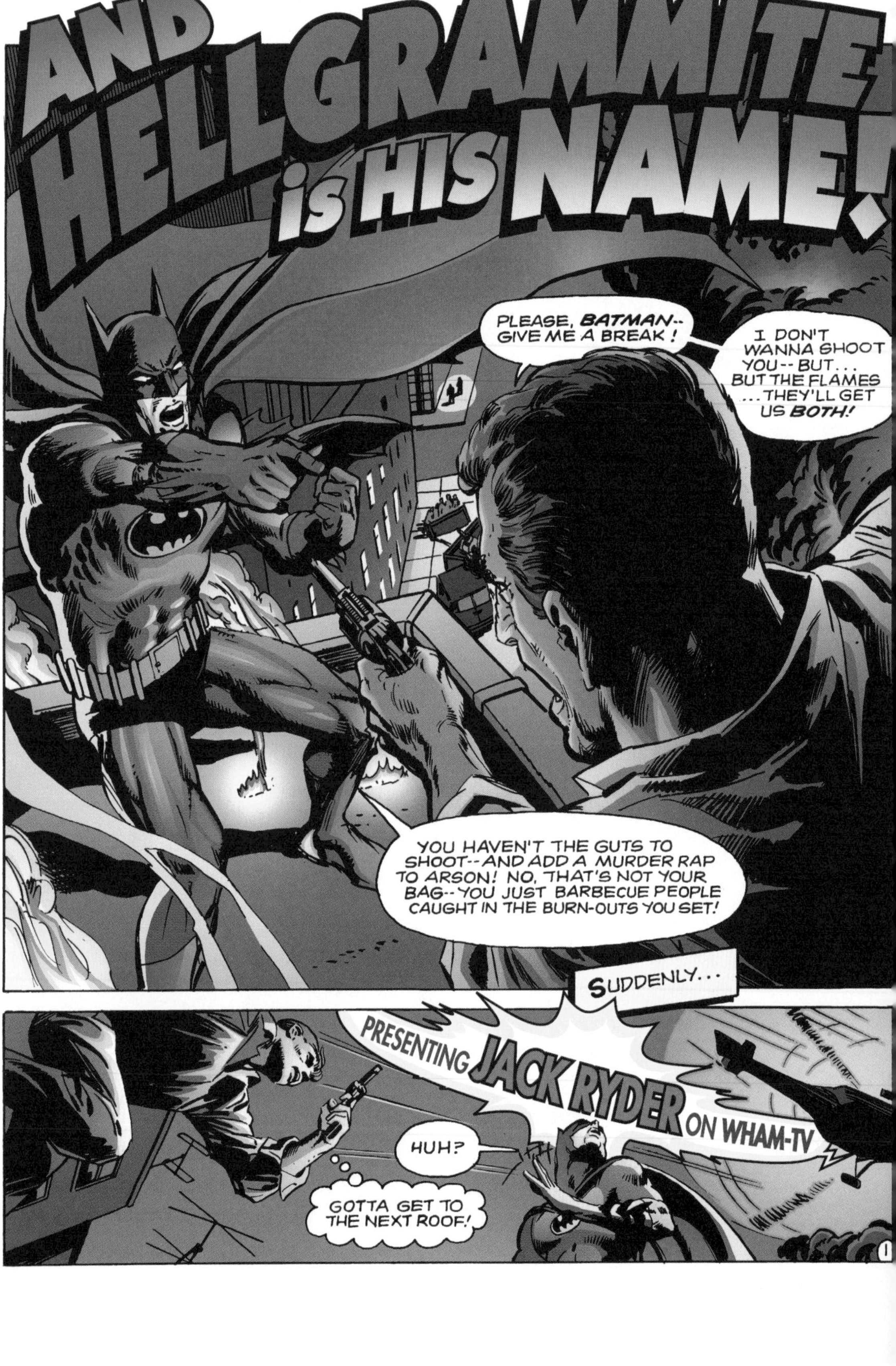
AND HELLGRAMMITE is HIS NAME!
PLEASE, BATMAN-- GIVE ME A BREAK!
I DON'T WANNA SHOOT YOU-- BUT... BUT THE FLAMES ...THEY'LL GET US BOTH!
YOU HAVEN'T THE GUTS TO SHOOT--AND ADD A MURDER RAP TO ARSON! NO, THAT'S NOT YOUR BAG--YOU JUST BARBECUE PEOPLE CAUGHT IN THE BURN-OUTS YOU SET!
SUDDENLY...
PRESENTING JACK RYDER ON WHAM-TV
HUH?
GOTTA GET TO THE NEXT ROOF!
1

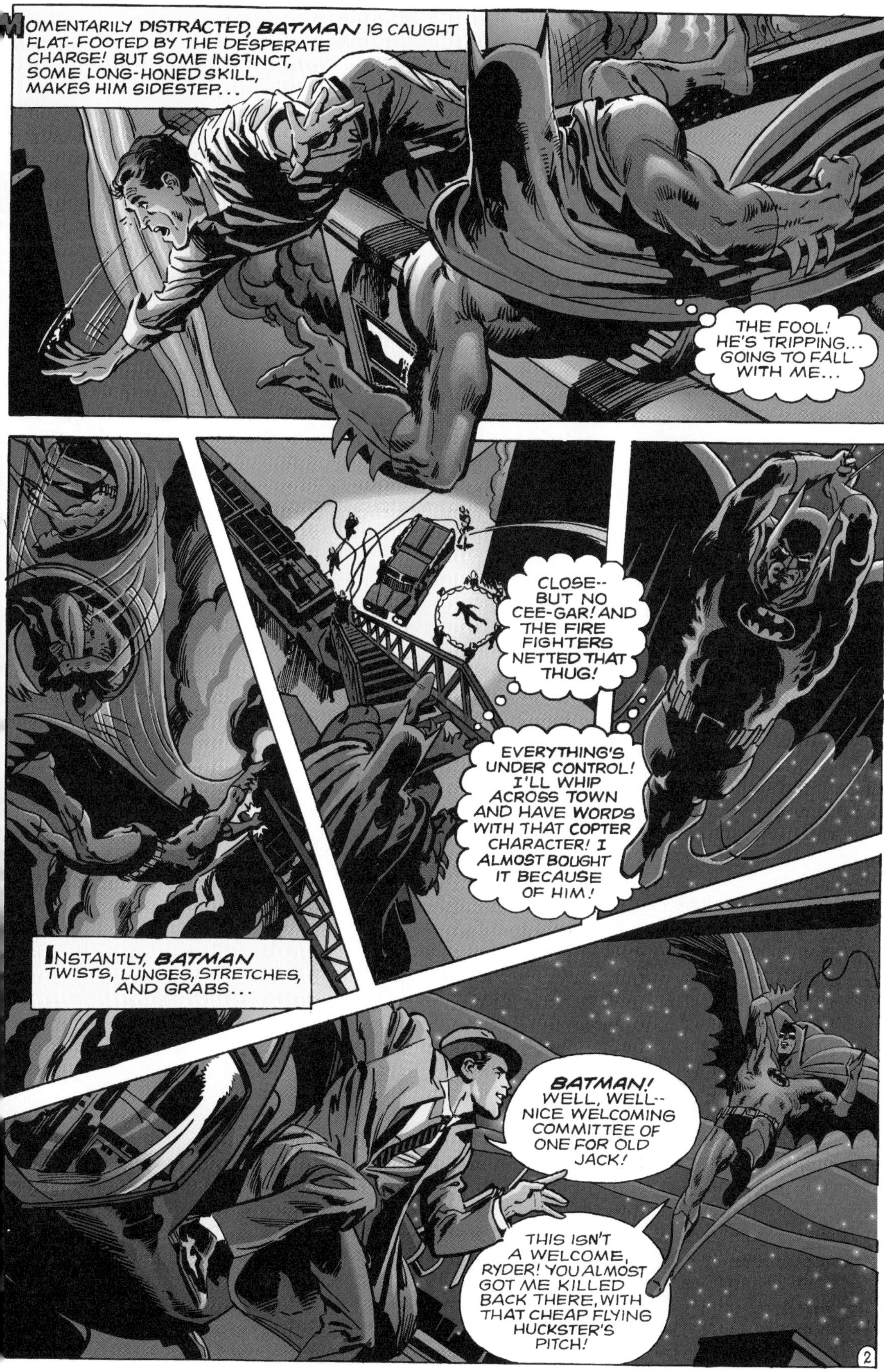
MOMENTARILY DISTRACTED, BATMAN IS CAUGHT FLAT-FOOTED BY THE DESPERATE CHARGE! BUT SOME INSTINCT, SOME LONG-HONED SKILL, MAKES HIM SIDESTEP...
THE FOOL! HE'S TRIPPING... GOING TO FALL WITH ME...
INSTANTLY, BATMAN TWISTS, LUNGES, STRETCHES, AND GRABS...
CLOSE-- BUT NO CEE-GAR! AND THE FIRE FIGHTERS NETTED THAT THUG!
EVERYTHING'S UNDER CONTROL! I'LL WHIP ACROSS TOWN AND HAVE WORDS WITH THAT COPTER CHARACTER! I ALMOST BOUGHT IT BECAUSE OF HIM!
BATMAN! WELL, WELL-- NICE WELCOMING COMMITTEE OF ONE FOR OLD JACK!
THIS ISN'T A WELCOME, RYDER! YOU ALMOST GOT ME KILLED BACK THERE, WITH THAT CHEAP FLYING HUCKSTER'S PITCH!
2

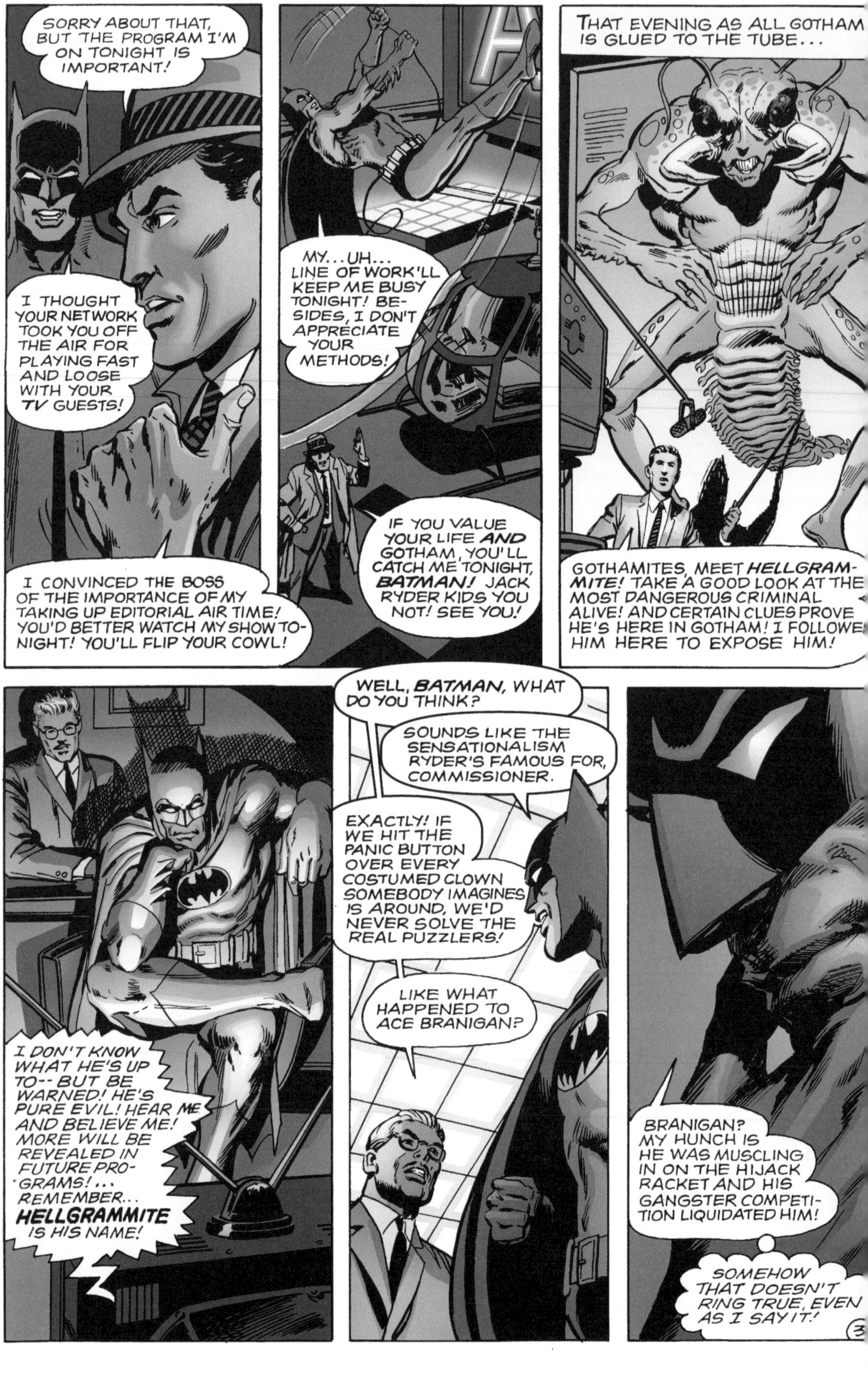
SORRY ABOUT THAT, BUT THE PROGRAM I'M ON TONIGHT IS IMPORTANT!
I THOUGHT YOUR NETWORK TOOK YOU OFF THE AIR FOR PLAYING FAST AND LOOSE WITH YOUR TV GUESTS!
I CONVINCED THE BOSS OF THE IMPORTANCE OF MY TAKING UP EDITORIAL AIR TIME! YOU'D BETTER WATCH MY SHOW TO-NIGHT! YOU'LL FLIP YOUR COWL!
MY...UH... LINE OF WORK'LL KEEP ME BUSY TONIGHT! BE-SIDES, I DON'T APPRECIATE YOUR METHODS!
IF YOU VALUE YOUR LIFE AND GOTHAM, YOU'LL CATCH ME TONIGHT, BATMAN! JACK RYDER KIDS YOU NOT! SEE YOU!
THAT EVENING AS ALL GOTHAM IS GLUED TO THE TUBE...
GOTHAMITES, MEET HELLGRAM-MITE! TAKE A GOOD LOOK AT THE MOST DANGEROUS CRIMINAL ALIVE! AND CERTAIN CLUES PROVE HE'S HERE IN GOTHAM! I FOLLOWE HIM HERE TO EXPOSE HIM!
I DON'T KNOW WHAT HE'S UP TO-- BUT BE WARNED! HE'S PURE EVIL! HEAR ME AND BELIEVE ME! MORE WILL BE REVEALED IN FUTURE PRO-GRAMS!... REMEMBER... HELLGRAMMITE IS HIS NAME!
WELL, BATMAN, WHAT DO YOU THINK?
SOUNDS LIKE THE SENSATIONALISM RYDER'S FAMOUS FOR, COMMISSIONER.
EXACTLY! IF WE HIT THE PANIC BUTTON OVER EVERY COSTUMED CLOWN SOMEBODY IMAGINES IS AROUND, WE'D NEVER SOLVE THE REAL PUZZLERS!
LIKE WHAT HAPPENED TO ACE BRANIGAN?
BRANIGAN? MY HUNCH IS HE WAS MUSCLING IN ON THE HIJACK RACKET AND HIS GANGSTER COMPETI-TION LIQUIDATED HIM!
SOMEHOW THAT DOESN'T RING TRUE, EVEN AS I SAY IT!
3

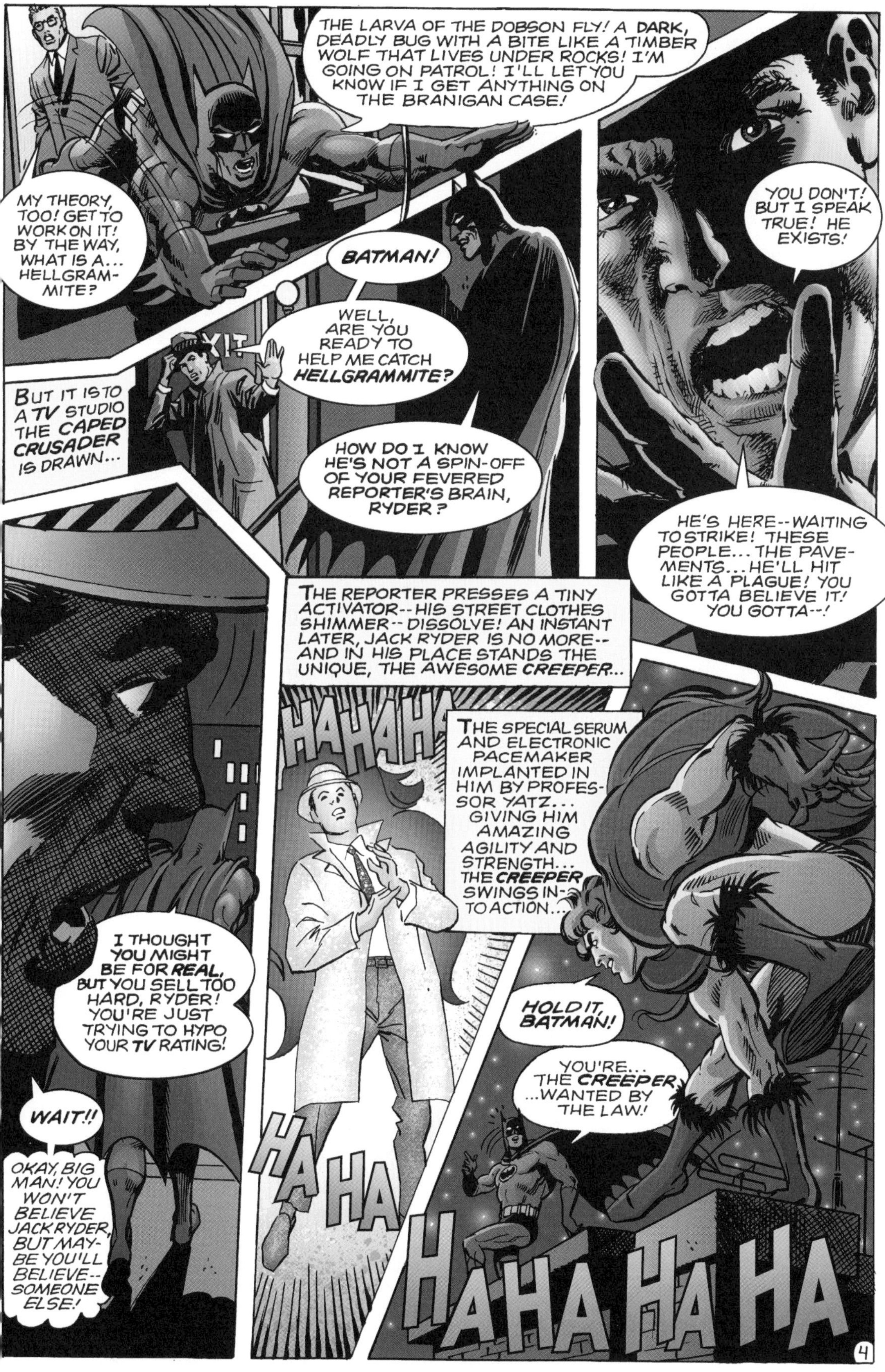

MY THEORY, TOO! GET TO WORK ON IT! BY THE WAY, WHAT IS A... HELLGRAMMITE?
THE LARVA OF THE DOBSON FLY! A DARK, DEADLY BUG WITH A BITE LIKE A TIMBER WOLF THAT LIVES UNDER ROCKS! I'M GOING ON PATROL! I'LL LET YOU KNOW IF I GET ANYTHING ON THE BRANIGAN CASE!
BUT IT IS TO A TV STUDIO THE CAPED CRUSADER IS DRAWN...
BATMAN!
WELL, ARE YOU READY TO HELP ME CATCH HELLGRAMMITE?
HOW DO I KNOW HE'S NOT A SPIN-OFF OF YOUR FEVERED REPORTER'S BRAIN, RYDER?
YOU DON'T! BUT I SPEAK TRUE! HE EXISTS!
HE'S HERE--WAITING TO STRIKE! THESE PEOPLE... THE PAVEMENTS... HE'LL HIT LIKE A PLAGUE! YOU GOTTA BELIEVE IT! YOU GOTTA--!
I THOUGHT YOU MIGHT BE FOR REAL, BUT YOU SELL TOO HARD, RYDER! YOU'RE JUST TRYING TO HYPO YOUR TV RATING!
WAIT!!
OKAY, BIG MAN! YOU WON'T BELIEVE JACK RYDER, BUT MAYBE YOU'LL BELIEVE--SOMEONE ELSE!
THE REPORTER PRESSES A TINY ACTIVATOR--HIS STREET CLOTHES SHIMMER--DISSOLVE! AN INSTANT LATER, JACK RYDER IS NO MORE--AND IN HIS PLACE STANDS THE UNIQUE, THE AWESOME CREEPER...
HAHAHAHA
THE SPECIAL SERUM AND ELECTRONIC PACEMAKER IMPLANTED IN HIM BY PROFESSOR YATZ... GIVING HIM AMAZING AGILITY AND STRENGTH... THE CREEPER SWINGS INTO ACTION...
HA HA HA
HOLD IT, BATMAN!
YOU'RE... THE CREEPER ...WANTED BY THE LAW!
HAHAHAHAHA
4

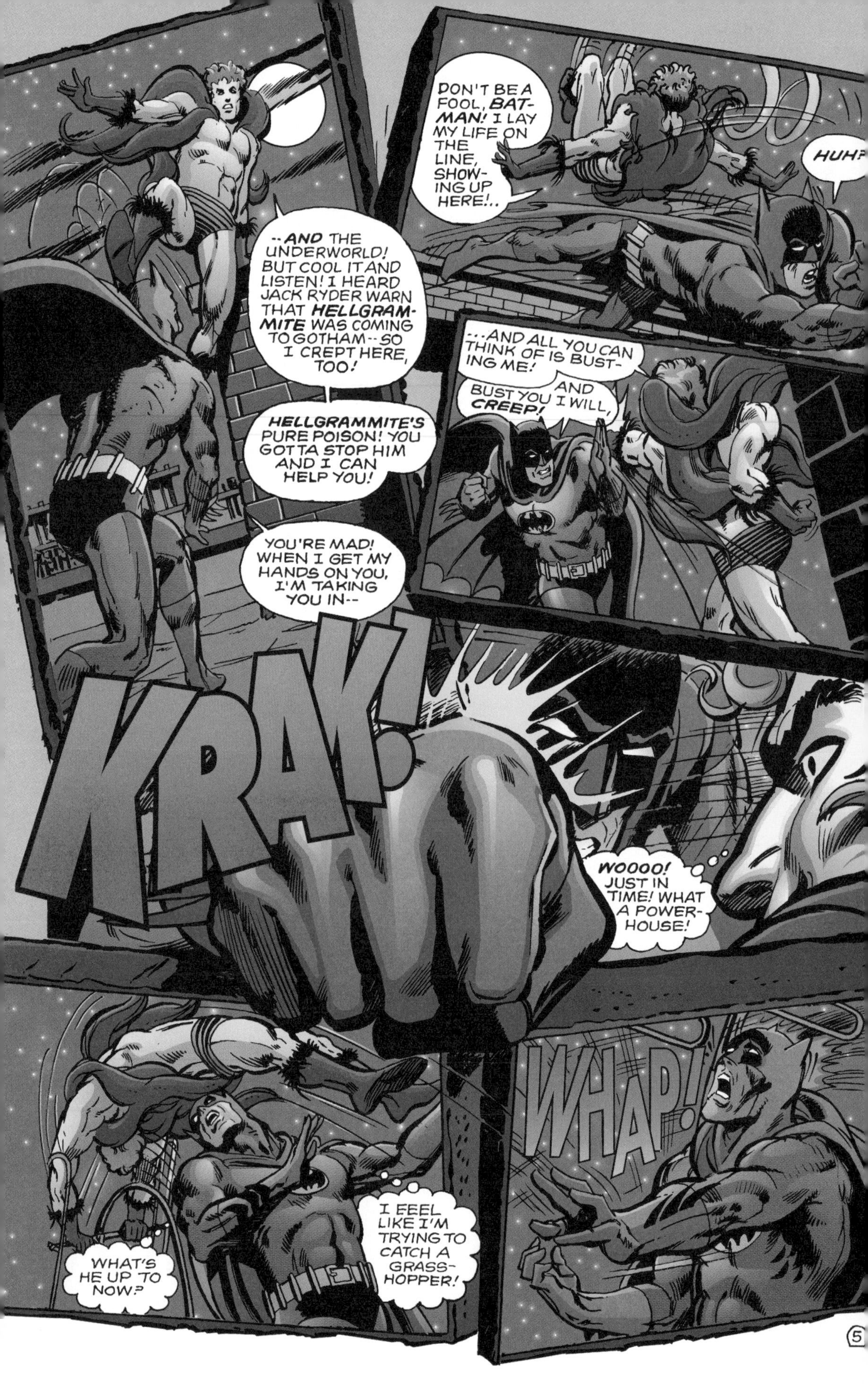
--AND THE UNDERWORLD! BUT COOL IT AND LISTEN! I HEARD JACK RYDER WARN THAT HELLGRAMMITE WAS COMING TO GOTHAM--SO I CREPT HERE, TOO!
HELLGRAMMITE'S PURE POISON! YOU GOTTA STOP HIM AND I CAN HELP YOU!
YOU'RE MAD! WHEN I GET MY HANDS ON YOU, I'M TAKING YOU IN--
DON'T BE A FOOL, BATMAN! I LAY MY LIFE ON THE LINE, SHOWING UP HERE!..
HUH?
...AND ALL YOU CAN THINK OF IS BUSTING ME!
AND BUST YOU I WILL, CREEP!
KRAK!
WOOOO! JUST IN TIME! WHAT A POWERHOUSE!
WHAT'S HE UP TO NOW?
I FEEL LIKE I'M TRYING TO CATCH A GRASSHOPPER!
WHAP!
5

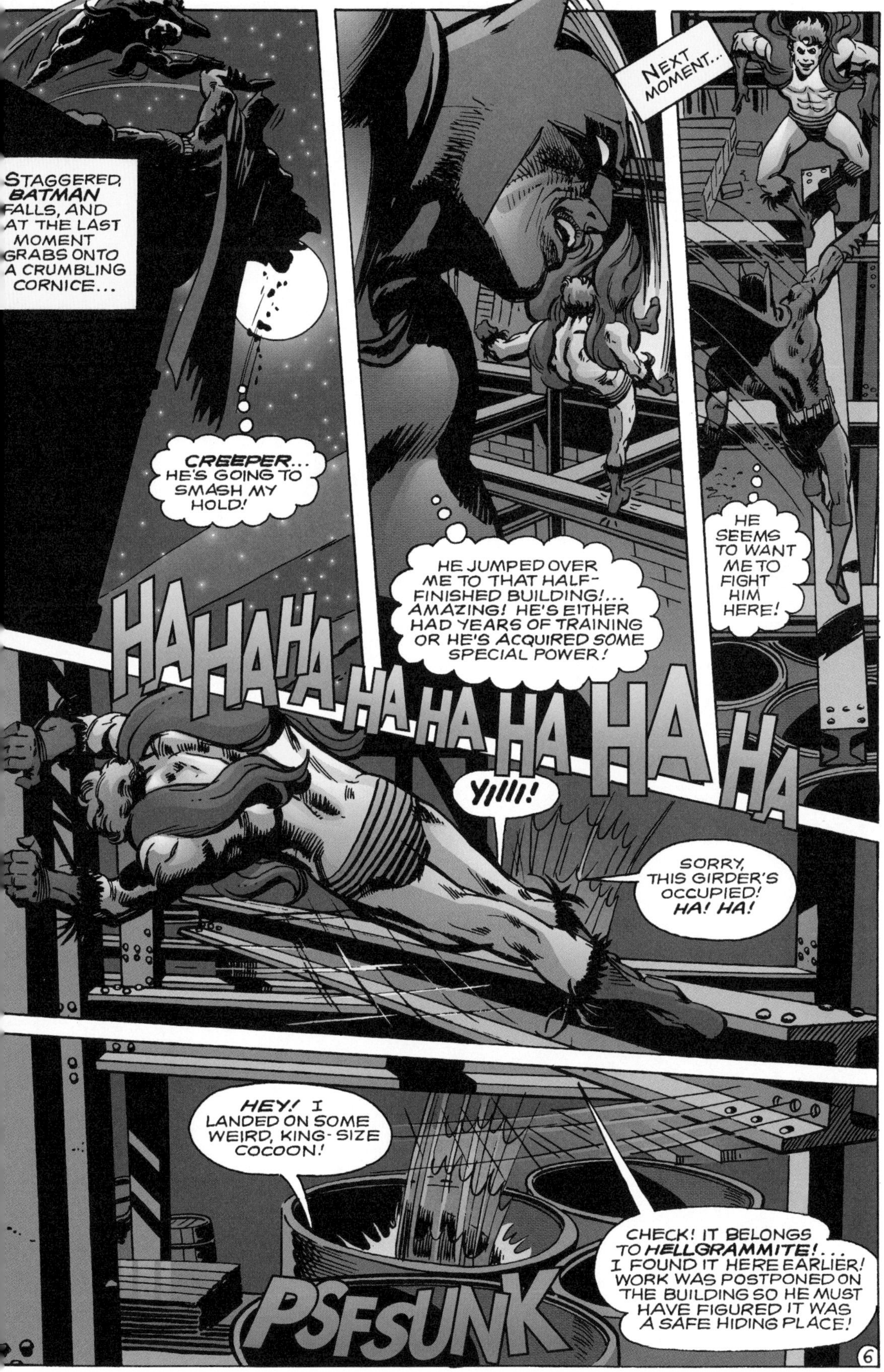
STAGGERED, BATMAN FALLS, AND AT THE LAST MOMENT GRABS ONTO A CRUMBLING CORNICE...
CREEPER... HE'S GOING TO SMASH MY HOLD!
HE JUMPED OVER ME TO THAT HALF-FINISHED BUILDING!... AMAZING! HE'S EITHER HAD YEARS OF TRAINING OR HE'S ACQUIRED SOME SPECIAL POWER!
NEXT MOMENT...
HE SEEMS TO WANT ME TO FIGHT HIM HERE!
HAHAHA HA HA HA HA HA HA
YIIII!
SORRY, THIS GIRDER'S OCCUPIED! HA! HA!
HEY! I LANDED ON SOME WEIRD, KING-SIZE COCOON!
CHECK! IT BELONGS TO HELLGRAMMITE!... I FOUND IT HERE EARLIER! WORK WAS POSTPONED ON THE BUILDING SO HE MUST HAVE FIGURED IT WAS A SAFE HIDING PLACE!
PSFSUNK
6

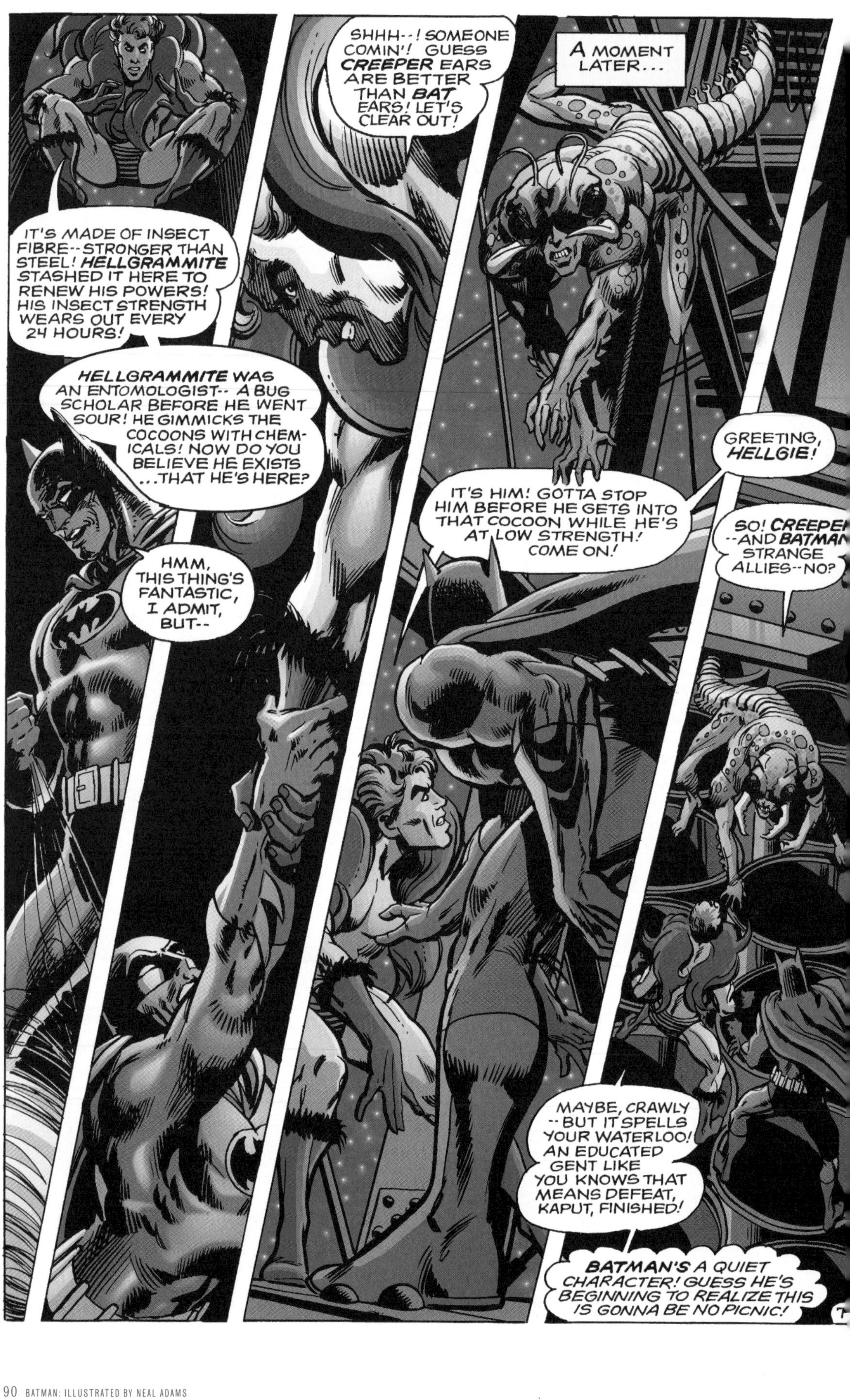
IT'S MADE OF INSECT FIBRE--STRONGER THAN STEEL! HELLGRAMMITE STASHED IT HERE TO RENEW HIS POWERS! HIS INSECT STRENGTH WEARS OUT EVERY 24 HOURS!
HELLGRAMMITE WAS AN ENTOMOLOGIST-- A BUG SCHOLAR BEFORE HE WENT SOUR! HE GIMMICKS THE COCOONS WITH CHEMICALS! NOW DO YOU BELIEVE HE EXISTS ...THAT HE'S HERE?
HMM, THIS THING'S FANTASTIC, I ADMIT, BUT--
SHHH--! SOMEONE COMIN'! GUESS CREEPER EARS ARE BETTER THAN BAT EARS! LET'S CLEAR OUT!
A MOMENT LATER...
IT'S HIM! GOTTA STOP HIM BEFORE HE GETS INTO THAT COCOON WHILE HE'S AT LOW STRENGTH! COME ON!
GREETING, HELLGIE!
SO! CREEPE --AND BATMA STRANGE ALLIES--NO?
MAYBE, CRAWLY --BUT IT SPELLS YOUR WATERLOO! AN EDUCATED GENT LIKE YOU KNOWS THAT MEANS DEFEAT, KAPUT, FINISHED!
BATMAN'S A QUIET CHARACTER! GUESS HE'S BEGINNING TO REALIZE THIS IS GONNA BE NO PICNIC!

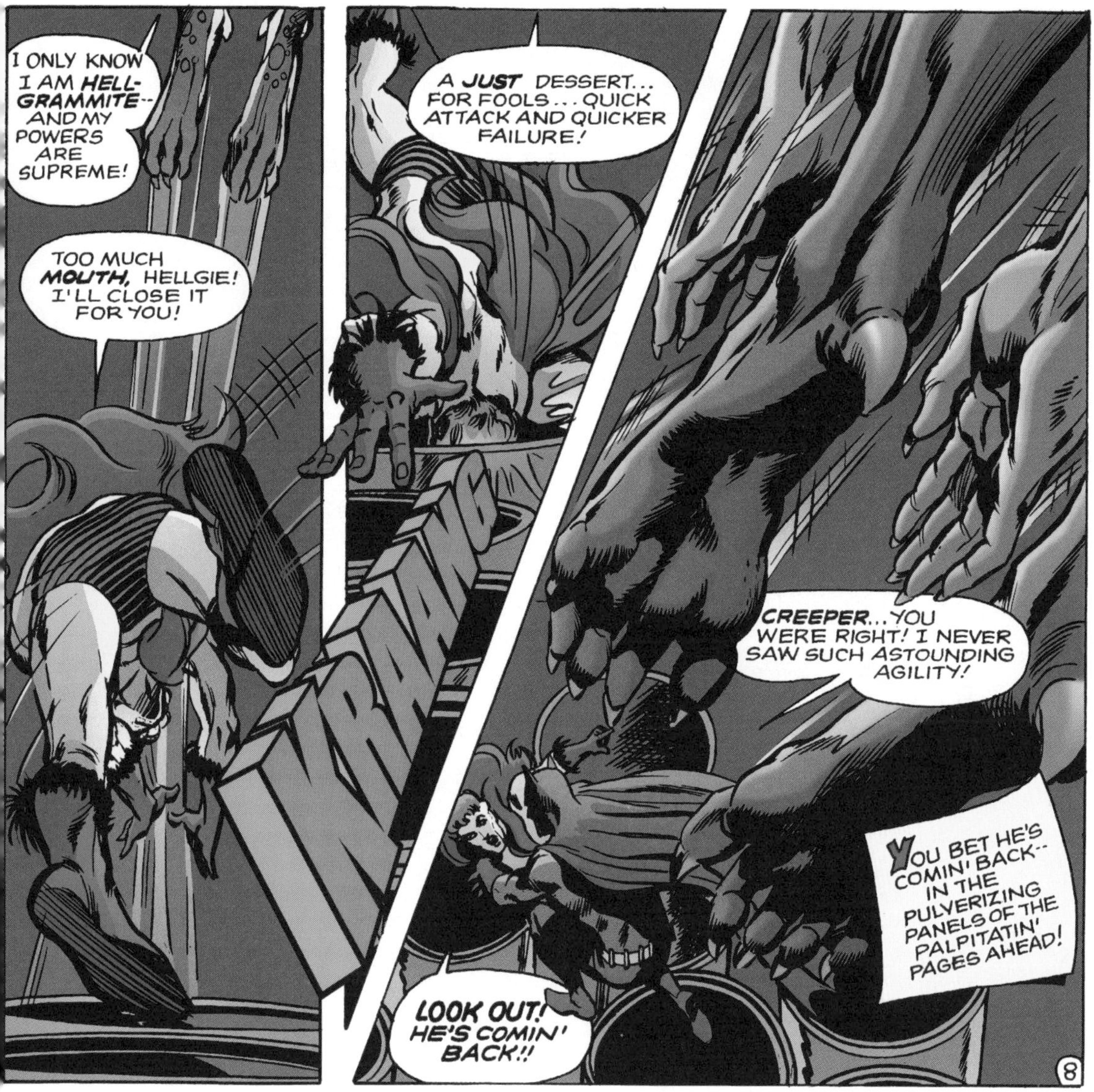
I ONLY KNOW I AM HELL-GRAMMITE-- AND MY POWERS ARE SUPREME!
TOO MUCH MOUTH, HELLGIE! I'LL CLOSE IT FOR YOU!
A JUST DESSERT... FOR FOOLS... QUICK ATTACK AND QUICKER FAILURE!
WRAANG
CREEPER... YOU WERE RIGHT! I NEVER SAW SUCH ASTOUNDING AGILITY!
LOOK OUT! HE'S COMIN' BACK!!
YOU BET HE'S COMIN' BACK-- IN THE PULVERIZING PANELS OF THE PALPITATIN' PAGES AHEAD!
8

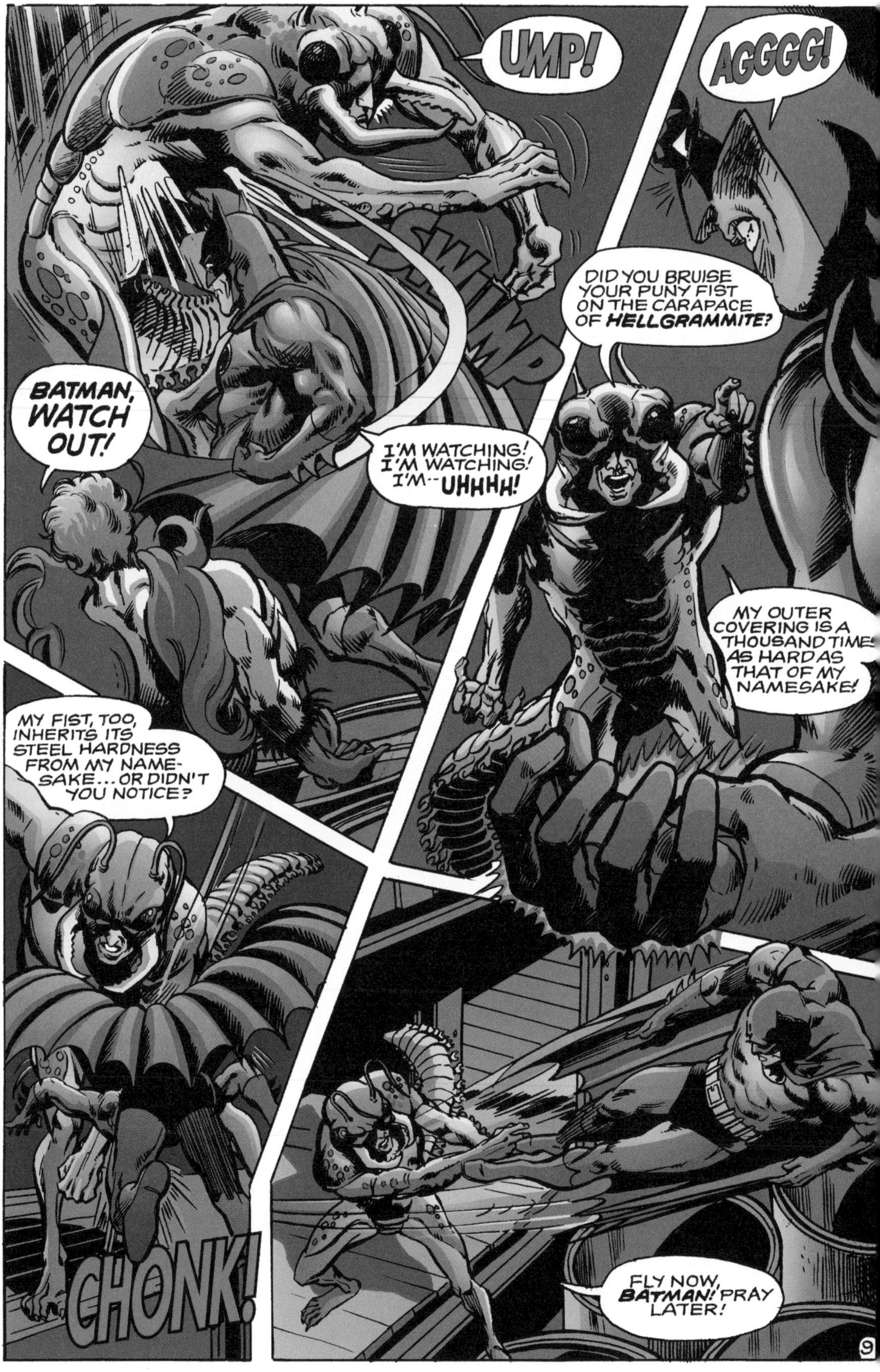
UMP!
SWHAMP
BATMAN, WATCH OUT!
I'M WATCHING! I'M WATCHING! I'M--UHHHH!
AGGGG!
DID YOU BRUISE YOUR PUNY FIST ON THE CARAPACE OF **HELLGRAMMITE?**
MY OUTER COVERING IS A THOUSAND TIMES AS HARD AS THAT OF MY NAMESAKE!
MY FIST, TOO, INHERITS ITS STEEL HARDNESS FROM MY NAME-SAKE... OR DIDN'T YOU NOTICE?
CHONK!
FLY NOW, **BATMAN!** PRAY LATER!
9

SOME INSTINCT, SOME DEEP REFLEX FOR SURVIVAL SAVES THE *MASKED MANHUNTER*...

GOT IT! WHEW! NEXT STOP WOULD'VE BEEN HALF WAY ACROSS GOTHAM!

CREEPER! WHERE'S *HELL-GRAMMITE?*

GONE! THAT INSECT POWER HE HAS IS THE SAME THAT ALLOWS AN ANT TO CARRY 50 TIMES ITS OWN WEIGHT!

...OR A LOCUST LEAP 30 TIMES ITS OWN LENGTH ... *CRAZY!*

I BELIEVE YOU NOW! RYDER WAS RIGHT-- HE'S A FANTASTIC THREAT! BUT WHY IS HE HERE?

HEY, SIRENS! IT'S THE POLICE! I'D BETTER LEAVE!

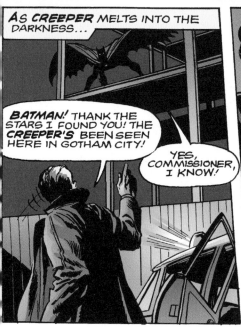

AS *CREEPER* MELTS INTO THE DARKNESS...

BATMAN! THANK THE STARS I FOUND YOU! THE *CREEPER'S* BEEN SEEN HERE IN GOTHAM CITY!

YES, COMMISSIONER, I KNOW!

HE'S DANGEROUS AND HE'S GOT TO BE BROUGHT IN:-- DROP EVERYTHING ELSE! I WANT HIM -- *TOP PRIORITY!* UNDERSTAND?

AS THE SIRENS WAIL AWAY INTO A DISTANT PURR...

WELL, YOU HEARD THE MAN! BRING ME IN!

I HEARD! BUT IF I TAKE OFF AFTER YOU, WHAT ABOUT *HELL-GRAMMITE?* GORDON DOESN'T BELIEVE HE EXISTS!

SO YOU GOT YOURSELF A PROBLEM, FELLA!

10

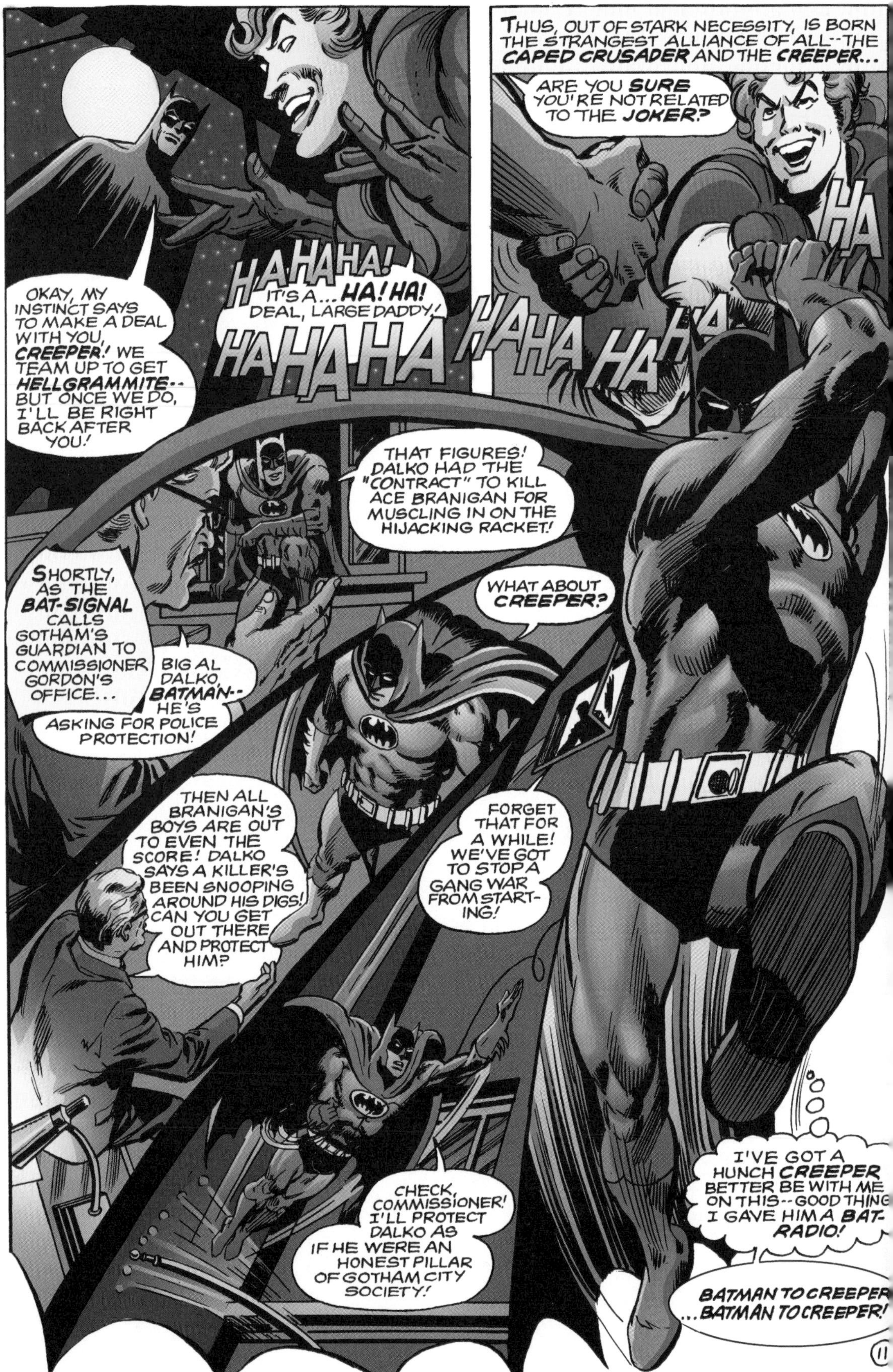

OKAY, MY INSTINCT SAYS TO MAKE A DEAL WITH YOU, CREEPER! WE TEAM UP TO GET HELLGRAMMITE-- BUT ONCE WE DO, I'LL BE RIGHT BACK AFTER YOU!
HAHAHA! IT'S A... HA! HA! DEAL, LARGE DADDY!
HAHAHA
THUS, OUT OF STARK NECESSITY, IS BORN THE STRANGEST ALLIANCE OF ALL--THE CAPED CRUSADER AND THE CREEPER...
ARE YOU SURE YOU'RE NOT RELATED TO THE JOKER?
HA
HAHA HA HA
SHORTLY, AS THE BAT-SIGNAL CALLS GOTHAM'S GUARDIAN TO COMMISSIONER GORDON'S OFFICE...
BIG AL DALKO, BATMAN-- HE'S ASKING FOR POLICE PROTECTION!
THAT FIGURES! DALKO HAD THE "CONTRACT" TO KILL ACE BRANIGAN FOR MUSCLING IN ON THE HIJACKING RACKET!
THEN ALL BRANIGAN'S BOYS ARE OUT TO EVEN THE SCORE! DALKO SAYS A KILLER'S BEEN SNOOPING AROUND HIS DIGS! CAN YOU GET OUT THERE AND PROTECT HIM?
WHAT ABOUT CREEPER?
FORGET THAT FOR A WHILE! WE'VE GOT TO STOP A GANG WAR FROM STARTING!
CHECK, COMMISSIONER! I'LL PROTECT DALKO AS IF HE WERE AN HONEST PILLAR OF GOTHAM CITY SOCIETY!
I'VE GOT A HUNCH CREEPER BETTER BE WITH ME ON THIS--GOOD THING I GAVE HIM A BAT-RADIO!
BATMAN TO CREEPER ...BATMAN TO CREEPER!
11

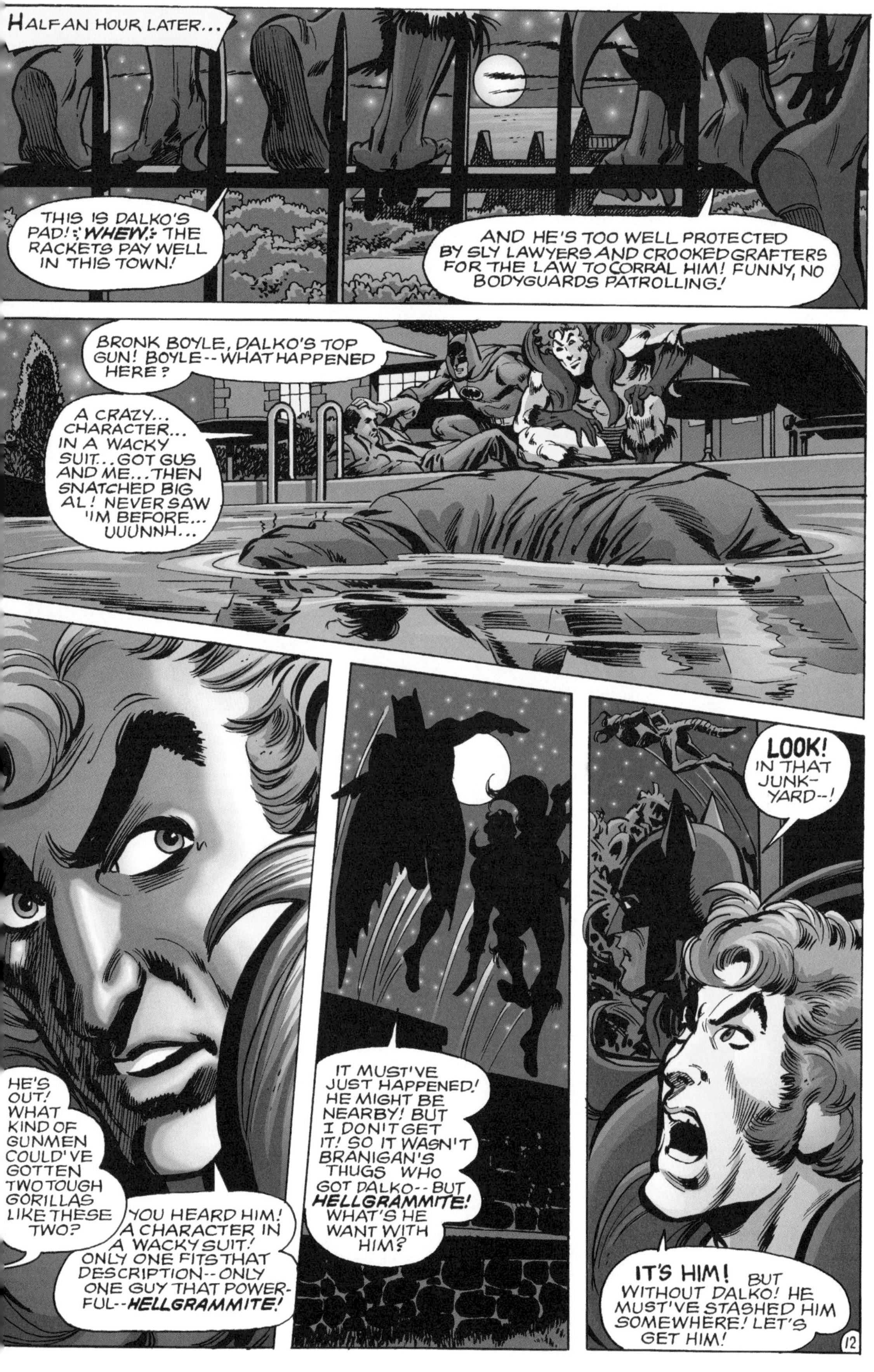
HALF AN HOUR LATER...
THIS IS DALKO'S PAD! WHEW! THE RACKETS PAY WELL IN THIS TOWN!
AND HE'S TOO WELL PROTECTED BY SLY LAWYERS AND CROOKED GRAFTERS FOR THE LAW TO CORRAL HIM! FUNNY, NO BODYGUARDS PATROLLING!
BRONK BOYLE, DALKO'S TOP GUN! BOYLE--WHAT HAPPENED HERE?
A CRAZY... CHARACTER... IN A WACKY SUIT...GOT GUS AND ME...THEN SNATCHED BIG AL! NEVER SAW 'IM BEFORE... UUUNNH...
HE'S OUT! WHAT KIND OF GUNMEN COULD'VE GOTTEN TWO TOUGH GORILLAS LIKE THESE TWO?
YOU HEARD HIM! A CHARACTER IN A WACKY SUIT! ONLY ONE FITS THAT DESCRIPTION--ONLY ONE GUY THAT POWERFUL--HELLGRAMMITE!
IT MUST'VE JUST HAPPENED! HE MIGHT BE NEARBY! BUT I DON'T GET IT! SO IT WASN'T BRANIGAN'S THUGS WHO GOT DALKO--BUT HELLGRAMMITE! WHAT'S HE WANT WITH HIM?
LOOK! IN THAT JUNK-YARD--!
IT'S HIM! BUT WITHOUT DALKO! HE MUST'VE STASHED HIM SOMEWHERE! LET'S GET HIM!
12

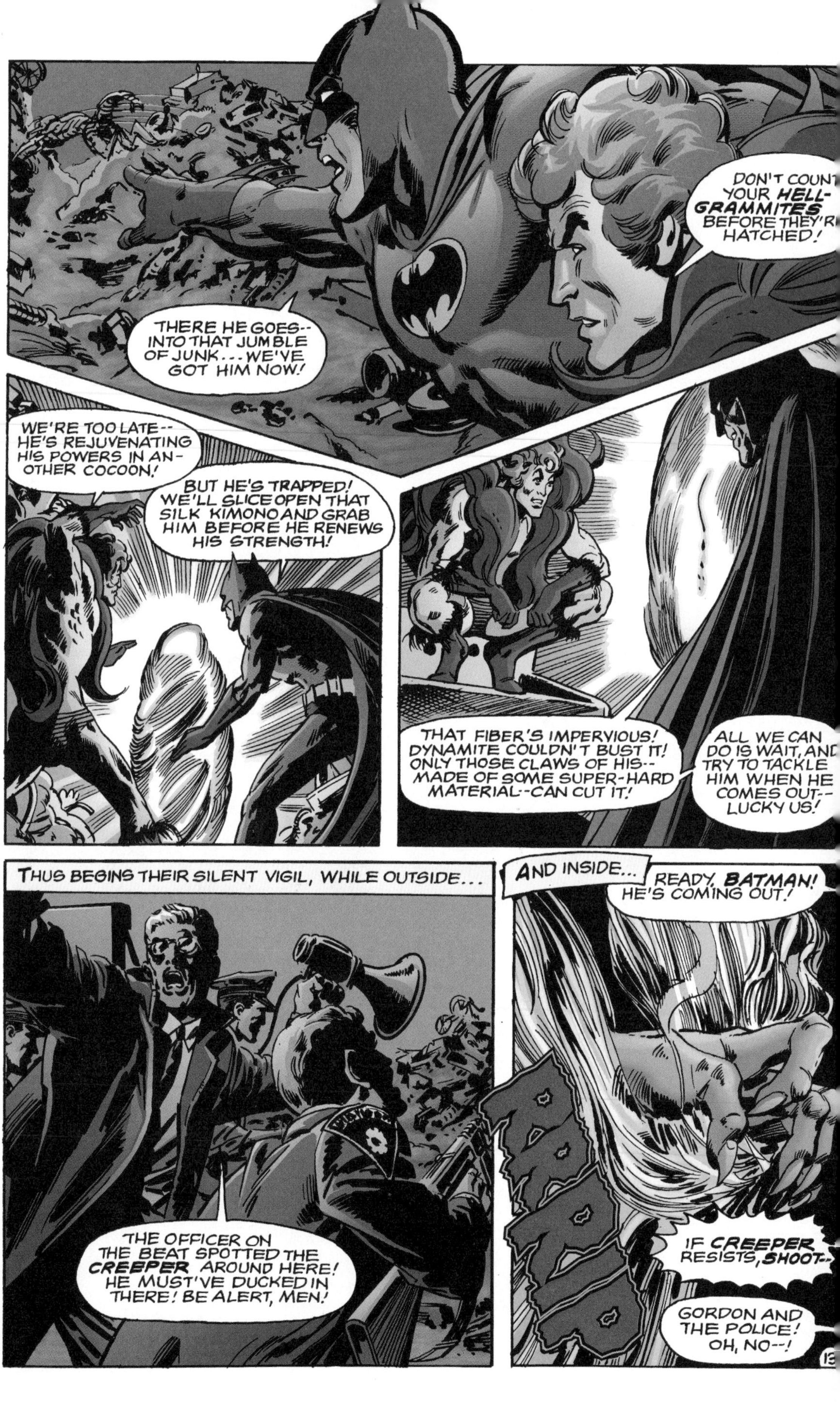
DON'T COUNT YOUR HELL-GRAMMITES BEFORE THEY'R HATCHED!
THERE HE GOES-- INTO THAT JUMBLE OF JUNK... WE'VE GOT HIM NOW!
WE'RE TOO LATE-- HE'S REJUVENATING HIS POWERS IN AN-OTHER COCOON!
BUT HE'S TRAPPED! WE'LL SLICE OPEN THAT SILK KIMONO AND GRAB HIM BEFORE HE RENEWS HIS STRENGTH!
THAT FIBER'S IMPERVIOUS! DYNAMITE COULDN'T BUST IT! ONLY THOSE CLAWS OF HIS-- MADE OF SOME SUPER-HARD MATERIAL--CAN CUT IT!
ALL WE CAN DO IS WAIT, AND TRY TO TACKLE HIM WHEN HE COMES OUT-- LUCKY US!
THUS BEGINS THEIR SILENT VIGIL, WHILE OUTSIDE...
THE OFFICER ON THE BEAT SPOTTED THE CREEPER AROUND HERE! HE MUST'VE DUCKED IN THERE! BE ALERT, MEN!
AND INSIDE...
READY, BATMAN! HE'S COMING OUT!
IF CREEPER RESISTS, SHOOT--
GORDON AND THE POLICE! OH, NO--!
13

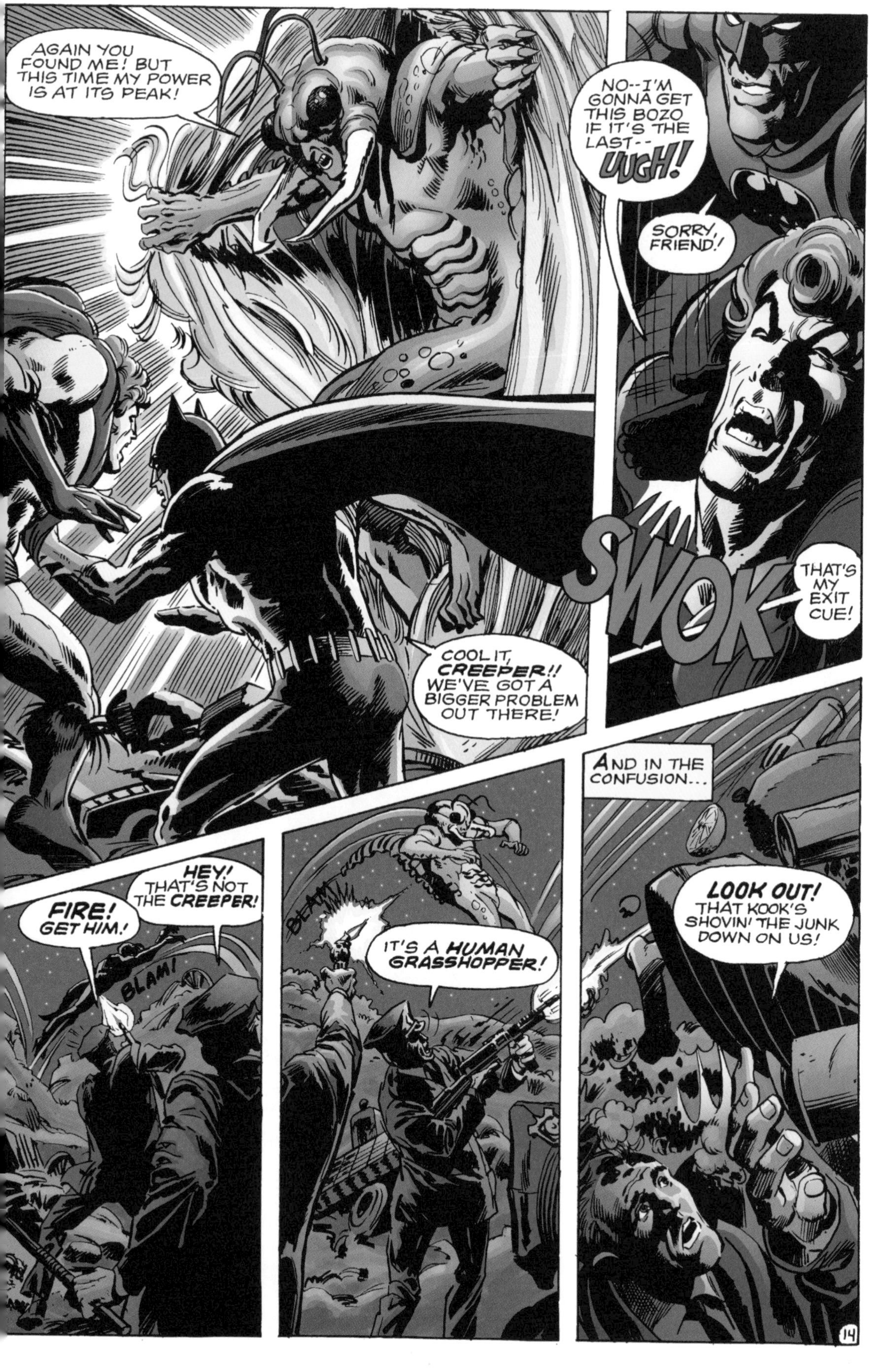
AGAIN YOU FOUND ME! BUT THIS TIME MY POWER IS AT ITS PEAK!
COOL IT, CREEPER!! WE'VE GOT A BIGGER PROBLEM OUT THERE!
NO--I'M GONNA GET THIS BOZO IF IT'S THE LAST--
UUGH!
SORRY, FRIEND!
SWOK
THAT'S MY EXIT CUE!
FIRE! GET HIM!
HEY! THAT'S NOT THE CREEPER!
BLAM!
BLAM
IT'S A HUMAN GRASSHOPPER!
AND IN THE CONFUSION...
LOOK OUT! THAT KOOK'S SHOVIN' THE JUNK DOWN ON US!
14

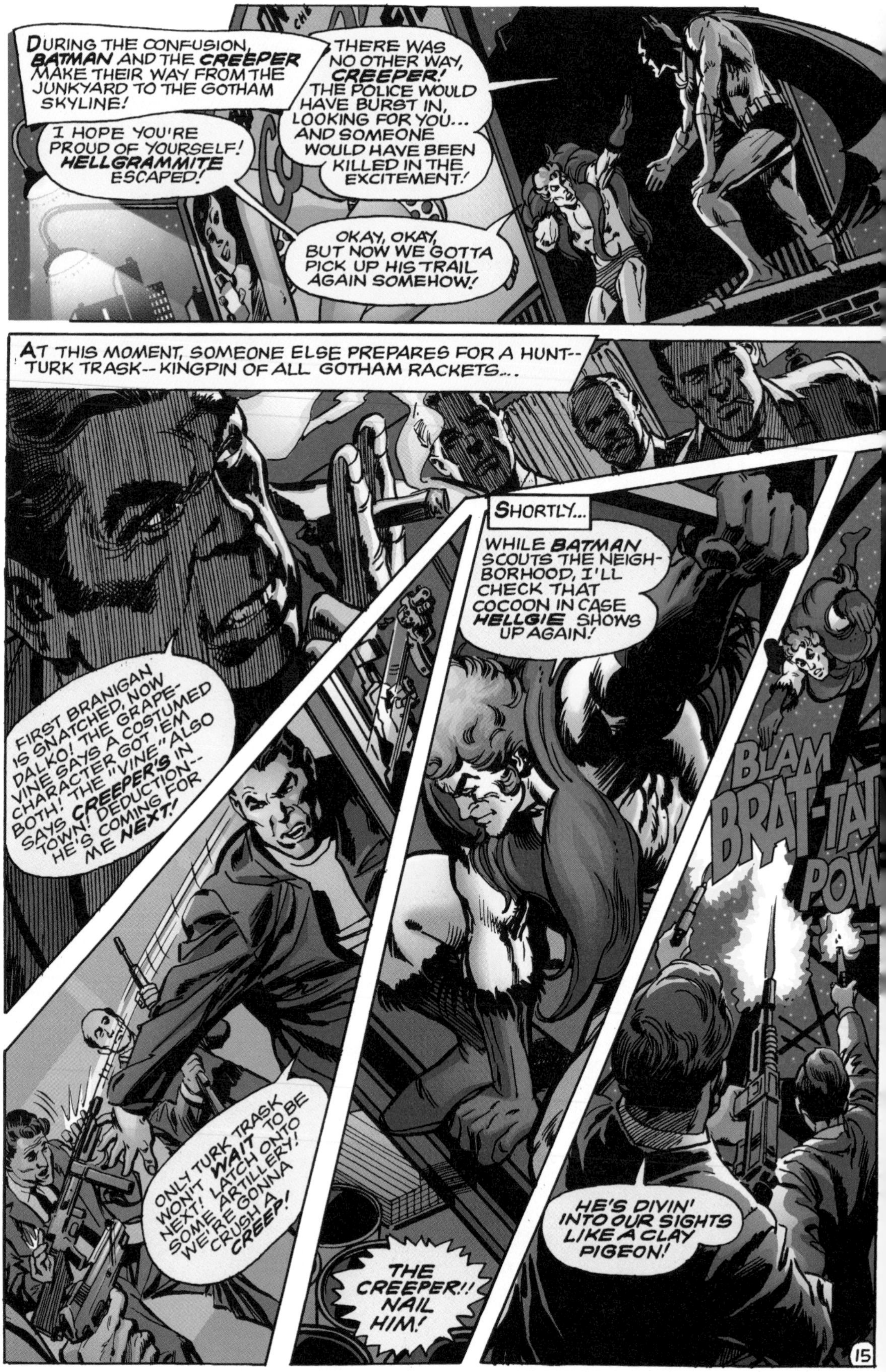
DURING THE CONFUSION, BATMAN AND THE CREEPER MAKE THEIR WAY FROM THE JUNKYARD TO THE GOTHAM SKYLINE!
THERE WAS NO OTHER WAY, CREEPER! THE POLICE WOULD HAVE BURST IN, LOOKING FOR YOU... AND SOMEONE WOULD HAVE BEEN KILLED IN THE EXCITEMENT!
I HOPE YOU'RE PROUD OF YOURSELF! HELLGRAMMITE ESCAPED!
OKAY, OKAY, BUT NOW WE GOTTA PICK UP HIS TRAIL AGAIN SOMEHOW!
AT THIS MOMENT, SOMEONE ELSE PREPARES FOR A HUNT-- TURK TRASK-- KINGPIN OF ALL GOTHAM RACKETS...
FIRST BRANIGAN IS SNATCHED, NOW DALKO! THE GRAPEVINE SAYS A COSTUMED CHARACTER GOT 'EM BOTH! THE "VINE" ALSO SAYS CREEPER'S IN TOWN! DEDUCTION-- HE'S COMING FOR ME NEXT!
ONLY TURK TRASK WON'T WAIT TO BE NEXT! LATCH ONTO SOME ARTILLERY! WE'RE GONNA CRUSH A CREEP!
SHORTLY...
WHILE BATMAN SCOUTS THE NEIGHBORHOOD, I'LL CHECK THAT COCOON IN CASE HELLGIE SHOWS UP AGAIN!
THE CREEPER!! NAIL HIM!
BLAM
BRAT-TAT
POW
HE'S DIVIN' INTO OUR SIGHTS LIKE A CLAY PIGEON!
15

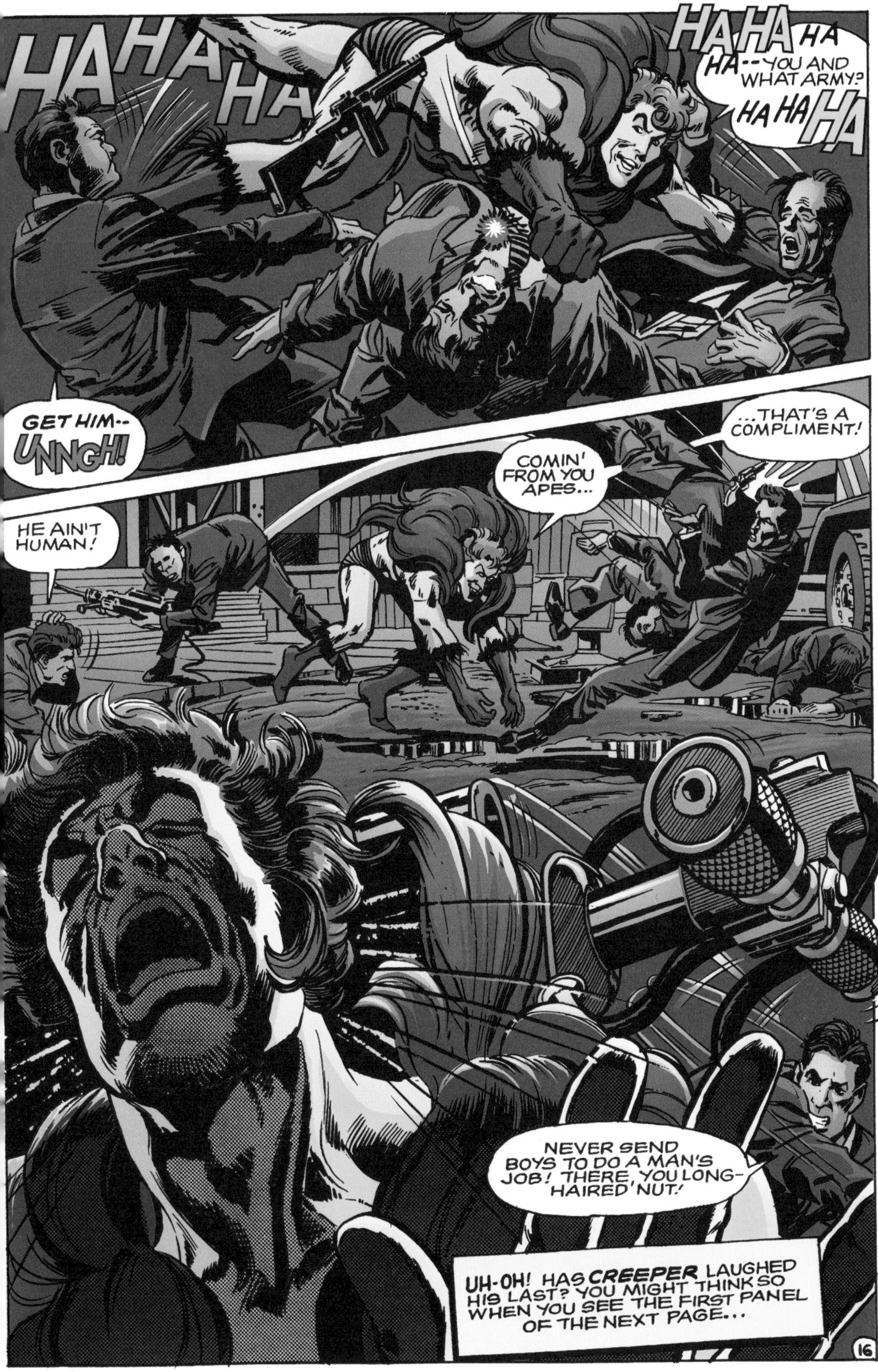

HAHAHAHA
HAHA HA HA--YOU AND WHAT ARMY? HA HA HA HA
GET HIM-- UNNGH!
...THAT'S A COMPLIMENT!
COMIN' FROM YOU APES...
HE AIN'T HUMAN!
NEVER SEND BOYS TO DO A MAN'S JOB! THERE, YOU LONG-HAIRED NUT!
UH-OH! HAS CREEPER LAUGHED HIS LAST? YOU MIGHT THINK SO WHEN YOU SEE THE FIRST PANEL OF THE NEXT PAGE...
16

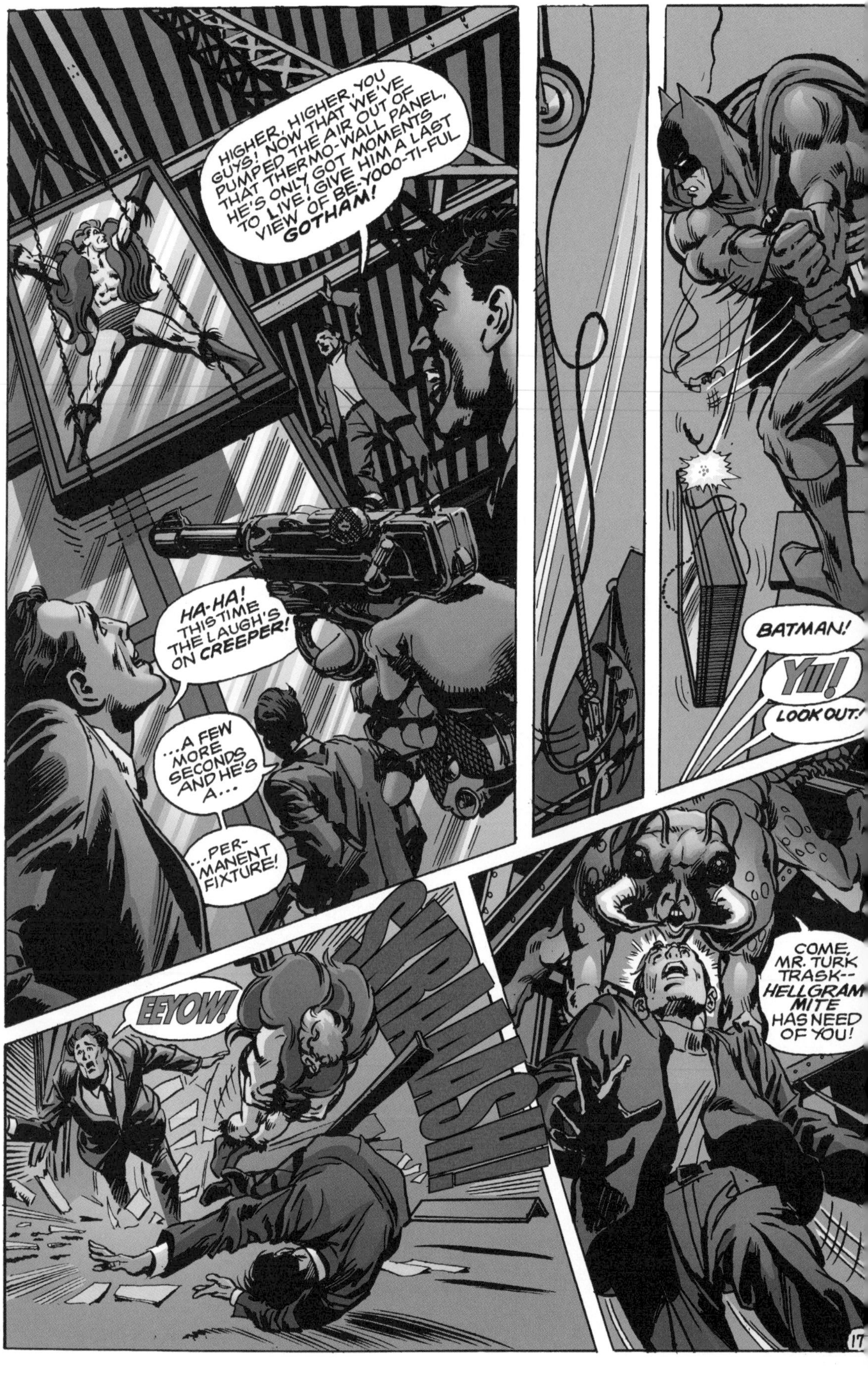
HIGHER, HIGHER, YOU GUYS! NOW THAT WE'VE PUMPED THE AIR OUT OF THAT THERMO-WALL PANEL, HE'S ONLY GOT MOMENTS TO LIVE! GIVE HIM A LAST VIEW OF BE-YOOO-TI-FUL GOTHAM!
HA-HA! THIS TIME THE LAUGH'S ON CREEPER!
...A FEW MORE SECONDS AND HE'S A...
...PER-MANENT FIXTURE!
BATMAN!
YII!
LOOK OUT!
EEYOW!
SKRAASH!
COME, MR. TURK TRASK-- HELLGRAM MITE HAS NEED OF YOU!
17

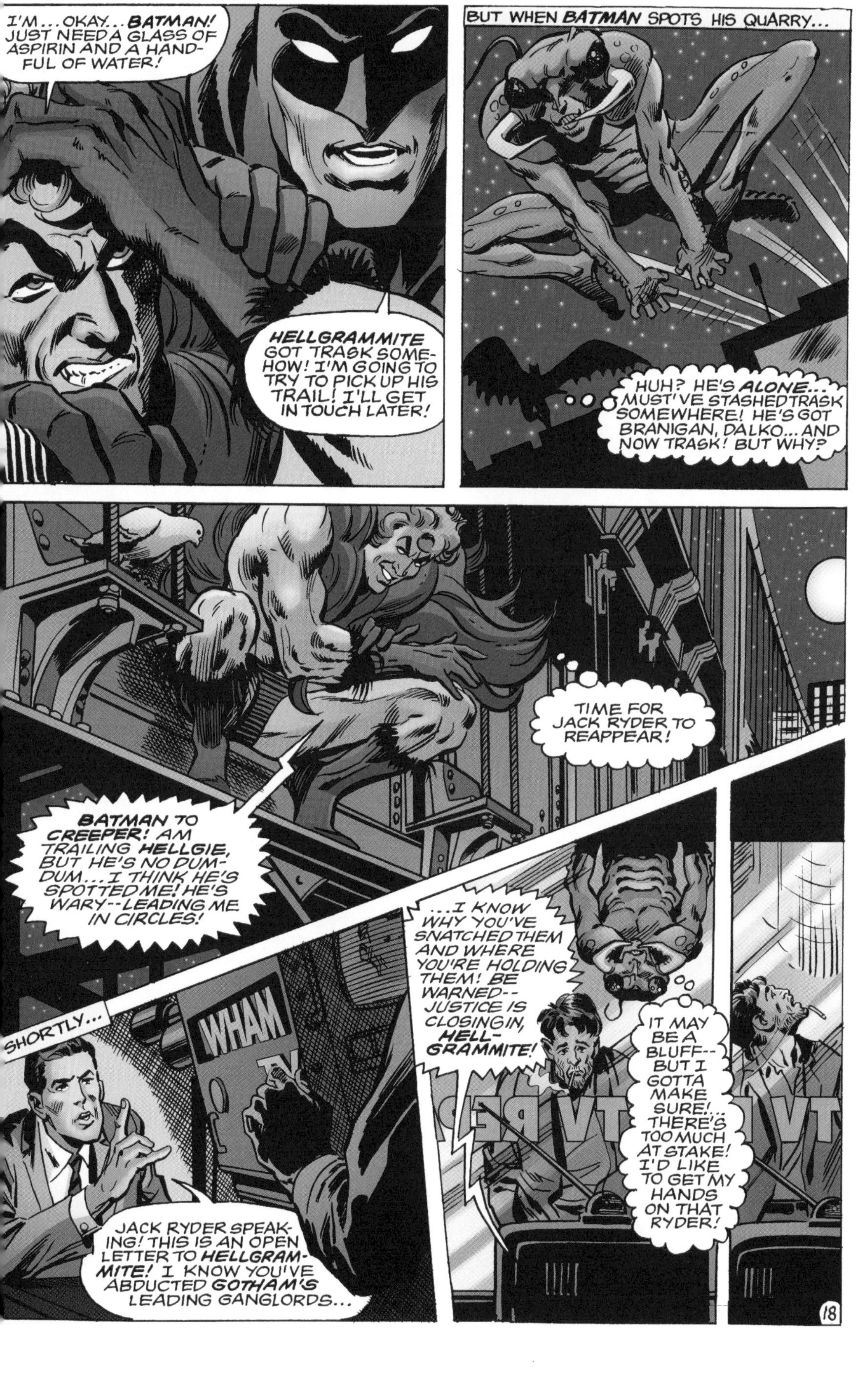
I'M... OKAY... BATMAN! JUST NEED A GLASS OF ASPIRIN AND A HANDFUL OF WATER!
HELLGRAMMITE GOT TRASK SOMEHOW! I'M GOING TO TRY TO PICK UP HIS TRAIL! I'LL GET IN TOUCH LATER!
BUT WHEN BATMAN SPOTS HIS QUARRY...
HUH? HE'S ALONE... MUST'VE STASHED TRASK SOMEWHERE! HE'S GOT BRANIGAN, DALKO... AND NOW TRASK! BUT WHY?
TIME FOR JACK RYDER TO REAPPEAR!
BATMAN TO CREEPER! AM TRAILING HELLGIE, BUT HE'S NO DUM-DUM... I THINK HE'S SPOTTED ME! HE'S WARY--LEADING ME IN CIRCLES!
SHORTLY...
WHAM
JACK RYDER SPEAKING! THIS IS AN OPEN LETTER TO HELLGRAMMITE! I KNOW YOU'VE ABDUCTED GOTHAM'S LEADING GANGLORDS...
...I KNOW WHY YOU'VE SNATCHED THEM AND WHERE YOU'RE HOLDING THEM! BE WARNED--JUSTICE IS CLOSING IN, HELLGRAMMITE!
IT MAY BE A BLUFF--BUT I GOTTA MAKE SURE!... THERE'S TOO MUCH AT STAKE! I'D LIKE TO GET MY HANDS ON THAT RYDER!
18

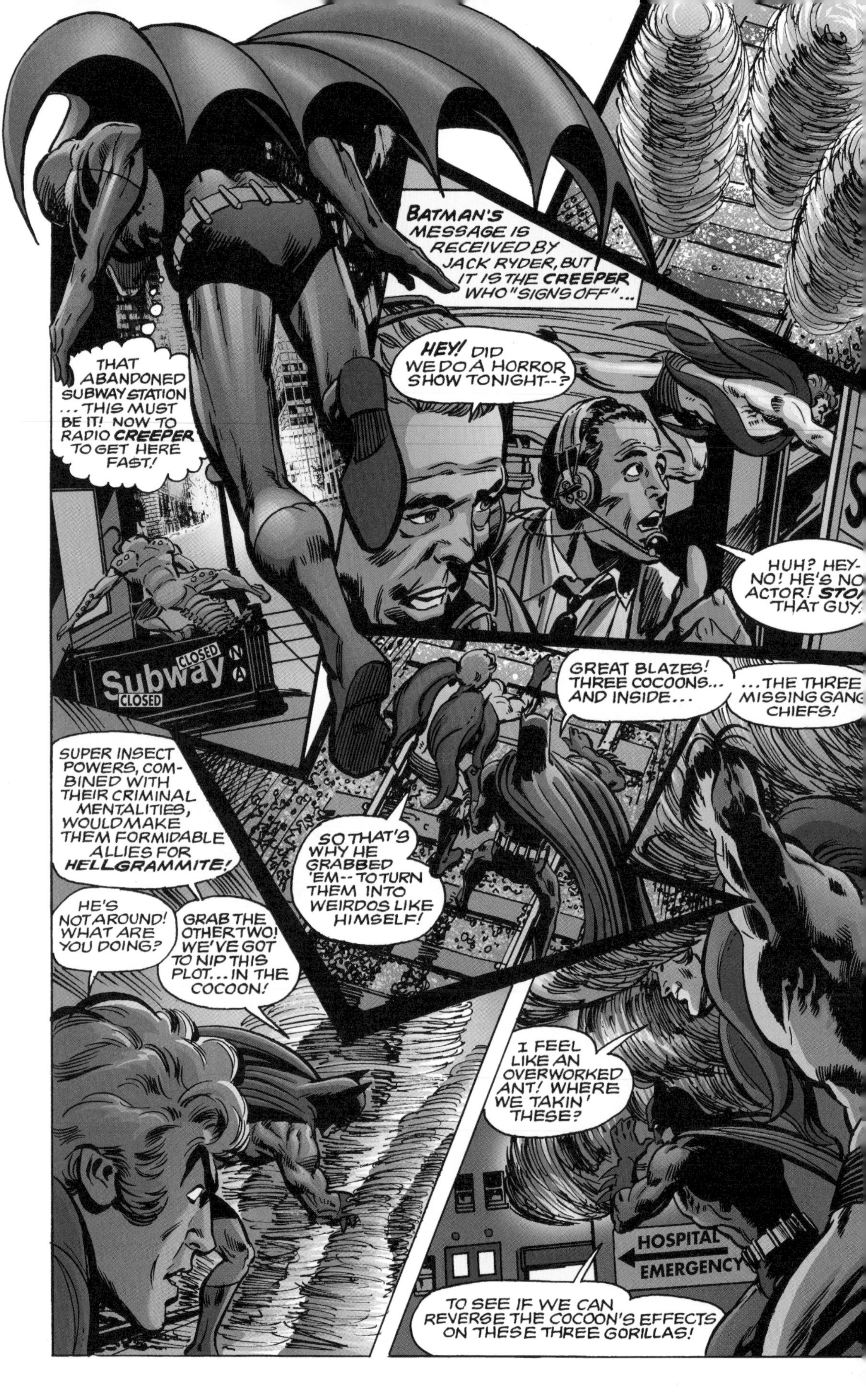
BATMAN'S MESSAGE IS RECEIVED BY JACK RYDER, BUT IT IS THE CREEPER WHO "SIGNS OFF"...
THAT ABANDONED SUBWAY STATION ...THIS MUST BE IT! NOW TO RADIO CREEPER TO GET HERE FAST!
HEY! DID WE DO A HORROR SHOW TONIGHT--?
HUH? HEY- NO! HE'S NO ACTOR! STO THAT GUY
Subway
CLOSED
CLOSED
N
A
GREAT BLAZES! THREE COCOONS... AND INSIDE...
...THE THREE MISSING GANG CHIEFS!
SUPER INSECT POWERS, COMBINED WITH THEIR CRIMINAL MENTALITIES, WOULD MAKE THEM FORMIDABLE ALLIES FOR HELLGRAMMITE!
SO THAT'S WHY HE GRABBED 'EM--TO TURN THEM INTO WEIRDOS LIKE HIMSELF!
HE'S NOT AROUND! WHAT ARE YOU DOING?
GRAB THE OTHER TWO! WE'VE GOT TO NIP THIS PLOT...IN THE COCOON!
I FEEL LIKE AN OVERWORKED ANT! WHERE WE TAKIN' THESE?
HOSPITAL
EMERGENCY
TO SEE IF WE CAN REVERSE THE COCOON'S EFFECTS ON THESE THREE GORILLAS!

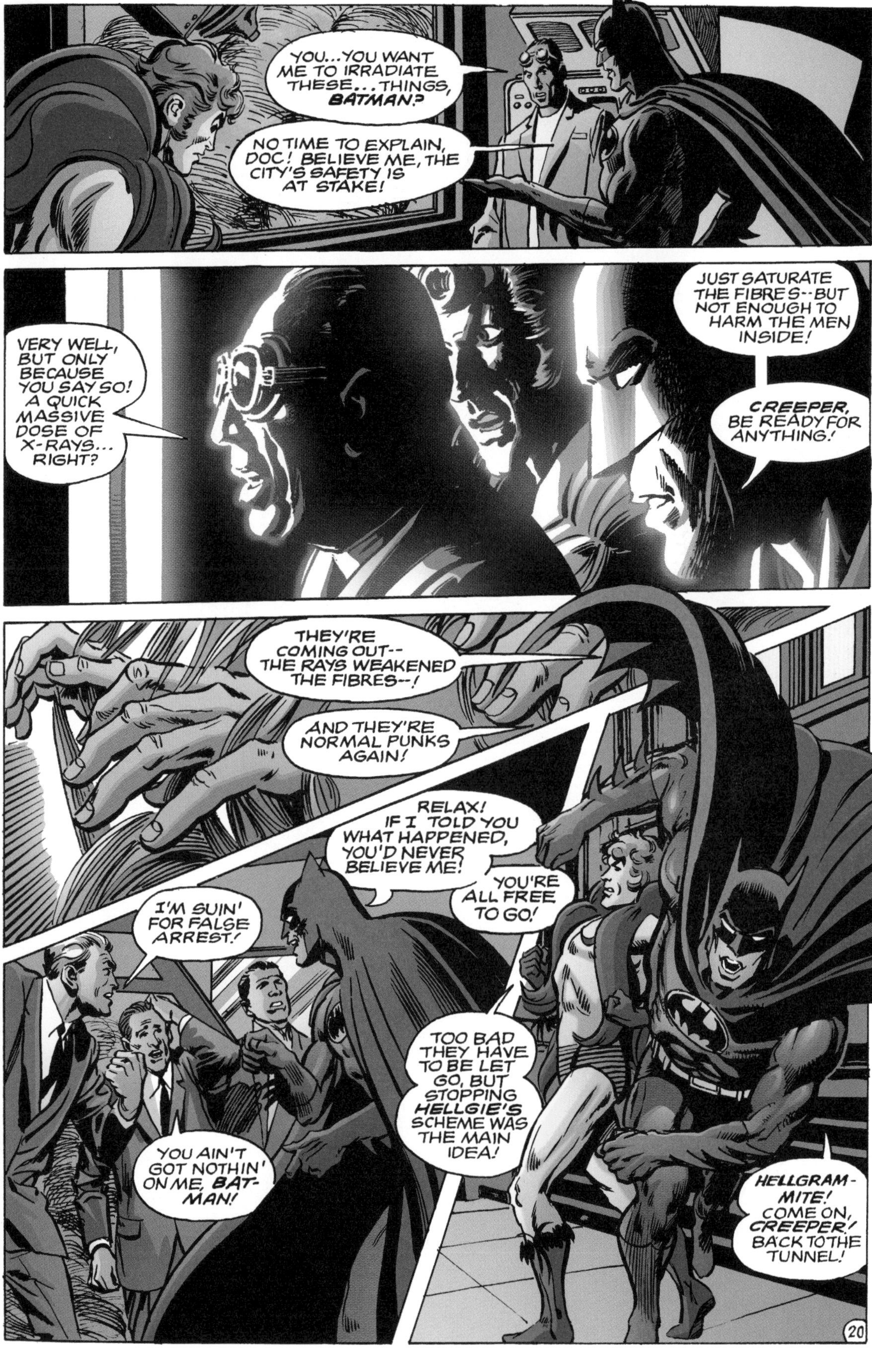
YOU...YOU WANT ME TO IRRADIATE THESE...THINGS, BATMAN?
NO TIME TO EXPLAIN, DOC! BELIEVE ME, THE CITY'S SAFETY IS AT STAKE!
VERY WELL, BUT ONLY BECAUSE YOU SAY SO! A QUICK MASSIVE DOSE OF X-RAYS... RIGHT?
JUST SATURATE THE FIBRES--BUT NOT ENOUGH TO HARM THE MEN INSIDE!
CREEPER, BE READY FOR ANYTHING!
THEY'RE COMING OUT-- THE RAYS WEAKENED THE FIBRES--!
AND THEY'RE NORMAL PUNKS AGAIN!
RELAX! IF I TOLD YOU WHAT HAPPENED, YOU'D NEVER BELIEVE ME!
YOU'RE ALL FREE TO GO!
I'M SUIN' FOR FALSE ARREST!
TOO BAD THEY HAVE TO BE LET GO, BUT STOPPING HELLGIE'S SCHEME WAS THE MAIN IDEA!
YOU AIN'T GOT NOTHIN' ON ME, BAT-MAN!
HELLGRAM-MITE! COME ON, CREEPER! BACK TO THE TUNNEL!
20

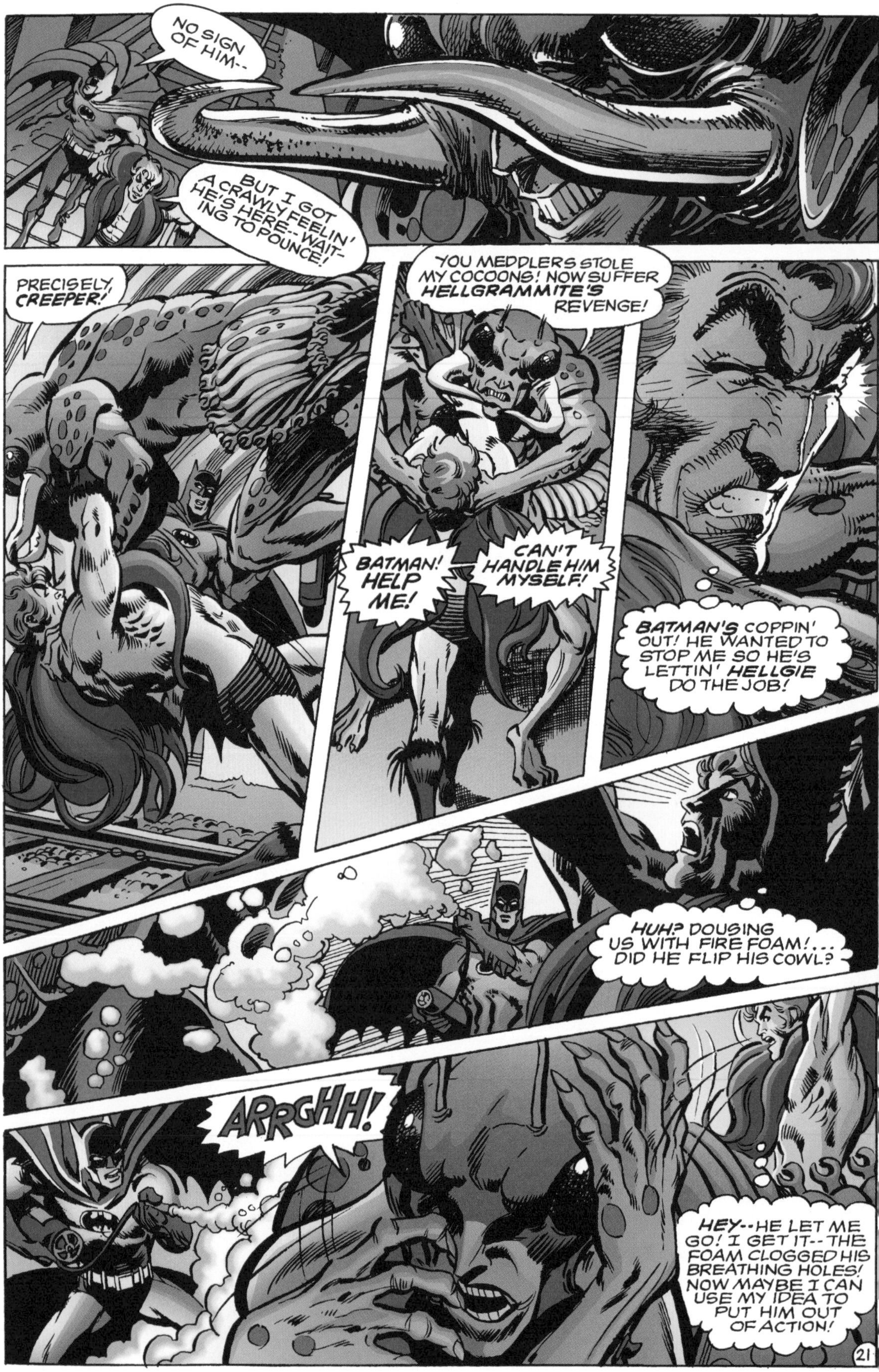
NO SIGN OF HIM--
BUT I GOT A CRAWLY FEELIN' HE'S HERE--WAITING TO POUNCE!
PRECISELY, CREEPER!
YOU MEDDLERS STOLE MY COCOONS! NOW SUFFER HELLGRAMMITE'S REVENGE!
BATMAN! HELP ME!
CAN'T HANDLE HIM MYSELF!
BATMAN'S COPPIN' OUT! HE WANTED TO STOP ME SO HE'S LETTIN' HELLGIE DO THE JOB!
HUH? DOUSING US WITH FIRE FOAM!... DID HE FLIP HIS COWL?
ARRGHH!
HEY--HE LET ME GO! I GET IT--THE FOAM CLOGGED HIS BREATHING HOLES! NOW MAYBE I CAN USE MY IDEA TO PUT HIM OUT OF ACTION!
21

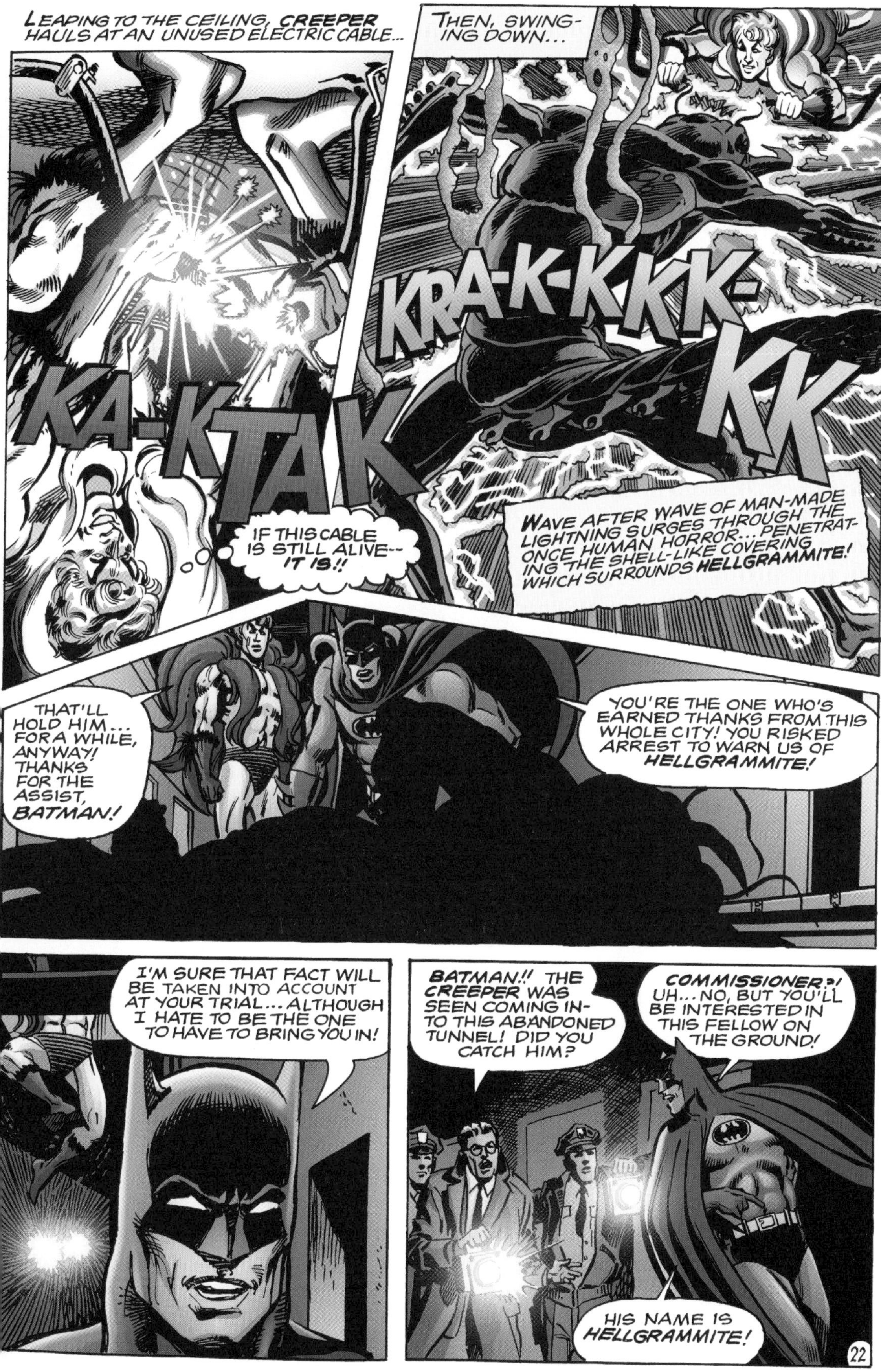
LEAPING TO THE CEILING, CREEPER HAULS AT AN UNUSED ELECTRIC CABLE...
KA-KTAK
IF THIS CABLE IS STILL ALIVE-- IT IS!!
THEN, SWING-ING DOWN...
KRA-K-K-K-K-KK
WAVE AFTER WAVE OF MAN-MADE LIGHTNING SURGES THROUGH THE ONCE HUMAN HORROR... PENETRAT-ING THE SHELL-LIKE COVERING WHICH SURROUNDS HELLGRAMMITE!
THAT'LL HOLD HIM... FOR A WHILE, ANYWAY! THANKS FOR THE ASSIST, BATMAN!
YOU'RE THE ONE WHO'S EARNED THANKS FROM THIS WHOLE CITY! YOU RISKED ARREST TO WARN US OF HELLGRAMMITE!
I'M SURE THAT FACT WILL BE TAKEN INTO ACCOUNT AT YOUR TRIAL... ALTHOUGH I HATE TO BE THE ONE TO HAVE TO BRING YOU IN!
BATMAN!! THE CREEPER WAS SEEN COMING IN-TO THIS ABANDONED TUNNEL! DID YOU CATCH HIM?
COMMISSIONER?! UH... NO, BUT YOU'LL BE INTERESTED IN THIS FELLOW ON THE GROUND!
HIS NAME IS HELLGRAMMITE!
22

WHILE YOU TAKE HIM IN, I'LL TRY TO GET A LINE ON *CREEPER!* BUT I HAVE A...HUNCH ...HE SKIPPED TOWN! THERE'S NOTHING IN *GOTHAM* TO INTEREST A MADMAN LIKE HIM, ANYWAY!

HA HA HA HA HA HA HA HA HA HA HA HA HA HA HA HA HA HA

The END

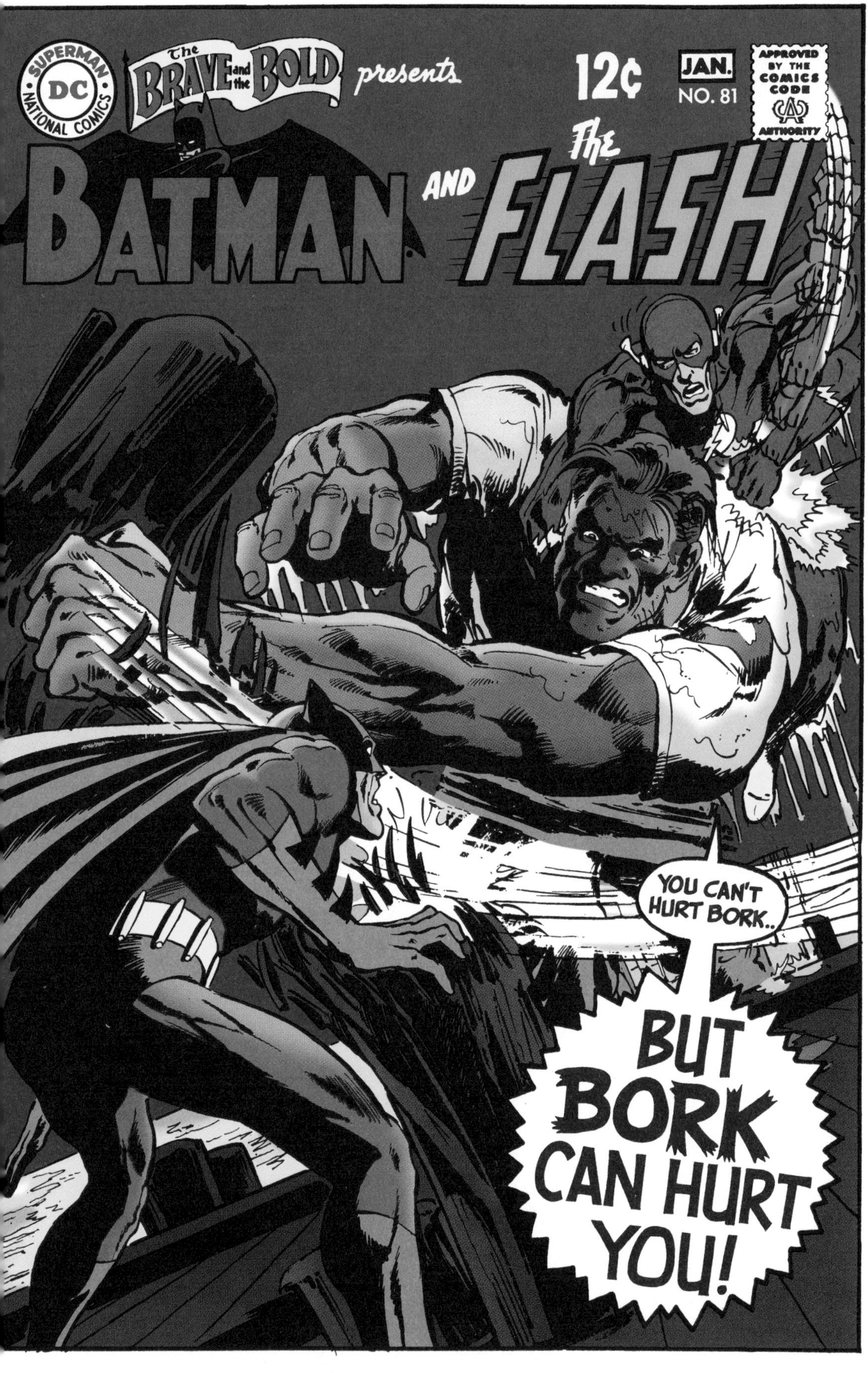
SUPERMAN
DC
NATIONAL COMICS
The BRAVE and the BOLD presents
12¢
JAN.
NO. 81
APPROVED BY THE COMICS CODE AUTHORITY
BATMAN AND THE FLASH
YOU CAN'T HURT BORK..
BUT BORK CAN HURT YOU!

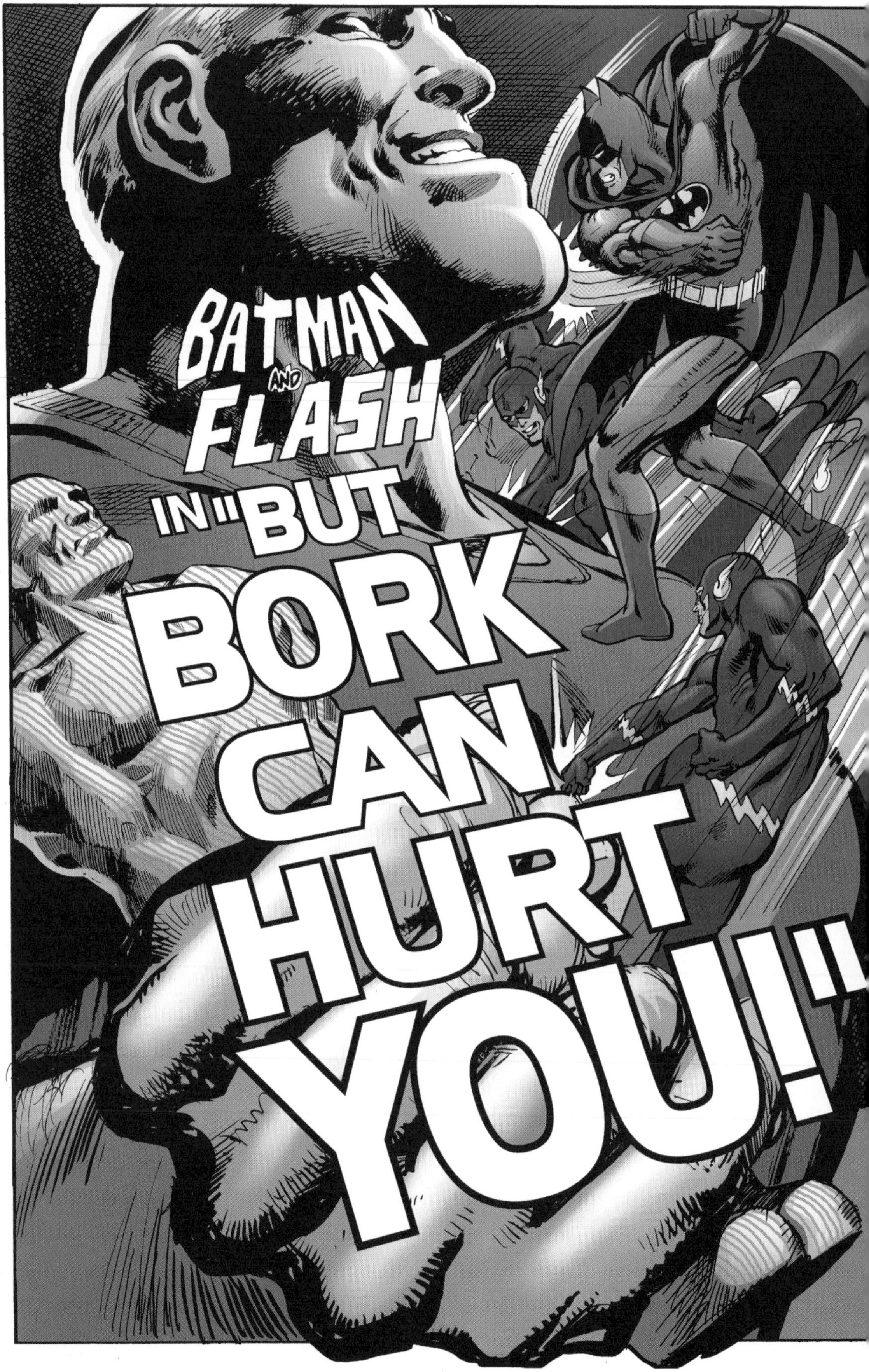
BATMAN AND FLASH
IN "BUT BORK CAN HURT YOU!"

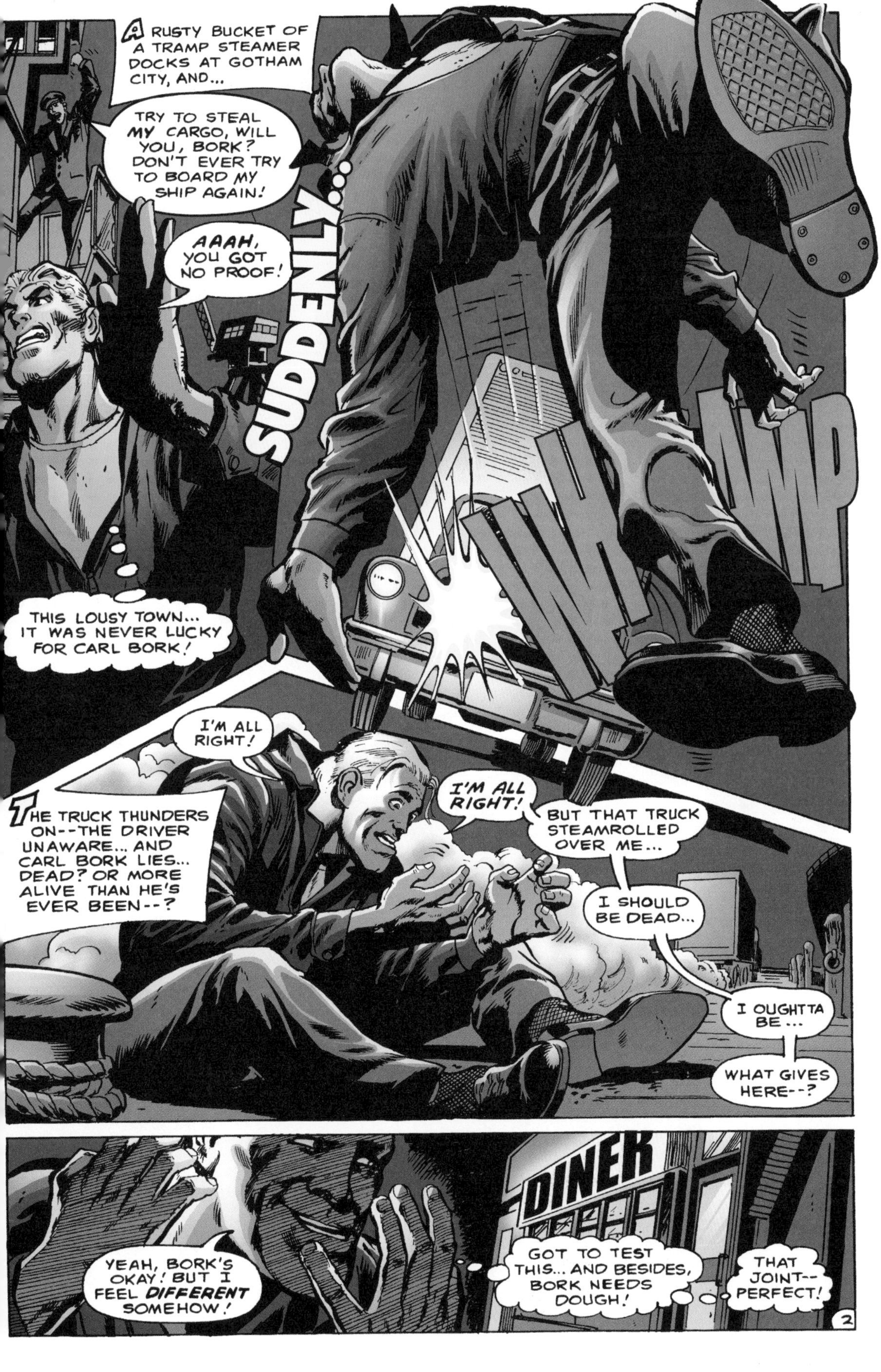
A RUSTY BUCKET OF A TRAMP STEAMER DOCKS AT GOTHAM CITY, AND...
TRY TO STEAL MY CARGO, WILL YOU, BORK? DON'T EVER TRY TO BOARD MY SHIP AGAIN!
AAAH, YOU GOT NO PROOF!
SUDDENLY...
THIS LOUSY TOWN... IT WAS NEVER LUCKY FOR CARL BORK!
WHAMP
I'M ALL RIGHT!
THE TRUCK THUNDERS ON--THE DRIVER UNAWARE... AND CARL BORK LIES... DEAD? OR MORE ALIVE THAN HE'S EVER BEEN--?
I'M ALL RIGHT!
BUT THAT TRUCK STEAMROLLED OVER ME...
I SHOULD BE DEAD...
I OUGHTTA BE...
WHAT GIVES HERE--?
YEAH, BORK'S OKAY! BUT I FEEL DIFFERENT SOMEHOW!
DINER
GOT TO TEST THIS... AND BESIDES, BORK NEEDS DOUGH!
THAT JOINT--PERFECT!
2

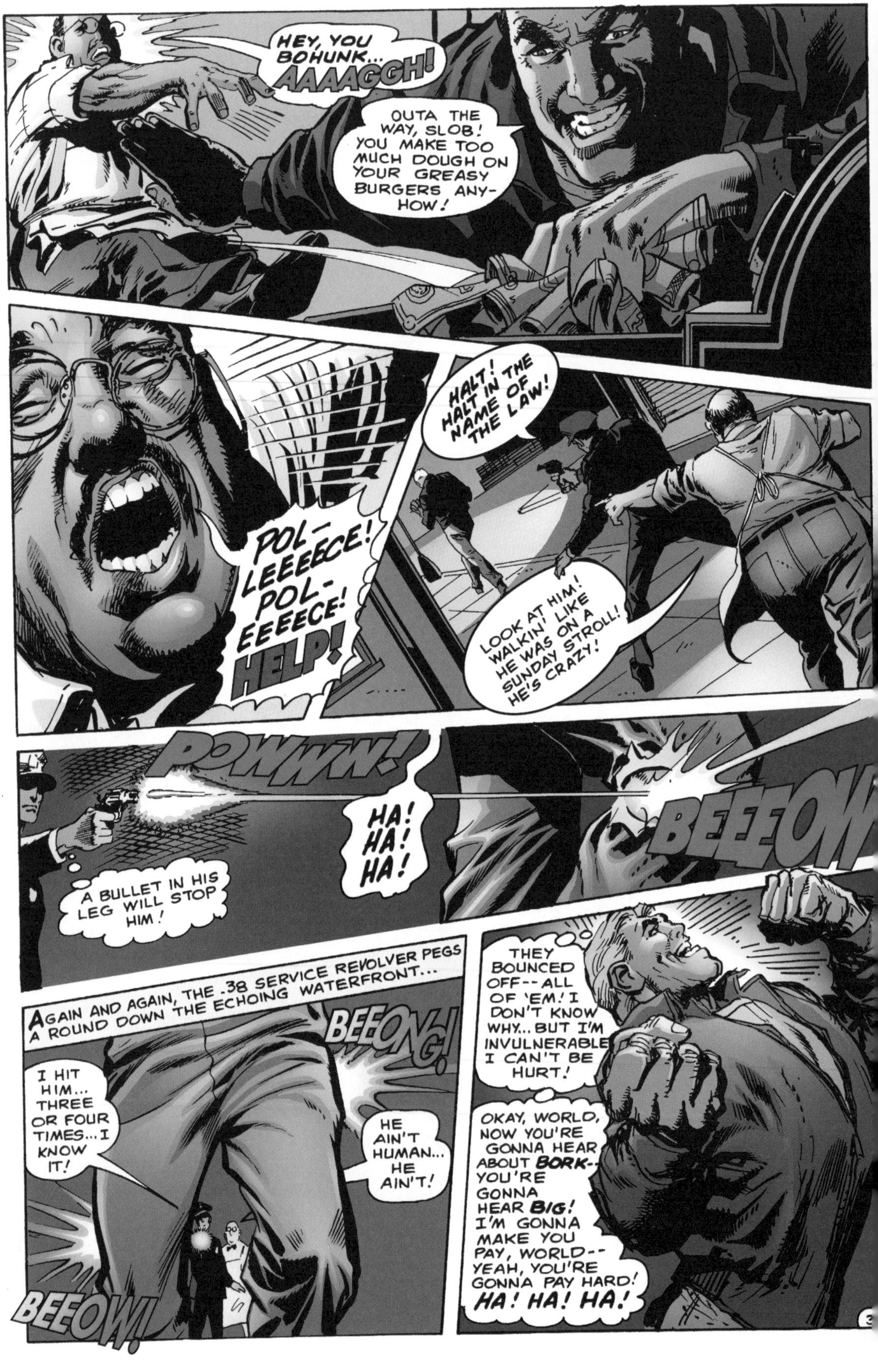
HEY, YOU BOHUNK... AAAAGGH!
OUTA THE WAY, SLOB! YOU MAKE TOO MUCH DOUGH ON YOUR GREASY BURGERS ANY-HOW!
POL-LEEEECE! POL-EEEECE! HELP!
HALT! HALT IN THE NAME OF THE LAW!
LOOK AT HIM! WALKIN' LIKE HE WAS ON A SUNDAY STROLL! HE'S CRAZY!
POWWW!
A BULLET IN HIS LEG WILL STOP HIM!
HA! HA! HA!
BEEEOW
AGAIN AND AGAIN, THE .38 SERVICE REVOLVER PEGS A ROUND DOWN THE ECHOING WATERFRONT...
BEEONG!
I HIT HIM... THREE OR FOUR TIMES... I KNOW IT!
HE AIN'T HUMAN... HE AIN'T!
BEEOW!
THEY BOUNCED OFF-- ALL OF 'EM! I DON'T KNOW WHY... BUT I'M INVULNERABLE! I CAN'T BE HURT!
OKAY, WORLD, NOW YOU'RE GONNA HEAR ABOUT BORK-- YOU'RE GONNA HEAR BIG! I'M GONNA MAKE YOU PAY, WORLD-- YEAH, YOU'RE GONNA PAY HARD! HA! HA! HA!

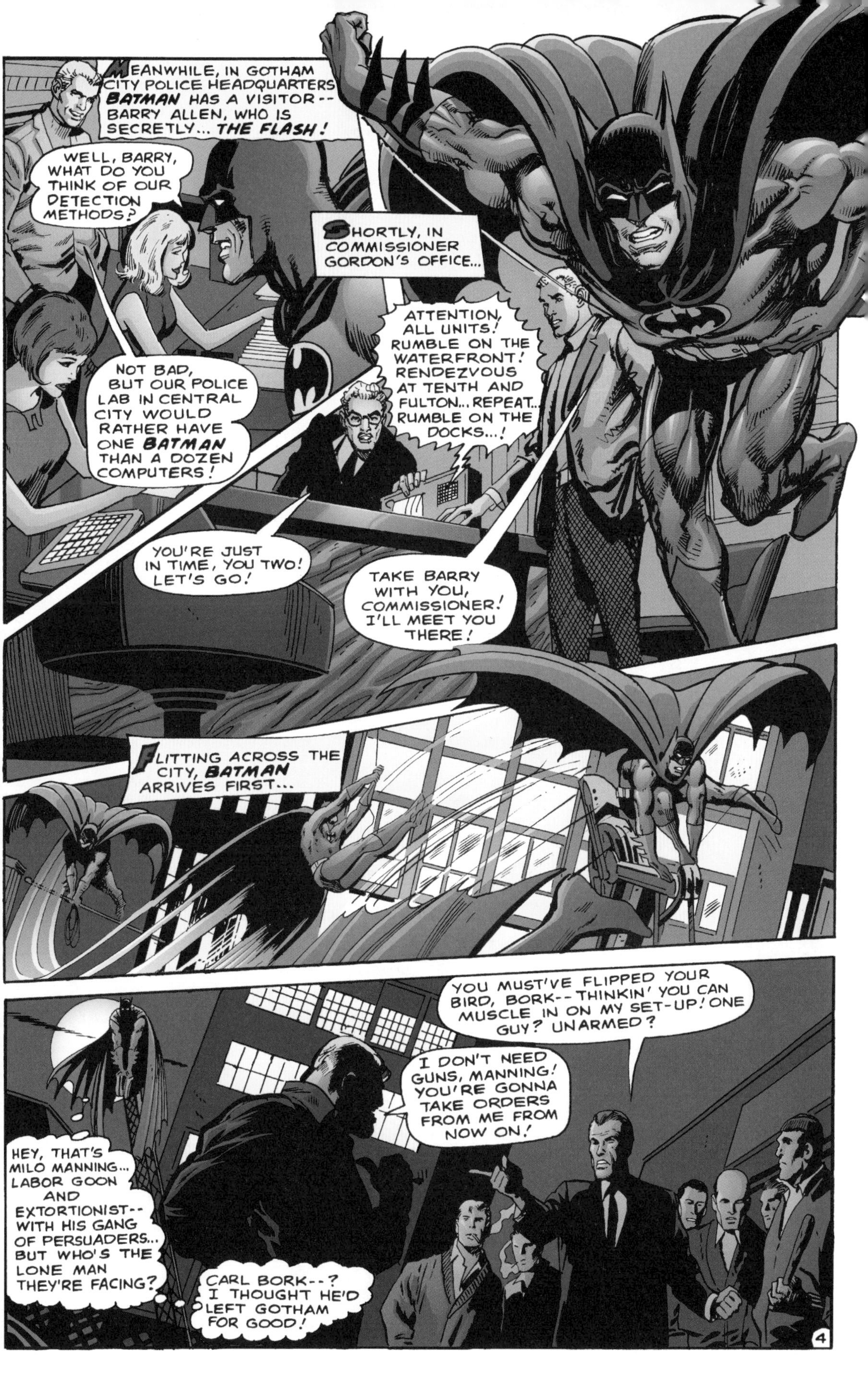
MEANWHILE, IN GOTHAM CITY POLICE HEADQUARTERS BATMAN HAS A VISITOR-- BARRY ALLEN, WHO IS SECRETLY... THE FLASH!
WELL, BARRY, WHAT DO YOU THINK OF OUR DETECTION METHODS?
NOT BAD, BUT OUR POLICE LAB IN CENTRAL CITY WOULD RATHER HAVE ONE BATMAN THAN A DOZEN COMPUTERS!
SHORTLY, IN COMMISSIONER GORDON'S OFFICE...
ATTENTION, ALL UNITS! RUMBLE ON THE WATERFRONT! RENDEZVOUS AT TENTH AND FULTON... REPEAT... RUMBLE ON THE DOCKS...!
YOU'RE JUST IN TIME, YOU TWO! LET'S GO!
TAKE BARRY WITH YOU, COMMISSIONER! I'LL MEET YOU THERE!
FLITTING ACROSS THE CITY, BATMAN ARRIVES FIRST...
YOU MUST'VE FLIPPED YOUR BIRD, BORK-- THINKIN' YOU CAN MUSCLE IN ON MY SET-UP! ONE GUY? UNARMED?
I DON'T NEED GUNS, MANNING! YOU'RE GONNA TAKE ORDERS FROM ME FROM NOW ON!
HEY, THAT'S MILO MANNING... LABOR GOON AND EXTORTIONIST-- WITH HIS GANG OF PERSUADERS... BUT WHO'S THE LONE MAN THEY'RE FACING?
CARL BORK--? I THOUGHT HE'D LEFT GOTHAM FOR GOOD!
4

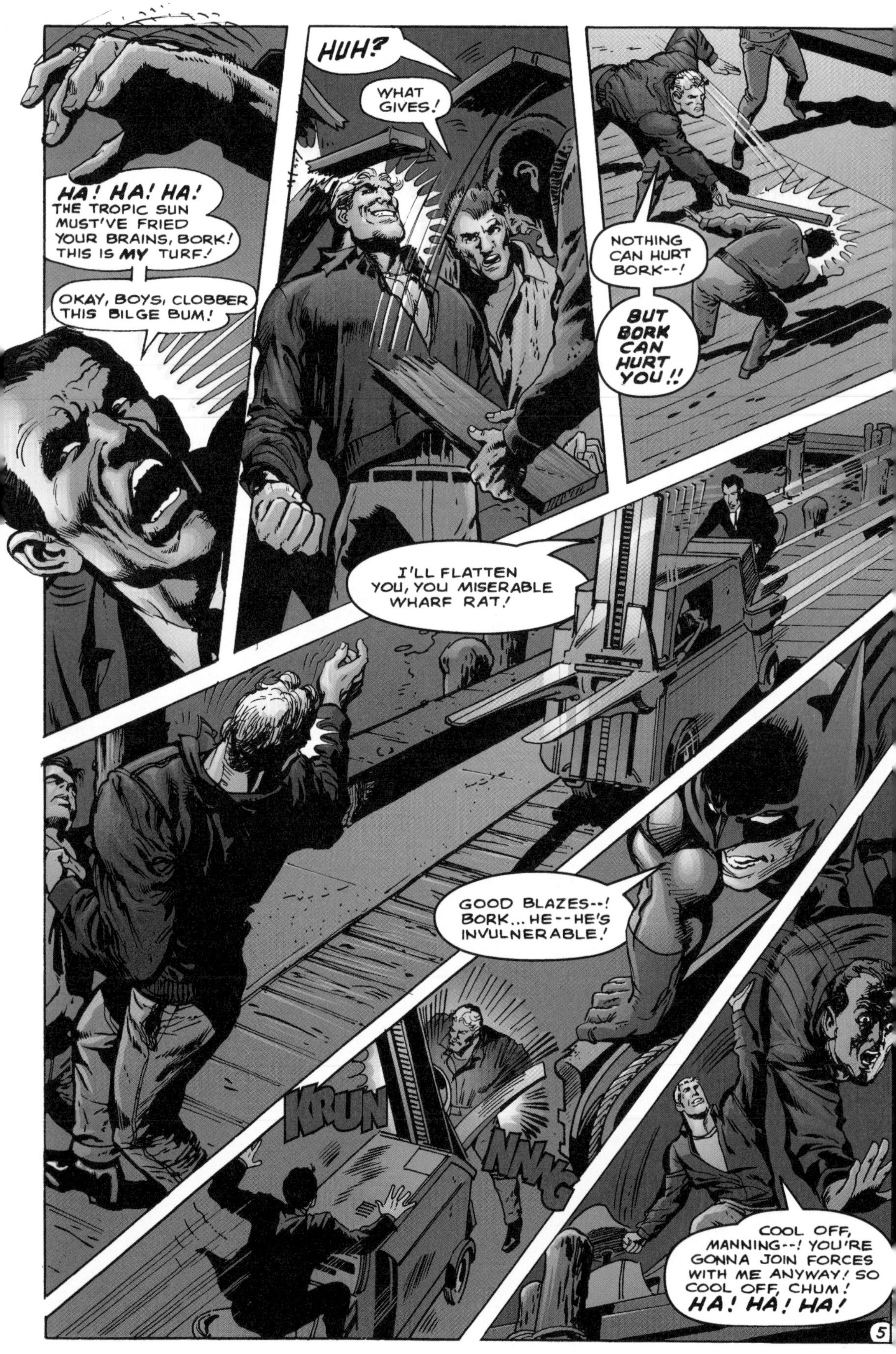
HA! HA! HA! THE TROPIC SUN MUST'VE FRIED YOUR BRAINS, BORK! THIS IS MY TURF!
OKAY, BOYS, CLOBBER THIS BILGE BUM!
HUH?
WHAT GIVES!
NOTHING CAN HURT BORK--!
BUT BORK CAN HURT YOU!!
I'LL FLATTEN YOU, YOU MISERABLE WHARF RAT!
GOOD BLAZES--! BORK... HE--HE'S INVULNERABLE!
KRUN
NNNG
COOL OFF, MANNING--! YOU'RE GONNA JOIN FORCES WITH ME ANYWAY! SO COOL OFF, CHUM! HA! HA! HA!
5

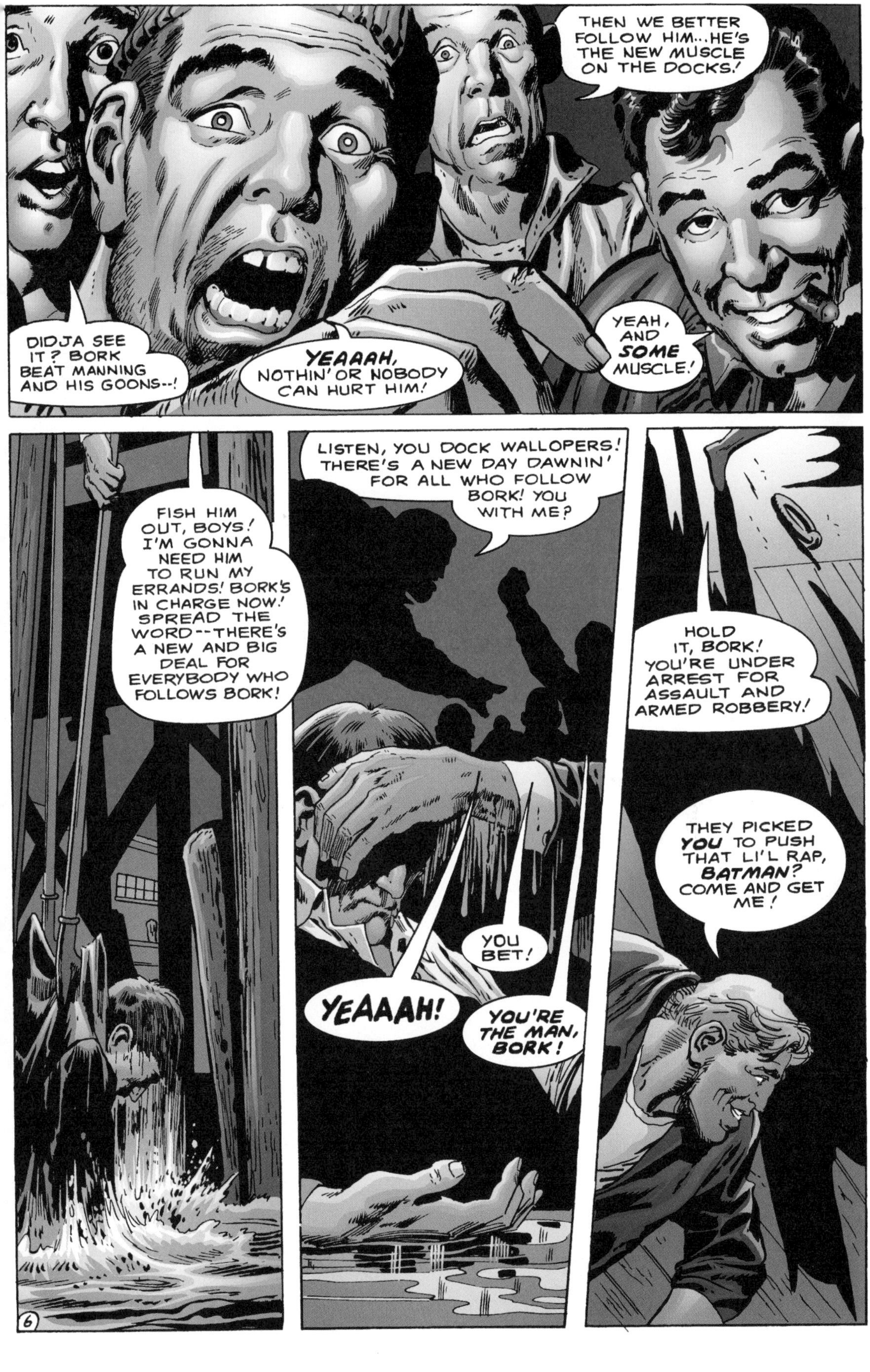
THEN WE BETTER FOLLOW HIM...HE'S THE NEW MUSCLE ON THE DOCKS!
DIDJA SEE IT? BORK BEAT MANNING AND HIS GOONS--!
YEAAAH, NOTHIN' OR NOBODY CAN HURT HIM!
YEAH, AND SOME MUSCLE!
FISH HIM OUT, BOYS! I'M GONNA NEED HIM TO RUN MY ERRANDS! BORK'S IN CHARGE NOW! SPREAD THE WORD--THERE'S A NEW AND BIG DEAL FOR EVERYBODY WHO FOLLOWS BORK!
6
LISTEN, YOU DOCK WALLOPERS! THERE'S A NEW DAY DAWNIN' FOR ALL WHO FOLLOW BORK! YOU WITH ME?
YOU BET!
YEAAAH!
YOU'RE THE MAN, BORK!
HOLD IT, BORK! YOU'RE UNDER ARREST FOR ASSAULT AND ARMED ROBBERY!
THEY PICKED YOU TO PUSH THAT LI'L RAP, BATMAN? COME AND GET ME!

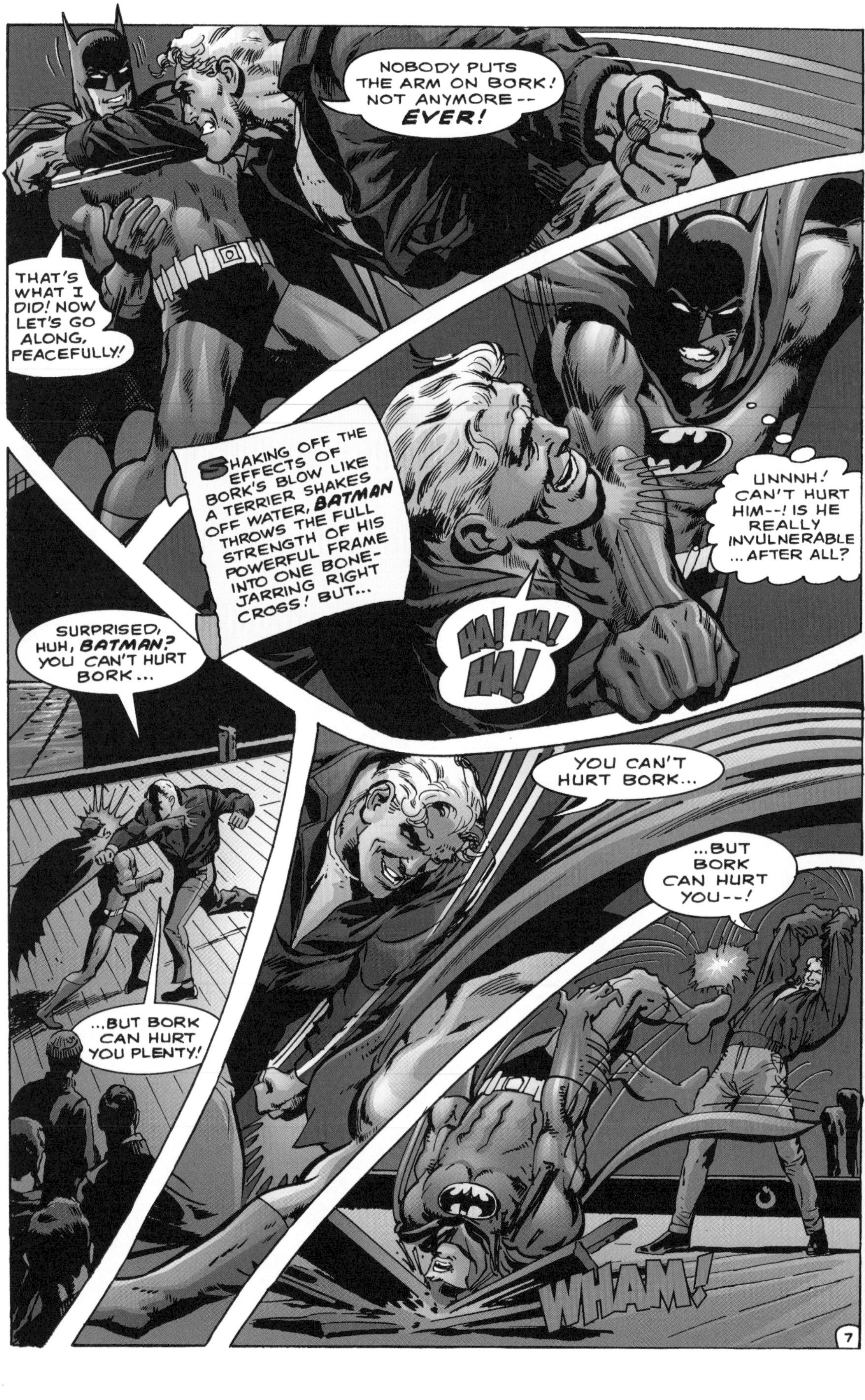
NOBODY PUTS THE ARM ON BORK! NOT ANYMORE -- EVER!
THAT'S WHAT I DID! NOW LET'S GO ALONG, PEACEFULLY!
SHAKING OFF THE EFFECTS OF BORK'S BLOW LIKE A TERRIER SHAKES OFF WATER, BATMAN THROWS THE FULL STRENGTH OF HIS POWERFUL FRAME INTO ONE BONE-JARRING RIGHT CROSS! BUT...
UNNNH! CAN'T HURT HIM--! IS HE REALLY INVULNERABLE ...AFTER ALL?
HA! HA! HA!
SURPRISED, HUH, BATMAN? YOU CAN'T HURT BORK...
...BUT BORK CAN HURT YOU PLENTY!
YOU CAN'T HURT BORK...
...BUT BORK CAN HURT YOU--!
WHAM!
7

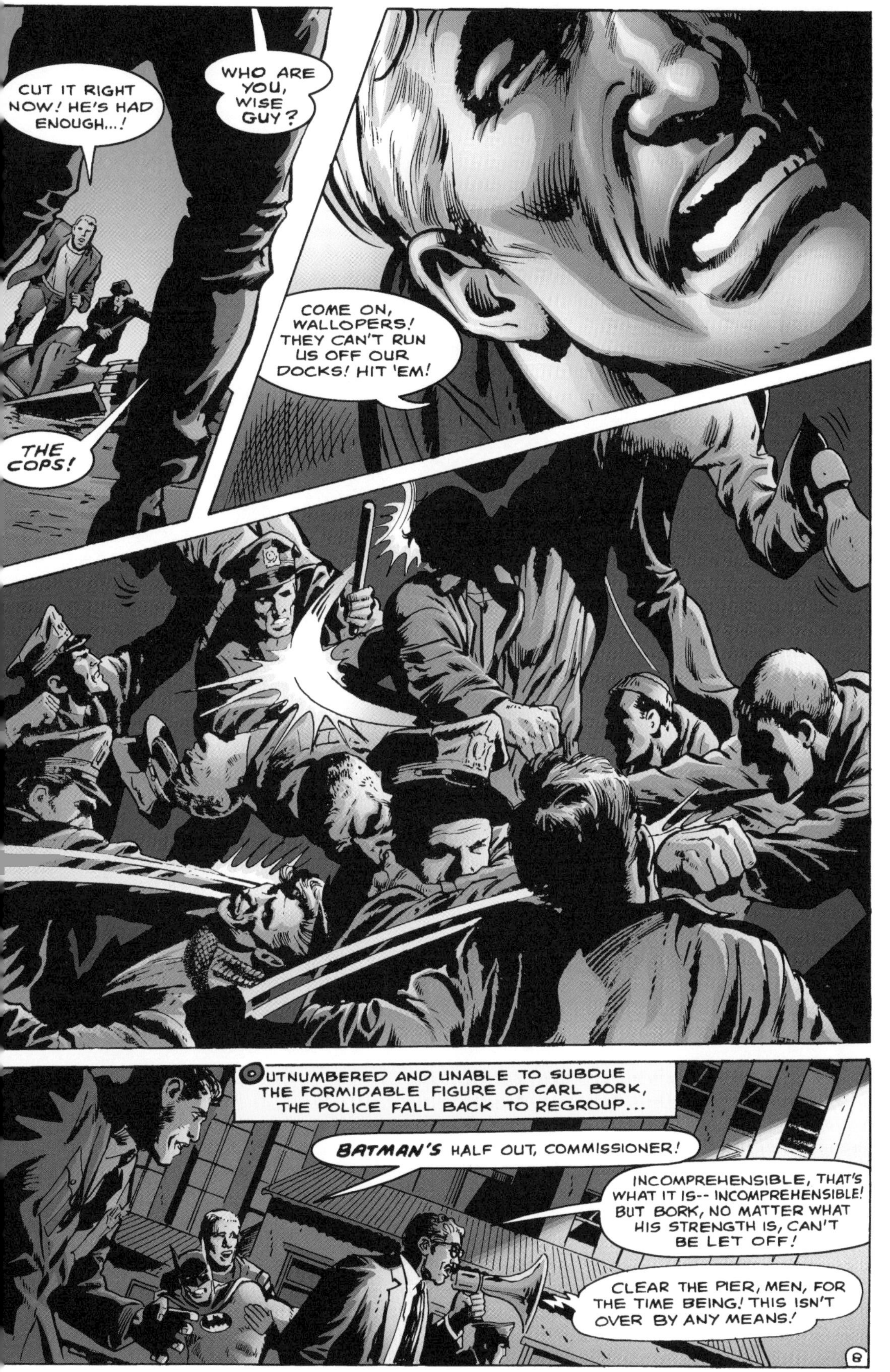
CUT IT RIGHT NOW! HE'S HAD ENOUGH...!
WHO ARE YOU, WISE GUY?
THE COPS!
COME ON, WALLOPERS! THEY CAN'T RUN US OFF OUR DOCKS! HIT 'EM!
OUTNUMBERED AND UNABLE TO SUBDUE THE FORMIDABLE FIGURE OF CARL BORK, THE POLICE FALL BACK TO REGROUP...
BATMAN'S HALF OUT, COMMISSIONER!
INCOMPREHENSIBLE, THAT'S WHAT IT IS-- INCOMPREHENSIBLE! BUT BORK, NO MATTER WHAT HIS STRENGTH IS, CAN'T BE LET OFF!
CLEAR THE PIER, MEN, FOR THE TIME BEING! THIS ISN'T OVER BY ANY MEANS!
8

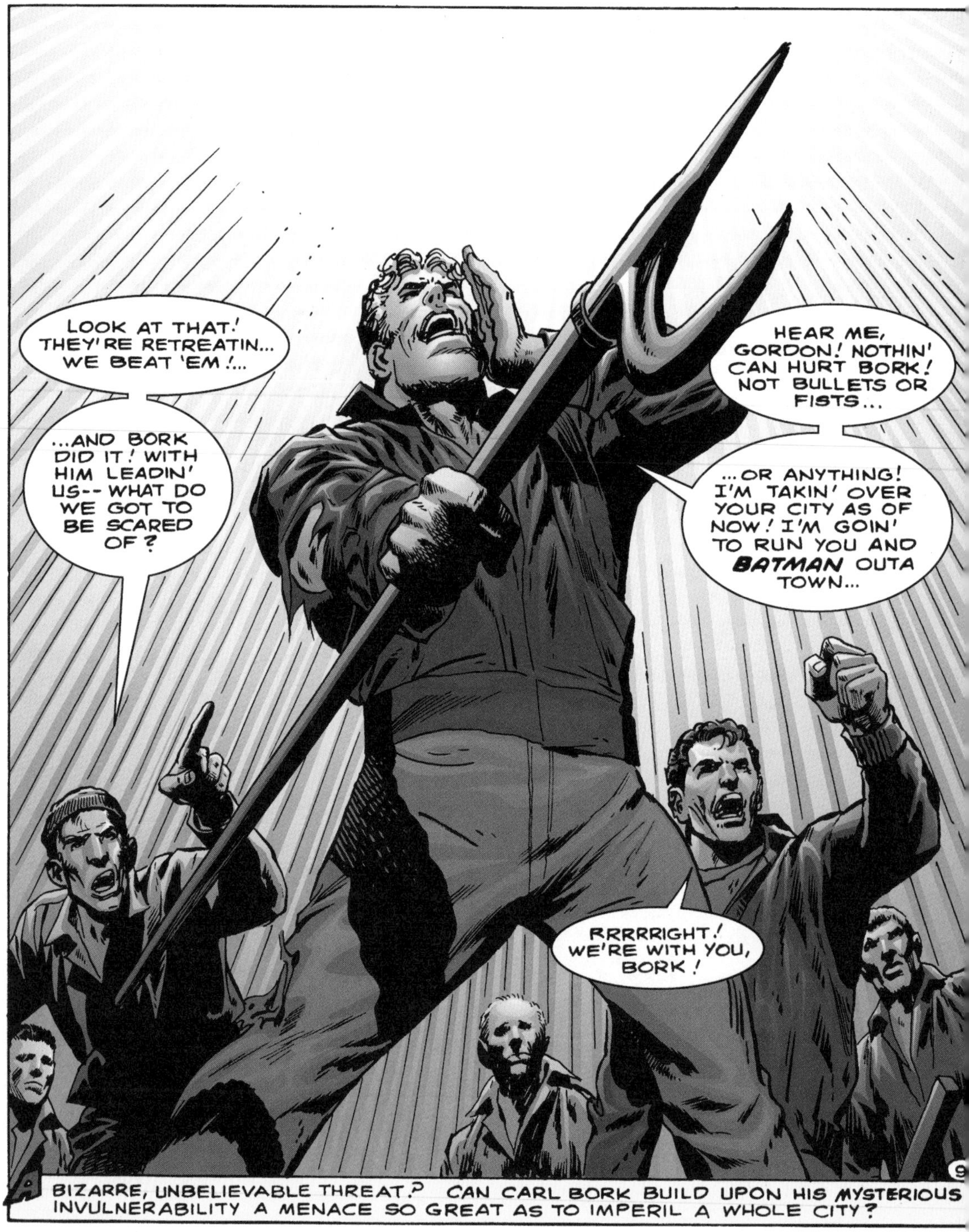
LOOK AT THAT! THEY'RE RETREATIN... WE BEAT 'EM!...
...AND BORK DID IT! WITH HIM LEADIN' US-- WHAT DO WE GOT TO BE SCARED OF?
HEAR ME, GORDON! NOTHIN' CAN HURT BORK! NOT BULLETS OR FISTS...
...OR ANYTHING! I'M TAKIN' OVER YOUR CITY AS OF NOW! I'M GOIN' TO RUN YOU AND BATMAN OUTA TOWN...
RRRRRIGHT! WE'RE WITH YOU, BORK!
9
A BIZARRE, UNBELIEVABLE THREAT? CAN CARL BORK BUILD UPON HIS MYSTERIOUS INVULNERABILITY A MENACE SO GREAT AS TO IMPERIL A WHOLE CITY?

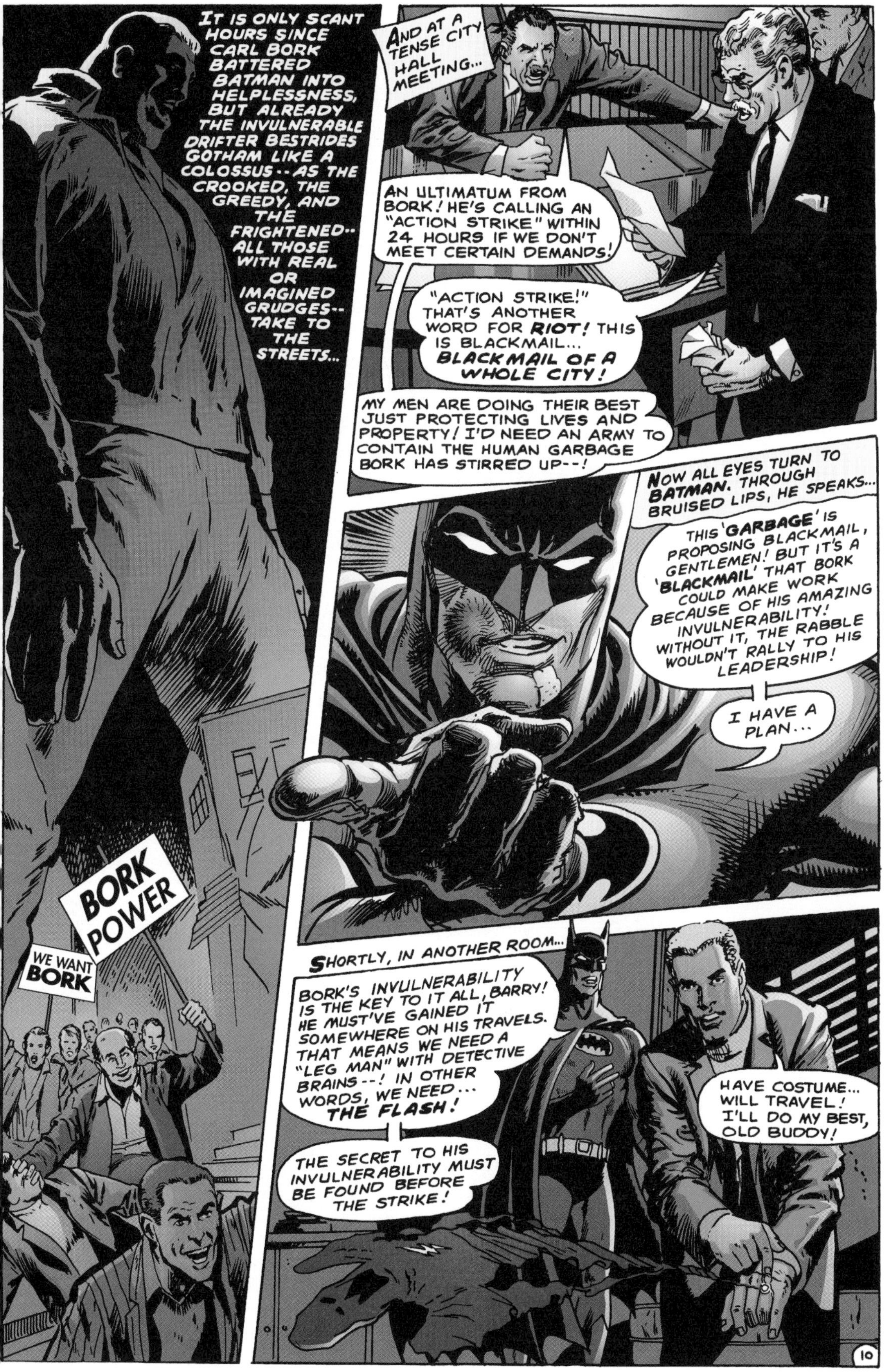
IT IS ONLY SCANT HOURS SINCE CARL BORK BATTERED BATMAN INTO HELPLESSNESS, BUT ALREADY THE INVULNERABLE DRIFTER BESTRIDES GOTHAM LIKE A COLOSSUS--AS THE CROOKED, THE GREEDY, AND THE FRIGHTENED--ALL THOSE WITH REAL OR IMAGINED GRUDGES--TAKE TO THE STREETS...
BORK POWER
WE WANT BORK
AND AT A TENSE CITY HALL MEETING...
AN ULTIMATUM FROM BORK! HE'S CALLING AN "ACTION STRIKE" WITHIN 24 HOURS IF WE DON'T MEET CERTAIN DEMANDS!
"ACTION STRIKE!" THAT'S ANOTHER WORD FOR RIOT! THIS IS BLACKMAIL... BLACKMAIL OF A WHOLE CITY!
MY MEN ARE DOING THEIR BEST JUST PROTECTING LIVES AND PROPERTY! I'D NEED AN ARMY TO CONTAIN THE HUMAN GARBAGE BORK HAS STIRRED UP--!
NOW ALL EYES TURN TO BATMAN. THROUGH BRUISED LIPS, HE SPEAKS...
THIS 'GARBAGE' IS PROPOSING BLACKMAIL, GENTLEMEN! BUT IT'S A 'BLACKMAIL' THAT BORK COULD MAKE WORK BECAUSE OF HIS AMAZING INVULNERABILITY! WITHOUT IT, THE RABBLE WOULDN'T RALLY TO HIS LEADERSHIP!
I HAVE A PLAN...
SHORTLY, IN ANOTHER ROOM...
BORK'S INVULNERABILITY IS THE KEY TO IT ALL, BARRY! HE MUST'VE GAINED IT SOMEWHERE ON HIS TRAVELS. THAT MEANS WE NEED A "LEG MAN" WITH DETECTIVE BRAINS--! IN OTHER WORDS, WE NEED... THE FLASH!
THE SECRET TO HIS INVULNERABILITY MUST BE FOUND BEFORE THE STRIKE!
HAVE COSTUME... WILL TRAVEL! I'LL DO MY BEST, OLD BUDDY!
10

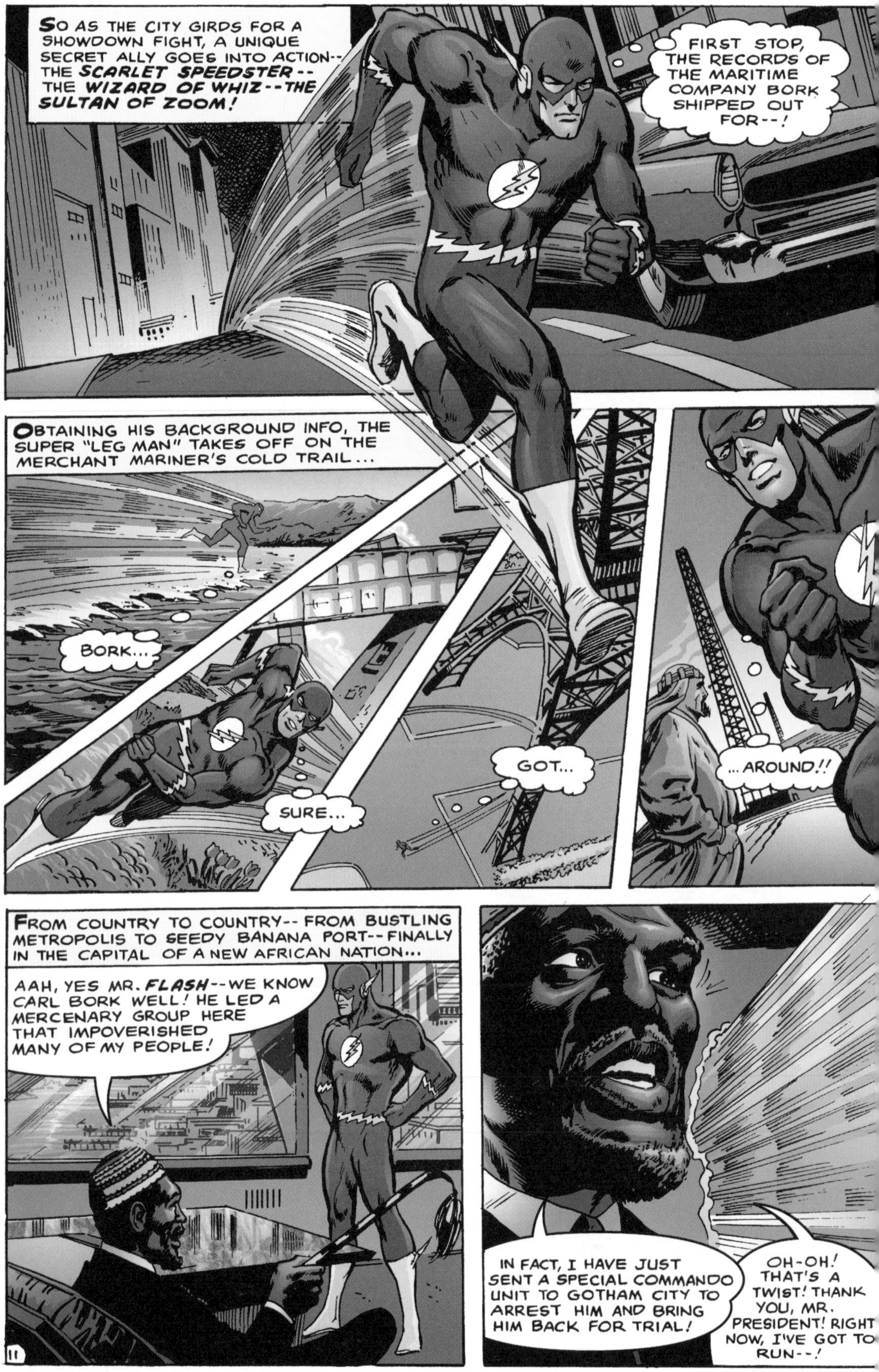

SO AS THE CITY GIRDS FOR A SHOWDOWN FIGHT, A UNIQUE SECRET ALLY GOES INTO ACTION-- THE SCARLET SPEEDSTER -- THE WIZARD OF WHIZ -- THE SULTAN OF ZOOM!
FIRST STOP, THE RECORDS OF THE MARITIME COMPANY BORK SHIPPED OUT FOR--!
OBTAINING HIS BACKGROUND INFO, THE SUPER "LEG MAN" TAKES OFF ON THE MERCHANT MARINER'S COLD TRAIL...
BORK...
SURE...
GOT...
...AROUND!!
FROM COUNTRY TO COUNTRY-- FROM BUSTLING METROPOLIS TO SEEDY BANANA PORT-- FINALLY IN THE CAPITAL OF A NEW AFRICAN NATION...
AAH, YES MR. FLASH--WE KNOW CARL BORK WELL! HE LED A MERCENARY GROUP HERE THAT IMPOVERISHED MANY OF MY PEOPLE!
IN FACT, I HAVE JUST SENT A SPECIAL COMMANDO UNIT TO GOTHAM CITY TO ARREST HIM AND BRING HIM BACK FOR TRIAL!
OH-OH! THAT'S A TWIST! THANK YOU, MR. PRESIDENT! RIGHT NOW, I'VE GOT TO RUN--!
11

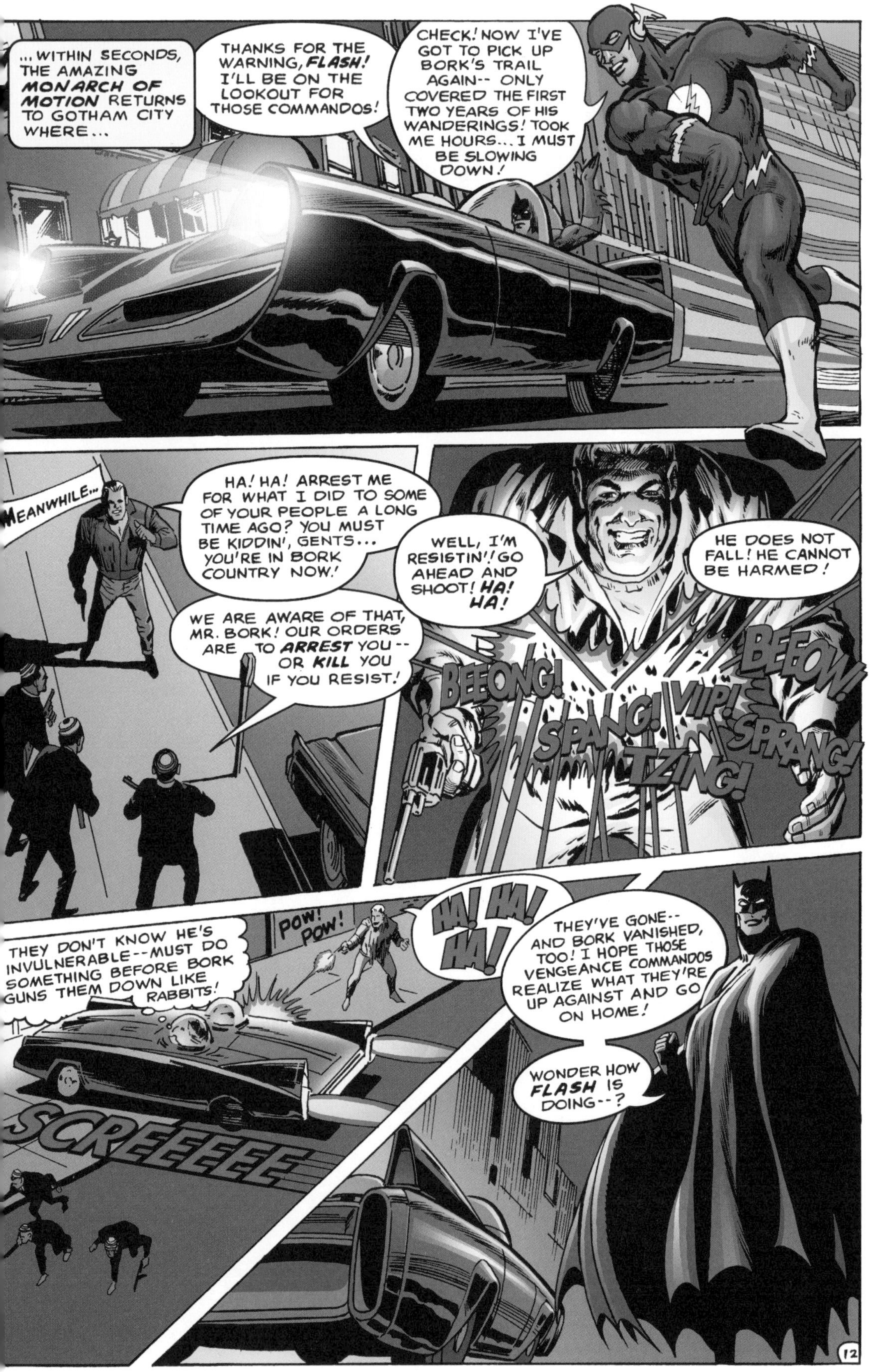
...WITHIN SECONDS, THE AMAZING MONARCH OF MOTION RETURNS TO GOTHAM CITY WHERE...
THANKS FOR THE WARNING, FLASH! I'LL BE ON THE LOOKOUT FOR THOSE COMMANDOS!
CHECK! NOW I'VE GOT TO PICK UP BORK'S TRAIL AGAIN-- ONLY COVERED THE FIRST TWO YEARS OF HIS WANDERINGS! TOOK ME HOURS... I MUST BE SLOWING DOWN!
MEANWHILE...
HA! HA! ARREST ME FOR WHAT I DID TO SOME OF YOUR PEOPLE A LONG TIME AGO? YOU MUST BE KIDDIN', GENTS... YOU'RE IN BORK COUNTRY NOW!
WE ARE AWARE OF THAT, MR. BORK! OUR ORDERS ARE TO ARREST YOU-- OR KILL YOU IF YOU RESIST!
WELL, I'M RESISTIN'! GO AHEAD AND SHOOT! HA! HA!
HE DOES NOT FALL! HE CANNOT BE HARMED!
BEEONG!
SPANG!
VIIP!
BEEOW!
SPRANG!
TZING!
THEY DON'T KNOW HE'S INVULNERABLE--MUST DO SOMETHING BEFORE BORK GUNS THEM DOWN LIKE RABBITS!
POW! POW!
HA! HA! HA!
SCREEEEEE
THEY'VE GONE-- AND BORK VANISHED, TOO! I HOPE THOSE VENGEANCE COMMANDOS REALIZE WHAT THEY'RE UP AGAINST AND GO ON HOME!
WONDER HOW FLASH IS DOING--?
12

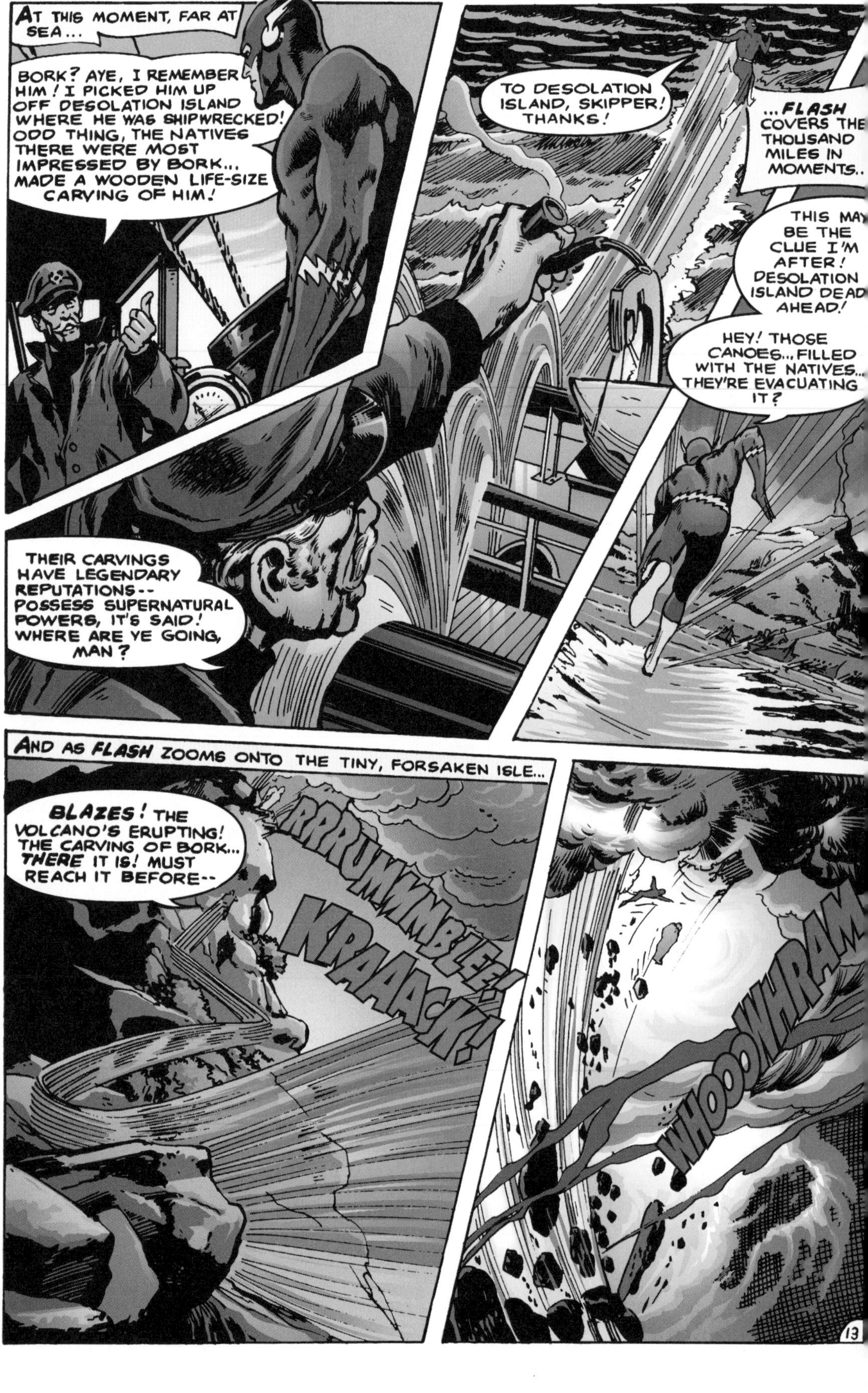
AT THIS MOMENT, FAR AT SEA...
BORK? AYE, I REMEMBER HIM! I PICKED HIM UP OFF DESOLATION ISLAND WHERE HE WAS SHIPWRECKED! ODD THING, THE NATIVES THERE WERE MOST IMPRESSED BY BORK... MADE A WOODEN LIFE-SIZE CARVING OF HIM!
THEIR CARVINGS HAVE LEGENDARY REPUTATIONS-- POSSESS SUPERNATURAL POWERS, IT'S SAID! WHERE ARE YE GOING, MAN?
TO DESOLATION ISLAND, SKIPPER! THANKS!
...FLASH COVERS THE THOUSAND MILES IN MOMENTS..
THIS MAY BE THE CLUE I'M AFTER! DESOLATION ISLAND DEAD AHEAD!
HEY! THOSE CANOES...FILLED WITH THE NATIVES... THEY'RE EVACUATING IT?
AND AS FLASH ZOOMS ONTO THE TINY, FORSAKEN ISLE...
BLAZES! THE VOLCANO'S ERUPTING! THE CARVING OF BORK... THERE IT IS! MUST REACH IT BEFORE--
RRRUMMMBLE!
KRAAACK!
WHOOOMHRAM
13

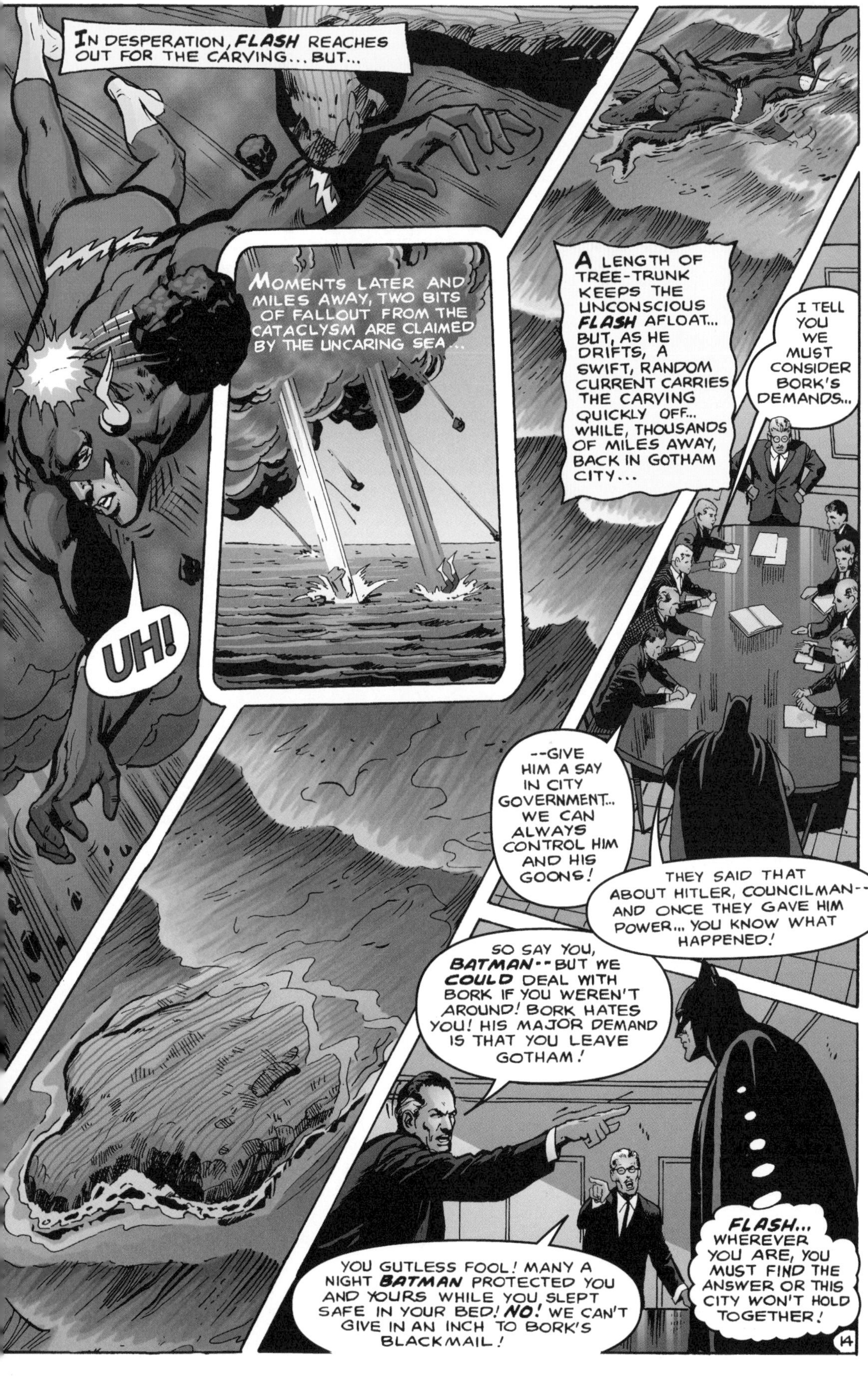
IN DESPERATION, FLASH REACHES OUT FOR THE CARVING... BUT...
UH!
MOMENTS LATER AND MILES AWAY, TWO BITS OF FALLOUT FROM THE CATACLYSM ARE CLAIMED BY THE UNCARING SEA...
A LENGTH OF TREE-TRUNK KEEPS THE UNCONSCIOUS FLASH AFLOAT... BUT, AS HE DRIFTS, A SWIFT, RANDOM CURRENT CARRIES THE CARVING QUICKLY OFF... WHILE, THOUSANDS OF MILES AWAY, BACK IN GOTHAM CITY...
I TELL YOU WE MUST CONSIDER BORK'S DEMANDS...
--GIVE HIM A SAY IN CITY GOVERNMENT... WE CAN ALWAYS CONTROL HIM AND HIS GOONS!
THEY SAID THAT ABOUT HITLER, COUNCILMAN-- AND ONCE THEY GAVE HIM POWER... YOU KNOW WHAT HAPPENED!
SO SAY YOU, BATMAN-- BUT WE COULD DEAL WITH BORK IF YOU WEREN'T AROUND! BORK HATES YOU! HIS MAJOR DEMAND IS THAT YOU LEAVE GOTHAM!
YOU GUTLESS FOOL! MANY A NIGHT BATMAN PROTECTED YOU AND YOURS WHILE YOU SLEPT SAFE IN YOUR BED! NO! WE CAN'T GIVE IN AN INCH TO BORK'S BLACKMAIL!
FLASH... WHEREVER YOU ARE, YOU MUST FIND THE ANSWER OR THIS CITY WON'T HOLD TOGETHER!
14

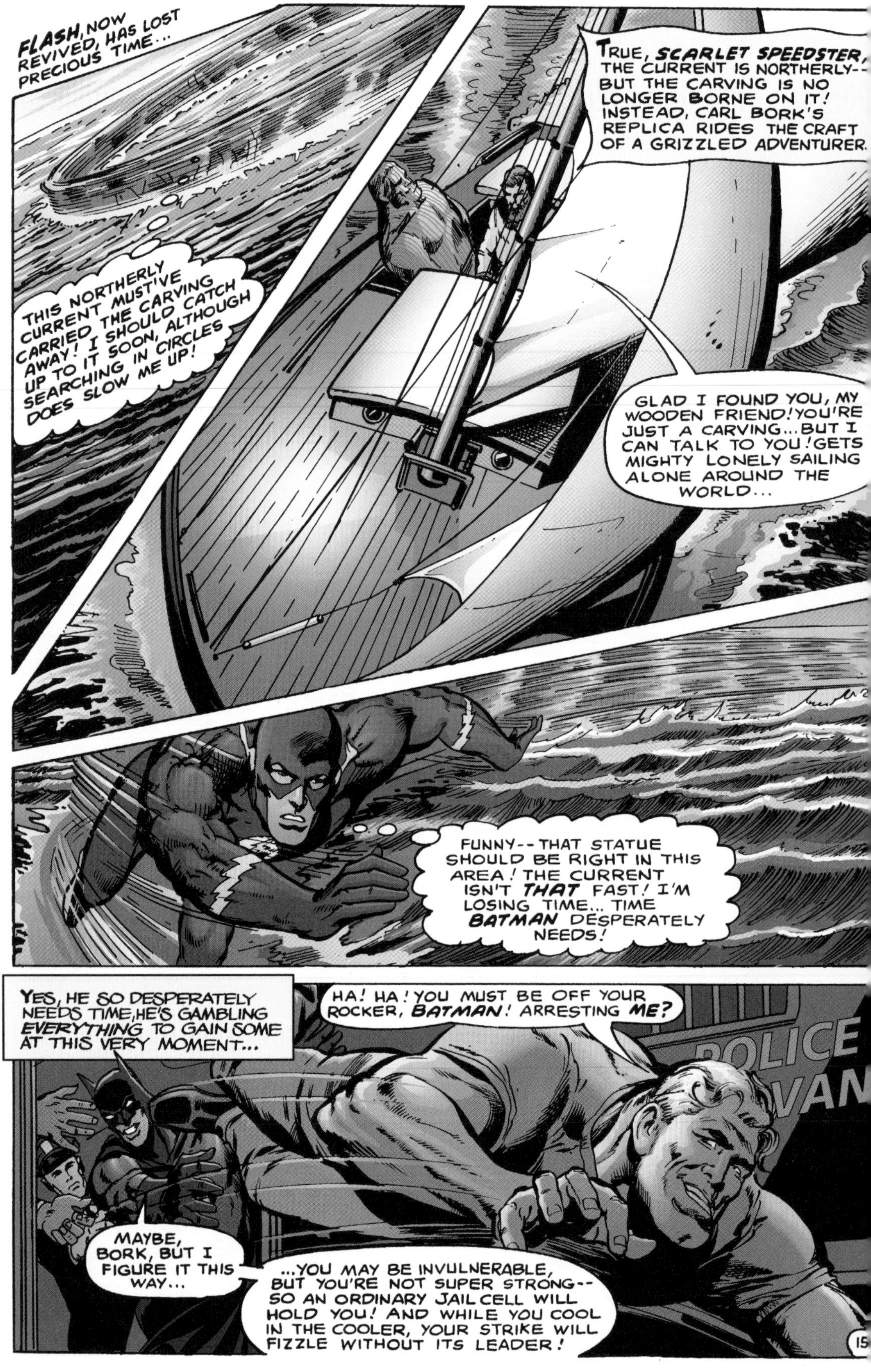
FLASH, NOW REVIVED, HAS LOST PRECIOUS TIME...
THIS NORTHERLY CURRENT MUST'VE CARRIED THE CARVING AWAY! I SHOULD CATCH UP TO IT SOON, ALTHOUGH SEARCHING IN CIRCLES DOES SLOW ME UP!
TRUE, SCARLET SPEEDSTER, THE CURRENT IS NORTHERLY-- BUT THE CARVING IS NO LONGER BORNE ON IT! INSTEAD, CARL BORK'S REPLICA RIDES THE CRAFT OF A GRIZZLED ADVENTURER.
GLAD I FOUND YOU, MY WOODEN FRIEND! YOU'RE JUST A CARVING... BUT I CAN TALK TO YOU! GETS MIGHTY LONELY SAILING ALONE AROUND THE WORLD...
FUNNY--THAT STATUE SHOULD BE RIGHT IN THIS AREA! THE CURRENT ISN'T THAT FAST! I'M LOSING TIME... TIME BATMAN DESPERATELY NEEDS!
YES, HE SO DESPERATELY NEEDS TIME, HE'S GAMBLING EVERYTHING TO GAIN SOME AT THIS VERY MOMENT...
HA! HA! YOU MUST BE OFF YOUR ROCKER, BATMAN! ARRESTING ME?
POLICE VAN
MAYBE, BORK, BUT I FIGURE IT THIS WAY...
...YOU MAY BE INVULNERABLE, BUT YOU'RE NOT SUPER STRONG-- SO AN ORDINARY JAIL CELL WILL HOLD YOU! AND WHILE YOU COOL IN THE COOLER, YOUR STRIKE WILL FIZZLE WITHOUT ITS LEADER!
15

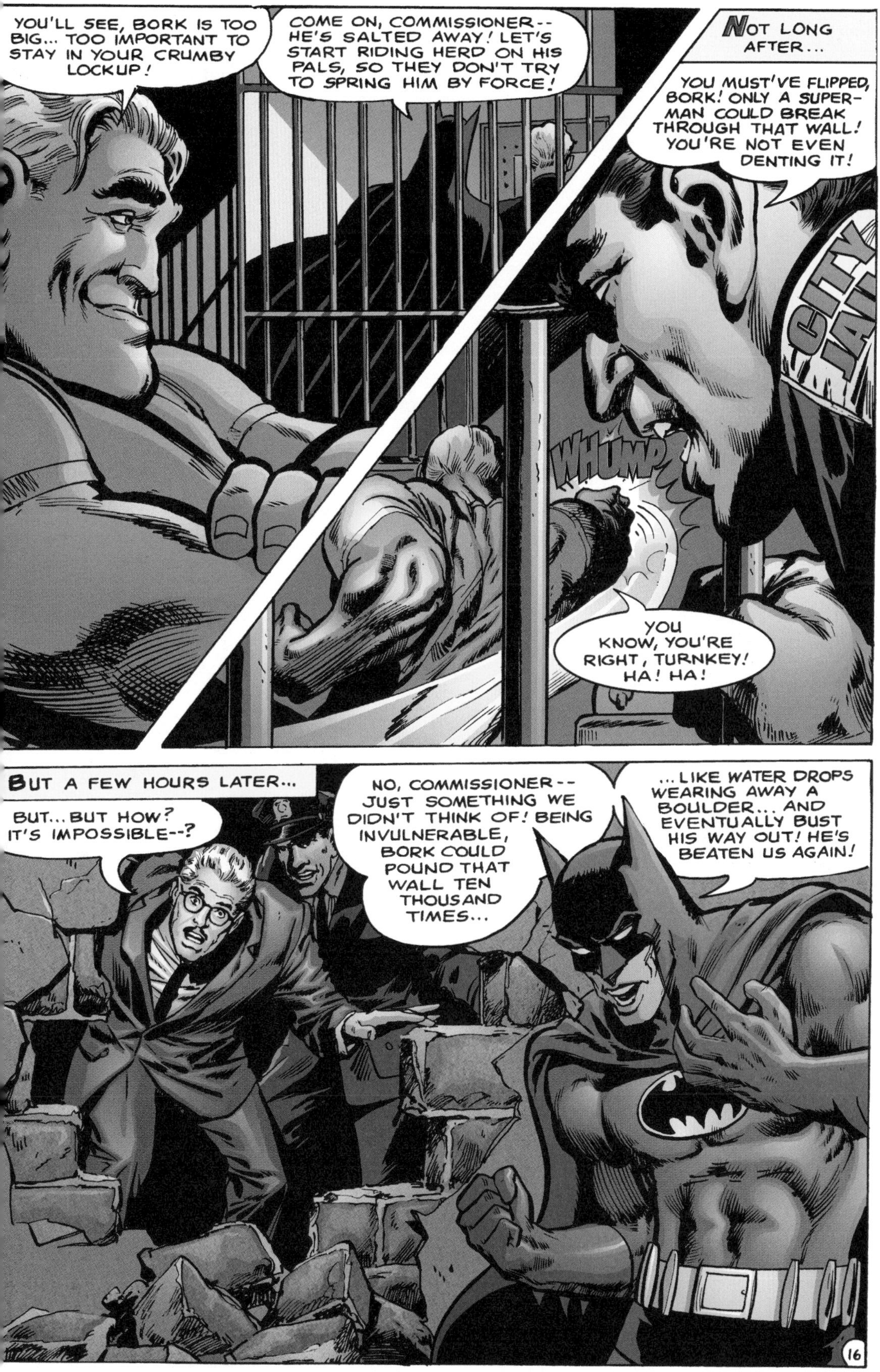

YOU'LL SEE, BORK IS TOO BIG... TOO IMPORTANT TO STAY IN YOUR CRUMBY LOCKUP!
COME ON, COMMISSIONER-- HE'S SALTED AWAY! LET'S START RIDING HERD ON HIS PALS, SO THEY DON'T TRY TO SPRING HIM BY FORCE!
NOT LONG AFTER...
YOU MUST'VE FLIPPED, BORK! ONLY A SUPER-MAN COULD BREAK THROUGH THAT WALL! YOU'RE NOT EVEN DENTING IT!
CITY JAIL
WHUMP
YOU KNOW, YOU'RE RIGHT, TURNKEY! HA! HA!
BUT A FEW HOURS LATER...
BUT... BUT HOW? IT'S IMPOSSIBLE--?
NO, COMMISSIONER-- JUST SOMETHING WE DIDN'T THINK OF! BEING INVULNERABLE, BORK COULD POUND THAT WALL TEN THOUSAND TIMES...
...LIKE WATER DROPS WEARING AWAY A BOULDER... AND EVENTUALLY BUST HIS WAY OUT! HE'S BEATEN US AGAIN!
16

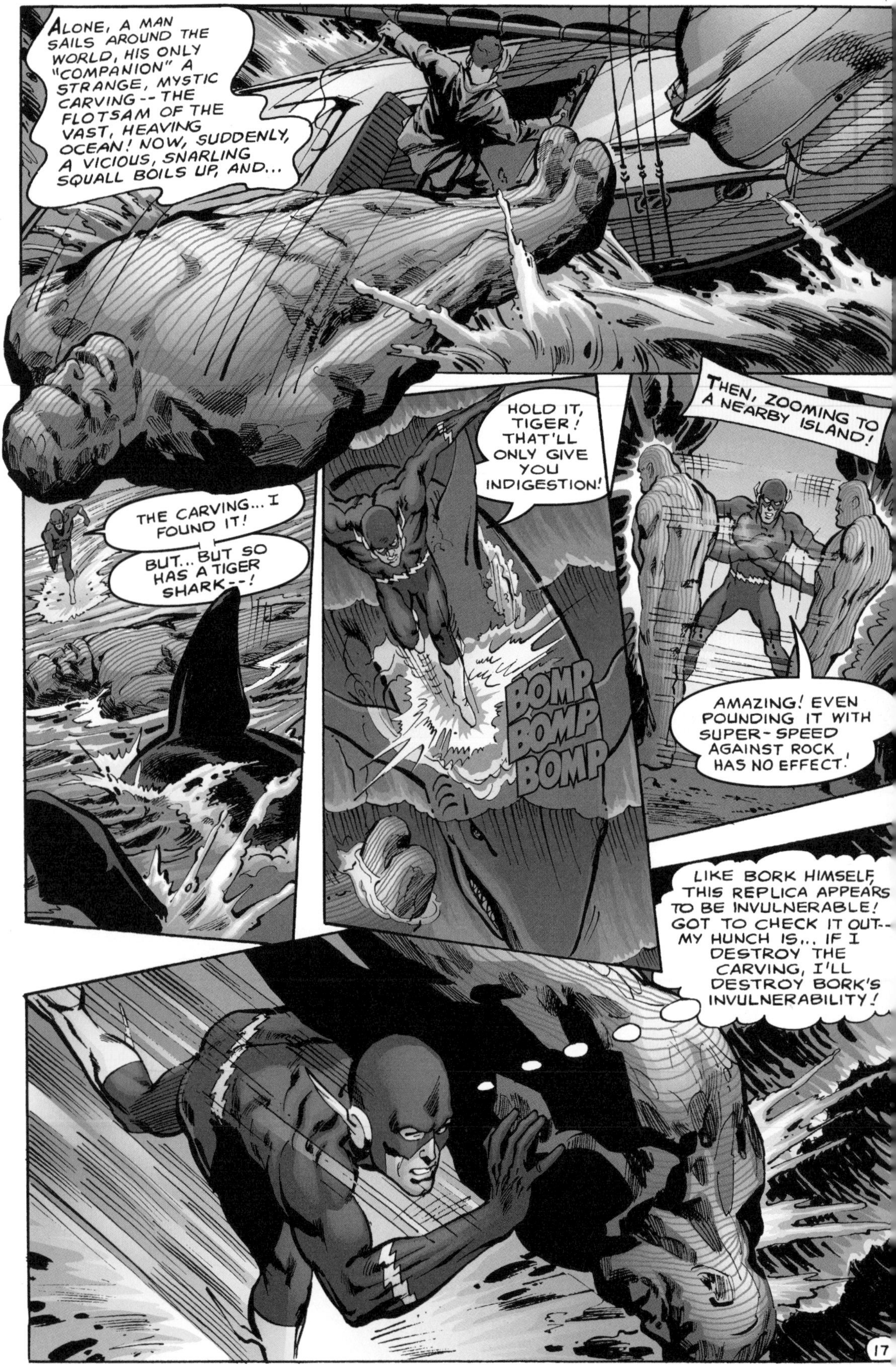
ALONE, A MAN SAILS AROUND THE WORLD, HIS ONLY "COMPANION" A STRANGE, MYSTIC CARVING -- THE FLOTSAM OF THE VAST, HEAVING OCEAN! NOW, SUDDENLY, A VICIOUS, SNARLING SQUALL BOILS UP, AND...
THE CARVING... I FOUND IT!
BUT... BUT SO HAS A TIGER SHARK--!
HOLD IT, TIGER! THAT'LL ONLY GIVE YOU INDIGESTION!
BOMP BOMP BOMP
THEN, ZOOMING TO A NEARBY ISLAND!
AMAZING! EVEN POUNDING IT WITH SUPER-SPEED AGAINST ROCK HAS NO EFFECT!
LIKE BORK HIMSELF, THIS REPLICA APPEARS TO BE INVULNERABLE! GOT TO CHECK IT OUT-- MY HUNCH IS... IF I DESTROY THE CARVING, I'LL DESTROY BORK'S INVULNERABILITY!
17

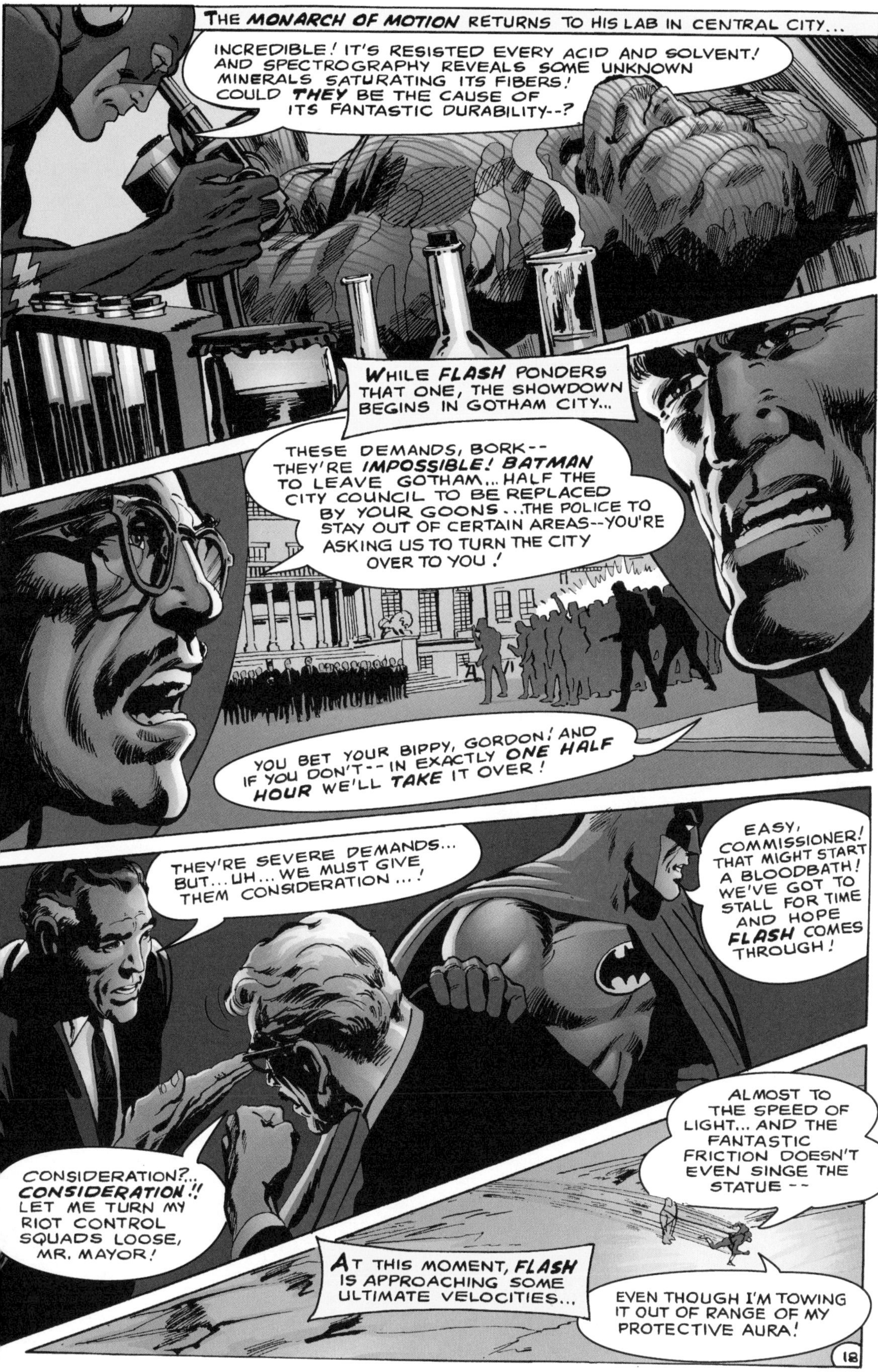
THE MONARCH OF MOTION RETURNS TO HIS LAB IN CENTRAL CITY...
INCREDIBLE! IT'S RESISTED EVERY ACID AND SOLVENT! AND SPECTROGRAPHY REVEALS SOME UNKNOWN MINERALS SATURATING ITS FIBERS! COULD THEY BE THE CAUSE OF ITS FANTASTIC DURABILITY--?
WHILE FLASH PONDERS THAT ONE, THE SHOWDOWN BEGINS IN GOTHAM CITY...
THESE DEMANDS, BORK-- THEY'RE IMPOSSIBLE! BATMAN TO LEAVE GOTHAM... HALF THE CITY COUNCIL TO BE REPLACED BY YOUR GOONS... THE POLICE TO STAY OUT OF CERTAIN AREAS--YOU'RE ASKING US TO TURN THE CITY OVER TO YOU!
YOU BET YOUR BIPPY, GORDON! AND IF YOU DON'T-- IN EXACTLY ONE HALF HOUR WE'LL TAKE IT OVER!
THEY'RE SEVERE DEMANDS... BUT... UH... WE MUST GIVE THEM CONSIDERATION...!
CONSIDERATION?... CONSIDERATION!! LET ME TURN MY RIOT CONTROL SQUADS LOOSE, MR. MAYOR!
EASY, COMMISSIONER! THAT MIGHT START A BLOODBATH! WE'VE GOT TO STALL FOR TIME AND HOPE FLASH COMES THROUGH!
AT THIS MOMENT, FLASH IS APPROACHING SOME ULTIMATE VELOCITIES...
ALMOST TO THE SPEED OF LIGHT... AND THE FANTASTIC FRICTION DOESN'T EVEN SINGE THE STATUE --
EVEN THOUGH I'M TOWING IT OUT OF RANGE OF MY PROTECTIVE AURA!
18

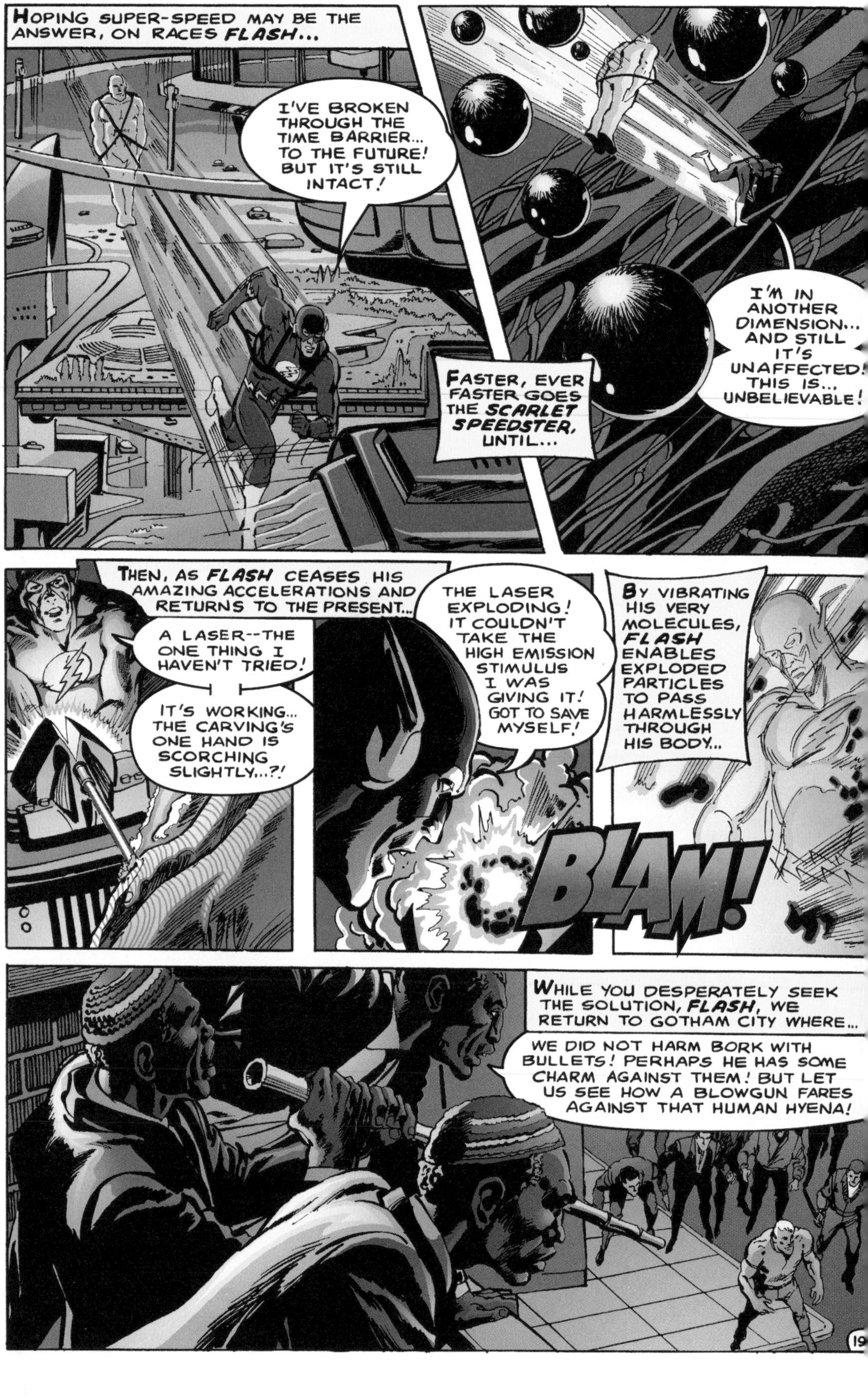
HOPING SUPER-SPEED MAY BE THE ANSWER, ON RACES FLASH...
I'VE BROKEN THROUGH THE TIME BARRIER... TO THE FUTURE! BUT IT'S STILL INTACT!
FASTER, EVER FASTER GOES THE SCARLET SPEEDSTER, UNTIL...
I'M IN ANOTHER DIMENSION... AND STILL IT'S UNAFFECTED! THIS IS... UNBELIEVABLE!
THEN, AS FLASH CEASES HIS AMAZING ACCELERATIONS AND RETURNS TO THE PRESENT...
A LASER--THE ONE THING I HAVEN'T TRIED!
IT'S WORKING... THE CARVING'S ONE HAND IS SCORCHING SLIGHTLY...?!
THE LASER EXPLODING! IT COULDN'T TAKE THE HIGH EMISSION STIMULUS I WAS GIVING IT! GOT TO SAVE MYSELF!
BLAM!
BY VIBRATING HIS VERY MOLECULES, FLASH ENABLES EXPLODED PARTICLES TO PASS HARMLESSLY THROUGH HIS BODY...
WHILE YOU DESPERATELY SEEK THE SOLUTION, FLASH, WE RETURN TO GOTHAM CITY WHERE...
WE DID NOT HARM BORK WITH BULLETS! PERHAPS HE HAS SOME CHARM AGAINST THEM! BUT LET US SEE HOW A BLOWGUN FARES AGAINST THAT HUMAN HYENA!
19

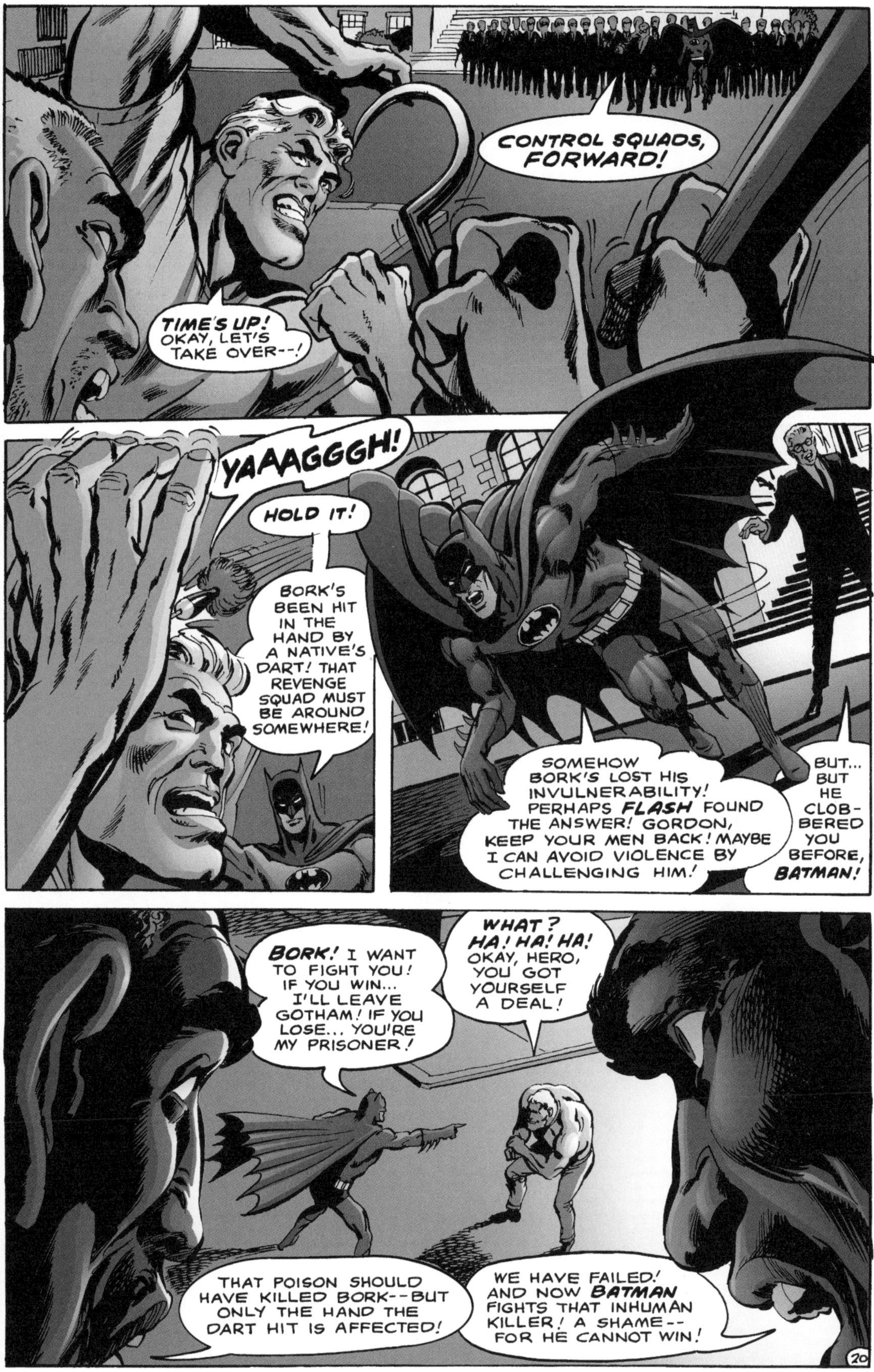
CONTROL SQUADS, FORWARD!
TIME'S UP! OKAY, LET'S TAKE OVER--!
YAAAGGGH!
HOLD IT!
BORK'S BEEN HIT IN THE HAND BY A NATIVE'S DART! THAT REVENGE SQUAD MUST BE AROUND SOMEWHERE!
SOMEHOW BORK'S LOST HIS INVULNERABILITY! PERHAPS FLASH FOUND THE ANSWER! GORDON, KEEP YOUR MEN BACK! MAYBE I CAN AVOID VIOLENCE BY CHALLENGING HIM!
BUT... BUT HE CLOBBERED YOU BEFORE, BATMAN!
BORK! I WANT TO FIGHT YOU! IF YOU WIN... I'LL LEAVE GOTHAM! IF YOU LOSE... YOU'RE MY PRISONER!
WHAT? HA! HA! HA! OKAY, HERO, YOU GOT YOURSELF A DEAL!
THAT POISON SHOULD HAVE KILLED BORK--BUT ONLY THE HAND THE DART HIT IS AFFECTED!
WE HAVE FAILED! AND NOW BATMAN FIGHTS THAT INHUMAN KILLER! A SHAME--FOR HE CANNOT WIN!
20

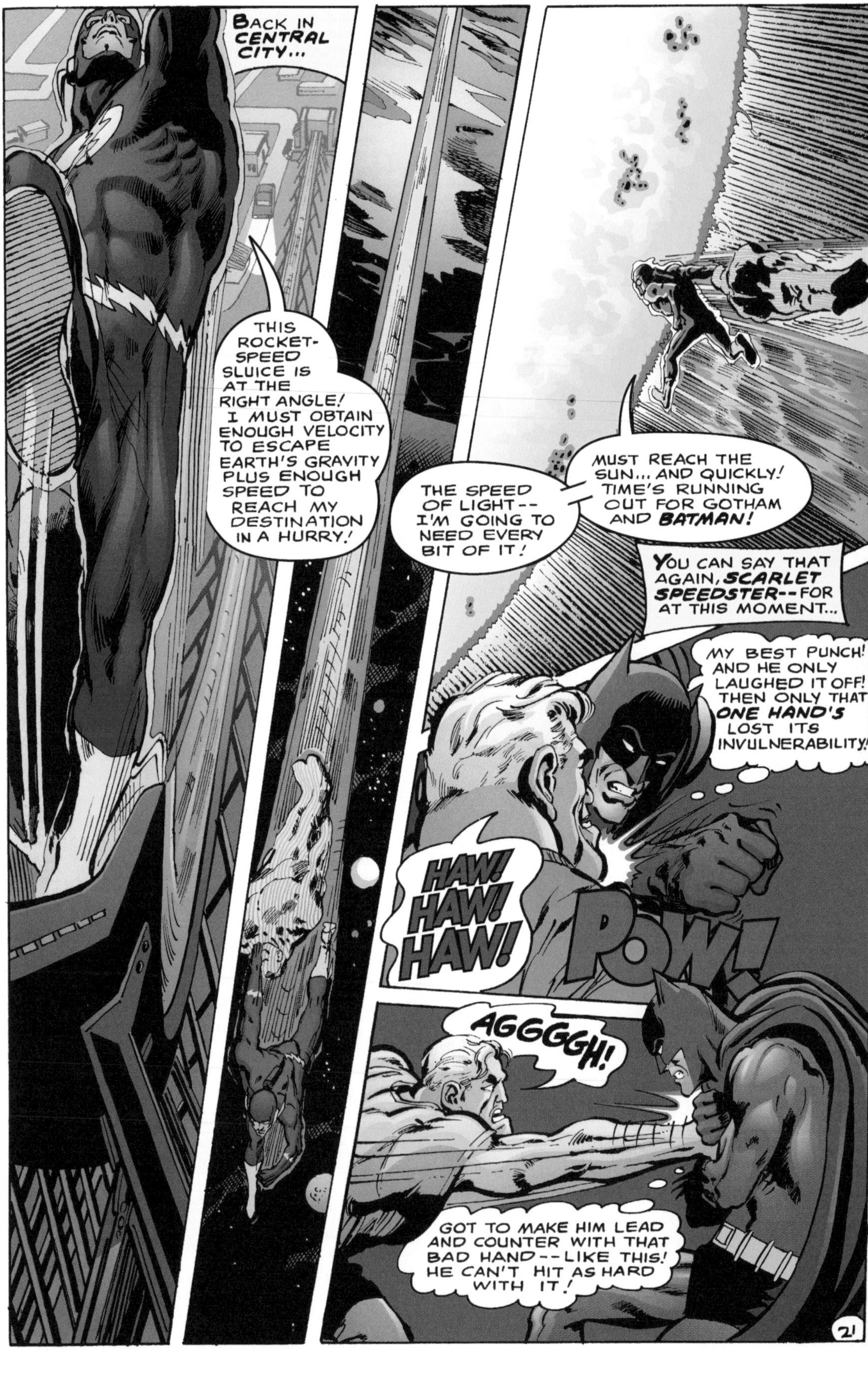
BACK IN CENTRAL CITY...
THIS ROCKET-SPEED SLUICE IS AT THE RIGHT ANGLE! I MUST OBTAIN ENOUGH VELOCITY TO ESCAPE EARTH'S GRAVITY PLUS ENOUGH SPEED TO REACH MY DESTINATION IN A HURRY!
THE SPEED OF LIGHT-- I'M GOING TO NEED EVERY BIT OF IT!
MUST REACH THE SUN... AND QUICKLY! TIME'S RUNNING OUT FOR GOTHAM AND BATMAN!
YOU CAN SAY THAT AGAIN, SCARLET SPEEDSTER--FOR AT THIS MOMENT...
MY BEST PUNCH! AND HE ONLY LAUGHED IT OFF! THEN ONLY THAT ONE HAND'S LOST ITS INVULNERABILITY!
HAW! HAW! HAW!
POW!
AGGGGH!
GOT TO MAKE HIM LEAD AND COUNTER WITH THAT BAD HAND--LIKE THIS! HE CAN'T HIT AS HARD WITH IT!
21

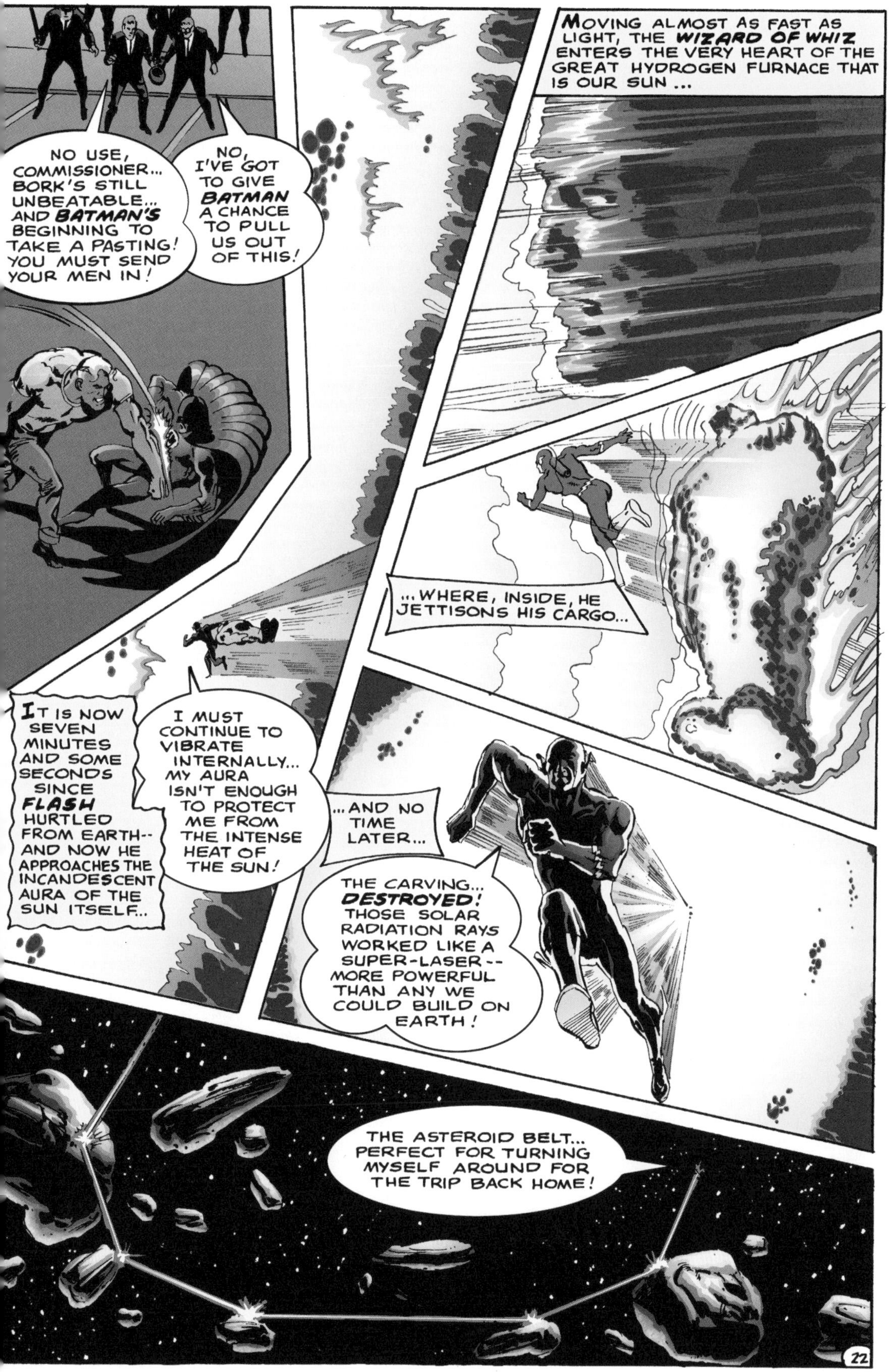
MOVING ALMOST AS FAST AS LIGHT, THE WIZARD OF WHIZ ENTERS THE VERY HEART OF THE GREAT HYDROGEN FURNACE THAT IS OUR SUN ...
NO USE, COMMISSIONER... BORK'S STILL UNBEATABLE... AND BATMAN'S BEGINNING TO TAKE A PASTING! YOU MUST SEND YOUR MEN IN!
NO, I'VE GOT TO GIVE BATMAN A CHANCE TO PULL US OUT OF THIS!
...WHERE, INSIDE, HE JETTISONS HIS CARGO...
IT IS NOW SEVEN MINUTES AND SOME SECONDS SINCE FLASH HURTLED FROM EARTH-- AND NOW HE APPROACHES THE INCANDESCENT AURA OF THE SUN ITSELF..
I MUST CONTINUE TO VIBRATE INTERNALLY... MY AURA ISN'T ENOUGH TO PROTECT ME FROM THE INTENSE HEAT OF THE SUN!
...AND NO TIME LATER...
THE CARVING... DESTROYED! THOSE SOLAR RADIATION RAYS WORKED LIKE A SUPER-LASER-- MORE POWERFUL THAN ANY WE COULD BUILD ON EARTH!
THE ASTEROID BELT... PERFECT FOR TURNING MYSELF AROUND FOR THE TRIP BACK HOME!
22

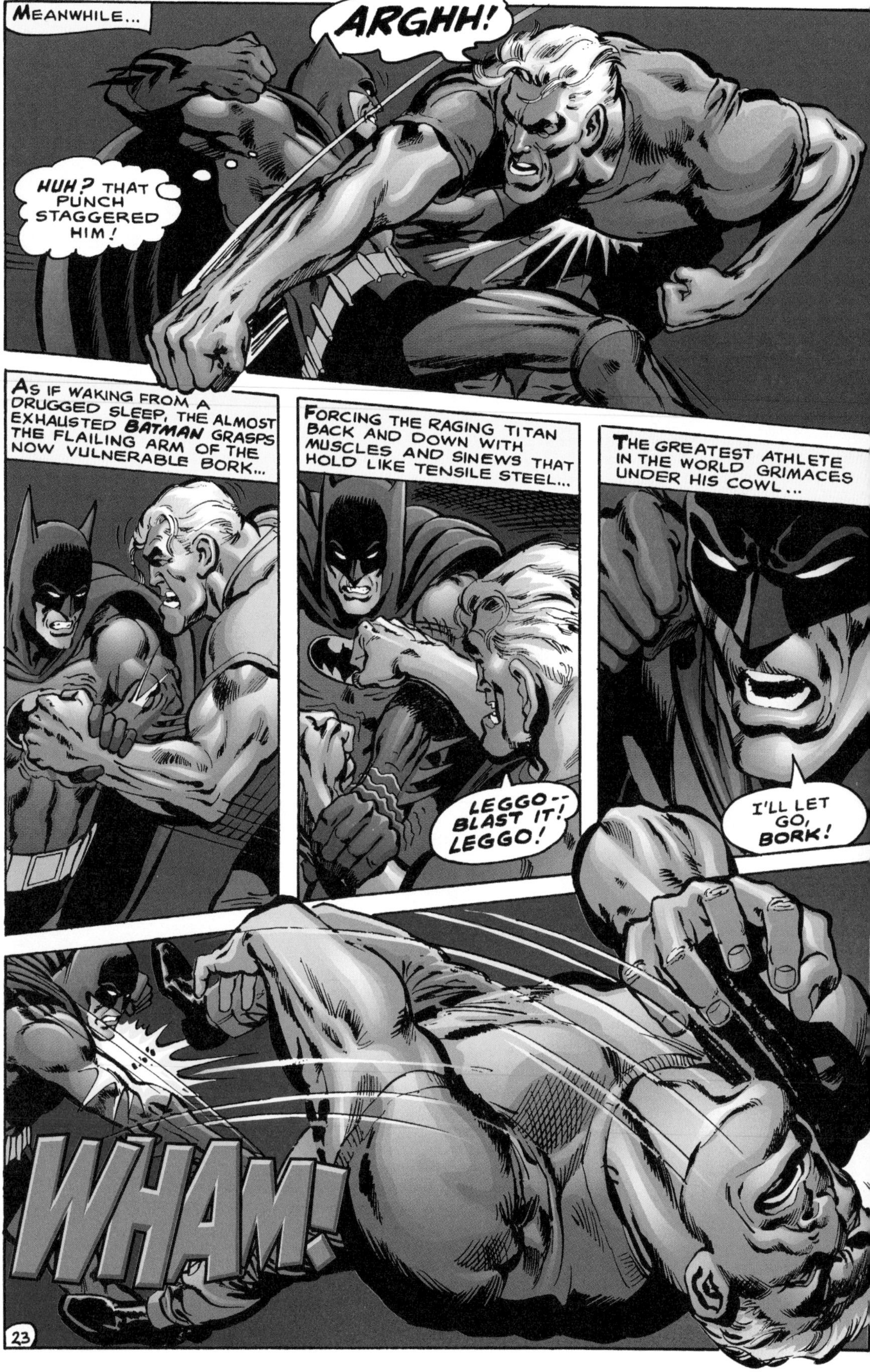

MEANWHILE...
ARGHH!
HUH? THAT PUNCH STAGGERED HIM!
AS IF WAKING FROM A DRUGGED SLEEP, THE ALMOST EXHAUSTED BATMAN GRASPS THE FLAILING ARM OF THE NOW VULNERABLE BORK...
FORCING THE RAGING TITAN BACK AND DOWN WITH MUSCLES AND SINEWS THAT HOLD LIKE TENSILE STEEL...
LEGGO-- BLAST IT! LEGGO!
THE GREATEST ATHLETE IN THE WORLD GRIMACES UNDER HIS COWL...
I'LL LET GO, BORK!
WHAM!
23

THEIR UNBEATABLE LEADER A SENSELESS HEAP, THE MOB WAVERS AND BREAKS, AS...

MOVE OUT!! CLEAR THE STREETS!

YOU DID IT, *BATMAN*... THANK THE STARS!

THANK *FLASH*, COMMISSIONER! HE MUST'VE FOUND THE ANSWER TO BORK'S INVULNERABILITY!

THE COURTS FELT THAT THE AFRICAN NATION HAS A PRIOR CLAIM TO DEAL JUSTICE TO HIM! BESIDES, IF ONE OF THEM HADN'T HIT HIM WITH THE DART AND TIPPED ME HE WAS LOSING HIS POWERS... TIME WOULD'VE RUN OUT FOR GOTHAM CITY!

WELL, TIME'S SURE RUN OUT FOR CARL BORK!

THE END. 24

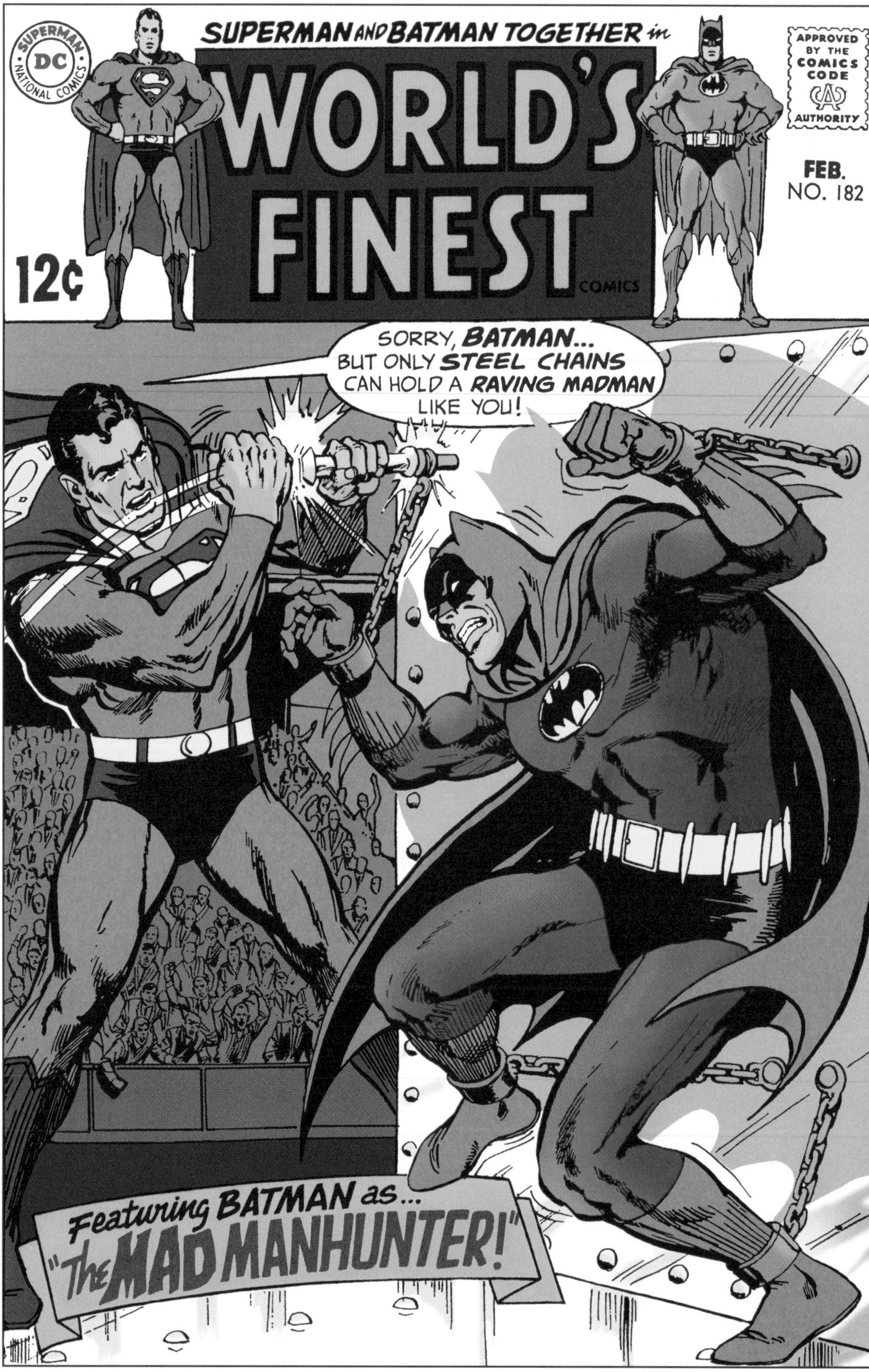
SUPERMAN AND BATMAN TOGETHER in
WORLD'S FINEST
COMICS
SUPERMAN
DC
NATIONAL COMICS
APPROVED BY THE COMICS CODE AUTHORITY
FEB.
NO. 182
12¢
SORRY, BATMAN... BUT ONLY STEEL CHAINS CAN HOLD A RAVING MADMAN LIKE YOU!
Featuring BATMAN as...
"The MAD MANHUNTER!"

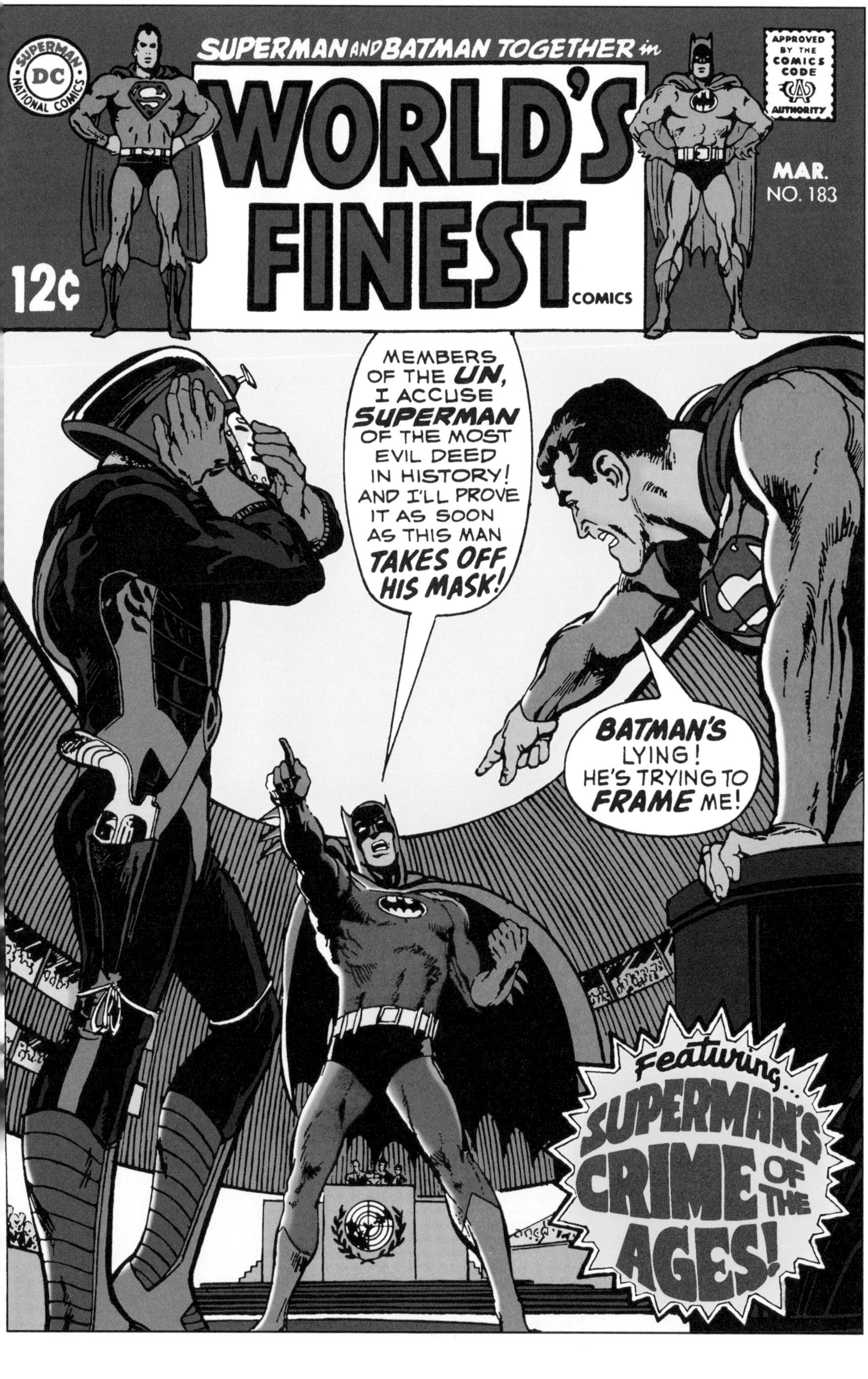
SUPERMAN AND BATMAN TOGETHER in
WORLD'S FINEST
COMICS
12¢
MAR.
NO. 183
APPROVED BY THE COMICS CODE AUTHORITY
SUPERMAN DC NATIONAL COMICS
MEMBERS OF THE UN, I ACCUSE SUPERMAN OF THE MOST EVIL DEED IN HISTORY! AND I'LL PROVE IT AS SOON AS THIS MAN TAKES OFF HIS MASK!
BATMAN'S LYING! HE'S TRYING TO FRAME ME!
Featuring... SUPERMAN'S CRIME OF THE AGES!

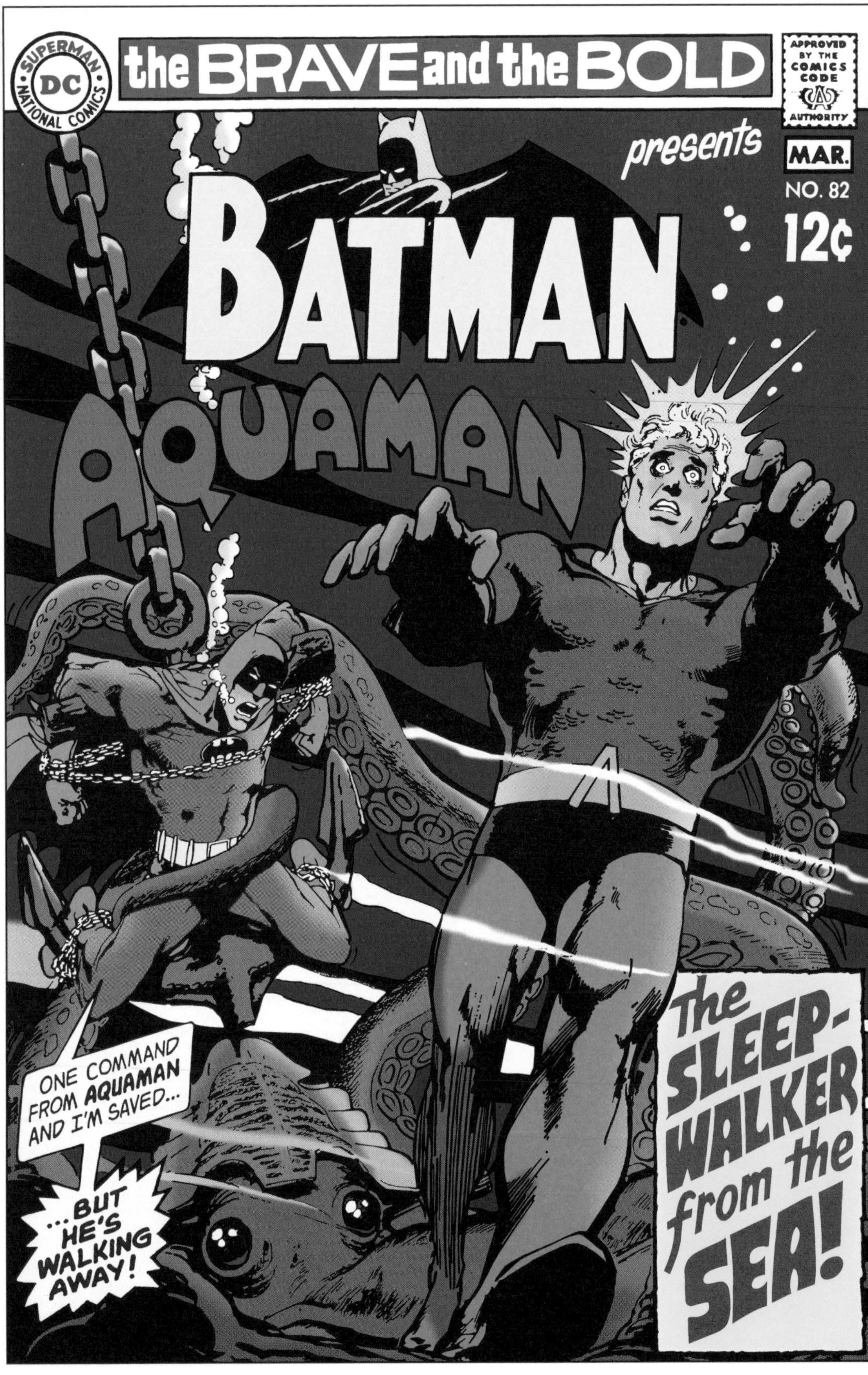

DC SUPERMAN NATIONAL COMICS
the BRAVE and the BOLD
APPROVED BY THE COMICS CODE AUTHORITY
presents
MAR.
NO. 82
12¢
BATMAN
AQUAMAN
ONE COMMAND FROM AQUAMAN AND I'M SAVED...
...BUT HE'S WALKING AWAY!
The SLEEP-WALKER from the SEA!

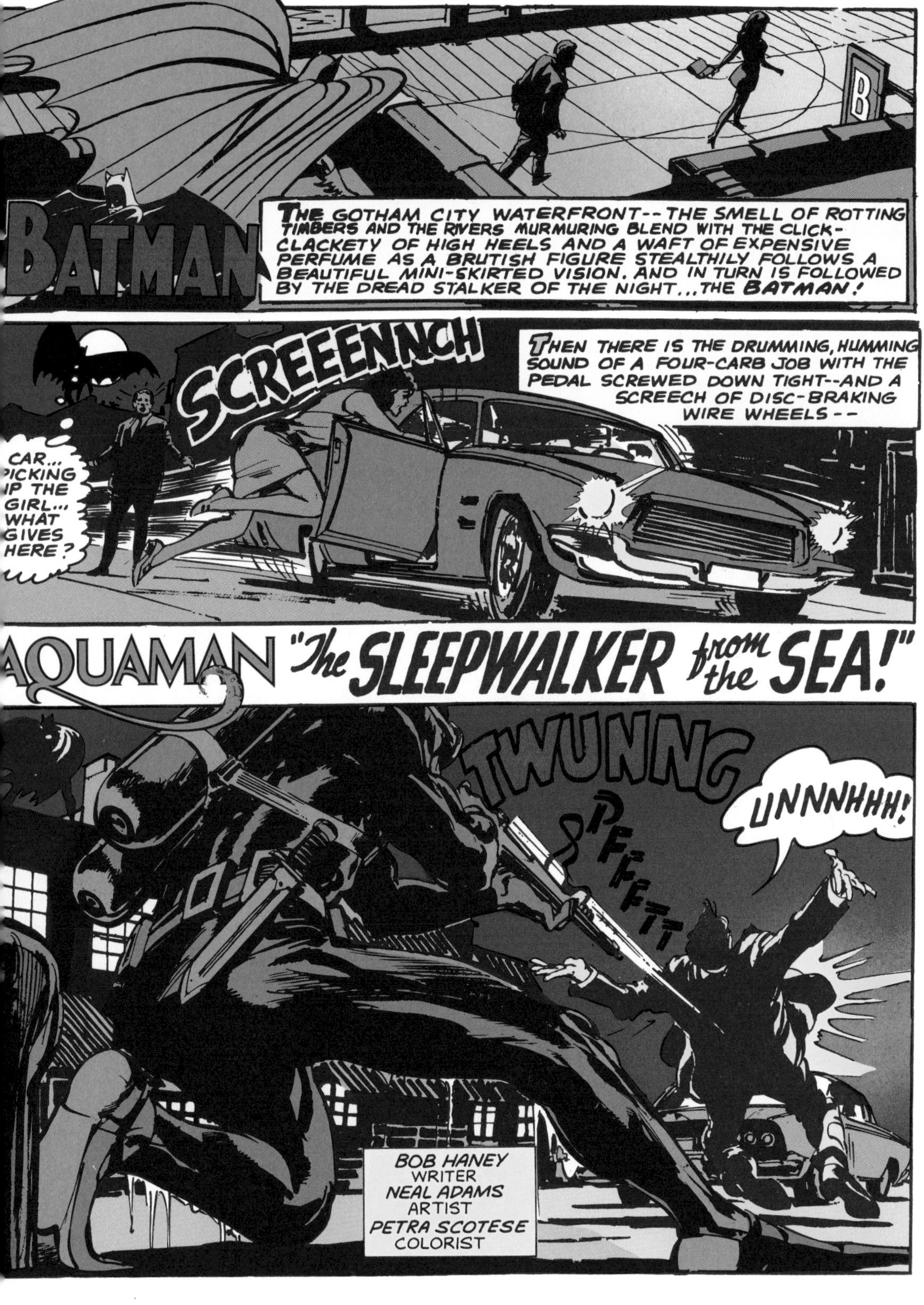
BATMAN
THE GOTHAM CITY WATERFRONT--THE SMELL OF ROTTING TIMBERS AND THE RIVERS MURMURING BLEND WITH THE CLICK-CLACKETY OF HIGH HEELS AND A WAFT OF EXPENSIVE PERFUME AS A BRUTISH FIGURE STEALTHILY FOLLOWS A BEAUTIFUL MINI-SKIRTED VISION. AND IN TURN IS FOLLOWED BY THE DREAD STALKER OF THE NIGHT...THE BATMAN!
SCREEENNCH
THEN THERE IS THE DRUMMING, HUMMING SOUND OF A FOUR-CARB JOB WITH THE PEDAL SCREWED DOWN TIGHT--AND A SCREECH OF DISC-BRAKING WIRE WHEELS--
CAR... PICKING UP THE GIRL... WHAT GIVES HERE?
AQUAMAN "The SLEEPWALKER from the SEA!"
TWUNNG
UNNNHHH!
PFFFTT
BOB HANEY WRITER
NEAL ADAMS ARTIST
PETRA SCOTESE COLORIST

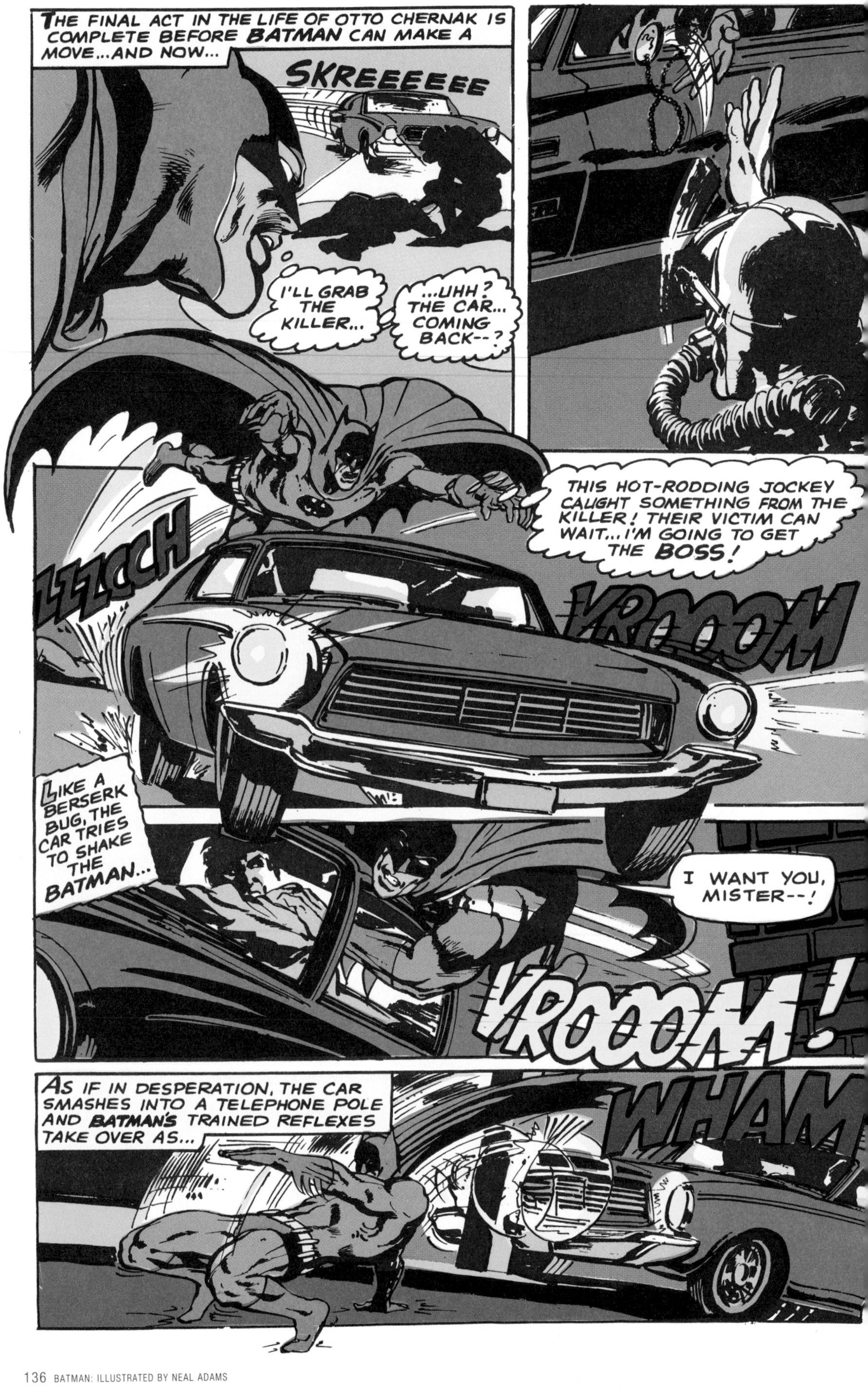
THE FINAL ACT IN THE LIFE OF OTTO CHERNAK IS COMPLETE BEFORE BATMAN CAN MAKE A MOVE...AND NOW...
SKREEEEEEE
I'LL GRAB THE KILLER...
...UHH? THE CAR... COMING BACK--?
THIS HOT-RODDING JOCKEY CAUGHT SOMETHING FROM THE KILLER! THEIR VICTIM CAN WAIT...I'M GOING TO GET THE BOSS!
ZZZCCH
VROOOOM
LIKE A BERSERK BUG, THE CAR TRIES TO SHAKE THE BATMAN...
I WANT YOU, MISTER--!
VROOOM!
AS IF IN DESPERATION, THE CAR SMASHES INTO A TELEPHONE POLE AND BATMAN'S TRAINED REFLEXES TAKE OVER AS...
WHAM

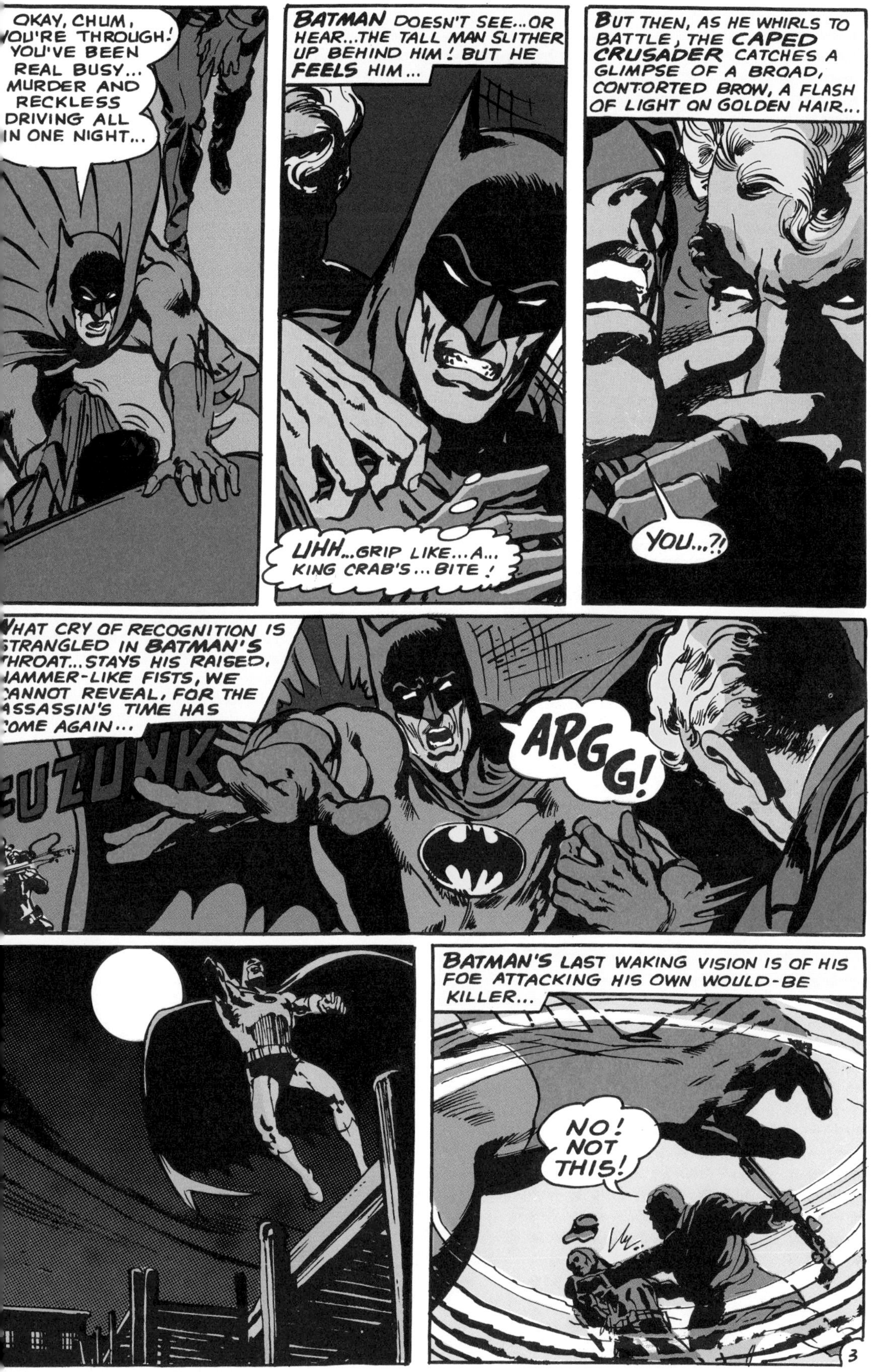
OKAY, CHUM, YOU'RE THROUGH! YOU'VE BEEN REAL BUSY... MURDER AND RECKLESS DRIVING ALL IN ONE NIGHT...
BATMAN DOESN'T SEE...OR HEAR...THE TALL MAN SLITHER UP BEHIND HIM! BUT HE FEELS HIM...
UHH...GRIP LIKE...A... KING CRAB'S...BITE!
BUT THEN, AS HE WHIRLS TO BATTLE, THE CAPED CRUSADER CATCHES A GLIMPSE OF A BROAD, CONTORTED BROW, A FLASH OF LIGHT ON GOLDEN HAIR...
YOU...?!
WHAT CRY OF RECOGNITION IS STRANGLED IN BATMAN'S THROAT...STAYS HIS RAISED, HAMMER-LIKE FISTS, WE CANNOT REVEAL, FOR THE ASSASSIN'S TIME HAS COME AGAIN...
ARGG!
BATMAN'S LAST WAKING VISION IS OF HIS FOE ATTACKING HIS OWN WOULD-BE KILLER...
NO! NOT THIS!
3

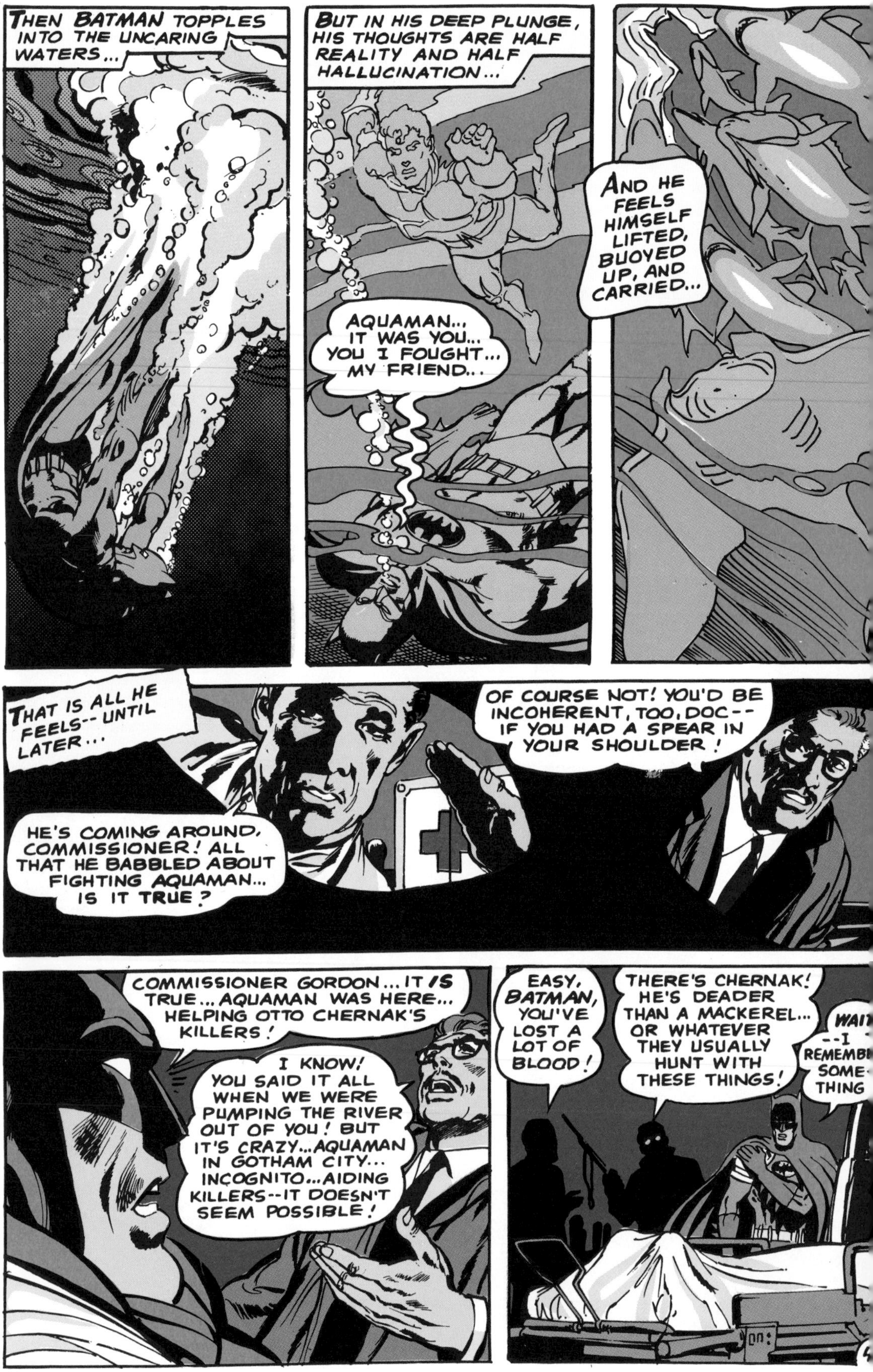
THEN BATMAN TOPPLES INTO THE UNCARING WATERS...
BUT IN HIS DEEP PLUNGE, HIS THOUGHTS ARE HALF REALITY AND HALF HALLUCINATION...
AQUAMAN... IT WAS YOU... YOU I FOUGHT... MY FRIEND...
AND HE FEELS HIMSELF LIFTED, BUOYED UP, AND CARRIED...
THAT IS ALL HE FEELS-- UNTIL LATER...
HE'S COMING AROUND, COMMISSIONER! ALL THAT HE BABBLED ABOUT FIGHTING AQUAMAN... IS IT TRUE?
OF COURSE NOT! YOU'D BE INCOHERENT, TOO, DOC-- IF YOU HAD A SPEAR IN YOUR SHOULDER!
COMMISSIONER GORDON... IT IS TRUE... AQUAMAN WAS HERE... HELPING OTTO CHERNAK'S KILLERS!
I KNOW! YOU SAID IT ALL WHEN WE WERE PUMPING THE RIVER OUT OF YOU! BUT IT'S CRAZY... AQUAMAN IN GOTHAM CITY... INCOGNITO... AIDING KILLERS--IT DOESN'T SEEM POSSIBLE!
EASY, BATMAN, YOU'VE LOST A LOT OF BLOOD!
THERE'S CHERNAK! HE'S DEADER THAN A MACKEREL... OR WHATEVER THEY USUALLY HUNT WITH THESE THINGS!
WAI
--I
REMEMB
SOME-
THING

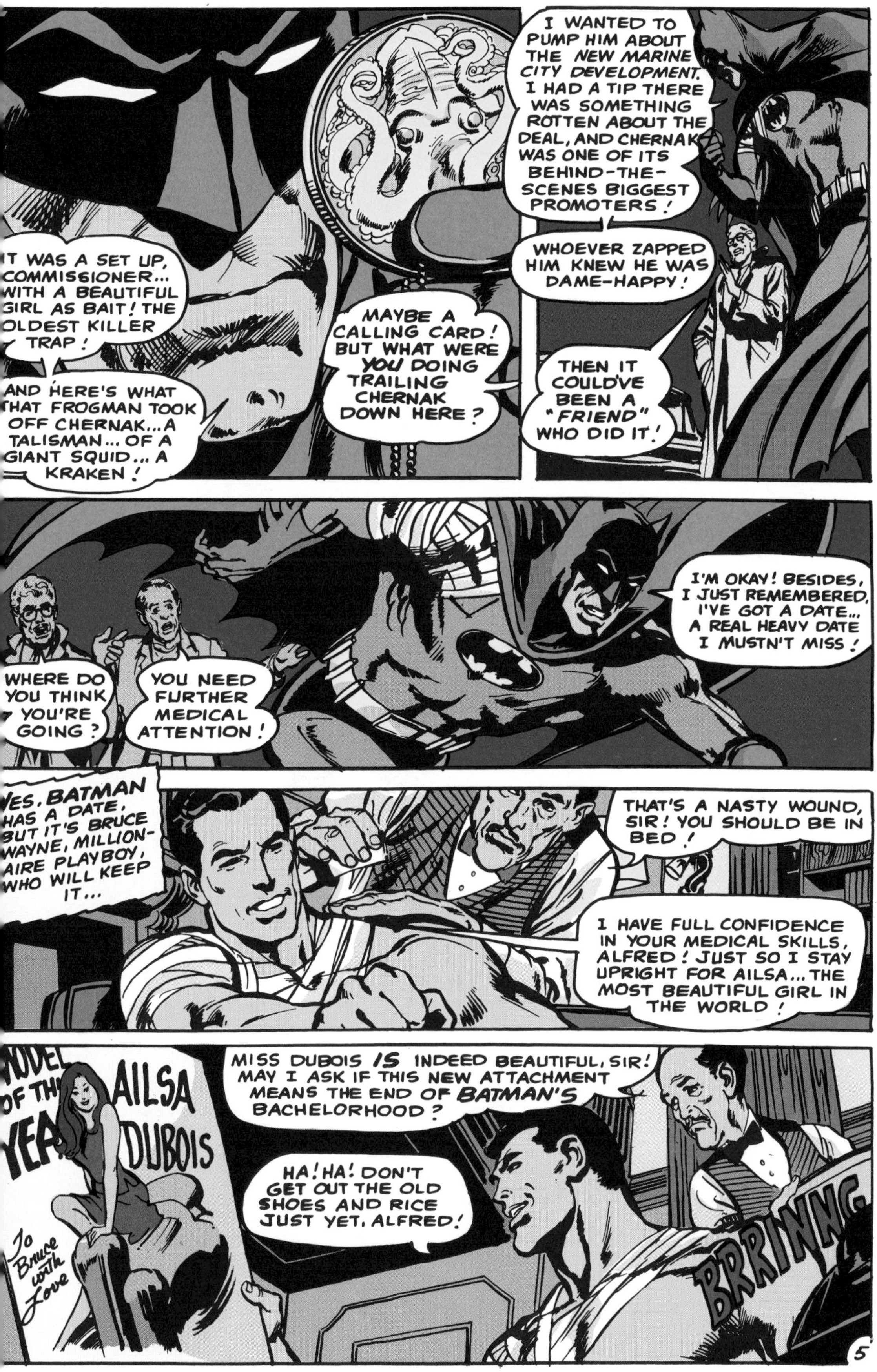
IT WAS A SET UP, COMMISSIONER... WITH A BEAUTIFUL GIRL AS BAIT! THE OLDEST KILLER TRAP!
AND HERE'S WHAT THAT FROGMAN TOOK OFF CHERNAK... A TALISMAN... OF A GIANT SQUID... A KRAKEN!
MAYBE A CALLING CARD! BUT WHAT WERE YOU DOING TRAILING CHERNAK DOWN HERE?
I WANTED TO PUMP HIM ABOUT THE NEW MARINE CITY DEVELOPMENT. I HAD A TIP THERE WAS SOMETHING ROTTEN ABOUT THE DEAL, AND CHERNAK WAS ONE OF ITS BEHIND-THE-SCENES BIGGEST PROMOTERS!
WHOEVER ZAPPED HIM KNEW HE WAS DAME-HAPPY!
THEN IT COULD'VE BEEN A "FRIEND" WHO DID IT!
WHERE DO YOU THINK YOU'RE GOING?
YOU NEED FURTHER MEDICAL ATTENTION!
I'M OKAY! BESIDES, I JUST REMEMBERED, I'VE GOT A DATE... A REAL HEAVY DATE I MUSTN'T MISS!
YES, BATMAN HAS A DATE, BUT IT'S BRUCE WAYNE, MILLIONAIRE PLAYBOY, WHO WILL KEEP IT...
THAT'S A NASTY WOUND, SIR! YOU SHOULD BE IN BED!
I HAVE FULL CONFIDENCE IN YOUR MEDICAL SKILLS, ALFRED! JUST SO I STAY UPRIGHT FOR AILSA... THE MOST BEAUTIFUL GIRL IN THE WORLD!
AILSA DUBOIS
To Bruce with Love
MISS DUBOIS IS INDEED BEAUTIFUL, SIR! MAY I ASK IF THIS NEW ATTACHMENT MEANS THE END OF BATMAN'S BACHELORHOOD?
HA! HA! DON'T GET OUT THE OLD SHOES AND RICE JUST YET, ALFRED!
BRRINNG
5

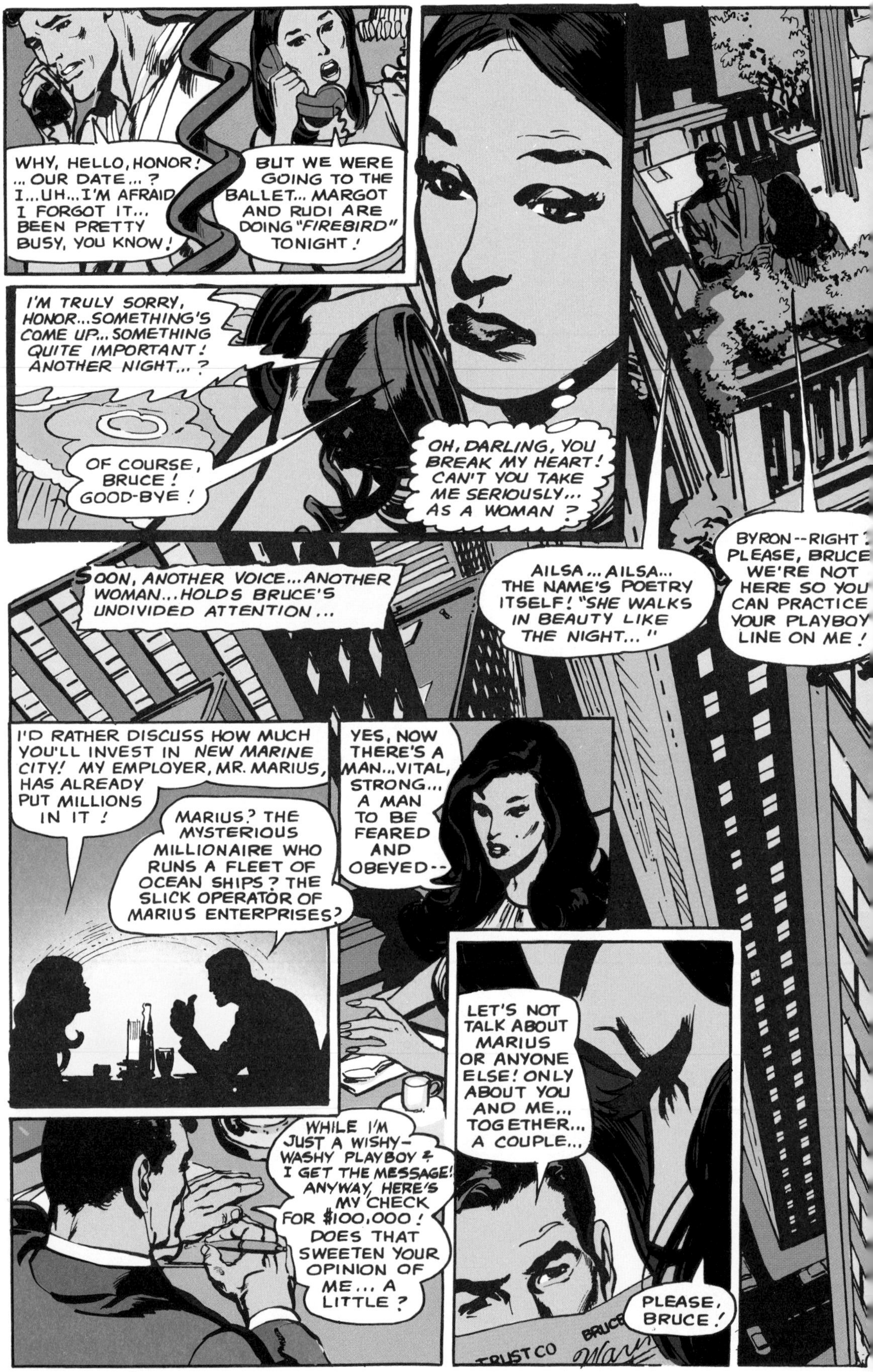
WHY, HELLO, HONOR! ... OUR DATE...? I...UH...I'M AFRAID I FORGOT IT... BEEN PRETTY BUSY, YOU KNOW!
BUT WE WERE GOING TO THE BALLET... MARGOT AND RUDI ARE DOING "FIREBIRD" TONIGHT!
I'M TRULY SORRY, HONOR...SOMETHING'S COME UP...SOMETHING QUITE IMPORTANT! ANOTHER NIGHT...?
OF COURSE, BRUCE! GOOD-BYE!
OH, DARLING, YOU BREAK MY HEART! CAN'T YOU TAKE ME SERIOUSLY... AS A WOMAN?
SOON, ANOTHER VOICE...ANOTHER WOMAN...HOLDS BRUCE'S UNDIVIDED ATTENTION...
AILSA... AILSA... THE NAME'S POETRY ITSELF! "SHE WALKS IN BEAUTY LIKE THE NIGHT..."
BYRON--RIGHT? PLEASE, BRUCE WE'RE NOT HERE SO YOU CAN PRACTICE YOUR PLAYBOY LINE ON ME!
I'D RATHER DISCUSS HOW MUCH YOU'LL INVEST IN NEW MARINE CITY! MY EMPLOYER, MR. MARIUS, HAS ALREADY PUT MILLIONS IN IT!
MARIUS? THE MYSTERIOUS MILLIONAIRE WHO RUNS A FLEET OF OCEAN SHIPS? THE SLICK OPERATOR OF MARIUS ENTERPRISES?
YES, NOW THERE'S A MAN...VITAL, STRONG... A MAN TO BE FEARED AND OBEYED--
WHILE I'M JUST A WISHY-WASHY PLAYBOY & I GET THE MESSAGE! ANYWAY, HERE'S MY CHECK FOR $100,000! DOES THAT SWEETEN YOUR OPINION OF ME... A LITTLE?
LET'S NOT TALK ABOUT MARIUS OR ANYONE ELSE! ONLY ABOUT YOU AND ME... TOGETHER... A COUPLE...
PLEASE, BRUCE!
TRUST CO
BRUCE

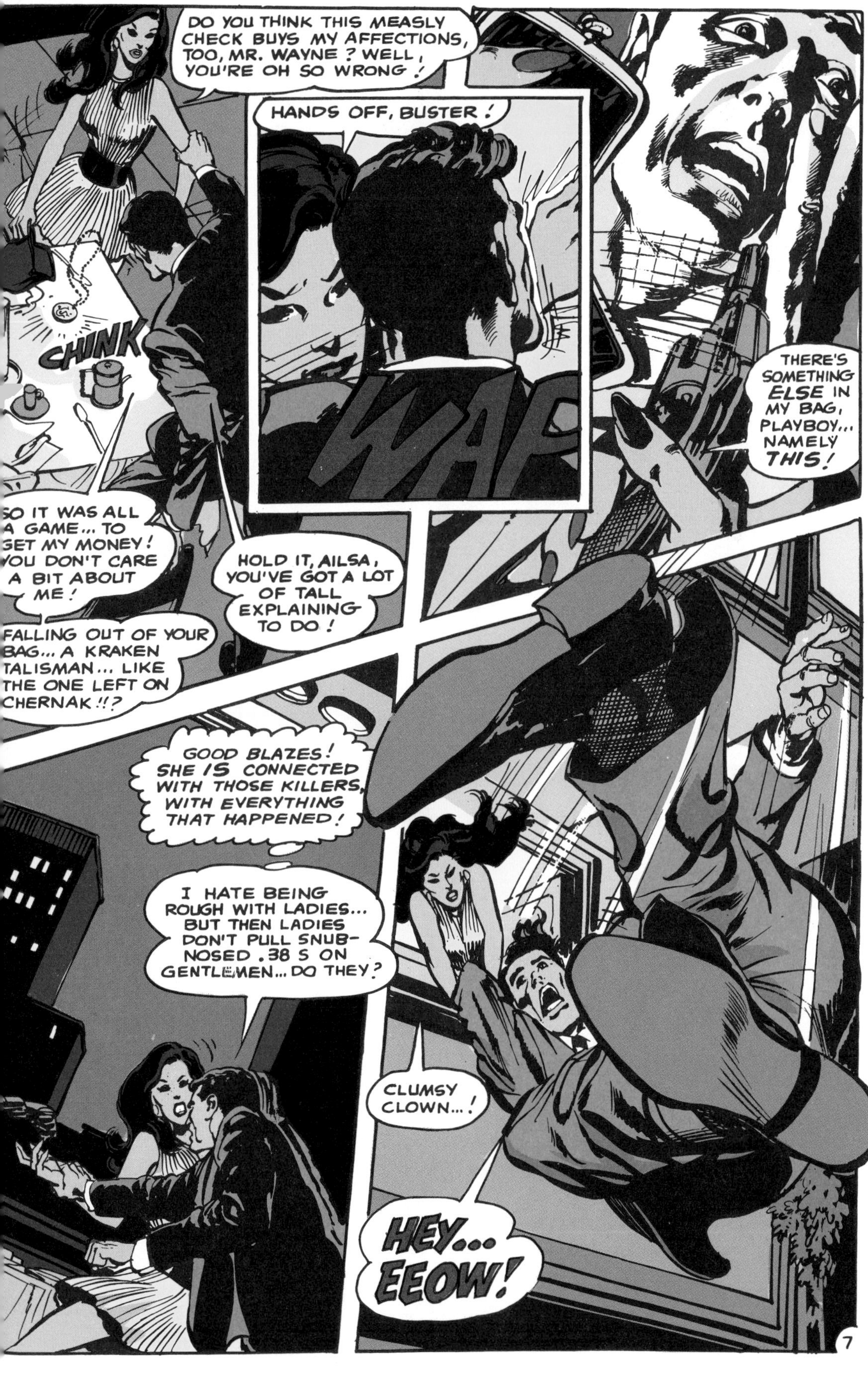
DO YOU THINK THIS MEASLY CHECK BUYS MY AFFECTIONS, TOO, MR. WAYNE ? WELL, YOU'RE OH SO WRONG !
CHINK
HANDS OFF, BUSTER !
WAP
THERE'S SOMETHING ELSE IN MY BAG, PLAYBOY... NAMELY THIS!
SO IT WAS ALL A GAME... TO GET MY MONEY! YOU DON'T CARE A BIT ABOUT ME!
HOLD IT, AILSA, YOU'VE GOT A LOT OF TALL EXPLAINING TO DO !
FALLING OUT OF YOUR BAG... A KRAKEN TALISMAN... LIKE THE ONE LEFT ON CHERNAK !!?
GOOD BLAZES! SHE IS CONNECTED WITH THOSE KILLERS, WITH EVERYTHING THAT HAPPENED!
I HATE BEING ROUGH WITH LADIES... BUT THEN LADIES DON'T PULL SNUB-NOSED .38 S ON GENTLEMEN... DO THEY?
CLUMSY CLOWN...!
HEY... EEOW!
7

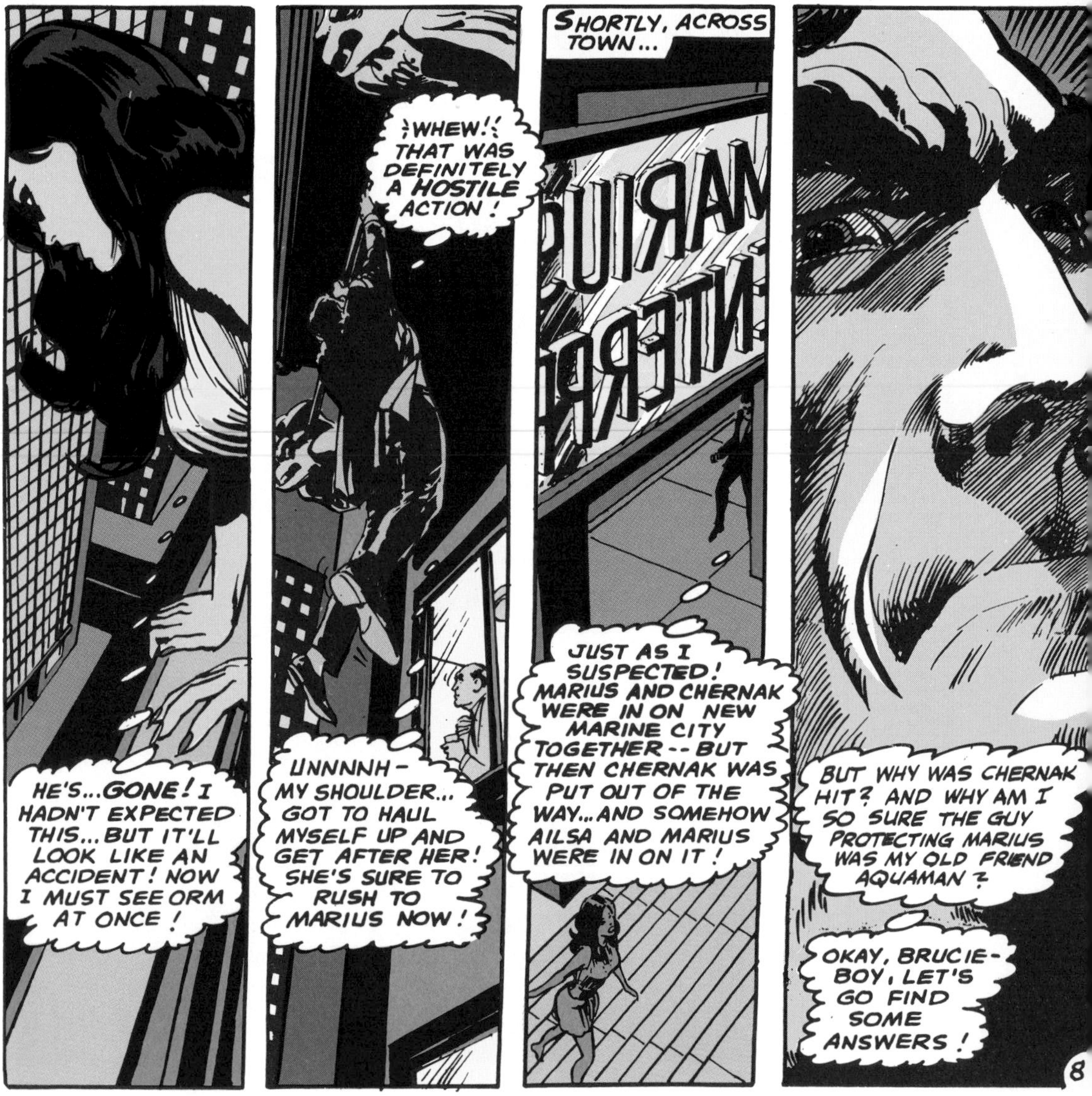
HE'S...GONE! I HADN'T EXPECTED THIS... BUT IT'LL LOOK LIKE AN ACCIDENT! NOW I MUST SEE ORM AT ONCE!
¡WHEW!¡ THAT WAS DEFINITELY A HOSTILE ACTION!
UNNNNH– MY SHOULDER... GOT TO HAUL MYSELF UP AND GET AFTER HER! SHE'S SURE TO RUSH TO MARIUS NOW!
SHORTLY, ACROSS TOWN...
JUST AS I SUSPECTED! MARIUS AND CHERNAK WERE IN ON NEW MARINE CITY TOGETHER -- BUT THEN CHERNAK WAS PUT OUT OF THE WAY... AND SOMEHOW AILSA AND MARIUS WERE IN ON IT!
BUT WHY WAS CHERNAK HIT? AND WHY AM I SO SURE THE GUY PROTECTING MARIUS WAS MY OLD FRIEND AQUAMAN?
OKAY, BRUCIE-BOY, LET'S GO FIND SOME ANSWERS!
8

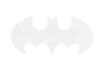

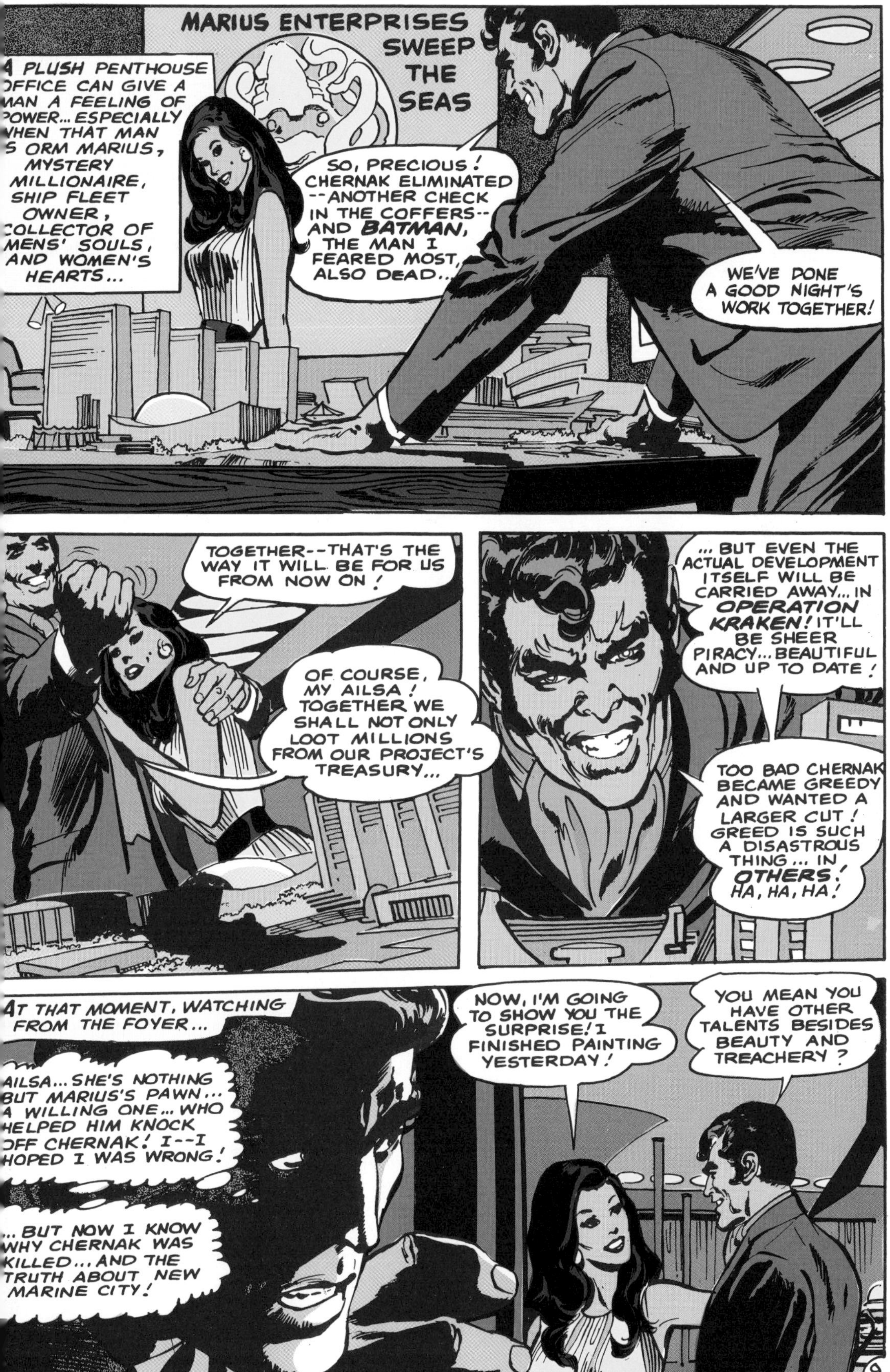
MARIUS ENTERPRISES SWEEP THE SEAS
A PLUSH PENTHOUSE OFFICE CAN GIVE A MAN A FEELING OF POWER... ESPECIALLY WHEN THAT MAN IS ORM MARIUS, MYSTERY MILLIONAIRE, SHIP FLEET OWNER, COLLECTOR OF MENS' SOULS, AND WOMEN'S HEARTS...
SO, PRECIOUS! CHERNAK ELIMINATED --ANOTHER CHECK IN THE COFFERS-- AND BATMAN, THE MAN I FEARED MOST, ALSO DEAD...
WE'VE DONE A GOOD NIGHT'S WORK TOGETHER!
TOGETHER--THAT'S THE WAY IT WILL BE FOR US FROM NOW ON!
OF COURSE, MY AILSA! TOGETHER WE SHALL NOT ONLY LOOT MILLIONS FROM OUR PROJECT'S TREASURY...
... BUT EVEN THE ACTUAL DEVELOPMENT ITSELF WILL BE CARRIED AWAY... IN OPERATION KRAKEN! IT'LL BE SHEER PIRACY... BEAUTIFUL AND UP TO DATE!
TOO BAD CHERNAK BECAME GREEDY AND WANTED A LARGER CUT! GREED IS SUCH A DISASTROUS THING... IN OTHERS! HA, HA, HA!
AT THAT MOMENT, WATCHING FROM THE FOYER...
AILSA... SHE'S NOTHING BUT MARIUS'S PAWN... A WILLING ONE... WHO HELPED HIM KNOCK OFF CHERNAK! I--I HOPED I WAS WRONG!
... BUT NOW I KNOW WHY CHERNAK WAS KILLED... AND THE TRUTH ABOUT NEW MARINE CITY!
NOW, I'M GOING TO SHOW YOU THE SURPRISE! I FINISHED PAINTING YESTERDAY!
YOU MEAN YOU HAVE OTHER TALENTS BESIDES BEAUTY AND TREACHERY?
9

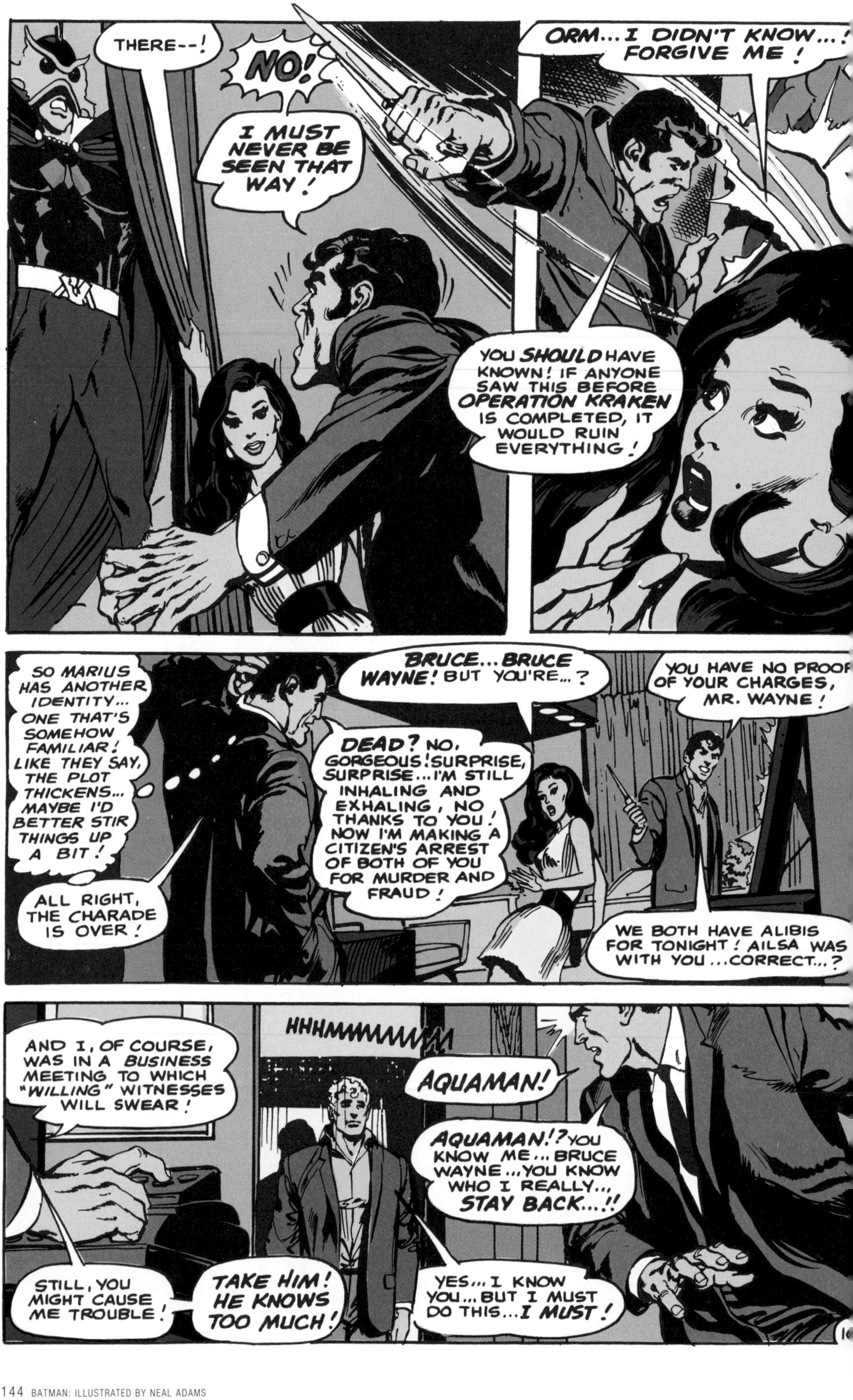

THERE--!
NO!
I MUST NEVER BE SEEN THAT WAY!
ORM... I DIDN'T KNOW...! FORGIVE ME!
YOU SHOULD HAVE KNOWN! IF ANYONE SAW THIS BEFORE OPERATION KRAKEN IS COMPLETED, IT WOULD RUIN EVERYTHING!
SO MARIUS HAS ANOTHER IDENTITY... ONE THAT'S SOMEHOW FAMILIAR! LIKE THEY SAY, THE PLOT THICKENS... MAYBE I'D BETTER STIR THINGS UP A BIT!
ALL RIGHT, THE CHARADE IS OVER!
BRUCE... BRUCE WAYNE! BUT YOU'RE...?
DEAD? NO, GORGEOUS! SURPRISE, SURPRISE... I'M STILL INHALING AND EXHALING, NO THANKS TO YOU! NOW I'M MAKING A CITIZEN'S ARREST OF BOTH OF YOU FOR MURDER AND FRAUD!
YOU HAVE NO PROOF OF YOUR CHARGES, MR. WAYNE!
WE BOTH HAVE ALIBIS FOR TONIGHT! AILSA WAS WITH YOU... CORRECT...?
AND I, OF COURSE, WAS IN A BUSINESS MEETING TO WHICH "WILLING" WITNESSES WILL SWEAR!
STILL, YOU MIGHT CAUSE ME TROUBLE!
TAKE HIM! HE KNOWS TOO MUCH!
HHHMMMMMMM
AQUAMAN!
AQUAMAN!? YOU KNOW ME... BRUCE WAYNE... YOU KNOW WHO I REALLY..., STAY BACK...!!
YES... I KNOW YOU... BUT I MUST DO THIS... I MUST!

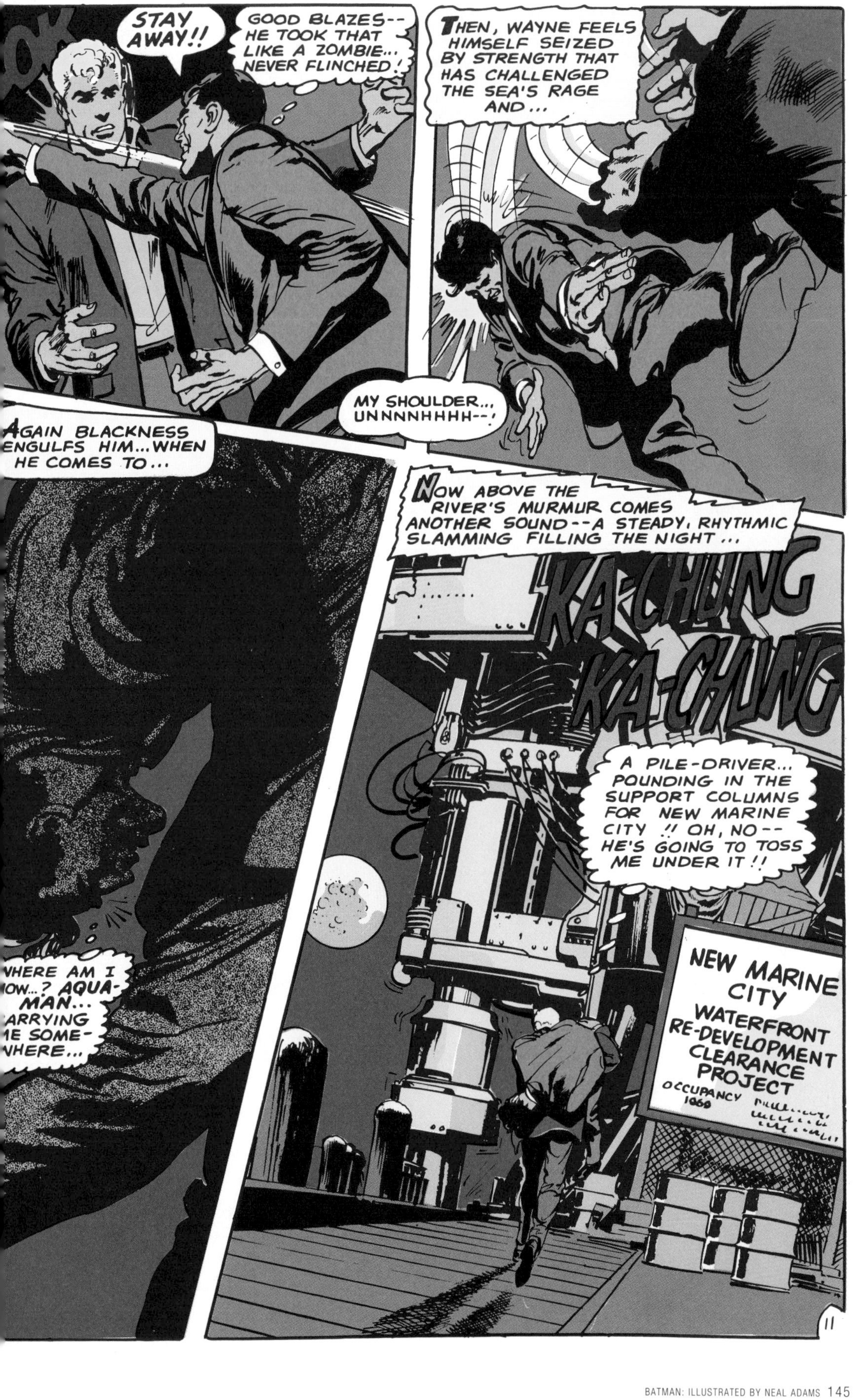
STAY AWAY!!
GOOD BLAZES-- HE TOOK THAT LIKE A ZOMBIE... NEVER FLINCHED!
THEN, WAYNE FEELS HIMSELF SEIZED BY STRENGTH THAT HAS CHALLENGED THE SEA'S RAGE AND...
MY SHOULDER..., UNNNNHHHH--!
AGAIN BLACKNESS ENGULFS HIM... WHEN HE COMES TO...
NOW ABOVE THE RIVER'S MURMUR COMES ANOTHER SOUND--A STEADY, RHYTHMIC SLAMMING FILLING THE NIGHT...
KA-CHUNG KA-CHUNG
A PILE-DRIVER... POUNDING IN THE SUPPORT COLUMNS FOR NEW MARINE CITY !! OH, NO-- HE'S GOING TO TOSS ME UNDER IT !!
NEW MARINE CITY
WATERFRONT RE-DEVELOPMENT CLEARANCE PROJECT
OCCUPANCY 1969
11

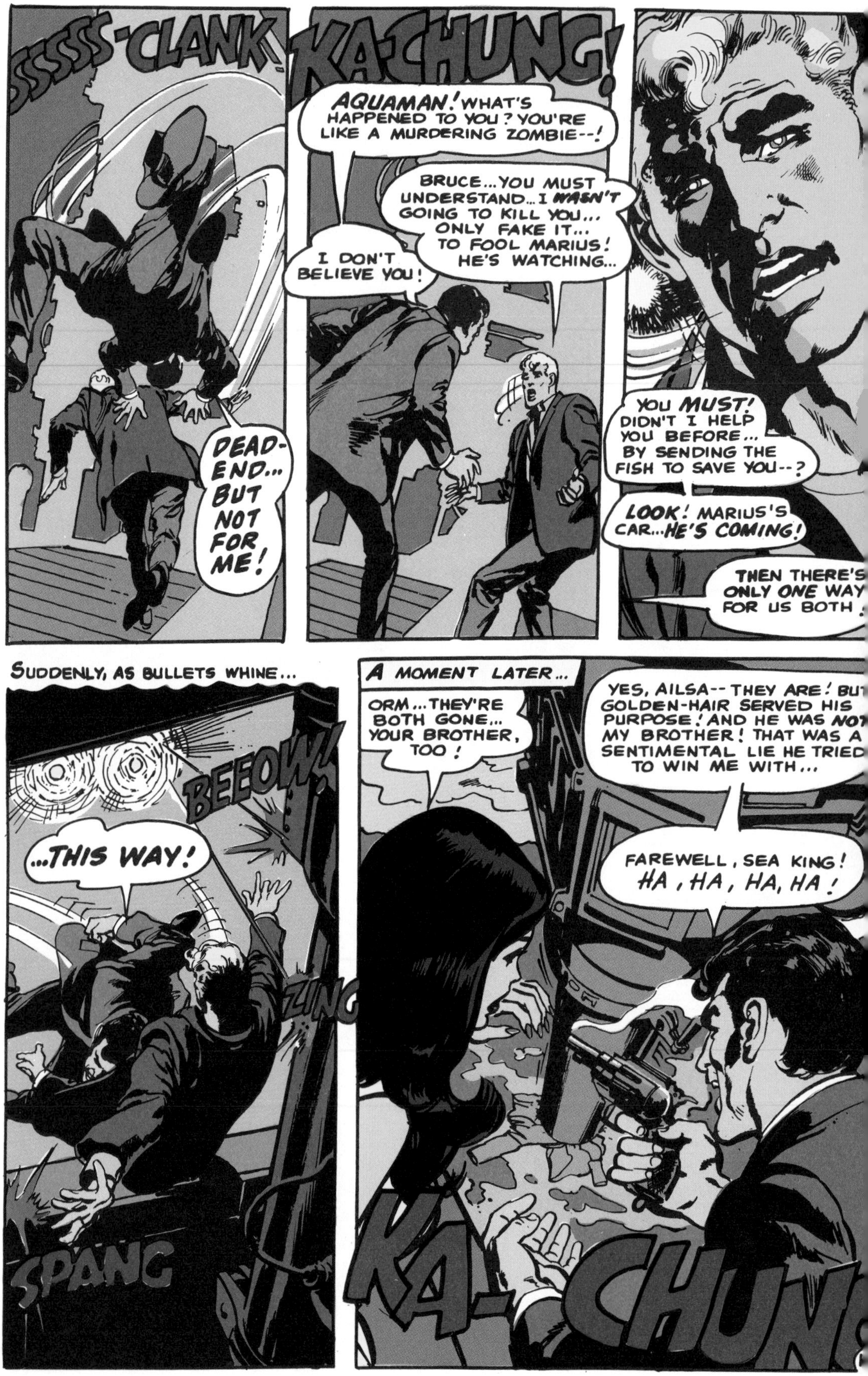
SSSSSS-CLANK
DEAD-END... BUT NOT FOR ME!
KA-CHUNG!
AQUAMAN! WHAT'S HAPPENED TO YOU? YOU'RE LIKE A MURDERING ZOMBIE--!
BRUCE... YOU MUST UNDERSTAND... I WASN'T GOING TO KILL YOU... ONLY FAKE IT... TO FOOL MARIUS! HE'S WATCHING...
I DON'T BELIEVE YOU!
YOU MUST! DIDN'T I HELP YOU BEFORE... BY SENDING THE FISH TO SAVE YOU--?
LOOK! MARIUS'S CAR... HE'S COMING!
THEN THERE'S ONLY ONE WAY FOR US BOTH
SUDDENLY, AS BULLETS WHINE...
BEEOW!
...THIS WAY!
ZING
SPANG
A MOMENT LATER...
ORM... THEY'RE BOTH GONE... YOUR BROTHER, TOO!
YES, AILSA--THEY ARE! BUT GOLDEN-HAIR SERVED HIS PURPOSE! AND HE WAS NOT MY BROTHER! THAT WAS A SENTIMENTAL LIE HE TRIED TO WIN ME WITH...
FAREWELL, SEA KING! HA, HA, HA, HA!
KA-CHUN

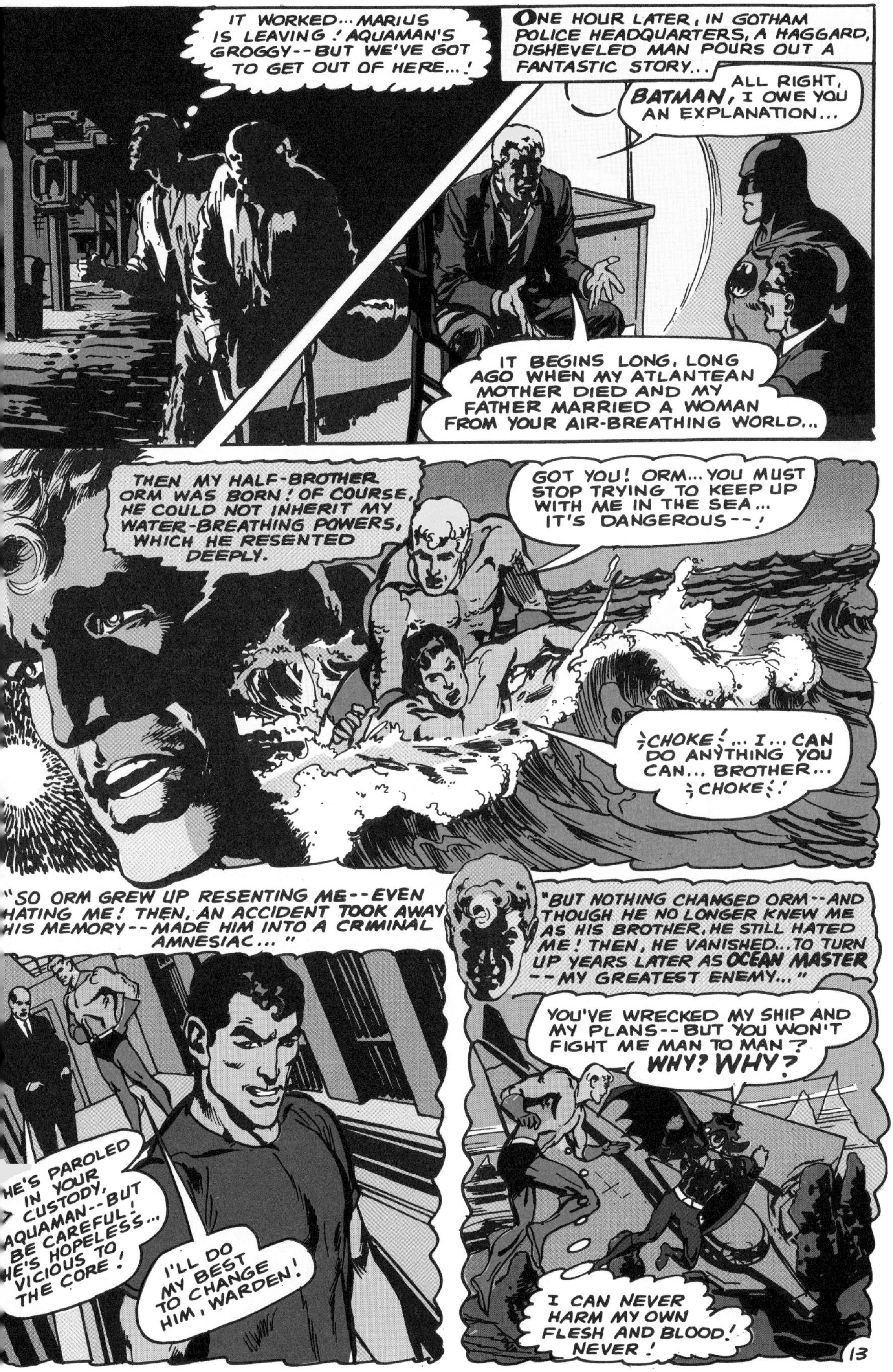
IT WORKED... MARIUS IS LEAVING! AQUAMAN'S GROGGY--BUT WE'VE GOT TO GET OUT OF HERE...!
ONE HOUR LATER, IN GOTHAM POLICE HEADQUARTERS, A HAGGARD, DISHEVELED MAN POURS OUT A FANTASTIC STORY...
ALL RIGHT, BATMAN, I OWE YOU AN EXPLANATION...
IT BEGINS LONG, LONG AGO WHEN MY ATLANTEAN MOTHER DIED AND MY FATHER MARRIED A WOMAN FROM YOUR AIR-BREATHING WORLD...
THEN MY HALF-BROTHER ORM WAS BORN! OF COURSE, HE COULD NOT INHERIT MY WATER-BREATHING POWERS, WHICH HE RESENTED DEEPLY.
GOT YOU! ORM... YOU MUST STOP TRYING TO KEEP UP WITH ME IN THE SEA... IT'S DANGEROUS--!
CHOKE! ... I... CAN DO ANYTHING YOU CAN... BROTHER... CHOKE!
"SO ORM GREW UP RESENTING ME--EVEN HATING ME! THEN, AN ACCIDENT TOOK AWAY HIS MEMORY--MADE HIM INTO A CRIMINAL AMNESIAC..."
"BUT NOTHING CHANGED ORM--AND THOUGH HE NO LONGER KNEW ME AS HIS BROTHER, HE STILL HATED ME! THEN, HE VANISHED...TO TURN UP YEARS LATER AS OCEAN MASTER--MY GREATEST ENEMY..."
HE'S PAROLED IN YOUR CUSTODY, AQUAMAN--BUT BE CAREFUL! HE'S HOPELESS... VICIOUS TO THE CORE!
I'LL DO MY BEST TO CHANGE HIM, WARDEN!
YOU'VE WRECKED MY SHIP AND MY PLANS--BUT YOU WON'T FIGHT ME MAN TO MAN? WHY? WHY?
I CAN NEVER HARM MY OWN FLESH AND BLOOD! NEVER!
13

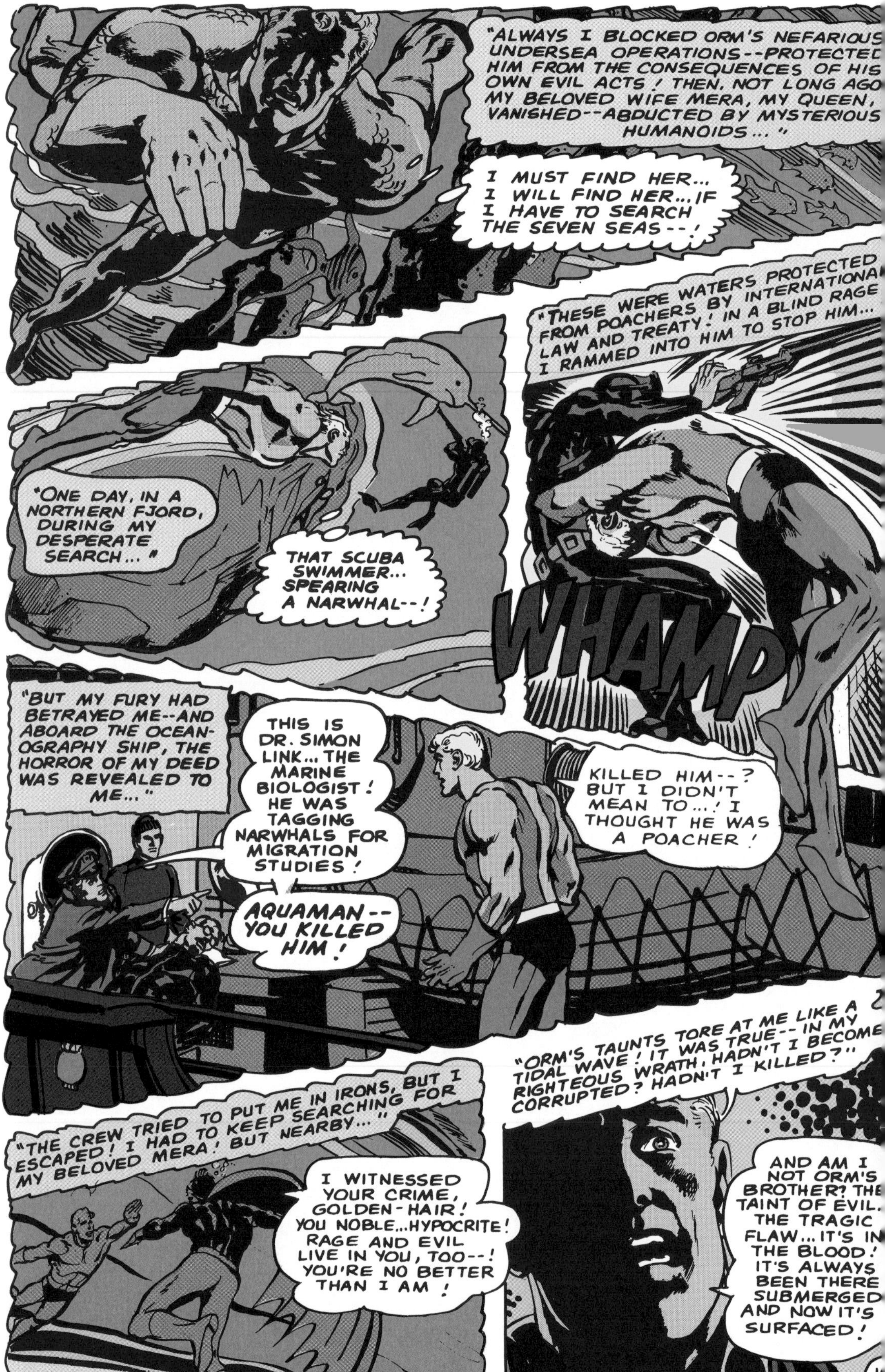
"ALWAYS I BLOCKED ORM'S NEFARIOUS UNDERSEA OPERATIONS--PROTECTED HIM FROM THE CONSEQUENCES OF HIS OWN EVIL ACTS! THEN, NOT LONG AGO MY BELOVED WIFE MERA, MY QUEEN, VANISHED--ABDUCTED BY MYSTERIOUS HUMANOIDS..."
I MUST FIND HER... I WILL FIND HER... IF I HAVE TO SEARCH THE SEVEN SEAS--!
"ONE DAY, IN A NORTHERN FJORD, DURING MY DESPERATE SEARCH..."
THAT SCUBA SWIMMER... SPEARING A NARWHAL--!
"THESE WERE WATERS PROTECTED FROM POACHERS BY INTERNATIONAL LAW AND TREATY! IN A BLIND RAGE I RAMMED INTO HIM TO STOP HIM..."
WHAMP
"BUT MY FURY HAD BETRAYED ME--AND ABOARD THE OCEANOGRAPHY SHIP, THE HORROR OF MY DEED WAS REVEALED TO ME..."
THIS IS DR. SIMON LINK... THE MARINE BIOLOGIST! HE WAS TAGGING NARWHALS FOR MIGRATION STUDIES!
AQUAMAN--YOU KILLED HIM!
KILLED HIM--? BUT I DIDN'T MEAN TO...! I THOUGHT HE WAS A POACHER!
"THE CREW TRIED TO PUT ME IN IRONS, BUT I ESCAPED! I HAD TO KEEP SEARCHING FOR MY BELOVED MERA! BUT NEARBY..."
I WITNESSED YOUR CRIME, GOLDEN-HAIR! YOU NOBLE...HYPOCRITE! RAGE AND EVIL LIVE IN YOU, TOO--! YOU'RE NO BETTER THAN I AM!
"ORM'S TAUNTS TORE AT ME LIKE A TIDAL WAVE! IT WAS TRUE--IN MY RIGHTEOUS WRATH, HADN'T I BECOME CORRUPTED? HADN'T I KILLED?"
AND AM I NOT ORM'S BROTHER? THE TAINT OF EVIL, THE TRAGIC FLAW... IT'S IN THE BLOOD! IT'S ALWAYS BEEN THERE SUBMERGED AND NOW IT'S SURFACED!

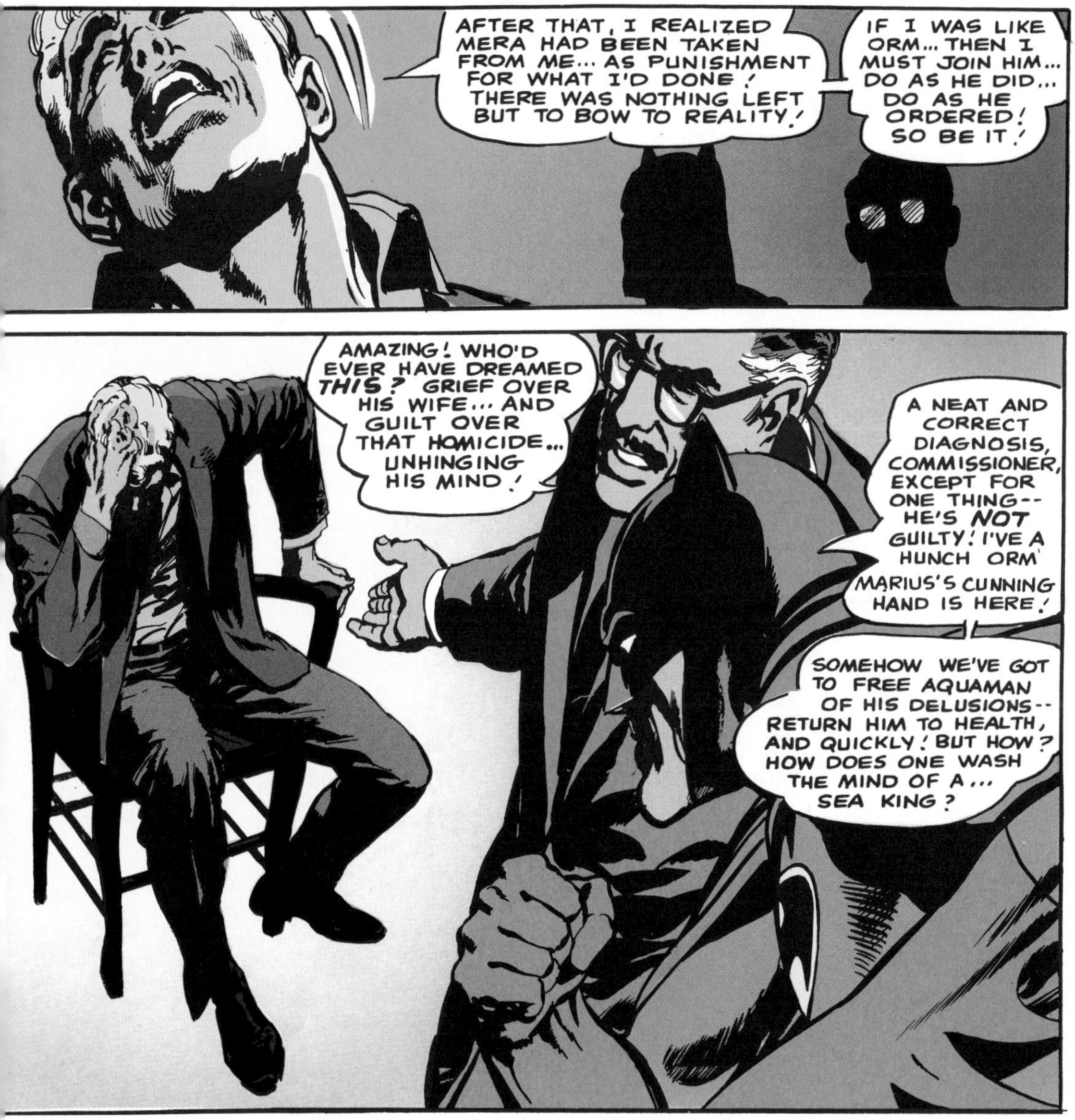
AFTER THAT, I REALIZED MERA HAD BEEN TAKEN FROM ME... AS PUNISHMENT FOR WHAT I'D DONE! THERE WAS NOTHING LEFT BUT TO BOW TO REALITY!
IF I WAS LIKE ORM... THEN I MUST JOIN HIM... DO AS HE DID... DO AS HE ORDERED! SO BE IT!
AMAZING! WHO'D EVER HAVE DREAMED THIS? GRIEF OVER HIS WIFE... AND GUILT OVER THAT HOMICIDE... UNHINGING HIS MIND!
A NEAT AND CORRECT DIAGNOSIS, COMMISSIONER, EXCEPT FOR ONE THING-- HE'S NOT GUILTY! I'VE A HUNCH ORM MARIUS'S CUNNING HAND IS HERE!
SOMEHOW WE'VE GOT TO FREE AQUAMAN OF HIS DELUSIONS-- RETURN HIM TO HEALTH, AND QUICKLY! BUT HOW? HOW DOES ONE WASH THE MIND OF A... SEA KING?

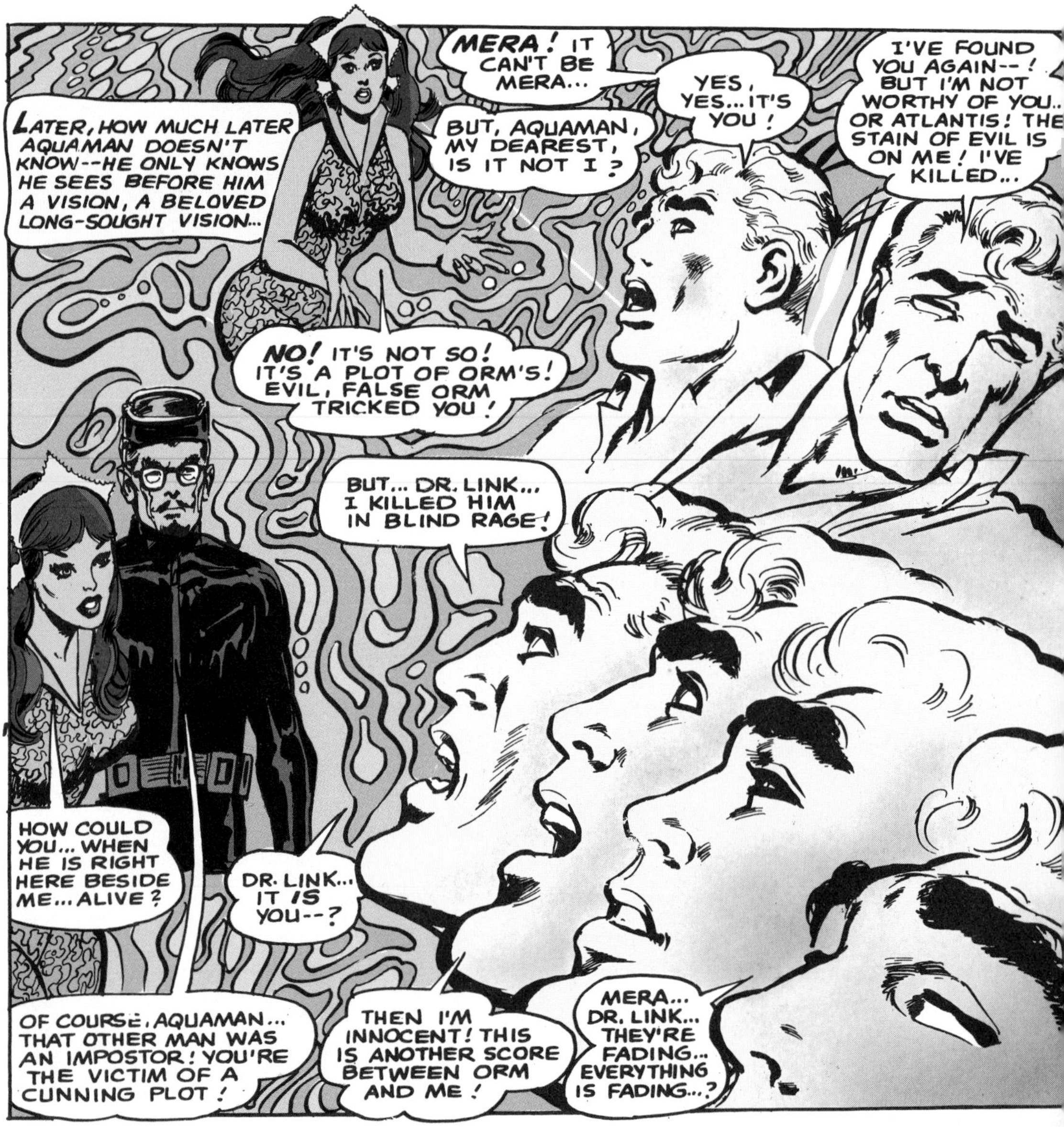
LATER, HOW MUCH LATER AQUAMAN DOESN'T KNOW--HE ONLY KNOWS HE SEES BEFORE HIM A VISION, A BELOVED LONG-SOUGHT VISION...
MERA! IT CAN'T BE MERA...
BUT, AQUAMAN, MY DEAREST, IS IT NOT I?
YES, YES... IT'S YOU!
I'VE FOUND YOU AGAIN--! BUT I'M NOT WORTHY OF YOU.. OR ATLANTIS! THE STAIN OF EVIL IS ON ME! I'VE KILLED...
NO! IT'S NOT SO! IT'S A PLOT OF ORM'S! EVIL, FALSE ORM TRICKED YOU!
BUT... DR. LINK... I KILLED HIM IN BLIND RAGE!
HOW COULD YOU... WHEN HE IS RIGHT HERE BESIDE ME... ALIVE?
DR. LINK... IT IS YOU--?
OF COURSE, AQUAMAN... THAT OTHER MAN WAS AN IMPOSTOR! YOU'RE THE VICTIM OF A CUNNING PLOT!
THEN I'M INNOCENT! THIS IS ANOTHER SCORE BETWEEN ORM AND ME!
MERA... DR. LINK... THEY'RE FADING... EVERYTHING IS FADING...?

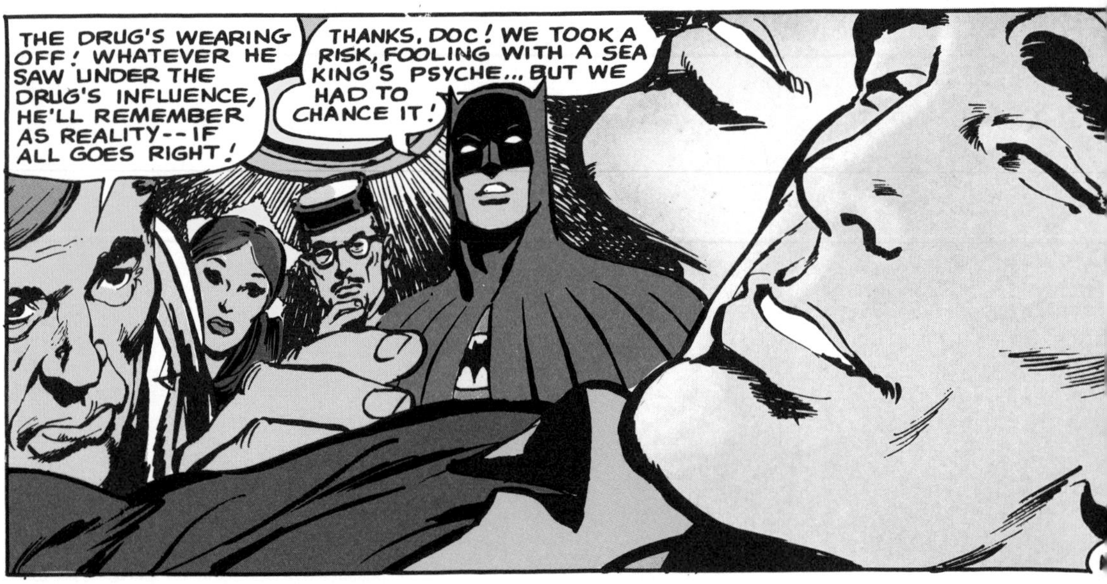
THE DRUG'S WEARING OFF! WHATEVER HE SAW UNDER THE DRUG'S INFLUENCE, HE'LL REMEMBER AS REALITY--IF ALL GOES RIGHT!
THANKS, DOC! WE TOOK A RISK, FOOLING WITH A SEA KING'S PSYCHE... BUT WE HAD TO CHANCE IT!

YOU WERE GREAT AS DR. LINK, COMMISSIONER. HONOR... WE COULDN'T HAVE DONE IT WITHOUT YOU! THANKS!

I DID IT FOR YOU... AND AQUAMAN, *BATMAN!* WHEN YOU SEE BRUCE WAYNE AGAIN, TELL HIM HE'S A FOOL AND I'VE CLOSED OUT THE PLAYBOY PHASE OF MY LIFE... FOREVER!

I'LL... TELL HIM!

BATMAN! COMMISSIONER GORDON! WHY ARE WE WASTING TIME? ORM... ORM MARIUS MUST BE STOPPED!

I HAVE ONE CONDITION -- ORM MUST *NOT* BE HARMED... EVEN IF IT MEANS HE ESCAPES!

WHAT? I CAN'T GUARANTEE THAT... HE'S A CRIMINAL... A COLD-HEARTED KILLER--!

COMMISSIONER... WE'VE NO CHOICE! AQUAMAN, *I'LL* GUARANTEE YOUR BROTHER'S SAFETY! NOW LET'S GO-!

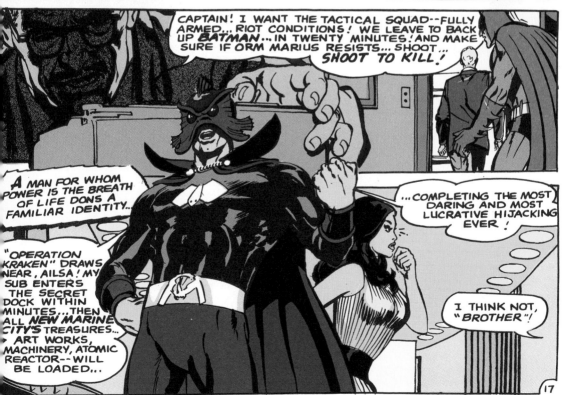

CAPTAIN! I WANT THE TACTICAL SQUAD--FULLY ARMED... RIOT CONDITIONS! WE LEAVE TO BACK UP *BATMAN*... IN TWENTY MINUTES! AND MAKE SURE IF ORM MARIUS RESISTS... SHOOT... *SHOOT TO KILL!*

A MAN FOR WHOM POWER IS THE BREATH OF LIFE DONS A FAMILIAR IDENTITY...

"OPERATION KRAKEN" DRAWS NEAR, AILSA! MY SUB ENTERS THE SECRET DOCK WITHIN MINUTES... THEN ALL *NEW MARINE CITY'S* TREASURES... ART WORKS, MACHINERY, ATOMIC REACTOR-- WILL BE LOADED...

...COMPLETING THE MOST DARING AND MOST LUCRATIVE HIJACKING EVER!

I THINK NOT, "BROTHER"!

(17)

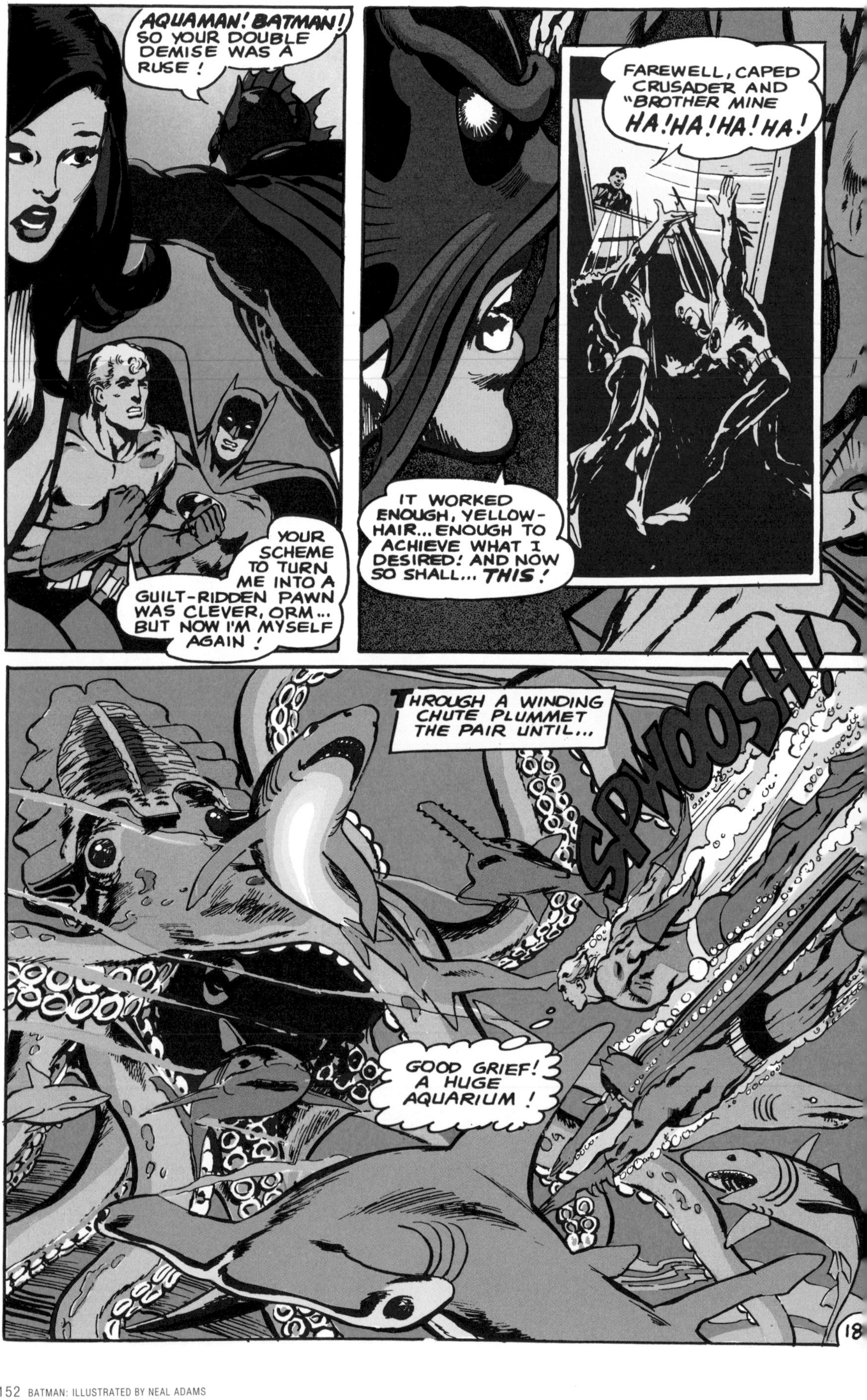
AQUAMAN! BATMAN! SO YOUR DOUBLE DEMISE WAS A RUSE!
YOUR SCHEME TO TURN ME INTO A GUILT-RIDDEN PAWN WAS CLEVER, ORM... BUT NOW I'M MYSELF AGAIN!
IT WORKED ENOUGH, YELLOW-HAIR... ENOUGH TO ACHIEVE WHAT I DESIRED! AND NOW SO SHALL... THIS!
FAREWELL, CAPED CRUSADER AND "BROTHER MINE"
HA! HA! HA! HA!
THROUGH A WINDING CHUTE PLUMMET THE PAIR UNTIL...
SPWOOSH!
GOOD GRIEF! A HUGE AQUARIUM!
18

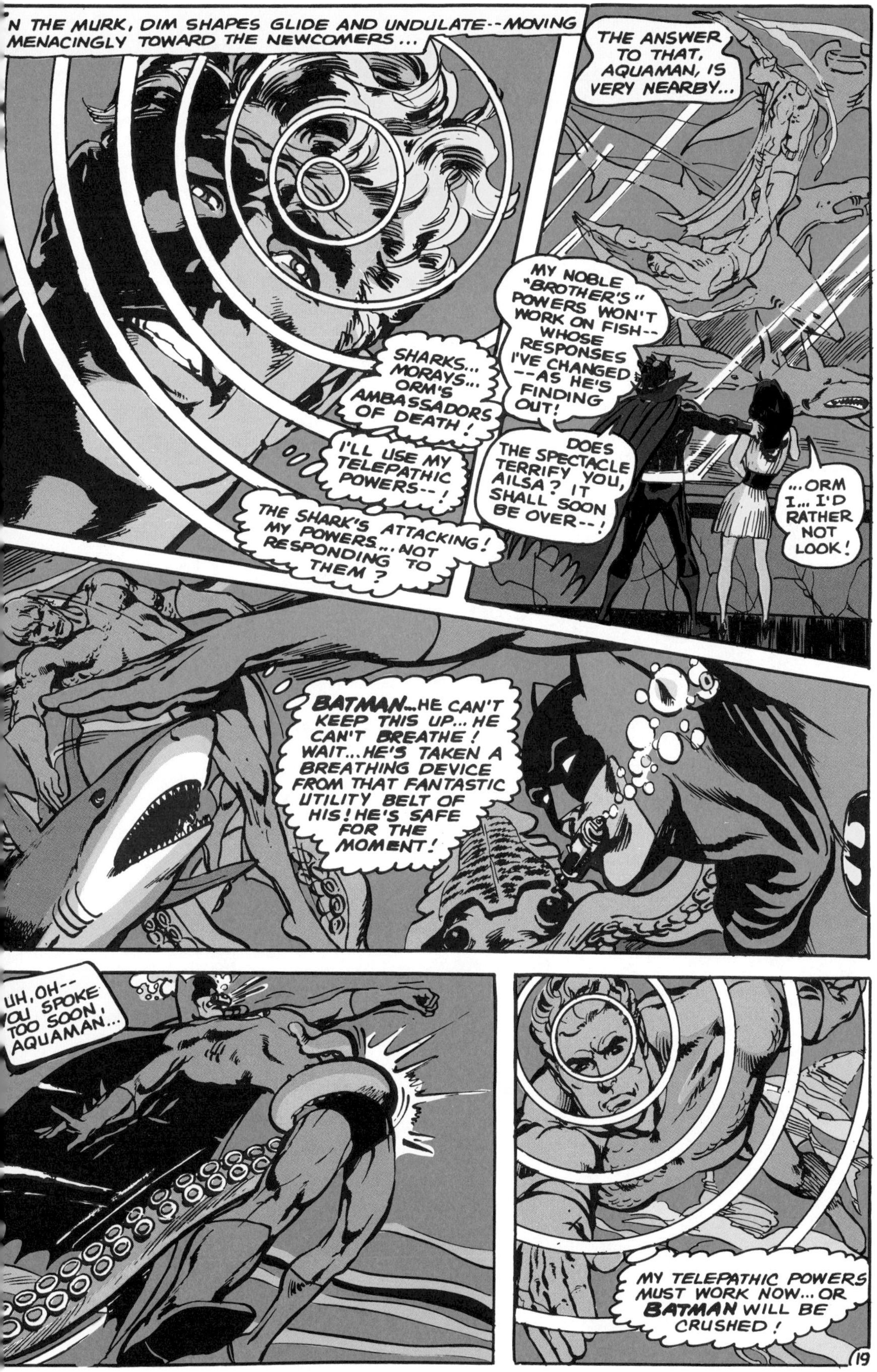

N THE MURK, DIM SHAPES GLIDE AND UNDULATE--MOVING MENACINGLY TOWARD THE NEWCOMERS...
SHARKS... MORAYS... ORM'S AMBASSADORS OF DEATH!
I'LL USE MY TELEPATHIC POWERS--!
THE SHARK'S ATTACKING! MY POWERS... NOT RESPONDING TO THEM?
THE ANSWER TO THAT, AQUAMAN, IS VERY NEARBY...
MY NOBLE "BROTHER'S" POWERS WON'T WORK ON FISH-- WHOSE RESPONSES I'VE CHANGED --AS HE'S FINDING OUT!
DOES THE SPECTACLE TERRIFY YOU, AILSA? IT SHALL SOON BE OVER--!
...ORM I... I'D RATHER NOT LOOK!
BATMAN...HE CAN'T KEEP THIS UP... HE CAN'T BREATHE! WAIT...HE'S TAKEN A BREATHING DEVICE FROM THAT FANTASTIC UTILITY BELT OF HIS! HE'S SAFE FOR THE MOMENT!
UH, OH-- OU SPOKE TOO SOON, AQUAMAN...
MY TELEPATHIC POWERS MUST WORK NOW... OR BATMAN WILL BE CRUSHED!
19

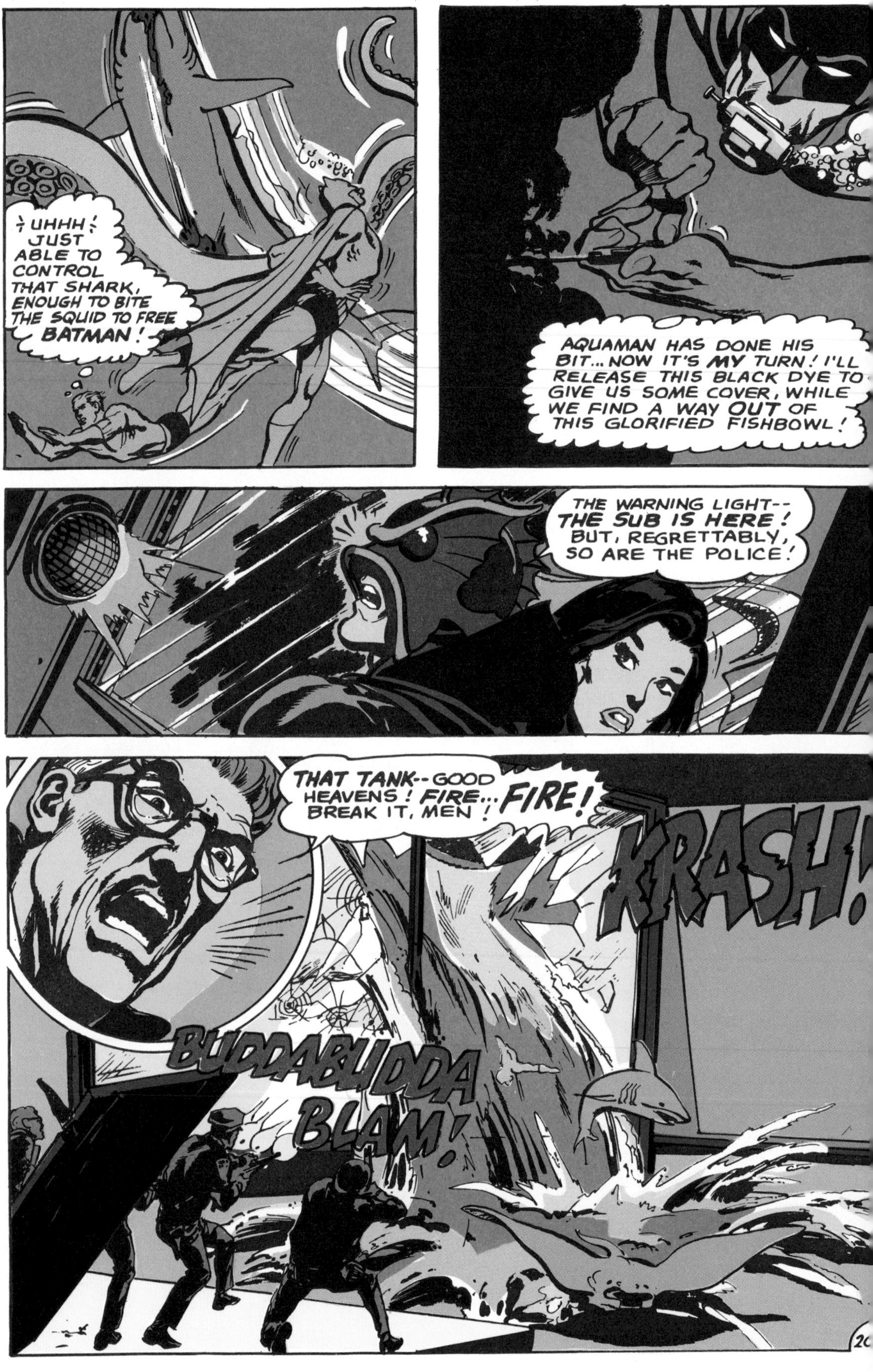
-UHHH- JUST ABLE TO CONTROL THAT SHARK, ENOUGH TO BITE THE SQUID TO FREE BATMAN!
AQUAMAN HAS DONE HIS BIT... NOW IT'S MY TURN! I'LL RELEASE THIS BLACK DYE TO GIVE US SOME COVER, WHILE WE FIND A WAY OUT OF THIS GLORIFIED FISHBOWL!
THE WARNING LIGHT-- THE SUB IS HERE! BUT, REGRETTABLY, SO ARE THE POLICE!
THAT TANK--GOOD HEAVENS! FIRE... BREAK IT, MEN! FIRE!
KRASH!
BUDDABUDDA BLAM!

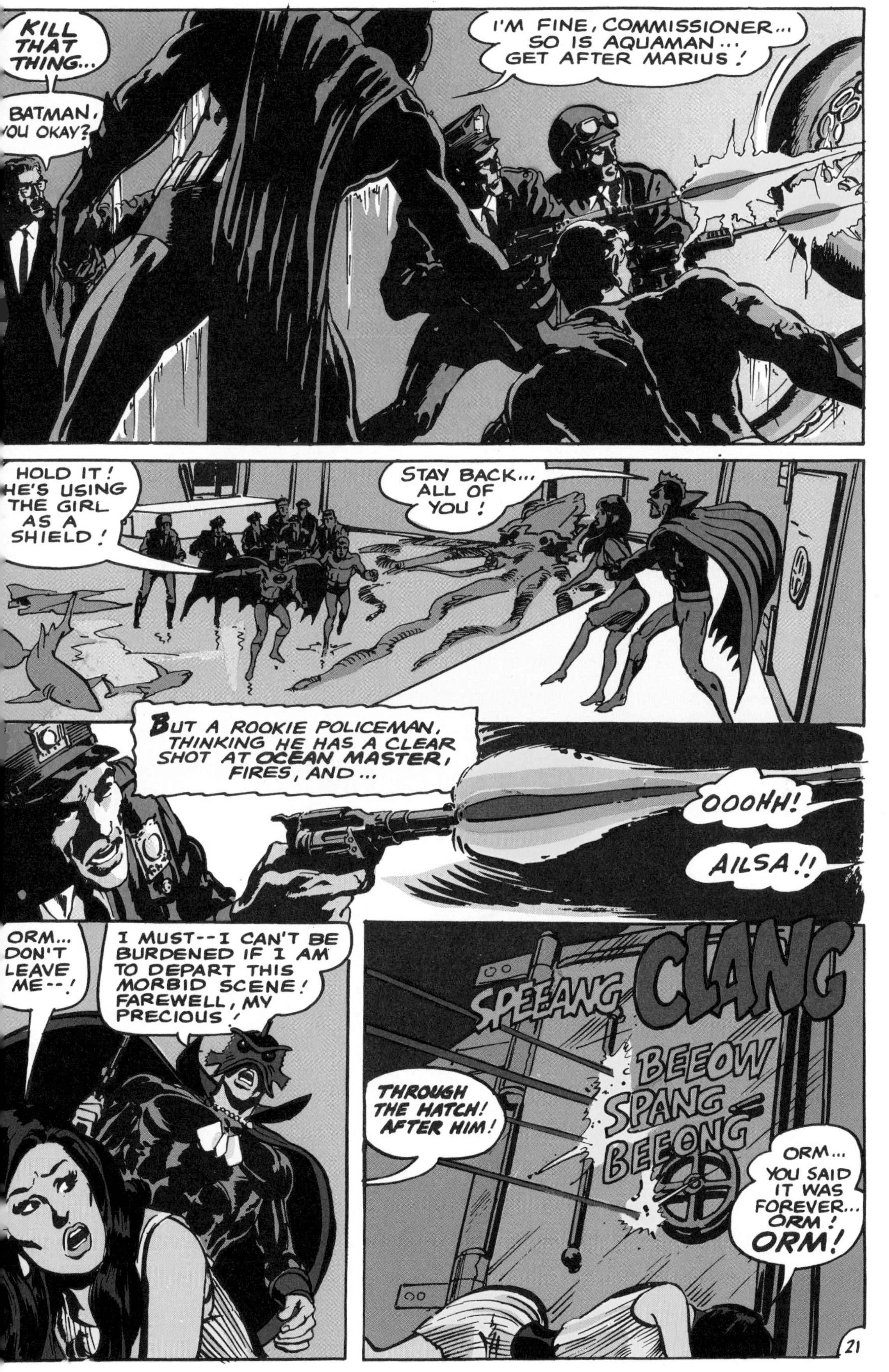
KILL THAT THING...
BATMAN, YOU OKAY?
I'M FINE, COMMISSIONER... SO IS AQUAMAN... GET AFTER MARIUS!
HOLD IT! HE'S USING THE GIRL AS A SHIELD!
STAY BACK... ALL OF YOU!
BUT A ROOKIE POLICEMAN, THINKING HE HAS A CLEAR SHOT AT OCEAN MASTER, FIRES, AND...
OOOHH!
AILSA!!
ORM... DON'T LEAVE ME--!
I MUST--I CAN'T BE BURDENED IF I AM TO DEPART THIS MORBID SCENE! FAREWELL, MY PRECIOUS!
SPEEANG
CLANG
BEEOW
SPANG
BEEONG
THROUGH THE HATCH! AFTER HIM!
ORM... YOU SAID IT WAS FOREVER... ORM! ORM!
21

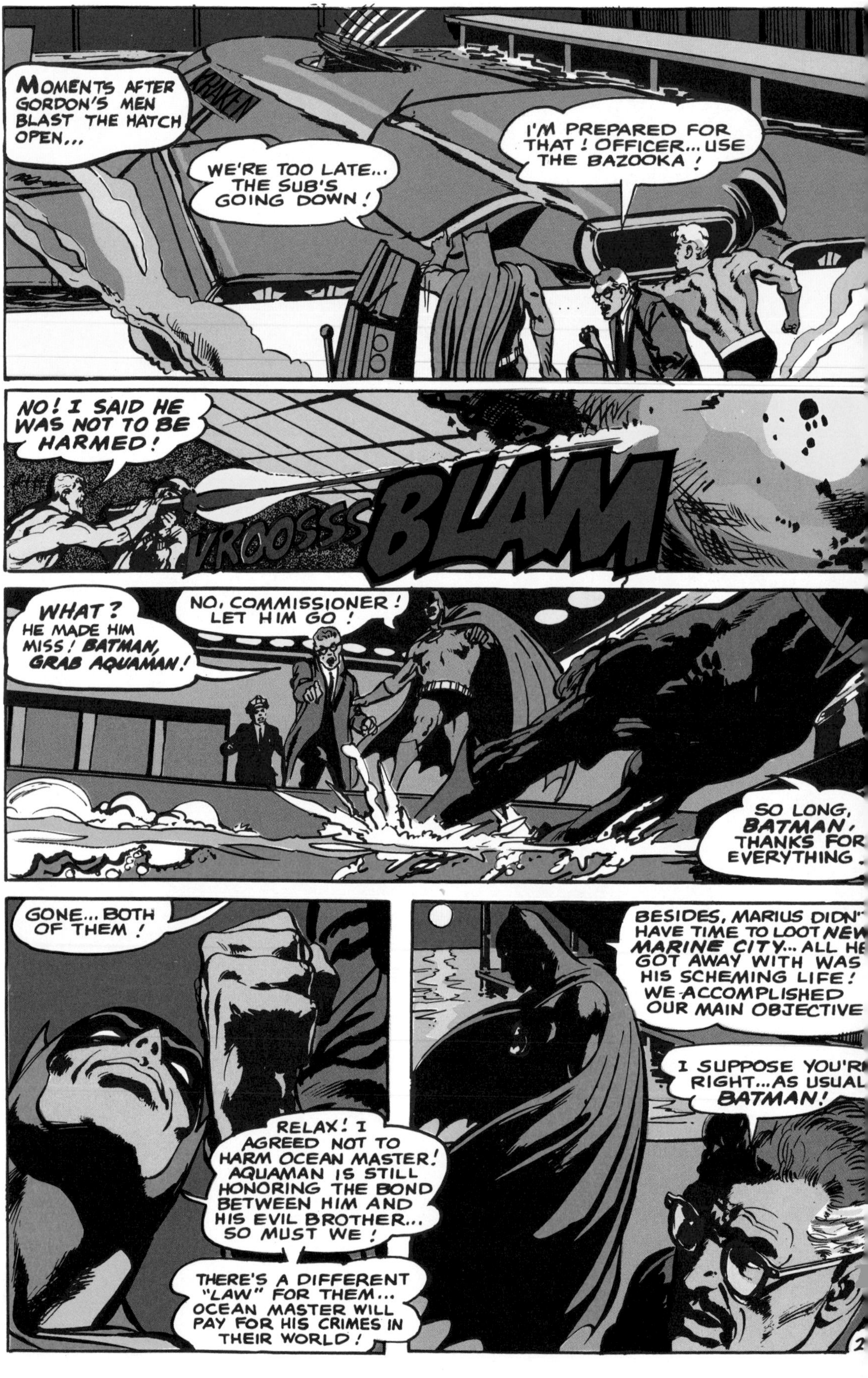
MOMENTS AFTER GORDON'S MEN BLAST THE HATCH OPEN...
KRAKEN
WE'RE TOO LATE... THE SUB'S GOING DOWN!
I'M PREPARED FOR THAT! OFFICER... USE THE BAZOOKA!
NO! I SAID HE WAS NOT TO BE HARMED!
VROOSSS
BLAM
WHAT? HE MADE HIM MISS! BATMAN, GRAB AQUAMAN!
NO, COMMISSIONER! LET HIM GO!
SO LONG, BATMAN, THANKS FOR EVERYTHING.
GONE... BOTH OF THEM!
RELAX! I AGREED NOT TO HARM OCEAN MASTER! AQUAMAN IS STILL HONORING THE BOND BETWEEN HIM AND HIS EVIL BROTHER... SO MUST WE!
THERE'S A DIFFERENT "LAW" FOR THEM... OCEAN MASTER WILL PAY FOR HIS CRIMES IN THEIR WORLD!
BESIDES, MARIUS DIDN'T HAVE TIME TO LOOT NEW MARINE CITY... ALL HE GOT AWAY WITH WAS HIS SCHEMING LIFE! WE ACCOMPLISHED OUR MAIN OBJECTIVE
I SUPPOSE YOU'RE RIGHT... AS USUAL, BATMAN!

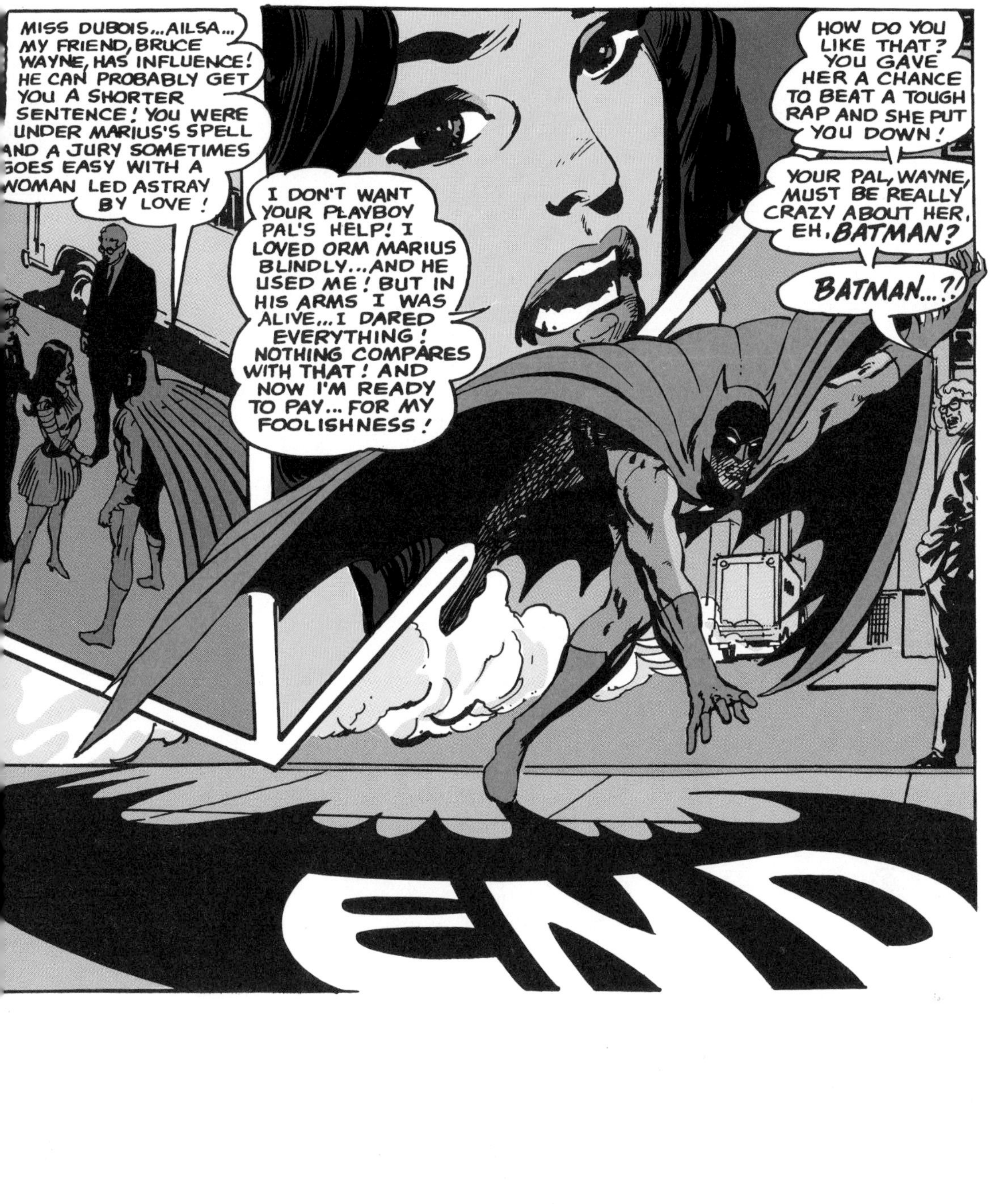
MISS DUBOIS...AILSA... MY FRIEND, BRUCE WAYNE, HAS INFLUENCE! HE CAN PROBABLY GET YOU A SHORTER SENTENCE! YOU WERE UNDER MARIUS'S SPELL AND A JURY SOMETIMES GOES EASY WITH A WOMAN LED ASTRAY BY LOVE!
I DON'T WANT YOUR PLAYBOY PAL'S HELP! I LOVED ORM MARIUS BLINDLY...AND HE USED ME! BUT IN HIS ARMS I WAS ALIVE...I DARED EVERYTHING! NOTHING COMPARES WITH THAT! AND NOW I'M READY TO PAY... FOR MY FOOLISHNESS!
HOW DO YOU LIKE THAT? YOU GAVE HER A CHANCE TO BEAT A TOUGH RAP AND SHE PUT YOU DOWN!
YOUR PAL, WAYNE, MUST BE REALLY CRAZY ABOUT HER, EH, BATMAN?
BATMAN...?!
END

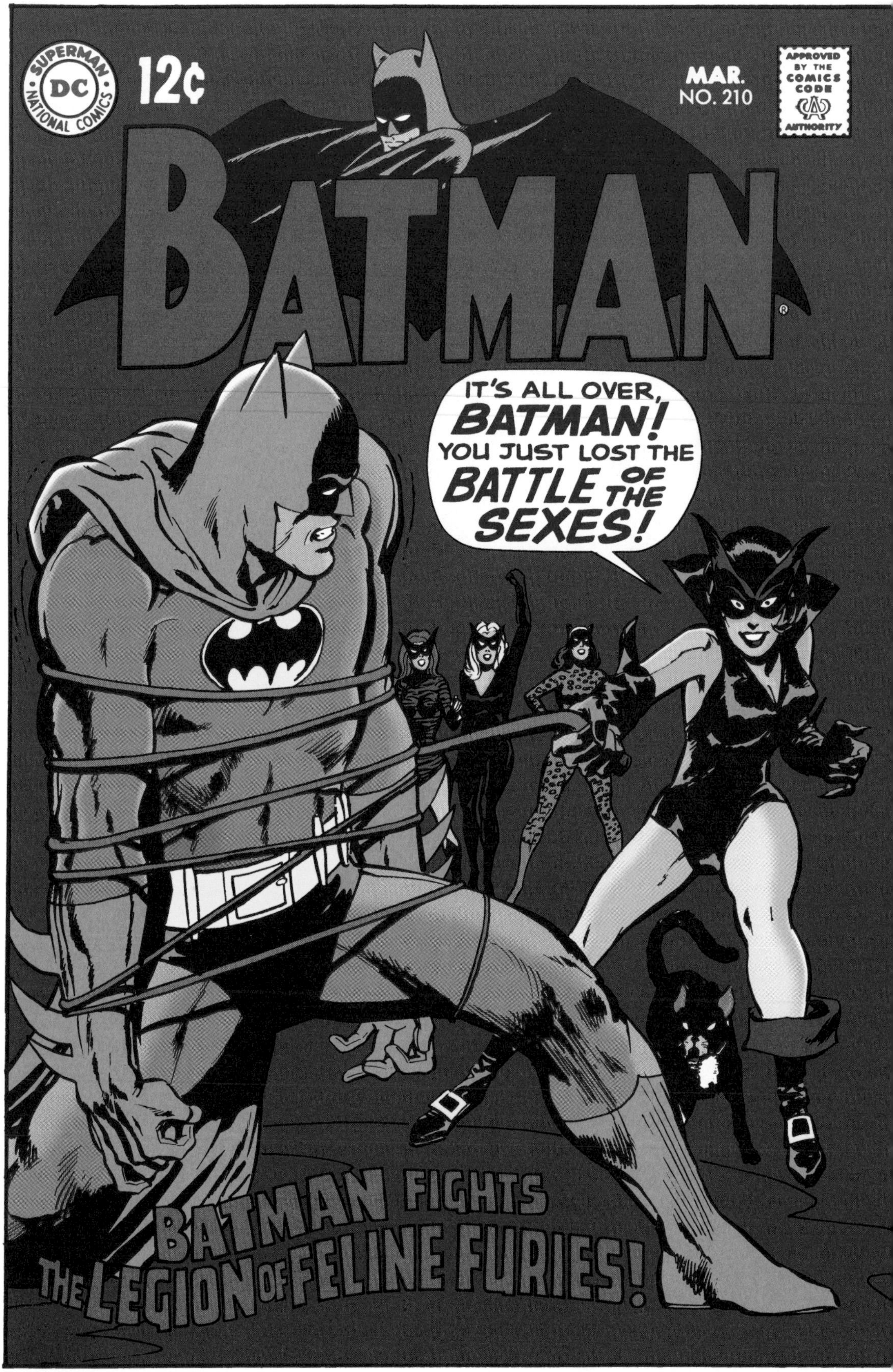
SUPERMAN DC NATIONAL COMICS
12¢
MAR.
NO. 210
APPROVED BY THE COMICS CODE AUTHORITY
BATMAN
IT'S ALL OVER, BATMAN! YOU JUST LOST THE BATTLE OF THE SEXES!
BATMAN FIGHTS THE LEGION OF FELINE FURIES!

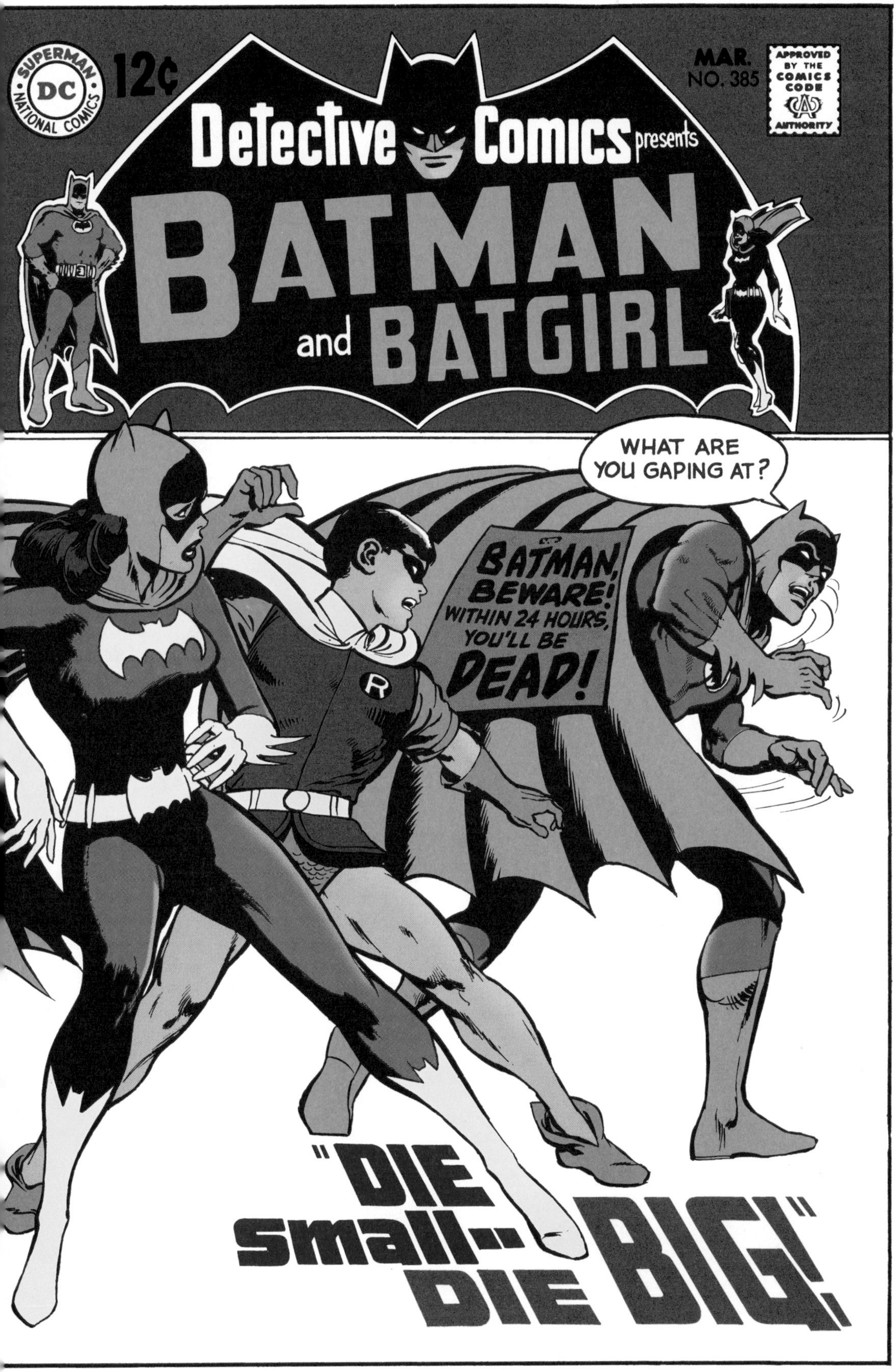
SUPERMAN DC NATIONAL COMICS
12¢
MAR. NO. 385
APPROVED BY THE COMICS CODE AUTHORITY
Detective Comics presents
BATMAN and BATGIRL
WHAT ARE YOU GAPING AT?
BATMAN, BEWARE! WITHIN 24 HOURS, YOU'LL BE DEAD!
"DIE small-- DIE BIG!"

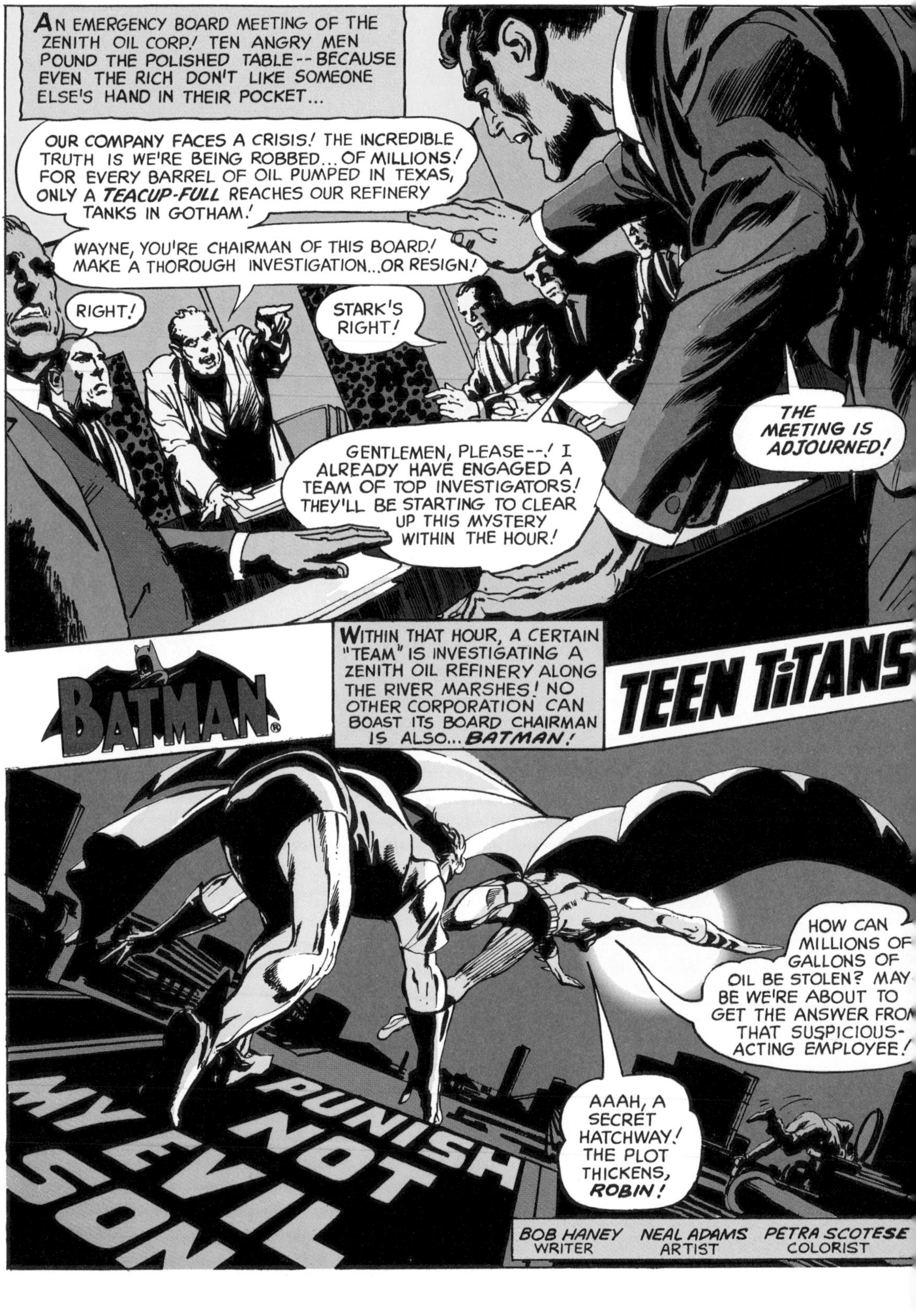

AN EMERGENCY BOARD MEETING OF THE ZENITH OIL CORP! TEN ANGRY MEN POUND THE POLISHED TABLE-- BECAUSE EVEN THE RICH DON'T LIKE SOMEONE ELSE'S HAND IN THEIR POCKET...
OUR COMPANY FACES A CRISIS! THE INCREDIBLE TRUTH IS WE'RE BEING ROBBED... OF MILLIONS! FOR EVERY BARREL OF OIL PUMPED IN TEXAS, ONLY A TEACUP-FULL REACHES OUR REFINERY TANKS IN GOTHAM!
WAYNE, YOU'RE CHAIRMAN OF THIS BOARD! MAKE A THOROUGH INVESTIGATION... OR RESIGN!
RIGHT!
STARK'S RIGHT!
GENTLEMEN, PLEASE--! I ALREADY HAVE ENGAGED A TEAM OF TOP INVESTIGATORS! THEY'LL BE STARTING TO CLEAR UP THIS MYSTERY WITHIN THE HOUR!
THE MEETING IS ADJOURNED!
BATMAN
WITHIN THAT HOUR, A CERTAIN "TEAM" IS INVESTIGATING A ZENITH OIL REFINERY ALONG THE RIVER MARSHES! NO OTHER CORPORATION CAN BOAST ITS BOARD CHAIRMAN IS ALSO... BATMAN!
TEEN TITANS
HOW CAN MILLIONS OF GALLONS OF OIL BE STOLEN? MAYBE WE'RE ABOUT TO GET THE ANSWER FROM THAT SUSPICIOUS-ACTING EMPLOYEE!
AAAH, A SECRET HATCHWAY! THE PLOT THICKENS, ROBIN!
PUNISH NOT MY EVIL SON!
BOB HANEY WRITER
NEAL ADAMS ARTIST
PETRA SCOTESE COLORIST

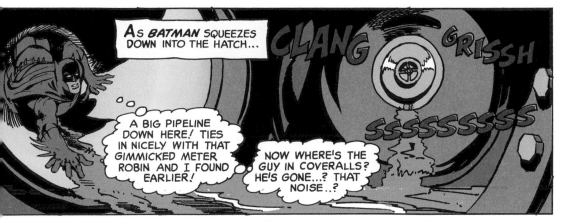

As **BATMAN** SQUEEZES DOWN INTO THE HATCH...

CLANG

GRISSH

SSSSSSSSS

A BIG PIPELINE DOWN HERE! TIES IN NICELY WITH THAT GIMMICKED METER ROBIN AND I FOUND EARLIER!

NOW WHERE'S THE GUY IN COVERALLS? HE'S GONE...? THAT NOISE..?

O EARS SHARPENED BY A THOUSAND AND ONE ANGER SOUNDS, THIS IS A NEW SIGNAL... OFT, SINISTER...

BWOOSH!

OIL! AND I'M CUT OFF FROM THE ESCAPE HATCH! I'M TRAPPED LIKE A RAT IN A SEWER--!

BATMAN HAS ONLY SECONDS TO FUMBLE FOR AN ITEM FROM HIS UBIQUITOUS UTILITY BELT TO ENABLE HIM TO BREATHE...

WHOOSH

BEFORE HE IS ENGULFED AND CARRIED ALONG IN AN ENVELOPING, VISCOUS VOID...

WHILE BOVE...

BWOOOSH!

OH NO! **BATMAN'S** BEEN WASHED AWAY IN AN OIL DELUGE! IF I DON'T FIND HIM FAST... HE'LL DROWN IN BLACK GOLD!

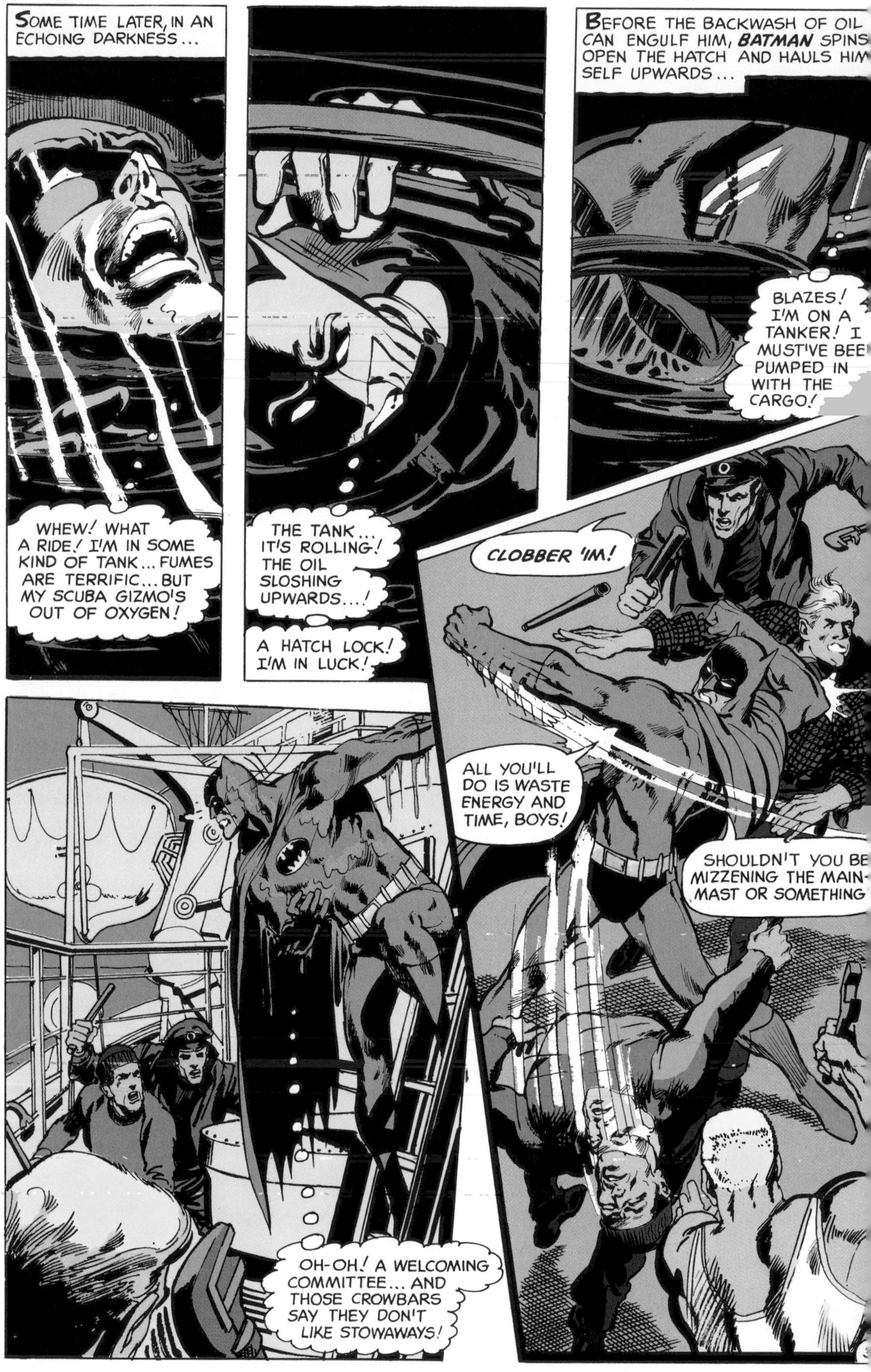
SOME TIME LATER, IN AN ECHOING DARKNESS...
WHEW! WHAT A RIDE! I'M IN SOME KIND OF TANK... FUMES ARE TERRIFIC... BUT MY SCUBA GIZMO'S OUT OF OXYGEN!
THE TANK... IT'S ROLLING! THE OIL SLOSHING UPWARDS...!
A HATCH LOCK! I'M IN LUCK!
BEFORE THE BACKWASH OF OIL CAN ENGULF HIM, BATMAN SPINS OPEN THE HATCH AND HAULS HIM SELF UPWARDS...
BLAZES! I'M ON A TANKER! I MUST'VE BEE PUMPED IN WITH THE CARGO!
OH-OH! A WELCOMING COMMITTEE... AND THOSE CROWBARS SAY THEY DON'T LIKE STOWAWAYS!
CLOBBER 'IM!
ALL YOU'LL DO IS WASTE ENERGY AND TIME, BOYS!
SHOULDN'T YOU BE MIZZENING THE MAIN-MAST OR SOMETHING

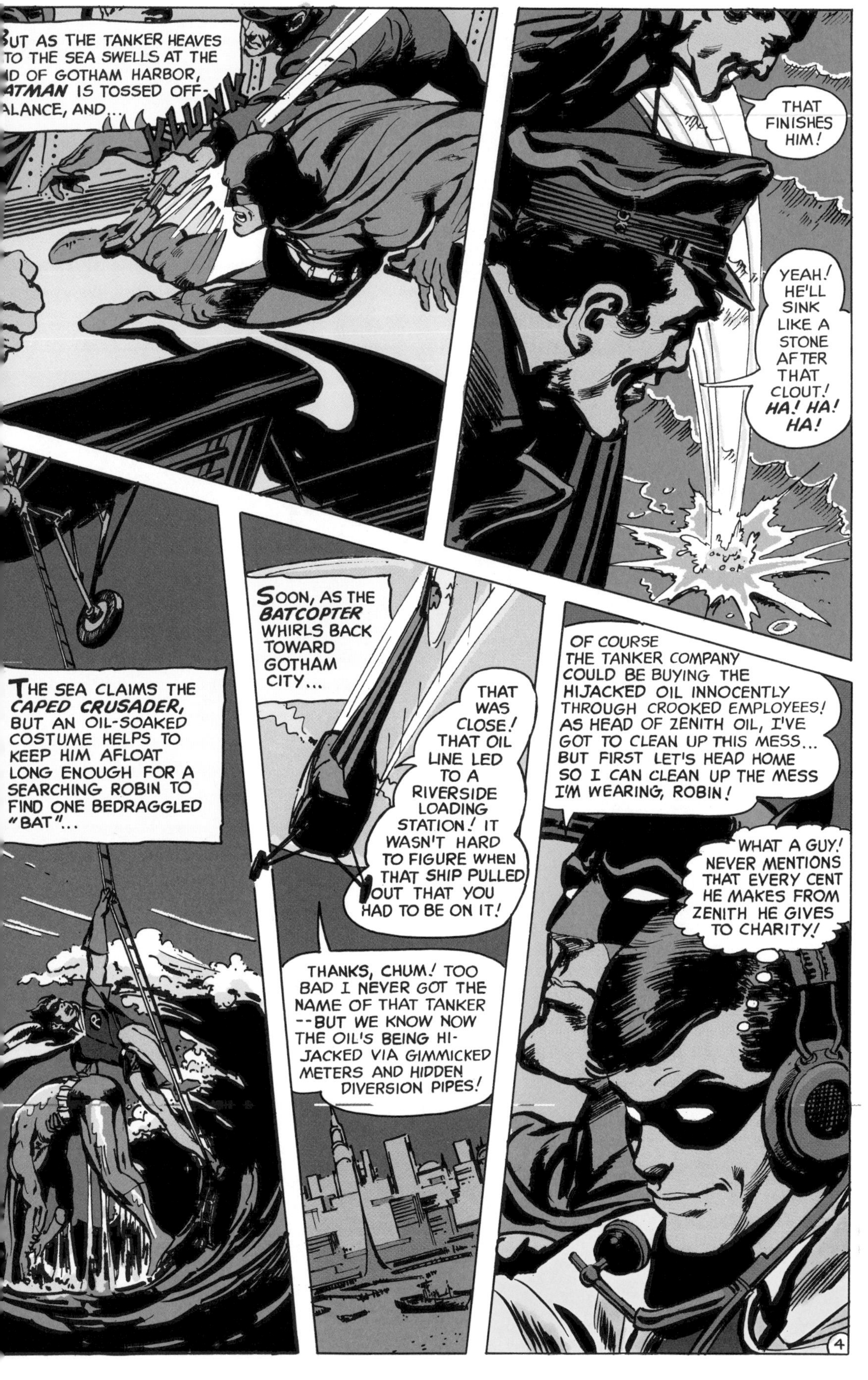
BUT AS THE TANKER HEAVES TO THE SEA SWELLS AT THE ND OF GOTHAM HARBOR, BATMAN IS TOSSED OFF-ALANCE, AND...
KLUNK
THAT FINISHES HIM!
YEAH! HE'LL SINK LIKE A STONE AFTER THAT CLOUT! HA! HA! HA!
THE SEA CLAIMS THE CAPED CRUSADER, BUT AN OIL-SOAKED COSTUME HELPS TO KEEP HIM AFLOAT LONG ENOUGH FOR A SEARCHING ROBIN TO FIND ONE BEDRAGGLED "BAT"...
SOON, AS THE BATCOPTER WHIRLS BACK TOWARD GOTHAM CITY...
THAT WAS CLOSE! THAT OIL LINE LED TO A RIVERSIDE LOADING STATION! IT WASN'T HARD TO FIGURE WHEN THAT SHIP PULLED OUT THAT YOU HAD TO BE ON IT!
THANKS, CHUM! TOO BAD I NEVER GOT THE NAME OF THAT TANKER --BUT WE KNOW NOW THE OIL'S BEING HI-JACKED VIA GIMMICKED METERS AND HIDDEN DIVERSION PIPES!
OF COURSE THE TANKER COMPANY COULD BE BUYING THE HIJACKED OIL INNOCENTLY THROUGH CROOKED EMPLOYEES! AS HEAD OF ZENITH OIL, I'VE GOT TO CLEAN UP THIS MESS... BUT FIRST LET'S HEAD HOME SO I CAN CLEAN UP THE MESS I'M WEARING, ROBIN!
WHAT A GUY! NEVER MENTIONS THAT EVERY CENT HE MAKES FROM ZENITH HE GIVES TO CHARITY!
4

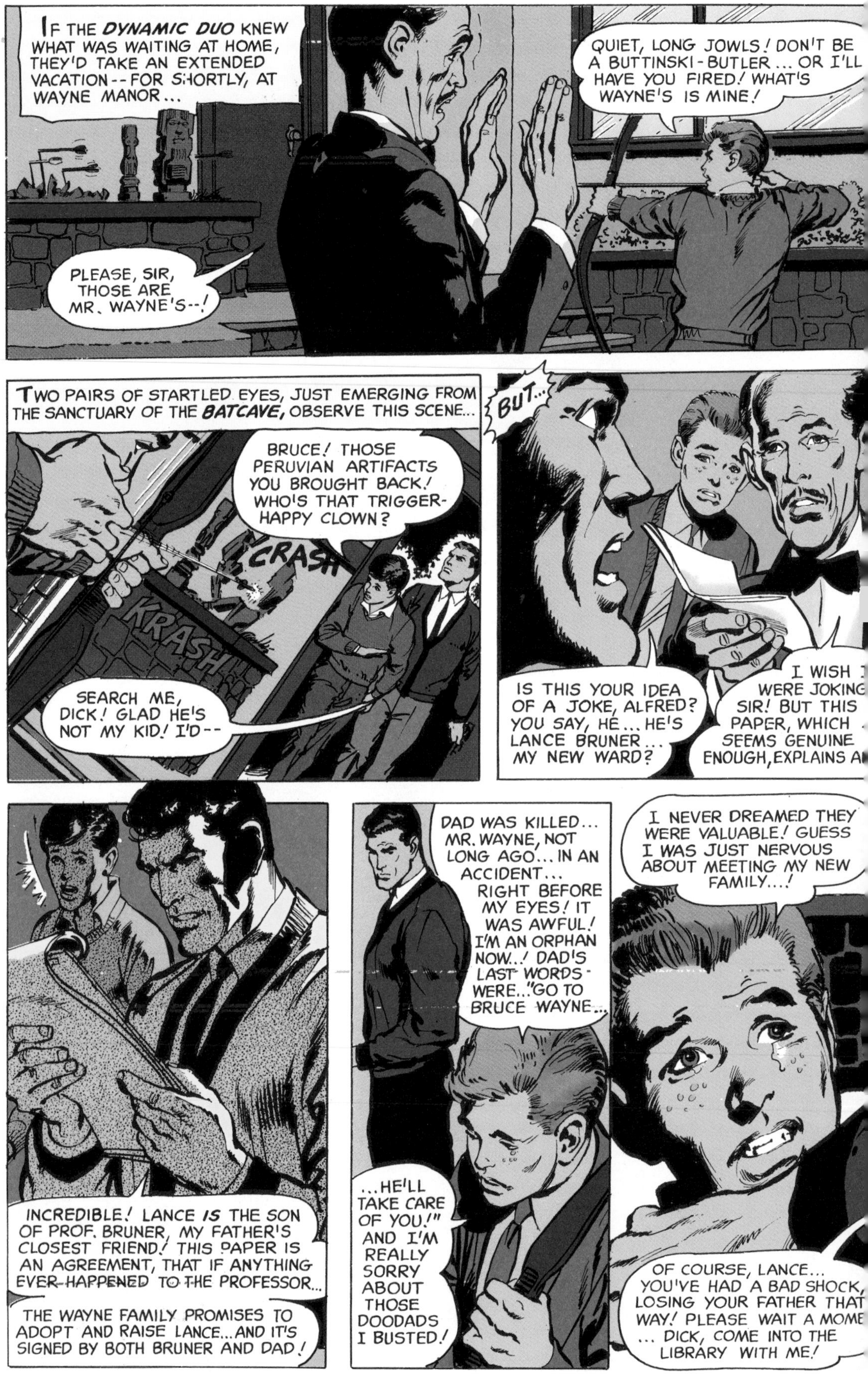
IF THE DYNAMIC DUO KNEW WHAT WAS WAITING AT HOME, THEY'D TAKE AN EXTENDED VACATION--FOR SHORTLY, AT WAYNE MANOR...
PLEASE, SIR, THOSE ARE MR. WAYNE'S--!
QUIET, LONG JOWLS! DON'T BE A BUTTINSKI-BUTLER... OR I'LL HAVE YOU FIRED! WHAT'S WAYNE'S IS MINE!
TWO PAIRS OF STARTLED EYES, JUST EMERGING FROM THE SANCTUARY OF THE BATCAVE, OBSERVE THIS SCENE...
BRUCE! THOSE PERUVIAN ARTIFACTS YOU BROUGHT BACK! WHO'S THAT TRIGGER-HAPPY CLOWN?
CRASH
KRASH
SEARCH ME, DICK! GLAD HE'S NOT MY KID! I'D--
BUT...
IS THIS YOUR IDEA OF A JOKE, ALFRED? YOU SAY, HE... HE'S LANCE BRUNER... MY NEW WARD?
I WISH I WERE JOKING SIR! BUT THIS PAPER, WHICH SEEMS GENUINE ENOUGH, EXPLAINS A
INCREDIBLE! LANCE IS THE SON OF PROF. BRUNER, MY FATHER'S CLOSEST FRIEND! THIS PAPER IS AN AGREEMENT, THAT IF ANYTHING EVER HAPPENED TO THE PROFESSOR...
THE WAYNE FAMILY PROMISES TO ADOPT AND RAISE LANCE...AND IT'S SIGNED BY BOTH BRUNER AND DAD!
DAD WAS KILLED... MR. WAYNE, NOT LONG AGO... IN AN ACCIDENT... RIGHT BEFORE MY EYES! IT WAS AWFUL! I'M AN ORPHAN NOW...! DAD'S LAST WORDS WERE..."GO TO BRUCE WAYNE...
...HE'LL TAKE CARE OF YOU!" AND I'M REALLY SORRY ABOUT THOSE DOODADS I BUSTED!
I NEVER DREAMED THEY WERE VALUABLE! GUESS I WAS JUST NERVOUS ABOUT MEETING MY NEW FAMILY...!
OF COURSE, LANCE... YOU'VE HAD A BAD SHOCK, LOSING YOUR FATHER THAT WAY! PLEASE WAIT A MOME ... DICK, COME INTO THE LIBRARY WITH ME!

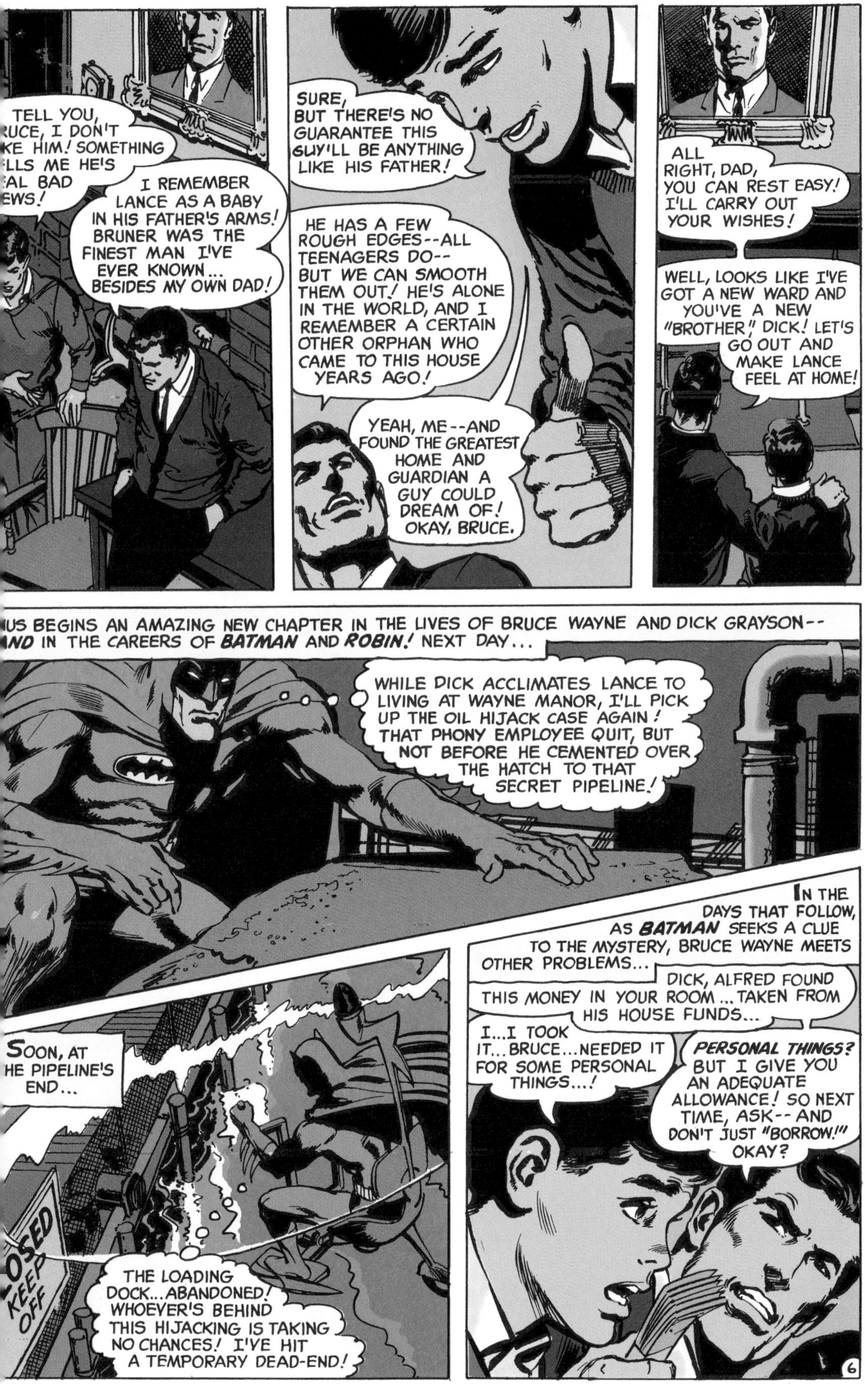

TELL YOU, RUCE, I DON'T KE HIM! SOMETHING LLS ME HE'S AL BAD EWS!
I REMEMBER LANCE AS A BABY IN HIS FATHER'S ARMS! BRUNER WAS THE FINEST MAN I'VE EVER KNOWN... BESIDES MY OWN DAD!
SURE, BUT THERE'S NO GUARANTEE THIS GUY'LL BE ANYTHING LIKE HIS FATHER!
HE HAS A FEW ROUGH EDGES--ALL TEENAGERS DO-- BUT WE CAN SMOOTH THEM OUT! HE'S ALONE IN THE WORLD, AND I REMEMBER A CERTAIN OTHER ORPHAN WHO CAME TO THIS HOUSE YEARS AGO!
YEAH, ME--AND FOUND THE GREATEST HOME AND GUARDIAN A GUY COULD DREAM OF! OKAY, BRUCE.
ALL RIGHT, DAD, YOU CAN REST EASY! I'LL CARRY OUT YOUR WISHES!
WELL, LOOKS LIKE I'VE GOT A NEW WARD AND YOU'VE A NEW "BROTHER," DICK! LET'S GO OUT AND MAKE LANCE FEEL AT HOME!
US BEGINS AN AMAZING NEW CHAPTER IN THE LIVES OF BRUCE WAYNE AND DICK GRAYSON-- ND IN THE CAREERS OF BATMAN AND ROBIN! NEXT DAY...
WHILE DICK ACCLIMATES LANCE TO LIVING AT WAYNE MANOR, I'LL PICK UP THE OIL HIJACK CASE AGAIN! THAT PHONY EMPLOYEE QUIT, BUT NOT BEFORE HE CEMENTED OVER THE HATCH TO THAT SECRET PIPELINE!
SOON, AT HE PIPELINE'S END...
OSED
KEEP OFF
THE LOADING DOCK... ABANDONED! WHOEVER'S BEHIND THIS HIJACKING IS TAKING NO CHANCES! I'VE HIT A TEMPORARY DEAD-END!
IN THE DAYS THAT FOLLOW, AS BATMAN SEEKS A CLUE TO THE MYSTERY, BRUCE WAYNE MEETS OTHER PROBLEMS...
DICK, ALFRED FOUND THIS MONEY IN YOUR ROOM... TAKEN FROM HIS HOUSE FUNDS...
I...I TOOK IT... BRUCE... NEEDED IT FOR SOME PERSONAL THINGS...!
PERSONAL THINGS? BUT I GIVE YOU AN ADEQUATE ALLOWANCE! SO NEXT TIME, ASK-- AND DON'T JUST "BORROW!" OKAY?
6

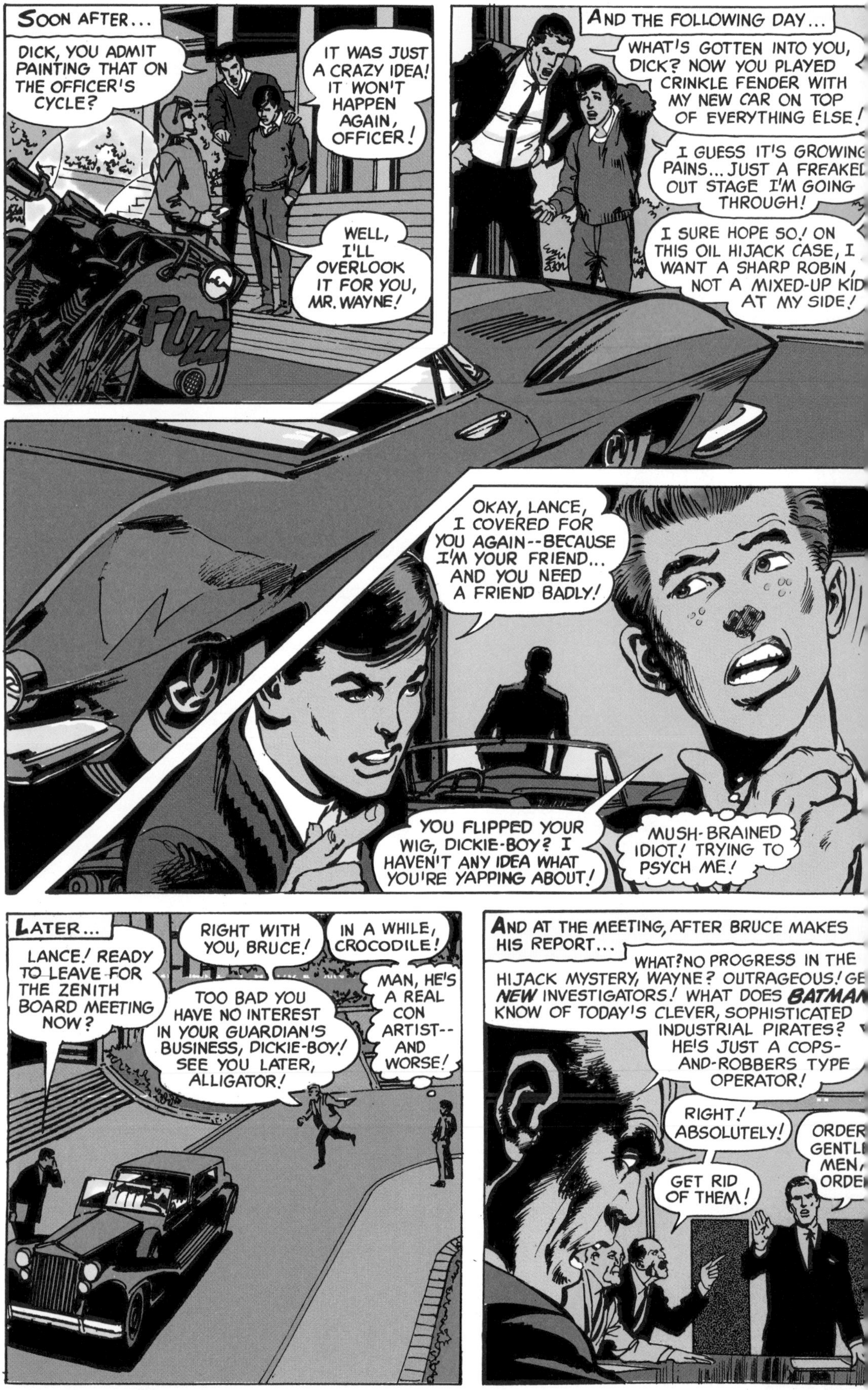

SOON AFTER...
DICK, YOU ADMIT PAINTING THAT ON THE OFFICER'S CYCLE?
IT WAS JUST A CRAZY IDEA! IT WON'T HAPPEN AGAIN, OFFICER!
WELL, I'LL OVERLOOK IT FOR YOU, MR. WAYNE!
FUZZ
AND THE FOLLOWING DAY...
WHAT'S GOTTEN INTO YOU, DICK? NOW YOU PLAYED CRINKLE FENDER WITH MY NEW CAR ON TOP OF EVERYTHING ELSE!
I GUESS IT'S GROWING PAINS... JUST A FREAKED OUT STAGE I'M GOING THROUGH!
I SURE HOPE SO! ON THIS OIL HIJACK CASE, I WANT A SHARP ROBIN, NOT A MIXED-UP KID AT MY SIDE!
OKAY, LANCE, I COVERED FOR YOU AGAIN--BECAUSE I'M YOUR FRIEND... AND YOU NEED A FRIEND BADLY!
YOU FLIPPED YOUR WIG, DICKIE-BOY? I HAVEN'T ANY IDEA WHAT YOU'RE YAPPING ABOUT!
MUSH-BRAINED IDIOT! TRYING TO PSYCH ME!
LATER...
LANCE! READY TO LEAVE FOR THE ZENITH BOARD MEETING NOW?
RIGHT WITH YOU, BRUCE!
TOO BAD YOU HAVE NO INTEREST IN YOUR GUARDIAN'S BUSINESS, DICKIE-BOY! SEE YOU LATER, ALLIGATOR!
IN A WHILE, CROCODILE!
MAN, HE'S A REAL CON ARTIST--AND WORSE!
AND AT THE MEETING, AFTER BRUCE MAKES HIS REPORT...
WHAT? NO PROGRESS IN THE HIJACK MYSTERY, WAYNE? OUTRAGEOUS! GE NEW INVESTIGATORS! WHAT DOES BATMAN KNOW OF TODAY'S CLEVER, SOPHISTICATED INDUSTRIAL PIRATES? HE'S JUST A COPS-AND-ROBBERS TYPE OPERATOR!
RIGHT! ABSOLUTELY!
GET RID OF THEM!
ORDER GENTL MEN, ORDE

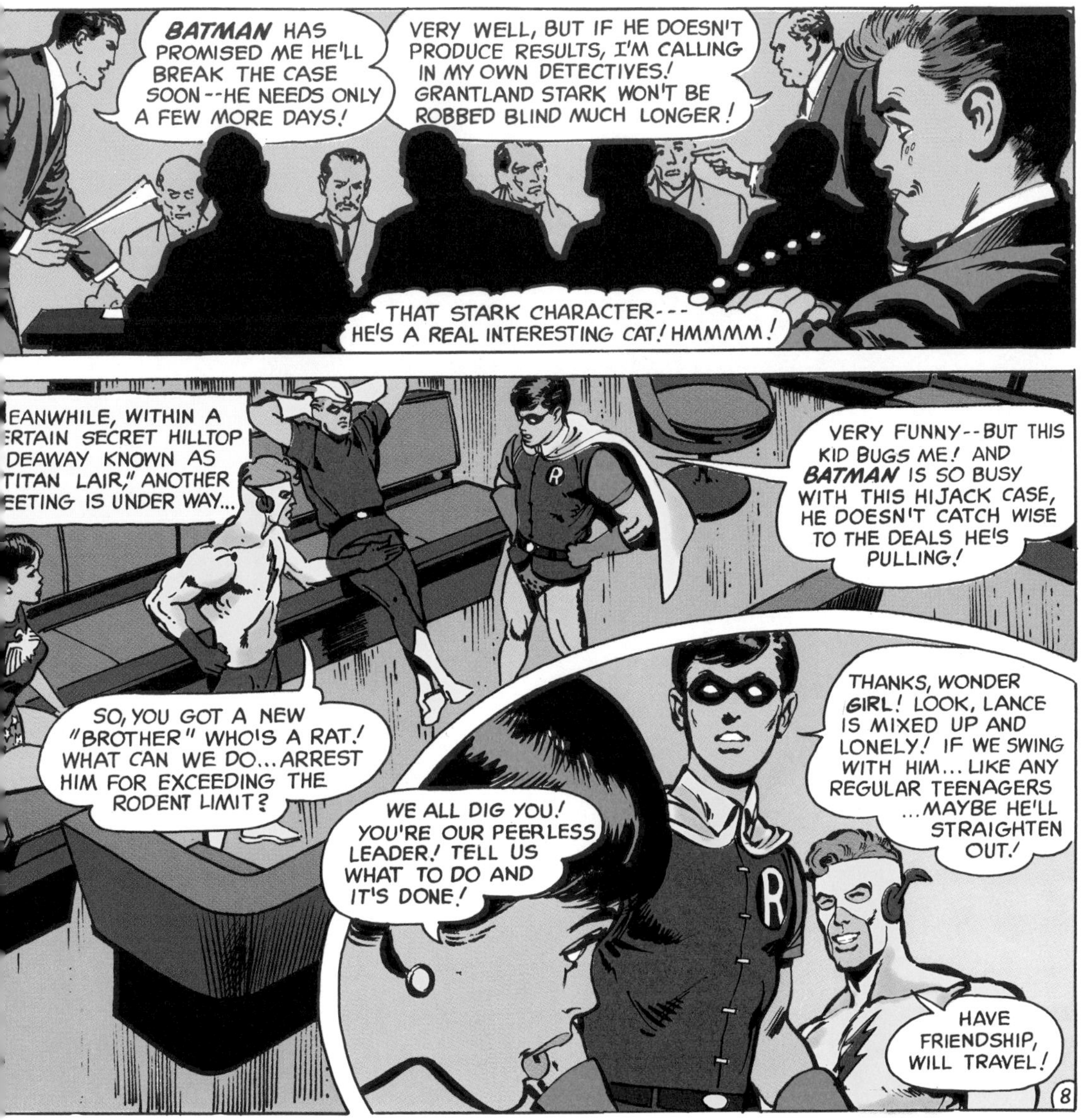
BATMAN HAS PROMISED ME HE'LL BREAK THE CASE SOON--HE NEEDS ONLY A FEW MORE DAYS!
VERY WELL, BUT IF HE DOESN'T PRODUCE RESULTS, I'M CALLING IN MY OWN DETECTIVES! GRANTLAND STARK WON'T BE ROBBED BLIND MUCH LONGER!
THAT STARK CHARACTER--- HE'S A REAL INTERESTING CAT! HMMMM!
EANWHILE, WITHIN A ERTAIN SECRET HILLTOP DEAWAY KNOWN AS TITAN LAIR," ANOTHER EETING IS UNDER WAY...
VERY FUNNY--BUT THIS KID BUGS ME! AND BATMAN IS SO BUSY WITH THIS HIJACK CASE, HE DOESN'T CATCH WISE TO THE DEALS HE'S PULLING!
SO, YOU GOT A NEW "BROTHER" WHO'S A RAT! WHAT CAN WE DO... ARREST HIM FOR EXCEEDING THE RODENT LIMIT?
WE ALL DIG YOU! YOU'RE OUR PEERLESS LEADER! TELL US WHAT TO DO AND IT'S DONE!
THANKS, WONDER GIRL! LOOK, LANCE IS MIXED UP AND LONELY! IF WE SWING WITH HIM... LIKE ANY REGULAR TEENAGERS ...MAYBE HE'LL STRAIGHTEN OUT!
HAVE FRIENDSHIP, WILL TRAVEL!
8

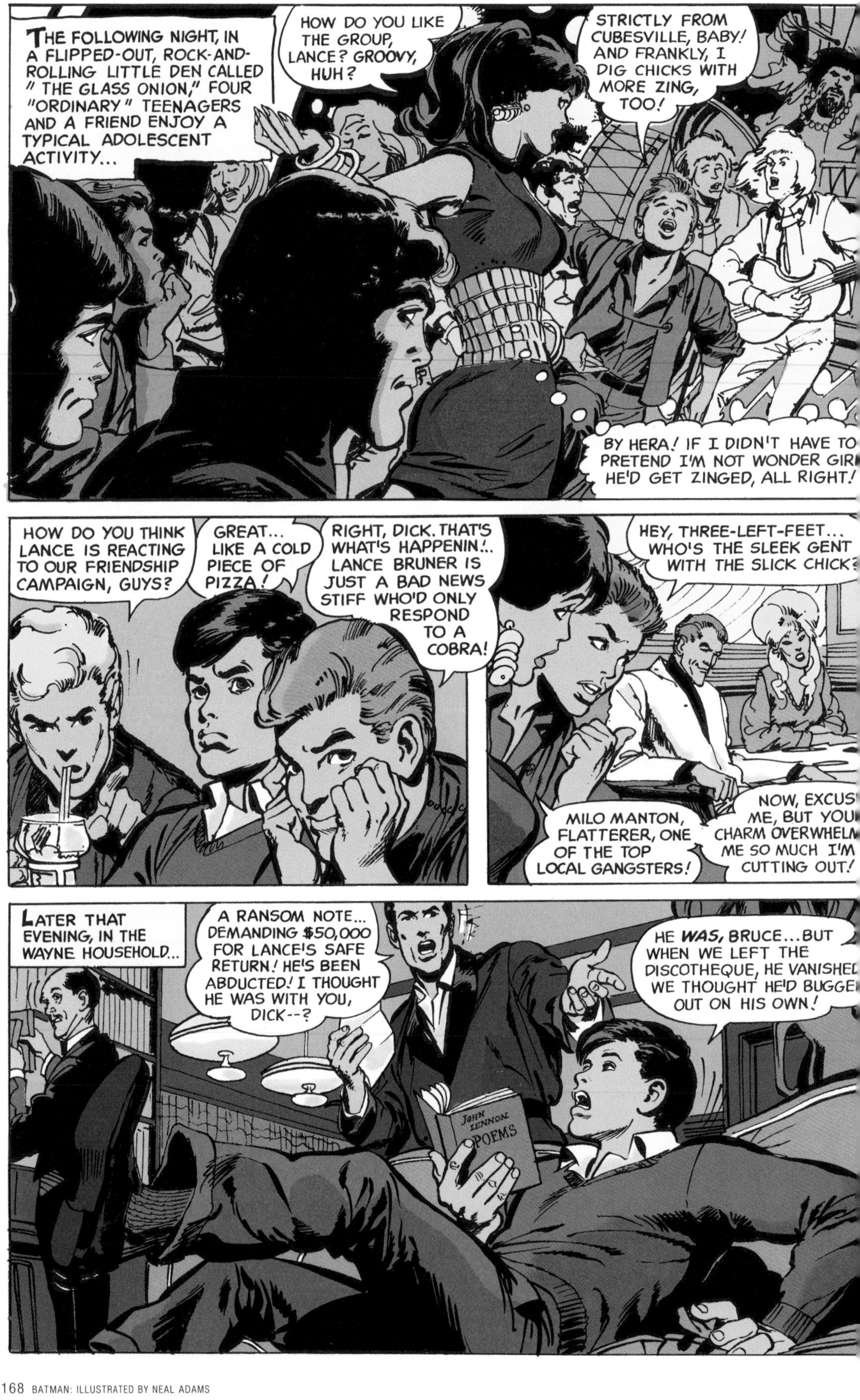
THE FOLLOWING NIGHT, IN A FLIPPED-OUT, ROCK-AND-ROLLING LITTLE DEN CALLED "THE GLASS ONION," FOUR "ORDINARY" TEENAGERS AND A FRIEND ENJOY A TYPICAL ADOLESCENT ACTIVITY...
HOW DO YOU LIKE THE GROUP, LANCE? GROOVY, HUH?
STRICTLY FROM CUBESVILLE, BABY! AND FRANKLY, I DIG CHICKS WITH MORE ZING, TOO!
BY HERA! IF I DIDN'T HAVE TO PRETEND I'M NOT WONDER GIR HE'D GET ZINGED, ALL RIGHT!
HOW DO YOU THINK LANCE IS REACTING TO OUR FRIENDSHIP CAMPAIGN, GUYS?
GREAT... LIKE A COLD PIECE OF PIZZA!
RIGHT, DICK. THAT'S WHAT'S HAPPENIN'.. LANCE BRUNER IS JUST A BAD NEWS STIFF WHO'D ONLY RESPOND TO A COBRA!
HEY, THREE-LEFT-FEET... WHO'S THE SLEEK GENT WITH THE SLICK CHICK?
MILO MANTON, FLATTERER, ONE OF THE TOP LOCAL GANGSTERS!
NOW, EXCUS ME, BUT YOU CHARM OVERWHELM ME SO MUCH I'M CUTTING OUT!
LATER THAT EVENING, IN THE WAYNE HOUSEHOLD...
A RANSOM NOTE... DEMANDING $50,000 FOR LANCE'S SAFE RETURN! HE'S BEEN ABDUCTED! I THOUGHT HE WAS WITH YOU, DICK--?
HE WAS, BRUCE... BUT WHEN WE LEFT THE DISCOTHEQUE, HE VANISHEI WE THOUGHT HE'D BUGGE OUT ON HIS OWN!
JOHN LENNON POEMS

SOMEONE KNOWS HE'S MY NEW WARD AND FIGURED I'D PAY FOR HIS RELEASE!

AS *BATMAN* AND ROBIN, WE COULD FIND HIM... I'M POSITIVE!

NO, IT MIGHT ENDANGER HIM! I COULDN'T LET ANYTHING HAPPEN TO LANCE! IT WOULD BE ON MY CONSCIENCE FOR THE REST OF MY LIFE! WE'LL HAVE TO PAY THE RANSOM!

SHORTLY, ON A DESERTED COUNTRY ROAD...

$50,000 FOR A BAD PENNY SEEMS HARDLY A FAIR TRADE!

AND NOT LONG AFTER...

HI, I'M BACK!

LANCE! THANK HEAVENS YOU'RE OKAY! TELL ME ALL ABOUT IT!

IT WAS ROUGH...THEY THREATENED TO KILL ME... I NEVER SAW THEIR FACES BUT I PLAYED IT COOL...

YEAH, HE'S BACK ALL RIGHT! LUCKY US! BUT I MUSTN'T GIVE UP TRYING TO CHANGE HIM! IT'D REALLY RACK BRUCE UP IF HE KNEW--! BETTER CALL ANOTHER MEETING OF THE TITANS!

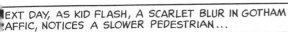

NEXT DAY, AS KID FLASH, A SCARLET BLUR IN GOTHAM TRAFFIC, NOTICES A SLOWER PEDESTRIAN...

WONDER WHAT ROBIN WANTS--? HUH? ENTERING THE BANK...IT'S LANCE BRUNER!

GOING INTO HIGH GEAR, THE JUNIOR WIZARD OF WHIZ VIBRATES INTO THE BANK, UNSEEN...

10

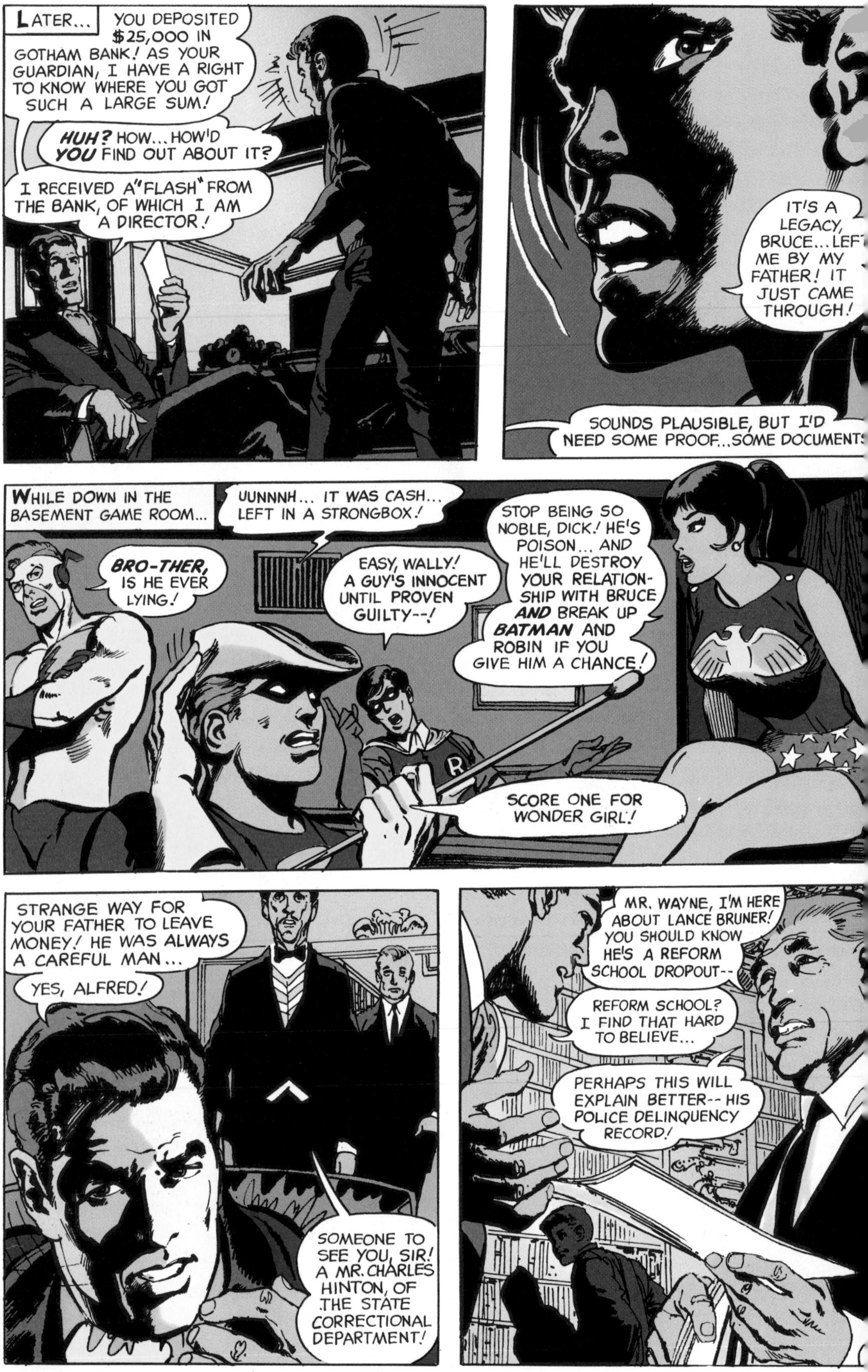
LATER...
YOU DEPOSITED $25,000 IN GOTHAM BANK! AS YOUR GUARDIAN, I HAVE A RIGHT TO KNOW WHERE YOU GOT SUCH A LARGE SUM!
HUH? HOW... HOW'D YOU FIND OUT ABOUT IT?
I RECEIVED A "FLASH" FROM THE BANK, OF WHICH I AM A DIRECTOR!
IT'S A LEGACY, BRUCE... LEFT ME BY MY FATHER! IT JUST CAME THROUGH!
SOUNDS PLAUSIBLE, BUT I'D NEED SOME PROOF... SOME DOCUMENTS
WHILE DOWN IN THE BASEMENT GAME ROOM...
UUNNNH... IT WAS CASH... LEFT IN A STRONGBOX!
BRO-THER, IS HE EVER LYING!
EASY, WALLY! A GUY'S INNOCENT UNTIL PROVEN GUILTY--!
STOP BEING SO NOBLE, DICK! HE'S POISON... AND HE'LL DESTROY YOUR RELATIONSHIP WITH BRUCE AND BREAK UP BATMAN AND ROBIN IF YOU GIVE HIM A CHANCE!
SCORE ONE FOR WONDER GIRL!
STRANGE WAY FOR YOUR FATHER TO LEAVE MONEY! HE WAS ALWAYS A CAREFUL MAN...
YES, ALFRED!
SOMEONE TO SEE YOU, SIR! A MR. CHARLES HINTON, OF THE STATE CORRECTIONAL DEPARTMENT!
MR. WAYNE, I'M HERE ABOUT LANCE BRUNER! YOU SHOULD KNOW HE'S A REFORM SCHOOL DROPOUT--
REFORM SCHOOL? I FIND THAT HARD TO BELIEVE...
PERHAPS THIS WILL EXPLAIN BETTER-- HIS POLICE DELINQUENCY RECORD!

LANCE, THIS RECORD... DOZENS OF INFRACTIONS! WHAT HAVE YOU TO SAY?

HE WAS ALSO KICKED OUT OF MILITARY ACADEMY! HIS FATHER DIED OF A BROKEN HEART, NOT IN AN ACCIDENT!

...LANCE BRUNER IS INCORRIGIBLE, MR. WAYNE! A BAD SEED! IT'S MY DUTY TO INFORM YOU OF THIS SINCE YOU ARE CONSIDERING LEGALLY ADOPTING HIM!

WERE **WE** EVER RIGHT ABOUT THAT CHARACTER!

SHHH! LET'S HEAR ON!

LANCE BRUNER, I AM EMPOWERED TO RETURN YOU TO LANESVILLE REFORMATORY TO--

NO! PLEASE! BRUCE... DON'T LET THEM DO THIS TO ME!

I BEG YOU, BRUCE! DON'T LET HIM TAKE ME AWAY! YEAH, IT'S TRUE... I DID ALL THOSE THINGS... INCLUDING THOSE BITS DICK TOOK THE RAP FOR, TOO! I... I EVEN ARRANGED FOR MILO MANTON TO KIDNAP ME... AND SPLIT THE RANSOM WITH HIM!

BUT IS IT MY FAULT I'M MESSED UP...WITH DAD ALWAYS AWAY ON EXPEDITIONS AND MOM DEAD SINCE I WAS ONLY TWO? I NEVER HAD ANYBODY TO SHOW ME THE RIGHT TRACK...STEER ME STRAIGHT...LIKE YOU, BRUCE!

I WANTED TO TELL YOU ABOUT MY PAST... BUT I WAS AFRAID TO SPOIL WHAT I FOUND HERE... RESPECT AND AFFECTION!

YOU PICKED AN ODD WAY OF RETURNING THAT AFFECTION, LANCE!

12

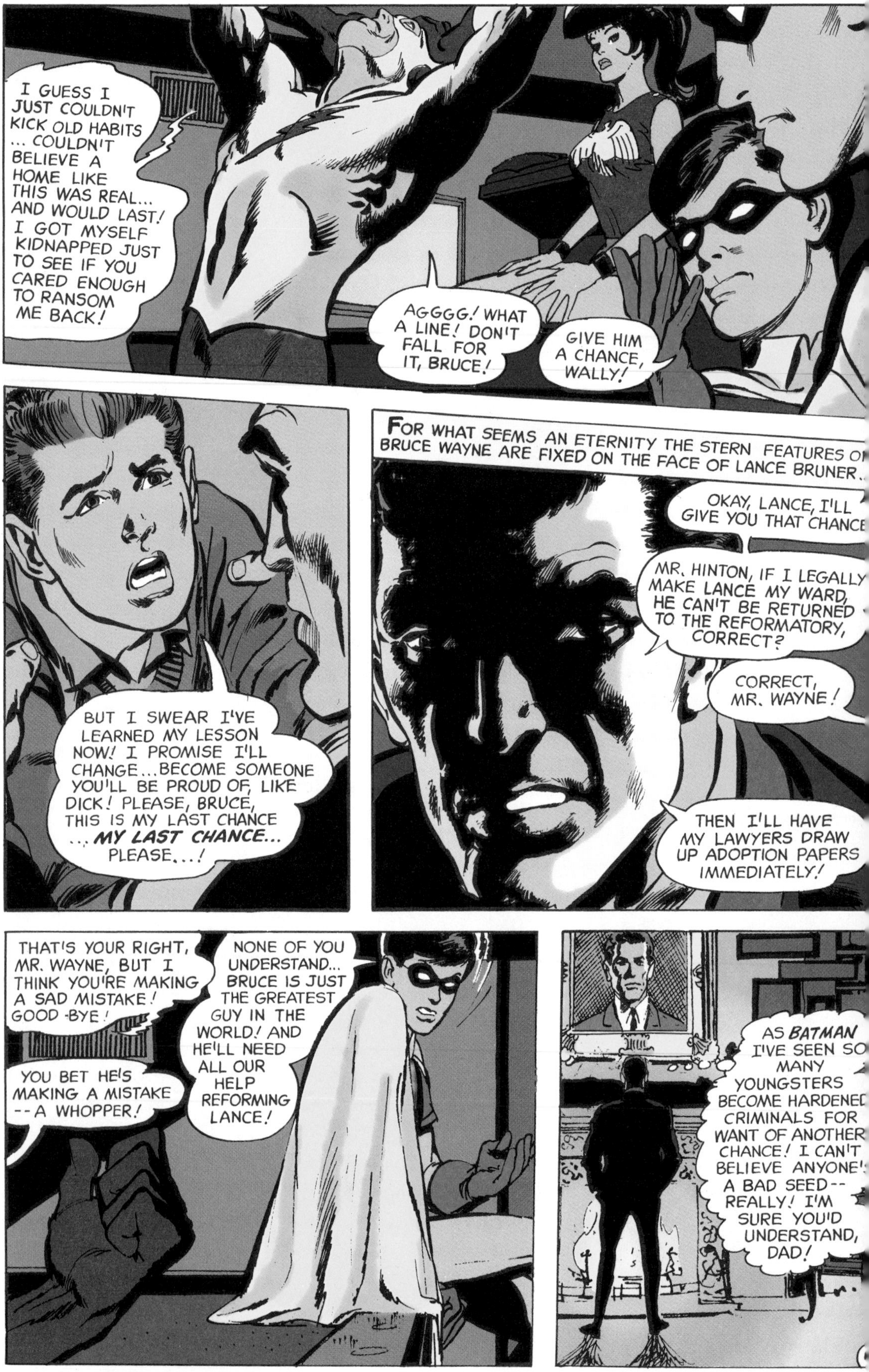
I GUESS I JUST COULDN'T KICK OLD HABITS ... COULDN'T BELIEVE A HOME LIKE THIS WAS REAL... AND WOULD LAST! I GOT MYSELF KIDNAPPED JUST TO SEE IF YOU CARED ENOUGH TO RANSOM ME BACK!
AGGGG! WHAT A LINE! DON'T FALL FOR IT, BRUCE!
GIVE HIM A CHANCE, WALLY!
BUT I SWEAR I'VE LEARNED MY LESSON NOW! I PROMISE I'LL CHANGE...BECOME SOMEONE YOU'LL BE PROUD OF, LIKE DICK! PLEASE, BRUCE, THIS IS MY LAST CHANCE ...MY LAST CHANCE... PLEASE...!
FOR WHAT SEEMS AN ETERNITY THE STERN FEATURES OF BRUCE WAYNE ARE FIXED ON THE FACE OF LANCE BRUNER..
OKAY, LANCE, I'LL GIVE YOU THAT CHANCE
MR. HINTON, IF I LEGALLY MAKE LANCE MY WARD, HE CAN'T BE RETURNED TO THE REFORMATORY, CORRECT?
CORRECT, MR. WAYNE!
THEN I'LL HAVE MY LAWYERS DRAW UP ADOPTION PAPERS IMMEDIATELY!
THAT'S YOUR RIGHT, MR. WAYNE, BUT I THINK YOU'RE MAKING A SAD MISTAKE! GOOD-BYE!
YOU BET HE'S MAKING A MISTAKE --A WHOPPER!
NONE OF YOU UNDERSTAND... BRUCE IS JUST THE GREATEST GUY IN THE WORLD! AND HE'LL NEED ALL OUR HELP REFORMING LANCE!
AS BATMAN I'VE SEEN SO MANY YOUNGSTERS BECOME HARDENED CRIMINALS FOR WANT OF ANOTHER CHANCE! I CAN'T BELIEVE ANYONE'S A BAD SEED-- REALLY! I'M SURE YOU'D UNDERSTAND, DAD!

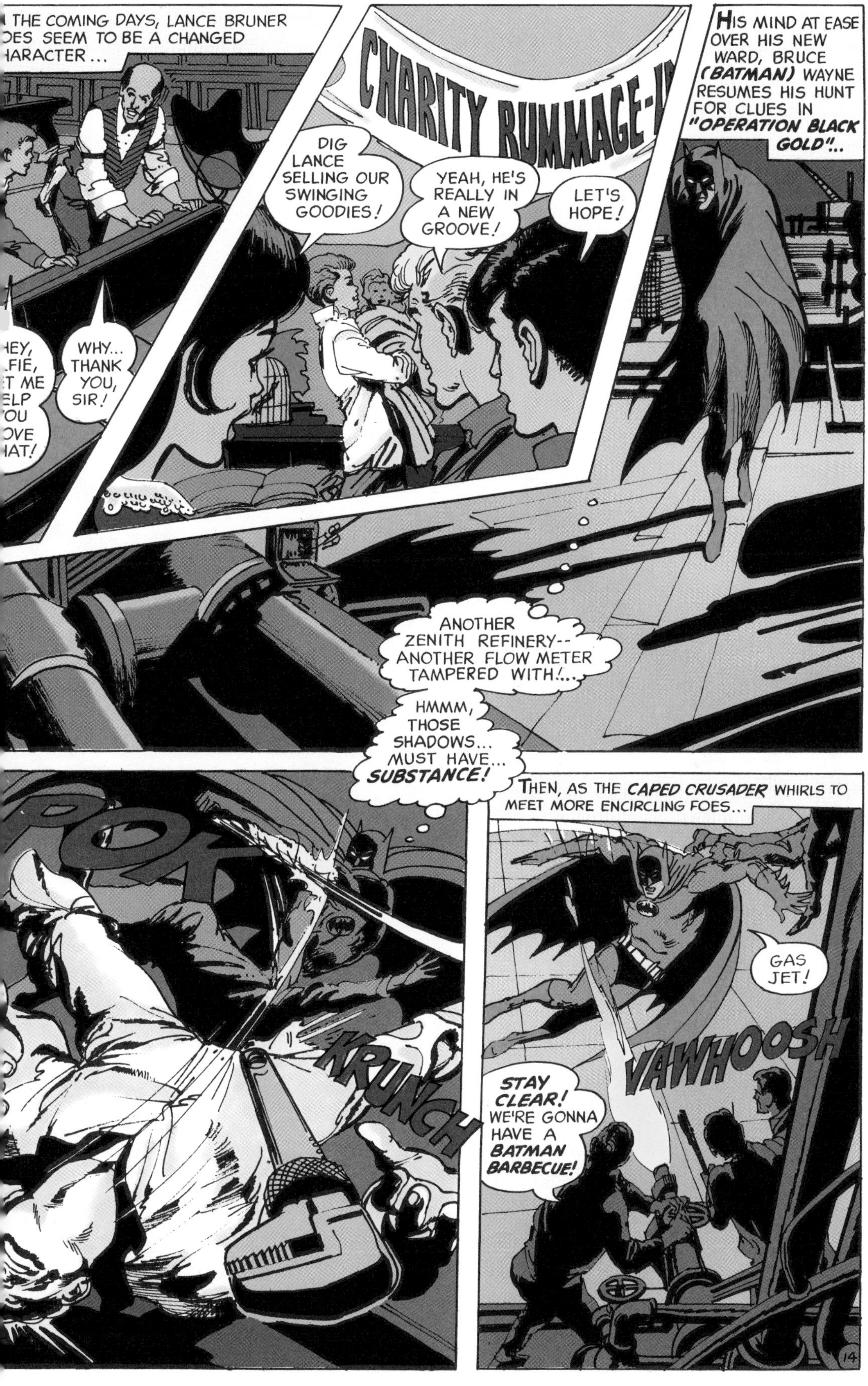

THE COMING DAYS, LANCE BRUNER
OES SEEM TO BE A CHANGED
HARACTER...
CHARITY RUMMAGE-
DIG LANCE SELLING OUR SWINGING GOODIES!
YEAH, HE'S REALLY IN A NEW GROOVE!
LET'S HOPE!
HIS MIND AT EASE OVER HIS NEW WARD, BRUCE (BATMAN) WAYNE RESUMES HIS HUNT FOR CLUES IN "OPERATION BLACK GOLD"!...
HEY,
FIE,
T ME
ELP
OU
OVE
HAT!
WHY... THANK YOU, SIR!
ANOTHER ZENITH REFINERY-- ANOTHER FLOW METER TAMPERED WITH!...
HMMM, THOSE SHADOWS... MUST HAVE... SUBSTANCE!
POK
KRUNCH
THEN, AS THE CAPED CRUSADER WHIRLS TO MEET MORE ENCIRCLING FOES...
GAS JET!
VAWHOOSH
STAY CLEAR! WE'RE GONNA HAVE A BATMAN BARBECUE!
14

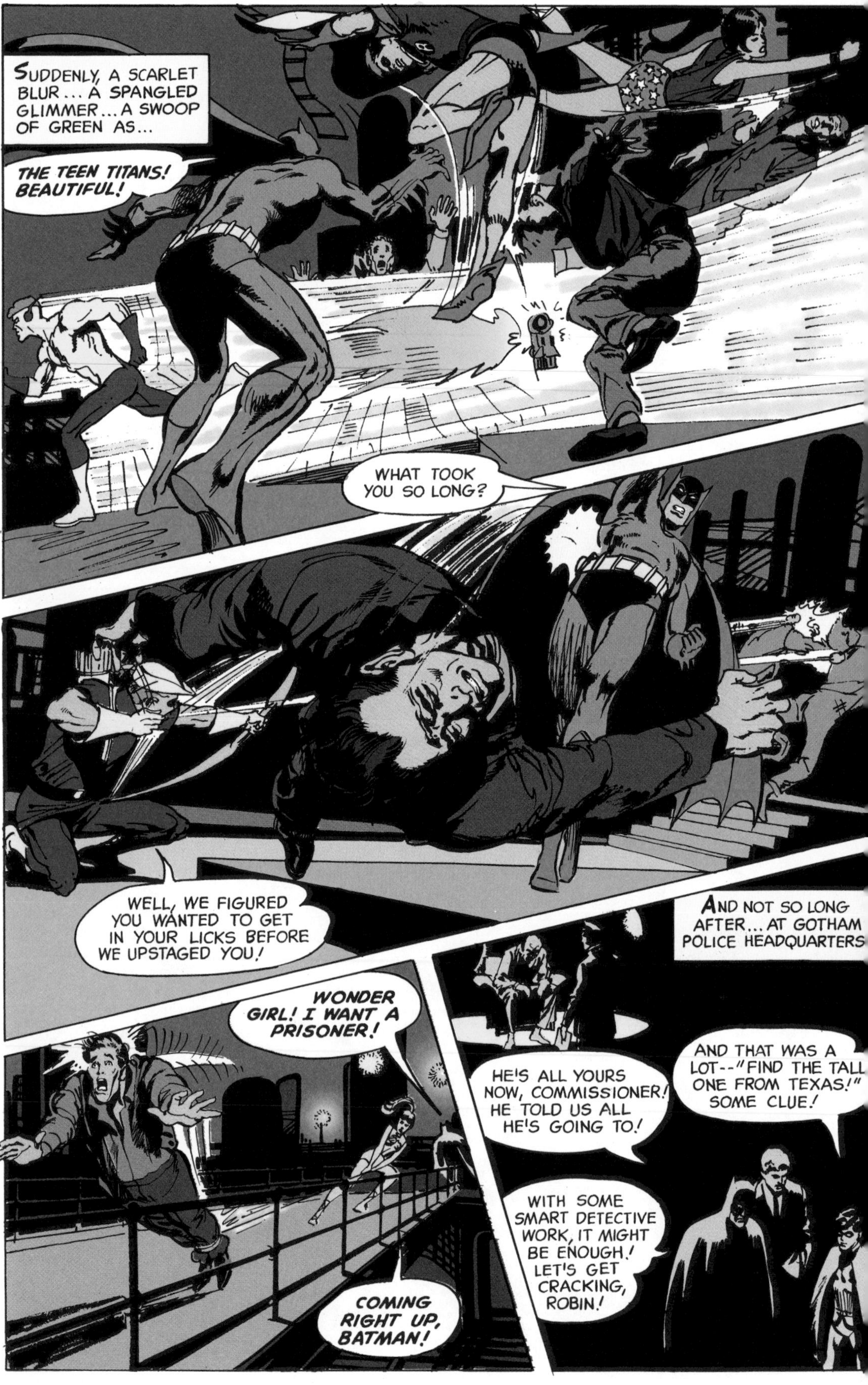
SUDDENLY, A SCARLET BLUR... A SPANGLED GLIMMER... A SWOOP OF GREEN AS...
THE TEEN TITANS! BEAUTIFUL!
WHAT TOOK YOU SO LONG?
WELL, WE FIGURED YOU WANTED TO GET IN YOUR LICKS BEFORE WE UPSTAGED YOU!
WONDER GIRL! I WANT A PRISONER!
COMING RIGHT UP, BATMAN!
AND NOT SO LONG AFTER... AT GOTHAM POLICE HEADQUARTERS
HE'S ALL YOURS NOW, COMMISSIONER! HE TOLD US ALL HE'S GOING TO!
AND THAT WAS A LOT--"FIND THE TALL ONE FROM TEXAS!" SOME CLUE!
WITH SOME SMART DETECTIVE WORK, IT MIGHT BE ENOUGH! LET'S GET CRACKING, ROBIN!

MEANTIME...

RRRRRR

BRUCE AND DICKIE-BOY... ALWAYS VANISHING SUDDENLY! ALFRED'S OUT SO I'LL SNOOP A BIT...!

HEY, A BUTTON OPENING A SECRET PANEL!? AND AN ELEVATOR SHAFT--!?

A CAVE...FULL OF GADGETS AND GIZMOS! THAT COWL AND CAPE! LANCE-BOY--YOU HIT IT... THE BIG PAYOLA! IT'S WILD BUT TRUE... MY EVER-LOVIN' FOOL OF A GUARDIAN IS... *BATMAN!* AND DICKIE-BOY... IS *ROBIN!*

I'VE GOT 'EM BOTH! I'LL MAKE 'EM PAY FOR HUMILIATING ME ...PATRONIZING ME... I'LL MAKE 'EM PAY THE MOST!

16

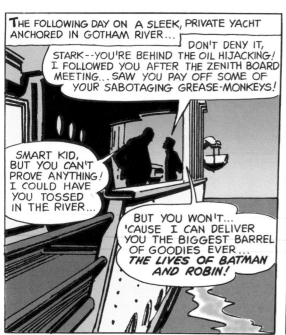

THE FOLLOWING DAY ON A SLEEK, PRIVATE YACHT ANCHORED IN GOTHAM RIVER...

DON'T DENY IT, STARK--YOU'RE BEHIND THE OIL HIJACKING! I FOLLOWED YOU AFTER THE ZENITH BOARD MEETING... SAW YOU PAY OFF SOME OF YOUR SABOTAGING GREASE-MONKEYS!

SMART KID, BUT YOU CAN'T PROVE ANYTHING! I COULD HAVE YOU TOSSED IN THE RIVER...

BUT YOU WON'T... 'CAUSE I CAN DELIVER YOU THE BIGGEST BARREL OF GOODIES EVER ... *THE LIVES OF BATMAN AND ROBIN!*

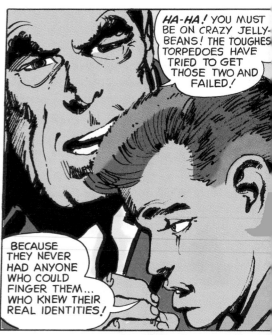

HA-HA! YOU MUST BE ON CRAZY JELLY-BEANS! THE TOUGHES[T] TORPEDOES HAVE TRIED TO GET THOSE TWO AND FAILED!

BECAUSE THEY NEVER HAD ANYONE WHO COULD FINGER THEM... WHO KNEW THEIR REAL IDENTITIES!

YOU MEAN, *YOU* KNOW WHO THEY ARE... CAN SET THEM UP? HOW? PROVE IT!

I GUARANTEE IT! I CAN'T TELL YOU HOW... YOU'LL HAVE TO TAKE MY WORD! BUT WHAT'VE YOU TO LOSE?

BATMAN AND THOSE TITANS ARE BREATHING TOO CLOSE! IF YOU CAN DELIVER, SONNY...WHAT DO YOU WANT-- MONEY FOR A NEW CAR, MAYBE?

NO PENNY-CANDY DEALS, STARK! $100,000 IN CASH DEPOSITED IN A SWISS BANK WHEN I SAY SO!

IT'S A DEAL, BRUNER! WISH I HA[D] A KID LIKE YOU--TOUGH, CLEVER...

NO THANKS, BIG DADDY, 'CAUSE STRANGE AS IT SOUNDS, I DON'T DIG YOU AT ALL! YOU'RE TOO MUCH LIKE ME!

"OUR ONLY CLUE TO THE HIJACK RING-- 'THE TALL ONE FROM TEXAS!' EVEN THE BATCOMPUTER'S DRAWN A BLANK CARD ON THAT!

AND THIS MAP OF OIL PIPELINES AND TANKER ROUTES IS NO GREAT HELP, OR....*IS IT!?*

BATMAN! LOOK!

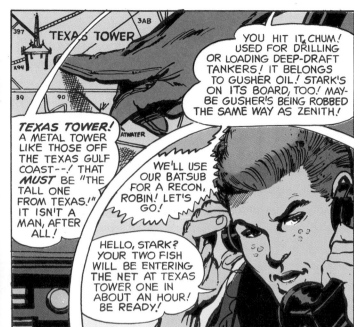

TEXAS TOWER

TEXAS TOWER! A METAL TOWER LIKE THOSE OFF THE TEXAS GULF COAST--! THAT *MUST* BE "THE TALL ONE FROM TEXAS!" IT ISN'T A MAN, AFTER ALL!

YOU HIT IT, CHUM! USED FOR DRILLING OR LOADING DEEP-DRAFT TANKERS! IT BELONGS TO GUSHER OIL! STARK'S ON ITS BOARD, TOO! MAYBE GUSHER'S BEING ROBBED THE SAME WAY AS ZENITH!

WE'LL USE OUR BATSUB FOR A RECON, ROBIN! LET'S GO!

HELLO, STARK? YOUR TWO FISH WILL BE ENTERING THE NET AT TEXAS TOWER ONE IN ABOUT AN HOUR! BE READY!

As THE BATSUB LEAVES ITS SECRET PEN AND MOVES UNSEEN OUT OF GOTHAM HARBOR...

I WANT TO SEE THIS MYSELF-- WATCH THEIR SMUG FACES WHEN THEY GET IT AND KNOW IT'S BEEN ME, LANCE BRUNER, WHO SENT THE MIGHTY DUO TO THEIR FINISH!

WE'RE NEAR THE TOWER, *BATMAN!* LOOK! A FLEXIBLE PIPELINE!

THE KIND USED IN INVASIONS TO CARRY FUEL TO A BEACH! LOOKS LIKE THE RIGHT TRACK, ROBIN!

18

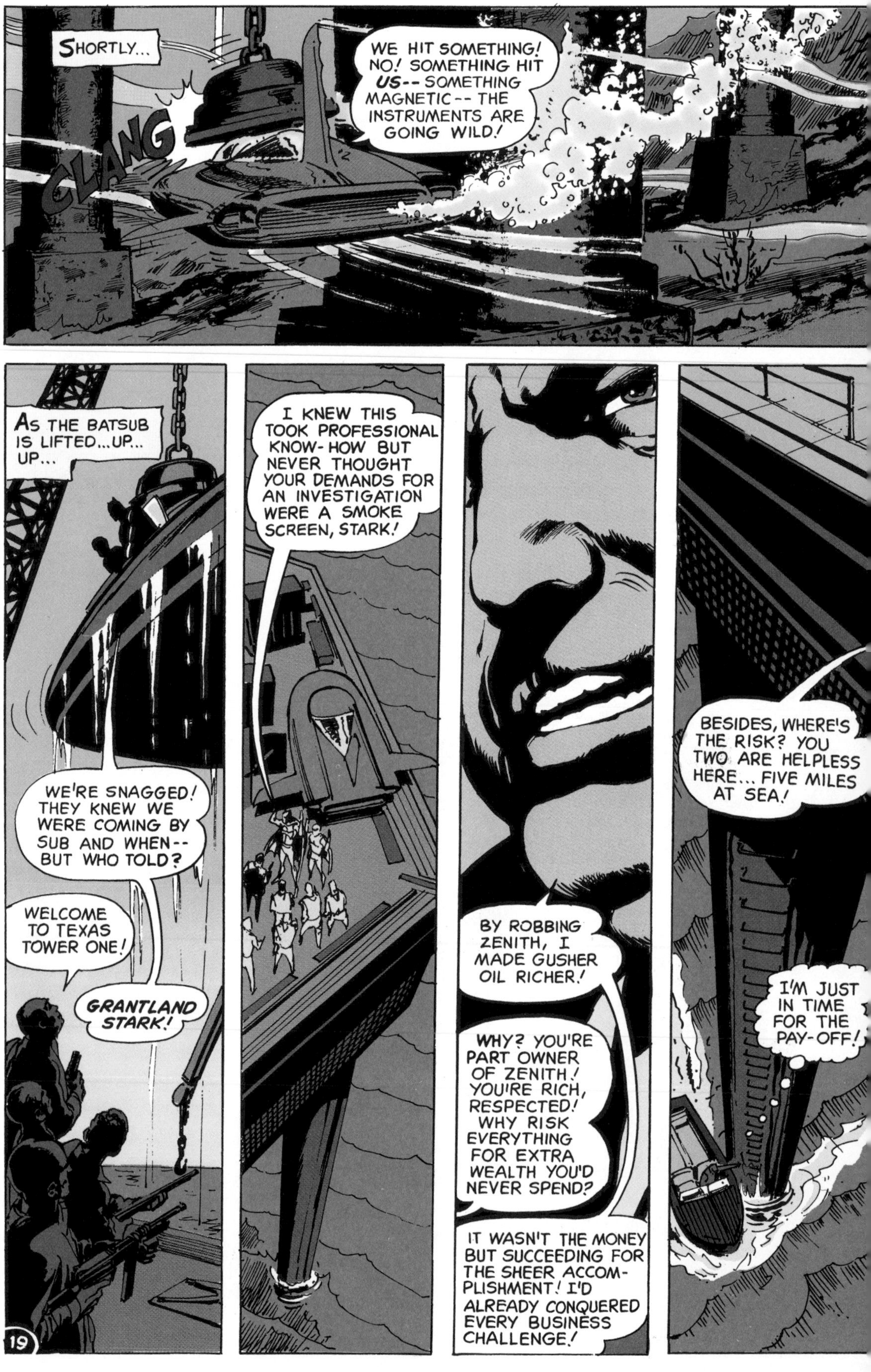
SHORTLY...
CLANG
WE HIT SOMETHING! NO! SOMETHING HIT US-- SOMETHING MAGNETIC-- THE INSTRUMENTS ARE GOING WILD!
AS THE BATSUB IS LIFTED...UP... UP...
WE'RE SNAGGED! THEY KNEW WE WERE COMING BY SUB AND WHEN-- BUT WHO TOLD?
WELCOME TO TEXAS TOWER ONE!
GRANTLAND STARK!
I KNEW THIS TOOK PROFESSIONAL KNOW-HOW BUT NEVER THOUGHT YOUR DEMANDS FOR AN INVESTIGATION WERE A SMOKE SCREEN, STARK!
BY ROBBING ZENITH, I MADE GUSHER OIL RICHER!
WHY? YOU'RE PART OWNER OF ZENITH! YOU'RE RICH, RESPECTED! WHY RISK EVERYTHING FOR EXTRA WEALTH YOU'D NEVER SPEND?
IT WASN'T THE MONEY BUT SUCCEEDING FOR THE SHEER ACCOMPLISHMENT! I'D ALREADY CONQUERED EVERY BUSINESS CHALLENGE!
BESIDES, WHERE'S THE RISK? YOU TWO ARE HELPLESS HERE... FIVE MILES AT SEA!
I'M JUST IN TIME FOR THE PAY-OFF!
19

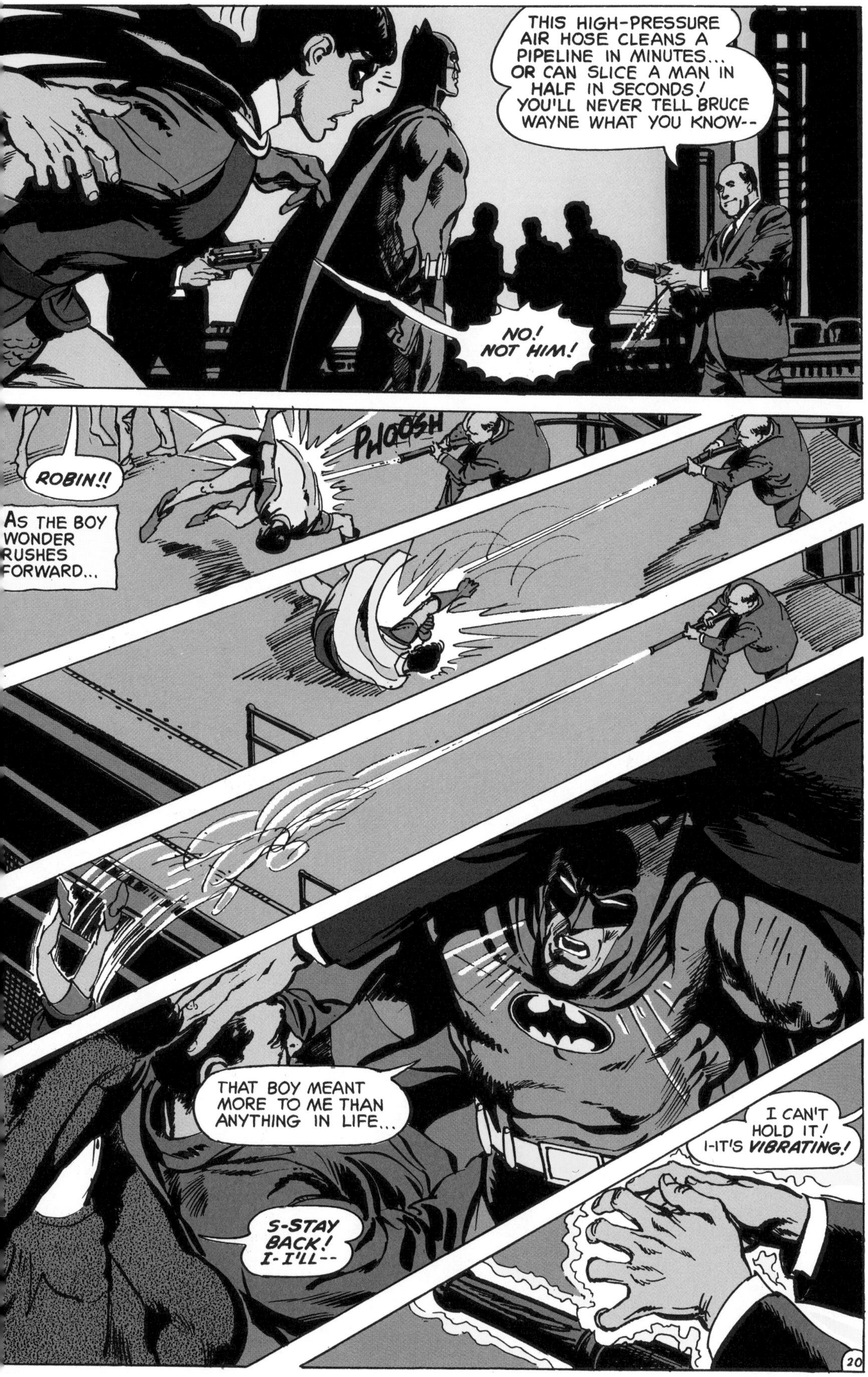
THIS HIGH-PRESSURE AIR HOSE CLEANS A PIPELINE IN MINUTES... OR CAN SLICE A MAN IN HALF IN SECONDS! YOU'LL NEVER TELL BRUCE WAYNE WHAT YOU KNOW--
NO! NOT HIM!
ROBIN!!
AS THE BOY WONDER RUSHES FORWARD...
PHOOSH
THAT BOY MEANT MORE TO ME THAN ANYTHING IN LIFE...
I CAN'T HOLD IT! I-IT'S VIBRATING!
S-STAY BACK! I-I'LL--
20

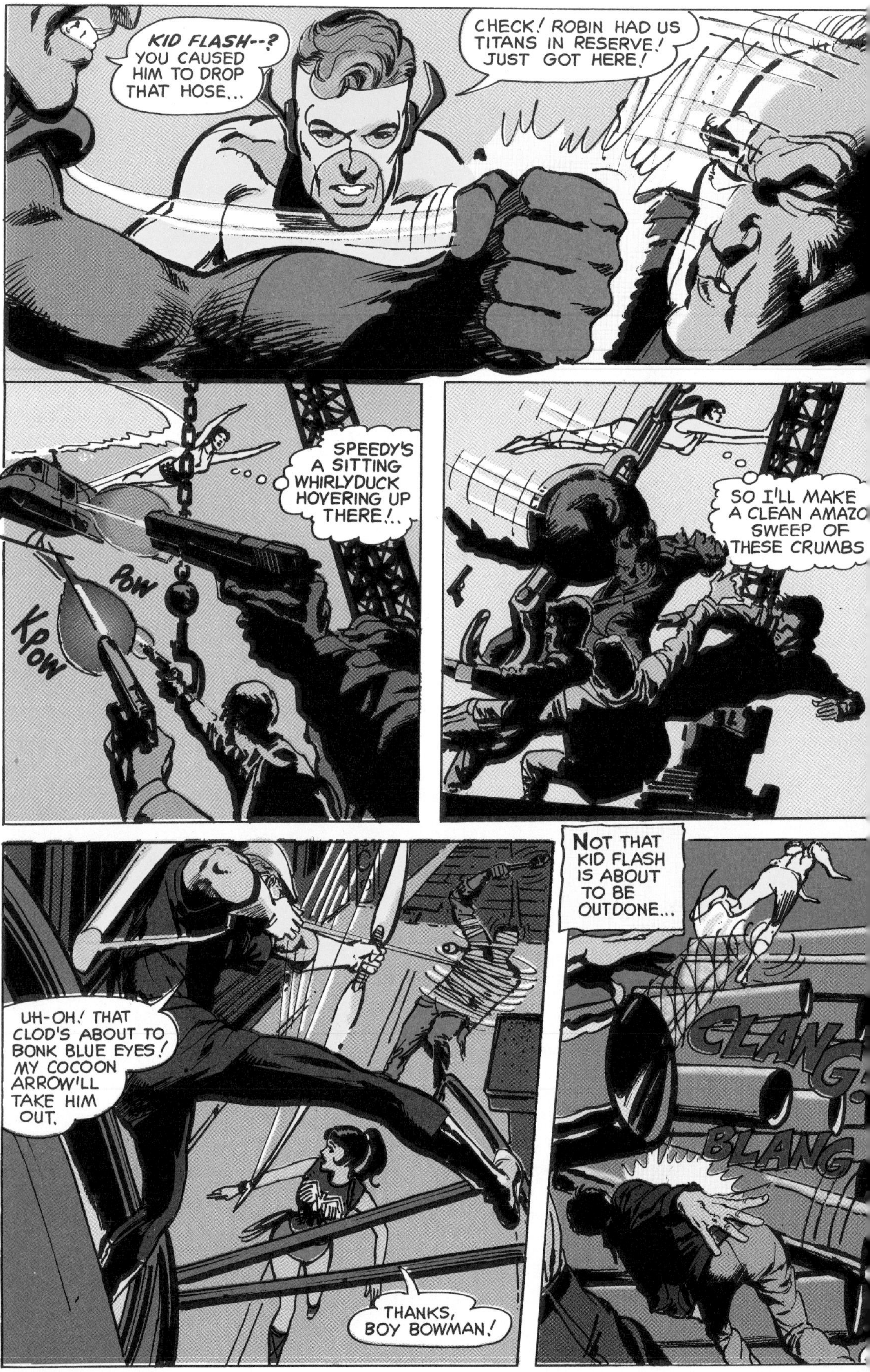
KID FLASH--? YOU CAUSED HIM TO DROP THAT HOSE...
CHECK! ROBIN HAD US TITANS IN RESERVE! JUST GOT HERE!
SPEEDY'S A SITTING WHIRLYDUCK HOVERING UP THERE!..
POW
KPOW
SO I'LL MAKE A CLEAN AMAZO SWEEP OF THESE CRUMBS
UH-OH! THAT CLOD'S ABOUT TO BONK BLUE EYES! MY COCOON ARROW'LL TAKE HIM OUT.
THANKS, BOY BOWMAN!
NOT THAT KID FLASH IS ABOUT TO BE OUTDONE...
CLANG
BLANG

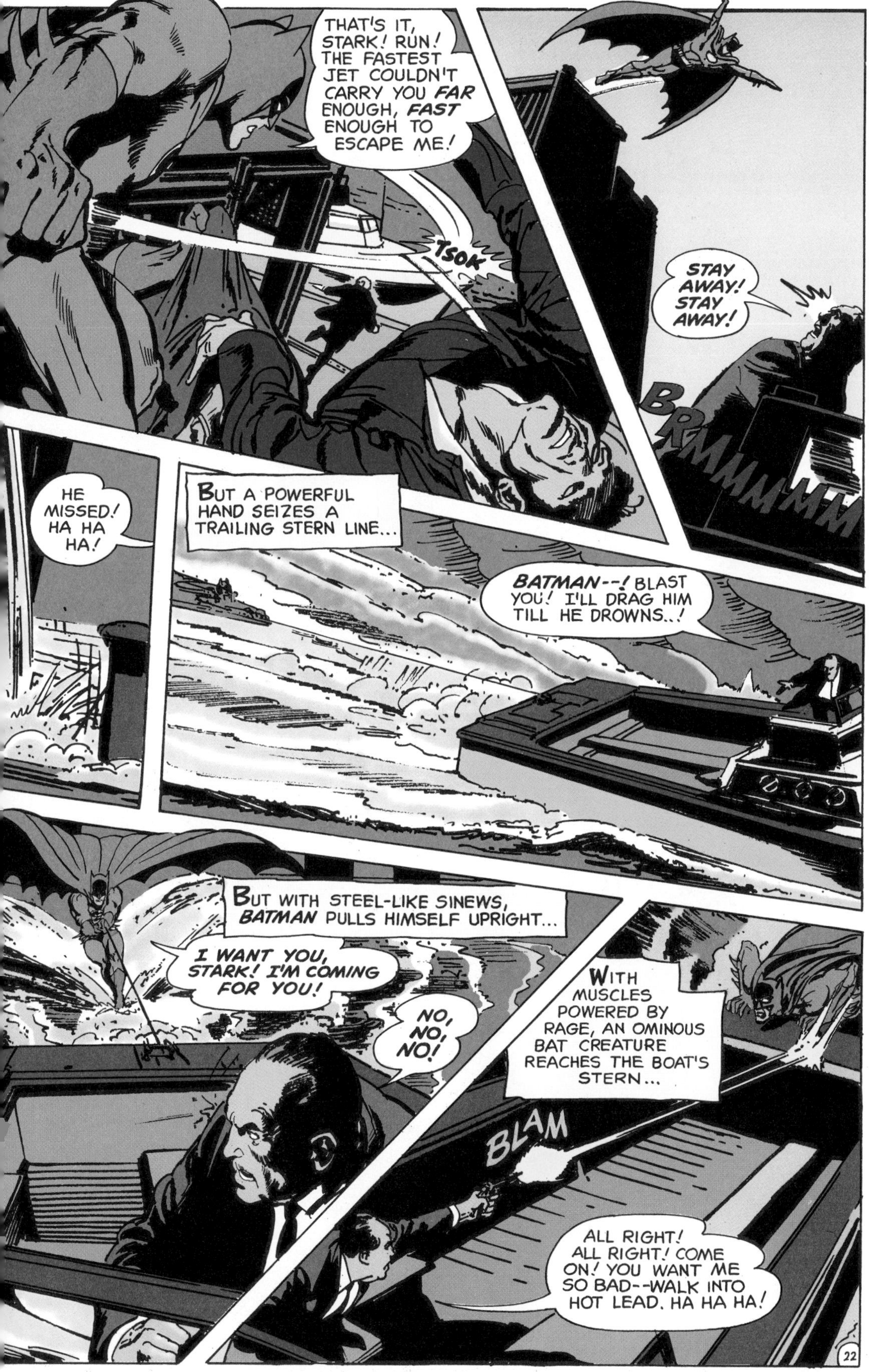
THAT'S IT, STARK! RUN! THE FASTEST JET COULDN'T CARRY YOU FAR ENOUGH, FAST ENOUGH TO ESCAPE ME!
TSOK
STAY AWAY! STAY AWAY!
BRMMMMMM
HE MISSED! HA HA HA!
BUT A POWERFUL HAND SEIZES A TRAILING STERN LINE...
BATMAN--! BLAST YOU! I'LL DRAG HIM TILL HE DROWNS..!
BUT WITH STEEL-LIKE SINEWS, BATMAN PULLS HIMSELF UPRIGHT...
I WANT YOU, STARK! I'M COMING FOR YOU!
NO, NO, NO!
WITH MUSCLES POWERED BY RAGE, AN OMINOUS BAT CREATURE REACHES THE BOAT'S STERN...
BLAM
ALL RIGHT! ALL RIGHT! COME ON! YOU WANT ME SO BAD--WALK INTO HOT LEAD. HA HA HA!
22

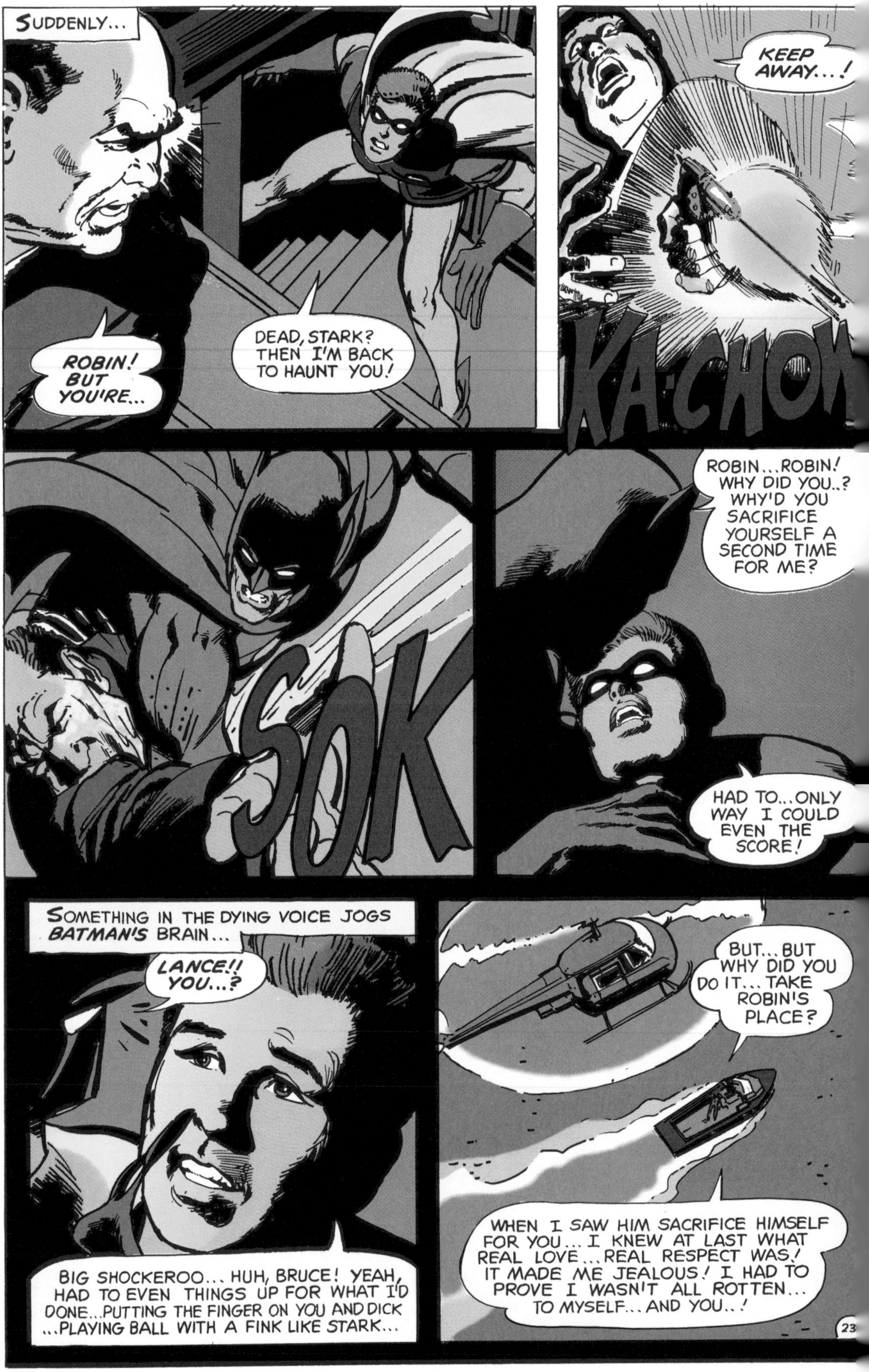
SUDDENLY...
ROBIN! BUT YOU'RE...
DEAD, STARK? THEN I'M BACK TO HAUNT YOU!
KEEP AWAY...!
KA-CHOM
SOK
ROBIN...ROBIN! WHY DID YOU..? WHY'D YOU SACRIFICE YOURSELF A SECOND TIME FOR ME?
HAD TO...ONLY WAY I COULD EVEN THE SCORE!
SOMETHING IN THE DYING VOICE JOGS BATMAN'S BRAIN...
LANCE!! YOU...?
BIG SHOCKEROO... HUH, BRUCE! YEAH, HAD TO EVEN THINGS UP FOR WHAT I'D DONE...PUTTING THE FINGER ON YOU AND DICK ...PLAYING BALL WITH A FINK LIKE STARK...
BUT...BUT WHY DID YOU DO IT... TAKE ROBIN'S PLACE?
WHEN I SAW HIM SACRIFICE HIMSELF FOR YOU... I KNEW AT LAST WHAT REAL LOVE...REAL RESPECT WAS! IT MADE ME JEALOUS! I HAD TO PROVE I WASN'T ALL ROTTEN... TO MYSELF... AND YOU...!
23

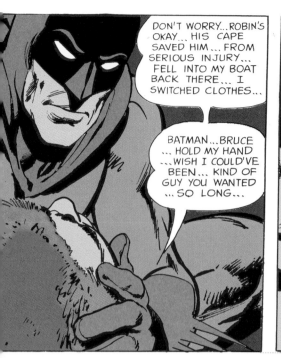

DON'T WORRY...ROBIN'S OKAY... HIS CAPE SAVED HIM... FROM SERIOUS INJURY... FELL INTO MY BOAT BACK THERE... I SWITCHED CLOTHES...

BATMAN...BRUCE ...HOLD MY HAND ...WISH I COULD'VE BEEN... KIND OF GUY YOU WANTED ...SO LONG...

SO LONG, LANCE... AND BELIEVE ME... YOU *WERE* THAT KIND OF HUMAN BEING ...DOWN DEEP INSIDE! YOU JUST NEVER HAD ENOUGH OF A CHANCE!

AND SO, LATER, IN THE PEACE OF WAYNE MANOR...

HE CAME INTO OUR LIVES LIKE A DESTRUCTIVE WHIRLWIND-- BUT HE LEFT IT IN A BLAZE OF HOPE! WE'LL NEVER FORGET HIM!

AND THANKS FOR *YOUR* HELP, TITANS!

ANYTIME!

THE END.

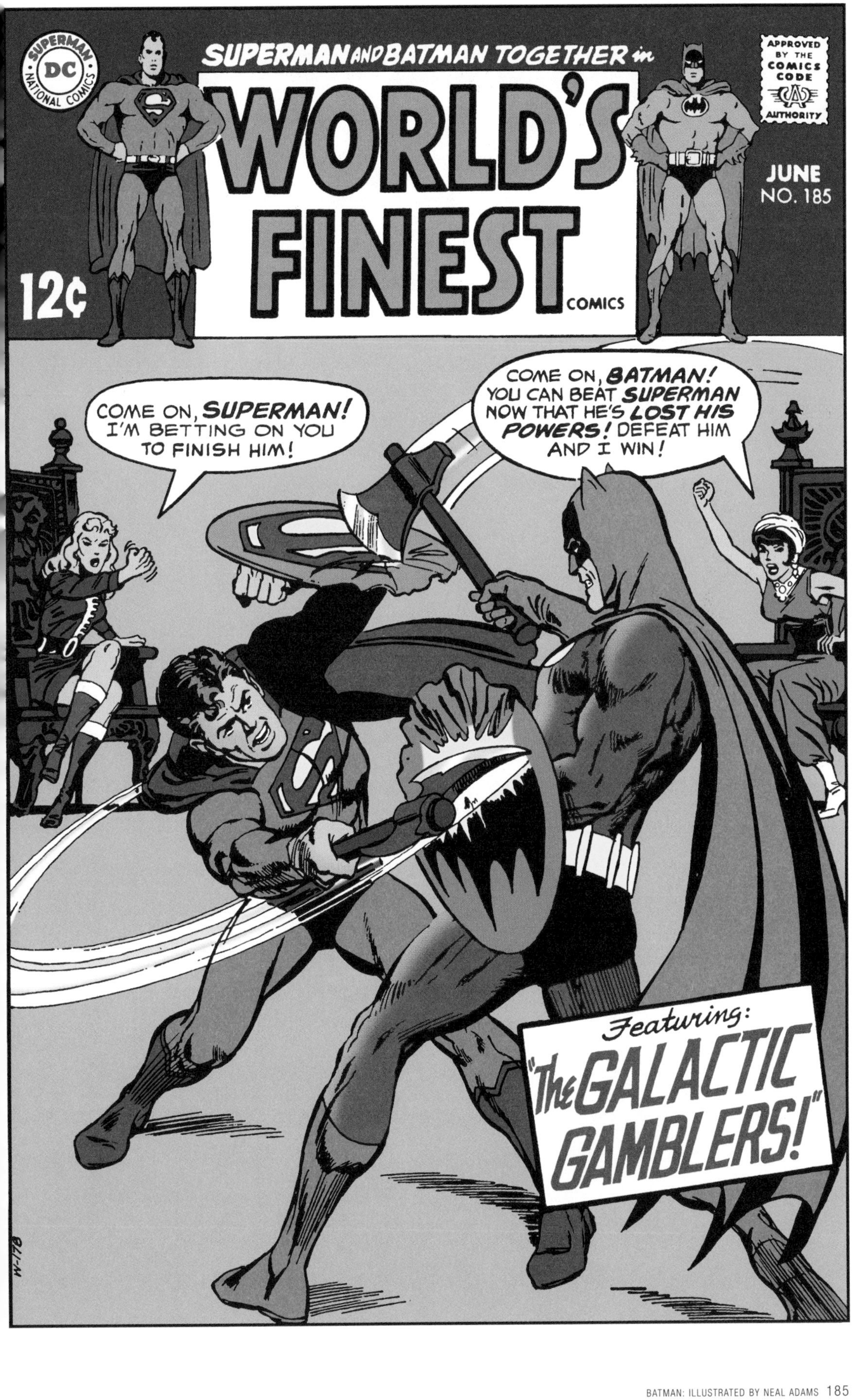
SUPERMAN
DC
NATIONAL COMICS
SUPERMAN AND BATMAN TOGETHER in
WORLD'S FINEST
COMICS
APPROVED BY THE COMICS CODE AUTHORITY
JUNE
NO. 185
12¢
COME ON, SUPERMAN! I'M BETTING ON YOU TO FINISH HIM!
COME ON, BATMAN! YOU CAN BEAT SUPERMAN NOW THAT HE'S LOST HIS POWERS! DEFEAT HIM AND I WIN!
Featuring:
"The GALACTIC GAMBLERS!"
W-178

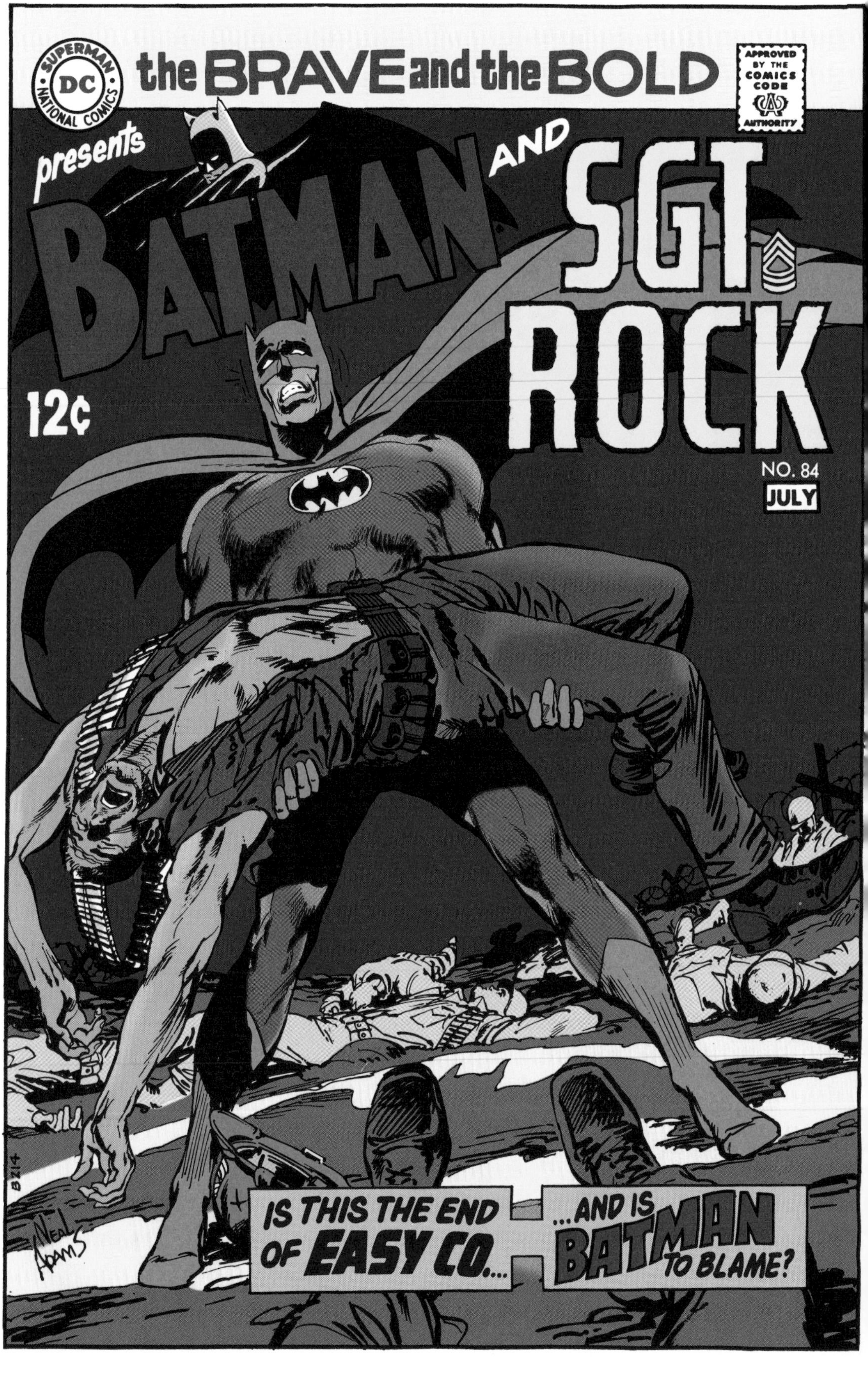
SUPERMAN
DC
NATIONAL COMICS
the BRAVE and the BOLD
APPROVED BY THE COMICS CODE AUTHORITY
presents
BATMAN AND SGT. ROCK
12¢
NO. 84
JULY
IS THIS THE END OF EASY CO...
...AND IS BATMAN TO BLAME?
NEAL ADAMS
B214

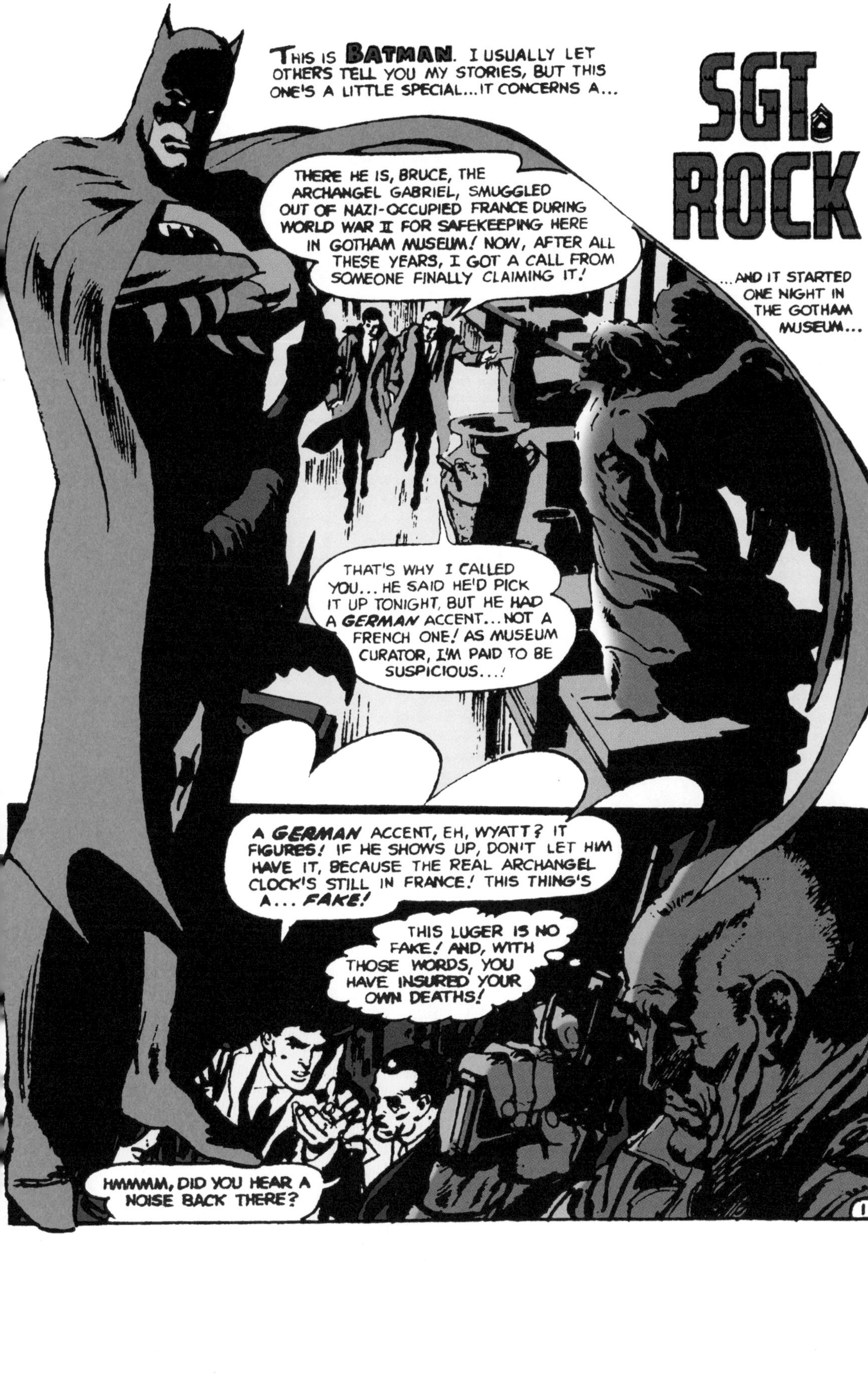
THIS IS BATMAN. I USUALLY LET OTHERS TELL YOU MY STORIES, BUT THIS ONE'S A LITTLE SPECIAL...IT CONCERNS A...
SGT. ROCK
THERE HE IS, BRUCE, THE ARCHANGEL GABRIEL, SMUGGLED OUT OF NAZI-OCCUPIED FRANCE DURING WORLD WAR II FOR SAFEKEEPING HERE IN GOTHAM MUSEUM! NOW, AFTER ALL THESE YEARS, I GOT A CALL FROM SOMEONE FINALLY CLAIMING IT!
...AND IT STARTED ONE NIGHT IN THE GOTHAM MUSEUM...
THAT'S WHY I CALLED YOU... HE SAID HE'D PICK IT UP TONIGHT, BUT HE HAD A GERMAN ACCENT...NOT A FRENCH ONE! AS MUSEUM CURATOR, I'M PAID TO BE SUSPICIOUS...!
A GERMAN ACCENT, EH, WYATT? IT FIGURES! IF HE SHOWS UP, DON'T LET HIM HAVE IT, BECAUSE THE REAL ARCHANGEL CLOCK'S STILL IN FRANCE! THIS THING'S A... FAKE!
THIS LUGER IS NO FAKE! AND, WITH THOSE WORDS, YOU HAVE INSURED YOUR OWN DEATHS!
HMMMM, DID YOU HEAR A NOISE BACK THERE?
1

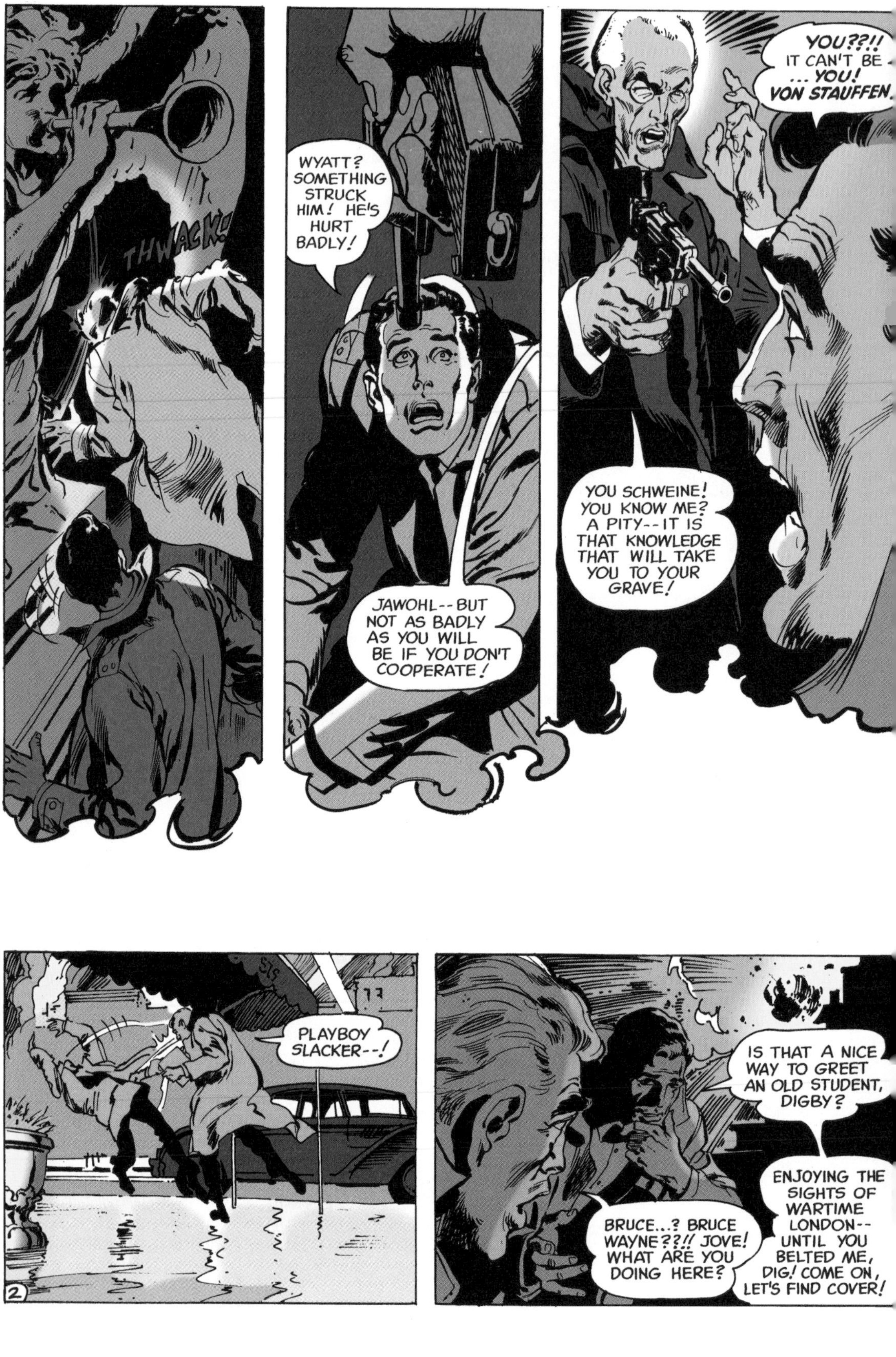
THWACK!
WYATT? SOMETHING STRUCK HIM! HE'S HURT BADLY!
JAWOHL--BUT NOT AS BADLY AS YOU WILL BE IF YOU DON'T COOPERATE!
YOU??!! IT CAN'T BE ... YOU! VON STAUFFEN.
YOU SCHWEINE! YOU KNOW ME? A PITY--IT IS THAT KNOWLEDGE THAT WILL TAKE YOU TO YOUR GRAVE!
2
PLAYBOY SLACKER--!
IS THAT A NICE WAY TO GREET AN OLD STUDENT, DIGBY?
BRUCE...? BRUCE WAYNE??!! JOVE! WHAT ARE YOU DOING HERE?
ENJOYING THE SIGHTS OF WARTIME LONDON--UNTIL YOU BELTED ME, DIG! COME ON, LET'S FIND COVER!

THEY SAY WHEN A MAN IS ABOUT TO DIE HIS WHOLE LIFE FLASHES BEFORE HIM, BUT MY LIFE HAS BEEN MORE CROWDED THAN MOST! ONE PART--ONE UNTOLD CHAPTER--WHICH BEGAN WITH THE WAIL OF SIRENS IN WARTIME LONDON... CAME TO ME: IN MY *CASE FILE* LABELED...

The ANGEL, the ROCK and the COWL!

WHEEEEOOO

YOU BLOOMIN' YOUNG IDIOT... TURN OFF THOSE LIGHTS! THERE'S A RAID ON!

IS THERE? NEXT YOU'LL TELL ME THERE'S A WAR ON, FRIEND!

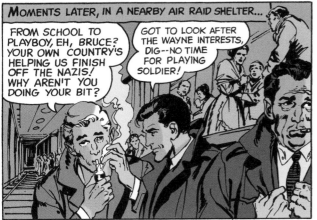

MOMENTS LATER, IN A NEARBY AIR RAID SHELTER...

FROM SCHOOL TO PLAYBOY, EH, BRUCE? YOUR OWN COUNTRY'S HELPING US FINISH OFF THE NAZIS! WHY AREN'T YOU DOING YOUR BIT?

GOT TO LOOK AFTER THE WAYNE INTERESTS, DIG--NO TIME FOR PLAYING SOLDIER!

CAN'T TELL HIM THAT, AS *BATMAN*, I'M WORKING FOR UNCLE SAM TRACKING DOWN WAR SABOTEURS--AND THAT I'M HERE OBSERVING BRITISH METHODS, USING MY WAYNE IDENTITY AS A COVER!

BUT I SURE WISH I COULD CHANGE THAT LOOK IN HIS EYE--!

ALL CLEAR! ALL CLEAR!

3

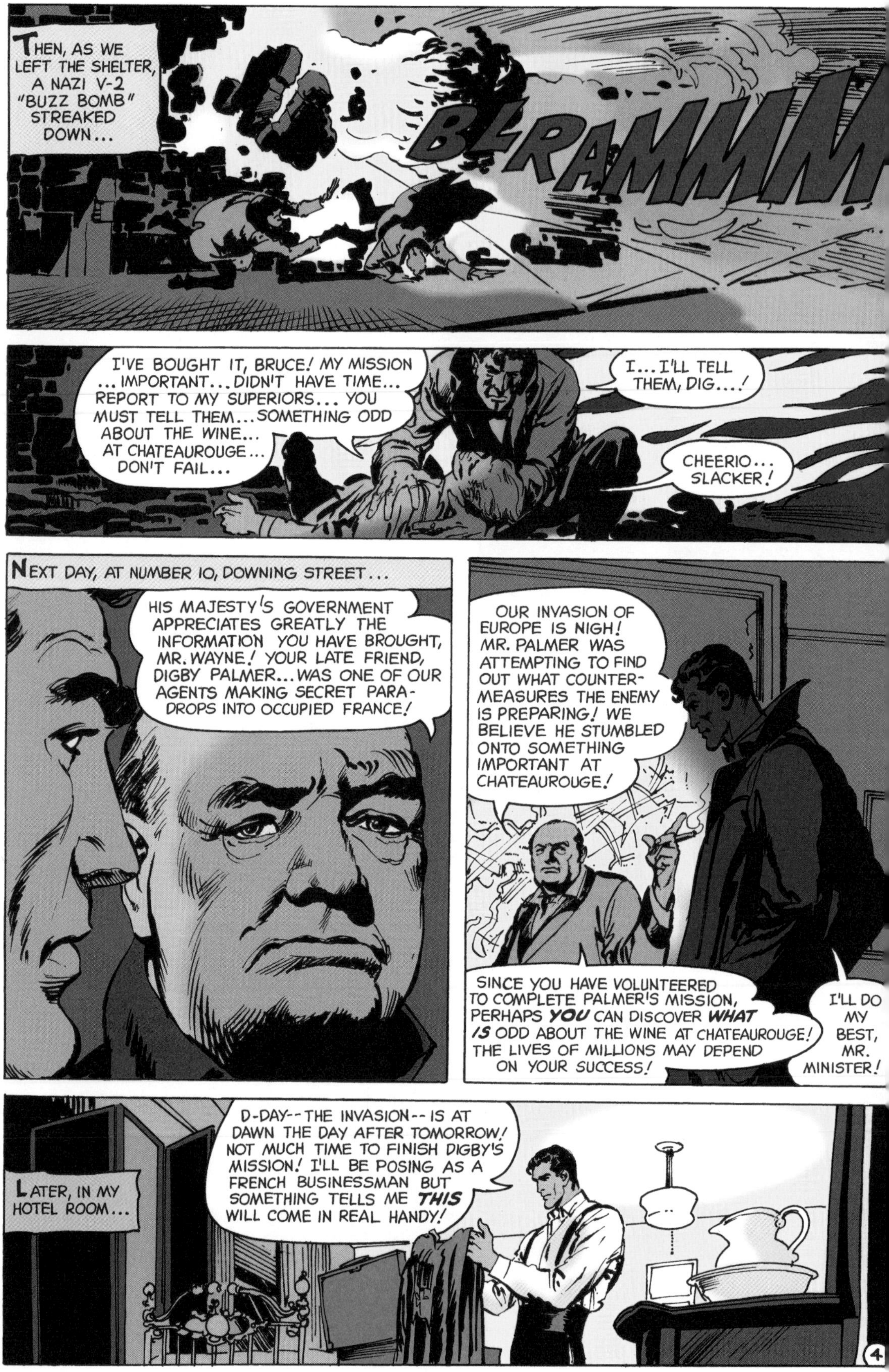
THEN, AS WE LEFT THE SHELTER, A NAZI V-2 "BUZZ BOMB" STREAKED DOWN...
BLRAMMMM
I'VE BOUGHT IT, BRUCE! MY MISSION ...IMPORTANT...DIDN'T HAVE TIME... REPORT TO MY SUPERIORS... YOU MUST TELL THEM...SOMETHING ODD ABOUT THE WINE... AT CHATEAUROUGE... DON'T FAIL...
I...I'LL TELL THEM, DIG...!
CHEERIO... SLACKER!
NEXT DAY, AT NUMBER 10, DOWNING STREET...
HIS MAJESTY'S GOVERNMENT APPRECIATES GREATLY THE INFORMATION YOU HAVE BROUGHT, MR. WAYNE! YOUR LATE FRIEND, DIGBY PALMER...WAS ONE OF OUR AGENTS MAKING SECRET PARA-DROPS INTO OCCUPIED FRANCE!
OUR INVASION OF EUROPE IS NIGH! MR. PALMER WAS ATTEMPTING TO FIND OUT WHAT COUNTER-MEASURES THE ENEMY IS PREPARING! WE BELIEVE HE STUMBLED ONTO SOMETHING IMPORTANT AT CHATEAUROUGE!
SINCE YOU HAVE VOLUNTEERED TO COMPLETE PALMER'S MISSION, PERHAPS YOU CAN DISCOVER WHAT IS ODD ABOUT THE WINE AT CHATEAUROUGE! THE LIVES OF MILLIONS MAY DEPEND ON YOUR SUCCESS!
I'LL DO MY BEST, MR. MINISTER!
LATER, IN MY HOTEL ROOM...
D-DAY--THE INVASION--IS AT DAWN THE DAY AFTER TOMORROW! NOT MUCH TIME TO FINISH DIGBY'S MISSION! I'LL BE POSING AS A FRENCH BUSINESSMAN BUT SOMETHING TELLS ME THIS WILL COME IN REAL HANDY!
4

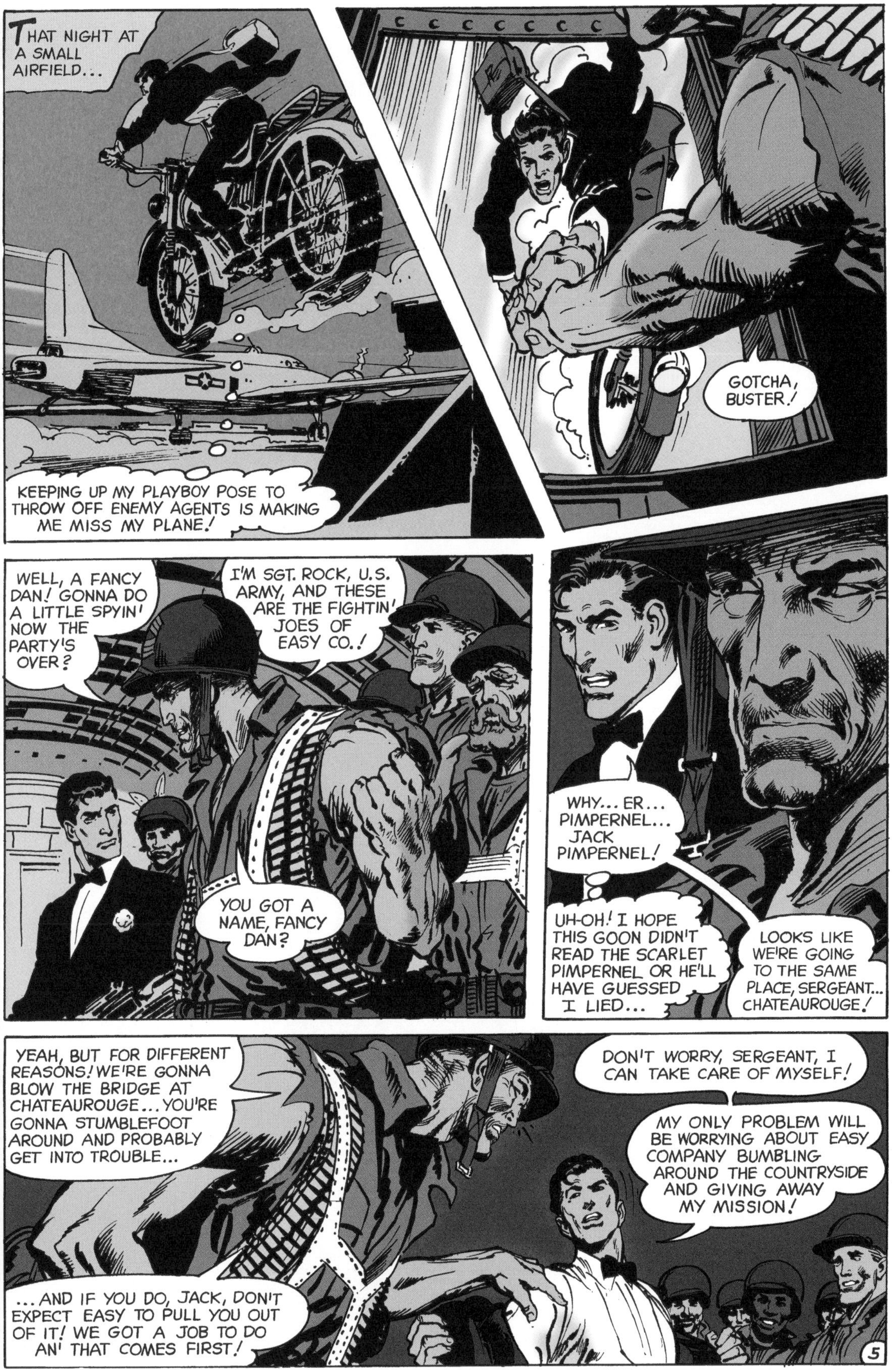
THAT NIGHT AT A SMALL AIRFIELD...
KEEPING UP MY PLAYBOY POSE TO THROW OFF ENEMY AGENTS IS MAKING ME MISS MY PLANE!
GOTCHA, BUSTER!
WELL, A FANCY DAN! GONNA DO A LITTLE SPYIN' NOW THE PARTY'S OVER?
I'M SGT. ROCK, U.S. ARMY, AND THESE ARE THE FIGHTIN' JOES OF EASY CO.!
YOU GOT A NAME, FANCY DAN?
WHY... ER... PIMPERNEL... JACK PIMPERNEL!
UH-OH! I HOPE THIS GOON DIDN'T READ THE SCARLET PIMPERNEL OR HE'LL HAVE GUESSED I LIED...
LOOKS LIKE WE'RE GOING TO THE SAME PLACE, SERGEANT... CHATEAUROUGE!
YEAH, BUT FOR DIFFERENT REASONS! WE'RE GONNA BLOW THE BRIDGE AT CHATEAUROUGE... YOU'RE GONNA STUMBLEFOOT AROUND AND PROBABLY GET INTO TROUBLE...
...AND IF YOU DO, JACK, DON'T EXPECT EASY TO PULL YOU OUT OF IT! WE GOT A JOB TO DO AN' THAT COMES FIRST!
DON'T WORRY, SERGEANT, I CAN TAKE CARE OF MYSELF!
MY ONLY PROBLEM WILL BE WORRYING ABOUT EASY COMPANY BUMBLING AROUND THE COUNTRYSIDE AND GIVING AWAY MY MISSION!
5

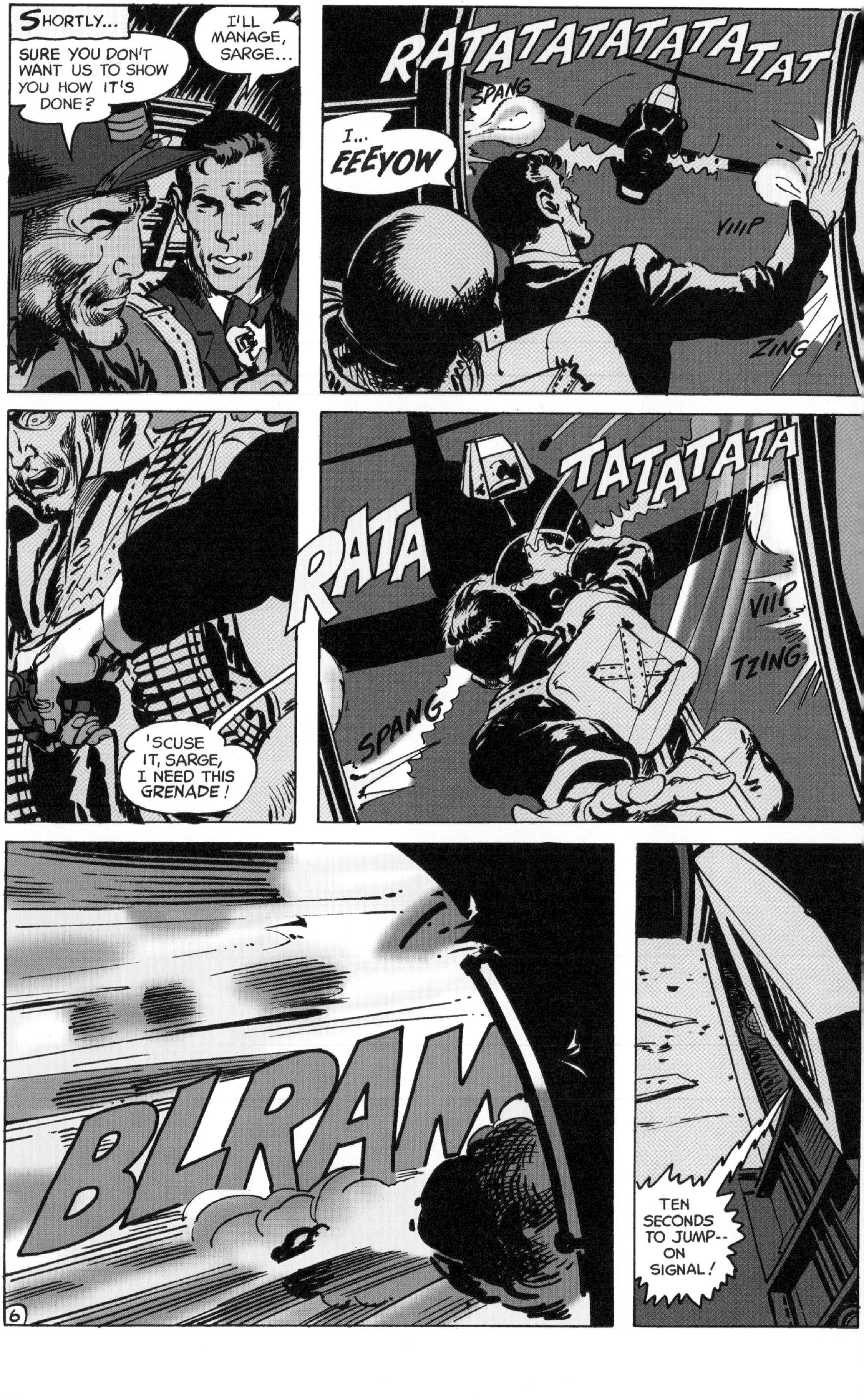
SHORTLY...
SURE YOU DON'T WANT US TO SHOW YOU HOW IT'S DONE?
I'LL MANAGE, SARGE...
RATATATATATATATAT
SPANG
I... EEEYOW
VIIIP
ZING
'SCUSE IT, SARGE, I NEED THIS GRENADE!
RATA
TATATATA
VIIP
TZING
SPANG
BLRAM
TEN SECONDS TO JUMP-- ON SIGNAL!
6

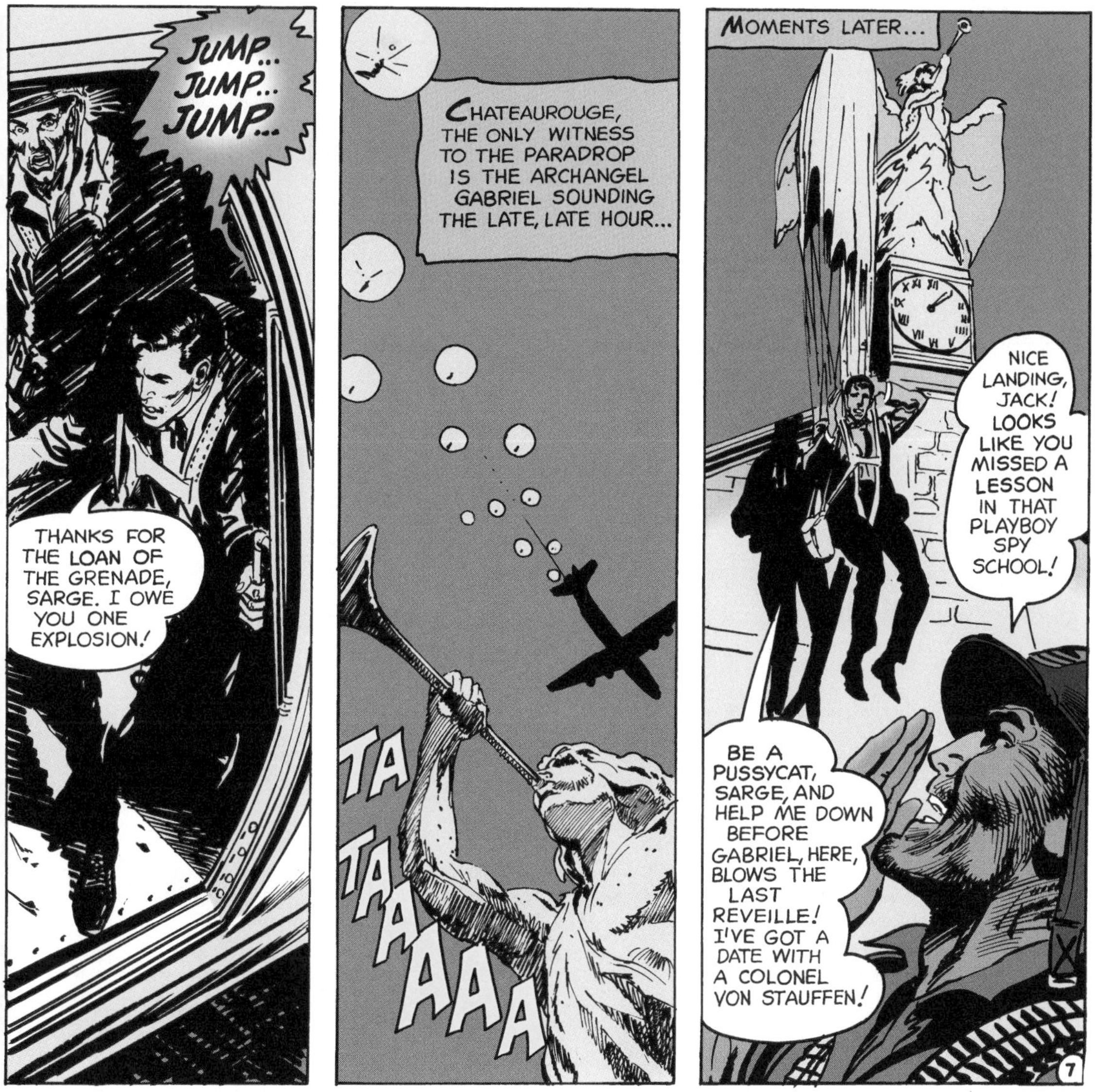
JUMP... JUMP... JUMP...
THANKS FOR THE LOAN OF THE GRENADE, SARGE. I OWE YOU ONE EXPLOSION!
CHATEAUROUGE, THE ONLY WITNESS TO THE PARADROP IS THE ARCHANGEL GABRIEL SOUNDING THE LATE, LATE HOUR...
TA TAAAAAA
MOMENTS LATER...
NICE LANDING, JACK! LOOKS LIKE YOU MISSED A LESSON IN THAT PLAYBOY SPY SCHOOL!
BE A PUSSYCAT, SARGE, AND HELP ME DOWN BEFORE GABRIEL, HERE, BLOWS THE LAST REVEILLE! I'VE GOT A DATE WITH A COLONEL VON STAUFFEN!
7

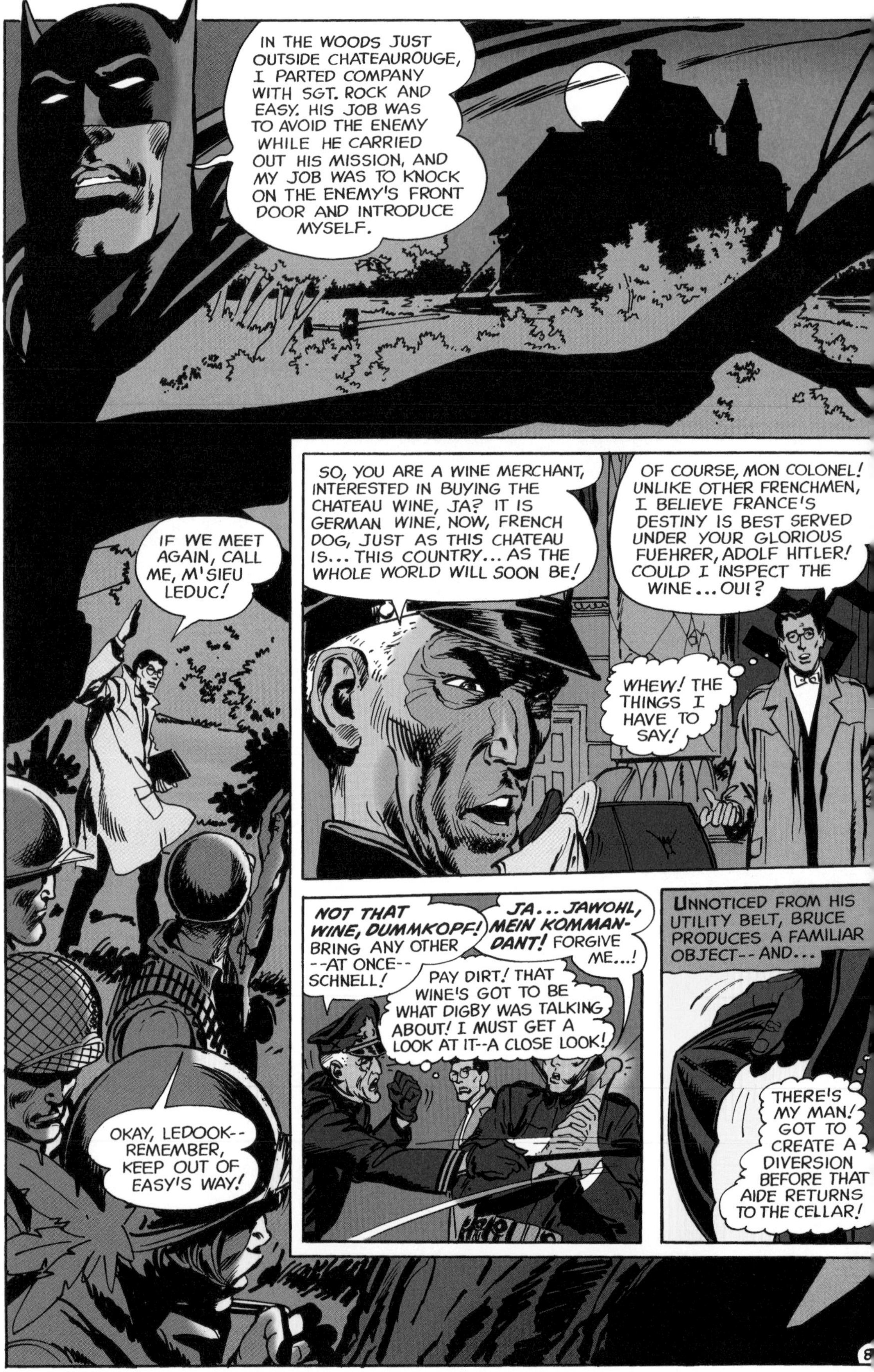
IN THE WOODS JUST OUTSIDE CHATEAUROUGE, I PARTED COMPANY WITH SGT. ROCK AND EASY. HIS JOB WAS TO AVOID THE ENEMY WHILE HE CARRIED OUT HIS MISSION, AND MY JOB WAS TO KNOCK ON THE ENEMY'S FRONT DOOR AND INTRODUCE MYSELF.
IF WE MEET AGAIN, CALL ME, M'SIEU LEDUC!
OKAY, LEDOOK--REMEMBER, KEEP OUT OF EASY'S WAY!
SO, YOU ARE A WINE MERCHANT, INTERESTED IN BUYING THE CHATEAU WINE, JA? IT IS GERMAN WINE, NOW, FRENCH DOG, JUST AS THIS CHATEAU IS... THIS COUNTRY... AS THE WHOLE WORLD WILL SOON BE!
OF COURSE, MON COLONEL! UNLIKE OTHER FRENCHMEN, I BELIEVE FRANCE'S DESTINY IS BEST SERVED UNDER YOUR GLORIOUS FUEHRER, ADOLF HITLER! COULD I INSPECT THE WINE... OUI?
WHEW! THE THINGS I HAVE TO SAY!
NOT THAT WINE, DUMMKOPF! BRING ANY OTHER--AT ONCE--SCHNELL!
JA... JAWOHL, MEIN KOMMANDANT! FORGIVE ME...!
PAY DIRT! THAT WINE'S GOT TO BE WHAT DIGBY WAS TALKING ABOUT! I MUST GET A LOOK AT IT--A CLOSE LOOK!
UNNOTICED FROM HIS UTILITY BELT, BRUCE PRODUCES A FAMILIAR OBJECT--AND...
THERE'S MY MAN! GOT TO CREATE A DIVERSION BEFORE THAT AIDE RETURNS TO THE CELLAR!
8

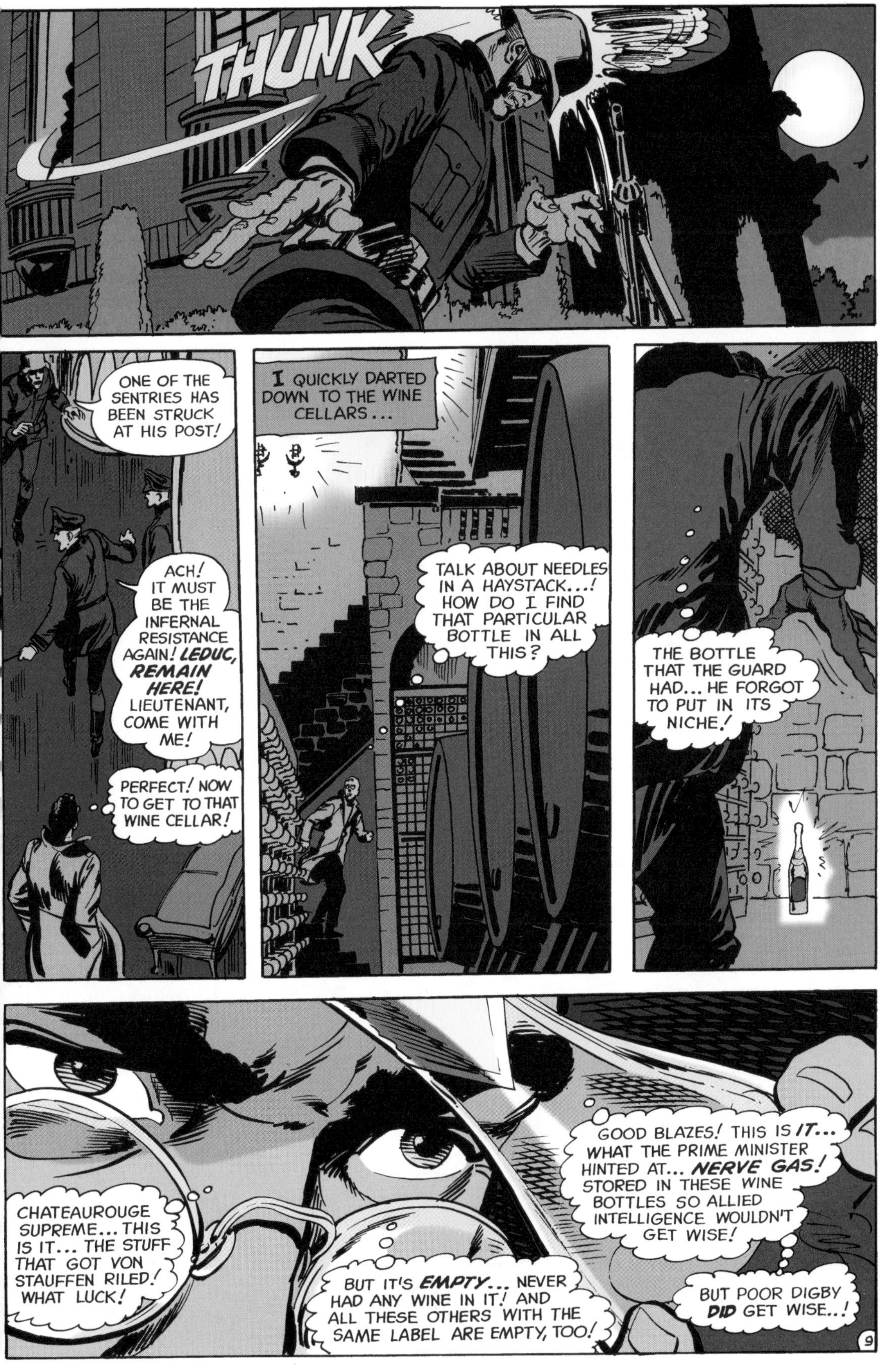
THUNK
ONE OF THE SENTRIES HAS BEEN STRUCK AT HIS POST!
ACH! IT MUST BE THE INFERNAL RESISTANCE AGAIN! LEDUC, REMAIN HERE! LIEUTENANT, COME WITH ME!
PERFECT! NOW TO GET TO THAT WINE CELLAR!
I QUICKLY DARTED DOWN TO THE WINE CELLARS...
TALK ABOUT NEEDLES IN A HAYSTACK...! HOW DO I FIND THAT PARTICULAR BOTTLE IN ALL THIS?
THE BOTTLE THAT THE GUARD HAD... HE FORGOT TO PUT IN ITS NICHE!
CHATEAUROUGE SUPREME... THIS IS IT... THE STUFF THAT GOT VON STAUFFEN RILED! WHAT LUCK!
BUT IT'S EMPTY... NEVER HAD ANY WINE IN IT! AND ALL THESE OTHERS WITH THE SAME LABEL ARE EMPTY, TOO!
GOOD BLAZES! THIS IS IT... WHAT THE PRIME MINISTER HINTED AT... NERVE GAS! STORED IN THESE WINE BOTTLES SO ALLIED INTELLIGENCE WOULDN'T GET WISE!
BUT POOR DIGBY DID GET WISE..!
9

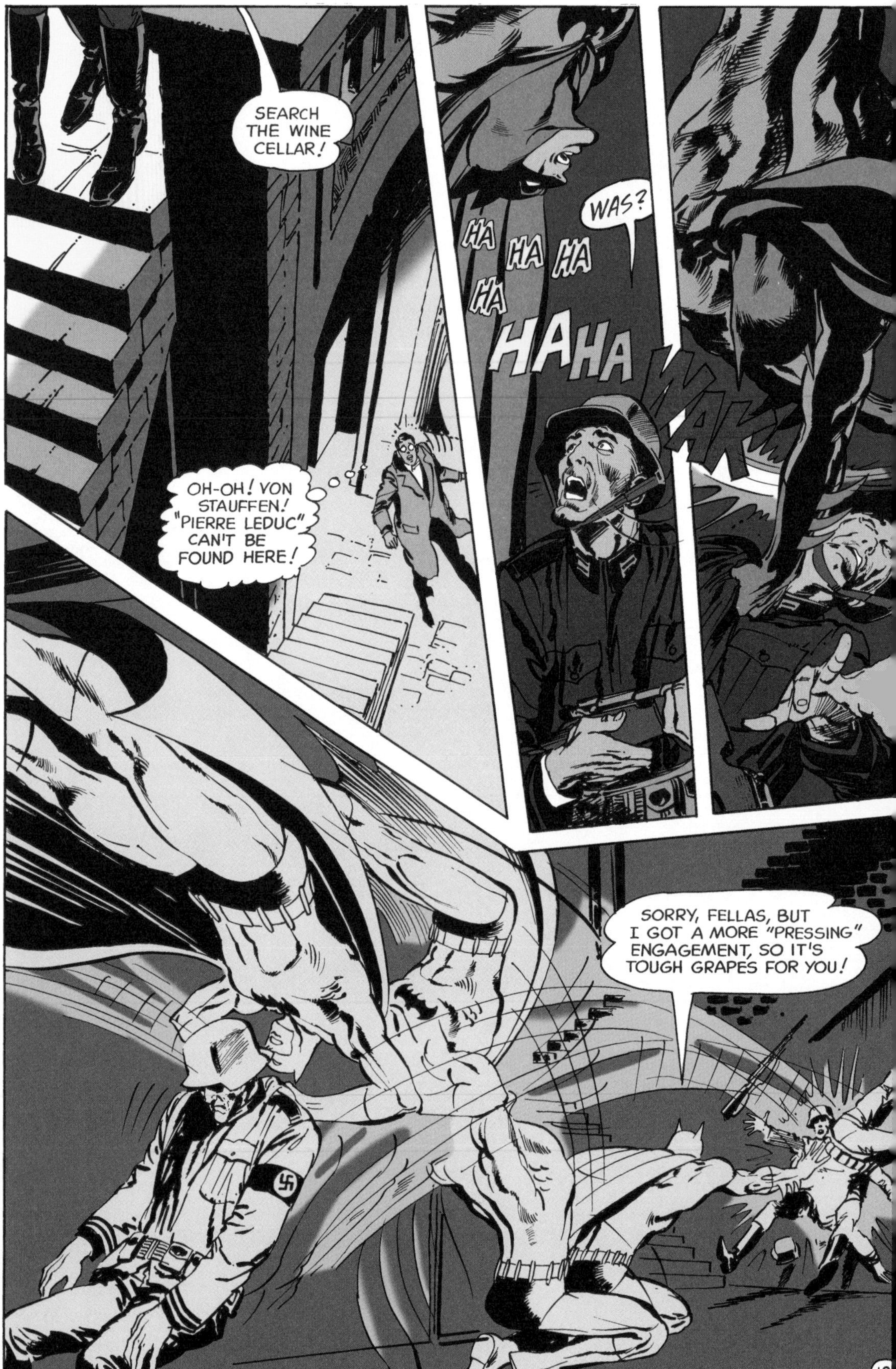
SEARCH THE WINE CELLAR!
OH-OH! VON STAUFFEN! "PIERRE LEDUC" CAN'T BE FOUND HERE!
HA HA HA HA HA
HAHA
WAS?
SORRY, FELLAS, BUT I GOT A MORE "PRESSING" ENGAGEMENT, SO IT'S TOUGH GRAPES FOR YOU!
10

I AGAIN BECAME "PIERRE LEDUC"...

I...I WAS HIDING, MON COLONEL...I WAS AFRAID THERE MIGHT BE SHOOTING!

YOU FRENCH SCHWEINE--ACH! BUT I HAVE MORE IMPORTANT PROBLEMS! IT MAY NOT BE THE FRENCH RESISTANCE BUT AMERIKANER SABOTEURS PREPARING THE WAY FOR THE INVASION! HANS, HERR. LEDUC IS LEAVING! LET HIM OUT!

ACHTUNG! IF ANY AMERIKANER SOLDIERS ARE SEEN, WE PUT *OPERATION BARBARIAN* INTO ACTION AT ONCE!

JAWOHL, HERR OBERST!

OPERATION BARBARIAN HAS TO BE THE NERVE GAS! VON STAUFFEN'S GETTING SUSPICIOUS...I MUST WARN SGT. ROCK!

WELL, WELL, IF IT AIN'T LITTLE JACK PIMPERNEL... THE SPY GUY! HOW'S THE PEEPHOLE DUTY, CHUM?

I CAME HERE TO TELL YOU TO LAY LOW... VON STAUFFEN'S GETTING WISE!

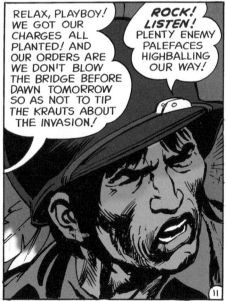

RELAX, PLAYBOY! WE GOT OUR CHARGES ALL PLANTED! AND OUR ORDERS ARE WE DON'T BLOW THE BRIDGE BEFORE DAWN TOMORROW SO AS NOT TO TIP THE KRAUTS ABOUT THE INVASION!

ROCK! LISTEN! PLENTY ENEMY PALEFACES HIGHBALLING OUR WAY!

11

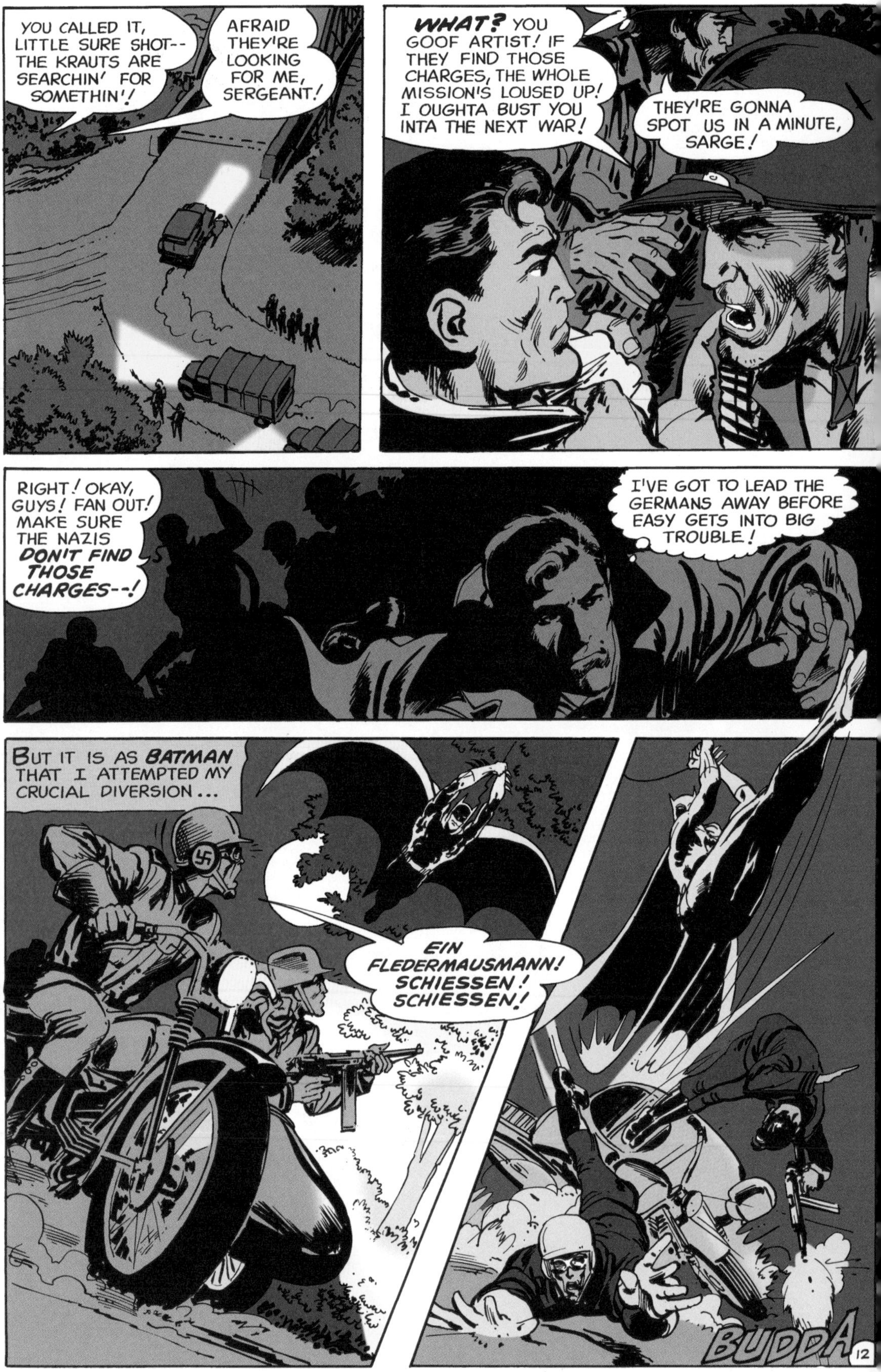

YOU CALLED IT, LITTLE SURE SHOT-- THE KRAUTS ARE SEARCHIN' FOR SOMETHIN'!
AFRAID THEY'RE LOOKING FOR ME, SERGEANT!
WHAT? YOU GOOF ARTIST! IF THEY FIND THOSE CHARGES, THE WHOLE MISSION'S LOUSED UP! I OUGHTA BUST YOU INTA THE NEXT WAR!
THEY'RE GONNA SPOT US IN A MINUTE, SARGE!
RIGHT! OKAY, GUYS! FAN OUT! MAKE SURE THE NAZIS DON'T FIND THOSE CHARGES--!
I'VE GOT TO LEAD THE GERMANS AWAY BEFORE EASY GETS INTO BIG TROUBLE!
BUT IT IS AS BATMAN THAT I ATTEMPTED MY CRUCIAL DIVERSION...
EIN FLEDERMAUSMANN! SCHIESSEN! SCHIESSEN!
BUDDA
12

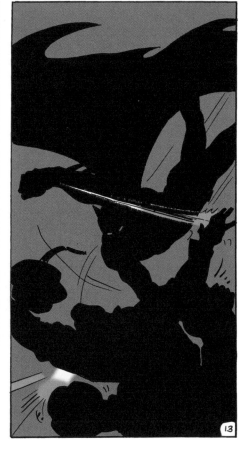

THEN, AS MORE TROOPS PURSUED ME...

ZING

ZIP

SPANG

GOOD! I'VE GOT THE HEAT OFF EASY! NOW TO GET BACK TO THE CHATEAU AND FIGURE A WAY TO CANCEL *OPERATION BARBARIAN!*

BUT AS I RAN ACROSS THE VILLAGE ROOFTOPS...

BLAZES! FRENCH HOSTAGES ABOUT TO BE EXECUTED--!

DESPERATE AS THIS MISSION WAS, I HAD TO DO SOMETHING TO STOP THE EXECUTION...

FLEDERMAUSMANN! SCHIESSEN!

BEEOW

SPANNG

I NEED YOU FOR COVER, GABE! I'M NOT BULLETPROOF YET!

...AND ONE WAY TO DO IT IS WITH MY *BATARANG!*

HIMMEL!

ZIP

KRAK

WAK

POK

WAS IST LOS?

13

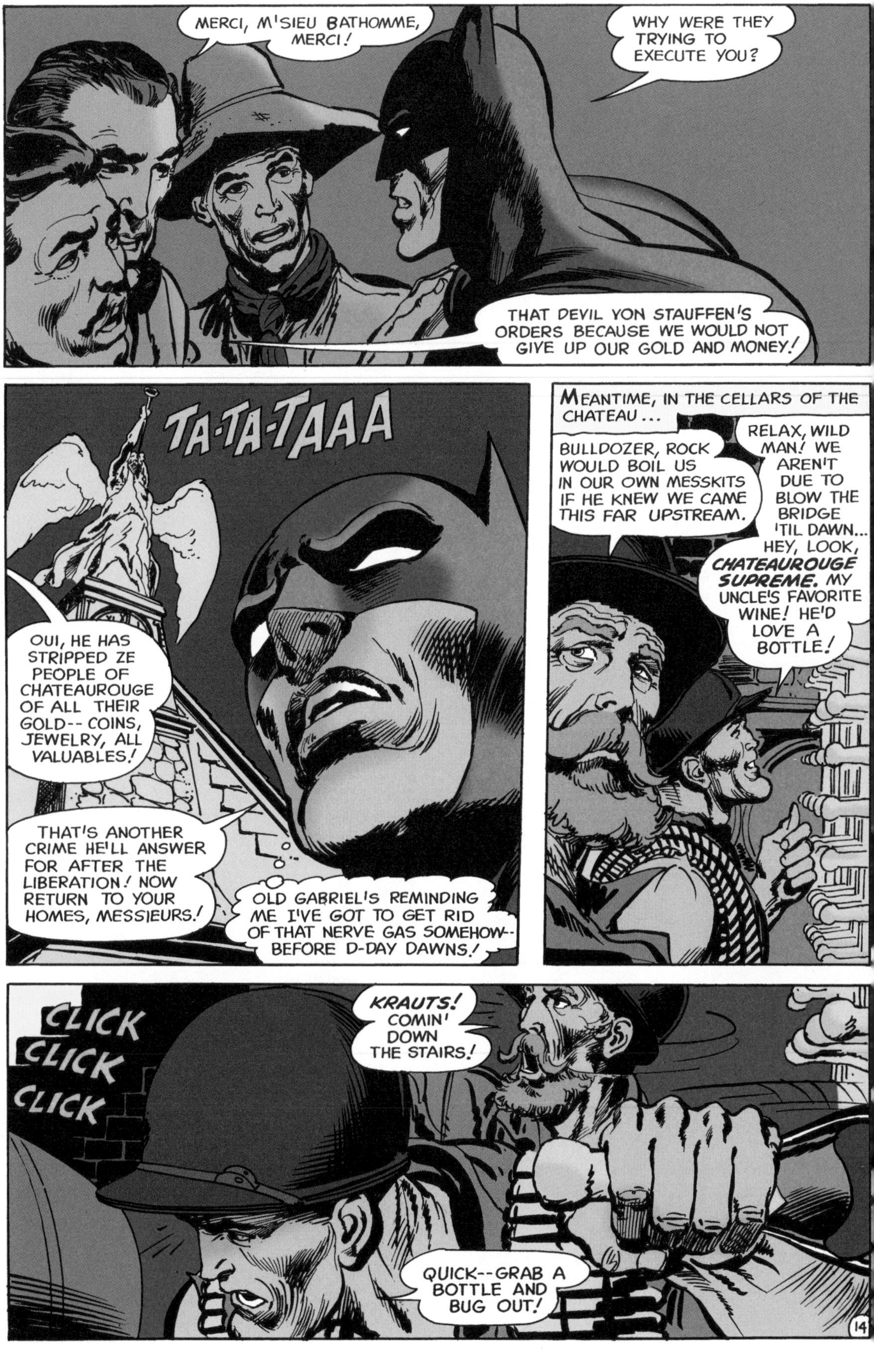
MERCI, M'SIEU BATHOMME, MERCI!
WHY WERE THEY TRYING TO EXECUTE YOU?
THAT DEVIL VON STAUFFEN'S ORDERS BECAUSE WE WOULD NOT GIVE UP OUR GOLD AND MONEY!
TA-TA-TAAA
OUI, HE HAS STRIPPED ZE PEOPLE OF CHATEAUROUGE OF ALL THEIR GOLD-- COINS, JEWELRY, ALL VALUABLES!
THAT'S ANOTHER CRIME HE'LL ANSWER FOR AFTER THE LIBERATION! NOW RETURN TO YOUR HOMES, MESSIEURS!
OLD GABRIEL'S REMINDING ME I'VE GOT TO GET RID OF THAT NERVE GAS SOMEHOW-- BEFORE D-DAY DAWNS!
MEANTIME, IN THE CELLARS OF THE CHATEAU...
BULLDOZER, ROCK WOULD BOIL US IN OUR OWN MESSKITS IF HE KNEW WE CAME THIS FAR UPSTREAM.
RELAX, WILD MAN! WE AREN'T DUE TO BLOW THE BRIDGE 'TIL DAWN... HEY, LOOK, CHATEAUROUGE SUPREME. MY UNCLE'S FAVORITE WINE! HE'D LOVE A BOTTLE!
CLICK
CLICK
CLICK
KRAUTS! COMIN' DOWN THE STAIRS!
QUICK--GRAB A BOTTLE AND BUG OUT!
14

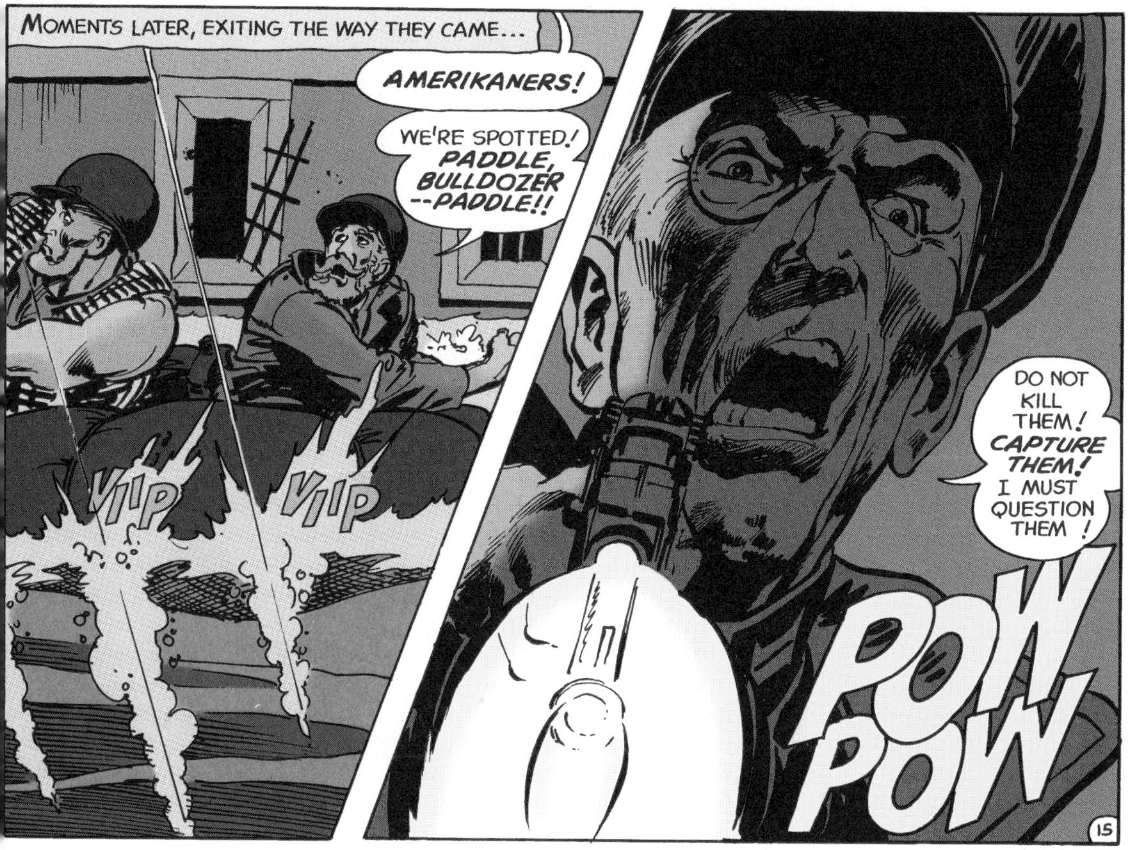
MOMENTS LATER, EXITING THE WAY THEY CAME...
AMERIKANERS!
WE'RE SPOTTED! PADDLE, BULLDOZER --PADDLE!!
VIIP
VIIP
DO NOT KILL THEM! CAPTURE THEM! I MUST QUESTION THEM!
POW
POW
15

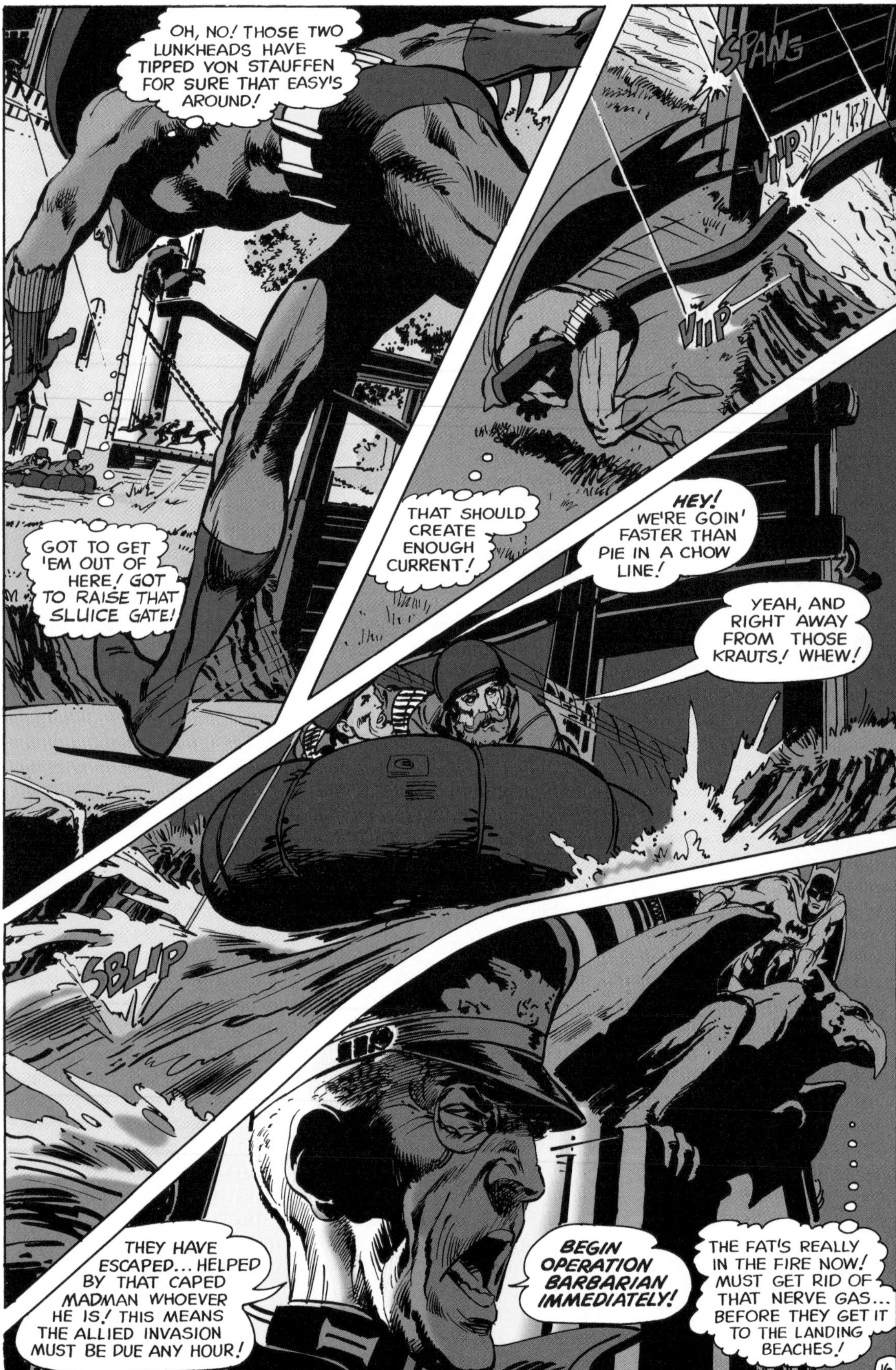
OH, NO! THOSE TWO LUNKHEADS HAVE TIPPED VON STAUFFEN FOR SURE THAT EASY'S AROUND!
GOT TO GET 'EM OUT OF HERE! GOT TO RAISE THAT SLUICE GATE!
SPANG
VIIP
VIIP
THAT SHOULD CREATE ENOUGH CURRENT!
HEY! WE'RE GOIN' FASTER THAN PIE IN A CHOW LINE!
YEAH, AND RIGHT AWAY FROM THOSE KRAUTS! WHEW!
SBLIP
THEY HAVE ESCAPED... HELPED BY THAT CAPED MADMAN WHOEVER HE IS! THIS MEANS THE ALLIED INVASION MUST BE DUE ANY HOUR!
BEGIN OPERATION BARBARIAN IMMEDIATELY!
THE FAT'S REALLY IN THE FIRE NOW! MUST GET RID OF THAT NERVE GAS... BEFORE THEY GET IT TO THE LANDING BEACHES!
16

WHAT'S THIS? TWO BOTTLES MISSING...! THOSE TWO CHUCKLEHEADS SWIPED THEM! I'VE GOT TO GET THEM BACK... BEFORE THAT GAS WIPES OUT ALL OF EASY CO.!

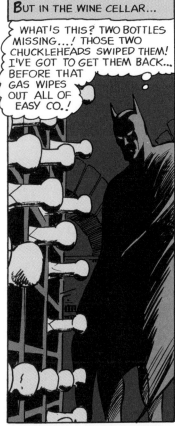

MEANWHILE... BULLDOZER AND WILD MAN ARE MISSIN'! COME ON--WE GOTTA FIND THOSE TWO APES BEFORE THE KRAUTS DO--OR THE WHOLE MISSION'S GOOFED!

HEY, WILD MAN, I JUST WANTED TO TASTE THIS, BUT I CAN'T GET THIS CRUMMY CORK OUT!

FORGET IT! I'LL BREAK THIS ONE OPEN AGAINST A TREE! SAVE THAT ONE FOR YOUR UNCLE!

HUH?

WHAT?

17

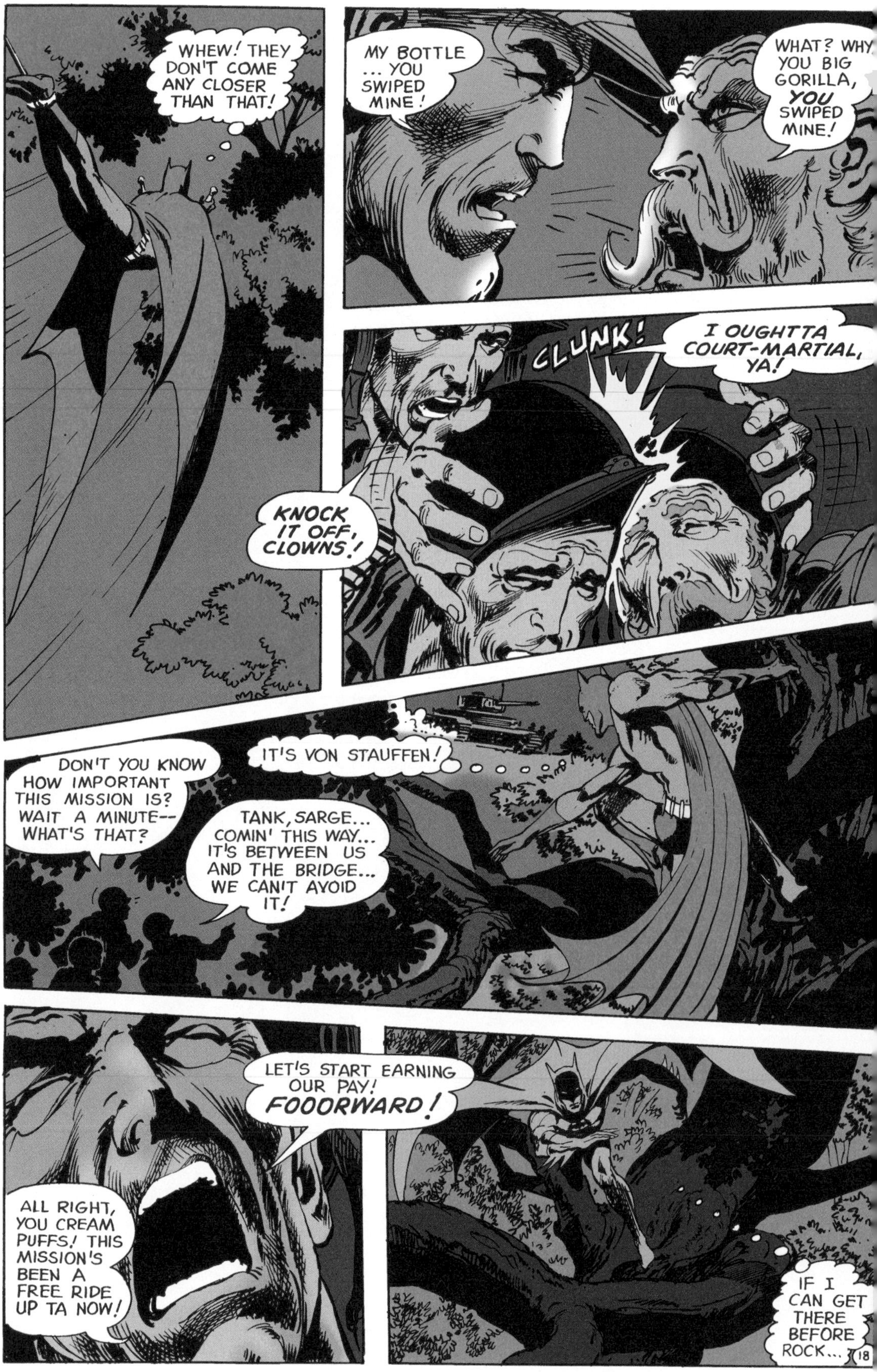

WHEW! THEY DON'T COME ANY CLOSER THAN THAT!
MY BOTTLE ... YOU SWIPED MINE!
WHAT? WHY YOU BIG GORILLA, YOU SWIPED MINE!
CLUNK!
I OUGHTTA COURT-MARTIAL, YA!
KNOCK IT OFF, CLOWNS!
IT'S VON STAUFFEN!
DON'T YOU KNOW HOW IMPORTANT THIS MISSION IS? WAIT A MINUTE-- WHAT'S THAT?
TANK, SARGE... COMIN' THIS WAY... IT'S BETWEEN US AND THE BRIDGE... WE CAN'T AVOID IT!
LET'S START EARNING OUR PAY! FOOORWARD!
ALL RIGHT, YOU CREAM PUFFS! THIS MISSION'S BEEN A FREE RIDE UP TA NOW!
IF I CAN GET THERE BEFORE ROCK...
18

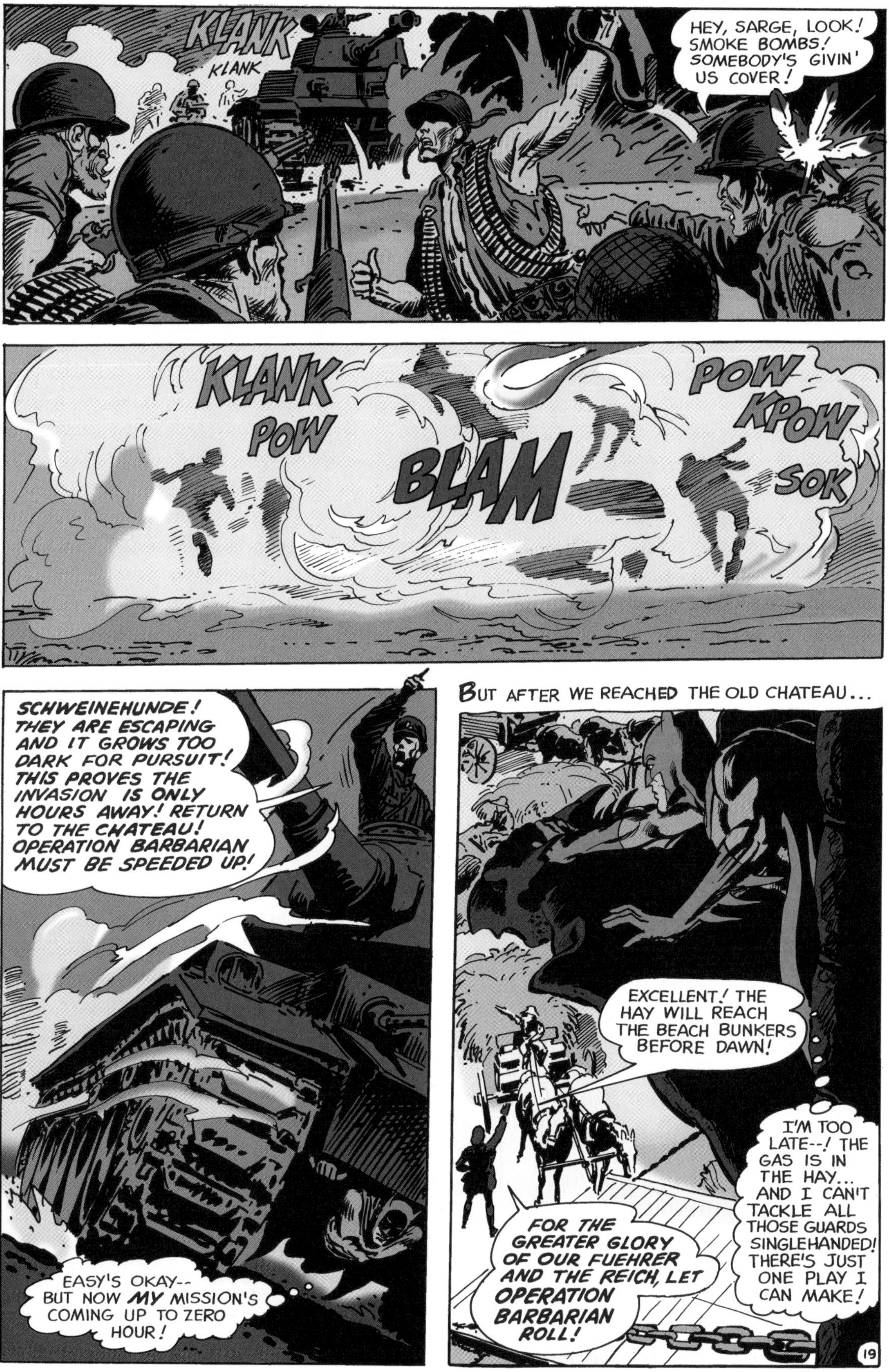
KLANK
KLANK
HEY, SARGE, LOOK! SMOKE BOMBS! SOMEBODY'S GIVIN' US COVER!
KLANK
POW
BLAM
POW
KPOW
SOK
SCHWEINEHUNDE! THEY ARE ESCAPING AND IT GROWS TOO DARK FOR PURSUIT! THIS PROVES THE INVASION IS ONLY HOURS AWAY! RETURN TO THE CHATEAU! OPERATION BARBARIAN MUST BE SPEEDED UP!
EASY'S OKAY-- BUT NOW MY MISSION'S COMING UP TO ZERO HOUR!
BUT AFTER WE REACHED THE OLD CHATEAU...
EXCELLENT! THE HAY WILL REACH THE BEACH BUNKERS BEFORE DAWN!
I'M TOO LATE--! THE GAS IS IN THE HAY... AND I CAN'T TACKLE ALL THOSE GUARDS SINGLEHANDED! THERE'S JUST ONE PLAY I CAN MAKE!
FOR THE GREATER GLORY OF OUR FUEHRER AND THE REICH, LET OPERATION BARBARIAN ROLL!
19

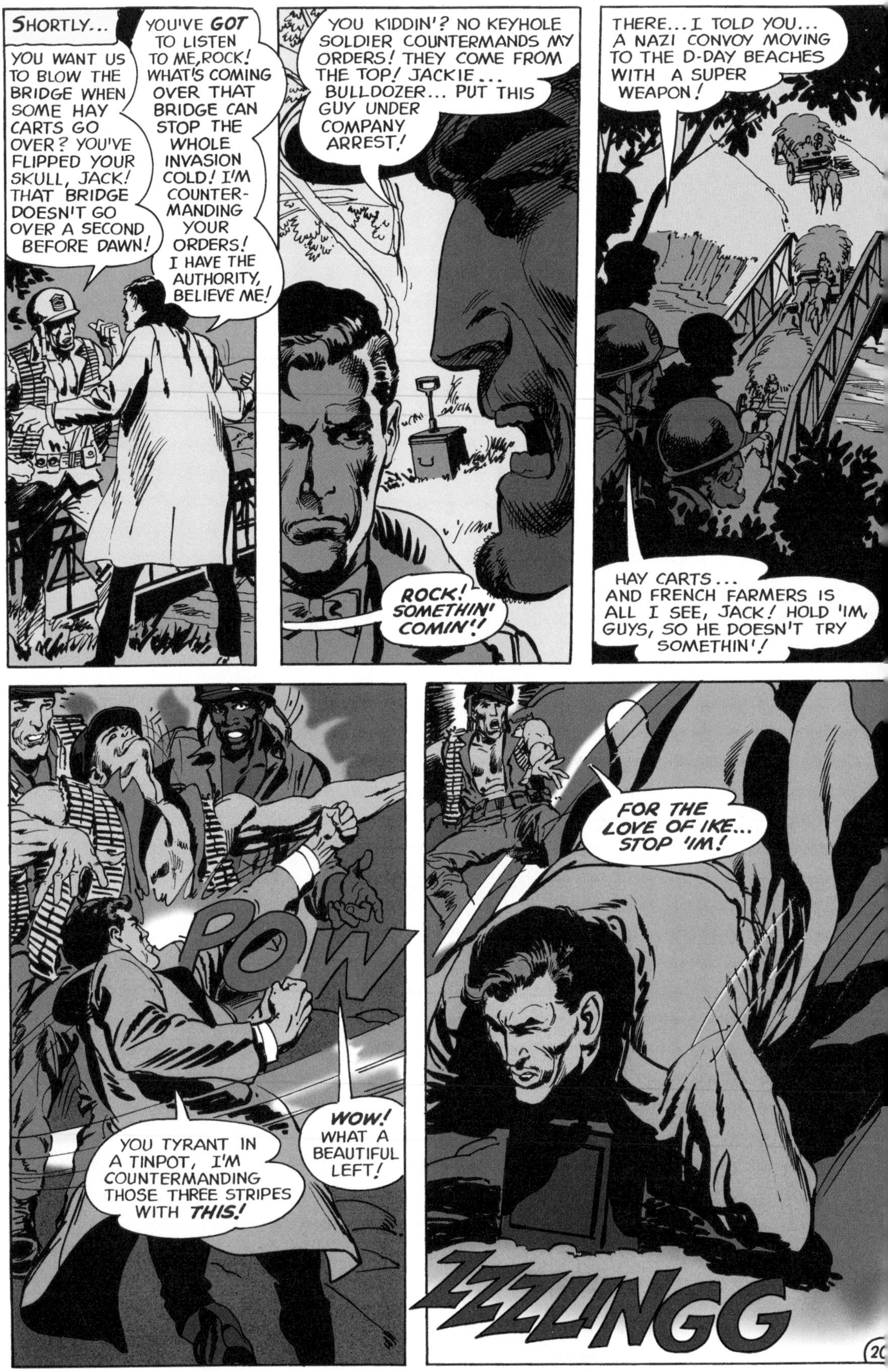
SHORTLY...
YOU WANT US TO BLOW THE BRIDGE WHEN SOME HAY CARTS GO OVER? YOU'VE FLIPPED YOUR SKULL, JACK! THAT BRIDGE DOESN'T GO OVER A SECOND BEFORE DAWN!
YOU'VE GOT TO LISTEN TO ME, ROCK! WHAT'S COMING OVER THAT BRIDGE CAN STOP THE WHOLE INVASION COLD! I'M COUNTER-MANDING YOUR ORDERS! I HAVE THE AUTHORITY, BELIEVE ME!
YOU KIDDIN'? NO KEYHOLE SOLDIER COUNTERMANDS MY ORDERS! THEY COME FROM THE TOP! JACKIE... BULLDOZER... PUT THIS GUY UNDER COMPANY ARREST!
ROCK! SOMETHIN' COMIN'!
THERE... I TOLD YOU... A NAZI CONVOY MOVING TO THE D-DAY BEACHES WITH A SUPER WEAPON!
HAY CARTS... AND FRENCH FARMERS IS ALL I SEE, JACK! HOLD 'IM, GUYS, SO HE DOESN'T TRY SOMETHIN'!
POW
YOU TYRANT IN A TINPOT, I'M COUNTERMANDING THOSE THREE STRIPES WITH THIS!
WOW! WHAT A BEAUTIFUL LEFT!
FOR THE LOVE OF IKE... STOP 'IM!
ZZZINGG
20

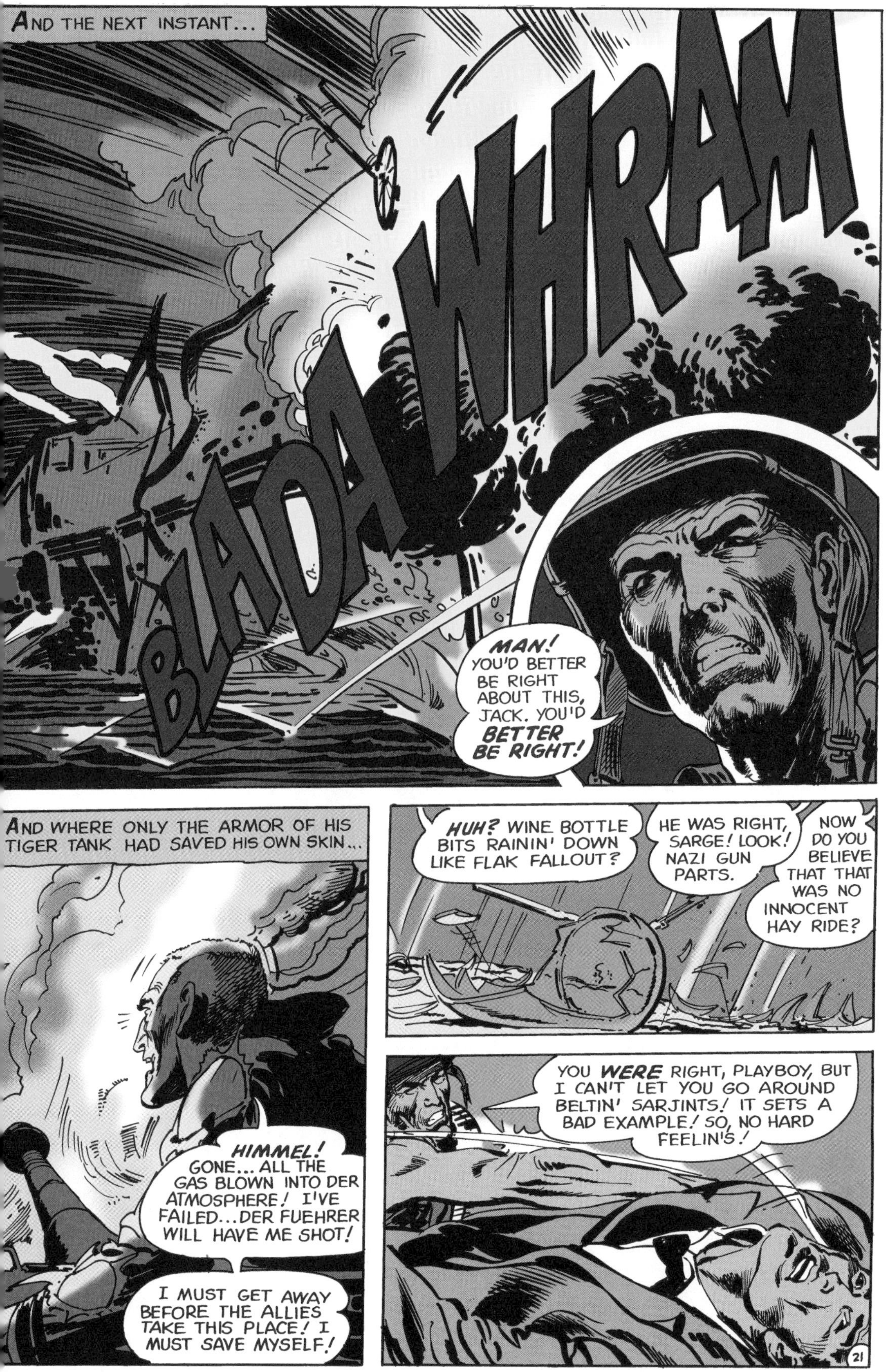
AND THE NEXT INSTANT...
BLAADA WHRAM
MAN! YOU'D BETTER BE RIGHT ABOUT THIS, JACK. YOU'D BETTER BE RIGHT!
AND WHERE ONLY THE ARMOR OF HIS TIGER TANK HAD SAVED HIS OWN SKIN...
HIMMEL! GONE... ALL THE GAS BLOWN INTO DER ATMOSPHERE! I'VE FAILED... DER FUEHRER WILL HAVE ME SHOT!
I MUST GET AWAY BEFORE THE ALLIES TAKE THIS PLACE! I MUST SAVE MYSELF!
HUH? WINE BOTTLE BITS RAININ' DOWN LIKE FLAK FALLOUT?
HE WAS RIGHT, SARGE! LOOK! NAZI GUN PARTS.
NOW DO YOU BELIEVE THAT THAT WAS NO INNOCENT HAY RIDE?
YOU WERE RIGHT, PLAYBOY, BUT I CAN'T LET YOU GO AROUND BELTIN' SARJINTS! IT SETS A BAD EXAMPLE! SO, NO HARD FEELIN'S!
21

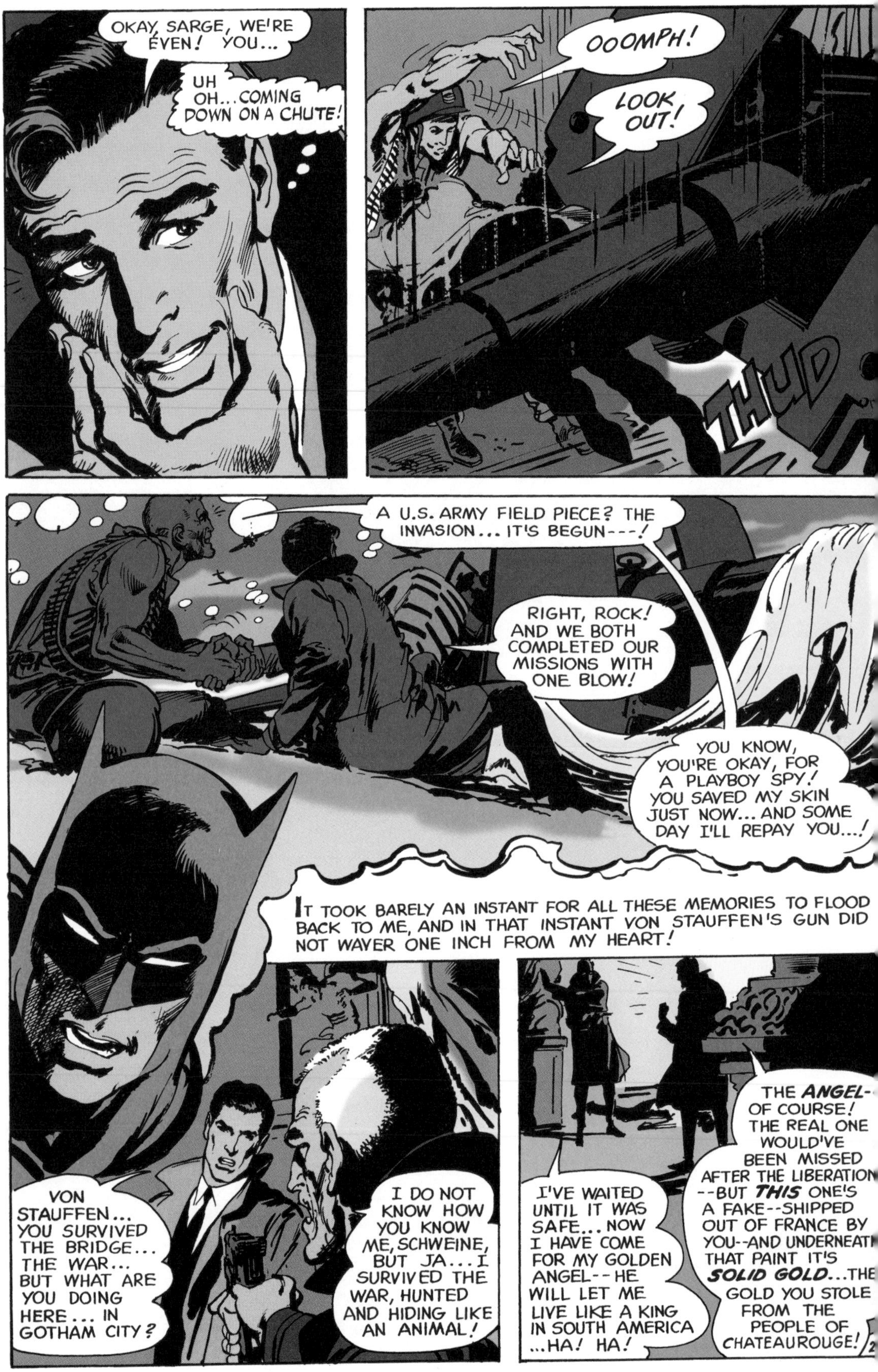
OKAY, SARGE, WE'RE EVEN! YOU...
UH OH...COMING DOWN ON A CHUTE!
OOOMPH!
LOOK OUT!
THUD
A U.S. ARMY FIELD PIECE? THE INVASION... IT'S BEGUN---!
RIGHT, ROCK! AND WE BOTH COMPLETED OUR MISSIONS WITH ONE BLOW!
YOU KNOW, YOU'RE OKAY, FOR A PLAYBOY SPY! YOU SAVED MY SKIN JUST NOW... AND SOME DAY I'LL REPAY YOU...!
IT TOOK BARELY AN INSTANT FOR ALL THESE MEMORIES TO FLOOD BACK TO ME, AND IN THAT INSTANT VON STAUFFEN'S GUN DID NOT WAVER ONE INCH FROM MY HEART!
VON STAUFFEN... YOU SURVIVED THE BRIDGE... THE WAR... BUT WHAT ARE YOU DOING HERE... IN GOTHAM CITY?
I DO NOT KNOW HOW YOU KNOW ME, SCHWEINE, BUT JA... I SURVIVED THE WAR, HUNTED AND HIDING LIKE AN ANIMAL!
I'VE WAITED UNTIL IT WAS SAFE... NOW I HAVE COME FOR MY GOLDEN ANGEL-- HE WILL LET ME LIVE LIKE A KING IN SOUTH AMERICA ...HA! HA!
THE ANGEL-OF COURSE! THE REAL ONE WOULD'VE BEEN MISSED AFTER THE LIBERATION --BUT THIS ONE'S A FAKE--SHIPPED OUT OF FRANCE BY YOU--AND UNDERNEATH THAT PAINT IT'S SOLID GOLD...THE GOLD YOU STOLE FROM THE PEOPLE OF CHATEAUROUGE!

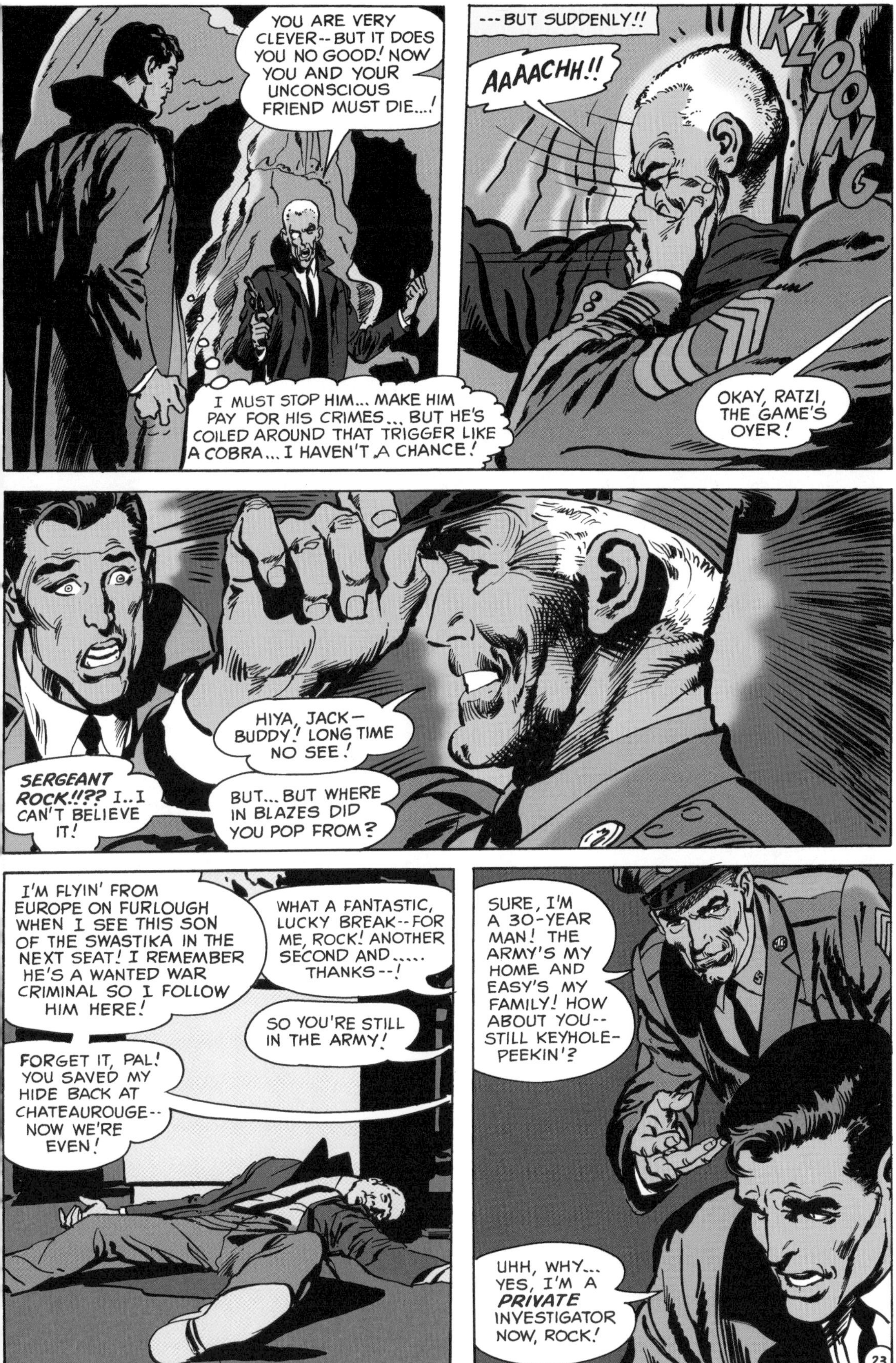
YOU ARE VERY CLEVER-- BUT IT DOES YOU NO GOOD! NOW YOU AND YOUR UNCONSCIOUS FRIEND MUST DIE...!
I MUST STOP HIM... MAKE HIM PAY FOR HIS CRIMES... BUT HE'S COILED AROUND THAT TRIGGER LIKE A COBRA... I HAVEN'T A CHANCE!
---BUT SUDDENLY!!
AAAACHH!!
KLOONG
OKAY, RATZI, THE GAME'S OVER!
SERGEANT ROCK!!?? I..I CAN'T BELIEVE IT!
HIYA, JACK-BUDDY! LONG TIME NO SEE!
BUT...BUT WHERE IN BLAZES DID YOU POP FROM?
I'M FLYIN' FROM EUROPE ON FURLOUGH WHEN I SEE THIS SON OF THE SWASTIKA IN THE NEXT SEAT! I REMEMBER HE'S A WANTED WAR CRIMINAL SO I FOLLOW HIM HERE!
WHAT A FANTASTIC, LUCKY BREAK--FOR ME, ROCK! ANOTHER SECOND AND..... THANKS--!
FORGET IT, PAL! YOU SAVED MY HIDE BACK AT CHATEAUROUGE-- NOW WE'RE EVEN!
SO YOU'RE STILL IN THE ARMY!
SURE, I'M A 30-YEAR MAN! THE ARMY'S MY HOME AND EASY'S MY FAMILY! HOW ABOUT YOU-- STILL KEYHOLE-PEEKIN'?
UHH, WHY... YES, I'M A *PRIVATE* INVESTIGATOR NOW, ROCK!
23

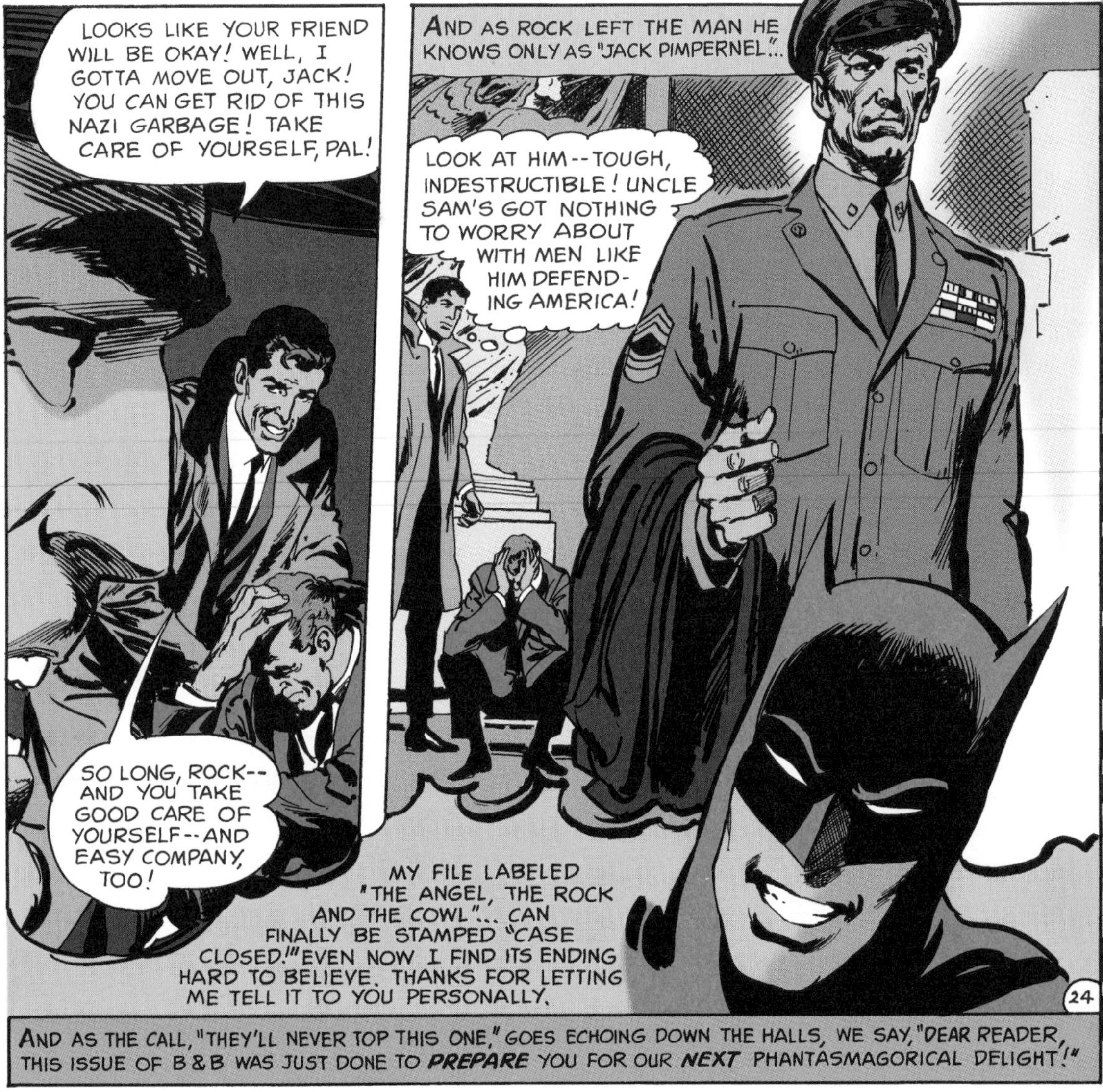
LOOKS LIKE YOUR FRIEND WILL BE OKAY! WELL, I GOTTA MOVE OUT, JACK! YOU CAN GET RID OF THIS NAZI GARBAGE! TAKE CARE OF YOURSELF, PAL!
SO LONG, ROCK-- AND YOU TAKE GOOD CARE OF YOURSELF--AND EASY COMPANY, TOO!
AND AS ROCK LEFT THE MAN HE KNOWS ONLY AS "JACK PIMPERNEL"...
LOOK AT HIM--TOUGH, INDESTRUCTIBLE! UNCLE SAM'S GOT NOTHING TO WORRY ABOUT WITH MEN LIKE HIM DEFENDING AMERICA!
MY FILE LABELED "THE ANGEL, THE ROCK AND THE COWL"... CAN FINALLY BE STAMPED "CASE CLOSED!" EVEN NOW I FIND ITS ENDING HARD TO BELIEVE. THANKS FOR LETTING ME TELL IT TO YOU PERSONALLY.
24
AND AS THE CALL, "THEY'LL NEVER TOP THIS ONE," GOES ECHOING DOWN THE HALLS, WE SAY, "DEAR READER, THIS ISSUE OF B&B WAS JUST DONE TO PREPARE YOU FOR OUR NEXT PHANTASMAGORICAL DELIGHT!"

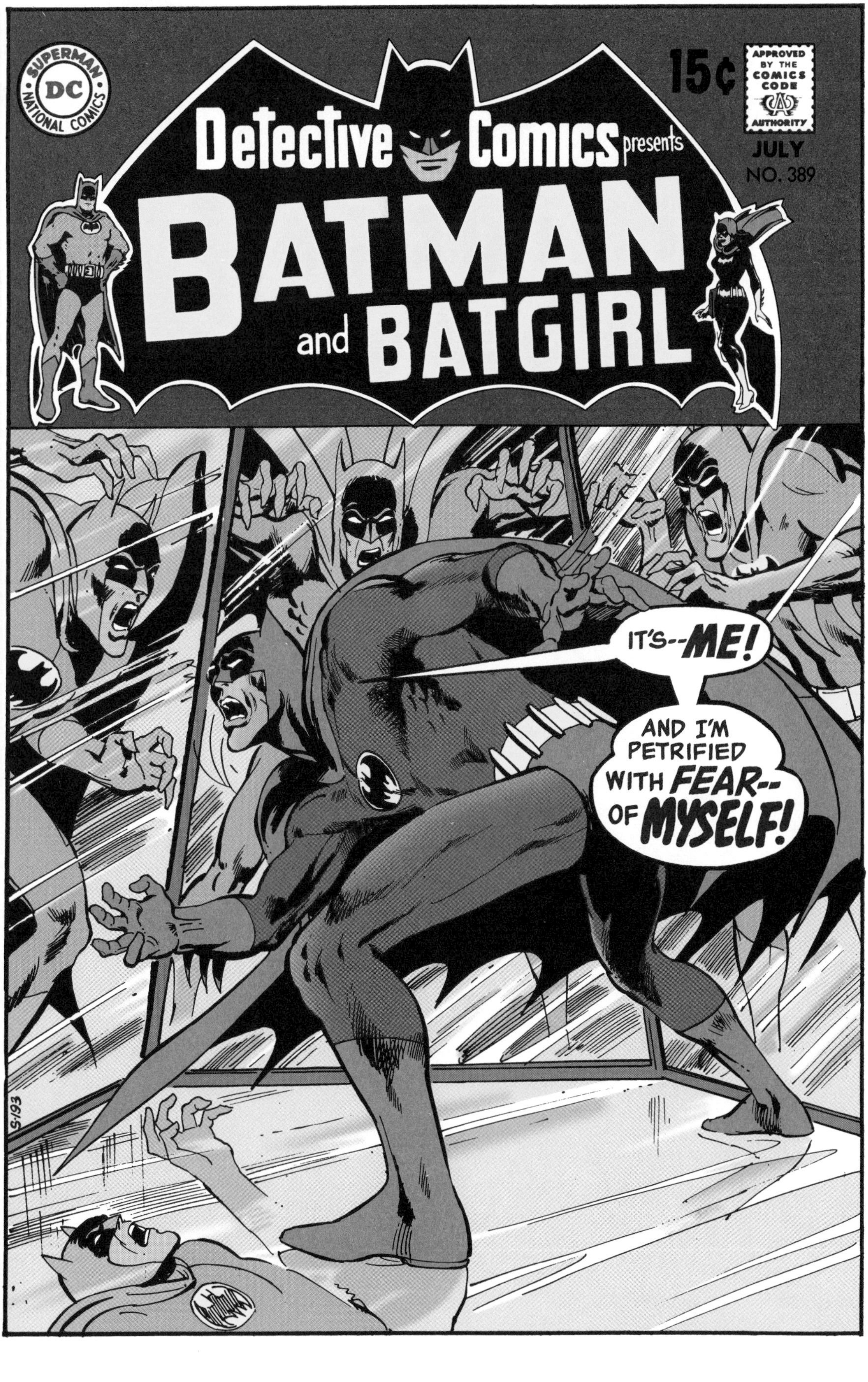
SUPERMAN DC NATIONAL COMICS
15¢
APPROVED BY THE COMICS CODE AUTHORITY
Detective Comics presents
JULY
NO. 389
BATMAN
and BATGIRL
IT'S--ME!
AND I'M PETRIFIED WITH FEAR-- OF MYSELF!
S-193

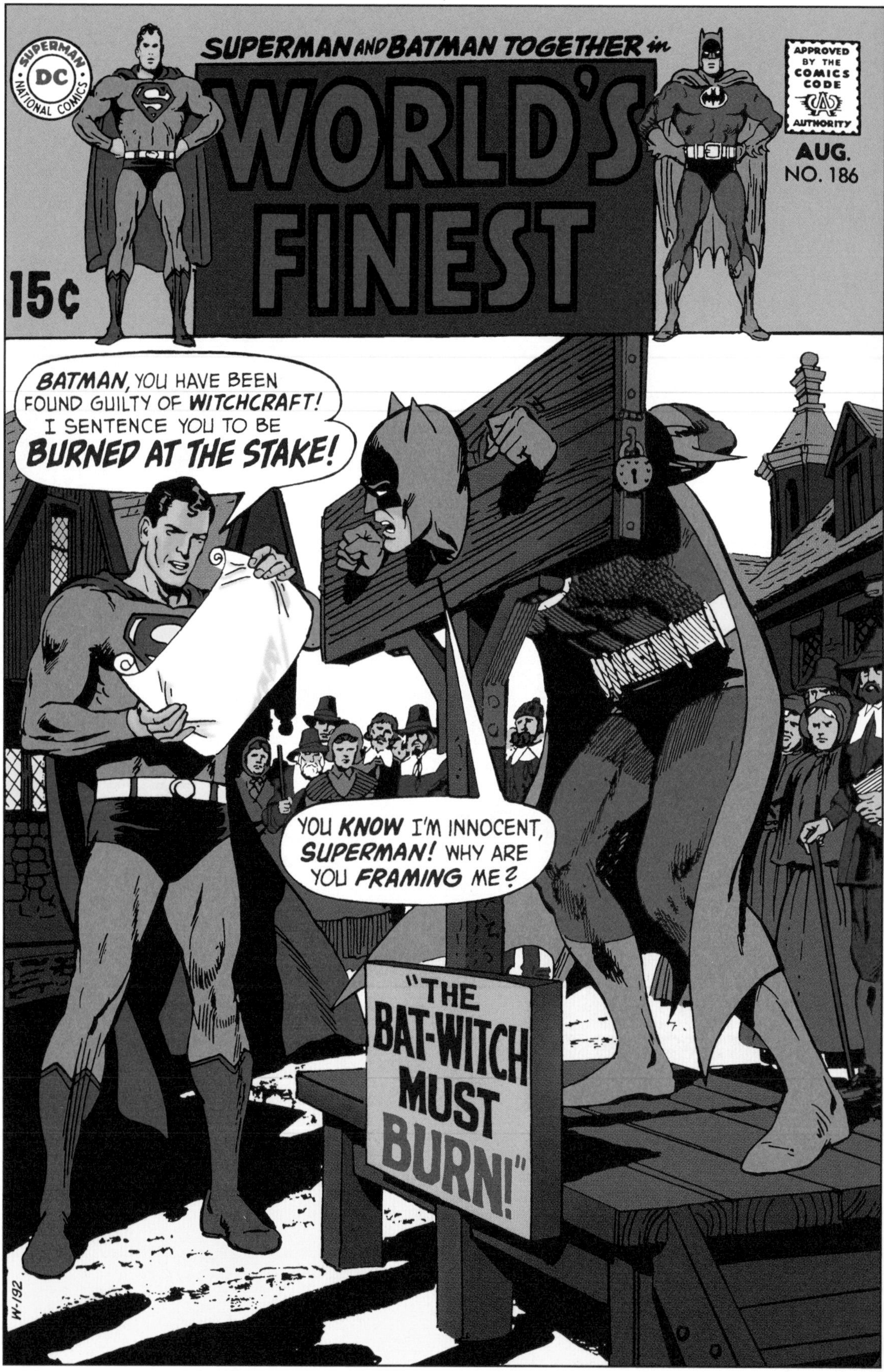
SUPERMAN AND BATMAN TOGETHER in
WORLD'S FINEST
SUPERMAN DC NATIONAL COMICS
APPROVED BY THE COMICS CODE AUTHORITY
AUG. NO. 186
15¢
BATMAN, YOU HAVE BEEN FOUND GUILTY OF WITCHCRAFT! I SENTENCE YOU TO BE BURNED AT THE STAKE!
YOU KNOW I'M INNOCENT, SUPERMAN! WHY ARE YOU FRAMING ME?
"THE BAT-WITCH MUST BURN!"
W-192

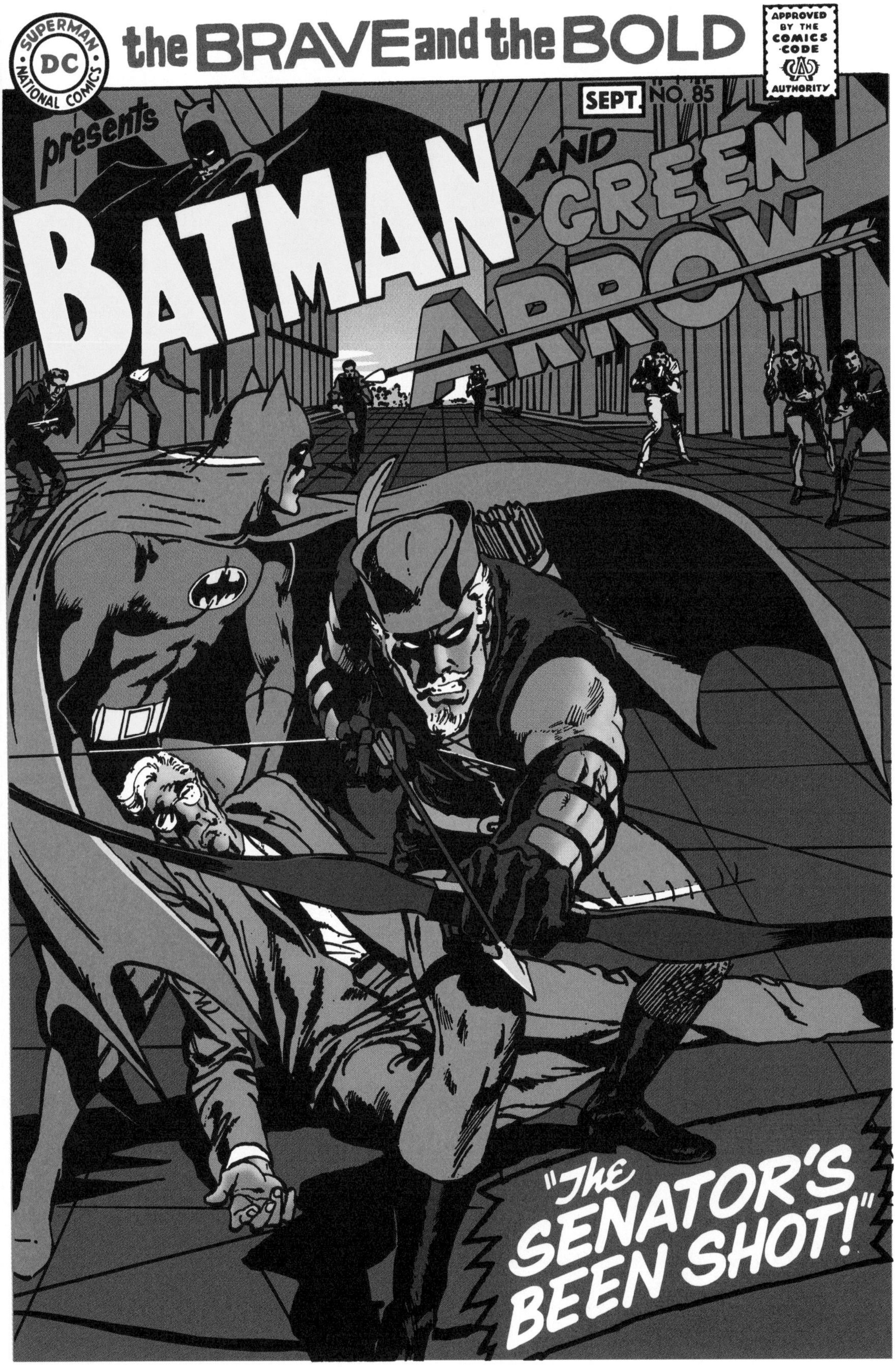
the BRAVE and the BOLD
SUPERMAN
DC
NATIONAL COMICS
APPROVED BY THE COMICS CODE AUTHORITY
SEPT. NO. 85
presents
BATMAN AND GREEN ARROW
"The SENATOR'S BEEN SHOT!"

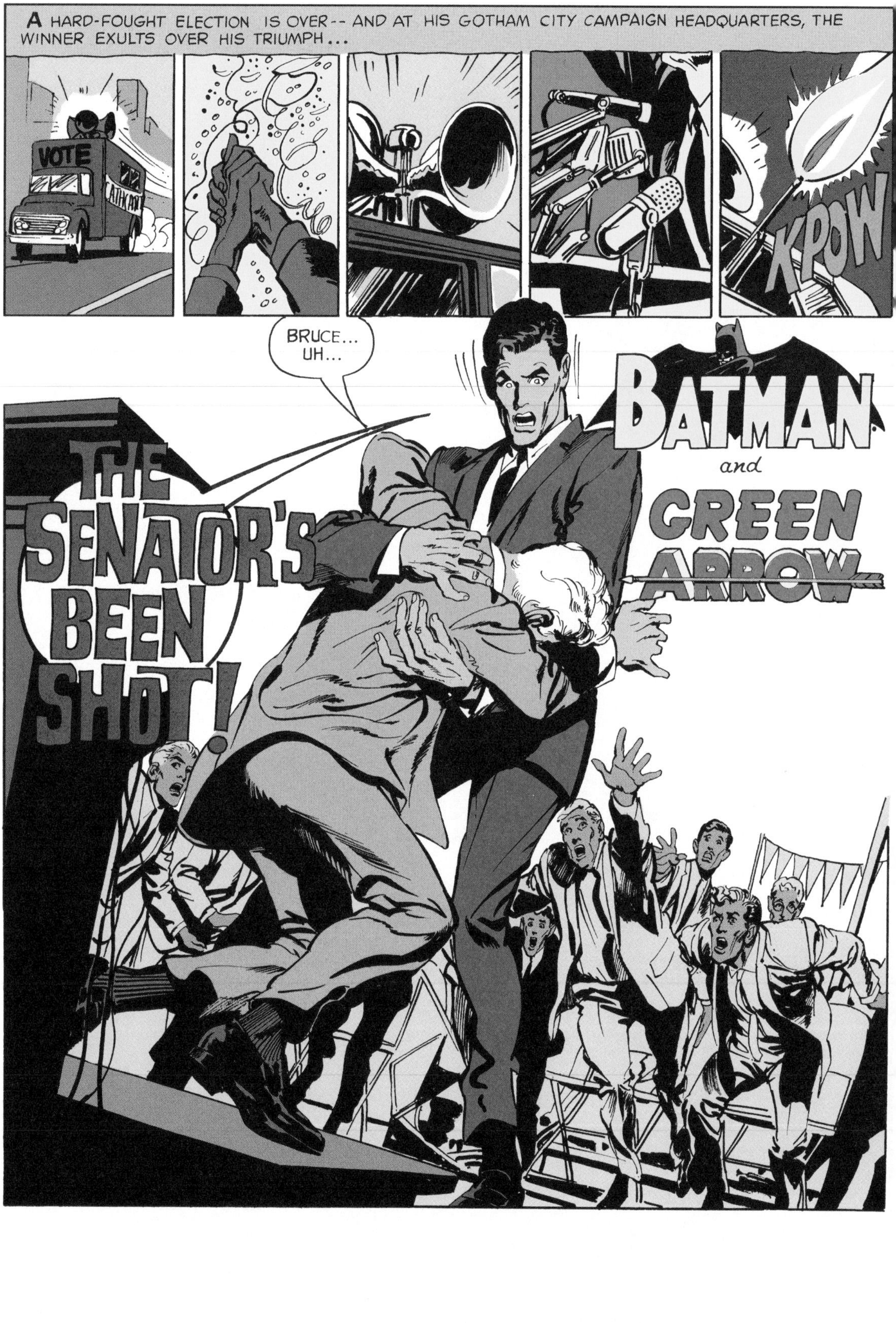
A HARD-FOUGHT ELECTION IS OVER-- AND AT HIS GOTHAM CITY CAMPAIGN HEADQUARTERS, THE WINNER EXULTS OVER HIS TRIUMPH...
VOTE
KPOW
BRUCE... UH...
THE SENATOR'S BEEN SHOT!
BATMAN
and
GREEN ARROW

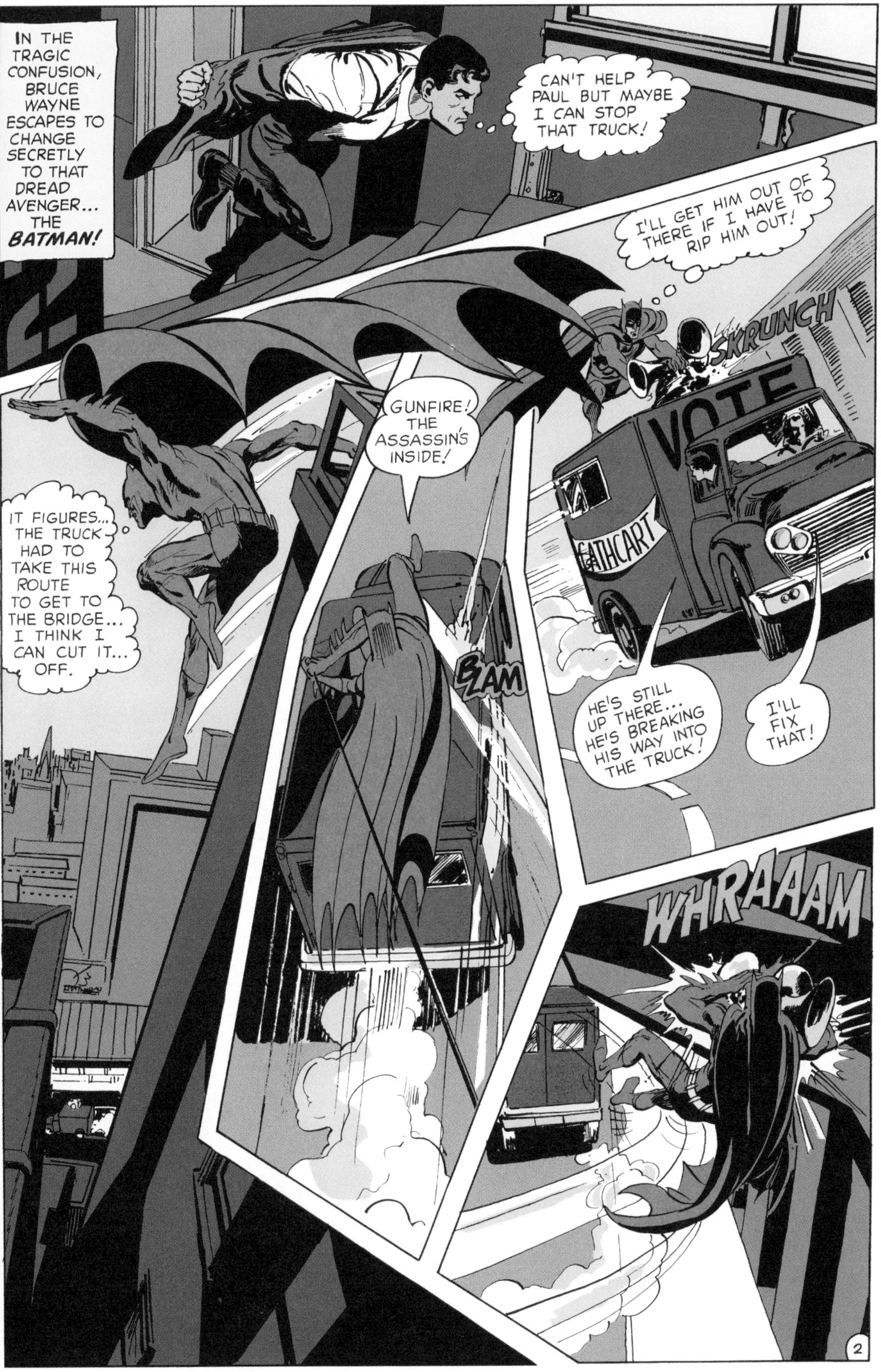
IN THE TRAGIC CONFUSION, BRUCE WAYNE ESCAPES TO CHANGE SECRETLY TO THAT DREAD AVENGER... THE BATMAN!
CAN'T HELP PAUL BUT MAYBE I CAN STOP THAT TRUCK!
I'LL GET HIM OUT OF THERE IF I HAVE TO RIP HIM OUT!
SKRUNCH
VOTE
DEATHCART
GUNFIRE! THE ASSASSIN'S INSIDE!
IT FIGURES... THE TRUCK HAD TO TAKE THIS ROUTE TO GET TO THE BRIDGE... I THINK I CAN CUT IT... OFF.
BLAM
HE'S STILL UP THERE... HE'S BREAKING HIS WAY INTO THE TRUCK!
I'LL FIX THAT!
WHRAAAM
2

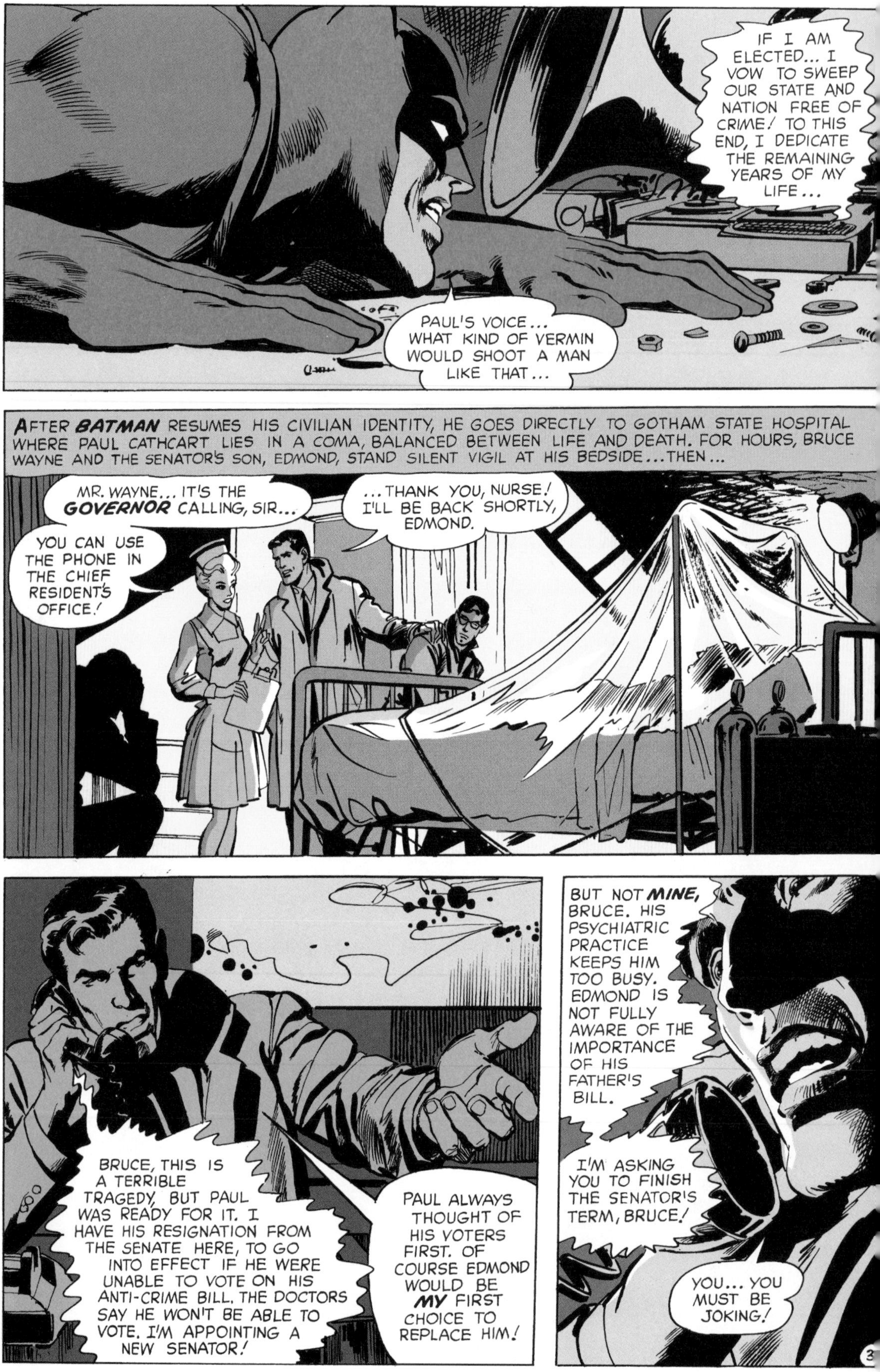
IF I AM ELECTED... I VOW TO SWEEP OUR STATE AND NATION FREE OF CRIME! TO THIS END, I DEDICATE THE REMAINING YEARS OF MY LIFE...
PAUL'S VOICE... WHAT KIND OF VERMIN WOULD SHOOT A MAN LIKE THAT...
AFTER BATMAN RESUMES HIS CIVILIAN IDENTITY, HE GOES DIRECTLY TO GOTHAM STATE HOSPITAL WHERE PAUL CATHCART LIES IN A COMA, BALANCED BETWEEN LIFE AND DEATH. FOR HOURS, BRUCE WAYNE AND THE SENATOR'S SON, EDMOND, STAND SILENT VIGIL AT HIS BEDSIDE...THEN...
MR. WAYNE... IT'S THE GOVERNOR CALLING, SIR...
YOU CAN USE THE PHONE IN THE CHIEF RESIDENT'S OFFICE!
...THANK YOU, NURSE! I'LL BE BACK SHORTLY, EDMOND.
BRUCE, THIS IS A TERRIBLE TRAGEDY, BUT PAUL WAS READY FOR IT. I HAVE HIS RESIGNATION FROM THE SENATE HERE, TO GO INTO EFFECT IF HE WERE UNABLE TO VOTE ON HIS ANTI-CRIME BILL. THE DOCTORS SAY HE WON'T BE ABLE TO VOTE. I'M APPOINTING A NEW SENATOR!
PAUL ALWAYS THOUGHT OF HIS VOTERS FIRST. OF COURSE EDMOND WOULD BE MY FIRST CHOICE TO REPLACE HIM!
BUT NOT MINE, BRUCE. HIS PSYCHIATRIC PRACTICE KEEPS HIM TOO BUSY. EDMOND IS NOT FULLY AWARE OF THE IMPORTANCE OF HIS FATHER'S BILL.
I'M ASKING YOU TO FINISH THE SENATOR'S TERM, BRUCE!
YOU... YOU MUST BE JOKING!

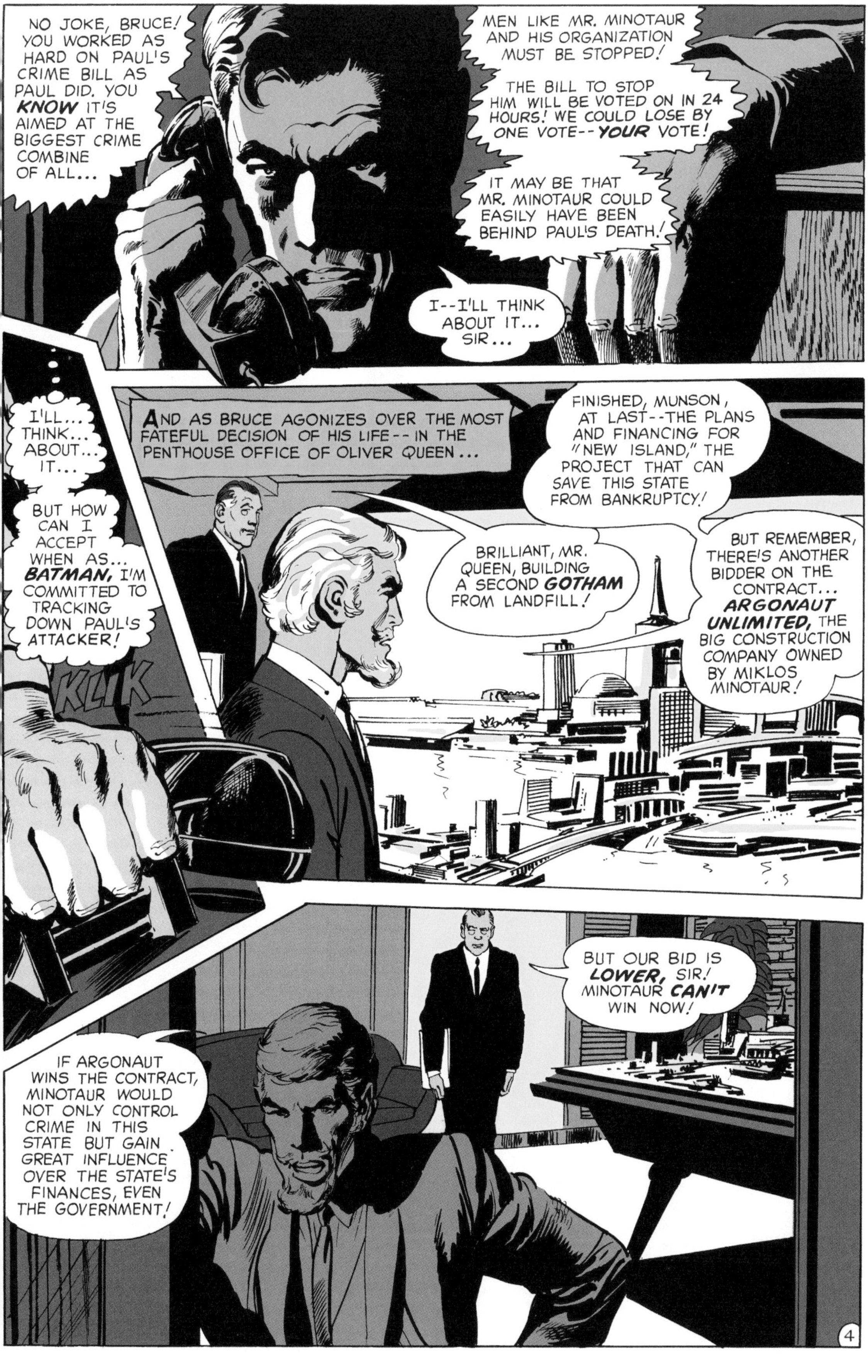
NO JOKE, BRUCE! YOU WORKED AS HARD ON PAUL'S CRIME BILL AS PAUL DID. YOU **KNOW** IT'S AIMED AT THE BIGGEST CRIME COMBINE OF ALL...
MEN LIKE MR. MINOTAUR AND HIS ORGANIZATION MUST BE STOPPED!
THE BILL TO STOP HIM WILL BE VOTED ON IN 24 HOURS! WE COULD LOSE BY ONE VOTE--**YOUR** VOTE!
IT MAY BE THAT MR. MINOTAUR COULD EASILY HAVE BEEN BEHIND PAUL'S DEATH!
I--I'LL THINK ABOUT IT... SIR...
I'LL... THINK... ABOUT... IT...
BUT HOW CAN I ACCEPT WHEN AS... **BATMAN,** I'M COMMITTED TO TRACKING DOWN PAUL'S ATTACKER!
KLIK
AND AS BRUCE AGONIZES OVER THE MOST FATEFUL DECISION OF HIS LIFE--IN THE PENTHOUSE OFFICE OF OLIVER QUEEN...
FINISHED, MUNSON, AT LAST--THE PLANS AND FINANCING FOR "NEW ISLAND," THE PROJECT THAT CAN SAVE THIS STATE FROM BANKRUPTCY!
BRILLIANT, MR. QUEEN, BUILDING A SECOND **GOTHAM** FROM LANDFILL!
BUT REMEMBER, THERE'S ANOTHER BIDDER ON THE CONTRACT... **ARGONAUT UNLIMITED,** THE BIG CONSTRUCTION COMPANY OWNED BY MIKLOS MINOTAUR!
BUT OUR BID IS **LOWER,** SIR! MINOTAUR **CAN'T** WIN NOW!
IF ARGONAUT WINS THE CONTRACT, MINOTAUR WOULD NOT ONLY CONTROL CRIME IN THIS STATE BUT GAIN GREAT INFLUENCE OVER THE STATE'S FINANCES, EVEN THE GOVERNMENT!
4

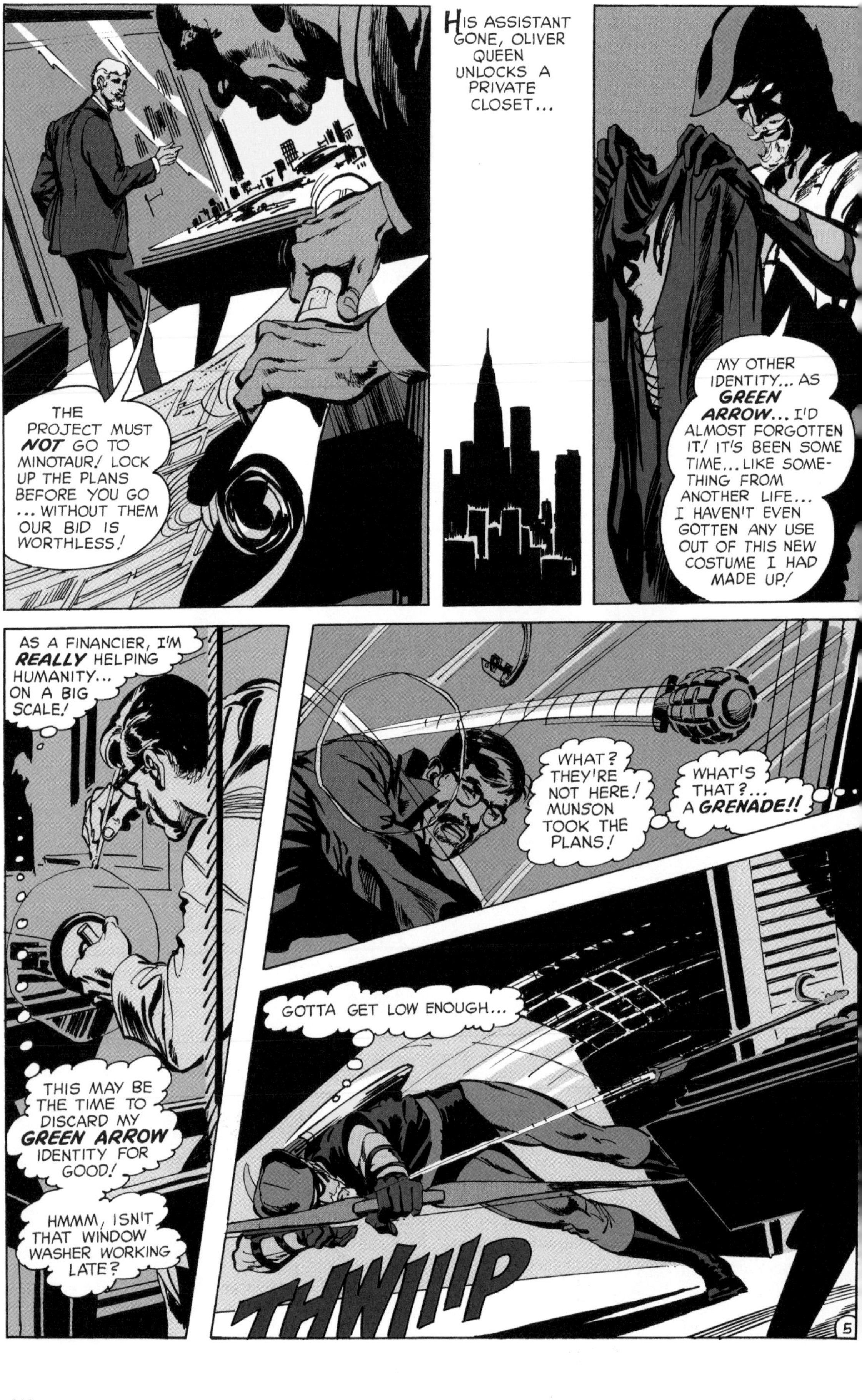

HIS ASSISTANT GONE, OLIVER QUEEN UNLOCKS A PRIVATE CLOSET...
THE PROJECT MUST NOT GO TO MINOTAUR! LOCK UP THE PLANS BEFORE YOU GO ... WITHOUT THEM OUR BID IS WORTHLESS!
MY OTHER IDENTITY... AS GREEN ARROW... I'D ALMOST FORGOTTEN IT! IT'S BEEN SOME TIME... LIKE SOMETHING FROM ANOTHER LIFE... I HAVEN'T EVEN GOTTEN ANY USE OUT OF THIS NEW COSTUME I HAD MADE UP!
AS A FINANCIER, I'M REALLY HELPING HUMANITY... ON A BIG SCALE!
WHAT? THEY'RE NOT HERE! MUNSON TOOK THE PLANS!
WHAT'S THAT?... A GRENADE!!
GOTTA GET LOW ENOUGH...
THIS MAY BE THE TIME TO DISCARD MY GREEN ARROW IDENTITY FOR GOOD!
HMMM, ISN'T THAT WINDOW WASHER WORKING LATE?
THWIIP
5

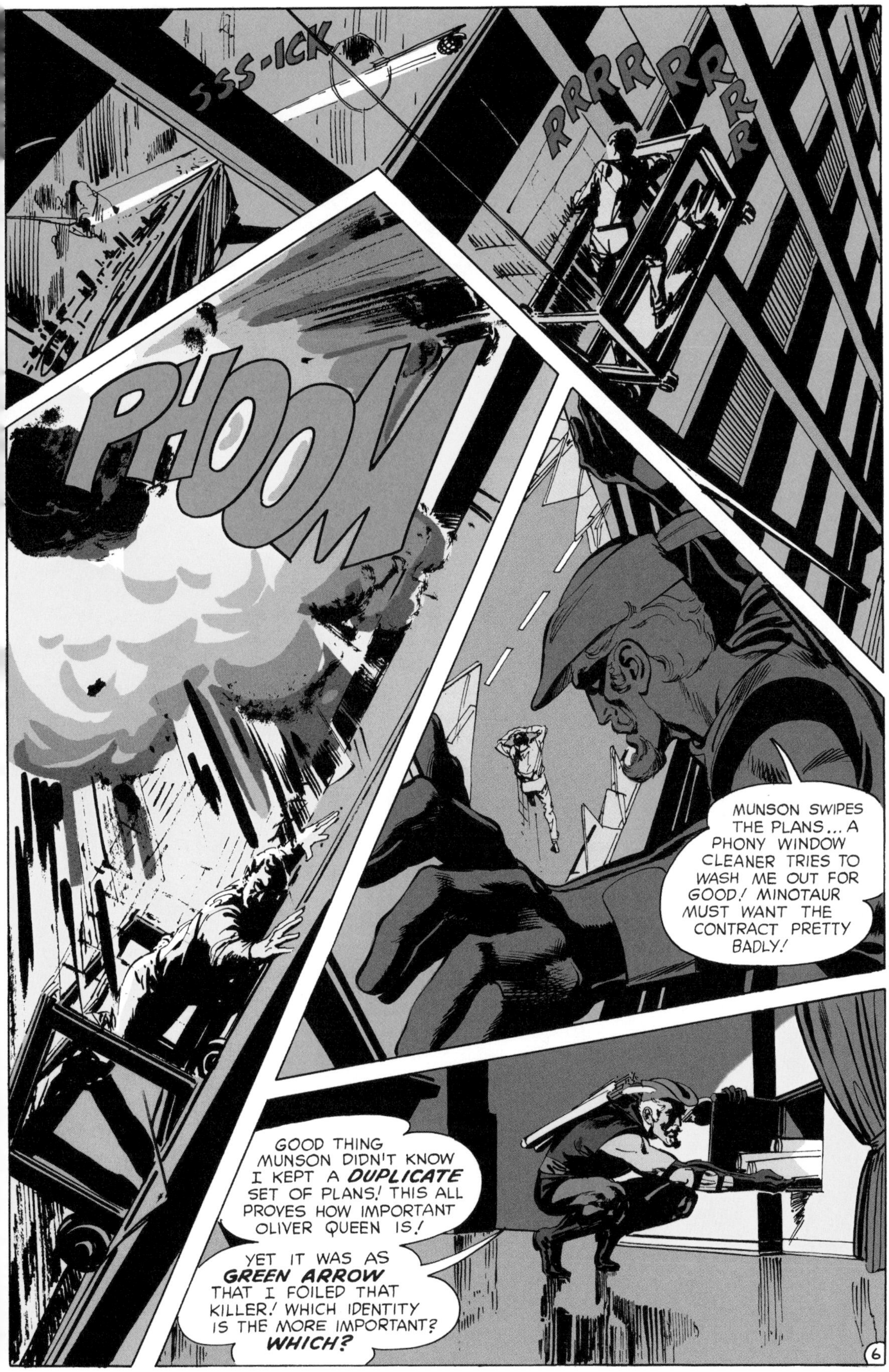
SSS-ICK
RRRRRRRR
PHOOM
MUNSON SWIPES THE PLANS... A PHONY WINDOW CLEANER TRIES TO WASH ME OUT FOR GOOD! MINOTAUR MUST WANT THE CONTRACT PRETTY BADLY!
GOOD THING MUNSON DIDN'T KNOW I KEPT A DUPLICATE SET OF PLANS! THIS ALL PROVES HOW IMPORTANT OLIVER QUEEN IS!
YET IT WAS AS GREEN ARROW THAT I FOILED THAT KILLER! WHICH IDENTITY IS THE MORE IMPORTANT? WHICH?
6

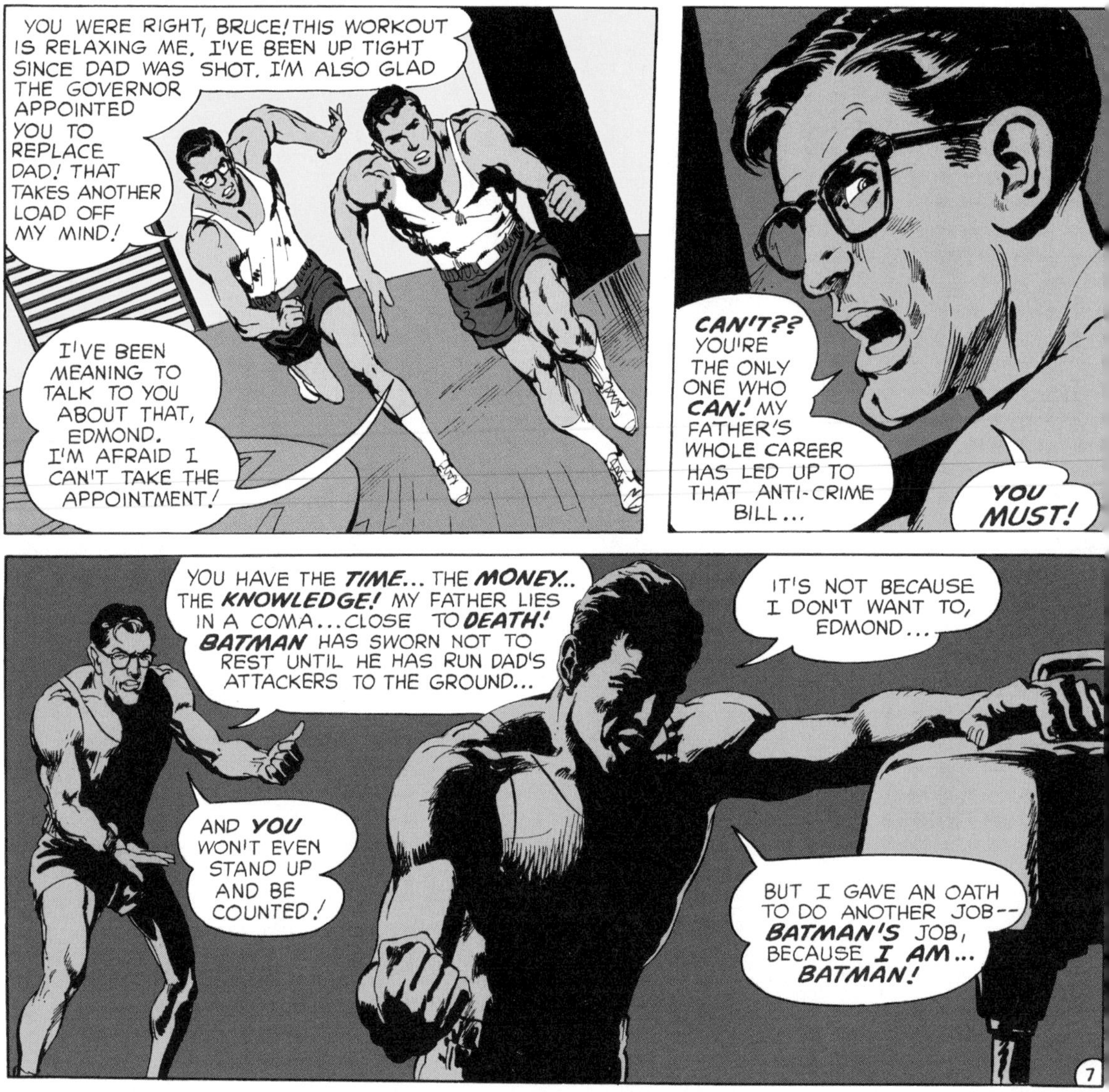
YOU WERE RIGHT, BRUCE! THIS WORKOUT IS RELAXING ME. I'VE BEEN UP TIGHT SINCE DAD WAS SHOT. I'M ALSO GLAD THE GOVERNOR APPOINTED YOU TO REPLACE DAD! THAT TAKES ANOTHER LOAD OFF MY MIND!
I'VE BEEN MEANING TO TALK TO YOU ABOUT THAT, EDMOND. I'M AFRAID I CAN'T TAKE THE APPOINTMENT!
CAN'T?? YOU'RE THE ONLY ONE WHO CAN! MY FATHER'S WHOLE CAREER HAS LED UP TO THAT ANTI-CRIME BILL...
YOU MUST!
YOU HAVE THE TIME... THE MONEY... THE KNOWLEDGE! MY FATHER LIES IN A COMA...CLOSE TO DEATH! BATMAN HAS SWORN NOT TO REST UNTIL HE HAS RUN DAD'S ATTACKERS TO THE GROUND...
AND YOU WON'T EVEN STAND UP AND BE COUNTED!
IT'S NOT BECAUSE I DON'T WANT TO, EDMOND...
BUT I GAVE AN OATH TO DO ANOTHER JOB-- BATMAN'S JOB, BECAUSE I AM... BATMAN!
7

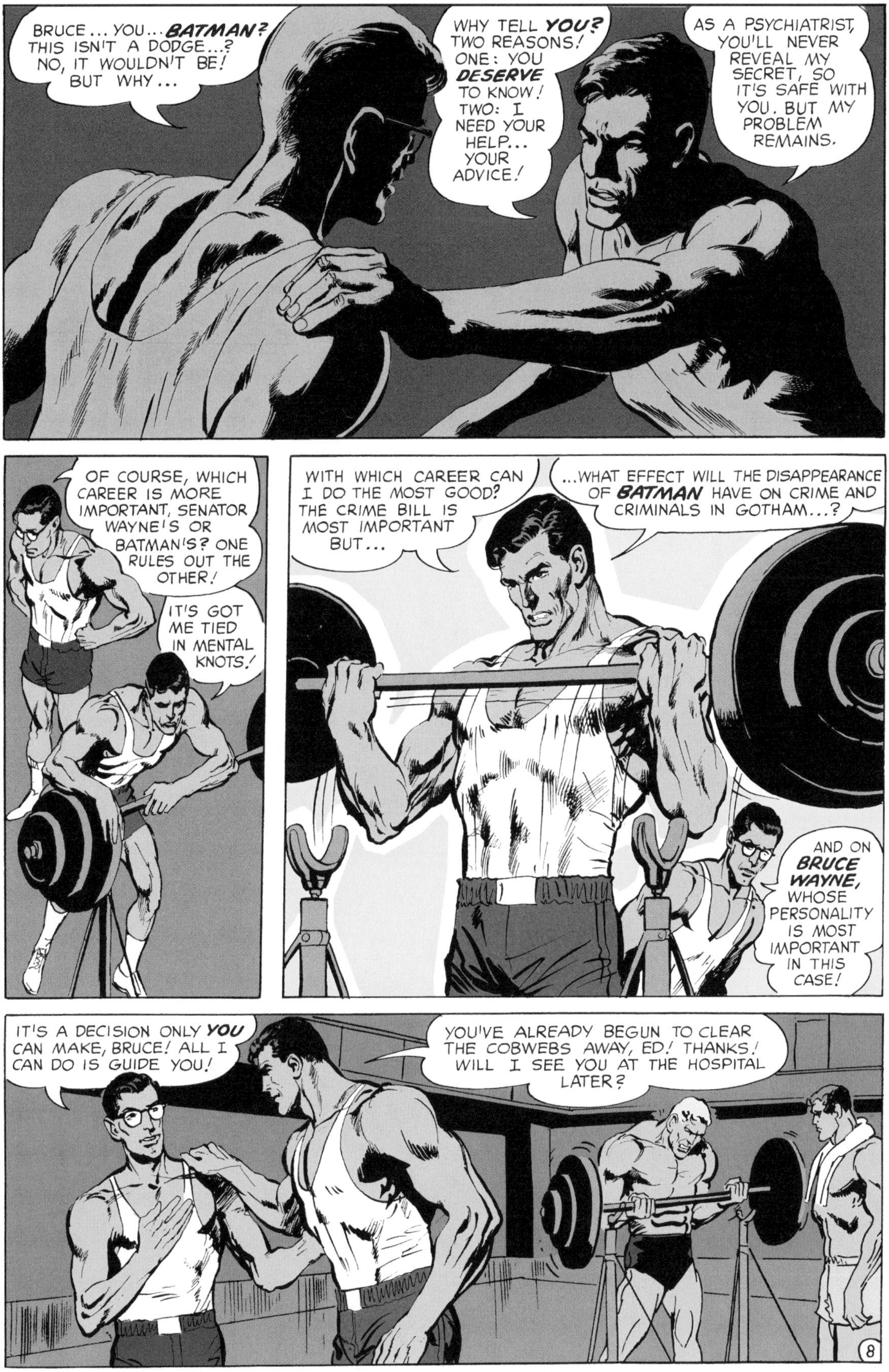
BRUCE... YOU... BATMAN? THIS ISN'T A DODGE...? NO, IT WOULDN'T BE! BUT WHY...
WHY TELL YOU? TWO REASONS! ONE: YOU DESERVE TO KNOW! TWO: I NEED YOUR HELP... YOUR ADVICE!
AS A PSYCHIATRIST, YOU'LL NEVER REVEAL MY SECRET, SO IT'S SAFE WITH YOU. BUT MY PROBLEM REMAINS.
OF COURSE, WHICH CAREER IS MORE IMPORTANT, SENATOR WAYNE'S OR BATMAN'S? ONE RULES OUT THE OTHER!
IT'S GOT ME TIED IN MENTAL KNOTS!
WITH WHICH CAREER CAN I DO THE MOST GOOD? THE CRIME BILL IS MOST IMPORTANT BUT...
...WHAT EFFECT WILL THE DISAPPEARANCE OF BATMAN HAVE ON CRIME AND CRIMINALS IN GOTHAM...?
AND ON BRUCE WAYNE, WHOSE PERSONALITY IS MOST IMPORTANT IN THIS CASE!
IT'S A DECISION ONLY YOU CAN MAKE, BRUCE! ALL I CAN DO IS GUIDE YOU!
YOU'VE ALREADY BEGUN TO CLEAR THE COBWEBS AWAY, ED! THANKS! WILL I SEE YOU AT THE HOSPITAL LATER?
8

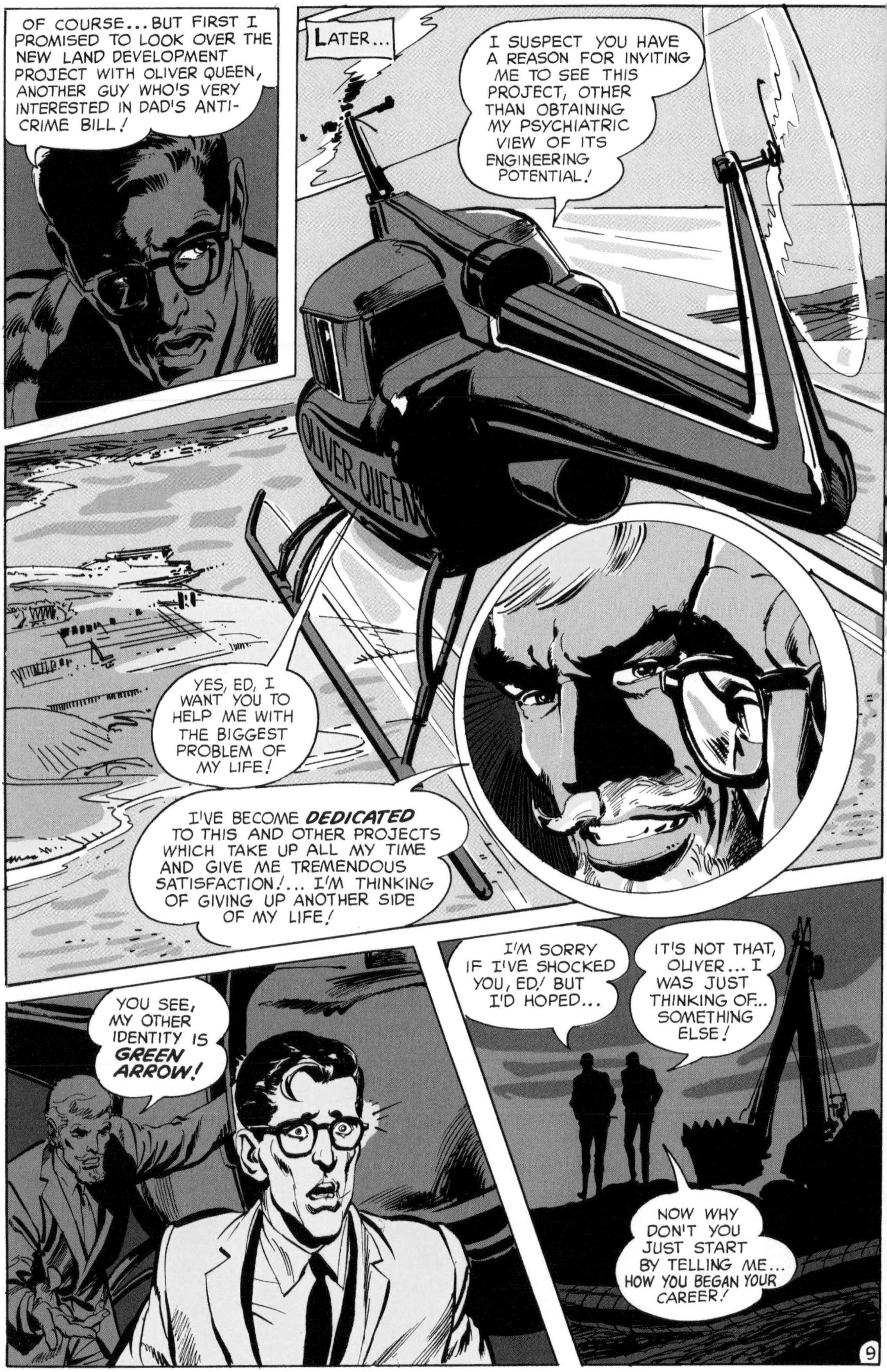

OF COURSE... BUT FIRST I PROMISED TO LOOK OVER THE NEW LAND DEVELOPMENT PROJECT WITH OLIVER QUEEN, ANOTHER GUY WHO'S VERY INTERESTED IN DAD'S ANTI-CRIME BILL!
LATER...
I SUSPECT YOU HAVE A REASON FOR INVITING ME TO SEE THIS PROJECT, OTHER THAN OBTAINING MY PSYCHIATRIC VIEW OF ITS ENGINEERING POTENTIAL!
OLIVER QUEEN
YES, ED, I WANT YOU TO HELP ME WITH THE BIGGEST PROBLEM OF MY LIFE!
I'VE BECOME **DEDICATED** TO THIS AND OTHER PROJECTS WHICH TAKE UP ALL MY TIME AND GIVE ME TREMENDOUS SATISFACTION!... I'M THINKING OF GIVING UP ANOTHER SIDE OF MY LIFE!
YOU SEE, MY OTHER IDENTITY IS **GREEN ARROW!**
I'M SORRY IF I'VE SHOCKED YOU, ED! BUT I'D HOPED...
IT'S NOT THAT, OLIVER... I WAS JUST THINKING OF... SOMETHING ELSE!
NOW WHY DON'T YOU JUST START BY TELLING ME... HOW YOU BEGAN YOUR CAREER!
9

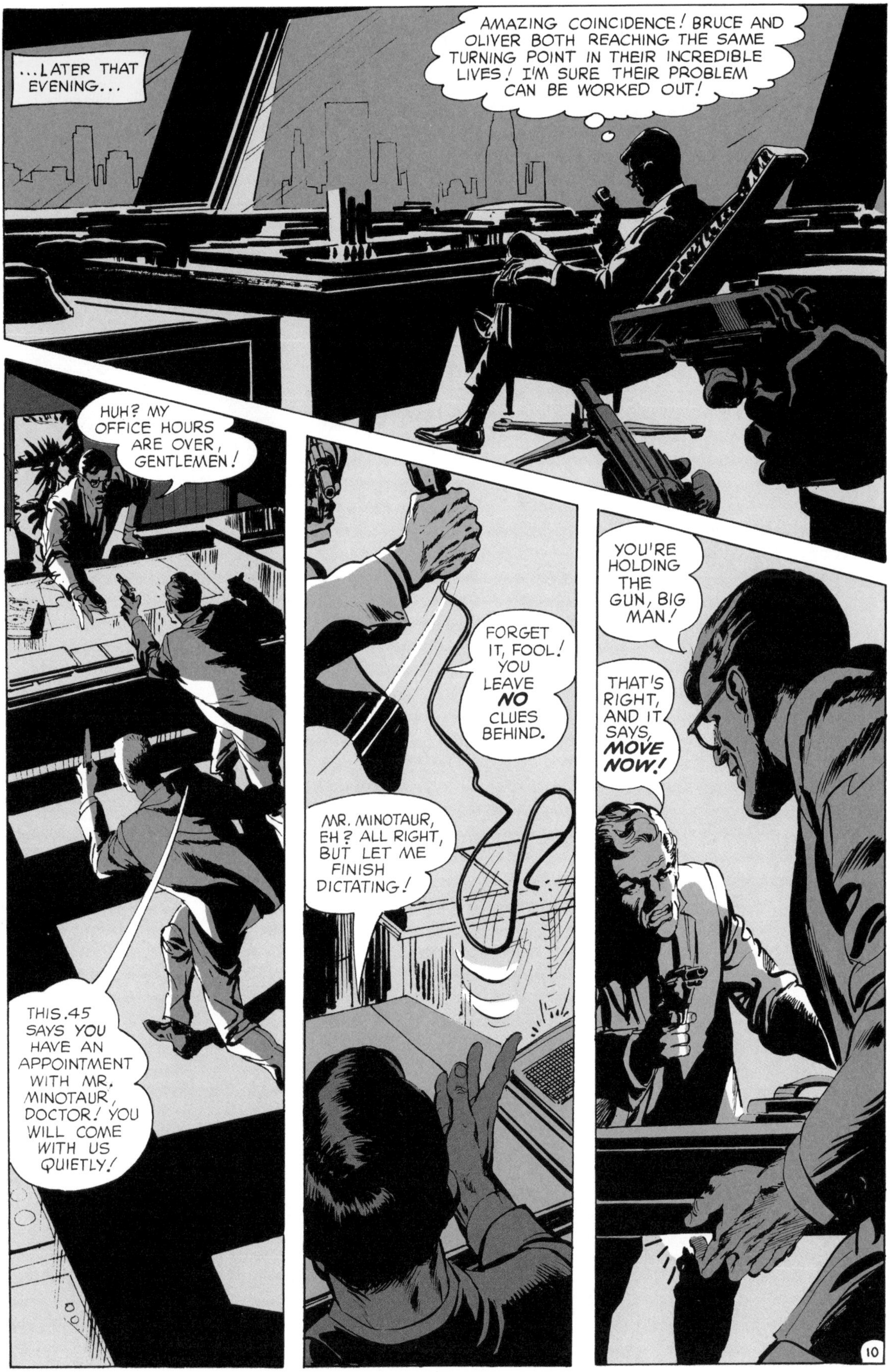
...LATER THAT EVENING...
AMAZING COINCIDENCE! BRUCE AND OLIVER BOTH REACHING THE SAME TURNING POINT IN THEIR INCREDIBLE LIVES! I'M SURE THEIR PROBLEM CAN BE WORKED OUT!
HUH? MY OFFICE HOURS ARE OVER, GENTLEMEN!
THIS .45 SAYS YOU HAVE AN APPOINTMENT WITH MR. MINOTAUR, DOCTOR! YOU WILL COME WITH US QUIETLY!
FORGET IT, FOOL! YOU LEAVE NO CLUES BEHIND.
MR. MINOTAUR, EH? ALL RIGHT, BUT LET ME FINISH DICTATING!
YOU'RE HOLDING THE GUN, BIG MAN!
THAT'S RIGHT, AND IT SAYS, MOVE NOW!
10

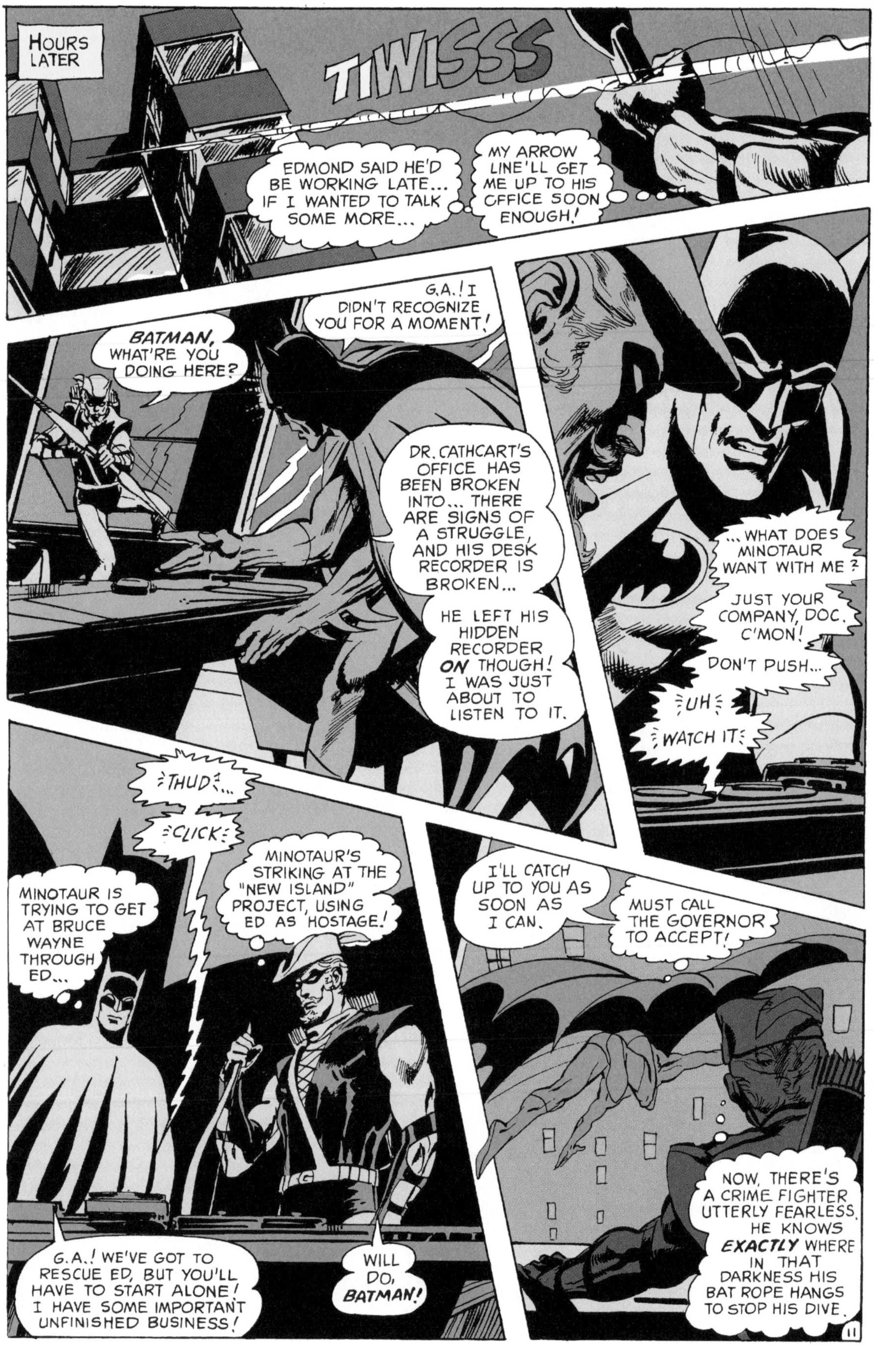
HOURS LATER
TIWISSS
EDMOND SAID HE'D BE WORKING LATE... IF I WANTED TO TALK SOME MORE...
MY ARROW LINE'LL GET ME UP TO HIS OFFICE SOON ENOUGH!
BATMAN, WHAT'RE YOU DOING HERE?
G.A.! I DIDN'T RECOGNIZE YOU FOR A MOMENT!
DR. CATHCART'S OFFICE HAS BEEN BROKEN INTO... THERE ARE SIGNS OF A STRUGGLE, AND HIS DESK RECORDER IS BROKEN...
HE LEFT HIS HIDDEN RECORDER ON THOUGH! I WAS JUST ABOUT TO LISTEN TO IT.
...WHAT DOES MINOTAUR WANT WITH ME?
JUST YOUR COMPANY, DOC. C'MON!
DON'T PUSH...
UH
WATCH IT
THUD...
CLICK
MINOTAUR IS TRYING TO GET AT BRUCE WAYNE THROUGH ED...
MINOTAUR'S STRIKING AT THE "NEW ISLAND" PROJECT, USING ED AS HOSTAGE!
G.A.! WE'VE GOT TO RESCUE ED, BUT YOU'LL HAVE TO START ALONE! I HAVE SOME IMPORTANT UNFINISHED BUSINESS!
WILL DO, BATMAN!
I'LL CATCH UP TO YOU AS SOON AS I CAN.
MUST CALL THE GOVERNOR TO ACCEPT!
NOW, THERE'S A CRIME FIGHTER UTTERLY FEARLESS. HE KNOWS EXACTLY WHERE IN THAT DARKNESS HIS BAT ROPE HANGS TO STOP HIS DIVE.
11

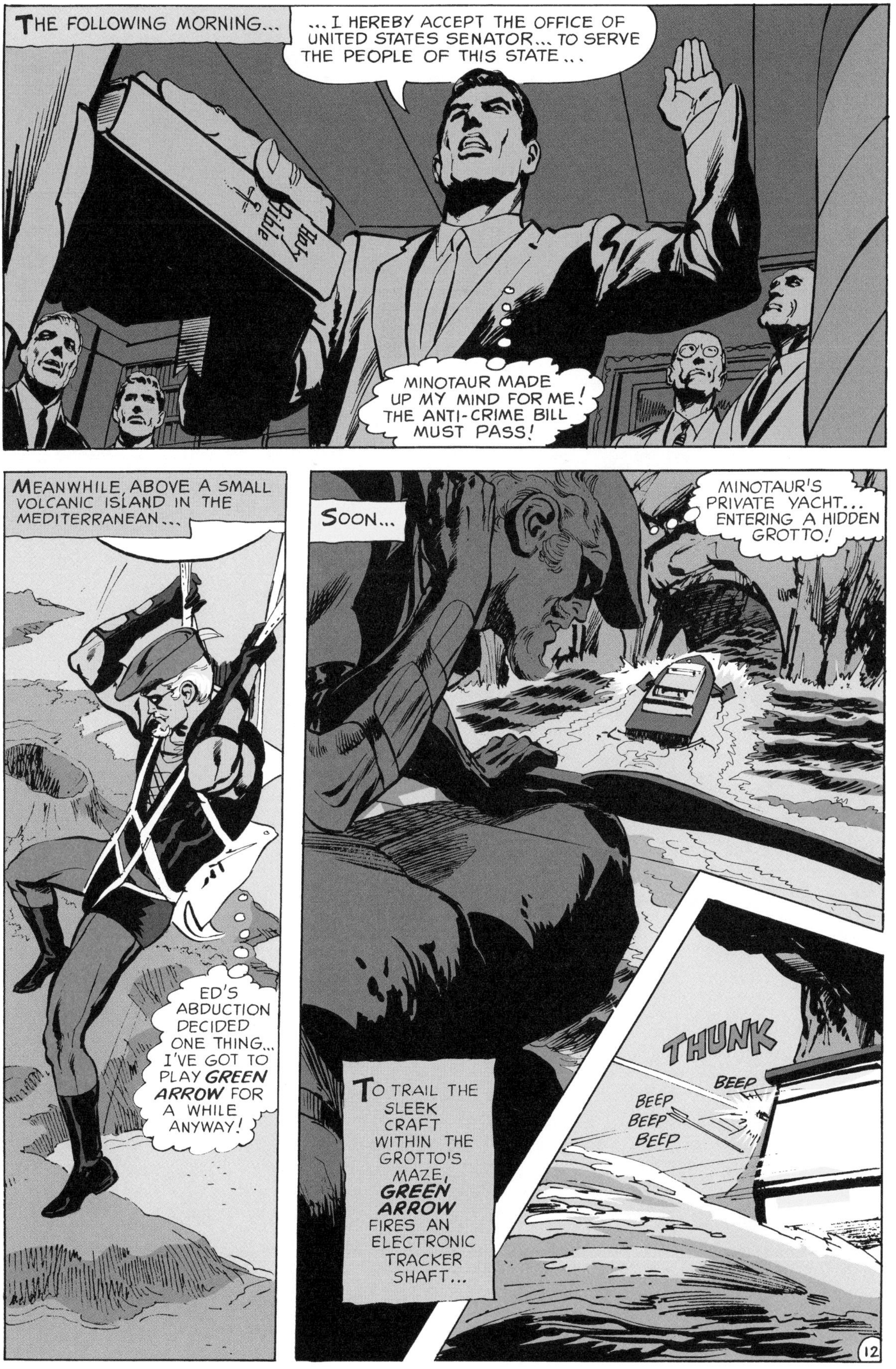

THE FOLLOWING MORNING...
...I HEREBY ACCEPT THE OFFICE OF UNITED STATES SENATOR... TO SERVE THE PEOPLE OF THIS STATE...
Holy Bible
MINOTAUR MADE UP MY MIND FOR ME! THE ANTI-CRIME BILL MUST PASS!
MEANWHILE, ABOVE A SMALL VOLCANIC ISLAND IN THE MEDITERRANEAN...
ED'S ABDUCTION DECIDED ONE THING... I'VE GOT TO PLAY GREEN ARROW FOR A WHILE ANYWAY!
SOON...
MINOTAUR'S PRIVATE YACHT... ENTERING A HIDDEN GROTTO!
TO TRAIL THE SLEEK CRAFT WITHIN THE GROTTO'S MAZE, GREEN ARROW FIRES AN ELECTRONIC TRACKER SHAFT...
THUNK
BEEP
BEEP
BEEP
BEEP
12

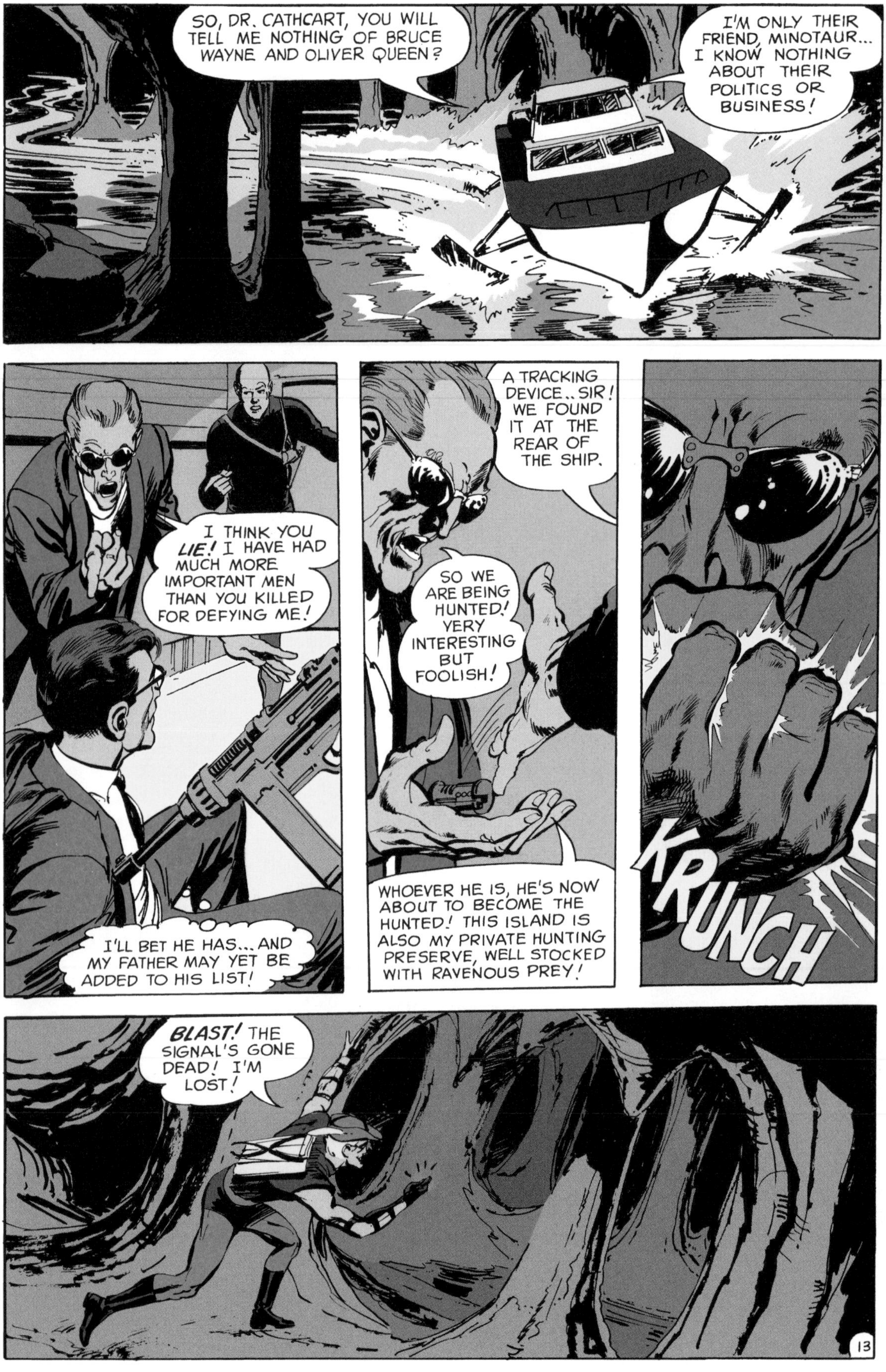
SO, DR. CATHCART, YOU WILL TELL ME NOTHING OF BRUCE WAYNE AND OLIVER QUEEN?
I'M ONLY THEIR FRIEND, MINOTAUR... I KNOW NOTHING ABOUT THEIR POLITICS OR BUSINESS!
I THINK YOU LIE! I HAVE HAD MUCH MORE IMPORTANT MEN THAN YOU KILLED FOR DEFYING ME!
I'LL BET HE HAS... AND MY FATHER MAY YET BE ADDED TO HIS LIST!
A TRACKING DEVICE.. SIR! WE FOUND IT AT THE REAR OF THE SHIP.
SO WE ARE BEING HUNTED! VERY INTERESTING BUT FOOLISH!
WHOEVER HE IS, HE'S NOW ABOUT TO BECOME THE HUNTED! THIS ISLAND IS ALSO MY PRIVATE HUNTING PRESERVE, WELL STOCKED WITH RAVENOUS PREY!
KRUNCH
BLAST! THE SIGNAL'S GONE DEAD! I'M LOST!
13

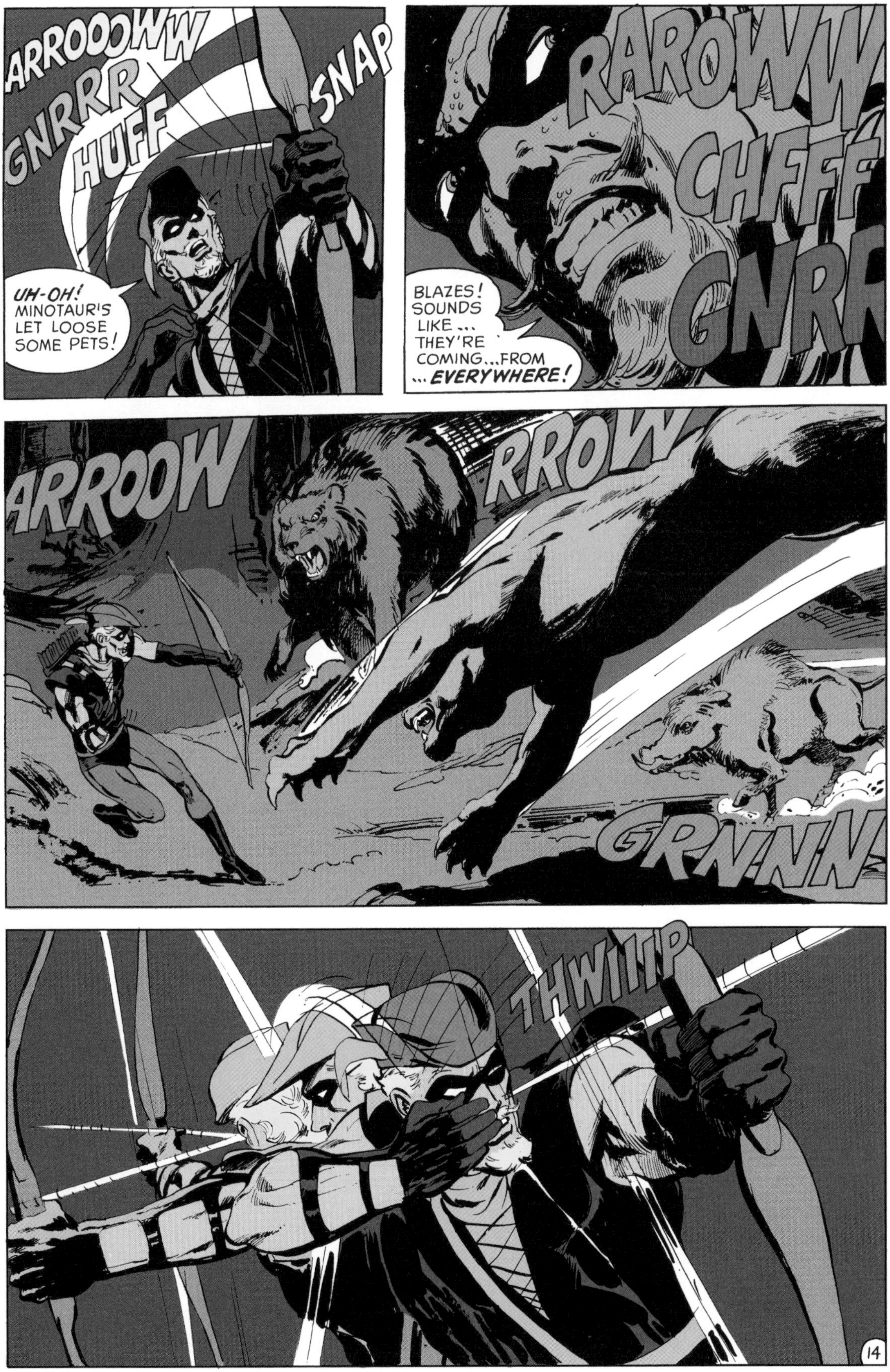
ARROOOWW
GNRRR
HUFF
SNAP
UH-OH! MINOTAUR'S LET LOOSE SOME PETS!
RAROWWW
CHFFF
GNRR
BLAZES! SOUNDS LIKE... THEY'RE COMING...FROM ...EVERYWHERE!
ARROOW
RROW
GRNNN
THWIIIP
14

SKREEOW
THWIIIIIP
SWIIIIIIP
RRUNT
ROOAR
15

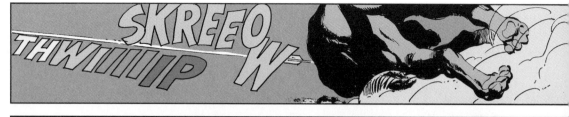

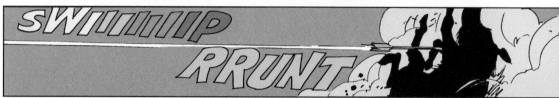

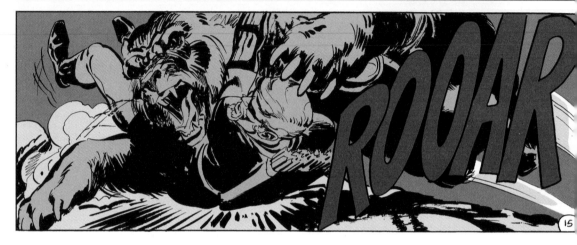

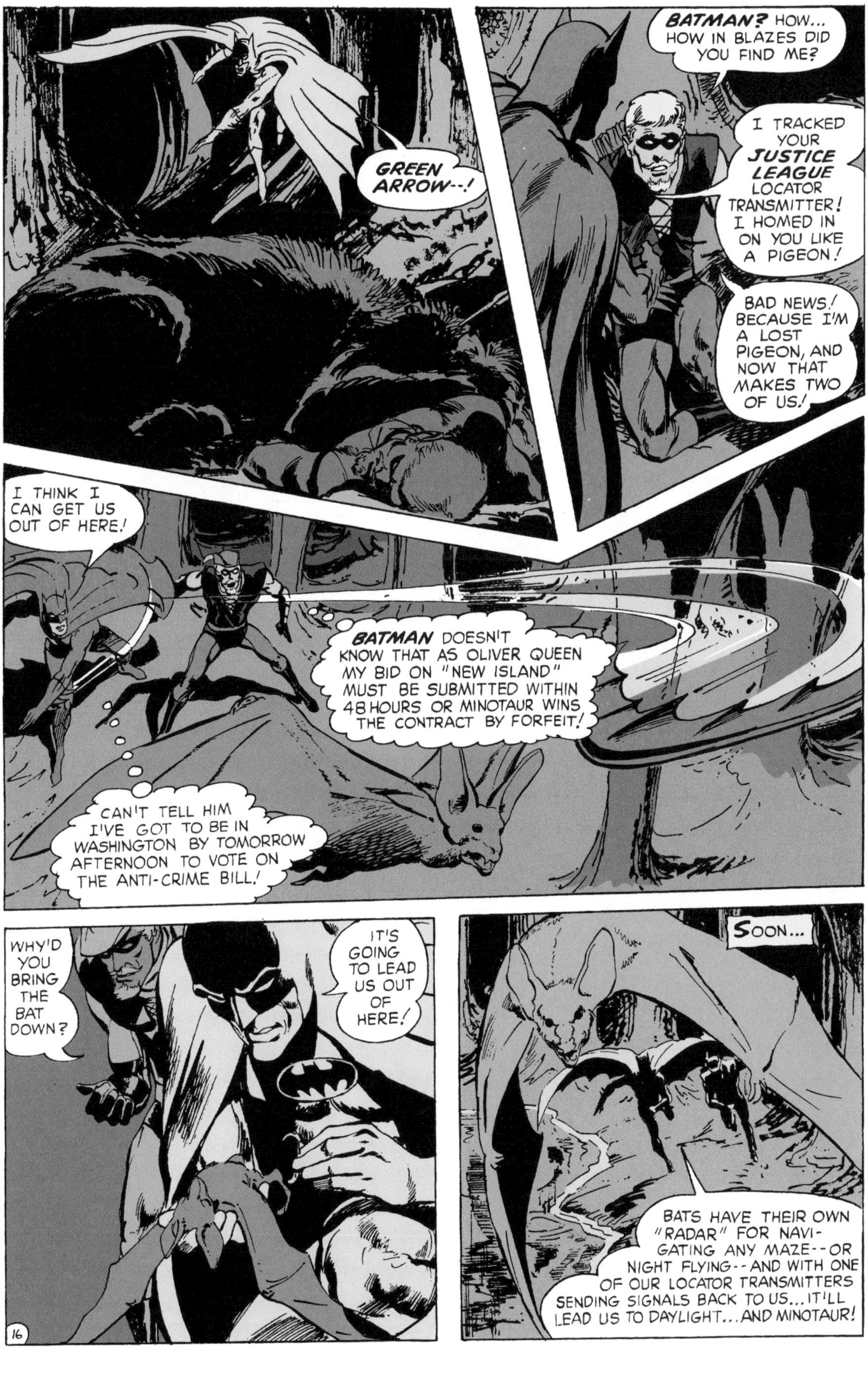
GREEN ARROW--!
BATMAN? HOW... HOW IN BLAZES DID YOU FIND ME?
I TRACKED YOUR JUSTICE LEAGUE LOCATOR TRANSMITTER! I HOMED IN ON YOU LIKE A PIGEON!
BAD NEWS! BECAUSE I'M A LOST PIGEON, AND NOW THAT MAKES TWO OF US!
I THINK I CAN GET US OUT OF HERE!
BATMAN DOESN'T KNOW THAT AS OLIVER QUEEN MY BID ON "NEW ISLAND" MUST BE SUBMITTED WITHIN 48 HOURS OR MINOTAUR WINS THE CONTRACT BY FORFEIT!
CAN'T TELL HIM I'VE GOT TO BE IN WASHINGTON BY TOMORROW AFTERNOON TO VOTE ON THE ANTI-CRIME BILL!
WHY'D YOU BRING THE BAT DOWN?
IT'S GOING TO LEAD US OUT OF HERE!
SOON...
BATS HAVE THEIR OWN "RADAR" FOR NAVI-GATING ANY MAZE--OR NIGHT FLYING--AND WITH ONE OF OUR LOCATOR TRANSMITTERS SENDING SIGNALS BACK TO US...IT'LL LEAD US TO DAYLIGHT...AND MINOTAUR!
16

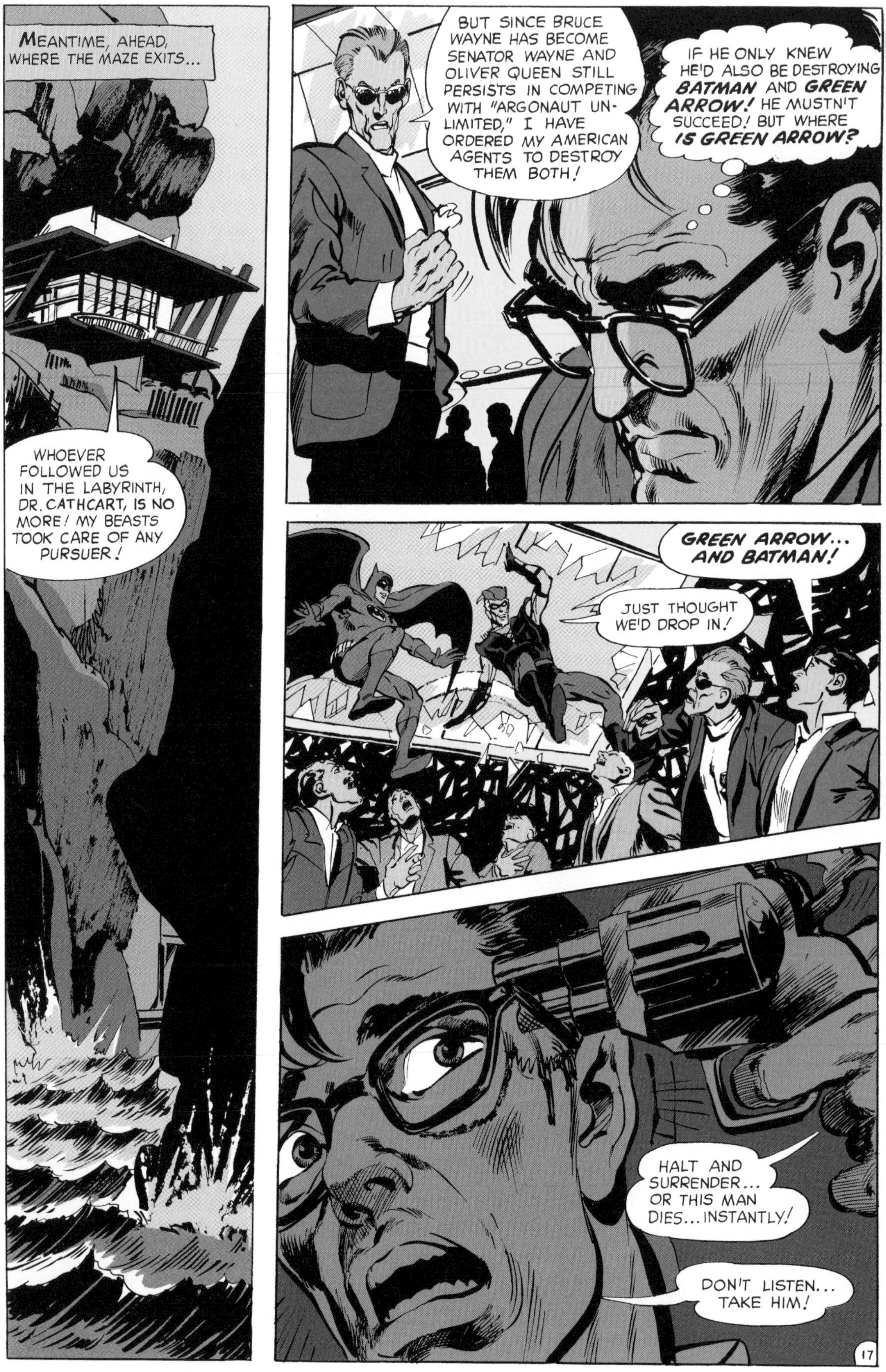
MEANTIME, AHEAD, WHERE THE MAZE EXITS...
WHOEVER FOLLOWED US IN THE LABYRINTH, DR. CATHCART, IS NO MORE! MY BEASTS TOOK CARE OF ANY PURSUER!
BUT SINCE BRUCE WAYNE HAS BECOME SENATOR WAYNE AND OLIVER QUEEN STILL PERSISTS IN COMPETING WITH "ARGONAUT UN-LIMITED," I HAVE ORDERED MY AMERICAN AGENTS TO DESTROY THEM BOTH!
IF HE ONLY KNEW HE'D ALSO BE DESTROYING BATMAN AND GREEN ARROW! HE MUSTN'T SUCCEED! BUT WHERE IS GREEN ARROW?
GREEN ARROW... AND BATMAN!
JUST THOUGHT WE'D DROP IN!
HALT AND SURRENDER... OR THIS MAN DIES... INSTANTLY!
DON'T LISTEN... TAKE HIM!
17

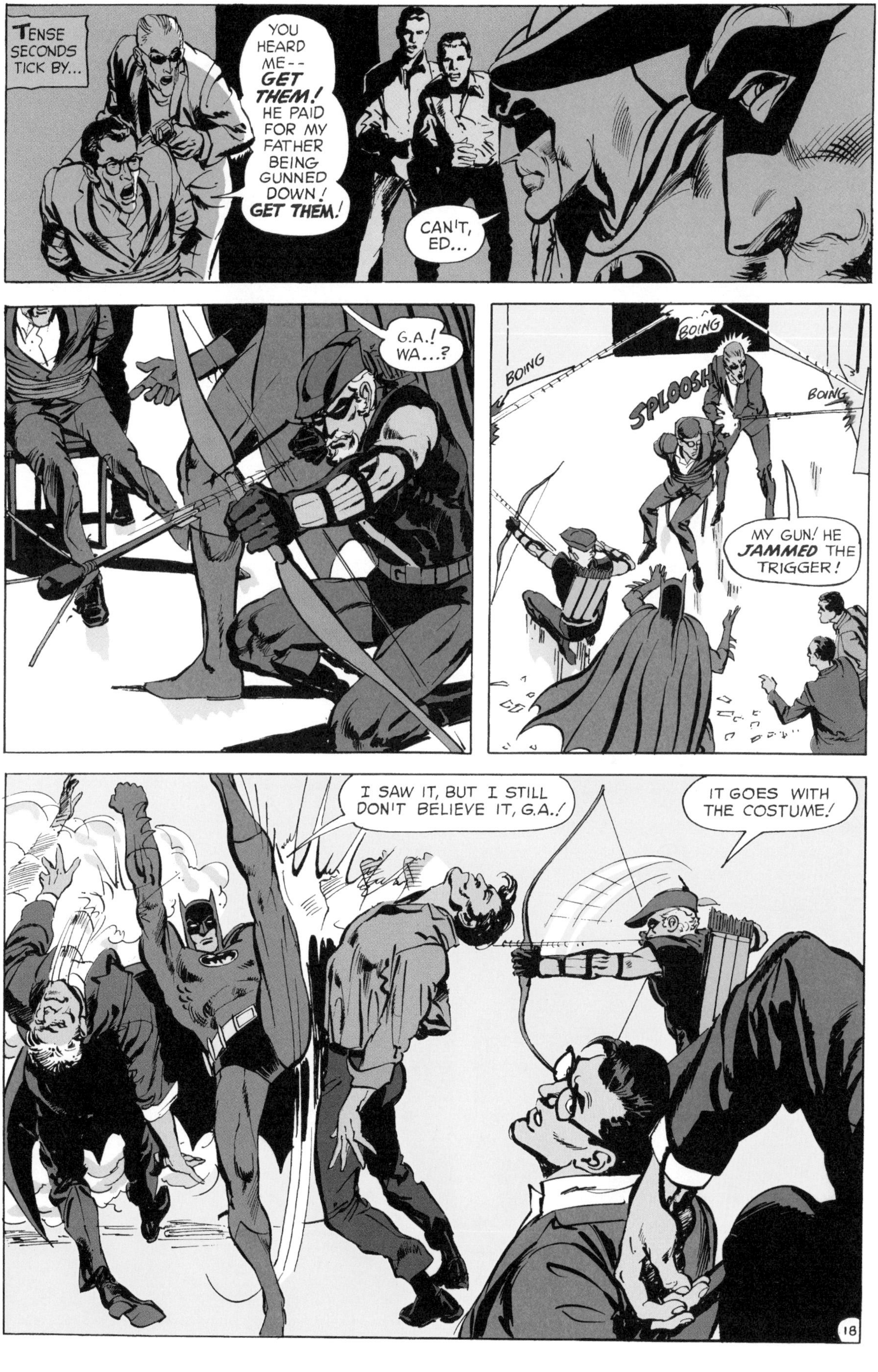
TENSE SECONDS TICK BY...
YOU HEARD ME-- GET THEM! HE PAID FOR MY FATHER BEING GUNNED DOWN! GET THEM!
CAN'T, ED...
G.A.! WA...?
BOING
BOING
SPLOOSH
BOING
MY GUN! HE JAMMED THE TRIGGER!
I SAW IT, BUT I STILL DON'T BELIEVE IT, G.A.!
IT GOES WITH THE COSTUME!
18

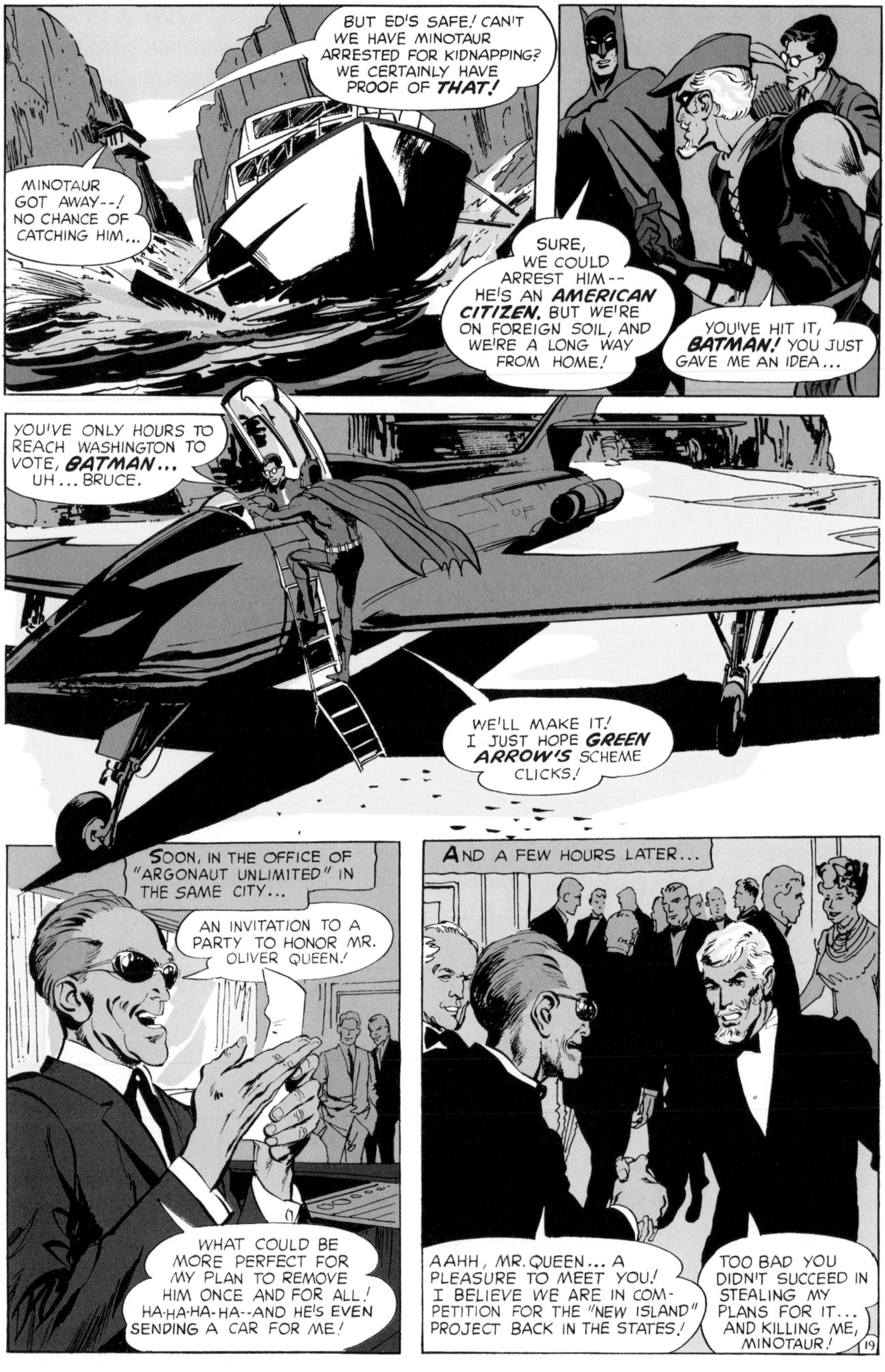
MINOTAUR GOT AWAY--! NO CHANCE OF CATCHING HIM...
BUT ED'S SAFE! CAN'T WE HAVE MINOTAUR ARRESTED FOR KIDNAPPING? WE CERTAINLY HAVE PROOF OF THAT!
SURE, WE COULD ARREST HIM-- HE'S AN AMERICAN CITIZEN. BUT WE'RE ON FOREIGN SOIL, AND WE'RE A LONG WAY FROM HOME!
YOU'VE HIT IT, BATMAN! YOU JUST GAVE ME AN IDEA...
YOU'VE ONLY HOURS TO REACH WASHINGTON TO VOTE, BATMAN... UH... BRUCE.
WE'LL MAKE IT! I JUST HOPE GREEN ARROW'S SCHEME CLICKS!
SOON, IN THE OFFICE OF "ARGONAUT UNLIMITED" IN THE SAME CITY...
AN INVITATION TO A PARTY TO HONOR MR. OLIVER QUEEN!
WHAT COULD BE MORE PERFECT FOR MY PLAN TO REMOVE HIM ONCE AND FOR ALL! HA-HA-HA-HA--AND HE'S EVEN SENDING A CAR FOR ME!
AND A FEW HOURS LATER...
AAHH, MR. QUEEN... A PLEASURE TO MEET YOU! I BELIEVE WE ARE IN COMPETITION FOR THE "NEW ISLAND" PROJECT BACK IN THE STATES!
TOO BAD YOU DIDN'T SUCCEED IN STEALING MY PLANS FOR IT... AND KILLING ME, MINOTAUR!
19

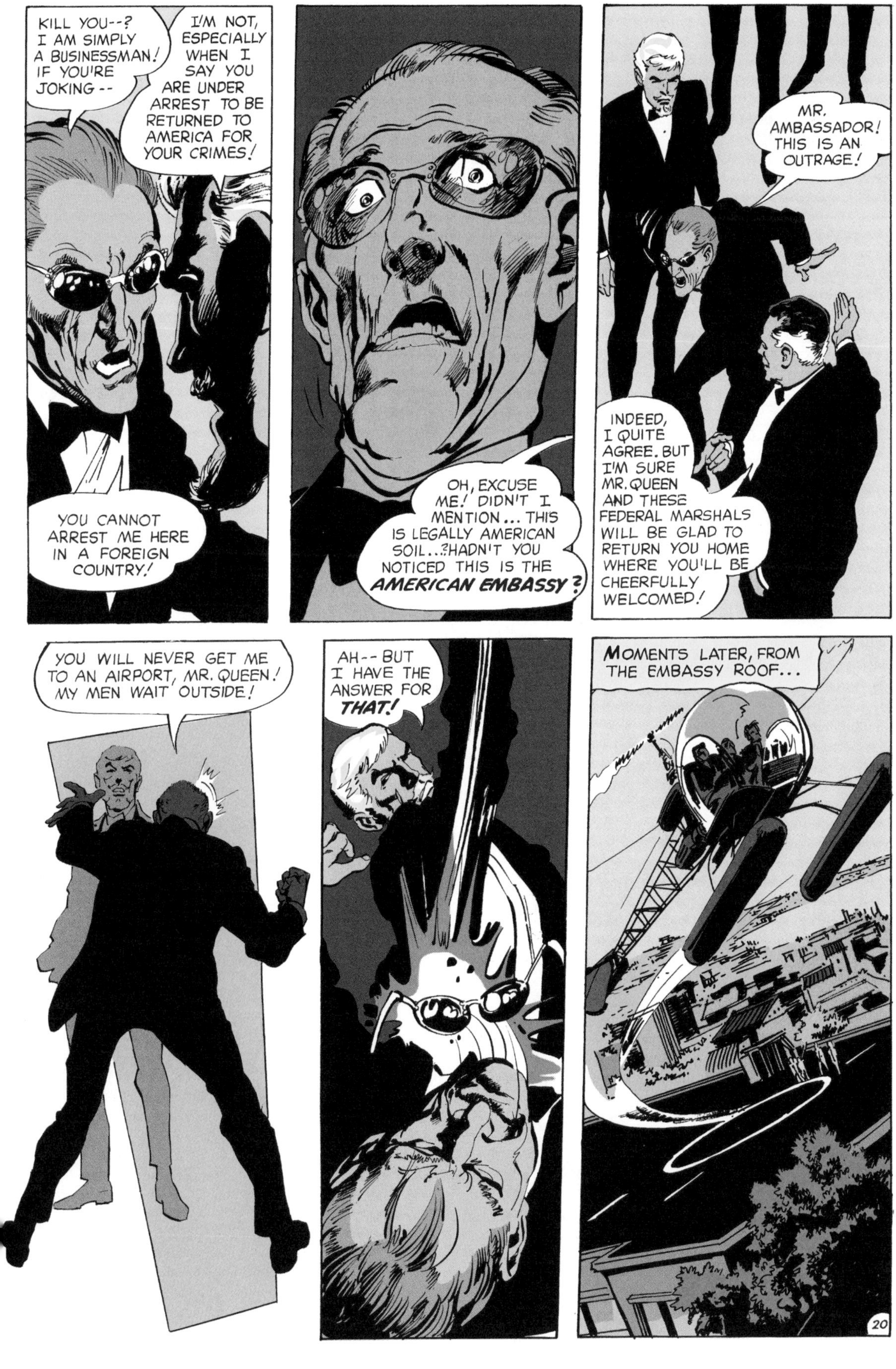
KILL YOU--? I AM SIMPLY A BUSINESSMAN! IF YOU'RE JOKING --
I'M NOT, ESPECIALLY WHEN I SAY YOU ARE UNDER ARREST TO BE RETURNED TO AMERICA FOR YOUR CRIMES!
YOU CANNOT ARREST ME HERE IN A FOREIGN COUNTRY!
OH, EXCUSE ME! DIDN'T I MENTION... THIS IS LEGALLY AMERICAN SOIL...?HADN'T YOU NOTICED THIS IS THE AMERICAN EMBASSY?
MR. AMBASSADOR! THIS IS AN OUTRAGE!
INDEED, I QUITE AGREE. BUT I'M SURE MR. QUEEN AND THESE FEDERAL MARSHALS WILL BE GLAD TO RETURN YOU HOME WHERE YOU'LL BE CHEERFULLY WELCOMED!
YOU WILL NEVER GET ME TO AN AIRPORT, MR. QUEEN! MY MEN WAIT OUTSIDE!
AH-- BUT I HAVE THE ANSWER FOR THAT!
MOMENTS LATER, FROM THE EMBASSY ROOF...
20

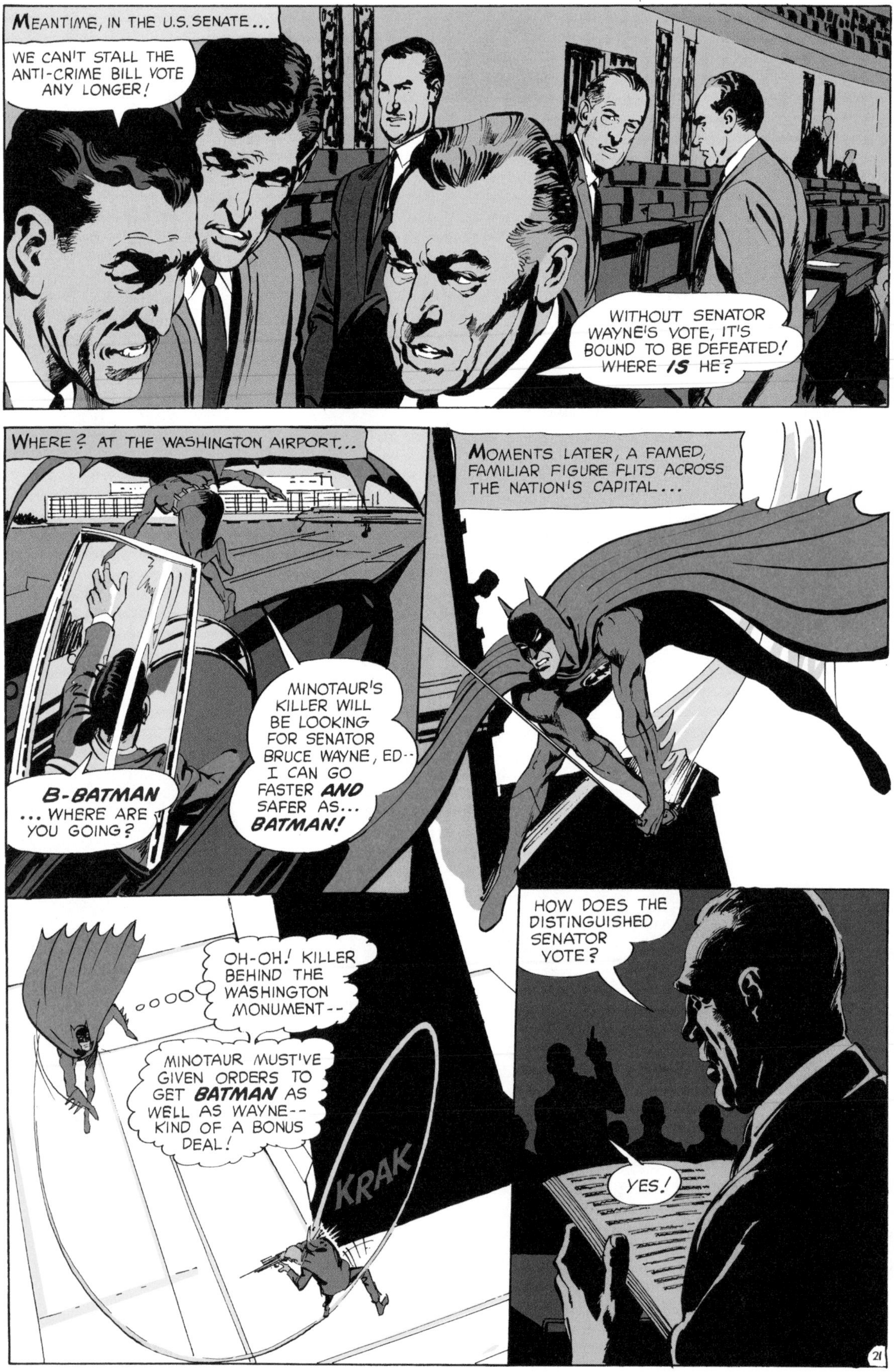
MEANTIME, IN THE U.S. SENATE...
WE CAN'T STALL THE ANTI-CRIME BILL VOTE ANY LONGER!
WITHOUT SENATOR WAYNE'S VOTE, IT'S BOUND TO BE DEFEATED! WHERE *IS* HE?
WHERE? AT THE WASHINGTON AIRPORT...
MINOTAUR'S KILLER WILL BE LOOKING FOR SENATOR BRUCE WAYNE, ED-- I CAN GO FASTER **AND** SAFER AS... **BATMAN!**
B-BATMAN ... WHERE ARE YOU GOING?
MOMENTS LATER, A FAMED, FAMILIAR FIGURE FLITS ACROSS THE NATION'S CAPITAL...
OH-OH! KILLER BEHIND THE WASHINGTON MONUMENT--
MINOTAUR MUST'VE GIVEN ORDERS TO GET **BATMAN** AS WELL AS WAYNE-- KIND OF A BONUS DEAL!
KRAK
HOW DOES THE DISTINGUISHED SENATOR VOTE?
YES!
21

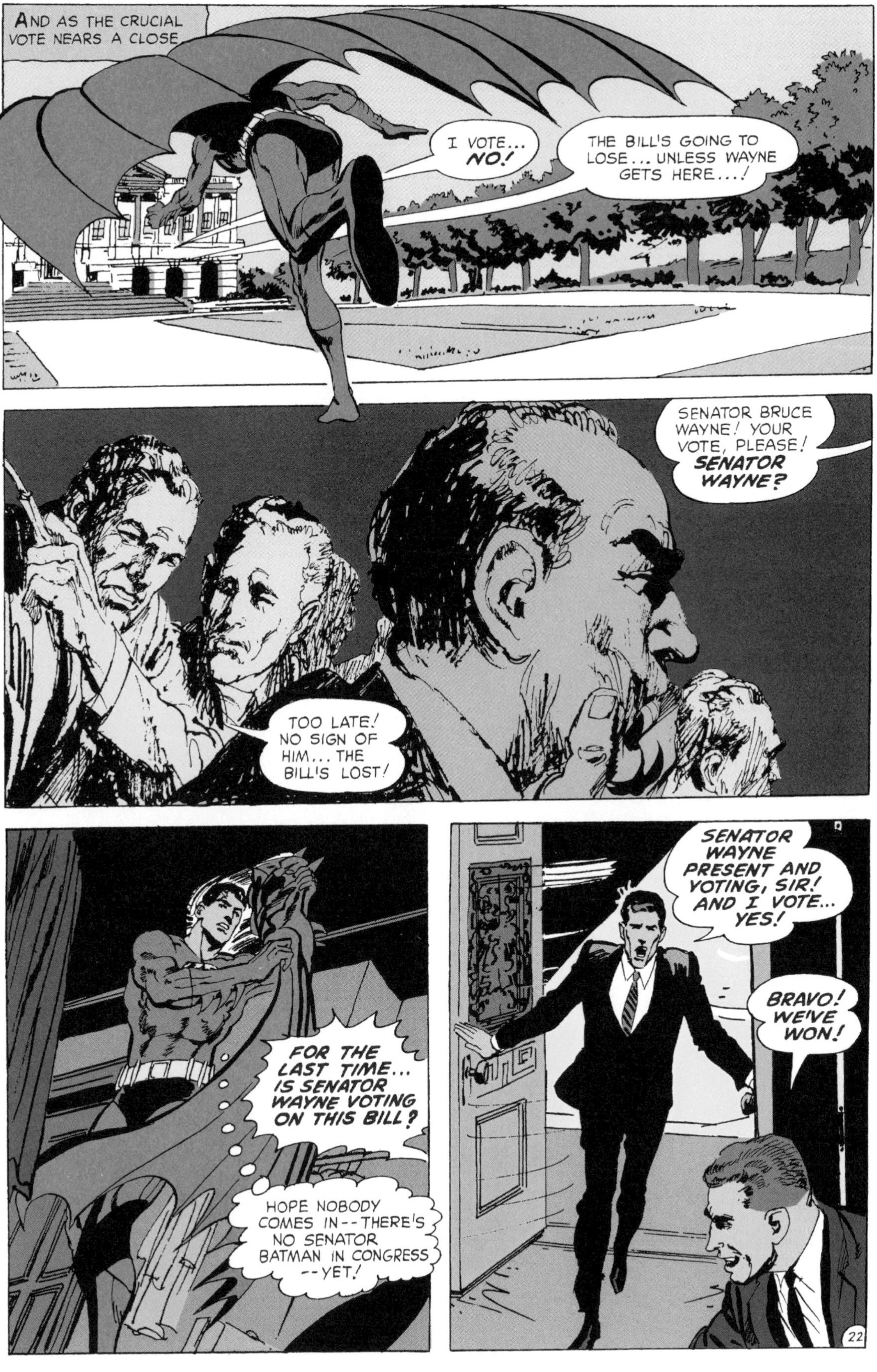
AND AS THE CRUCIAL VOTE NEARS A CLOSE
I VOTE... NO!
THE BILL'S GOING TO LOSE... UNLESS WAYNE GETS HERE...!
SENATOR BRUCE WAYNE! YOUR VOTE, PLEASE! SENATOR WAYNE?
TOO LATE! NO SIGN OF HIM... THE BILL'S LOST!
FOR THE LAST TIME... IS SENATOR WAYNE VOTING ON THIS BILL?
HOPE NOBODY COMES IN--THERE'S NO SENATOR BATMAN IN CONGRESS--YET!
SENATOR WAYNE PRESENT AND VOTING, SIR! AND I VOTE... YES!
BRAVO! WE'VE WON!
22

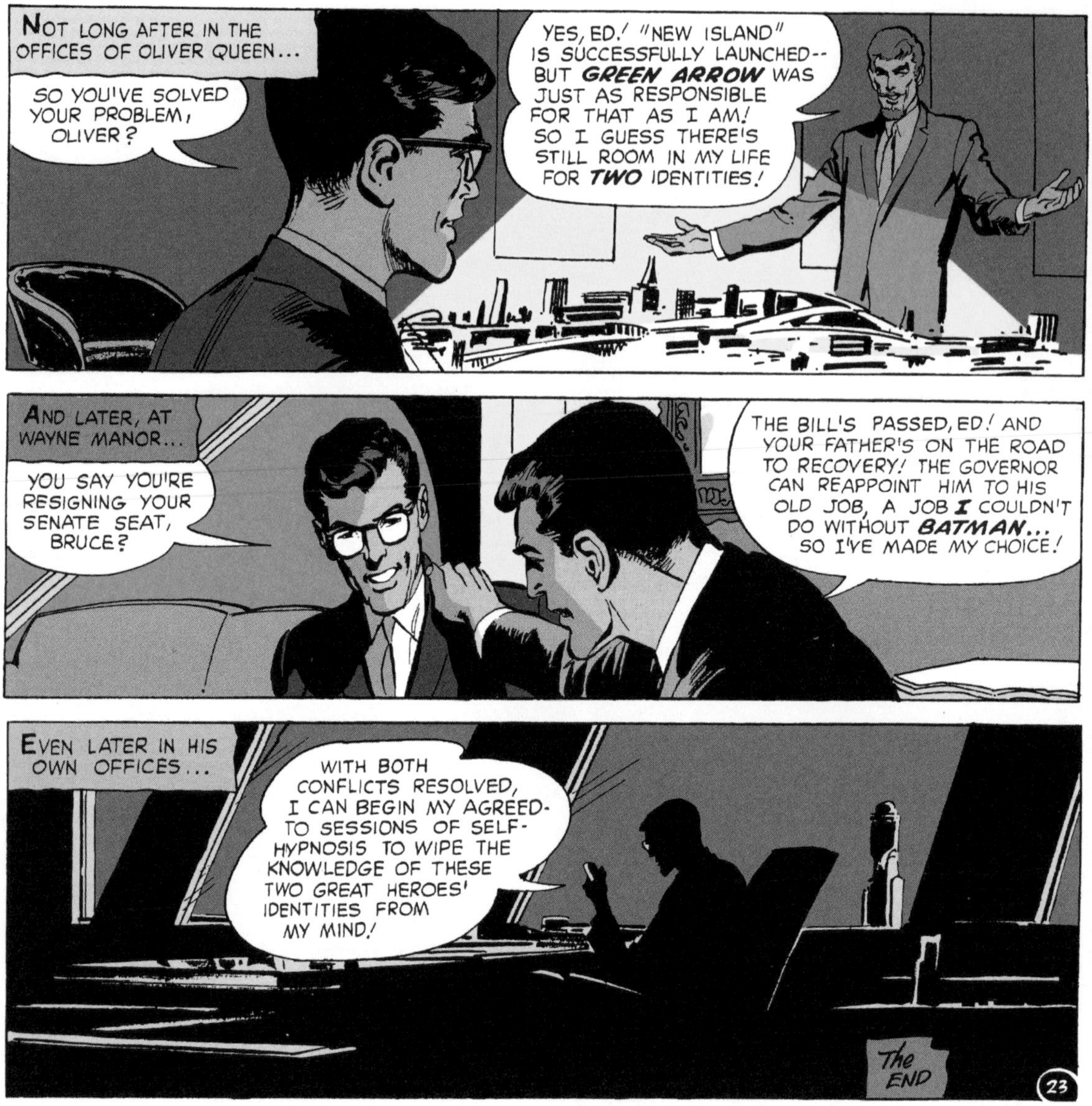
NOT LONG AFTER IN THE OFFICES OF OLIVER QUEEN...
SO YOU'VE SOLVED YOUR PROBLEM, OLIVER?
YES, ED! "NEW ISLAND" IS SUCCESSFULLY LAUNCHED-- BUT GREEN ARROW WAS JUST AS RESPONSIBLE FOR THAT AS I AM! SO I GUESS THERE'S STILL ROOM IN MY LIFE FOR TWO IDENTITIES!
AND LATER, AT WAYNE MANOR...
YOU SAY YOU'RE RESIGNING YOUR SENATE SEAT, BRUCE?
THE BILL'S PASSED, ED! AND YOUR FATHER'S ON THE ROAD TO RECOVERY! THE GOVERNOR CAN REAPPOINT HIM TO HIS OLD JOB, A JOB I COULDN'T DO WITHOUT BATMAN... SO I'VE MADE MY CHOICE!
EVEN LATER IN HIS OWN OFFICES...
WITH BOTH CONFLICTS RESOLVED, I CAN BEGIN MY AGREED-TO SESSIONS OF SELF-HYPNOSIS TO WIPE THE KNOWLEDGE OF THESE TWO GREAT HEROES' IDENTITIES FROM MY MIND!
The END
23

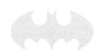

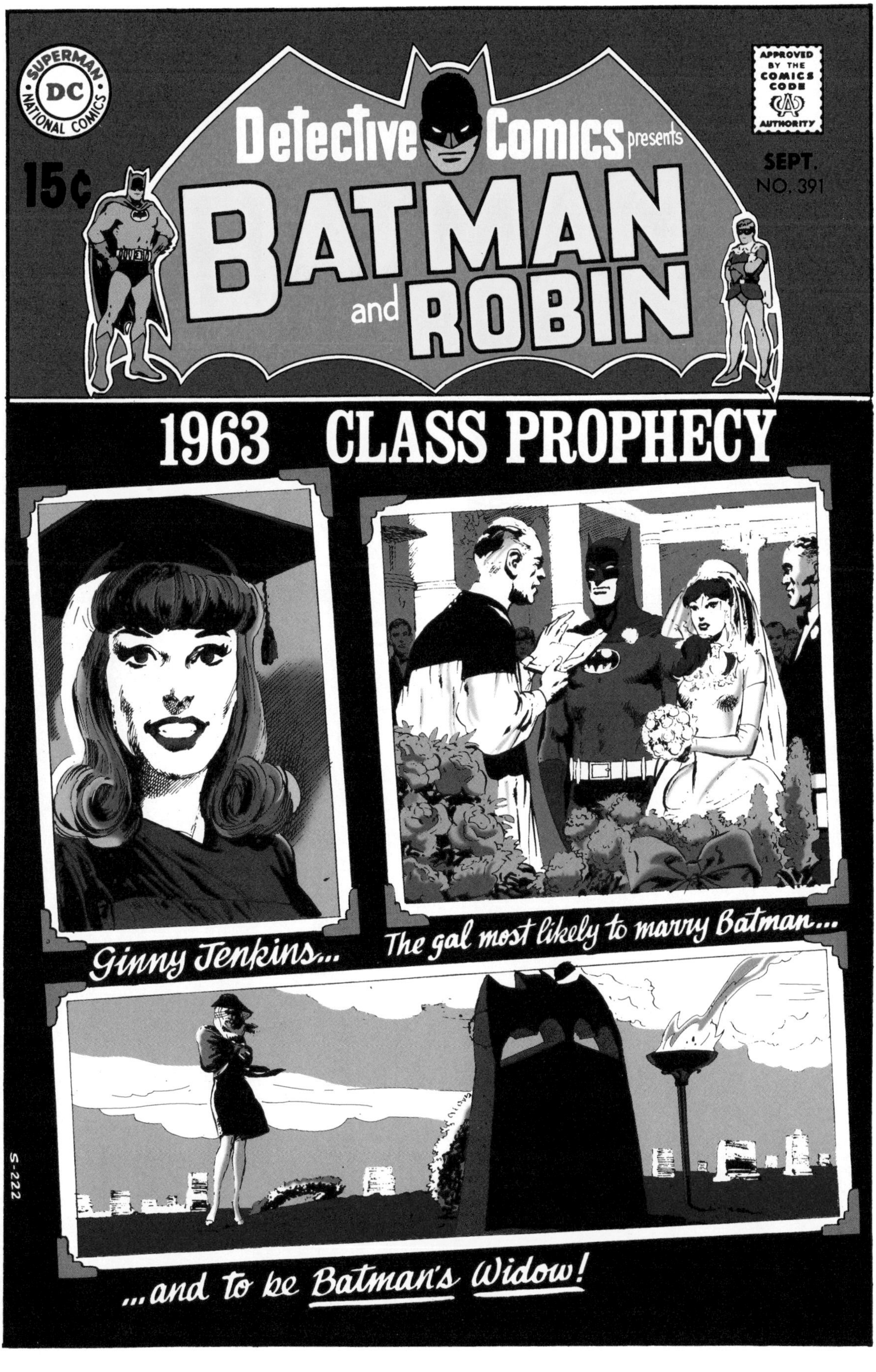
SUPERMAN DC NATIONAL COMICS
15¢
Detective Comics presents
BATMAN and ROBIN
APPROVED BY THE COMICS CODE AUTHORITY
SEPT. NO. 391
1963 CLASS PROPHECY
Ginny Jenkins...
The gal most likely to marry Batman...
...and to be Batman's Widow!
S-222

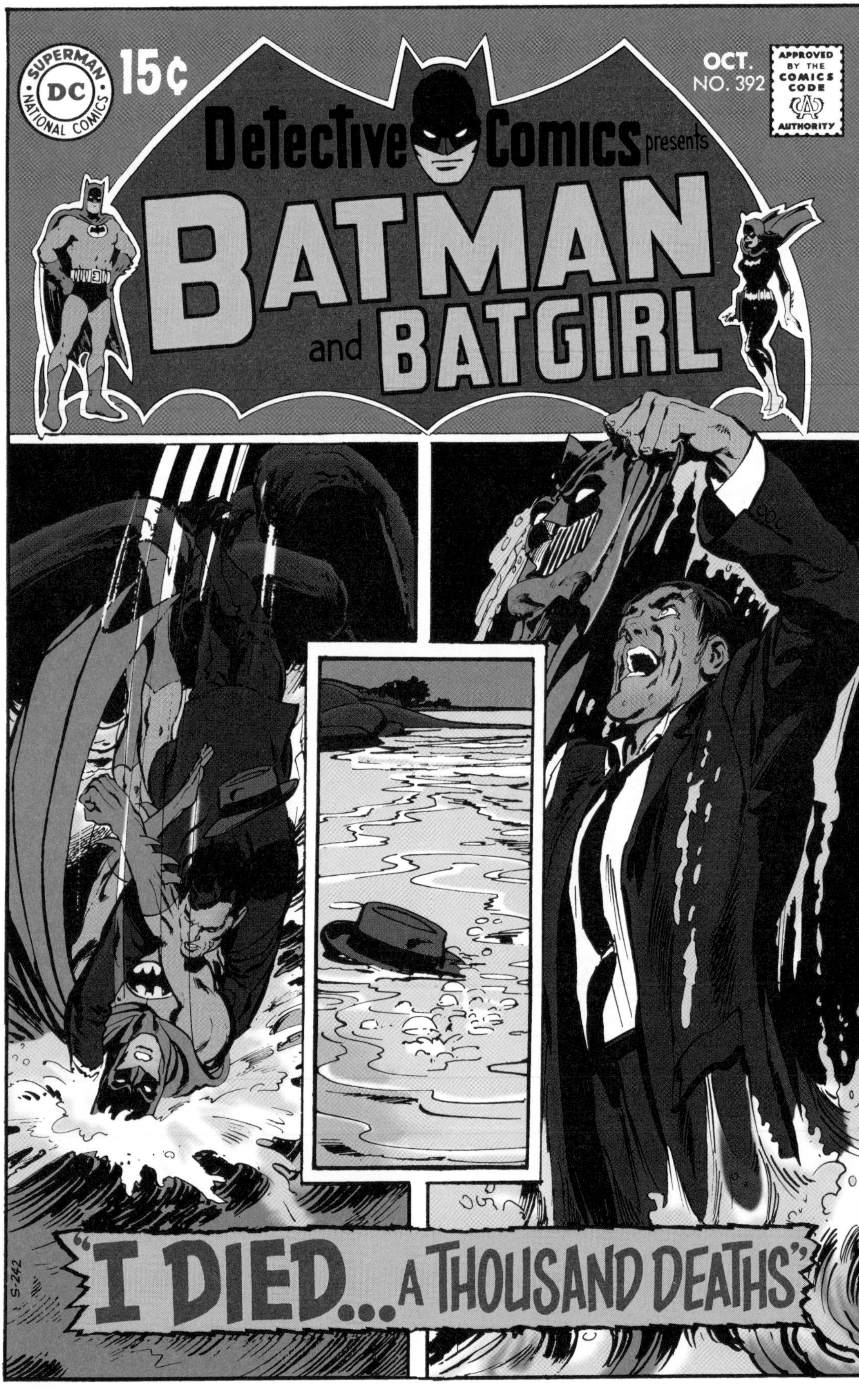
SUPERMAN DC NATIONAL COMICS
15¢
OCT.
NO. 392
APPROVED BY THE COMICS CODE AUTHORITY
Detective Comics presents
BATMAN
and BATGIRL
S-242
"I DIED... A THOUSAND DEATHS"

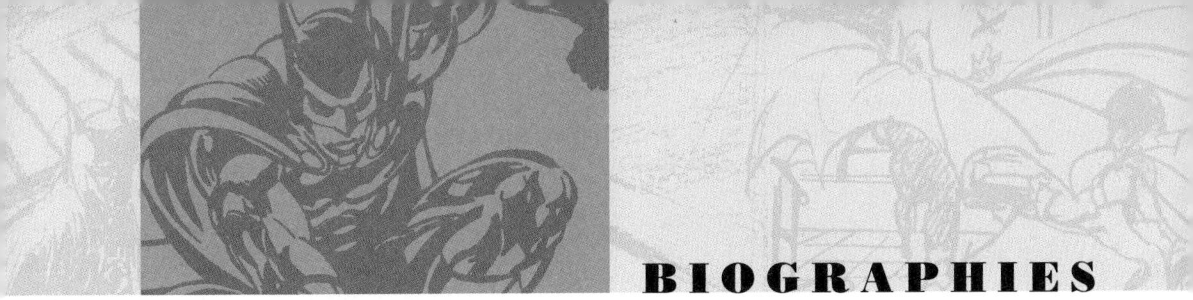

BIOGRAPHIES

NEAL ADAMS

Born on June 15, 1941 in New York City, Neal Adams began his comics career drawing pages for *The Archie Comics Joke Book* immediately after graduating from high school (and being turned down for work by DC Comics). Within a year, he was also drawing commercial illustration spots as well as background work and full pencil work on Howard Nostrand's *Bat Masterson* syndicated comic strip. Building on this early success, he landed a desk at Johnstone and Cushing, the country's leading "comics for advertising" studio. There Adams did comics for such advertisers as Norelco, Bell Telephone, General Electric, AT&T, Tandy Industries, and the United States National Guard.

At the age of 20, Adams began drawing the internationally syndicated comic strip based on the popular TV series *Ben Casey*, while at the same time "ghosting" other newspaper strips like Stan Drake's *The Heart of Juliet Jones, Peter Scratch, Rip Kirby,* and *Secret Agent X-9*. *Ben Casey* was a success, appearing in 161 newspapers worldwide, but after nearly four years on the strip Adams decided to change the direction of his career to illustration and spent six months carefully assembling a new portfolio of his work. However, when the portfolio disappeared from the first agency he left it with, he was forced to seek work in the comic-book field once again. After doing work for Jim Warren's horror publications, Adams tried DC once more — this time successfully.

Adams joined DC Comics in 1965 and became an overnight sensation by infusing a new visual vitality into longtime characters. Working closely with editorial director Carmine Infantino, Adams quickly became DC's preeminent cover artist, contributing radical and dynamic illustrations to nearly every title the company published. His first interior work was done for Bob Kanigher's war titles, followed by Elongated Man stories for Julie Schwartz, and, curiously enough, Jerry Lewis and Bob Hope comics. Next to come were four issues of THE SPECTRE, two of which Adams also wrote, and two issues of WORLD'S FINEST COMICS for Mort Weisinger. Adams then picked up a new feature from Infantino called DEADMAN, a title with which he would soon become closely identified. (Besides the two SPECTRE issues and most of DEADMAN, Adams's writing credits include a number of commercial comic books for Johnstone and Cushing, about a quarter of the writing on *Ben Casey*, and some short stories for both DC and Marvel.)

In the early 1970s Adams did pivotal runs on *The Avengers* and *The Uncanny X-Men* at Marvel Comics. But it was his DC work with writer Dennis O'Neil and inker Dick Giordano during this period that cemented Adams's reputation as a comics legend. The stories featuring Batman, Green Lantern, and Green Arrow broke new ground for mainstream comics and attracted major (and overwhelmingly positive) national media attention to the form.

Later in the 1970s, Adams and Giordano opened Continuity Associates, using their comic art experience to produce advertising artwork for clients around the world. Continuity became a training ground for new talent, mentored and encouraged by the two founders. During this time Adams also designed a three-part science-fiction epic adventure play, *Warp*, which was first staged in Chicago and then moved to Broadway. He earned a Drama Desk Award for his efforts, the only such award earned by a comic-book artist. In addition, Adams has been an outspoken supporter of creator's rights in the comics industry and was influential in convincing comic-book publishers to return original artwork to the artists who created it.

CARY BATES

Born in 1948 in Ohio, Cary Bates was, along with 13-year-old Jim Shooter, one of Mort Weisinger's teen wunderkinds, contributing story ideas and cover sketches to Weisinger when he was barely seventeen. In time, Weisinger encouraged Bates to submit scripts to DC, and as a Superman author Bates found himself with a steady job that lasted for nearly two decades. In the late 1980s, Bates — by then a story editor for the *Superboy* television series — left the comics field altogether to pursue a television and movie career, having left behind a vast body of work that forever defined him as one of the definitive Superman writers.

LEO DORFMAN

Most of Leo Dorfman's comic-book work went uncredited during his career, but he was a mainstay of Mort Weisinger's group, writing adventures of Superman, Lois Lane, Jimmy Olsen, Superboy, Supergirl, the Legion of Super-Heroes as well as the WORLD'S FINEST adventures of Batman and Robin. He also scripted Superboy tales for Filmation's 1966 Superman animated series and wrote extensively for Murray Boltinoff's mystery comics, notably GHOSTS. Dorfman died in the 1970s.

DICK GIORDANO

Dick Giordano was part of a creative team that helped change the face of comic books in the late 1960s and early 1970s. Along with writer Dennis O'Neil and penciller Neal Adams, Giordano helped bring Batman back to his roots as a dark, brooding "creature of the night" and brought relevance to comics in the pages of GREEN LANTERN. Giordano began his career as an artist for Charlton Comics in 1952 and became the company's editor-in-chief in 1965. In that capacity, he revamped the Charlton line by adding an emphasis on such heroes as the Question, Captain Atom, and the Blue Beetle. In 1967, Giordano came over to DC for a three-year stint as editor, bringing with him many of the

talents who would help shape the industry of the day, including Dennis O'Neil, Jim Aparo, and Steve Skeates. Winner of numerous industry awards, Giordano later returned to DC, rising to the position of Vice President-Executive Editor before "retiring" in 1993 to once again pursue a full-time career as penciller and inker.

BOB HANEY

Born in 1926, Bob Haney received an M.A. from Columbia University in New York. As a writer for DC he was the co-creator in the 1960s of the Doom Patrol, Eclipso, Metamorpho, and the original Teen Titans. In earlier days he also wrote for Fawcett, Fox, Harvey, Hillman, Quality, Ziff-Davis, Dell, St. John, and many other comics publishers. From the late 1950s through the 1960s he scripted many war stories for ALL-AMERICAN MEN OF WAR and STAR SPANGLED WAR STORIES, as well as THE BRAVE AND THE BOLD team-ups, BLACKHAWK, TOMAHAWK, Green Arrow, Suicide Squad, and others. He currently resides in Mexico.

CARMINE INFANTINO

The man most closely associated with the Silver Age Flash, Carmine Infantino began working in comics in the mid-1940s as the artist on such features as Green Lantern, Black Canary, Ghost Patrol... and the original Golden Age Flash. Infantino's unique style continued to grace a variety of super-hero, supernatural, and western features through-out the 1950s until he was tapped to pencil the 1956 revival of the Flash. While continuing to pencil the FLASH series, he also provided the art for other series, including Batman, the Elongated Man, and Adam Strange. Infantino became DC's editorial director in 1967 and, later, publisher before returning to freelancing in 1976, since which time he has pencilled and inked numerous features, including the *Batman* newspaper strip, GREEN LANTERN CORPS, and DANGER TRAIL. Infantino continues to contribute the occasional illustration to DC to this day.